Mark Spenik
Orryn Sledge

MW01053957

Microsoft® SQL Server 2000 DBA Survival Guide

SAMS

201 West 103rd Street, Indianapolis, Indiana 46290

Microsoft SQL Server 2000 DBA Survival Guide

International Standard Book Number: 0-672-32468-7

Library of Congress Catalog Card Number: 2002110541

Printed in the United States of America

First Printing: November 2002

05   04   03   02   4   3   2

Trademarks

All terms mentioned in this book that are known to be trademarks or service marks have been appropriately capitalized. Sams Publishing cannot attest to the accuracy of this information. Use of a term in this book should not be regarded as affecting the validity of any trademark or service mark.

Warning and Disclaimer

Every effort has been made to make this book as complete and as accurate as possible, but no warranty or fitness is implied. The information provided is on an "as is" basis.

Associate Publisher
Michael Stephens

Acquisitions Editor
Michelle Newcomb

Development Editor
Kevin Howard

Managing Editor
Charlotte Clapp

Project Editor
George E. Nedeff

Copy Editor
Rhonda Tinch-Mize

Indexer
Lisa Wilson

Proofreader
Linda Seifert

Technical Editor
J. Boyd Nolan

Team Coordinator
Pamalee Nelson

Multimedia Developer
Dan Scherf

Interior Designer
Gary Adair

Cover Designer
Alan Clements

Contents at a Glance

Introduction 1

Part I   Overview
   1   Role of the Database Administrator 9
   2   SQL Server Overview 23
   3   The Evolution of SQL Server 45

Part II   Installing and Upgrading SQL Server
   4   Planning an Installation or Upgrade 53
   5   Installing or Upgrading SQL Server 77

Part III   SQL Server Management and Configuration
   6   Enterprise Management Processes 111
   7   Configuring and Tuning SQL Server 139
   8   Managing Databases 165
   9   Managing SQL Server Users and Security 203

Part IV   Database Backup and Recovery
   10   Backup and Recovery 239

Part V   SQL Database Maintenance
   11   Developing a SQL Server Maintenance Plan 301
   12   Automating Database Administration Tasks 313

Part VI   Importing and Exporting Data
   13   Data Transformation Services 355
   14   Using BCP and Bulk Insert 397

Part VII   Troubleshooting
   15   Troubleshooting SQL Server 429

Part VIII   Architecture and Database Design

      16   Architecture Features...459

1-26   **17**   Database Design Issues..467

Part IX   Performance and Tuning

1-26   **18**   Understanding Indexes..483

2-2   **19**   Query Optimization...507

      20   Multiuser Issues..537

Part X   Transact-SQL

1-19   **21**   SQL Essentials...565

      22   Using Stored Procedures and Cursors......................593

Part XI   Advanced DBA Topics

2-23   **23**   SQL Server 2000 and the Internet...........................639

      24   Monitoring SQL Server..685

      25   SQL Mail..703

2-23   **26**   Using SQL-DMO..711

Part XII   Replication

      27   Replication..751

3-8   **28**   Transactional Replication..779

      29   Snapshot and Merge Replication.............................803

Part XIII   Data Warehousing

3-15   **30**   Introduction to Datawarehousing.............................835

      31   SQL 2000 Analysis Services....................................855

Part XIV   Appendixes

      A   Naming Conventions...895

      B   DBCC Commands...899

      C   SQL Server Resources..925

      Index...929

Table of Contents

Introduction   1

Part I   Overview

1   Role of the Database Administrator   9

Hardware 10

Network 10

Operating Systems 11

File/Print Server 11

Database Server 11

Who Does What? 11

    PC and Tech Support 12

    Network Administrator 12

    System Administrator 12

    Webmaster 12

    Database Administrator 12

What Is a Database Administrator? 13

Who Are the DBAs? 13

DBA Responsibilities 13

    Installing and Upgrading a SQL Server 14

    Monitoring the Database Server's Health and
      Tuning Accordingly 14

    Using Storage Properly 14

    Performing Backup and Recovery Duties 14

    Managing Database Users and Security 14

    Working with Developers 15

    Establishing and Enforcing Standards 15

    Transferring Data 15

    Replicating Data 15

    Data Warehousing 16

    Scheduling Events 16

    Capacity Planning 16

    Providing 24-Hour Access 16

    Learning Constantly 16

    Does It Pay to Be a DBA? 16

Tricks of the Trade...17
    Classes and Training..17
    On the Job...17
    Microsoft TechNet, Microsoft Developers Network, and Internet
      News Group..18
    Magazines and Books..18
    Certification...18
    Internet...19
How the DBA Interacts with Other Team Members...........19
    System Administrator and Network Administrator............19
    Developers...20
    Users...20
Summary...20

2   SQL Server Overview   23

Architecture..23
    Symmetric Multiprocessing (SMP)....................................23
    Operating System Support...24
    Network Independence...24
    Reliability...25
Operating System Integration..25
    Taskbar Integration..25
    Control Panel...25
    Event Viewer...25
    The Registry..27
    NT User Accounts..28
    Performance Monitor..28
Visual Administration Tools...29
    SQL Server Service Manager..29
    SQL Server Enterprise Manager.......................................30
    SQL Server Query Analyzer...31
    SQL Server Setup...31
    SQL Server Network Utility...32
    SQL Server Profiler..33
    Version Upgrade Wizard..34
SQL Server Companion Products...34
    Microsoft English Query..34
    Analysis Services..35

Nonvisual Administration Tools and Command-Line Tools 36
     BCP 36
     ISQL 37
     OSQL 38
     TEXTCOPY 38
Common SQL Server Objects 39
     Tables 39
     Rules 39
     Defaults 40
     User-Defined Data Types 40
     Views 40
     Triggers 41
     Stored Procedures 42
FAQ 42
Summary 43

3   The Evolution of SQL Server   45

History of SQL Server 45
What's New in Version 2000 46
     XML Support 46
     Multi-Instance Support 47
     Data Warehousing and Business Intelligence (BI)
        Improvements 47
     Windows 2000 Support 47
     Performance and Scalability Improvements 47
     Wizard Improvements 48
     Query Analyzer Improvements 48
     DTS Enhancement 48
     Transact-SQL Enhancements 49
Summary 49

Part II   Installing and Upgrading SQL Server

4   Planning an Installation or Upgrade   53

Developing an Installation Strategy and Plan 54
     Step 1: Determine System and User Requirements 54
     Step 2: Select the Right Platform 56

Step 3: Answer Required Questions and Understand Why
    They Are Important 64
Step 4: Install SQL Server 67
Developing an Upgrade Strategy and Plan 68
Upgrade/Installation Planning FAQ 74
Summary 74
The Upgrade Checklist 75

5   Installing or Upgrading SQL Server   77

Different Editions of SQL Server 78
Installing SQL Server 79
    SQL Server Installation Checklist 79
    Step 1: Running Setup 81
    Step 2: Select an Installation Option 82
    Step 3: Select Computer Install Method 82
    Step 4: Installation Type 82
    Step 5: User Information 83
    Step 6: License Agreement 83
    Step 7: Installation Type 84
    Step 8: Instance Name 85
    Step 9: Setup Type and File Location 86
    Step 10: Select Components to Install 87
    Step 11: Authentication Mode 87
    Step 12: Collation Setting 88
    Step 13: Network Libraries 88
    Step 13a: SQL Server, SQL Agent, MSDTC User Accounts,
        and Auto Start Services—Windows 2000 and NT Only 88
    Step 14: Start Copying Files 89
Starting and Stopping SQL Server 89
Installation Troubleshooting 91
    Error Log and Windows 2000/NT Application Log 91
    Start SQL Server from the Command Line 93
Upgrading SQL Server 95
    Upgrading SQL Server 7.0 to SQL Server 2000 96
    Upgrading SQL Server 6.5 101
Removing SQL Server 102
Installing Client Tools 103
Configuring Clients 104
Remote Installation 105
Installing Multiple Instances of SQL Server 106

Installation FAQ 106
Summary 107

Part III   SQL Server Management and Configuration

6   Enterprise Management Processes   111

Starting, Pausing, and Stopping SQL Server 111
Starting the SQL Server Enterprise Manager 112
Navigating the SQL Server Enterprise Manager 113
Registering a Server 113
Connecting to a Server 116
Disconnecting from a Server 118
Starting, Stopping, and Configuring SQL Server Agent 118
Starting, Stopping, and Configuring SQL Mail 119
Using the Enterprise Manager to Perform Common Tasks 120
    Manage Server Configurations 121
    Manage Logins 121
    Manage Server Roles 122
    Manage Databases 124
    Manage Database Users and Objects 124
    Generate SQL Scripts 126
    Manage Jobs 127
    Manage Alerts 129
    Manage Operators 129
    Monitor User Activity 132
    Manage Data Transformation Packages 132
    Manage Error Logs 134
SQL Server Query Analyzer 135
Starting and Stopping the Distributed Transaction
   Coordinator (DTC) 137
FAQ 137
Summary 138

7   Configuring and Tuning SQL Server   139

Configuring SQL Server 140
SQL Server 2000 Self-Tuning Features 147
    Memory 147
    Asynchronous Read Ahead 150

Configuration Parameters 150
    allow updates 150
    default language 151
    max text repl size 151
    nested triggers 152
    remote access 152
    remote login timeout 152
    remote query timeout 152
    remote proc trans 153
    show advanced options 153
    two digit year cutoff 153
    user_option 154
Advanced Configuration Parameters 154
    affinity mask 154
    awe enabled 154
    C2 Audit Mode 155
    cost threshold for parallelism 155
    cursor threshold 155
    default full-text language 156
    fill factor 156
    index create memory 157
    lightweight pooling 157
    locks 157
    max degree of parallelism 158
    max server memory 158
    max worker threads 158
    media retention 159
    min memory per query 159
    min server memory 159
    network packet size 159
    open objects 160
    priority boost 160
    query governor cost limit 161
    query wait 161
    recovery interval 161
    scan for startup procs 162
    set working set size 162
    user connections 162
Configuration FAQ 163
Summary 163

8   Managing Databases   **165**

A Database Primer 165

    What Is a Database? 165

    What Is the Transaction Log? 165

    How Databases and Operating System Datafiles Interact 167

Database Basics 168

    Creating a Database 168

    Viewing Information About a Database 174

    Setting Database Options 174

    Expanding the Database and Log Size 182

    Shrinking a Database and Log 186

    Renaming a Database 187

    Deleting a Database 188

    Moving Database Files 190

Additional Database Information 191

    Tip 1: Document the Database 192

    Tip 2: Take Advantage of the `model` Database 192

Filegroups 193

    Implementing a Filegroup During Database Creation 194

    Implementing a Filegroup for an Existing Database 194

    Adding Secondary Data Files to the Filegroup 195

    Place an Object on the Filegroup 196

    Creating an Index on a Filegroup 196

    Viewing Information About a Filegroup 197

Database FAQ 198

Summary 200

9   Managing SQL Server Users and Security   **203**

Introduction 203

An Overview of SQL Server's Security Model 204

    SQL Server Login 204

    Database User 205

    `guest` User 206

    Permissions 206

    Roles 208

Managing Logins 212

Managing Server Roles 215

Managing Database Access and Database Roles 216

Viewing and Modifying Login Information 219
Removing Logins 219
Changing a Password 220
Managing SQL Server Security 222
    Levels of Security 222
    Security Hierarchy 223
    Granting and Revoking Object Permissions 224
    Granting and Revoking Statement Permissions 228
Beyond Security Basics: Suggested Strategies 229
    Role-Based Security Management 229
    Views for Data Security 230
    Stored Procedures for Data Security 233
    Triggers for Audit Trails 233
Managing SQL Server Users and Security FAQ 234
Summary 236

Part IV   Database Backup and Recovery

10   Backup and Recovery   239

SQL Server 2000 Backups—Simplified with Recovery Models
  (But Few Changes Under the Covers) 240
    Recovery Models 241
    Simple Recovery 241
    Full Recovery 242
    Bulk-Logged Recovery 242
    What Is a Database Backup? 242
    What Is a Differential Backup? 243
    What Is a Transaction Log Backup? 243
What Is a File/Filegroup Backup? 244
    Selecting the Right Recovery Model for Your Database ... 245
Creating a Backup Device 246
Performing Database, Transaction Log, Differential, and
  File/File Group Backups 247
    The Steps to Perform a Backup 248
Understanding Log Truncation Options 255
    TRUNCATE_ONLY 255
    NO_LOG 256
    NO_TRUNCATE 256

Backup Wizard 257
Using Multiple Backup Devices (Striped Backups) and Media Sets 261
Full Recovery Model and Bulk Logged Recovery Model—
  Using Database Complete Backups and Transaction Log
  Backups to Restore a Database 262
    Day 1: Full Database Backup Occurs 264
    Day 2: Database Modified, Database Corrupted 264
    Using the Backups to Restore the Database 264
    Problem Resolution 264
    Using the Backups to Restore the Database 265
    Restore Example—Reality Check 267
    Using Differential Backups to Speed Up the Restore Time 267
Performing a Database Restore 267
Restoring the master Database 271
    Reattaching Database Files 273
Interactive Example of Losing and Restoring a Database 274
    Step 1: Create a Database 275
    Step 2: Create a Table 275
    Step 3: Create a Backup Device 275
    Step 4: Add Rows to the Table 276
    Step 5: Back Up the TestRestore Database 277
    Step 6: Add More Rows to the Table 277
    Step 7: Back Up the Transaction Log 277
    Step 8: Add More Rows to the Table 277
    Checkpoint: Backup Part of Exercise Completed 277
    Step 9: Shut Down SQL Server 278
    Step 10: Delete the Database Data File 278
    Step 11: Restart SQL Server 278
    Step 12: Restore the Database TestRestore 278
Creating a Backup Schedule 280
    Category 1: Actions that Warrant Dumping a Database 280
    Category 2: Scheduled Database Backups 281
Log Shipping Overview 283
    Log Shipping Requirements 284
    Setting-Up Log Shipping 285
    Modifying and Removing Log Shipping 290
    Monitoring and Troubleshooting Log Shipping 292
Backup and Restore FAQ 294
Summary 296

Part V   SQL Database Maintenance

11   Developing a SQL Server Maintenance Plan   301

Areas of Maintenance..301

SQL Server Maintenance...302

Database Maintenance...307

Table/Object Maintenance...308

Job Maintenance..308

Windows Maintenance..309

Maintenance Checklist..311

Maintenance FAQ...311

Summary...312

12   Automating Database Administration Tasks   313

Introduction...313

SQL Server Agent...313

Jobs...313

Alerts...329

Database Maintenance Plan Wizard..341

Automating Database Administration Tasks FAQ...............................351

Summary...351

Part VI   Importing and Exporting Data

13   Data Transformation Services   355

DTS and the Data Warehouse...356

DTS and OLE DB/ODBC..356

The DTS Framework..357

Packages...358

Connections..359

Tasks...359

Steps...360

The DTS Data Pump...361

Using the DTS Wizard...361

A DTS Wizard Example...362

Using the DTS Designer...370

Creating a DTS Package and Adding Simple Workflow..................371

Execute Process Task..372

Dynamic Properties Task...373

ActiveX Script Task 376
Execute SQL Task 377
FTP Task 378
Execute Package Task 379
What Are Workflow and Batch Processing? 379
How DTS Provides Workflow and Batch Processing
Capabilities 380
DTS Package Properties 380
Individual Task Workflow Properties 382
Using the Workflow ActiveX Script Property for Loop
Control and Conditions 385
Using DTS Packages 393
Running Packages from the Command Line 393
DTS Package Performance 393
The Data Transformation Services FAQ 394
Summary 396

14   **Using BCP and BULK INSERT**   **397**

BCP 398
BCP Syntax 399
Permissions Required to Run BCP 404
Character Mode Versus Native Mode 405
Interactive BCP 405
File Storage Type 406
Prefix Length 407
Field Length 407
Field Terminator 408
Format Files 408
Sample BCP Scripts 410
Simple Import 410
Simple Export 410
Comma-Delimited Import 411
Comma-Delimited Export 411
Fixed-Length Import 411
Fixed-Length Export 413
Skipped Fields on Import 413
Skipped Fields on Export 414

Modes of Operation 414
   Achieving Fast Mode BCP 415
   Why You Should Be Concerned with Which BCP Mode
    Is Running 415
BCP and Enforcement of Triggers, Rules, Defaults, Constraints, and
  Unique Indexes 417
Common BCP Traps 418
BCP Tips 418
BULK INSERT 421
BCP FAQ 424
Summary 424

Part VII   Troubleshooting

15   Troubleshooting SQL Server   429
SQL Error Messages 430
   Error Message Number 430
   Error Severity 431
   State Number 432
   Error Message 432
Using the Error Message Number to Resolve the Error 433
Deciphering the Error Log 436
Using the Event Viewer 438
Killing a Process 438
Viewing Detailed Process Activity 441
Using DBCC and Trace Statements to Troubleshoot 442
   Table/Index Fragmentation 444
Troubleshooting Applications 445
Other Sources of Help and Information 446
   Technical Support 446
   Microsoft TechNet and Microsoft Developer Network 447
   The Internet 448
   User Groups 448
Using the Performance Monitor for Trend Analysis 448
   Generating a Log File with the Performance Monitor 449
Troubleshooting FAQ 453
Summary 455

Part VIII   Architecture and Database Design

16   Architecture Features   459

SQL Server Thread Scheduling 460

What Is a Thread? 460

What Is a Context Switch? 460

What Is SMP? 461

SQL Server 6.x Thread Scheduling 461

SQL Server 2000 Thread Scheduling 461

Disk I/O and Data Management 462

Page Size 462

File Groups 463

Multiple Database Instances 464

Federated Database Servers 465

Other Enhancements 465

Read-Ahead Logic 466

Locking Enhancements 466

Summary 466

17   Database Design Issues   467

Problems that Can Arise from an Improperly Designed Database 467

Redundant Data 468

Limited Data Tracking 468

Inconsistent Data 469

Update Anomalies 469

Delete Anomalies 469

Insert Anomalies 470

Normalization 470

How to Normalize a Database 471

Denormalization 475

Performance 475

Ad Hoc Reporting 477

Denormalization Techniques 477

FAQ 480

Summary 480

Part IX   Performance and Tuning

18   Understanding Indexes   483

General Principle Behind Indexes 483
Structure of SQL Server Indexes 488
    Clustered Index 489
    Nonclustered Index 490
Data Modification and Index Performance Considerations 491
How to Create Indexes 492
Other Index Operations 498
    Indexes on Views and Computed Columns 498
    Viewing Indexes on Tables in a Database 498
    Renaming, Adding, or Deleting an Index 499
Suggested Index Strategies 501
    What to Index 501
    What Not to Index 502
    Clustered or Nonclustered Index 502
Letting SQL Server Help with Index Selection 503
Index FAQ 503
Summary 506

19   Query Optimization   507

What's a Query Optimizer? 507
What Are Statistics? 508
Basic Query Optimization Suggestions 511
Tools to Help Optimize a Query 511
    Index Tuning Wizard 512
    SQL Server Profiler 514
    Showplan 521
    Statistics I/O 523
    Statistics Time Tool 524
Reading Showplans 526
Overriding the Optimizer 529
    Index Hints 529
    The SET FORCEPLAN ON Command 530
Other Tuning Tricks 531
    Are You Trying to Tune an UPDATE, DELETE, or
        INSERT Query? 532
    Does the Query Reference a View? 532

Are the Datatypes Mismatched? 532
Does the Query Use a Nonsearch Argument? 533
Query Optimization FAQ 534
Summary 534

20   Multiuser Issues   537

Locks 537
Understanding SQL Server's Locking Behavior 539
Physical Locks 541
Lock Methods 543
Viewing Locks and Blocking 544
Tips to Help Minimize Locking and Prevent Deadlocks 551
Multiuser Configuration Options 557
Transaction Isolation Level 557
Explicit Locking 558
Multiuser FAQ 561
Summary 562

Part X   Transact-SQL

21   SQL Essentials   565

An Overview of Basic SQL Statements 566
SELECT 566
A Simple SELECT Statement 567
Adding the WHERE Clause 568
Adding the ORDER BY Clause 569
Using the WHERE Clause to Join Tables 571
Using the Join Operator to Join Tables 571
Aggregate Functions in SQL Statements 573
Use of the GROUP BY Clause 574
Use of the HAVING Clause 576
INSERT 577
Use of the INSERT Statement with a Value List 577
Use of the INSERT Statement with a SELECT Statement 578
UPDATE 578
Setting Columns to a Fixed Value with UPDATE Statement 579
Setting a Column Value Based on Existing Column Values 579
Setting a Column Based on Values in a Joined Table 579

DELETE 580

    Using DELETE to Delete All Rows from a Table 580

    Using DELETE to Delete Specific Rows from a Table 581

    Using a Subquery to Delete Rows Based on Values in a

    Different Table 581

CREATE TABLE 581

    Using CREATE TABLE to Create the authors Table 582

SELECT...INTO 583

    Using SELECT...INTO to Create a New authortitles Table 583

Distributed Queries 584

    Distributed Query Restrictions 585

    Adding a Linked Server 586

    Logon IDs 588

    Retrieving Data from a Linked Server 590

    Examples 591

    Linked Servers Pass Through Queries 592

Summary 592

22   Using Stored Procedures and Cursors   593

What Is a Stored Procedure? 593

Stored Procedure Pros and Cons 594

How to Create a Stored Procedure 595

How to Modify a Stored Procedure 600

Control-of-Flow Language 600

    The DECLARE Statement 601

    The GOTO Statement 602

    The BEGIN...END Statement 602

    The IF...ELSE Statement 602

    The WAITFOR Statement 603

    The RETURN Statement 603

    The WHILE, BREAK, and CONTINUE Statements 605

    The PRINT Statement 605

    The RAISERROR Statement 606

    Comments 606

Parameters Used with Stored Procedures 607

    Input Parameters 607

    Output Parameters 609

Commonly Used Global Variables 610

How to Debug a Stored Procedure 610
    Transact-SQL Debugger 611
    Transact-SQL Debug Statements 611
    Other Debugging Tools 612
What Is a Cursor? 613
Creating a Cursor 613
    Step 1: DECLARE the Cursor 613
    Step 2: OPEN the Cursor 616
    Step 3: FETCH from the Cursor 617
    Step 4: CLOSE or DEALLOCATE the Cursor 618
    Positional UPDATE and DELETE 618
    Global Variables 619
Putting It All Together 620
    Example 1: Loop Through a Table 620
    Example 2: Display Object Names and Object Types 622
Stored Procedure and Cursor FAQ 631
Summary 635

Part XI   Advanced DBA Topics

23   SQL Server 2000 and the Internet   639

SQL Server 2000 Web Publishing 641
    Using the Web Assistant 642
    Web Assistant Jobs 643
    Using the Web Assistant Wizard to Publish an HTML Page 644
    Using the Web Assistant Wizard to Publish Data to a
        Web Page 660
SQL Server 2000 and Managing Web Assistant Jobs 663
Advanced Template File Example 663
XML Integration 676
Retrieving XML Data 677
    Using XPath Queries 678
    XPath Queries Against XML-Data Reduced (XDR) Schema 679
Updating Information via XML 680
SQL Server and the Web FAQ 682
Summary 682

24   Monitoring SQL Server   685

Tools for Monitoring SQL Server 685
  System Monitor...685
  SQL Server Enterprise Manager..694
  SQL Server Profiler...695
Monitoring SQL Server FAQ 701
Summary 701

25   SQL Mail   703

Setting Up Your SQL Server as a Mail Client.............................703
Configuring SQL Mail 704
Configuring SQL Agent Mail 706
Using SQL Mail..706
  Sending Email from SQL Server...707
  Processing Incoming Email...708
SQL Mail FAQ...710
Summary 710

26   Using SQL-DMO   711

SQL Server's Object Model 714
Why Use SQL-DMO?..714
Creating Applications with SQL-DMO...715
  Using Visual Basic..715
  Required SQL-DMO Files...719
  SQL-DMO Checklist..719
Enhancing the SQL Server DBA Assistant...................................720
  What's in the SQL Server DBA Assistant? 721
  Connecting to SQL Server 721
  Filling a Combo Box with Databases......................................725
  Performing Table Maintenance..728
  Performing Table Exports Using Bulk Copy (BCP).....................731
Using SQL-DMO with Stored Procedures 736
  OLE Automation Procedures...736
  Transact SQL Examples 739
SQL-DMO FAQ...746
Summary 747

Part XII   Replication

27   Replication **751**

Replication Overview and Terminology 752
    Publish and Subscribe 753
    Publication and Articles 753
    Subscriptions Types (Push and Pull) 754
    Server Roles 754
    Replication Types 755
    Transactional Consistency 757
    The Problem That SQL Server 2000 Replication Cannot Solve 758
    Distribution Database 758
    An Overview of the SQL Server Replication Agents 759
    Synchronization Modes 760
Creating and Assigning the Distribution Database 761
Configuring Replication Distribution Options 764
Deleting a Distribution Database 765
Configuring Replication Publishing 767
    Adding a Publisher to a Distribution Database 767
    Enabling a Database for Publishing and Removing a
    Database from Publishing 769
Enabling Replication Subscribers 770
Using the Disabling Publishing and Distribution Wizard 771
Adding NonSQL Server (Heterogeneous) Subscribers 772
    Step 1: Create an ODBC Data Source Name (DSN) 773
    Step 2: Register the ODBC Source as a Subscribing Server 775
Upgrading SQL Server Replication 776
Replication FAQ 777
Summary 778

28   Transactional Replication **779**

Applicable Uses for Transactional Replication 779
Replication Agents 780
Replication Topology 781
    Central Publisher 781
    Central Publisher with Remote Distributor 781
    Republisher 783
    Central Subscriber 784

Immediate Updating Subscribers 785
    Triggers 785
    Stored Procedures 786
    Microsoft Distributed Transaction Coordinator 786
    Conflict Detection 786
    Loopback Detection 786
Recommended Topology for Updating Subscribers 787
Creating a Transaction Based Publication 787
Subscriptions 795
Custom Stored Procedures 795
Transforming Published Data 798
Inline Data Validation and Reinitialization 798
Generating Publication Scripts 799
Replicating Stored Procedures 799
Replication Monitor 800
Transactional Replication FAQ 801
Summary 802

29   **Snapshot and Merge Replication**   **803**
What Is Snapshot Replication? 804
    Snapshot Applications 804
    Snapshot Replication: Step by Step 805
    Planning and Special Design Considerations for Snapshot
        Replication 807
Setting Up a Snapshot Publication 808
    Name Conflicts 810
    Copy Objects to Destination 810
What Is Merge Replication? 811
    Merge Applications 811
    Merge Replication: Step by Step 812
    Merge Replication and Transactional Consistency 813
    Planning and Special Design Considerations for
        Merge Replication 815
Setting Up a Merge Publication 817
Merge Replication and Resolving Conflicts—Hands-on Example 817
    Step 1: Create a Database 818
    Step 2: Create a Merge Publication Called test_authors 818
    Step 3: Push the Publication 819

Step 4: Make Changes to the Information in One of the
Articles 823
Step 5: Replicate the Changes 824
Step 6: Deal with Conflicts 825
Troubleshooting Merge and Snapshot Replication 826
Additional Publication Options 827
General Tab 827
Status Tab 828
Snapshot Tab 828
Alternative Synchronization Partners 829
Replicating via the Web (Internet) 829
Replication FAQ 830
Summary 831

Part XIII   Data Warehousing

30   Introduction to Data Warehousing   835
Why Warehouse? 835
What Is a Data Warehouse? 836
Decision Support Systems (DSS) 837
Online Analytical Processing (OLAP) 837
Warehouse Data Versus Operational Data 838
Data Warehousing Components 839
What Is a Data Mart? 840
Warehouses Versus Marts 841
Transforming Operational Data 842
Data Integration or Consolidation 843
Ensuring Data Quality 843
Data Mapping and Matching 844
Summarization 844
Extracting, Loading, and Refreshing Data 845
Metadata 845
Planning the Warehouse Design 846
Top Down or Bottom Up? 846
Dimensional Modeling (Stars and Snowflakes) 847
Important Design Considerations 849
Managing a Data Warehouse or Data Mart 850

Microsoft and SQL Server 2000 Contributions to Data
  Warehousing 850
    Data Transformation Services 851
    Repository 852
    Analysis Services 852
  Data Warehousing FAQ 853
  Summary 854

31   SQL 2000 Analysis Services   855

What Is OLAP? 855
Understanding Multidimensional Data 856
The Microsoft Analysis Manager 857
Building an OLAP Database 858
    Creating the Data Source 859
    Defining the Dimensions 860
    Building the Cube 864
Data Storage in an OLAP Database 868
    MOLAP 868
    ROLAP 869
    HOLAP 869
Optimizing an OLAP Database 869
    Aggregations 870
    Partitions 878
Managing Multidimensional Data 878
    Processing the Cube 878
    Merging Partitions 880
    Client Write Back 880
    Securing Your OLAP Data 881
Microsoft SQL Server 2000 Analysis Services FAQ 890
Summary 891

Part XIV   Appendixes

A   Naming Conventions   895

B   DBCC Commands   899

Quick Reference 899
Reading the Output from DBCC Commands 902

Resolving Errors Reported by DBCC 903
Essential DBCC Commands 903
DBCC Commands for Verification 904
    CHECKALLOC 904
    CHECKCATALOG 905
    CHECKDB 905
    CHECKFILEGROUP 908
    CHECKIDENT 909
    CHECKTABLE 910
    DBREINDEX 911
    SHOWCONTIG 911
    UPDATEUSAGE 912
DBCC Commands to Return Process Information 914
DBCC Commands to Return Performance Monitor Statistics 915
Trace Flag Commands 917
Data Cache Commands 918
Transaction Commands 919
Other DBCC Commands 920
    SHOW_STATISTICS 920
    SHRINKDATABASE 921
    SHRINKFILE 922
    USEROPTIONS 923
    DBCC dllname (FREE) 923

C   SQL Server Resources   925

Index   929

About the Authors

Mark Spenik is the vice president of Enterprise Technologies at Venturi Technology Partners located in Richmond, VA. Mark, a graduate of George Mason University in Fairfax, VA., entered the computer industry in 1985. He has designed and coded large-scale applications and has consulted with numerous firms in application development, implementation, and migration. He has a broad programming background, including assembly language, C, C++, HTML, Active Server Pages, and Visual Basic. Mark is a Microsoft Certified Solution Developer (MCSD) and charter member, and is frequently invited to speak at various developer conferences and seminars. Mark has also coauthored or contributed to several books on Microsoft SQL Server or Visual Basic. Mark can be reached via the Internet `mspenik@venturi-partners.com`.

Orryn Sledge is a Practice Director with FullTilt in Pittsburgh, PA. He specializes in managing and developing large-scale eBusiness solutions. His background includes SQL Server, Microsoft's .NET platform, Plumtree, Oracle, and other popular eBusiness products. He has been actively involved with SQL Server consulting since 1992 and is a Microsoft Certified Solution Developer (MCSD). Orryn is also a frequent speaker at various Microsoft conferences and presentations. He can be reached at `osledge@fulltilt.com`.

Dedication

Mark's Dedication

In memory of Marge Meyer.

Orryn's Dedication

To my three wonderful children: Abigail, Emma, and Margarite.

Acknowledgments

Mark's Acknowledgments

I want to thank my wife and best friend Lisa for her patience and support while enduring the rigors of writing a book. To my family Bonnie, John, Denise, David, Kim, Adam, Chris, Gary, Debbie, Lisa, David, and all my nieces and nephews (whose numbers are steadily increasing), thanks for the support! The Meyer (Sam and Jonathan) and the Rimes (Denise and Pat) families for all their encouragement. To my father John and my late mother Anna Jane for being such remarkable role models.

Orryn's Acknowledgments

I would like to thank my wife and family for helping me through another book. Also, I would like to thank everyone at Sams Publishing for making this book a reality.

We Want to Hear from You!

As the reader of this book, *you* are our most important critic and commentator. We value your opinion and want to know what we're doing right, what we could do better, what areas you'd like to see us publish in, and any other words of wisdom you're willing to pass our way.

As an executive editor for Sams Publishing, I welcome your comments. You can email or write me directly to let me know what you did or didn't like about this book—as well as what we can do to make our books better.

Please note that I cannot help you with technical problems related to the *topic* of this book. We do have a User Services group, however, where I will forward specific technical questions related to the book.

When you write, please be sure to include this book's title and author as well as your name, email address, and phone number. I will carefully review your comments and share them with the author and editors who worked on the book.

Email: feedback@samspublishing.com

Mail: Michael Stephens
           Executive Editor
           Sams Publishing
           201 West 103rd Street
           Indianapolis, IN 46290 USA

For more information about this book or another Sams title, visit our Web site at www.samspublishing.com. Type the ISBN (excluding hyphens) or the title of a book in the Search field to find the page you're looking for.

Introduction

Welcome to the second edition of the *Microsoft SQL Server DBA Survival Guide*! Not only is SQL Server 2000 the best RDBMS ever released by Microsoft, We think you'll find that this is the best and most complete edition of the *Microsoft SQL Server DBA Survival Guide*! This is the second edition of the *SQL Server 2000 Survival Guide*, so we have been able to review and add new material based on our experience with the 2000 product since the products release. In this edition, we have added several step-by-step exercises, which actually walk you through real-world DBA scenarios such as performing backup and recoveries or data transformation services. We have also expanded the Frequently Asked Question (FAQ) section at the end of each technical chapter to try and answer common questions that we have received via email or while working with the product ourselves. We also decided to get some help from contributing authors on some of the new SQL Server 2000 features, which allowed us to focus on some of the core topics while allowing others to focus on a single topic to bring you a better survival guide.

We really do appreciate the emails, feedback, and praise we have received from the previous editions—Keep them coming!

Mark Spenik and Orryn Sledge

The Goals of This Book

The trick to becoming a good Microsoft DBA is to become familiar with the graphical front end, to understand what happens behind the scenes (that is, what happens when you push a particular button), and to have a good understanding of the product and your job. The goals of this book are as follows:

- To provide the knowledge and know-how to administrate a SQL Server database

- To appeal to all levels of DBAs: beginner, intermediate, and experienced

- To appeal to all levels of developers: beginner, intermediate, and experienced

- Offer any tips, tricks, and suggestions buried deep within the documentation

- Offer real-world insight and experience and to pass on any tips, tricks, or suggestions learned the hard way

- Provide checklists and examples for SQL Server DBA tasks

- Provide conventions and naming standards

- Provide insight into the tasks that make up a DBA's job description

The Organization of the Book

Not sure what a DBA is or what the responsibilities of a DBA are? Chapter 1, "Role of the Database Administrator," is for you.

Chapter 2, "SQL Server Overview," provides a high-level overview of SQL 2000 and its capabilities.

Chapter 4, "Planning an Installation or Upgrade," covers the planning steps required before you attempt a SQL Server upgrade or installation. Do you have all your bases covered in the event an upgrade fails? This chapter covers this topic and many more. Chapter 5, "Installing or Upgrading SQL Server," discusses the actual installation and upgrade process.

Chapter 6, "Enterprise Management Processes," provides a high-level explanation of the types of tasks that can be performed through the Enterprise Manager.

Need to configure SQL Server? Well not really with SQL Server 2000, but because there are still a few knobs to turn, check out Chapter 7, "Configuring and Tuning SQL Server."

Chapter 8, "Managing Databases," explains how to create, manage, and delete a database. The chapter includes a discussion about transaction logs and data files.

Chapter 9, "Managing SQL Server Users and Security," discusses user management and data security, which are quite different from previous versions of SQL Server.

Curious on how to use your backups to recover a database? Wonder how SQL Server 2000 has simplified the backup and recovery process? What happens if a database fails after a backup? Can you provide up-to-the-minute recovery? These are standard questions all new DBAs are faced with. See Chapter 10, "Backup and Recovery."

Can't get BCP to work? You're not alone—almost every DBA hits a snag or two when trying to work with BCP. Chapter 14, "Using BCP and Bulk Insert," discusses in detail how BCP works and provides numerous tips and examples on how to make BCP work.

Having performance problems with SQL Server? Look at Chapter 15, "Troubleshooting SQL Server."

New to relational databases? Chapter 17, "Database Design Issues," provides information on database design issues. Do indexes have you all tangled up? If so, don't miss Chapter 18, "Understanding Indexes."

Chapter 19, "Query Optimization," explains in easy-to-understand vernacular the inner workings of SQL Server's cost-based optimizer. When transactions are slow to process or you are experiencing blocking or deadlocks, you will want to refer to the tips and tricks in this chapter. Knowing how to read a showplan is a key element to diagnosing query performance problems. The hard part about reading a showplan is knowing what to look for because a lot of cryptic information is generated. This chapter explains what to look for in the output generated by a showplan, what the output really means, and how to improve performance based on showplan information.

I think every DBA has seen an application that runs fine when a single user is logged in to the system, but when multiple users log on, the system bogs down. With multi-user applications, issues such as blocking and deadlocks must be addressed. Chapter 20, "Multiuser Considerations," offers solutions that can reduce the headaches associated with a multiuser system. Be sure to read up on SQL Server 2000's new dynamic locking feature.

Do you want to learn more about stored procedures and cursors? Look at Chapter 22, "Using Stored Procedures and Cursors." This chapter provides a detailed discussion on these two topics and includes several examples the DBA can use to automate common tasks. Don't know SQL very well? Review the SQL primer in Chapter 21, "SQL Essentials."

What would a book be nowadays without a chapter on the Internet? See Chapter 23, "SQL Server 2000 and the Internet," to learn how to use Microsoft SQL Server to create Web pages.

SQL Server provides numerous tools to help diagnose and isolate bottlenecks. The secret is knowing how to effectively use these tools. For example, the Performance Monitor allows you to monitor over 40 different SQL Server counters and several hundred different operating system counters. Which counters do you look at? Chapter 24, "Monitoring SQL Server," guides you in the right direction if you are wondering which Performance Monitor counters you should analyze.

You already know that OLE is included with SQL Server, but what can you do with it? Chapter 26, "Using SQL-DMO," walks through the construction of an application that helps simplify database administration task using Visual Basic.

Not sure what Microsoft SQL Server's replication is all about? Having trouble installing the distribution database? Not sure what an updating subscriber is? Want to learn how to create disconnected applications using two-way merge replication? Want to know the difference between one-way and two-way replication? The DBA Survival Guide has got you covered with three chapters dedicated to SQL Server 200 replication (Chapters 27–29).

Not sure what data warehousing is or unfamiliar with the data warehousing terminology? See Chapter 30, "Introduction to Datawarehousing." Need to get information from other systems into your data warehouse? Check out Chapter 13, "Data Transformation Services." And above all, look at Chapter 31, "SQL 2000 Analysis Services."

Conventions Used in This Book

The following conventions are used in this book:

The `computer font` is used for commands, parameters, statements, and text you see onscreen.

A **`boldfaced computer font`** indicates text you type.

Italics indicate new terms or items of emphasis.

NOTE

Notes provide additional information pertinent to the current subject matter.

TIP

Tips offer useful hints and information.

CAUTION

Caution boxes present warnings and describe the consequences of particular actions.

STRANGER THAN FICTION!

Some say that truth is stranger than fiction. These boxes offer fun facts to know and tell that *are* stranger than fiction!

Web Site

Instead of including a CD with examples and other information, the *Microsoft SQL Server 2000 DBA Survival Guide* now has a Web site where you can download the information and find any updates to the book or useful tips. The web site for the book is `http://www.samspublishing.com`. Besides useful tips and updates to the book you will also find the following items on the web site for downloading:

- The SQL Server DBA Assistant
- SQL DTS Packages (from Chapter 13 "Data Transformation Services"

The SQL Server DBA Assistant

The SQL Server DBA Assistant is an application written in 32-bit Visual Basic 6.0. Using the SQL Server Assistant, you can perform the following tasks:

- Populate a combo box with database names

- Allow exporting of data using graphical BCP

- Perform table maintenance functions, including recompiling references, updating statistics checking identity column values, and using the DBCC `CheckTable` command

NOTE

The code in the application is discussed in detail in Chapter 26, "Using SQL-DMO."

Following are the prerequisites for using the SQL Server DBA Assistant:

- You must be running Windows NT 4.0, Windows 2000, Windows XP, or Windows 95/98.

- You must have the following files (included with the SQL Server Client Utilities Installation):

  `SQLDMO.HLP`—SQL-DMO help files, including object hierarchy

  `SQLDMO.DLL`—In-process SQL-DMO server

  `SQLDMO.rll`—Local resource file (Note: extension varies)

PART I

Overview

IN THIS PART

1 Role of the Database Administrator

2 SQL Server Overview

3 The Evolution of SQL Server

1

Role of the Database Administrator

by Mark Spenik

In this chapter, you learn about the person who manages and maintains relational database management systems (RDBMS), the database administrator (DBA). Just as SQL Server has evolved from the days of 4.21 to 2000, the role of the DBA has also evolved. SQL Server 2000 greatly simplifies many DBA tasks, such as backups, maintenance, and server configuration. SQL Server 2000 provides services that enable a DBA to easily set up jobs shared across multiple servers, so a single DBA can handle more database servers. However, although common DBA tasks have been eliminated or simplified, the role of the SQL Server 2000 DBA is more challenging than ever before. SQL Server 2000 runs on Windows 95, Windows NT 4.0, Windows 2000, Windows XP, and Windows 98 and can be used as the default engine for Microsoft Access, all of which will surely increase the number of SQL Servers in your organization. SQL Server 2000 adds advanced features like Heterogeneous Distributed queries, two-way update replication (merge), Data Transformation Services, federated database servers, and Data Warehousing!

This is a lot of information for a single person to be responsible for, but this chapter will help you learn the responsibilities of a DBA. Let's start by looking at the traditional role of a DBA and then examine the added responsibilities of SQL Server 2000. But first, acquaint yourself with the type of tasks and different roles required to maintain a simple network as shown in Figure 1.1.

IN THIS CHAPTER

- Hardware
- Network
- Operating Systems
- File/Print Server
- Database Server
- Who Does What?
- What Is a Database Administrator?
- Who Are the DBAs?
- DBA Responsibilities
- Tricks of the Trade
- How the DBA Interacts with Other Team Members

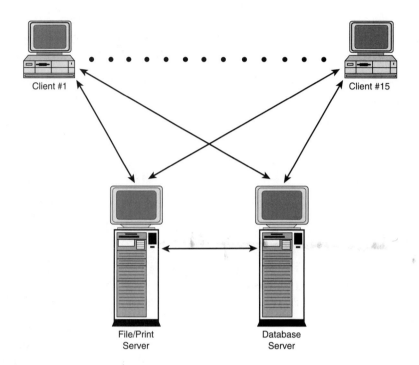

FIGURE 1.1   A small client/server network.

Hardware

Figure 1.1 shows a total of 15 client machines and 2 servers. Someone must be responsible for maintaining the physical machines to ensure that they are continually running. This person is responsible for routine maintenance and upgrades, such as adding more disk space and memory and installing or upgrading software packages.

Network

The 15 client machines communicate with the two servers over the *network*. The network consists of the hardware and software that ties all the machines together and includes the cabling, routers, repeaters, and network protocols (TCP/IP, Named Pipes, SPX/IPX, and so on). Again, someone must make sure that the network stays up and running. If the network goes down, none of the machines can talk to each other.

Operating Systems

All machines—clients and servers—use some sort of *operating system*. Because this is a book about Windows SQL Server, you can safely assume that the servers shown in Figure 1.1 are running Microsoft operating systems (Windows NT or Windows 2000) and that the clients are running Microsoft Windows, Microsoft Windows NT Workstation, Windows 2000 Professional, or Windows XP. Each client and server machine must be properly configured and set up.

File/Print Server

The *file/print server* needs general maintenance, backups, and upgrades to protect against the loss of data. Someone must be responsible for adding user accounts, installing new applications, and maintaining the stability of the file/print servers. After all, if the file and print server go down, users cannot perform their jobs.

Database Server

The *database server* requirements are similar to those of the file/print server. The difference is that the administration occurs with the RDBMS package. The database server must be set up and tuned correctly to produce the best performance. Database server tuning has been simplified quite a bit in SQL Server 2000, reducing the workload of a DBA. However the most important job of a DBA, protecting the data, remains. The data in the databases must be protected; if data is lost, your company could lose millions! It's the responsibility of the DBA to recover lost databases (under pressure and with peering eyes, of course!). Managing database security is another chief responsibility of the DBA. The DBA is responsible for adding users and restricting or permitting users and groups to view information in the database. Additional SQL Server 2000 capabilities, such as replication and data warehousing, add further responsibilities to the DBA.

Who Does What?

You might notice that even for a small network, there seems to be a lot of jobs and responsibilities behind keeping the whole network running. Imagine an enterprise network 10 to 100 times the size of the relatively small network used in this example with thousands of internal users and Internet users! So, who is responsible for which task? The answer to who does what can become quite complex because the size of an organization and the size of the enterprise network dictates who is responsible for each task. In some organizations, a single individual might wear many different hats. In other organizations, an individual's job might be more specialized. Roles and responsibilities are assigned from the company management. The following sections examine some of the general job titles and the responsibilities that accompany each position.

PC and Tech Support

The PC and tech support group is responsible for maintaining and setting up the hardware on the different client machines and sometimes on the server machines. If a new software package is installed or more disk space or memory must be added, the PC and tech support group is called in.

Network Administrator

The network administrator is responsible for maintaining the network. A network administrator makes sure that all the hardware components are working correctly and that the networking software is set up correctly. In many cases, the network administrator is also responsible for maintaining the network operating system.

System Administrator

The system administrator is responsible for maintaining the many different servers in the organization. The responsibilities include backup and recovery, maintaining user access and security, scheduling task and batch runs, and upgrading and maintaining the operating system.

Webmaster

The Webmaster is a recent addition to the project team. The Webmaster maintains various company Web sites (Internet or intranet). He is responsible for Web server maintenance and in many cases for setting standards, maintaining sites, and adding content produced by others to the production servers. Many Web-based applications build dynamic Web pages by pulling information from a database, so DBAs should expect to work with the Webmaster to provide him with the database access required for the Web-based applications.

Database Administrator

There is a lot more to being a DBA than just being responsible for the data; that is what you will concentrate on for the rest of the chapter!

> **NOTE**
>
> You might notice that a fine line separates job responsibilities (where one job starts and ends), such as the possible overlap of the network administrator and the system administrator. Depending on their size, most organizations divide the work realistically (that is, no one person has too many responsibilities). One of the most important things to remember is that it takes a team effort to keep a network healthy. Cooperation among the different individuals is a must.

What Is a Database Administrator?

In a very general sense, a *database administrator* is the individual responsible for maintaining the RDBMS system (in this book, Microsoft SQL Server). The DBA has many different responsibilities, but the overall goal of the DBA is to keep the server up at all times and to provide users with access to the required information when they need it. The DBA makes sure that the database is protected and that any chance of data loss is minimized.

Who Are the DBAs?

Who are the DBAs and how do you become one? A DBA can be someone who, from the start, has concentrated in the area of database design and administration. A DBA can be a programmer who, by default or by volunteering, took over the responsibility of maintaining a SQL Server during project development and enjoyed the job so much that he switched. A DBA can be a system administrator who was given the added responsibility of maintaining a SQL Server. DBAs can even come from unrelated fields, such as accounting or the help desk, and switch to Information Systems to become DBAs. To start your journey to becoming a Microsoft SQL Server DBA, you need the following:

- A good understanding of Microsoft Windows operating systems

- Knowledge of Structured Query Language (SQL)

- Sound database design

- General understanding of network architectures (for example, client/server, Internet/intranet, enterprise)

- Knowledge of Microsoft SQL Server

TIP

If you are part of a technical team looking for a Microsoft SQL Server DBA, do yourself a favor and volunteer. It is a great job; good DBAs are in demand and typically are paid more than developers.

DBA Responsibilities

The following sections examine the responsibilities of the database administrator and how they translate to various Microsoft SQL Server tasks.

Installing and Upgrading a SQL Server

The DBA is responsible for installing a SQL Server or upgrading an existing SQL Server. In the case of upgrading a SQL Server, the DBA is responsible for ensuring that if the upgrade is not successful, the SQL Server can be rolled back to an earlier release until the upgrade issues can be resolved. The DBA is also responsible for applying SQL Server service packs. A *service pack* is not a true upgrade, but an installation of the current version of software with various bug fixes and patches that have been resolved since the product's release.

Monitoring the Database Server's Health and Tuning Accordingly

Monitoring the health of the database server means making sure that the following is done:

- The server is running with optimal performance.

- The error log or event log is monitored for database errors.

- Databases have routine maintenance performed on them, and the overall system has periodic maintenance performed by the system administrator.

Using Storage Properly

SQL Server 2000 enables you to automatically grow the size of your databases and transaction logs, or you can choose to select a fixed size for the database and transaction log. Either way, maintaining the proper use of storage means monitoring space requirements and adding new storage space (disk drives) when required.

Performing Backup and Recovery Duties

Backup and recovery are the DBA's most critical tasks; they include the following aspects:

- Establishing standards and schedules for database backups

- Developing recovery procedures for each database

- Making sure that the backup schedules meet the recovery requirements

Managing Database Users and Security

With SQL Server 2000, the DBA works closely with the Windows NT administrator to add user NT logins to the database. In non-NT domains, the DBA adds user logins. The DBA is also responsible for assigning users to databases and determining the proper security level for each user. Within each database, the DBA is responsible for assigning permissions to the various database objects such as tables, views, and stored procedures.

Working with Developers

It is important for the DBA to work closely with development teams to assist in overall database design, such as creating normalized databases, helping developers tune queries, assigning proper indexes, and aiding developers in the creation of triggers and stored procedures. In the SQL Server 2000 environment, a good DBA will show the developers how to use and take advantage of the SQL Server Index Tuning Wizard and the SQL Server profiler.

> **TIP**
>
> I have too often seen DBAs who were content to sit back and watch developers make bad design and SQL Server decisions. I have also seen situations in which the DBA wanted to be involved in design decisions, but management prevented it because it was not the DBA's job. Don't be underutilized. If you are in this situation, show your management this tip! Take an active role in new project development. The entire team will benefit from your insight and knowledge!

Establishing and Enforcing Standards

The DBA should establish naming conventions and standards for the SQL Server and databases and make sure that everyone sticks to them.

Transferring Data

The DBA is responsible for importing and exporting data to and from the SQL Server. In the current trend to downsize and combine client/server systems with mainframe systems and Web technologies to create enterprise systems, importing data from the mainframe to SQL Server is a common occurrence that is about to become more common with the SQL Server 2000 Data Transformation Services (DTS). Good DTS DBAs will be in hot demand as companies struggle to move and translate legacy systems to enterprise systems.

Replicating Data

SQL Server 2000 has many different replication capabilities such as Merge replication (two-way disconnected replication) and queued replication. Managing and setting up replication topologies is a big undertaking for a DBA because of the complexities involved.

Data Warehousing

SQL Server 2000 has substantial data warehousing capabilities that require the DBA to learn an additional product (the Microsoft OLAP Server) and architecture. Data warehousing provides new and interesting challenges to the DBA and in some companies a new career as a warehouse specialist.

Scheduling Events

The database administrator is responsible for setting up and scheduling various events using Windows NT and SQL Server to aid in performing many tasks such as backups and replication.

Capacity Planning

The database administrator is responsible for capacity planning, which is making sure that the current servers have enough disk space and processing power to handle current and future business requirements. This is accomplished by monitoring the health and performance of the database servers and projecting and forecasting the potential growth and space requirements and current and future loads on the database servers based on current growth and performance patterns. DBAs will often recommend additional hardware or new database servers based on trends discovered while doing capacity planning.

Providing 24-Hour Access

The database server must stay up, and the databases must always be protected and online. Be prepared to perform some maintenance and upgrades after hours. Also be prepared to carry that dreaded beeper. If the database server should go down, be ready to get the server up and running. After all, that's your job.

Learning Constantly

To be a good DBA, you must continue to study and practice your mission-critical procedures, such as testing your backups by recovering to a test database. In this business, technology changes very fast, so you must continue learning about SQL Server, available client/servers, and database design tools. It is a neverending process.

Does It Pay to Be a DBA?

Okay, so here is a topic that was skipped in previous editions of the book: Does it pay to be a DBA? And how much? Well, it definitely does pay to be a DBA! DBAs continue to be in demand (like all IS professionals). SQL Server 2000 has the capability to increase Microsoft's RDBMS market share, which should mean a greater demand for SQL Server DBAs. DBAs tend to make more than your standard or great developer (but less than the gurus). Of course, this is always subject to change, but it has been true for the past several years.

So what are DBAs paid? It really would not be fair to put out a dollar figure because it varies from city to city and by the time this book has been published, it will have already changed. Ask around in some of the Internet user groups and check various salary surveys for your region and years of experience. You can find salary surveys at several Web-based job sites like http://www.salary.com, http://www.monster.com, or http://www.dice.com. But DBAs make good money. DBAs who possess one or more of the following skills will be in hot demand and can require top dollar for their services:

- Data Warehousing (HOT, HOT, HOT)
- Data Transformation Services
- Replication Architecture

Tricks of the Trade

Now that you understand the different responsibilities of a DBA, how can you learn the tricks of the trade? You are off to a good start by reading this book. The following sections examine some other ways to learn the tricks of the trade.

Classes and Training

Taking a Microsoft-certified SQL Server training class is very good way to get started. Find a class that gives you hands-on classroom training. The class can introduce you to many of the concepts and procedures required to maintain SQL Server. To find out about authorized Microsoft SQL Server training centers near you, call 1-800-SOL-PROV and ask for information on Microsoft Solution Provider Authorized Technical Education Centers. On the Internet, go to http://www.microsoft.com/mcp.

> **TIP**
>
> If you go to a class, make sure that when you return, you immediately start practicing what you learned in class. Most classes last three to five days; to retain the information, you must use it immediately.

On the Job

The real DBA training occurs on the job; that is where many DBAs learn. On-the-job training can be difficult when you are the only one learning a system with which no one else is familiar. Although some people have the luxury of a seasoned DBA to teach them the ropes, ultimately, all DBAs learn on the job.

TIP

Practice, practice, practice. Constantly practice different procedures and tasks, such as backing up and recovering data or importing data on a nonproduction server. When the day comes to perform the task, you will be well prepared.

Microsoft TechNet, Microsoft Developers Network, and Internet News Group

Take advantage of the vast knowledge base of articles Microsoft makes available on the TechNet and Microsoft Developers Network (MSDN) CDs. Many times, you can solve a problem simply by searching the two CDs (or DVDs) for the problem and possible resolution. You get online help by accessing the SQL Server News Group on the Internet. On the News Group, you can post problems and get help from other DBAs, or you can scan through the various messages posted and learn how to solve problems you have not yet encountered.

> The Microsoft SQL Server News Group can be found at
> `http://www.msdn.microsoft.com/sqlserver`.
>
> Microsoft's Web page for SQL Server is `http://www.Microsoft.com/SQL`.
>
> You can learn more about Microsoft TechNet by navigating the Internet to
> `http://www.microsoft.com/technet`.
>
> To learn more about the Microsoft Developers Network (MSDN), go to
> `http://www.msdn.microsoft.com`.

Magazines and Books

Subscribe to various database magazines that keep you abreast of topics such as the latest database design and development tools, relational database concepts, and SQL Server. Also search the bookstore for books on database design and SQL Server (like this book). Pinnacle Publishing publishes a magazine called the *Microsoft SQL Server Professional*; it can be accessed on the Internet at `http://www.pinnaclepublishing.com/sql`, or by fax at 1-206-251-5057. Another magazine that provides very good articles on SQL Server is *SQL Server Magazine*; reach the publishers at 1-800-621-1544 or on the Internet at `http://www.sqlmag.com`.

Certification

Microsoft offers certification for SQL Server DBAs in the form of the Microsoft Certified Database Administrator (MCDBA). I highly recommend certification for DBAs. Certification shows a potential or current employer that you have the basic knowledge to be a DBA. It is strongly recommended that you take the test to become certified. Certification does not replace experience and training, but it points out possible weaknesses in your understanding of SQL Server and gives you credibility (because you understand the concepts and procedures to maintain SQL Server). The requirements for the certification test change frequently, so the best way to learn about the MCDBA certification is to go to `http://www.microsoft.com/mcp`. To help you study and practice for the various tests, I highly recommend the Transcender tests, which are a series of computerized test that simulates the actual exams. You can learn more about Transcender tests at `http://www.transcender.com`.

TIP

We are often asked, "What do I need to do to pass certification? Will this book help?" Of course this book will help! Here are some words of advice about the certification test: Before taking the test, review the test outline for SQL Server (which is part of the Certification Roadmap). The certification test asks questions on only the topics listed in the test outline. Make sure that you are familiar with each of the topics.

Although managing a Microsoft SQL Server is a graphical experience, the test is likely to ask you about the command to create a database (instead of how to create a database using the Enterprise Manager). Make sure that you are familiar with the commands required to perform various administrative tasks.

Last, but not least, take the practice test that comes with the Certification Roadmap. The practice test gives you a general idea of the types of questions asked on the test. Do not take the real test until you do well on the practice test.

Internet

As you can tell from the previous sections, one of the best resources for SQL Server information is the Internet. Appendix C, "SQL Server Resources," provides you with a list of useful resources, especially Internet resources.

How the DBA Interacts with Other Team Members

Now that you have decided to become a DBA, how will you interact with other team members such as the system administrator, network administrator, developers, and users? Many times, these relationships are hard to determine because each organization has people filling one or many different roles. Based on earlier job descriptions, however, the following sections quickly examine the types of interaction you can expect.

System Administrator and Network Administrator

A DBA's interaction with the network administrator is mostly concerned with the type of network protocols that can be used and the network address or port number that can be used for the server. If users are complaining about query times and SQL Server is executing the queries very fast, you and the network administrator should examine possible networking problems.

The interaction of the system administrator and the DBA is much tighter than the interaction of the network administrator and the DBA. The system administrator is responsible for tuning the Windows server on which your SQL Server runs. The system administrator is responsible for adding the hard drives and storage space required for your databases. If you choose to use integrated user security with SQL Server, you must work with the system administrator to set up the correct Windows user accounts and groups. The different types of backup and recovery procedures for the Windows Server and the SQL Server should be worked out by both parties because, in some cases, the system administrator might have to restore a system drive that contains a database or database backup.

Developers

The interaction of DBAs with developers is where the greatest differences in organizations' definitions of a DBA are found. In some organizations, the DBA works very closely with the developers; in other organizations, the DBAs work very little with the developers and are stuck maintaining the developers' systems and designs without any input. To perform most efficiently, the DBA should work closely with the developers. After all, the DBA is the one maintaining the database side of the application, and in many cases, the DBA has the most experience in relational database design and tuning. The DBA should design, aid, or review any and all database designs for the organization. The DBA should also assist developers in selecting proper indexes and optimizing queries and stored procedures, as well as provide a source of information to the developers.

Users

In most organizations, the DBA's interaction with the users of the system is limited to user account maintenance, security, and database recovery requirements.

Summary

The role of the database administrator is very important in an organization. The job can be challenging and exciting. If you are a DBA or want to be a DBA, remember that it is important to constantly study SQL Server and database tools. Become certified and practice your backup and recovery procedures. The following is a list of the many duties and responsibilities of a DBA:

- Installing and upgrading SQL Server
- Applying SQL Server service packs

- Monitoring the database server's health and tuning it accordingly
- Using storage properly
- Backing up and recovering data
- Managing database users and security
- Establishing and enforcing standards
- Performing data transfer
- Setting up and maintaining data replication
- Data warehousing
- Setting up server scheduling
- Providing 24-hour access
- Working with development teams
- Learning!

2

SQL Server Overview

by Orryn Sledge

IN THIS CHAPTER

- Architecture
- Operating System Integration
- Visual Administration Tools
- SQL Server Companion Products
- Nonvisual Administration Tools and Command-Line Tools
- Common SQL Server Objects
- FAQ

SQL Server is a high-performance relational database system that is tightly integrated with the Windows operating systems. This arrangement allows SQL Server to take advantage of the features provided by the operating system. SQL Server is an excellent choice for meeting the challenging needs of today's complex client/server systems.

This chapter is designed to provide a broad overview of SQL Server's tools and features. Those new to SQL Server should use this chapter to gain a basic understanding of SQL Server's fundamental components.

Architecture

SQL Server's integration with the operating system provides the following important features:

- Symmetric multiprocessing (SMP)
- Portability
- Network independence
- Reliability

Symmetric Multiprocessing (SMP)

SMP allows SQL Server to increase performance through the use of additional processors. When running the Enterprise Edition of SQL Server 2000 on Windows 2000 Datacenter, it can effectively scale up to 32 processors and support up to 64GB of RAM. SQL Server can automatically run a query, in parallel, on two or more processors. All this occurs without user interaction; it also relieves administrators from the complexities of managing multiple processors.

NOTE

The Windows 9x version of SQL Server does not provide SMP support.

Operating System Support

SQL Server can run on numerous operating systems. SQL Server 2000 supports the operating systems shown in Table 2.1.

TABLE 2.1   Supported Operating Systems

SQL Server 2000 Version	Supported Operating System
Enterprise Edition	Windows 2000 Server, Windows 2000 Advanced Server, Windows 2000 Data Center Server, Microsoft Windows NT Server 4.0, and Microsoft Windows NT Server Enterprise Edition 4.0.
Standard Edition	Windows 2000 Server, Windows 2000 Advanced Server, Windows 2000 Data Center Server Microsoft Windows NT Server 4.0, and Microsoft Windows NT Server Enterprise Edition.
Personal Edition	Microsoft Windows XP, Windows Me, Windows 98, Windows NT Workstation 4.0, Windows 2000 Professional, Microsoft Windows NT Server 4.0, Windows 2000 Server.
Developer Edition	Microsoft Windows NT Workstation 4.0, Windows 2000 Professional, and all other Windows NT and Windows 2000 operating systems.
Client Tools only	Windows 2000, Microsoft Windows NT 4.0, Windows XP, Windows Me, and Windows 98.
Connectivity only	Windows 2000, Microsoft Windows NT 4.0, Windows XP, Windows Me, Windows 98, and Windows 95.

NOTE

In case you were wondering whether you could run SQL Server 2000 on that old 486 machine that has been lying around and collecting dust, the answer is no. The minimum processor requirement, as specified by Microsoft, is a Pentium 166 with 64MB of RAM. Maybe it's time to turn that old computer into something useful, such as a doorstop or yard art.

Network Independence

The Windows 2000 and the Windows 9x operating systems support several different types of network protocols. This level of support extends to the client-side connectivity of SQL Server. This enables you to choose the network protocol that best fits your present and future needs. TCP/IP, IPX/SPX, named pipes, AppleTalk, and Banyan Vines are currently supported.

Reliability

Windows 2000 and SQL Server provide crash protection, memory management, preemptive scheduling, and remote management. These types of features enable you to keep SQL Server up and running 24 hours a day, 7 days a week.

NOTE

Microsoft Cluster Server (MSCS, formerly known as Wolfpack) provides failover support for SQL Server 2000. This product provides an additional level of support for those organizations that require 100% up time. MSCS is an add-on product for Windows 2000 and is not included with SQL Server 2000.

Operating System Integration

SQL Server is designed to take advantage of the Windows 2000 and Windows 9x operating systems. This means that several common NT and Windows 9x components provide additional functionality to SQL Server.

NOTE

The majority of the topics discussed in this section are specific to the Windows 2000 version of SQL Server. The Windows 9x version provides similar operating system functionality.

Taskbar Integration

The status of SQL Server, SQL Server Service Manager, Microsoft DTC, and Microsoft Search are integrated with the taskbar in Windows 2000 and Windows 9x. From the taskbar, you can also start and stop the services listed.

Control Panel

SQL Server (MSSQLServer), SQL Server Agent (SQLServerAgent), Distributed Transaction Coordinator (MSDTC), and Microsoft Search (MSSearch) are defined as services in the NT Control Panel (see Figure 2.1). You use the Control Panel to start, stop, and monitor the status of SQL Server, SQL Server Agent, Distributed Transaction Coordinator, and Microsoft Search.

Event Viewer

The *Event Viewer* allows administrators to view and track information pertaining to SQL Server(see Figure 2.2). SQL Server logs the following types of messages to the Event Viewer: information, errors, and warnings.

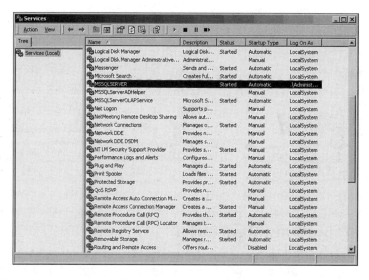

FIGURE 2.1 Integration with the Windows 2000 Control Panel.

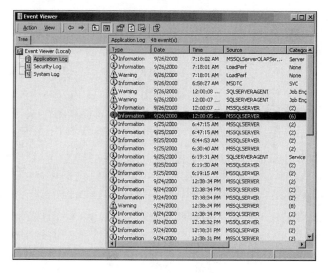

FIGURE 2.2 The Event Viewer.

TIP

In the Event Viewer, you can control the size of the event log. To control its size, right-click and select the Properties menu option. The Log Properties dialog box appears. From this dialog box, you can specify a maximum log size and the overwrite behavior.

Also, from within SQL Server, you can write your own messages to the event log. Use the extended stored procedure xp_logevent, as in the following syntax:

```
xp_logevent error_number, message, [severity]
```

The Registry

SQL Server configuration information is stored in a database called the *Registry*. To view and edit the Registry, run REGEDIT.EXE (see Figure 2.3). Normally, your software automatically maintains the Registry. You should change information in the Registry only when absolutely necessary. Otherwise, you might inadvertently introduce errors into your software and operating system.

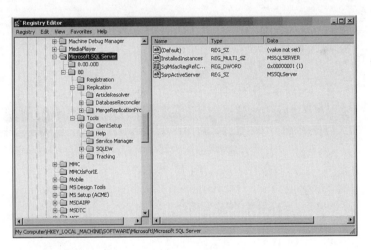

FIGURE 2.3 The Registry.

Following is the Registry key to SQL Server 2000:

```
HKEY_LOCAL_MACHINE
 \SOFTWARE
 \Microsoft
 \Microsoft SQL Server
```

NT User Accounts

Through *Windows 2000 Authentication,* SQL Server can use Windows 2000 user accounts and passwords (see Figure 2.4). This means that a single user account can be used to control access to NT and SQL Server. This significantly reduces account maintenance, eliminates duplication, and simplifies login procedures.

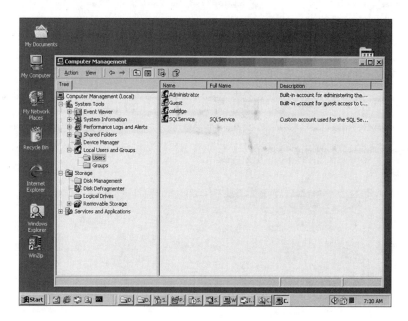

FIGURE 2.4   NT user accounts.

For more information on user accounts and *Windows 2000 Authentication,* see Chapter 9, "Managing SQL Server Users and Security."

Performance Monitor

The *Performance Monitor* provides graphical statistics about the performance of SQL Server and Windows 2000 (see Figure 2.5). For more information about using the Performance Monitor, see Chapter 24, "Monitoring SQL Server."

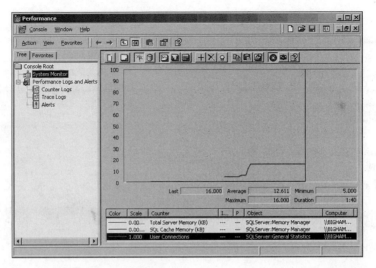

FIGURE 2.5   The Performance Monitor.

Visual Administration Tools

A primary goal of SQL Server 2000 is to provide administrators with easy-to-use graphical administration tools. The ease with which someone can administer SQL Server 2000 is a testimony to the success of Microsoft's development efforts.

The following tools enable you to easily set up, administer, and interact with SQL Server.

SQL Server Service Manager

From the SQL Server Service Manager, you can start, stop, and pause SQL Server, SQL Server Agent, Microsoft Distributed Transaction Coordinator, and Microsoft Search (see Figure 2.6).

FIGURE 2.6   The SQL Server Service Manager.

TIP

What is the purpose of the Pause button in the SQL Server Service Manager? This is a commonly asked question. By pausing the server, you can prevent users from logging in to SQL Server while still keeping it up and running. This makes the feature useful when you want to halt users from making new connections but allow existing connections to continue processing; it also allows users a chance to log off normally before bringing down the database.

NOTE

The SQL Server service can also be started through the Control Panel or from the command line by using the command `NET START MSSQLSERVER`. Additionally, SQL Server can be started independently from the Control Panel by running `SQLSERVR.EXE` from the command prompt (see Chapter 5, "Installing or Upgrading SQL Server," for more information on starting and stopping SQL Server).

SQL Server Enterprise Manager

As an administrator, you will probably spend the majority of your time interacting with SQL Server through the SQL Server Enterprise Manager. This is where you can administer multiple database servers through a single interface (see Figure 2.7).

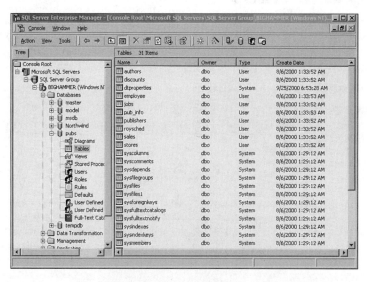

FIGURE 2.7   The SQL Server Enterprise Manager.

Using the Enterprise Manager, you can perform the following functions:

- Start, configure, or shut down the following services— SQL Server, SQL Agent, SQL Mail, Distributed Transaction Coordinator, and Microsoft Search
- Manage backups
- Manage databases
- Manage database maintenance tasks
- Manage logins and permissions
- Manage replication
- Manage tables, views, stored procedures, triggers, indexes, rules, defaults, and user-defined data types
- Schedule tasks
- Generate Web pages
- Generate SQL scripts

SQL Server Query Analyzer

SQL Server Query Analyzer is the Windows-based product used to execute SQL scripts (see Figure 2.8). The product also provides a color-coded query editor and a graphical execution plan. It does not provide graphical administration (use the SQL Server Enterprise Manager for graphical administration).

Using SQL Server Query Analyzer, you can perform the following functions:

- Execute and debug SQL statements
- Analyze query plans
- Display query statistics
- Perform index analysis

SQL Server Setup

Through SQL Setup, you can perform the following functions (see Figure 2.9):

- Set up SQL Server
- Configure an existing SQL Server installation
- Remove SQL Server

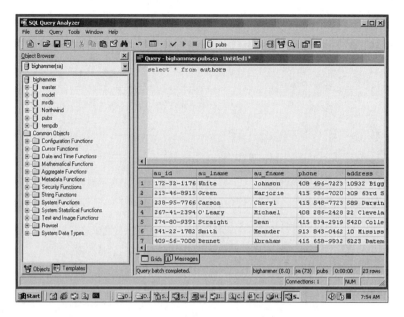

FIGURE 2.8   The SQL Server Query Analyzer.

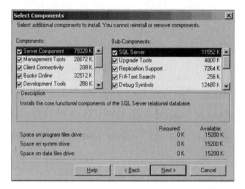

FIGURE 2.9   The SQL Server Setup.

SQL Server Network Utility

From the SQL Server Network Utility, you can perform the following functions (see Figure 2.10):

- Configure client-side connections
- Determine network library version information

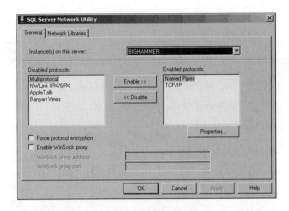

FIGURE 2.10　The SQL Server Network Utility.

SQL Server Profiler

SQL Server Profiler is a graphical tool that displays Transact-SQL activity for a selected server (see Figure 2.11). SQL Server Profiler can be used by an administrator or developer to probe user activity and to generate audit trails. The output from SQL Server Profiler can be saved as a script or as an activity log. See Chapter 24 for more information on SQL Server Profiler.

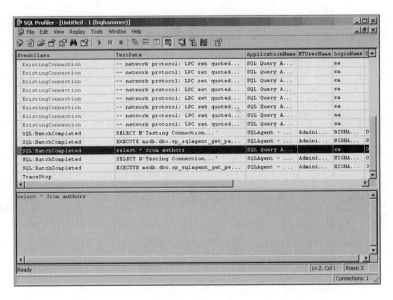

FIGURE 2.11　The SQL Server Profiler.

Version Upgrade Wizard

The Version Upgrade Wizard is used to upgrade 6.x databases to SQL Server 2000 (see Figure 2.12). This wizard exports the contents of a 6.x database and imports it into SQL Server 2000. Additionally, the wizard performs data- and object-level validation to ensure that the 6.x database is properly migrated to 2000. See Chapter 5 for more information on the Version Upgrade Wizard.

FIGURE 2.12   The Version Upgrade Wizard.

SQL Server Companion Products

SQL Server 2000 includes companion products that are designed to integrate with Microsoft's goals of simplifying data access and providing an integrated data warehousing solution. The following are the companion products:

- Microsoft English Query
- Analysis Services

Microsoft English Query

Microsoft English Query is a tool that can translate English syntax into SQL statements (see Figure 2.13). For example, a user can enter the following question: "Who wrote *The Gourmet Microwave?*" Microsoft English Query automatically translates the English syntax into the following SQL statement:

```
select distinct dbo.authors.au_fname as "First Name",
➡ dbo.authors.au_lname as "Last Name" from dbo.titles,
➡ dbo.titleauthor, dbo.authors where
➡dbo.titles.title='The Gourmet Microwave'
➡and dbo.titles.title_id=dbo.titleauthor.title_id
➡and dbo.titleauthor.au_id=dbo.authors.au_id
```

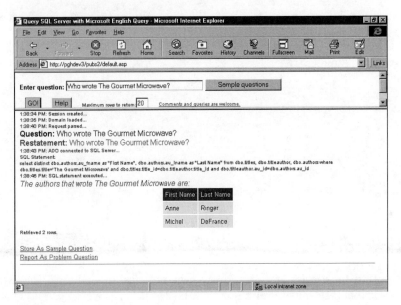

FIGURE 2.13   Microsoft English Query.

Analysis Services

With Analysis Services, you can build and manage OLAP databases that are used to perform multidimensional database analysis (see Figure 2.14). Dimensions, cubes, and partitions are key components of this OLAP product. See Chapter 31, "SQL 2000 Analysis Services," for more information on the OLAP Manager.

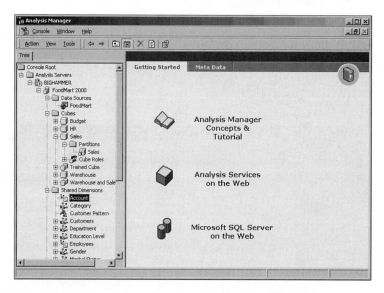

FIGURE 2.14   Analysis Services.

Nonvisual Administration Tools and Command-Line Tools

A DBA probably spends the majority of his or her time using the visual administration tools included with SQL Server. However, there are several nonvisual administration tools that a DBA might also use: BCP, ISQL, OSQL, TEXTCOPY, and ODBCPING.

BCP

BCP stands for *Bulk Copy Program.* It is a command-line utility that enables you to import and export data to and from SQL Server. The advantage of BCP is that it is fast. Users new to SQL Server are often amazed at how quickly it operates. The drawback of BCP is that it can be difficult to use.

By default, BCP.EXE is installed in the C:\Program Files\Microsoft SQL Server\MSSQL\Binn directory of SQL Server. The syntax for BCP is shown in Listing 2.1. For more information on BCP, see Chapter 14, "Using BCP and BULK INSERT."

LISTING 2.1   Syntax for BCP

```
bcp dbtable {in | out | format} datafile
    [-m maxerrors]              [-f formatfile]          [-e errfile]
    [-F firstrow]               [-L lastrow]             [-b batchsize]
    [-n native type]           [-c character type]       [-w wide character type]
    [-N keep non-text native] [-6 6x file format]        [-q quoted identifier]
    [-C code page specifier]  [-t field terminator]      [-r row terminator]
```

LISTING 2.1   Continued

```
[-i inputfile]              [-o outfile]              [-a packetsize]
[-S server name]            [-U username]             [-P password]
[-T trusted connection]     [-v version]
[-k keep null values]       [-E keep identity values]
[-h "load hints"]
```

NOTE

BCP switches are case sensitive.

ISQL

ISQL is a command-line utility used for executing queries. ISQL communicates with SQL Server through db-library. With the advent of graphical administration tools for SQL Server, the importance of ISQL has diminished. Most people prefer to perform day-to-day administration tasks from the SQL Server Enterprise Manager instead of using ISQL.

ISQL's minimal overhead, however, makes it useful for processing noninteractive routines such as nightly batch jobs.

By default, ISQL.EXE is installed in the `C:\Program Files\Microsoft SQL Server\MSSQL\Binn` directory. The syntax for ISQL is shown in Listing 2.2.

LISTING 2.2   Syntax for ISQL

```
isql [-U login id] [-e echo input] [-x max text size]
  [-p print statistics] [-b On error batch abort] [-n remove numbering]
  [-c cmdend] [-h headers] [-w columnwidth] [-s colseparator]
  [-m errorlevel] [-t query timeout] [-l login timeout]
  [-L list servers] [-a packetsize]
  [-H hostname] [-P password]
  [-q "cmdline query"] [-Q "cmdline query" and exit]
  [-S server] [-d use database name]
  [-r msgs to stderr] [-E trusted connection]
  [-i inputfile] [-o outputfile]
  [-O use Old ISQL behavior disables the following]
          <EOF> batch processing
          Auto console width scaling
          Wide messages
          default errorlevel is -1 vs 1
  [-? show syntax summary]
```

NOTE

ISQL switches are case sensitive.

OSQL

OSQL is a command-line utility used for executing queries. OSQL communicates with SQL Server through ODBC. OSQL is similar to ISQL except for the communication layer.

By default, OSQL.EXE is installed in the C:\Program Files\Microsoft SQL Server\MSSQL\Binn directory. The syntax for OSQL is shown in Listing 2.3.

LISTING 2.3   Syntax for OSQL

```
osql [-U login id]        [-P password]
  [-S server]             [-H hostname]          [-E trusted connection]
  [-d use database name] [-l login timeout]     [-t query timeout]
  [-h headers]            [-s colseparator]      [-w columnwidth]
  [-a packetsize]         [-e echo input]
  [-L list servers]       [-c cmdend]
  [-q "cmdline query"]    [-Q "cmdline query" and exit]
  [-n remove numbering]   [-m errorlevel]
  [-r msgs to stderr]
  [-i inputfile]          [-o outputfile]
  [-p print statistics]   [-b On error batch abort]
  [-O use Old ISQL behavior disables the following]
      <EOF> batch processing
      Auto console width scaling
      Wide messages
      default errorlevel is -1 vs 1
  [-? show syntax summary]
```

TEXTCOPY

TEXTCOPY is a command-line utility used for importing and exporting image files with SQL Server.

By default, TEXTCOPY.EXE is installed in the C:\Program Files\Microsoft SQL Server\MSSQL\Binn directory.

Following is the syntax for TEXTCOPY:

```
TEXTCOPY [/S [sqlserver]] [/U [login]] [/P [password]]
  [/D [database]] [/T table] [/C column] [/W"where clause"]
  [/F file] [{/I | /O}] [/K chunksize] [/Z] [/?]
```

Common SQL Server Objects

SQL Server uses the term *object* to describe a database component. Common database objects include tables, rules, defaults, user-defined data types, views, triggers, and stored procedures.

> **NOTE**
>
> Do not be mislead by the term *object*. SQL Server is *not* an object-oriented database.

Tables

A *table* is used to store data. It is organized in a row/column manner (see Figure 2.15). You can retrieve, modify, and remove data from a table by using the SQL language.

stor_id	stor_name	stor_address	city	state	zip	last_update
7066	Barnum's	567 Pasadena Ave.	Tustin	CA	92789	8/1/1995 4:25 PM
7067	News & Brews	577 First St.	Los Gatos	CA	96745	8/15/1995 3:00 PM
7131	Doc-U-Mat	24-A Avrogado Way	Remulade	WA	98014	3/11/1995 1:00 PM
8042	Bookbeat	679 Carson St.	Portland	CA	89076	4/25/1995 3:00 PM

FIGURE 2.15   An example of a table.

Rules

A *rule* is used to enforce a data constraint (see Figure 2.16). Rules are column specific and cannot perform table lookups. Generally, rules are used to enforce simple business constraints.

stor_id	stor_name	stor_address	city	state	zip	last_update
7066	Barnum's	567 Pasadena Ave.	Tustin	CA	92789	8/1/1995 4:25 PM
7067	News & Brews	577 First St.	Los Gatos	CA	96745	8/15/1995 3:00 PM
7131	Doc-U-Mat	24-A Avrogado Way	Remulade	WA	98014	3/11/1995 1:00 PM
8042	Bookbeat	679 Carson St.	Portland	CA	89076	4/25/1995 3:00 PM

Business Rule: All store ids must be between 1 and 9999.

SQL Server Translation: CREATE RULE stor_id_rule AS
@stor_id > = 1 AND @stor_id < = 9999

sp_bindrule stor_id_rule, 'stores. stor_id'

FIGURE 2.16   An example of a rule.

> **NOTE**
>
> An alternative to creating a rule is to use the CHECK constraint. Another alternative to creating a rule is to use a trigger.

Defaults

Defaults are used to populate a column with a default value when a value is not supplied (see Figure 2.17).

Business Rule: If store address is not known when adding a new record, enter "unknown."

SQL Server Translation: CREATE DEFAULT stor_address_default AS
'unknown'

sp_bindefault stor_address_default, 'stores, stor_address'

FIGURE 2.17   An example of defaults.

> **NOTE**
>
> An alternative to creating a default is to use the DEFAULT constraint.

User-Defined Data Types

With a *user-defined data type*, you can create a custom, reusable data type based on an existing SQL Server data type (see Figure 2.18). By implementing user-defined data types, you can ensure data type consistency.

Business Rule: Store id is an integer and can not be null.

SQL Server Translation: sp_addtype stor_id_data type, 'integer,' 'not null'

CREATE TABLE stores (stor_id stor_id_datatype,
stor_name char (35).

FIGURE 2.18   An example of a user-defined data type.

Views

A *view* is a virtual table that looks and feels like a real table. Views limit the amount of data a user can see and modify. Views can be used to control user access to data and to simplify data presentation (see Figure 2.19).

stor_id	stor_name	stor_address	city	state	zip	last_update
7066	Barnum's	567 Pasadena Ave.	Tustin	CA	92789	8/1/1995 4:25 PM
7067	News & Brews	577 First St.	Los Gatos	CA	96745	8/15/1995 3:00 PM
7131	Doc-U-Mat	24-A Avrogado Way	Remulade	WA	98014	3/11/1995 1:00 PM
8042	Bookbeat	679 Carson St.	Portland	CA	89076	4/25/1995 3:00 PM
8100	Johnston	unknown	Fairfax	VA	23294	

Business Rule: End-users can only see the stor_name column

SQL Server Translation: CREATE VIEW end_user_view AS
SELECT stor_name
FROM stores

SELECT * FROM end_user_view

stor_name
Barnum's
News & Brews
Doc-U-Mat
Bookbeat
Johnston

Output from view

FIGURE 2.19   An example of a view.

Triggers

A *trigger* is a user-defined collection of Transact-SQL commands that is automatically executed when an INSERT, DELETE, or UPDATE is executed against a table (see Figure 2.20). Triggers are flexible and powerful, which makes them useful for enforcing business rules, referential integrity, and data integrity. Triggers can be column, row, or table specific.

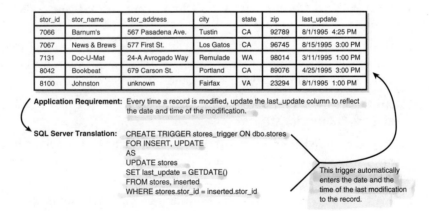

stor_id	stor_name	stor_address	city	state	zip	last_update
7066	Barnum's	567 Pasadena Ave.	Tustin	CA	92789	8/1/1995 4:25 PM
7067	News & Brews	577 First St.	Los Gatos	CA	96745	8/15/1995 3:00 PM
7131	Doc-U-Mat	24-A Avrogado Way	Remulade	WA	98014	3/11/1995 1:00 PM
8042	Bookbeat	679 Carson St.	Portland	CA	89076	4/25/1995 3:00 PM
8100	Johnston	unknown	Fairfax	VA	23294	8/1/1995 1:00 PM

Application Requirement: Every time a record is modified, update the last_update column to reflect the date and time of the modification.

SQL Server Translation: CREATE TRIGGER stores_trigger ON dbo.stores
FOR INSERT, UPDATE
AS
UPDATE stores
SET last_update = GETDATE()
FROM stores, inserted
WHERE stores.stor_id = inserted.stor_id

This trigger automatically enters the date and the time of the last modification to the record.

FIGURE 2.20   An example of a trigger.

Stored Procedures

A *stored procedure* is a compiled SQL program (see Figure 2.21). Within a stored procedure, you can embed conditional logic (if/else logic), declare variables, pass parameters, and perform other programming tasks.

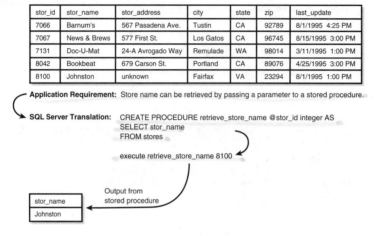

stor_id	stor_name	stor_address	city	state	zip	last_update
7066	Barnum's	567 Pasadena Ave.	Tustin	CA	92789	8/1/1995 4:25 PM
7067	News & Brews	577 First St.	Los Gatos	CA	96745	8/15/1995 3:00 PM
7131	Doc-U-Mat	24-A Avrogado Way	Remulade	WA	98014	3/11/1995 1:00 PM
8042	Bookbeat	679 Carson St.	Portland	CA	89076	4/25/1995 3:00 PM
8100	Johnston	unknown	Fairfax	VA	23294	8/1/1995 1:00 PM

Application Requirement: Store name can be retrieved by passing a parameter to a stored procedure.

SQL Server Translation: CREATE PROCEDURE retrieve_store_name @stor_id integer AS
SELECT stor_name
FROM stores

execute retrieve_store_name 8100

Output from stored procedure

stor_name
Johnston

FIGURE 2.21   An example of a stored procedure.

FAQ

The following are some of the common questions asked by DBAs about SQL Server:

Q What is the difference between the NT and the Windows 9x versions of SQL Server?

A The two products are virtually identical. The main difference is that Windows 9x does not support the following features: SMP support, asynchronous I/O support, and Windows 2000 Authentication security.

Q Can I use SQL Server Enterprise Manager, version 2000, to administer 7.x versions of SQL Server?

A Yes, you can use Enterprise Manager, version 2000, to administer a 7.0 version of SQL Server. You can also use the Query Analyzer, version 2000, to manage a 7.0 database.

Q Can I use SQL Server Enterprise Manager on a Windows 9x client to manage SQL Server running on NT?

A Yes, SQL Server Enterprise Manager on a Windows 9x client can be used to administer SQL Server on NT.

Summary

The following is summary information for this chapter:

- The Enterprise Manager is used to administer SQL Server. From this console, you can administer multiple database servers through a single interface. Tasks— such as starting and stopping SQL Server, managing databases, managing backups, managing permissions, and others—are performed through this interface.

- The Enterprise Manager is part of the Microsoft Management Console (MMC). This console is also used to manage products via snap-ins, such as Exchange, Microsoft Transaction Server, and other products through a single interface.

- SQL Server 2000 supports the Windows 2000 and Windows 9x operating systems. The functionality in each version of SQL Server is nearly identical, and each product uses the same code base.

- SQL Server 2000 is integrated with NT's Control Panel through the following services: SQL Server (MSSQLServer), SQL Server Agent (SQLServerAgent), Distributed Transaction Coordinator (MSDTC), and Microsoft Search.

- Information about SQL Server is stored in the following Registry key:

```
HKEY_LOCAL_MACHINE
 \SOFTWARE
 \Microsoft
 \Microsoft SQL Server
```

- SQL Server Query Analyzer is used to perform the following functions: execute SQL statements, analyze query plans, display query statistics, and perform index analysis.

- SQL Server Profiler is a tool that graphically traces activity. The information generated by the SQL Server Profiler is often used to probe user activity, troubleshoot queries, and generate audit trails.

- Microsoft English Query is a tool that can translate English syntax into SQL statements.

- Microsoft Analysis Services provides multidimensional database analysis. This is a key component to Microsoft's data warehousing strategy.

- A table is used to store data and is organized in a row/column manner.

- A trigger is a user-defined collection of Transact-SQL commands that is automatically executed when an INSERT, DELETE, or UPDATE is executed against a table.

- A stored procedure is a compiled program that contains Transact-SQL statements.

3

The Evolution of SQL Server

IN THIS CHAPTER

• History of SQL Server

• What's New in Version 2000

by Orryn Sledge

Microsoft SQL Server 2000 is a significant release because it continues to build upon the framework Microsoft created with SQL Server 7.0. It has become the database of choice for e-Business and data warehousing initiatives, and it continues to set the standard for performance, ease-of-use, and out-of-the-box functionality. Also, SQL Server 2000 is a supporting component to the Microsoft.NET strategy. Those administrators who are upgrading from previous versions will be very pleased with the 2000 product and all that it has to offer.

History of SQL Server

In 1988, Microsoft released its first version of SQL Server. It was designed for the OS/2 platform and was developed jointly by Microsoft and Sybase. During the early 1990s, Microsoft began to develop a new version of SQL Server for the NT platform. While it was under development, Microsoft decided that SQL Server should be tightly coupled with the NT operating system. In 1992, Microsoft assumed core responsibility for the future of SQL Server for NT. In 1993, Windows NT 3.1 and SQL Server 4.2 for NT were released. Microsoft's philosophy of combining a high-performance database with an easy-to-use interface proved to be very successful. Microsoft quickly became the second most popular vendor of high-end relational database software. In 1994, Microsoft and Sybase formally ended their partnership. In 1995, Microsoft released version 6.0 of SQL Server. This release was a major rewrite of SQL Server's core technology. Version 6.0 substantially improved performance, provided built-in replication, and delivered centralized administration. In 1996, Microsoft released version 6.5 of SQL Server. This version brought significant enhancements to the existing technology and provided several new features. In 1997, Microsoft released version 6.5 Enterprise Edition. In 1998, Microsoft released version 7.0 of SQL Server, which was a complete rewrite of the database engine. In 2000, Microsoft released SQL Server 2000. SQL Server version 2000 is Microsoft's most significant release of SQL Server to date. This version further builds upon the SQL Server 7.0 framework. According to the SQL Server development team, the changes to the database engine are designed to provide an architecture that will last for the next 10 years.

Rather than listing all the new features and enhancements found in 2000, I've decided to list my favorite changes. The remainder of this chapter is dedicated to discussing these new features found in version 2000.

What's New in Version 2000

Several of the key features found in SQL Server 2000 are as follows:

- XML Support
- Multi-Instance Support
- Data Warehousing/Business Intelligence Improvements
- Windows 2000 Support
- Performance and Scalability Improvements
- Wizard Improvements
- Query Analyzer Improvements
- DTS Improvements
- Transact SQL Enhancements

XML Support

XML is becoming the standard in which businesses communicate and share information. SQL Server 2000 provides extensive XML support. XML support is easy to setup and access. Once you are up and running with XML, you can store XML inside a table, query the XML data through Transact-SQL statements, and even join XML data to relational data through a SQL statement.

Multi-Instance Support

Multi-Instance support enables multiple copies of the SQL Server engine to run on the same machine. Microsoft has finally caught up to Oracle on this feature. This is a great feature in that it enables a DBA to combine multiple environments such as development, test, and production onto one machine. Also, this is big win for ASP and ISPs in that they can host multiple applications on the same machine.

Data Warehousing and Business Intelligence (BI) Improvements

Microsoft continues to build out its BI offering through SQL Server 2000 and its Analysis Services (previously named OLAP Services in version 7.0). Analysis Services provides OLAP analysis over the Web through accessing and linking cubes via the Internet. Additionally, SQL Server 2000 includes Data Mining tools and support for Web-related analysis. For example, when SQL Server is combined with Commerce Server 2000, you can perform data mining on click-streams, purchasing patterns, and other types of information.

Windows 2000 Support

SQL Server 2000 is tightly integrated with Windows 2000. SQL Server 2000 automatically registers itself with the Active Directory. This enables someone to search for SQL 2000 servers in an organization, manage databases directly from the Active Directory service, and perform other functions.

SQL Server 2000 is also integrated with Windows 2000 through the Kerberos security mechanism. Furthermore, SQL Server takes advantage of the performance improvements found in Windows 2000. When running Windows 2000 Datacenter and SQL Server 2000 Enterprise Edition, SQL Server can scale up to 32 processors and 64GB of RAM.

Performance and Scalability Improvements

SQL Server 2000 continues to produce record-setting performance numbers on the Intel–based platform. SQL Server 2000 is the first Microsoft product to enable the data tier to be portioned across multiple servers. This is accomplished through distributed partitioned views, which enables the workload to be distributed across multiple servers. Distributed portioned views are a key component of Microsoft's scale-up-and-out strategy.

Also, SQL Server 2000 provides other performance enhancements such as DBCC improvements, indexed views, and index reorganization. DBCC operations can now take advantage of multiple processors (Enterprise Edition only). Indexed views are a big plus for data warehousing. Furthermore, index reorganization can now take place with a minimal performance impact.

DBCC = Data Base Consistancy Checker

Wizard Improvements

SQL Server 2000 provides two very useful wizards: Copy Database Wizard and Log Shipping Wizard (Enterprise Edition only).

The Copy Database Wizard automates the steps to copy a database. This is very useful when setting up test environments, moving databases, and sharing databases.

The Log Shipping Wizard automates log shipping. It enables you to copy and apply transaction logs to a standby server. This is useful when creating a standby server. Previously, the Log Shipping utility was found in the SQL Server 7.0 resource kit and was script based. Now it is directly integrated with the Enterprise Edition and automates the scripting process.

Query Analyzer Improvements

The Query Analyzer is full of productivity enhancements. The following lists my favorite improvements:

- **Integrated Debugger**—Finally, the SQL Server has an integrated debugger! This is great for DBAs and developers who have to debug stored procedures. No longer do you have to use the Visual Studio debugger (which did not always work).

- **Object Browser**—The Object Browser provides a hierarchical view of objects. For example, you can drill into a database, table, column, or other types of objects. After drilling into the object, you can drag and drop the object name into a SQL statement.

- **Object Search**—The Object Search enables keyword searching across databases, tables, stored procedures, and other objects.

- **Templates**— With this feature, you can create custom templates or use the standard templates—for example, whether you always include a code header in your stored procedures, save the code header as a template, or use the template to create the stored procedure. This ensures consistency and reduces cut-and-pasting.

DTS Enhancement

DTS has been improved to preserve primary key and foreign key constraints. This is useful when migrating tables from other RDBMS. Additionally, a DTS package can be saved as a Visual Basic project. By adding the package to SourceSafe, you gain version control for your DTS packages.

Transact-SQL Enhancements

Transact-SQL has been enhanced to support *user-definable functions (UDFs)*. This enables you to store your logic in a common routine. Also, Transact-SQL has been enhanced to support declarative referential integrity.

Summary

As you can see from this chapter, SQL Server 2000 has been significantly enhanced. For a full listing of all the enhancements found in SQL Server 2000, I suggest reading the What's New section in SQL Server's Books Online.

As with any enterprise product, several administrative tasks must be dealt with in a production environment. The remainder of this book is designed to help you effectively manage those tasks.

PART II

Installing and Upgrading SQL Server

IN THIS PART

4 Planning an Installation or Upgrade

5 Installing or Upgrading SQL Server

4

Planning an Installation or Upgrade

by Mark Spenik

IN THIS CHAPTER

- Developing an Installation Strategy and Plan

- Developing an Upgrade Strategy and Plan

- Upgrade/Installation Planning FAQ

In this chapter, you develop plans and strategies to help you correctly install or upgrade SQL Server. Why bother with a planning stage? Why not just skip right to the installation or upgrade? SQL Server installation and upgrading is a simple process, but, by planning, you can make the correct decisions that affect the performance and operation of SQL Server before the installation. When upgrading, you can never make too many plans to limit server downtime and protect your database against problems encountered during the upgrade. Additionally, the SQL Server 2000 upgrade process is different from any previous version's upgrade process and provides you with more options. Whether you are upgrading or planning a new installation, the first step of the process is the installation of SQL Server 2000. Start by examining installation strategies and plans, and then tackle the subject of upgrade strategies and plans.

NOTE

Installing SQL Server has been simplified. You can get by during the installation process by answering a few simple questions such as your name and company. However, I still think it is important to understand what happens during installation and what defaults you are accepting if you do not select custom install.

Developing an Installation Strategy and Plan

Developing an installation plan starts with the assessment of the requirements of your business or users, includes the selection and purchase of the hardware, and finishes with making decisions about specific SQL Server options. Begin by determining user and system requirements. After the requirements have been determined, you examine possible hardware configurations and SQL Server options. You then create a checklist to use during system installation, and, finally, you install SQL Server.

Step 1: Determine System and User Requirements

How do you determine the hardware system requirements and user requirements for SQL Server? You ask questions and do some homework. Start with the user requirements or business requirements. Based on the requirements of the users or business, you can determine the size and type of hardware system you need to meet the requirements. Start with the following questions:

- What is the purpose or goal of the system?

- What are the database requirements?(for example, How many transactions?)

- What are the user or business requirements?

- How much money will it cost?

NOTE

One decision you won't have to make is whether to use UNIX, NetWare, or Windows NT. Microsoft SQL Server 2000 is supported on Windows 2000, Windows XP, Windows NT Server 4.0, Windows NT Workstation 4.0, and Windows 9x. If you have decided to use Microsoft SQL Server, the operating system war is already over; it will be a Microsoft operating system! For a database that handles multiple users, use Windows NT Server or Windows 2000; for laptop or mobile users, use Windows 9x. NT workstation can be used on high-end laptops or desktops, or for developers working with their own copy of SQL Server during the development process.

The following sections expand on each of the preceding questions to help you determine the type of system you need.

What Is the Intended Use of the System?

The first questions you might ask yourself are what the system is for and how many concurrent users the system must accommodate. (For example, is the system for a single department with 10 users or for a very large Web-based database system with several thousand users?) A system supporting more users requires more memory, disk space, and processing power. Is the system a dedicated SQL Server system, or does it perform other activities such as file and printing services? Is the system replacing another system because of downsizing or right-sizing? If it is replacing an existing system, you already have a lot of information available to you (such as the current load on the system and the current system's shortcomings). Is the system a production system or a development/test system? You want more fault tolerance and more storage capability on a production server than you typically need on a development server.

What Are the Database Requirements?

What are the database requirements for the system? Will the SQL Server primarily support decision support systems or transaction systems? How heavy is the expected transaction load? If the system is transaction driven, try to determine the number of expected transactions per day and how the transactions will be processed. For example, is the server idle for eight hours and does it then process all the transactions during a few hours, or does it process the transactions evenly throughout the day? What is the expected size of the database? Are you moving databases from another system to SQL Server because of downsizing or right-sizing? If so, you should be able to obtain information such as the current database size, expected database size, and the transaction load of the system from the current system. You also need to determine the type of transactions that occur on the system. For example, are 90% of the transactions disk reads or are they primarily disk writes. This information is crucial when trying to determine the proper drive configuration for your system. If you can determine the expected peak transaction load and the number of reads and writes, you can use the disk drive I/O times to compute the number and type of drives required.

TIP

If you have the means, dedicate a machine for SQL Server. Then you can tune the hardware to give the best SQL Server performance.

What Are the Users' Requirements and Expectations?

It is always important to understand the requirements and expectations of the individuals who use SQL Server. What type of query response time do the users expect? How many users will be logged on to SQL Server at one time? What are the backup and storage requirements of the users or business? After you understand the users' expectations, determine whether you can provide them with a system that meets their expectations. You might need to bring them back to earth to face the reality of what their systems can do.

How Much Does It Cost?

Maybe this question should be listed first! In the real world, the difference between the system you need and the system you get is the amount of money you have available to spend on the system. (Enough said!) The good news is that system prices are steadily dropping, making the server you need more affordable.

Step 2: Select the Right Platform

After you obtain the answers and information to the questions described in "Step 1: Determine System and User Requirements," you are ready to select the hardware platform for your SQL Server. For this discussion, the hardware platform is divided into four areas:

- Hardware (including the processor or processors and peripherals)
- Memory
- Disk drives
- File system

The following sections examine each area and the type of decisions you need to make regarding each subject.

Hardware

When determining which hardware platform to use, check the Windows NT Hardware Compatibility List to make sure that the brand and model of the machine you are considering is on the list. If the brand and model you are interested in is not on the compatibility list, download the latest list from the Microsoft Web site at `http://www.microsoft.com/windows2000/server/howtobuy/upgrading/compat/defa ult.asp`. If the machine is still not listed, check with the manufacturer. It is always good to let the vendor know when you are purchasing the machine that you plan to use the machine as a database server. Mention that you plan to use Microsoft SQL Server as the database engine and ask if there are any known issues or problems with using the selected platform with SQL Server.

TIP

Save yourself a lot of problems and potential headaches by using only the machines approved for Microsoft Windows NT. Although you might get other machines to work, I have seen the difficulty involved and the potential for failing to get the machine up and running when using unapproved platforms and configurations.

So, how do you determine the correct hardware platform for your business or organization? Start with cost and examine hardware platforms within your budget. There is no point in wasting your time researching hardware platforms you can't afford.

Use the information you gathered earlier, such as the expected number of transactions during a given time period, and talk to the hardware manufacturers or integrators to see whether the platform you are considering can meet those goals and requirements. Check for SQL Server benchmarks on the particular platform and ask to speak to other clients currently using the platform. Consider other factors such as manufacturer reliability, service, and maintenance. These three factors are extremely important if the machine runs into a hardware problem and you are faced with downtime. Consider expandability—for example, will you require multiple processors in the future? If so, can the current platform be expanded to accept more processors?

DO I NEED SMP (SYMMETRIC MULTIPLE PROCESSORS)?

Right out of the box, Windows NT 4.0 supports up to four processors. Windows 2000 Advanced Server supports eight processors, and Windows 2000 DataCenter supports up to 32 processors. SQL Server can take advantage of these processors without any special add-ons or configuration changes. In theory, a perfect scalable SMP machine would scale 100%, meaning that if your SQL Server performed 20 transactions per second and you added a second processor, you would increase the number of transactions to 40 per second. The scalability of systems varies widely and can range from nearly 100% to below 60%. Check with the manufacturer.

What does it mean to you and SQL Server? If you are performing heavy transaction database processing, you can expect your transaction performance to increase with the scalability of the system. If you perform 10 transactions per second and add a second processor on a system that provides 80% scalability, you can expect roughly 18 transactions per second. SMP works very well for transaction-based systems.

What if you primarily do decision support (such as database queries)? In the 6.x version of SQL Server, adding a second processor might not have been the best way to improve your system performance. In decision-support systems, the queries are I/O bound and not processor bound, so adding additional processors does not provide the same substantial performance gain you get with transaction-based systems. However, with SQL Server 2000, adding additional processors in a decision-support environment enables you to take advantage of SQL Server 2000's parallel query capabilities, which can greatly decrease the time required to run long-running queries. SQL Server 2000 has many features that can take advantage of a SMP system whether it is transaction based or decision-support based. That's why I would recommend starting with a SMP machine if you can fit it into your budget!

Scaling Up or Scaling Out?   SQL Server 2000 adds another option to the hardware selection process, which is *scaling out* (that is picking a platform that allows you to add more disk drives, memory server and processors) . Buying a server that allows you to scale out is really smart planning for the future. If the workload or number of users is greater than anticipated or grows over time, you can purchase additional components to handle the increased workload without buying a brand new server. If it is in the budget, I always recommend purchasing hardware that allows users to scale out in the future. Scale out solutions, which are actually adding multiple servers and spreading out the database across multiple servers using SQL Server federated servers (discussed in Chapter 16 "Architecture and Database Design"), require more planning and the application must be written or modified to use distributed partitioned views. It should be noted that using federated servers, Microsoft has been able to achieve the top rated TPC marks. Federated servers work well when the I/O and data can be evenly spread across multiple servers. If you use federated database servers do not expect to achieve higher query performance than you would with a single server, some queries may require information from the other servers which must be merged with the final results.

Memory

A common theme in this book is *giving SQL Server enough memory*. Not because SQL Server is an inefficient memory hog, but because SQL Server uses memory very intelligently. Extra memory can provide you with some very cost-effective performance enhancements. The minimum memory requirement of SQL Server is 32MB. (See the tip later in this section for comments on the minimum amount.)

You are no longer required to configure and tune SQL Server's memory usage. SQL Server 2000 dynamically adjusts the amount of memory it uses based on its current requirements and the requirements of the system on which it is running.

Regardless of the amount of memory you start with, after SQL Server is up and running, you can monitor SQL Server to more accurately determine your memory requirements.

> **TIP**
>
> The cost of memory has plummeted to the point where memory is now cheap! Do yourself a favor and get database servers that start with a fair amount of memory. A few years back, I would have said start with 128MB and then tune up. With current memory prices, I now recommend starting with 256MB to 512MB, depending on your budget and user requirements. SQL Server uses memory very effectively, and giving it enough memory to cache a fair amount of data pages in memory means improved performance. If you are planning to use SQL Server for a laptop and merge replication, 32MB of memory works but 64MB works even better.

Disk Drives

One of the most important system decisions you can make is the type of disk drives and disk controllers you select. Selecting the proper disk system has a big impact on the overall performance of the SQL Server system and the type of data fault tolerance used to protect the databases.

Before you get into the specifics, you want to select fast disk drives and smart controller cards to take advantage of Windows NT multitasking and asynchronous read-ahead features. When buying disk drives for a database server, consider using more, smaller physical drives rather than one large physical drive. Doing so enables you to spread your databases and transaction logs over several different physical devices. If you are considering buying one 12GB hard drive, for example, reconsider and purchase three 4GB hard drives or six 2GB hard drives.

Just as important as the speed of your hard disk system is the fault tolerance offered in modern disk drive systems. You want the best protection for your databases with optimum performance. One option available to you is the use of *RAID (Redundant Array of Inexpensive Disks)* disk drive configurations. RAID disk configurations use several disk drives to build a single logical striped drive. Logically, a striped drive is a single drive; physically, the logical drive spans many different disk drives. *Striping the drives* allows files and devices to span multiple physical devices.

By spreading the data over several physical drives, RAID configurations offer excellent performance. Another benefit of some RAID configurations is fault tolerance and recovery. A RAID 5 configuration can lose a single disk drive and recover all the data on the lost drive. When a new drive is added, the RAID configuration rebuilds the lost drive on the new drive. A RAID 5 system offers good protection and performance for your databases. RAID configurations can be hardware-based solutions or Windows NT software-based solutions. Hardware-based RAID solutions are typically faster than software-based RAID solutions, here are descriptions of the most common types of RAID disk configurations:

RAID 0   In a RAID 0 configuration, the data is spread across multiple drives (disk striping). RAID 0 performs well for both reads and writes but it lacks redundancy. Essentially a single drive failure would cause you to lose all information across the RAID array so RAID 0 is not recommended for SQL Server installations.

RAID 1   RAID 1 is also known as "disk mirroring." In a RAID 1 configuration, there is no disk striping. All information is copied to a single drive and the contents of that drive are copied to another drive for fault tolerance. RAID 1 configurations work well for sequential write operations like those used by the transaction log. RAID 1 has redundancy so that a drive can fail and the database stays active. The problem with RAID 1 is the cost. To achieve 10GB of usable space requires 20GB of purchased space (RAID 1 requires two times the drive space to achieve the desired space). RAID 1 is recommended for SQL Server transaction logs.

RAID 5   A RAID 5 configuration uses disk striping with parity. Like RAID 0, the data is spread across multiple drives but RAID 5 also computes and stores parity information for the data across the drives as well. The parity information is used to re-create the disk information in case of a disk failure. Essentially, RAID 5 can with stand a single drive failure. The drive can be replaced with a new drive and the information from the lost drive can be re-created using the parity. RAID 5 is very popular because it offers fault tolerance at a low price. To determine the number of drives required for RAID 5 is N-1. So if you have five 2GB hard drives (a total of 10GB) in a RAID 5 configuration you would have 8GB of usable space (2GB is used to store parity information). The downside of RAID 5 is the write performance. Additional time is required to compute the parity and then the parity must be written to disk. RAID 5 has very good performance for database read operations and is recommended for databases where the majority of transactions are read based. For systems that perform frequent or many write operations, RAID 5 is not the best candidate. You should also avoid using RAID 5 for transaction logs because transaction logs are not read and (except on start up) and are primarily sequential writes.

RAID 10   A RAID 10 configuration is a cross between RAID 0 and RAID 1. Like a RAID 0 configuration, data is striped evenly across all the drives, and the drive set is then mirrored (for example, a mirrored disk stripe). The write performance for RAID 10 is far superior to that of RAID 5 and the READ performance between RAID 5 and RAID 10 is similar and like RAID 5, RAID 10 offers fault tolerance. RAID 10 is the ideal configuration for databases that have frequent writes. The drawback to RAID 10 is the cost. Like RAID 1, you will need twice the number of disks.

File System

When working with Windows NT, should you use *NTFS (New Technology File System)* or *FAT (File Allocation Table)*? From a performance standpoint, it does not really matter. (The performance difference between the two file systems is negligible.) In general, NTFS performs faster in read operations, and FAT performs faster in write operations. If you use the NTFS file system, you can take advantage of Windows NT security.

TIP
I typically recommend NTFS on Windows NT systems, which enables you to take advantage of NT security and auditing features.

The Right Platform

The right platform for SQL Server is the best system you can afford that does the SQL Server processing you require! A good configuration for a SQL Server system used primarily for queries and reports (that is mostly read operations) is shown in Figure 4.1: a computer configured with one or many processors and starting with 256MB of memory. Use a RAID 5 stripe set disk configuration for the databases; place the transaction logs on a RAID 1 (disk mirroring) stripe set, and place the operating system and SQL Server on a nonstriped drive or a RAID 1 stripe set. What makes this a good configuration? SQL Server 2000 is designed to take advantage of SMP systems with features such as parallel queries. The RAID 5 disk configuration for the databases gives you fault tolerance, and the RAID 5 configuration is very fast in performing disk-read operations. RAID 5 also takes care of spreading the data across multiple drives.

The RAID 1 configuration for the logs is desirable because a transaction log is used only for sequential writes and does not benefit from RAID 5's fast disk reads. RAID 5 is slower than RAID 1 when performing sequential writes because of the time required to compute and write out the parity data, and the RAID 1 configuration offers you fault tolerance. For a system that has frequent write operations, replace the RAID 5 configuration with a RAID 10 configuration for the best performance with fault tolerance. How could either system be enhanced? Add additional stripe sets or more memory. Additional stripe sets can give you additional logical drives so that you can place a table on one logical drive and its index on another. For the memory requirements, monitor your SQL Server and determine the correct amount of memory for your server. More memory enables you to cache more data without having to go to the disk to retrieve the information. 256MB of memory is a good starting point, if you have the budget start with.

The Microsoft Recommended Software and Hardware Requirements

Now that you have decided what you want the system to do and have begun to select your hardware configuration, take a look at the minimum SQL Server 2000 configurations as suggested by Microsoft. Remember, these are the minimum hardware platform requirements. As you work with these products, you will learn that the minimum suggested processor and memory requirements run the software but don't give great performance. Whenever possible, use the best processor you can afford. More important than the processor is the memory. Start with more than the minimum memory requirements; after all, SQL Server loves memory!

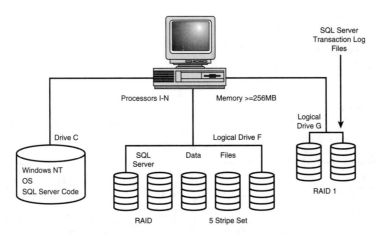

FIGURE 4.1   A typical SQL Server hardware configuration.

Supported Hardware Platforms   The following hardware platforms are supported by SQL Server 2000:

> Intel and compatible systems—minimum recommended processor—Pentium 166 MHz or higher

SQL Server Editions   SQL Server comes in many different editions. The following is a list of the SQL Server editions. (For more detail, see Chapter 5, "Installing or Upgrading SQL Server.")

- **Enterprise Edition**—Supports the largest of enterprise database solutions such as large scale Web sites, OLTP applications, and large data warehousing systems.

- **Standard Edition**—Supports large scale applications and Web sites. Lacks some of the scalability features of the Enterprise Edition. For example, the standard edition can support a maximum of 8 CPUs on Windows NT 4.0 Enterprise Edition, but the Enterprise Edition supports 32 CPUs on the Windows 2000 datacenter.

- **Personal Edition**—Used by laptop/mobile users. Can also be used by developers.

- **Developer Edition**—Used by developer's creating SQL Server–based solutions.

- **Database Engine Option**—Previously called MSDE. Allows developers using such tools as Microsoft Access to use the SQL Server engine for database development.

- **CE Edition**—Used by handheld devices running Windows CE.

Memory   The following is the minimum memory requirements for SQL Server 2000:

> A minimum of 64MB of RAM on most systems (32MB for the Personal Edition on Windows 9x.)

Operating Systems   SQL Server 2000 supports the following operating systems:

- Windows 95 or later (includes Windows 95 OSR2 and Windows 98)
- Windows NT 4.0 Server, Service Pack 4 or later
- Windows NT 4.0 Workstation, Service Pack 4 or later
- Windows NT 4.0 Enterprise Edition
- Windows 2000 Standard Server
- Windows 2000 Advanced Server
- Windows 2000 Professional
- Windows XP Professional
- Windows 2000 Data Center Server

Disk Space Requirements   SQL Server has several different installation options, such as Install Client Utilities Only, Typical Installation, and Compact Installation, to name a few. The estimated disk space requirements for these various options are as follows (not including the Analysis Server):

- Full Installation, 270MB
- Typical Installation, 250MB
- Minimum Installation, 95MB
- Management Tools Only, 95MB

As far as disk space goes, the numbers listed are the required amounts to install SQL Server and the system databases. They do not include the size required for your various user databases or for any other applications you might want to install. When you are looking at disk requirements, don't forget to add in the anticipated size of your user databases. If the server does not have a tape backup unit, add additional space (about the same amount for user databases) to allow disk backups of your databases.

> **NOTE**
>
> IE 5.0 must be installed before you can install SQL Server 2000.

Step 3: Answer Required Questions and Understand Why They Are Important

When you begin a new SQL Server installation or an upgrade from SQL Server 6.x or 7.0 to 2000, you are asked several questions such as your name and company name. You should be able to answer these questions with no problem, and with SQL Server 2000, that's about all you have to answer to install the product! However, if you select a custom install, you are asked to answer other questions that affect SQL Server performance, maintenance, and behavior. If you select the typical or compact installation, you won't be asked these questions, but you should be familiar with them and with the defaults used by SQL Server when making these selections. Examine the following installation topics in more detail to help you make the correct choices for your SQL Server:

- Data File Location
- Instance Name
- Collation Setting
- Network
- SQL Server and SQL Server Agent Windows NT User Accounts

Data File Location

During installation, you are asked to give the drive and path to install the SQL Server system databases. The system databases are as follows:

- master—SQL Server's configuration database
- model—Serves as a template on which other databases are created
- tempdb—Temporary storage area
- msdb—Scheduling database and SQL Server Agent database
- Northwind—Example database
- pubs—Sample database

The default location used for the data files is the SQL Server root directory, \Program Files\Microsoft SQL Server\MSSQL, sub-directory DATA. You can change the location of these files or leave them on the default location (\Program Files\Microsoft

SQL Server\MSSQL). Select a drive that has enough space to allow these databases to expand. The master, msdb, model, and pubs databases typically do not grow rapidly (adding several megabytes a day). However, tempdb is a different story. SQL Server 2000 allows tempdb to automatically expand if the database's configured size is exceeded. When SQL Server is shut down and restarted, tempdb automatically shrinks to its initial configured size. For this reason, it is wise to select a drive or stripe set for tempdb that has room for the database to expand, as well as a drive or stripe set that provides you with good performance.

Instance Name

SQL Server 2000 allows you to install multiple instances of the SQL Server database engine. If you are only installing a single instance of SQL Server, you can take the default name (which is the computer name). If you want to install multiple instances of SQL Server, you will need to use different unique names for each of the instances. Instance names are not case sensitive and cannot exceed 16 characters. The first character of the name must be a letter, underscore, number sign, or ampersand.

Collation Setting

SQL Server 2000 does not require you to select the sort order and character set for your server and a separate Unicode collation setting. Instead, you select the collation name and the sort rules to use for your data, including the Unicode data. The collation setting determines how the data is sorted and compared; for example, you can have non–case-sensitive comparisons or binary comparisons. Collation settings also include the character set used by the data. The character set is the set of valid characters (uppercase letters, lowercase letters, and symbols) that can be represented by the database server. Unicode data is double the size of any ANSI character. The possible number of characters represented by an ANSI character is 256, whereas a Unicode character can represent up to 65,536 different characters. During SQL Server setup, SQL Server will check the Windows collation setting and default the database to the specific Windows collation. It is recommended that you keep the default setting.

CAUTION

Changing the collation setting after SQL Server has been installed requires rebuilding the master database and user databases. It will also prevent you from being able to recover databases with backups made prior to the change.

Network

Because SQL Server supports many different network options simultaneously, clients running TCP/IP can connect to SQL Server along with clients using IPX/SPX—all at the same time. SQL Server installs different network libraries during installation to handle network communication with other servers and client workstations. SQL

Server 2000 installs TCP/IP, multiprotocol, and the named-pipes protocol (not available in Windows 9x installations) by default. You have the option during installation (and after) to install one or more network libraries. Keep in mind that the type of network support you select determines the security mode that you can use for SQL Server. Before you examine the network libraries available to you, look at the two different security modes:

- **Windows NT Authentication**—Takes advantage of Windows NT user security and account mechanisms. Windows NT Authentication requires a trusted connection and can be implemented over the named-pipes protocol or multiprotocol network protocols. Note: Windows NT Authentication is not supported with Windows 95/98 clients.

- **Mixed**—Enables users to connect via Windows NT Authentication or SQL Server Authentication. Using SQL Server Authentication, an individual logging on to SQL Server supplies a username and a password that is validated by SQL Server against a system table. Users implementing trusted connections (named-pipes or multiprotocol) can log in using Windows NT Authentication; users from trusted or nontrusted connections (any network protocol supported by SQL Server) can log in using standard security.

The following sections describe the network options available for SQL Server 2000.

Named-Pipes Protocol   The named-pipes protocol is the default protocol installed with SQL Server. Named-pipes allows for interprocess communication locally or over networks and is used in NT networks.

Multiprotocol   The multiprotocol uses Windows NT *Remote Procedure Call (RPC)* mechanisms for communication and requires no setup parameters. Multiprotocol currently supports NWLINK IPX/SPX, TCP/IP, and named-pipes. Multiprotocol enables users of IPX/SPX and TCP/IP protocols to take advantage of Windows NT Authentication.

NWLink IPX/SPX Protocol   IPX/SPX is the familiar network protocol used for Novell networks. If you select NWLink IPX/SPX during installation, you are prompted for the Novell Bindery service name to register SQL Server.

TCP/IP Protocol   TCP/IP is a popular communications protocol used by the Internet. If you select TCP/IP, you are asked to provide a TCP/IP port number for SQL Server to use for client connections. The default port number and the official Internet Assigned Number Authority socket number for Microsoft SQL Server is 1433.

Banyan Vines   Banyan Vines is another popular PC-based network system. Support for Banyan Vines is included only on Intel-based SQL Server systems. If you install Banyan Vines, you are prompted for a valid street talk name that must first be created using the Vines program MSERVICE.

AppleTalk ADSP Protocol   AppleTalk ADSP enables Apple Macintosh clients to connect to SQL Server using AppleTalk. If you select AppleTalk, you are prompted for the AppleTalk service object name.

SQL Server and SQL Server Agent Windows NT User Accounts

The SQL Executive was first introduced in SQL Server 6.0. In SQL Server 2000, the SQL Executive is called the SQL Server Agent. The SQL Server Agent is the service responsible for managing SQL Server tasks such as replication, events, alerts, and job scheduling. During system installation and upgrade, you are required to assign a NT system user account for the SQL Server Agent and for SQL Server. If you use the local system account, you do not have to create a new NT user account. However, you will not be able to perform tasks with other servers—such as replication, backups to network drives, SQL mail, or shared heterogeneous joins—because the local system account has no network access rights. SQL Server also requires a Windows NT account.

It is recommended that you set up a Windows NT domain user account for SQL Server and for the SQL Server Agent. Then you can access files on other servers, such as a Novell NetWare server or NT server and perform server-to-server replication and scheduling. You can use the same Windows NT domain user for both SQL Server and the SQL Server Agent or create a separate account for each. If you are planning to upgrade your SQL Server 2000 installation, you will need to use a domain account for SQL Server. When you or your NT administrator create the domain user account(s) for SQL Server and the SQL Server Agent, make sure that the following is true for the user:

- The account has Password Never Expires set.
- The account is a member of the SQL Server's local Administrators group.

The account must have the following advanced user rights selected:

Log On As a Service

NOTE

If you are installing on Windows 95 or later, SQL Server does not use an NT user account for SQL Server or the SQL Server Agent. Both services use the identity of the user currently logged in to the Windows 9x machine.

Step 4: Install SQL Server

The next step is to read Chapter 5 and begin the installation process. Use the following worksheet to help you prepare for the installation; use the worksheet later as a reference:

```
┌─────────────────────────────────────────────────────────────────────┐
│                                                                       │
│   SQL Server Installation WorkSheet                                   │
│                                          Installation Date:           │
│                                          Installed By:                │
│   Name:                                                               │
│   Company:                                                            │
│   Product ID:                                                         │
│   # of Client Licenses:                                               │
│   SQL Server Installation Path:                                       │
│   Master database Path:                                               │
│   Master Database Size:                                               │
│   Collation Setting:                                                  │
│                                                                       │
│                                                                       │
│   Network Support                                                     │
│   _X_ Named Pipes            ___ TCP/IP                               │
│   ___ NWLink IPX/SPX         ___ Banyan Vines      ___ Apple Talk ADSP│
│   Auto Start SQL Server at Boot Time                                  │
│   Yes    No                                                           │
│   Auto Start SQL Server Agent at Boot Time                            │
│   Yes    No                                                           │
│   SQL Server Agent and SQL Server Log On Account                      │
│                                                                       │
└─────────────────────────────────────────────────────────────────────┘
```

Developing an Upgrade Strategy and Plan

The plan and strategy for an upgrade is different from the plan and strategy for a new installation. In an upgrade, you have already decided on a platform and are currently running SQL Server. You might have many large production databases and hundreds of users who depend on the databases, or you might have small development databases with a few users. In many ways, upgrading an existing SQL Server is more critical than installing a new SQL Server. The existing SQL Server contains data being used and depended on by your organization.

With your organization depending on these databases, it is easy to see why it is important to develop a plan that enables you to upgrade to the new release with the least amount of risk. If the upgrade is not successful, your plan should allow you to return the system to its pre-upgrade state.

MARK AND ORRYN'S FIRST RULE OF UPGRADING

Never under estimate the difficulty of an upgrade. Remember Mark and Orryn's first rule of upgrading:

Expect something to go wrong.

When it does, make sure that you can get the system back up and running to its previous state. Creating an upgrade plan is essential. I was once involved with what was to be a simple upgrade for a banking organization that gave me a six-hour window to get its high-powered, multiprocessor SQL Server upgraded from SQL Server 4.21 to SQL Server 4.21a. No problem, right? After all, the upgrade was not even a major revision number—just a revision letter. Nothing could go wrong...NOT! Five hours later, when the SQL Server still was not working correctly and tech support was trying to resolve the problem, we opted to restore the system to the pre-upgrade state. After the SQL Server was restored, it did not work either! It appears that the problem had to do with the SQL Server Registry entries. This was not a problem because our upgrade plan called for backing up the system Registry. After the Registry was restored, the SQL Server was up and running with no problems, and the upgrade was pushed off to another day, awaiting information from tech support.

The moral of this story is to never underestimate the potential problems that might be encountered during an upgrade, and be overly cautious. It's better to have too many files backed up and ready to restore than not enough.

SQL Server 2000 greatly simplifies the upgrade process by providing DBAs with a lot of flexibility and options when upgrading from version 7.0—not to mention that SQL Server 2000 can run simultaneously alongside SQL Server 7.0 and SQL Server 6.5. Let's look at the different possibilities available for a SQL Server 2000 upgrade.

Upgrade the Existing 7.0 SQL Server (Single Computer)

If you choose to upgrade a SQL Server 7.0 installation, SQL Server 2000 will replace the 7.0 files with SQL Server 2000 and upgrade the databases. In this situation, all the databases are upgraded at once, and you are running SQL Server 2000. To fall back to SQL Server 7.0 would require you to uninstall SQL Server 2000, reinstall SQL Server 7.0, and then restore the databases from 7.0 backups.

Install SQL Server 2000 and Then Upgrade the Existing SQL Server (Single Computer)

You can choose to install SQL Server 2000 alongside a SQL Server 7.0 or SQL Server 6.5 installation and then selectively upgrade the databases. The two versions can run simultaneously. To upgrade a SQL Server 7.0 database to SQL Server 2000, use the Copy Database Wizard. To upgrade a SQL Server 6.5 database, use the SQL Server 2000 Version Upgrade Wizard to export your 6.5 databases to disk, tape, or network drives and then import them into SQL Server 2000. Because SQL Server 2000 can run alongside SQL Server 6.5 and SQL Server 7.0, you and your users will have access to the 2000 server as well as the 7.0 or 6.5 server before and after the upgrade.

NOTE

If you are using SQL Server 6.0, you can upgrade your database to SQL Server 6.5 and then use the SQL Server 2000 Upgrade Wizard, or you can upgrade your 6.0 database to SQL Server 7.0 and then upgrade to SQL Server 2000. SQL Server 2000 can't upgrade a SQL Server 6.0 installation directly.

Installing a New SQL Server 2000 Computer to Migrate Existing 7.0 or 6.5 Databases (Two Computers)

In this upgrade process, you are dealing with two machines. Because you are not installing SQL Server 2000 on the same machine as SQL Server 6.5 or SQL Server 7.0, you are in a good upgrade position. You can migrate all your databases at once or a few at a time. You and your users will have access to the 7.0 server and the 6.x server after the upgrade process because the 7.0 and 6.5 servers are on different computers.

Copy Database Wizard

If you choose to load an instance of SQL Server 2000 alongside your SQL Server 7.0 instance instead of upgrading, you can migrate your 7.0 databases one at a time or in groups, using the SQL Server 2000 Copy Database Wizard. The Copy Database Wizard allows you to keep your 7.0 database server running and available while performing the upgrade. (The database being upgraded must be set to read-only mode.) The Copy Database Wizard also allows you to copy login, user information along with jobs for a particular database. The process works only with SQL Server 7.0 databases and uses the attach and detach features of SQL Server 7.0 and 2000 to migrate the databases.

General Version Upgrade Wizard Information

If you have two computers, you can access both databases after the upgrade process has ended. When upgrading on a single machine, the state of your SQL Server 6.5—after the SQL Server 7.0 Version Upgrade Wizard completes—depends on the method selected to transfer the databases. If you have enough disk space on your server to install SQL Server 7.0 without removing SQL Server 6.x's data devices, you can use a direct pipeline to transfer the data. The direct pipeline approach is the best approach to take when performing an upgrade. The direct pipeline approach transfers the data and objects in memory from SQL Server 6.x to SQL Server 7.0, leaving the SQL Server 6.x intact. The direct pipeline approach also offers the best upgrade performance. If you do not have enough disk space to upgrade without removing your SQL Server 6.x databases first, you will have to export the SQL Server 6.x data and objects to tape or a network drive. The tape drive option is the faster of the two options; however, if you don't have a tape drive, use the network drive option.

Version Upgrade Wizard Steps with Tape Drive and Network Drive Options for Migrating SQL Server 6.5 Databases

The following steps are taken by the Version Upgrade Wizard when using a tape drive or network drive to migrate a SQL Server 6.5 database to SQL Server 2000:

1. Exports 6.x. objects.

2. Shuts down SQL Server 6.x.

3. Exports 6.x data.

4. Backs up and deletes 6.x devices.

5. Starts SQL Server 2000.

6. Imports SQL Server 6.5 objects into SQL Server 2000.

7. Imports SQL Server 6.5 data into SQL Server 2000.

Version Upgrade Wizard Steps Using the Direct Pipeline Options for Migrating SQL Server 6.5 Databases

The following steps are taken by the Version Upgrade Wizard when using a direct pipeline to migrate a SQL Server 6.5 database to SQL Server 2000:

1. Exports SQL Server 6.x objects.

2. Shuts down SQL Server 6.x.

3. Starts SQL Server 2000.

4. Imports SQL Server 6.x objects.

5. Exports and imports data from SQL Server 6.x to SQL Server 2000.

The Upgrade Plan

Before you begin to upgrade an existing SQL Server installation, it is important to create an upgrade plan. For SQL Server 7.0 users, your available options—such as a full upgrade or side-by-side installation and then using the copy database wizard—present you with different fall-back options. For a SQL Server 6.5 installation, you also have the side-by-side installation option as well as the total upgrade option. With SQL Server 6.5, the Upgrade Wizard provides different mechanisms for recovery from data loss. Regardless, you should have the capabilities to recover the databases if the upgrade fails for some reason.

TIP

When performing an upgrade, use the direct pipeline transfer mechanism of the Version Upgrade Wizard, if possible. The direct pipeline offers the best performance and leaves your 6.x databases intact.

The following sections provide you with an example of an upgrade plan to upgrade an existing SQL Server installation to SQL Server 2000.

1. **Determine whether you have the required disk space.**

   Make sure that you have the required amounts of disk space to upgrade your existing SQL Server. Upgrading SQL Server 7.0 to SQL Server 2000 does not require any additional space. But if you want to do a side-by-side installation of SQL Server 7.0 and SQL Server 2000, you might need between 95MB and 190MB, depending on the type of SQL Server 2000 installation you select. As a rough estimate, you need 1.5 times your current database's size in disk space to perform a direct pipeline. If you are upgrading a SQL Server 4.2x installation, you need to upgrade to 6.5 first.

2. **Make sure that NT and SQL Server have the proper service packs installed.**

   SQL Server 2000 requires NT Service Pack 5 or later, for Windows NT. The SQL Server 6.5 server must be on Service Pack 3 or later. Windows 2000 or Windows 9x do not require any service packs.

3. **Estimate downtime and schedule the upgrade with users.**

   Estimate the amount of time you expect the upgrade to take and then double it! Remember that the larger the database, the longer the upgrade takes. Don't forget to give yourself time to perform any necessary backups before the upgrade begins, time to test the upgraded server, and time to handle any possible problems—including going back to the original installation, if necessary. After you have determined the amount of time required to perform the upgrade, schedule a date with your users to perform the upgrade. If you have a Microsoft Technical Support contract, notify tech support of your upgrade plans and check for any last minute instructions or known problems.

On the day of the upgrade, follow these steps:

1. **Perform database maintenance.**

   Before backing up the databases, perform the following DBCC commands on each database: CHECKDB, NEWALLOC, and CHECKCATALOG.

2. **Back up all databases.**

   Perform SQL Server backups on the databases, including the master database. If possible, shut down SQL Server and use the Windows NT backup facilities to back up the SQL Server directories, including all the SQL Server devices for possible restoration.

3. **Back up the NT Registry.**

   Back up the NT System Registry again, in case you need to restore the system to the original SQL Server installation (see Chapter 5 to see how to back up the NT Registry).

4. **Make sure that no SQL Server applications are executing.**

   Before upgrading the SQL Server, make sure that no one is using SQL Server.

5. **Upgrade the server.**

   Run the setup program and select the Upgrade SQL Server option.

The Fall-Back Plan

A SQL Server upgrade is a straightforward process, but because you are usually dealing with valuable data and systems that can be down only for a limited time, upgrades should be treated with extreme caution and care. Just as important as a good upgrade plan is a good fall-back plan, in case the upgrade does not go as smoothly as you hoped. Here are some suggestions on how to protect yourself. Above all, make sure that you have the backups (tapes and so on) to return your SQL Server to its earlier state if necessary.

CAUTION

Always make sure that you have a valid backup of the Windows NT System Registry before starting any upgrade.

Suggestion 1: Complete System Backup Recovery Plan   If possible, shut down the SQL Server before the upgrade and perform a backup of the SQL Server directories and all the data devices. You must shut down SQL Server to back up files that the SQL Server is using, such as devices. If the upgrade fails for some reason, you can restore the SQL Server directories, devices, and the NT Registry, returning your system to its earlier setup.

Suggestion 2: Complete Database Backups—Reinstall Previous Version   Perform SQL Server database backups on the databases, including the master. Make sure that you have all the valid SQL Server configuration information such as the server name, character set, sort order, network configuration, and device and database layouts. If you cannot get the SQL Server 6.5 upgrade to work correctly, having the database dumps and the required SQL Server information enables you to reinstall your previous SQL Server system and reload your databases if necessary.

Suggestion 3: Complete System Backup and Database Backups   Perform suggestions 1 and 2. You can never be too careful!

Suggestion 4: Slow Migration—Multiple Instances   If you have the disk space, memory, and processing power, you can install an instance of SQL Server 2000 alongside your existing SQL Server installation. Allow both services to execute and then selectively migrate your databases from previous versions to SQL Server 2000.

When you have completed the migration and testing, you can shut down and remove the old version of SQL Server.

The bottom line is that the information and data completely recover your system if the upgrade fails. Play it safe. Have a backup plan to use if the backup plan fails!

Upgrade/Installation Planning FAQ

The following are some frequently asked questions about upgrade and installation planning:

Q My company typically purchases hardware RAID 5 servers for SQL Server. However, I'm bringing up an application that is purely transaction based (lots of writes, updates, and deletes). Is RAID 5 the best hardware configuration from a performance standpoint for transaction-based systems? (Note: I want fault tolerance!)

A When it comes to pure transaction-based systems with fault tolerance, a RAID 10 (disk mirroring) is better from a performance standpoint than RAID 5. RAID 5 is slower than RAID 10 when performing writes (because of the checksum computation and additional write), but faster than RAID 1 when performing reads. Because transaction-based systems are write intensive, RAID 10 offers better performance.

Q If I have replication setup, do I need to do anything special when upgrading?

A Make sure that you upgrade the distribution server first, publishers second, and subscribers last.

Q Can I install SQL Server on an NT Server that is also a Primary or Backup Domain Controller?

A Yes, you can install SQL Server on a PDC or BDC. However, it is not recommended, and you are much better off if you can dedicate a machine to SQL Server. If you must use your PDC or BDC, add more memory and, if possible, additional processors.

Summary

This chapter helps prepare you for a SQL Server upgrade or installation. In the next chapter, you walk through the installation and upgrade process.

The Upgrade Checklist

Use the following checklist to help prepare for a SQL Server upgrade. Check off each item on the list as it is completed. Perform each step in order from top to bottom.

- ❑ Have free disk space: 90MB, compact install; 180MB, typical; 190MB, full
- ❑ Install NT Service Pack 5 or later
- ❑ Install SQL Server 6.5 Service Pack 3 or later
- ❑ Shut down all applications or services that use SQL Server

Estimated Down Time:_____hours

- ❑ Alert users
- ❑ Have fall-back recovery plan in place
- ❑ Have another fall-back recovery plan in place in case fall-back plan fails
- ❑ Maintain SQL Server DBCC commands of *all* databases
- ❑ Perform SQL Server backup of *all* databases
- ❑ Perform SQL Server backup of master database
- ❑ Back up Windows NT System Registry
- ❑ Perform operating system backup of SQL Server directories and files (including devices)
- ❑ Make sure that no users are on the system
- ❑ Make sure that no applications are using SQL Server
- ❑ Start the SQL Server upgrade

5

Installing or Upgrading SQL Server

by Mark Spenik

IN THIS CHAPTER

- Installing SQL Server
- Starting and Stopping SQL Server
- Installation Troubleshooting
- Upgrading SQL Server
- Removing SQL Server
- Installing Client Tools
- Configuring Clients
- Installation FAQ

In this chapter, you walk through the actual installation and upgrade of SQL Server as well as the installation of software for the client PCs. Take a look at what the SQL Server installation program actually loads onto your computer. Following are the directories created from the SQL Server root directory (MSSQL) during installation:

- **BACKUP**—Default backup directory
- **BINN**—SQL Server, Dynamic Link Library files (DLLs), and client executable files as well as online help files
- **DATA**—SQL Server system database files
- **INSTALL**—Installation scripts and output files
- **JOBS**—Temporary storage location for job output files
- **LOG**—Error log files
- **REPLDATA**—Replication synchronization task working directory
- **Upgrade**—Files used by the Version Upgrade Wizard to upgrade 6.x databases
- **FTDATA**—Full text catalog files (only if using Full Text search)

The following services are installed:

- **MSSQLServer** (SQL Server)
- **SQLServerAgent** (SQL Server Agent)
- **MSSQLServerADHelper** (Active Directory Integration)

The following utilities are installed:

- **SQL Service Manager**— Used to start and stop SQL Server

- **Query Analyzer**—Utility to issue SQL queries

- **SQL Enterprise Manager**—Primary tool used to manage SQL Server and SQL Server objects

- **SQL Client Network Utility**—Used to set up SQL Server connection information and check versions of the database (db)-library installed

- **SQL Server Profiler**—Utility to monitor and record database activity

- **Version Upgrade Wizard**—Utility to upgrade SQL Server 6.x databases to 2000

- **Server Network Utility**—Used to add additional protocols to SQL Server

- **Import and Export Utility**—Allows you to create DTS packages for importing and exporting data

- **BCP**—Bulk Copy Utility to import and export flat files with SQL Server

Different Editions of SQL Server

SQL Server now comes in the following editions:

Personal

Standard

Developer

Windows CE

Desktop engine (MSDE)

Enterprise

All the editions of SQL Server share the majority of SQL Server 2000 features and are built on the same code base. Installing and using each edition is the same; for example, you can manage all editions with the Enterprise Manager. The key differences are where in your enterprise each edition fits in. The personal edition is for Windows 9.x or Windows NT workstations, and can be used by developers or mobile users. The Developer edition is targeted at the enterprise developer. It provides you with all the advanced features found in the Enterprise edition of SQL Server but runs on NT Workstation and Windows 2000 Professional. The Personal edition has the majority of SQL Server 2000 features found in the Standard, Developer, and Enterprise editions with some limitations. For example, the Personal version will only scale across two processors, and it supports full merge and snapshot replication. But, it can only act as a subscriber for transactional replication. The Standard edition does not support the following SQL Server 2000 features found in the Enterprise and Developer editions:

Failover clusters

Extended memory addressing

Parallel DBCC

Parallel Create Index

Indexed Views

Federated Database Servers

Enhanced Read-ahead and Scan

System Area Network Support (SAN)

The major differences between the Standard edition and the Enterprise edition are the scalability and fault tolerance. The Enterprise edition supports failover clustering, extended memory, and more processors than the Standard edition, which lacks failover clustering and extended memory support.

Installing SQL Server

Before installing SQL Server, make sure that you have read the documentation regarding installation that ships with SQL Server 2000. Also, make sure that your system meets the minimum requirements. To help you with your installation, use the following worksheet.

NOTE

Before you can install SQL Server 2000, you must install IE 5.0. IE 5.0 is located on the SQL Server CD; select SQL Server Prerequisites from the startup screen from the SQL Server 2000 installation program.

SQL Server Installation Checklist

Check off the following items as you complete or verify them:

Hardware and PC Setup:

- ❏ Computer is Intel (32-bit x86) Pentium 166 MHz or higher and is on the Windows NT Hardware Compatibility list.

- ❏ Memory: 64M (32M on Windows 9.*x*).

- ❏ Operating System: Windows XP, Windows 2000, Windows NT 4.0 Server or Workstation Service pack 5 or greater, Windows 9.*x* or later.

- ❏ Free disk space depending on the installation

    Minimum   95MB

    Typical   250MB

    Full   270MB

    on the hard drive to which SQL Server is to be installed. Note: For upgrades using 6.5 direct pipeline, you need about 1.5 times your current database size in disk space.

File System: ❏ FAT
                    ❏ NTFS

Computer Name:

SQL Server Options (Check or fill in)

User Name:_____Company Name:_____Product ID:_____

SQL Server Root Directory:_____

Program File Location: _____

Program Data Files Location: _____

Selected Collation Setting:_____

Network Protocols:

❏ Named-Pipes (Default, except Win 95)	❏ Multiprotocol (default)
❏ NWLink IPX/SPX (default Win 95 and 98)	❏ TCP/IP Sockets
❏ Banyan VINES	❏ AppleTalk ADSP
Books OnLine Installed:	❏ No (Requires anadditional 1M to 15M) ❏ Yes

Auto-Start Options:

- ❏ SQL Server

- ❏ SQL Server Agent

IE 5.0 or greater Installed: _____

Windows NT User Accounts (Not Available on Windows 95 or Later):

MSSQL Server User Account: _____ (Required for SQL Server network access for features such as ODBC replication or Web page generation)

SQL Server Agent User Account: _____

> **TIP**
>
> The installation of SQL Server can cause you problems if you try to install it with a user account that does not have the correct NT permissions to create new directories and files. If you get the error message `Can't create directory`, make sure that you are using an account with the correct privileges. Try creating the directory with File Manager. If you have the correct privileges, you will be able do so; otherwise, use a different account that has the correct permissions.

Step 1: Running Setup

Installing SQL Server requires running the setup program, located on the SQL Server 2000 CD. The CD contains several directories: The autorun file is located in the root directory of the CD.

Run the setup program (if autorun has not already displayed the setup program shown in Figure 5.1).

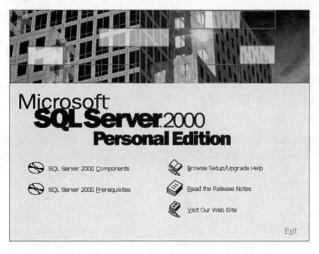

FIGURE 5.1   The SQL Server Setup Start window.

Step 2: Select an Installation Option

If you have already installed IE 5.0 and any required service packs and viewed the release notes, you are ready to begin your SQL Server installation. Click the SQL Server 2000 Components option shown in Figure 5.1; the Install Components dialog box opens (see Figure 5.2).

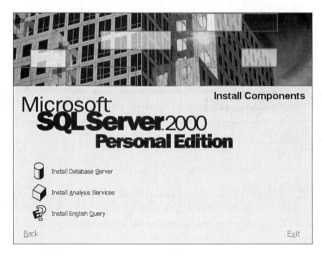

FIGURE 5.2   SQL Server 2000 Install Components dialog box.

To install the standard SQL Server, select Install Database Server. To install the OLAP server, click Install Analysis Services, and to install English Query, click Install English Query. For this walkthrough, select Install Database Server. The SQL Server 2000 Installation Wizard's welcome dialog box appears. To continue the installation process, click the Next button.

Step 3: Select Computer Install Method

The Computer Name dialog box, shown in Figure 5.3, opens.

For a new SQL Server 2000 installation, the Computer Name defaults to the PC name. Select the type of SQL Server installation you want: local, remote, or Virtual Server (only available with Microsoft Cluster Services). Make your selection and click the Next button; the Installation Selection dialog box, shown in Figure 5.4, appears.

Step 4: Installation Type

Most users take the default setting to Create a new instance of SQL Server, or install Client Tools. This option will install SQL Server and the Client Tools. If you want to create an installation script (an .ISS file) that allows you to perform unattended SQL

Server 2000 installations, if you want to rebuild the Registry (set Registry settings without installing SQL Server), or if you want to make changes to an existing SQL Server cluster (such as add or remove a cluster), select Advanced Options shown in Figure 5.4. For this walkthrough, take the default setting and click the Next button.

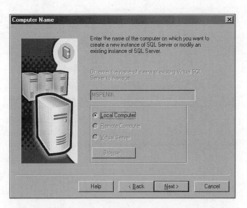

FIGURE 5.3   The SQL Server Computer Name dialog box.

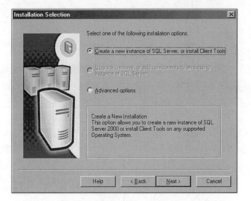

FIGURE 5.4   SQL Server Installation Selection dialog box.

Step 5: User Information

The User Information dialog box shown in Figure 5.5 appears. Fill in your name and company, and then click the Next button.

Step 6: License Agreement

The SQL Server Software License Agreement dialog box appears. For the Standard and Enterprise editions of SQL Server 2000, the dialog box looks slightly different from that shown in Figure 5.6. With the Standard and Enterprise editions, you need to also select a licensing mode. SQL Server 2000 supports two licensing modes: per seat mode and per processor. Per seat mode requires a license for any device that connects to SQL Server. Per processor mode allows unlimited connections but requires a license for each processor installed. You can add seats or processors after installation, but you can't change the licensing mode after installation. For this example using the Personal edition, read through the agreement and click the Yes button.

FIGURE 5.5   The User Information dialog box.

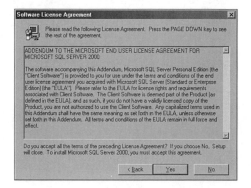

FIGURE 5.6   SQL Server Software License Agreement dialog box.

Step 7: Installation Type

The Installation Definition dialog box shown in Figure 5.7 appears. To install an instance of SQL Server 2000 and the Client Tools, select the Server and Client Tools radio button. To install only the Client Tools, select the Client Tools Only radio button. To install network libraries and Microsoft's Data Access components, select the Connectivity Only radio button. For this example, select the Server and Client Tools radio button and click the Next button.

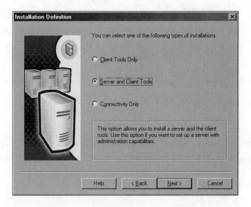

FIGURE 5.7   Installation Definition dialog box.

Step 8: Instance Name

The Instance Name dialog box shown in Figure 5.8 appears. For a default installation, leave the Default check box checked. If you want to create a named instance of SQL Server 2000, uncheck the box and enter an instance name in the Instance Name text box. When you have made your choice, click the Next button.

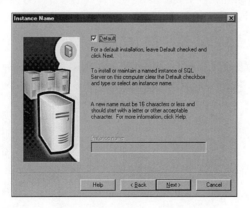

FIGURE 5.8   Instance Name dialog box.

Step 9: Setup Type and File Location

The Setup Type dialog box shown in Figure 5.9 appears. Select the type of installation you want to perform. The Typical installation installs SQL Server 2000 with the standard defaults. The standard defaults are as follows:

- **Program Location**: C:\Program Files\Microsoft SQL Server

- **Data Files**: C:\Program Files\Microsoft SQL Server

- **Network**: TCP/IP (Windows 9.*x*), named-pipes Windows NT

- **Books OnLine Installed**

The Typical installation includes all management tools and online documentation but does not include full text search, development tools, or samples. The Minimum installation installs only the essential SQL Server 2000 components, which requires about 65MB of disk space and does not include the online documentation or all the management tools. The Custom installation is similar to the Typical installation; however, you can modify features such as the code page and network libraries and add additional components like full text search, development tools, and samples. To change the default location of SQL Server program files or data files, click the Browse buttons and select a new drive or directory. The default location is C:\Program Files\Microsoft SQL Server. The drive and directory you select is where SQL Server installs the initial SQL Server databases and file groups for the program files as well as the database data and log files for the data files. The Setup Type dialog box, shown in Figure 5.9, displays the required amount of disk space for the program files and data files as well as the available space on the selected drives. To continue, click the Next button. For this walkthrough, the Custom option is selected; if you select Typical or Minimum, skip to step 11.

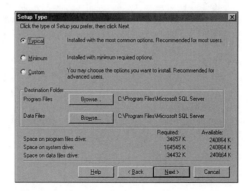

FIGURE 5.9   SQL Server Setup Type dialog box.

Step 10: Select Components to Install

The SQL Server Select Components dialog box shown in Figure 5.10 appears. Select the check boxes beside the options you want to install. To skip installation of a particular option, clear the option box. When you have made all your selections, click the Next button.

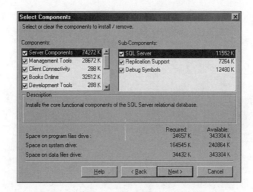

FIGURE 5.10   SQL Server Select Components dialog box.

Step 11: Authentication Mode

The Authentication Mode dialog box appears. Select the appropriate authentication mode—mixed or Windows—by selecting the proper radio button. When using the Personal Edition of SQL Server on Windows 9.*x*, the Windows Authentication mode radio button is disabled. Enter a password and password confirmation for the SQL Server sa user account (mixed mode) in the Enter password and Confirm password text boxes. For a blank password (not recommended), check the Blank Password check box shown in Figure 5.11. Click the Next button to continue. (Note: If you selected Typical or Minimum, skip to step 14).

FIGURE 5.11   The Authentication Mode dialog box.

Step 12: Collation Setting

The Collation Settings dialog box, shown in Figure 5.12, appears. Use the drop-down box to select a collation designator or the list box to select a collation. The collation setting will default based on your Windows collation setting; it is recommended that you take the default for collation setting. After you have made your selection, click the Next button.

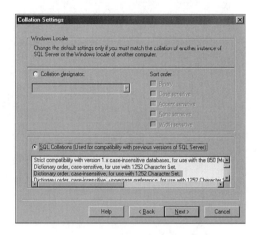

FIGURE 5.12   SQL Server Collation Settings dialog box.

CAUTION

Refer to Chapter 4, "Planning an Installation or Upgrade," on the importance of select-ing the proper collation setting from the start. Changing the collation requires exporting the data from the databases, rebuilding the databases, and then reloading the data.

Step 13: Network Libraries

The SQL Server Network Libraries dialog box, shown in Figure 5.13, appears. To add additional network protocols, select the check box located besides the protocol. To remove a protocol, clear the check box. After you have made your selection, click the Next button.

Step 13a: SQL Server, SQL Agent, MSDTC User Accounts, and Auto Start Services—Windows 2000 and NT Only

If you are installing SQL Server on a Windows 2000 or NT machine, you are prompted by a dialog box that enables you to assign a domain user account to SQL Server. The default is to use the system local account. If you do not assign a specific

account to the SQL Server Agent and MSDTC, they use the same account as SQL
Server. You are also prompted to restart SQL Server and the SQL Agent automatically
if the NT server is shut down and restarted. After you have made your selections,
click the Next button.

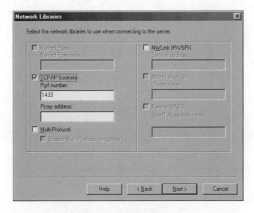

FIGURE 5.13   SQL Server Network Libraries dialog box.

TIP

It is recommended that you assign a domain user account to SQL Server. Without a domain
user account, SQL Server cannot use replication, SQL mail, or the Version Upgrade Wizard. It
is also recommended that you auto-start both SQL Server and SQL Agent so that if you lose
power, you won't be called in the middle of the night because an application cannot connect
to the database.

Step 14: Start Copying Files

The final dialog box is the SQL Server Start Copying Files dialog box, shown in
Figure 5.14. Click the Next button to start the SQL Server installation. Then it's wait-
and-watch time as SQL Server is installed, the system databases are created, and the
program group is created. When the installation is completed, you are shown a
completion dialog box and told that the machine must be rebooted to complete the
installation. To reboot now, click OK. Otherwise, select Reboot Later and click OK.
Congratulations! You have just successfully installed SQL Server 2000.

Starting and Stopping SQL Server

If you checked the Auto Boot options for SQL Server and the SQL Agent, the two
services start automatically when the server reboots. The easiest way to start, stop,

pause, or check the status of SQL Server and SQL Agent is to use the SQL Server Service Manager (see Figure 5.15).

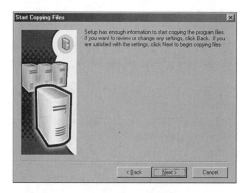

FIGURE 5.14   SQL Server Start Copying Files dialog box.

FIGURE 5.15   The SQL Server Service Manager.

The SQL Server Service Manager is located in the Microsoft SQL Server program group, which was created during the installation or upgrade. To start the SQL Server Service Manager, double-click its icon. If SQL Server is running, the indicator light is green. If the service is stopped, the indicator light is red. To start SQL Server, first select the instance of SQL Server you want to start in the Server combo box, shown in Figure 5.15. Next, select SQL Server in the Services combo box, shown in Figure 5.15 and click the arrow button next to the Start/Continue label. To stop SQL Server, click the red box next to the Stop label. To pause SQL Server, click the double-bar next to the Pause label. Pausing SQL Server does not halt queries in process; it prevents new users from logging in to SQL Server. When SQL Server is paused, users currently logged in to SQL Server can continue to work as normal.

Controlling the SQL Server Agent and MSDTC is the same as controlling SQL Server, except that you cannot pause the SQL Server Agent or MSDTC. To perform stop, start, and status checks on SQL Server Agent or MSDTC, use the drop-down Services list box and select SQLServerAgent or MSDTC instead of MSSQLServer.

NOTE

The service name for Microsoft SQL Server 2000 is *MSSQLServer*.

Installation Troubleshooting

As stated earlier, the installation process for SQL Server is straightforward; however, even in the most straightforward operations, problems can and do occur. Ideally, you should be provided with error messages that pinpoint your problem. In some cases, you will have to do some debugging and observation to determine what has gone wrong. In the worst cases, you might find yourself on the telephone with tech support trying to determine the problem.

Some of the common errors encountered during an installation or upgrade are improper Windows NT permissions or insufficient disk space. If you receive an error message telling you that you can't create a directory or file, you probably have a permissions problem. Switch to an account with the correct permissions. If the installation fails, check your disk space to make sure that you have enough free space to install SQL Server.

TIP

Okay, I've done so many of these installations that I've lost count! Where have I encountered problems? Well, the most common problem I've encountered is trying to install SQL Server when something is using another file that SQL Server wants to install—for instance, a new ODBC driver manager or in the case of an upgrade, the SQL Server 7.0 Service Manager tray icon. It helps to shut down other services while installing. I've also run into problems in which the domain user account assigned to SQL Server was not set up correctly (for example, a local administrator, log on as service, and so on). I can say that most of the time, I have experienced no problems at all.

What can you do if you have completed an installation and your SQL Server does not work? You have to start debugging and try to determine the problem. The best place to start is the SQL Server error log.

Error Log and Windows 2000/NT Application Log

The error log, located on the SQL Server root directory in the directory \LOG, is a text file used to log audit and error information for SQL Server.

The Windows 2000 or NT application log is a system log used by applications and Windows 2000 and NT to log audit and error information. The application log contains the same information as the SQL Server error log, except that only SQL Server writes to the error log, but any Windows NT application can write to the application log. You can configure SQL Server to write to both logs (the default) or to either log.

TIP

When I try to read consecutive error or audit messages, I find that the SQL Server error log is easier to view than the Windows NT application log. However, one benefit of the Windows NT application log is that error messages are highlighted with a stop sign icon and are easy to find.

Following is an example of an SQL Server error log entry during system startup:

```
2000-10-19 22:18:56.49 server    Microsoft SQL Server  2000
- 8.00.194 (Intel X86)
    Aug  6 2000 00:57:48
    Copyright (c) 1988-2000 Microsoft Corporation
    Personal Edition on Windows 4.10 (Build 1998:  )


2000-10-19 22:18:56.54 server    Copyright (C) 1988-2000 Microsoft Corporation.
2000-10-19 22:18:56.54 server    All rights reserved.
2000-10-19 22:18:56.54 server    Server Process ID is -726989.
2000-10-19 22:18:56.54 server    Logging SQL Server messages in
file 'D:\Program Files\Microsoft SQL Server\MSSQL$TRIOLGY\log\ERRORLOG'.
2000-10-19 22:18:56.75 server    SQL Server is starting at priority class
'normal'(1 CPU detected).
2000-10-19 22:18:57.39 server    SQL Server configured for thread mode
processing.
2000-10-19 22:18:57.54 server    Using dynamic lock
allocation. [500] Lock Blocks, [1000] Lock Owner Blocks.
2000-10-19 22:18:57.94 spid3     Starting up database 'master'.
2000-10-19 22:18:59.04 spid5     Starting up database 'model'.
2000-10-19 22:19:00.63 server    SQL server listening on TCP,
TCP, Shared Memory.
2000-10-19 22:19:00.78 server    SQL server listening
on 172.16.14.113:1067, 127.0.0.1:1067, 172.16.14.113:1112, 127.0.0.1:1112.
2000-10-19 22:19:00.91 server    SQL Server is ready for client connections
2000-10-19 22:19:01.09 spid3     Server name is 'MSPENIK\TRIOLGY'.
2000-10-19 22:19:01.14 spid3     Skipping startup of clean database id 4
2000-10-19 22:19:01.14 spid3     Skipping startup of clean database id 5
2000-10-19 22:19:01.14 spid3     Skipping startup of clean database id 6
2000-10-19 22:19:01.33 spid5     Clearing tempdb database.
2000-10-19 22:19:02.92 spid5     Starting up database 'tempdb'.
2000-10-19 22:19:03.44 spid3     Recovery complete.
```

You can view the error log using any text file editor, such as Windows Notepad or SQL Server Enterprise Manager. You can view the Windows 2000 or NT application log using the Event Viewer.

Scan through the error log or application log and look for possible error messages. Every time you stop and restart SQL Server, a new error log is started. SQL Server archives the error logs by saving the previous six error log files (by default, SQL Server 2000 allows you to configure the number of archived error logs), which are named as follows (where X is 1 through 6, and the current error log is ERRORLOG):

ERRORLOG.X

Start SQL Server from the Command Line

If you are having trouble starting SQL Server from the Windows 2000 or NT Service Manager or the SQL Server Service Manager after an installation or upgrade, try starting SQL Server from the command line. Starting SQL Server from the command line is a great way to debug because the messages usually logged to the error log or Windows NT application log are displayed directly in the DOS command window. To start SQL Server from the command line, enter the following:

sqlservr `<command line options>`

Not all the command-line options are discussed here, but read on to find out about a few of the important options you can use to help get your SQL Server debugged and up and running. When starting SQL Server from the command line, make sure that you are in the proper BINN directory for the instance you want to start. For example, to start the default instance, you should be in the \MSSQL\BINN directory. To start any instance other than the default, you should be in the \MSSQL$Instance_Name\BINN directory.

-s
The -s option specifies the instance name you want to start. Without the -s option, the default instance is started.

-d
The -d option specifies the path and filename of the master database file.

-l
The -l option specifies the path and filename of the master transaction log file.

-e
The -e option specifies the path and filename of the error log file.

-c

The -c option starts SQL Server independent of the Windows NT Service Control Manager.

> **TIP**
>
> The -c option is supposed to quicken SQL Server startup time by bypassing the Windows NT Service Control Manager. If you are having problems starting SQL Server, include the -c option to help further isolate the problem. I was working with one upgraded SQL Server installation in which the NT Service Control Manager kept shutting down SQL Server every time it started. By specifying the -c option, I was able to get the server up and correct the problem. The only drawback is that you cannot stop the SQL Server with any of the conventional methods (such as the SQL Server Service Manager). SQL Server can be halted by logging off of Windows NT or pressing Ctrl+C in the DOS command window running SQL Server. When you press Ctrl+C, you are prompted with a message asking if you want to shut down the server. Select Y to shut down the server.

-m

The -m option enables you to start SQL Server in single-user mode, which means that only one user can log in to SQL Server. Use the -m option when restoring databases or trying to fix suspect or corrupted databases.

-T

The -T option allows you to start SQL Server with a trace flag.

-f

The -f option enables you to start SQL Server in a minimal configuration. Use the -f option only when SQL Server does not start because of a configuration parameter problem.

-v

The -v option displays the server version number.

-x

The -x option disables the gathering of CPU statistics.

-g

The -g option allows you to specify in megabytes an amount of memory to reserve for other in-process applications.

-O

The -O option signals SQL Server that DCOM (Distributed COM) is not required. This feature disables the use of Distributed Queries.

-y

The -y option allows you to specify an error number that, if it occurs, SQL Server 2000 will write a stack trace to the error log. You can have multiple -y options to support multiple error numbers.

Following is an example of how to start the default instance of SQL Server from the command line using some of the preceding options:

```
sqlservr -c -dc:\mssql7\data\master.mdf -lc:\mssql7\data\master.ldf -e
➡ dc:\mssql7\log\errorlog -f
```

Upgrading SQL Server

As stated in Chapter 4, SQL Server 2000 gives you two different options for upgrading a server. The first option is to perform an actual upgrade of a SQL Server 7.0 database, which replaces the SQL Server 7.0 instance with SQL Server 2000 and upgrades the data files to SQL Server 2000. The second option is to leave SQL Server 7.0 intact and install a new instance of SQL Server 2000 alongside SQL Server 7.0. You can then use the Copy Database Wizard to upgrade databases from SQL Server 7.0 to SQL Server 2000.

For SQL Server 6.5, the upgrade process is done via the Version Upgrade Wizard. All the databases can be migrated at one time, or you can selectively upgrade them one at a time. The Version Upgrade Wizard provides a very easy user interface to migrate your SQL Server 6.x databases to SQL Server 2000. The Version Upgrade Wizard is extremely smart. At any step in the process, you can pause or halt the wizard. You can then later pick up where you left off, or you can restart the process. If you pick up from where you left off, the wizard does not redo things that have already been completed successfully. For example, each table is treated as an individual transaction. If the wizard successfully completes the export and import of Table A but fails on Table B, halt the process and correct the problem and then restart the process. The wizard does not redo Table A because it was exported and imported successfully; instead it begins with Table B (where you left off).

As a reminder, make sure that you have done the following before performing an upgrade:

- Performed database backups

- Backed up SQL Server files, devices, and directories

- Backed up the NT Registry

- Reviewed the release notes

- Have adequate disk space to perform the upgrade

Upgrading SQL Server 7.0 to SQL Server 2000

After you have taken all the pre-upgrade actions required (such as backing up your databases), you are ready to perform an upgrade. When upgrading from SQL Server 7.0 to SQL Server 2000, you have the following two options:

- Upgrade the SQL Server 7.0 instance to SQL Server 2000

- Install a new instance of SQL Server 2000 to run alongside SQL Server 7.0

Upgrade the SQL Server 7.0 Instance to SQL Server 2000

When upgrading SQL Server 7.0 to SQL Server 2000, no additional drive space is required. The upgrade process is very simple and mimics the installation process. When you reach "Step 4: Installation Type" of the installation process, you need to manually select Upgrade, Remove, or Add Components to an Existing Instance of SQL Server in the Installation Selection dialog box shown in Figure 5.16.

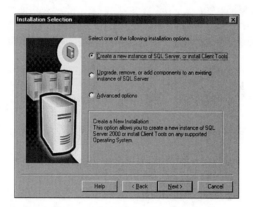

FIGURE 5.16   Installation Selection dialog box.

Your SQL Server 7.0 installation will be upgraded along with your databases to SQL Server 2000.

TIP

After upgrading SQL Server 7.0 to SQL Server 2000, it is recommended that you update statistics on all the database upgrades and repopulate the full-text catalogs even if you have auto updated statistics turned on. Doing both procedures after an upgrade can greatly improve performance in SQL Server 2000 because Sever 2000 is better at collecting statistics than 7.0. Doing it manually (even if auto stats is on) allows you to know exactly when the statistics were updated.

Install a New Instance of SQL Server 2000 to Run Alongside SQL Server 7.0
Installing a new instance of SQL Server 2000 alongside a SQL Server 7 installation requires the same amount of disk space required by a new SQL Server 2000 installation, plus enough space to migrate the existing 7.0 databases. The only difference in the installation process when installing a new instance of SQL Server 2000 to an existing 7.0 or 2000 server is to add an instance name in the Instance Name dialog box, shown in Figure 5.17.

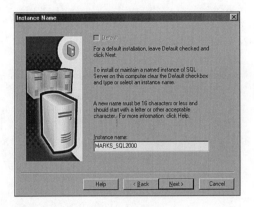

FIGURE 5.17   The Instance Name dialog box.

After an instance of SQL Server 2000 is installed alongside a SQL Server 7.0 instance, use the SQL Server 2000 Enterprise Manager and other SQL 2000 utilities to access the 7.0 instance and the 2000 instance. To upgrade a database from a 7.0 instance to a SQL Server 2000 instance, use the Copy Database Wizard.

Copy Database Wizard   You can use the Copy Database Wizard to copy databases from SQL Server 7.0 to SQL Server 2000 or from SQL Server 2000 to SQL Server 2000. The instance of SQL Server can be on the same computer or on different computers. Using the Copy Database Wizard, you can selectively copy one or more databases to SQL Server 2000. The Copy Database Wizard detaches the database from the source server, copies the files to the destination server, and then reattaches the database at the destination server. You can copy the database, which leaves it intact at the source server or move the database, which removes the files from the source server. Using the wizard on Windows 2000 or NT 4.0 requires that you use an account that is part of the sysadmin role and must have NT administrator rights. You can't copy a database from a source to a destination server if a database with the same name already exists on the destination server. Also, the database being moved can't have any active sessions.

To use the Copy Database Wizard using the Enterprise Manager, perform the following:

1. From the Enterprise Manager, select Tools and then select Wizards. The Select Wizard dialog box appears.

2. View the Management wizards by clicking the + sign. Select Copy Database Wizard and click the OK button. The Welcome to the Copy Database Wizard dialog box appears. Click the Next button.

3. The Select a Source Server dialog box, shown in Figure 5.18, appears. Select the source server of the database(s) to copy using the Source Server combo box. After you have selected the source server, click the Next button.

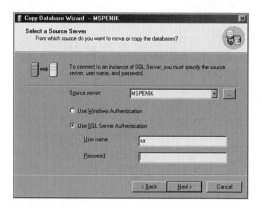

FIGURE 5.18   The Select a Source Server dialog box.

4. The Select a Destination Server dialog box, shown in Figure 5.19, appears. Select the destination server of the database(s) to copy the databases to using the Destination Server combo box. After you have selected the source server, click the Next button.

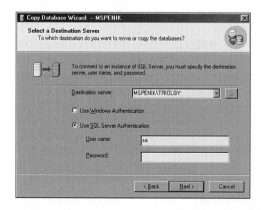

FIGURE 5.19   The Select a Destination Server dialog box.

5. The Select the Databases to Move or Copy dialog box, shown in Figure 5.20, appears. Check the database(s) you want to move or copy by selecting the check box by the database to move or copy. After you have selected the databases, click the Next button.

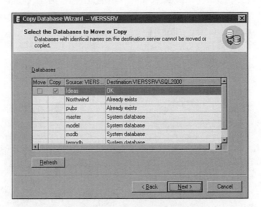

FIGURE 5.20   The Select the Databases to Move or Copy dialog box.

6. The Database File Location dialog box, shown in Figure 5.21, appears. This dialog box shows and allows you to modify the location of the database filename to be copied or moved. A green check in the Status column means that the file can be moved or copied. A red X means that there might not be enough space on the destination drive(s) or that there is a conflicting filename. To continue, click the Next button.

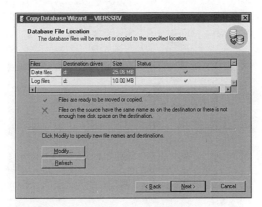

FIGURE 5.21   The Database File Location dialog box.

7. The Select Related Objects dialog box, shown in Figure 5.22, appears. This dialog box allows you to copy related SQL Server objects that are not part of the database(s) being moved but that reside in the master and msdb databases like user logins, jobs, user-defined error messages, and shared stored procedures located in the master database. You can choose to copy all of them or select the objects you want copied (that is jobs, logins, and so on). After you have made your selections, click the Next button.

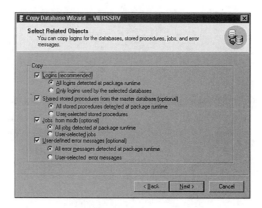

FIGURE 5.22   The Select Related Objects dialog box.

8. The Schedule the DTS Package dialog box, shown in Figure 5.23, appears. Using this dialog box, you can choose to run the copy or move the database immediately or schedule it to run at another time. When you have made your choice, the database(s) will be moved or copied immediately or at the scheduled time. You can then test your applications that use the databases to verify that they work appropriately with SQL Server 2000.

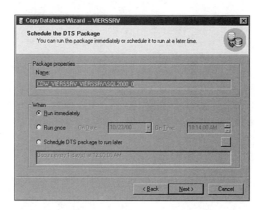

FIGURE 5.23   The Schedule the DTS Package dialog box.

Upgrading SQL Server 6.5

Upgrading a 6.5 server to SQL Server 2000 is a slightly more complicated process than upgrading a SQL Server 7.0 database. For starters, SQL Server 7.0 and SQL Server 2000 have different page sizes and data structures than SQL Server 6.5, so the 6.5 data files are not upgraded. Instead, data is copied from SQL Server 6.5 into SQL Server 2000. Also, SQL Server 6.5 will have possible compatibility issues with various functions and T-SQL (see the question regarding compatibility settings in this chapter's FAQ). The requirements and Version Upgrade Wizard are discussed in detail in Chapter 4. To launch the Version Upgrade Wizard, from the Windows start menu select Programs, and then SQL Server Switch—SQL Server Upgrade Wizard. Follow the steps in the Version Upgrade Wizard to upgrade your 6.5 databases to SQL Server 2000.

6.5 Upgrade Troubleshooting

The Version Upgrade Wizard provides useful and easy-to-access information regarding errors that occur during the upgrade process. If an error does occur during the upgrade process, you will get an Informational Files Found dialog box, shown in Figure 5.24.

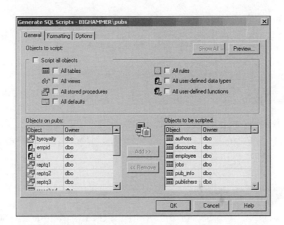

FIGURE 5.24   Informational Files Found dialog box.

You can then select to view the information files to see what problem occurred with the particular object. You can then try to correct the problem and resume or redo the upgrade process.

Upgrade Subdirectories and Contents

To troubleshoot the upgrade process, it helps to know how the upgrade subdirectories are created and what the contents of each directory are. The main upgrade directory is the subdirectory UPGRADE located off the main SQL Server directory.

Whenever you perform an upgrade, a subdirectory that has the following format is created off the upgrade directory:

```
Machine name_date_time
```

For example, on the MAS server, the full path is

```
C:\MSSQL\UPGRADE\MAS_041898_125255
```

This directory contains the following:

- **.OUT files**—For each stage of the upgrade process
- **.OK files**—For all scripts run on 6.x and 7.0
- **.ERR files**—Errors encountered during a stage in the upgrade process

The upgrade subdirectory created whenever you run the upgrade process also has a subdirectory for each database upgraded with the following naming convention:

```
Number Database Name
```

For example, the full path of the database Finance is as follows:

```
C:\MSSQL\UPGRADE\KSCSINC_041898_125255\001Finance
```

This subdirectory contains the following:

- **.OK files**—For each successful object transfer
- **Script files**—For each database object with file extensions based on the type of object (for example, Table = .tab, stored procedure = .prc, and so on)

Removing SQL Server

If you want to remove SQL Server installation, do not delete the SQL Server directories. To remove an instance of SQL Server 2000, use the Windows control panel. Select Add/Remove programs from the Windows control panel. The Add/Remove Programs Properties dialog box, shown in Figure 5.25 appears. Scroll down to the SQL Server 2000 instance you want to remove, select the instance name, and click OK. This will remove the SQL Server instance. To remove all instances, repeat the removal process for each instance.

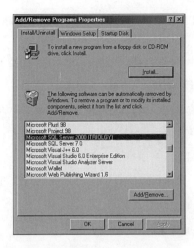

FIGURE 5.25   Add/Remove Programs Properties dialog box.

Installing Client Tools

SQL Server provides several different tools that allow computers acting as clients to connect to SQL Server. The following are the current 32-bit operating systems supported by the SQL Server Client Tools:

- Microsoft Windows NT Server version 4.0

- Microsoft Windows NT Workstation version 4.0

- Microsoft Windows 2000 Professional

- Microsoft Windows 2000 Server

- Microsoft Windows 2000 Advanced Server

- Microsoft Windows XP

- Microsoft Windows 98

- Microsoft Windows 95

If you are using one of these 32-bit operating systems, you can install the following tools:

- **SQL Server Query Analyzer**—Utility to issue SQL queries

- **SQL Enterprise Manager**—Primary tool used to manage SQL Server and SQL Server objects

- **Client Network Utility**—Utility to set up SQL Server connection information and check versions of the db-library installed

- **Version Upgrade Wizard**—Utility to convert 6.x databases to 2000

- **SQL Server Profiler**—Utility to monitor and record database activity

- **MS DTC**—Microsoft Distributed Transaction Coordinator client support

- **SQL Server Web Assistant**—Creates HTML files as the result of a query

- **ODBC Drivers**—Installs other ODBC drivers for replication use

- **BCP**—Bulk Copy Utility to import and export flat files with SQL Server

Configuring Clients

Now that you have the client utilities installed, you are ready to connect to SQL Server. SQL Server clients establish connections with SQL Server over named-pipes using dynamic server names. SQL Server clients can connect over named-pipes or any of the Microsoft-supplied protocols, including TCP/IP sockets and IPX/SPX.

Typically, you can connect to SQL Server from a client utility without any special configuration. When using ISQL/W or the SQL Enterprise Manager, click the List Servers to get a list of the active SQL Servers.

To connect to SQL Server that is using a different network protocol or listening on an alternative named-pipe, you can set up an entry for the SQL Server using the Add button located on the Alias tab of the Client Network Utility dialog box (see Figure 5.26).

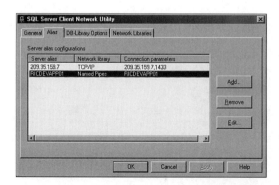

FIGURE 5.26   The Alias tab of the SQL Server Client Network Utility dialog box.

To add a new client configuration, click the Add button and enter the server name in the Server Alias text box. Select the network used to communicate with the server by checking the proper radio button. Selecting the network assigns the correct DLL to the server entry. The network DLLs for each operating system are listed in Table 5.1.

TABLE 5.1   SQL Server Net Libraries

Network Protocol	Windows NT/95 DLL	MS-DOS TSR
Named-pipes	DBNMPNTW	DBNMPIPE.EXE
NWLink IPX/SPX	DBMSSPXN	DBMSSPX.EXE
Banyan VINES	DBMSVINN	DBMSVINE.EXE
TCP/IP Sockets	DBMSSOCN	None
Multiprotocol	DBMSRPCN	None

Click the OK button to add the new server.

WHAT ABOUT ODBC?

If you are trying to connect to SQL Server using the Open Database Connectivity standard (ODBC), remember that the Client Configuration utility does not set up ODBC data sources for applications such as Microsoft Access or PowerBuilder. You must run the ODBC setup program that ships with the application or the operating system. You can test an ODBC connection using the DOS-based utility osql, which is located in the SQL Server BINN directory.

Remote Installation

You can install SQL Server on a different machine than the installation program is running on. This feature is called remote installation. To install SQL Server on a remote machine you must be logged in to the machine you are running the SQL Server setup program from with a user account that has administrative privileges on the remote computer. Of course both computers must be running Windows NT or Windows 2000. The remote installation process is the same as the regular installation process with the exception of selecting a remote computer by selecting the Remote Computer radio button shown in Figure 5.3 and clicking the Browse button, which brings up the dialog box of computers on the network. Select the one on which you want to install SQL Server remotely and the installation process will continue on as normal. The only other information you will be asked for that is not part of the regular installation process is the username, password and, domain for the SQL Server account on the remote computer and the path on the remote computer to install SQL Server.

Installing Multiple Instances of SQL Server

One of the new features of SQL Server 2000 is the ability to install multiple instances of SQL Server on the same computer. Multiple instances of SQL Server means that more than one copy of SQL Server exists on the same computer. Multiple instances run simultaneously and independently of one another. Client applications connect to each instance of SQL Server. Essentially using instances is like having SQL Server on different physical servers except that the multiple instances live on the same server sharing the same CPU, disk space, and memory resources. You are allowed to have one default installation of SQL Server, which takes the name of the computer as its default name. If SQL Server is not installed on the server, you can skip the default instance and create a named instance. If SQL Server is already installed, then you must use a named instance for the installation. SQL Server 2000 can support up to 16 instances on the same machine (assuming the hardware has the capacity to support it). Instance names cannot exceed 16 characters and must begin with a letter, underscore, or ampersand and can contain letters, numbers, or characters. To connect to a named instance of SQL Server, you must include the computer network name and the instance name. For example if the computer network name is BigServer and the instance name is Finance, you would refer to the instance as BigServer/Finance. The SQL Server installation files and data files are also placed in directories that use the instance name, for example the instance Finance would be found in:

```
Program Files\Microsoft SQL Server\MSSQL$Finance
```

Installation FAQ

Q When using the SQL Server Manager, what does Pause do?

A When you pause SQL Server, current users are allowed to continue to work, but any new logons are denied.

Q SQL Server 6.5 had an option used with setup.exe that allowed you to rebuild SQL Server's Registry entries. Does such a thing exist in 2000?

A Rebuilding SQL Server's Registry entry is no longer hidden in the setup program. SQL Server setup (installation program) allows you to rebuild the Registry for SQL Server services.

Q What are service packs, and how do I install them?

A After a product releases, problems or bugs might occur. These are reported to Microsoft. Microsoft tracks down the problem and fixes it. After several changes have been made, a service pack is released to correct the problems on existing SQL Servers. Service packs replace DLLs and exe files. Typically a readme file, which tells you how to install the service pack, accompanies the service pack. Service packs are cumulative as well. For example, if the latest service pack is 2 and you never installed service pack 1, you have to install only service pack 2 because it contains the changes from service pack 1.

Q Does SQL Server 2000 still support compatibility modes?

A Each SQL Server 2000 database has a compatibility mode property that allows you to set up compatibility from SQL Server 6.0 to SQL Server 2000. The compatibility modes tell SQL Server how to respond to different T-SQL statements. In 6.5 mode, the following would be a valid statement:

```
Select * from authors where state = NULL
```

The statement would return all authors with a NULL state. The previous statement would return no rows in SQL Server 7.0 or SQL Server 2000 and would need to be rewritten as follows:

```
Select * from authors where state Is NULL
```

The compatibility mode allows you to upgrade your 6.x applications and obtain the overall benefits of SQL Server 2000 without having to rewrite your applications. Check the SQL Server 2000 Books Online and the Microsoft Web sites for issues surrounding 6.x to 2000 compatibility issues. Although compatibility mode works well with standard T-SQL, some functions do behave differently in 2000 regardless of the mode.

Summary

You now have completed the chapters on installing and upgrading SQL Server. The remaining chapters in this book teach you how to perform database administration tasks, such as database backups, SQL Server tuning and configuration, and many other activities.

PART III

SQL Server Management and Configuration

IN THIS PART

6 Enterprise Management Processes

7 Configuring and Tuning SQL Server

8 Managing Databases

9 Managing SQL Server Users and Security

6

Enterprise Management Processes

by Orryn Sledge

This chapter provides an overview of the SQL Server Enterprise Manager and how to use it to perform common tasks. It also covers other commonly used products such as the Service Manager and the Query Analyzer.

Starting, Pausing, and Stopping SQL Server

Before discussing the Enterprise Manager, verify that SQL Server is started. To start, pause, or stop SQL Server, double-click the Service Manager icon in the Microsoft SQL Server group (see Figure 6.1). The SQL Server Service Manager dialog box appears (see Figure 6.2). From this dialog box, you can start, pause, or stop SQL Server.

TIP

SQL Server can also be started, paused, and stopped from the Task Tray icon (see Figure 6.3) in Windows NT and Windows 9x. The following are valid actions for the task tray icon:

- Double-click the icon in the task tray to open the SQL Server Service Manager dialog box. From the SQL Server Service Manager dialog box, you can start, pause, and stop SQL Server.

- Right-click the Task Tray icon. From the right-mouse menu, select the SQL Server service to start, pause, and stop SQL Server.

IN THIS CHAPTER

- Starting, Pausing, and Stopping SQL Server

- Starting the SQL Server Enterprise Manager

- Navigating the SQL Server Enterprise Manager

- Registering a Server

- Connecting to a Server

- Disconnecting from a Server

- Starting, Stopping, and Configuring SQL Server Agent

- Starting, Stopping, and Configuring SQL Mail

- Using the Enterprise Manager to Perform Common Tasks

- SQL Server Query Analyzer

- Starting and Stopping the Distributed Transaction Coordinator (DTC)

- FAQ

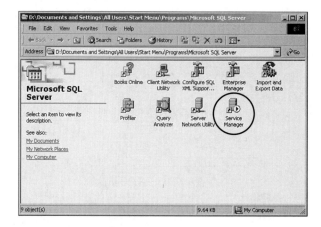

FIGURE 6.1   The Service Manager icon.

FIGURE 6.2   The SQL Server Service Manager dialog box.

FIGURE 6.3   Task tray icon.

Starting the SQL Server Enterprise Manager

To start the SQL Server Enterprise Manager, double-click the Enterprise Manager icon in the Microsoft SQL Server group (see Figure 6.4).

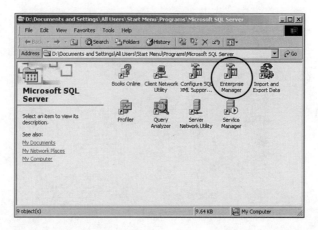

FIGURE 6.4   The Enterprise Manager icon.

Navigating the SQL Server Enterprise Manager

Because of its graphical interface, the SQL Server Enterprise Manager minimizes the number of commands required to administer a server. Following are common methods of navigation in the SQL Server Enterprise Manager:

- Menu items
- Double-click
- Right-click
- Drag and drop

Registering a Server

When you *register a server,* you provide the SQL Server Enterprise Manager with a server name and user login with which to connect to the SQL Server database engine.

Follow these steps to register a server:

1. From the Enterprise Manager, click the Register Server icon. The Register SQL Server Wizard dialog box appears.

2. From the Register SQL Server Wizard dialog box (see Figure 6.5), click the Next button to continue.

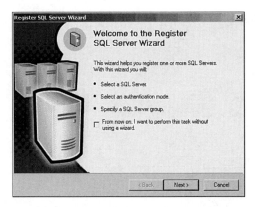

FIGURE 6.5   The Register SQL Server Wizard.

3. From the Select a SQL Server dialog box (see Figure 6.6), select the name of a
   server and click the Add button to add the server to the Added Servers list (if
   the server does not appear in the list, you can also type the name of the
   server). Click the Next button to continue.

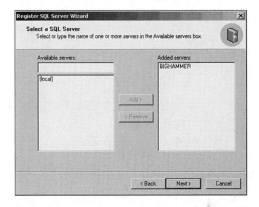

FIGURE 6.6   Select a server.

4. Select the type of authentication mode to use (see Figure 6.7): Windows
   Authentication or SQL Server Authentication. Windows Authentication offers
   the advantage of having to maintain only a Windows NT login account and
   password. With SQL Server Authentication, you must maintain a network
   account as well as a SQL Server account and password.

   If you are using SQL Server Authentication, enter the login ID and password.

   Click the Next button to continue.

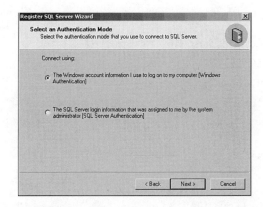

FIGURE 6.7   Select an authentication mode.

5. Select a server group or create a new server group (see Figure 6.8). Click the Next button to continue.

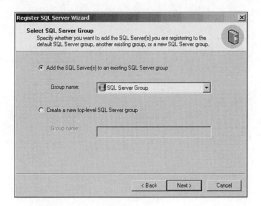

FIGURE 6.8   Select a SQL Server group.

6. Click the Finish button to register the server with the SQL Server Enterprise Manager (see Figure 6.9).

7. The Register SQL Server Messages dialog box appears (see Figure 6.10). Click the Close button to complete this operation.

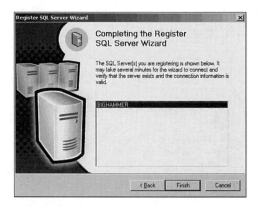

FIGURE 6.9   Completing the Register SQL Server Wizard.

FIGURE 6.10   The Register SQL Server Messages dialog box.

Connecting to a Server

After you open the SQL Server Enterprise Manager and start SQL Server, perform the following to connect to a server.

1. Click the plus (+) sign next to the Microsoft SQL Servers folder.

2. Click the plus (+) sign next to the group that contains the registered server you want to connect with (usually this is the SQL Server Group).

3. Click the plus (+) sign next to the server name.

If a connection is successfully made, server folders will appear below the server name (see Figure 6.11).

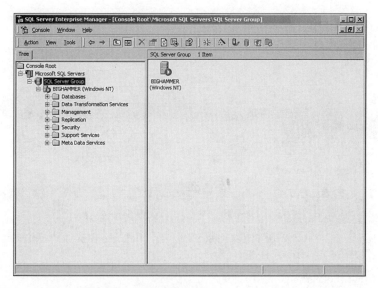

FIGURE 6.11 A successful server connection.

NOTE

If you are unable to establish a connection to SQL Server from the SQL Server Enterprise Manager, make sure that the MSSQLServer service is currently running. (See the topic "Starting, Pausing, and Stopping SQL Server" in this chapter for more information.)

If the MSSQLServer service is running and you are still unable to connect to SQL Server, verify the security mode, logon name, and password used to connect to SQL Server. To verify this information, right-click the server. From the right-mouse menu, select the Edit SQL Server Registration menu option. The Registered SQL Server Properties dialog box appears. From this dialog box, verify the connection information.

If you are still unable to connect, verify the network protocol used to connect with SQL Server versus the network protocols in use by the server. To verify the client protocol in use, open the Client Network Utility (found in the Microsoft SQL Server Program Group) and review the default network library and other network library settings. To verify the server protocol in use, open the Server Network Utility (found in the Microsoft SQL Server Program Group) and review the active server network libraries. Compare the server information to the client information.

If you are running TCP/IP on the client and on the server, try pinging the server from a command window by using `ping` `ipaddress`. This will tell you if you are properly networked to the server. If you are unable to ping the server, you have a networking problem. You must get the networking problem fixed before you can connect to SQL Server.

Disconnecting from a Server

To disconnect from a server, select the server and right-click. From the shortcut menu, select Disconnect.

> **NOTE**
>
> You are automatically disconnected from SQL Server when you close the SQL Server Enterprise Manager.

Starting, Stopping, and Configuring SQL Server Agent

Follow these steps to start, stop, or configure SQL Server Agent:

1. From the SQL Server Enterprise Manager, click the plus (+) sign next to the server to manage SQL Server Agent.

2. Click the Management folder.

3. Right-click the SQL Server Agent icon (see Figure 6.12). From the right-mouse menu, select Start to start the service, select Stop to stop the service, or select Properties (see Figure 6.13) to configure the service.

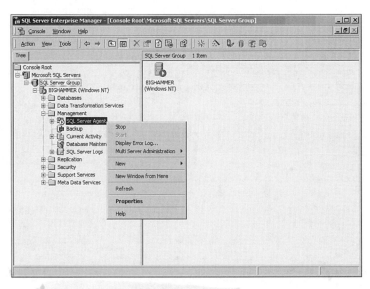

FIGURE 6.12   SQL Server Agent right-mouse menu.

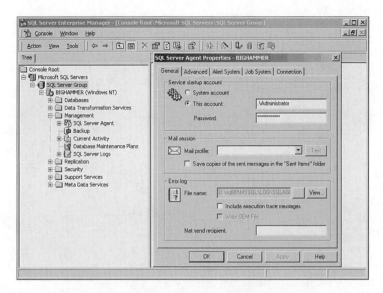

FIGURE 6.13   The SQL Server Agent Properties dialog box.

Starting, Stopping, and Configuring SQL Mail

Follow these steps to start, stop, or configure SQL Mail:

1. From the SQL Server Enterprise Manager, click the plus (+) sign next to the server to manage SQL Mail.

2. Click the Support Services folder.

3. Right-click the SQL Mail icon (see Figure 6.14). From the right-mouse menu, select Start to start the service, select Stop to stop the service, or select Properties (see Figure 6.15) to configure the service.

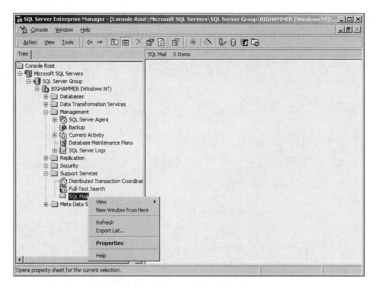

FIGURE 6.14   SQL Mail right-mouse menu.

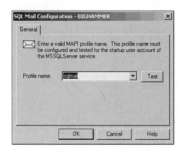

FIGURE 6.15   SQL Mail Configuration dialog box.

Using the Enterprise Manager to Perform Common Tasks

The following sections provide brief descriptions of how to perform common administration tasks from the SQL Server Enterprise Manager. Many of these tasks are explained in greater detail in other sections of this book.

Manage Server Configurations

Follow these steps to configure a server:

1. From the SQL Server Enterprise Manager, right-click the server you want to configure.

2. From the menu, select the Properties menu option. The SQL Server Properties dialog box appears (see Figure 6.16). From this dialog box, you can configure server options by selecting the corresponding tab.

FIGURE 6.16   SQL Server Properties dialog box.

Manage Logins

Follow these steps to manage logins:

1. From the SQL Server Enterprise Manager, click the plus (+) sign next to the server to manage logins.

2. Click the Security folder.

3. Click the Logins icon. The Result pane appears with login information. Right-click in the Result pane to add, edit, and delete logins (see Figures 6.17 and 6.18).

Refer to Chapter 9, "Managing SQL Server Users and Security," for more information on managing logins.

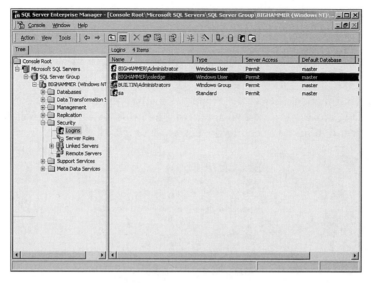

FIGURE 6.17   The Result pane with login information.

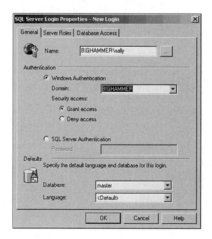

FIGURE 6.18   The Login Properties dialog box.

Manage Server Roles

Server roles delegate responsibility for server-wide operations. Follow these steps to manage server roles:

1. From the SQL Server Enterprise Manager, click the plus (+) sign next to the server to manage server roles.

2. Click the Security folder.

3. Click the Server Roles icon. The Result pane appears with server roles (see Figure 6.19). Double-click a server role. The corresponding Server Role Properties dialog box appears. From this dialog box, you can add, edit, and delete members of a server role (see Figure 6.20).

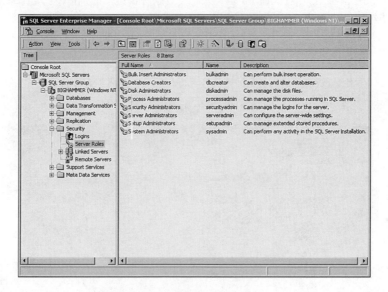

FIGURE 6.19   The Server Role Result pane.

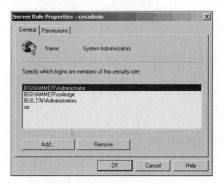

FIGURE 6.20   The Server Role Properties dialog box.

Refer to Chapter 9 for more information on server roles.

Manage Databases

Follow these steps to create, manage, and delete a database:

1. From the SQL Server Enterprise Manager, click the plus (+) sign next to the server to manage a database.

2. Open the Databases folder by clicking the plus (+) sign next to the Databases folder. From this folder, you can create a new database, edit an existing database, or delete a database by right-clicking a database (see Figures 6.21 and 6.22).

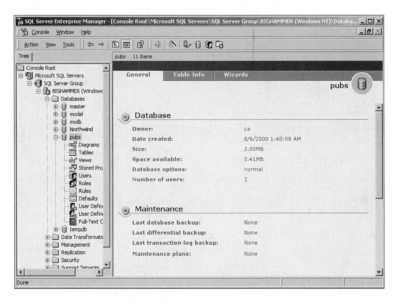

FIGURE 6.21   The Databases folder.

Refer to Chapter 8, "Managing Databases," for more information on managing databases.

Manage Database Users and Objects

Follow these steps to create, manage, and delete database objects such as database users, database roles, tables, SQL Server views, stored procedures, rules, defaults, user-defined datatypes, database diagrams, and full-text catalogs:

1. From the SQL Server Enterprise Manager, click the plus (+) sign next to the server to manage database users and objects.

2. Open the Database folder by clicking the plus (+) sign next to the Databases folder. Open the database that contains the objects you want to work with by clicking the plus (+) sign next to the corresponding database.

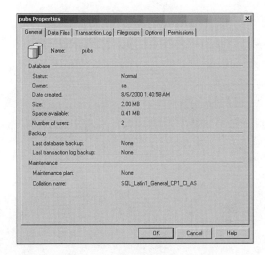

FIGURE 6.22   The Database Properties dialog box.

3. From this folder (see Figure 6.23), you can manage diagrams, tables, views, stored procedures, users, roles, rules, defaults, user defined data types, and full-text catalogs. For example, to manage a table, click the Tables folder. From the Results pane, right-click a table. From the right-mouse menu, select the Design Table menu option. This action opens the Design Table dialog box that can be used to create and alter table designs (see Figure 6.24).

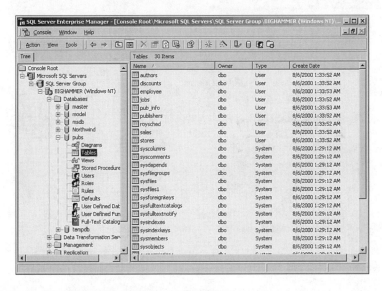

FIGURE 6.23   Manage database users and objects.

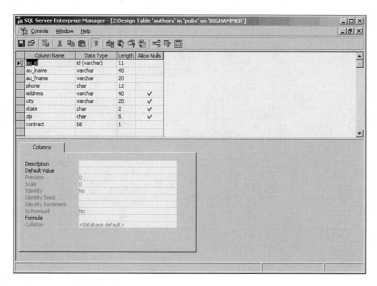

FIGURE 6.24   The Design Table dialog box.

Generate SQL Scripts

From the SQL Server Enterprise Manager, you can generate SQL scripts that contain the data definition language used to create an object in a database. This enables you to reverse-engineer existing objects.

TIP

SQL Scripts are also useful for performing keyword searches. Suppose that you want to determine how many stored procedures reference the column au_id. An easy way to determine this is to generate the data definition language for all the tables in the database and then search with a text editor for au_id.

Another use for generating SQL scripts is to store object information in a source code control tool such as Microsoft SourceSafe. This is a great way to manage different versions of application code and SQL Server code.

Follow these steps to generate SQL scripts:

1. From the SQL Server Enterprise Manager, click the plus (+) sign next to the server to generate SQL scripts.

2. Open the Database folder by clicking the plus (+) sign next to the Databases folder. Right-click the database that contains the objects you want to work with.

3. From the right-mouse menu, select the All Tasks menu option.

4. From the All Tasks menu option, select the Generate SQL Script option. This action displays the Generate SQL Script dialog box. From this dialog box, you can generate the appropriate SQL syntax (see Figures 6.25 and 6.26). From this dialog box, you can also preview the script by clicking on the Preview command button.

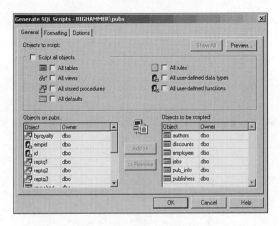

FIGURE 6.25   The Generate SQL Script dialog box.

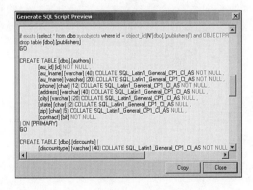

FIGURE 6.26   Sample output from the Generate SQL Scripts dialog box.

Manage Jobs

Jobs are tasks scheduled to automatically run at preset time intervals. The SQL Server Agent manages these jobs. Database backups, transaction log backups, and DBCC commands are just a few types of administrative jobs that can be automated by the SQL Server Agent. To manage jobs, follow these steps:

1. From the SQL Server Enterprise Manager, click the plus (+) sign next to the server to manage jobs.

2. Click the plus (+) sign next to the Management folder.

3. Click the plus (+) sign next to the SQL Server Agent icon.

4. Click the Jobs icon. The Result pane appears with job information. Right-click in the Result pane to start, stop, add, edit, and delete jobs (see Figures 6.27 and 6.28).

NOTE

If your job will not start, make sure that SQL Server Agent is running. Otherwise, the job will never run.

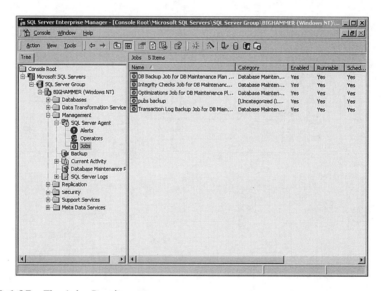

FIGURE 6.27   The Jobs Result pane.

Refer to Chapter 12, "Automating Database Administration Tasks," for more information on jobs.

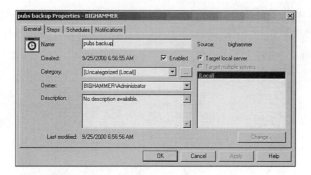

FIGURE 6.28   The Job Properties dialog box.

Manage Alerts

Alerts are notifications of errors and predefined conditions. Alerts can notify operators through email and pages of these conditions. The SQL Server Agent manages these alerts. Alerts are designed to provide a proactive approach to database administration. To manage alerts, follow these steps:

1. From the SQL Server Enterprise Manager, click the plus (+) sign next to the server to manage alerts.

2. Click the plus (+) sign next to the Management folder.

3. Click the plus (+) sign next to the SQL Server Agent icon.

4. Click the Alerts icon. The Result pane appears with alert information. Right-click in the Result pane to add, edit, and delete alerts (see Figures 6.29 and 6.30).

Refer to Chapter 12, for more information on alerts.

Manage Operators

Operators are recipients of alerts and notifications. The SQL Server Agent manages these operators. To manage operators, follow these steps:

1. From the SQL Server Enterprise Manager, click the plus (+) sign next to the server to manage operators.

2. Click the plus (+) sign next to the Management folder.

3. Click the plus (+) sign next to the SQL Server Agent icon.

4. Click the Operators icon. The Result pane appears with operator information. Right-click in the Result pane to add, edit, and delete operators (see Figures 6.31 and 6.32).

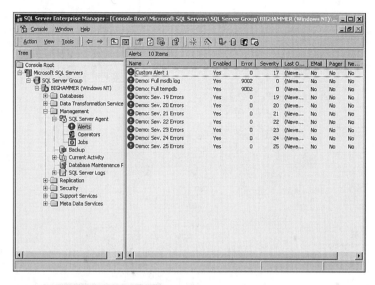

FIGURE 6.29   The Alert Result pane.

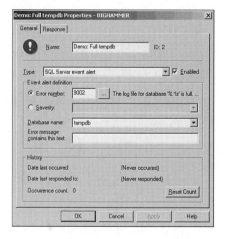

FIGURE 6.30   The Alert Properties dialog box.

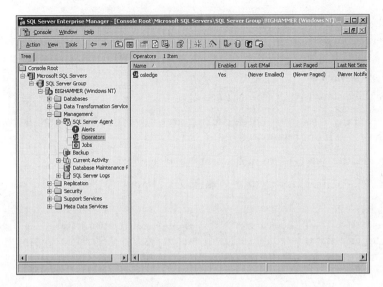

FIGURE 6.31   The Operator Result pane.

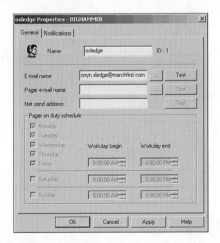

FIGURE 6.32   Operator Properties dialog box.

Refer to Chapter 12 for more information on operators.

Monitor User Activity

SQL Server provides a console within the SQL Server Enterprise Manager that monitors user activity. This information is often useful to pinpoint query problems and isolate bottlenecks.

Follow these steps to monitor user activity:

1. From the SQL Server Enterprise Manager, click the plus (+) sign next to the server to monitor user activity.

2. Click the plus (+) sign next to the Management folder.

3. Click the plus (+) sign next to the Current Activity icon.

4. Click one of the following icons: Process Info, Locks/Process ID, Locks/Object. The Result pane appears with the corresponding information. Right-click in the Result pane to send a message to the process, view detailed information about the process, or kill the process.

Refer to Chapter 20, "Multiuser Considerations," for more information on monitoring user activity.

Manage Data Transformation Packages

Data transformation packages are import and export programs. These programs transform data through OLE DB, ODBC, and user-defined validation rules.

Follow these steps to manage data transformation packages:

1. From the SQL Server Enterprise Manager, click the plus (+) sign next to the server to manage data transformation packages.

2. Click the plus (+) sign next to the Data Transformation Services folder.

3. Click the plus (+) sign next to the Local Packages icon or the Repository Packages icon. The Result pane appears with the corresponding information. Right-click in the Result pane to add, edit, delete, and execute data transformation packages (see Figure 6.33). Double-click the package to modify its content (see Figure 6.34).

Refer to Chapter 13, "Data Transformation Services," for more information on data transformation packages.

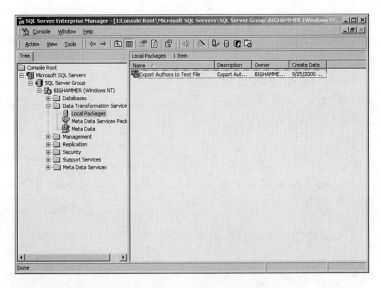

FIGURE 6.33   The Data Transformation Packages Result pane.

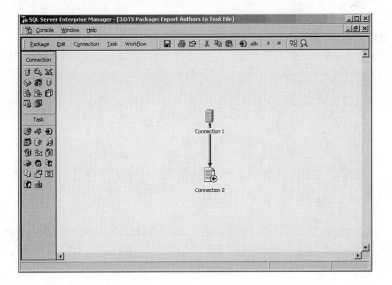

FIGURE 6.34   Sample DTS Package.

Manage Error Logs

Error logs provide detailed information about SQL Server. This information is often used to troubleshoot SQL Server errors and problems.

Follow these steps to manage error logs:

1. From the SQL Server Enterprise Manager, click the plus (+) sign next to the server to manage error logs.

2. Click the plus (+) sign next to the Management folder.

3. Click the SQL Server Logs folder. The Result pane appears with error log information (see Figure 6.35). Double-click an error log to display its contents (see Figure 6.36).

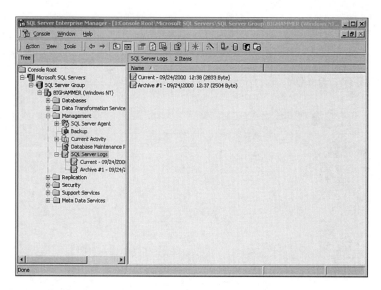

FIGURE 6.35   The Error Log Result pane.

Refer to Chapters 11, "Developing a SQL Server Maintenance Plan," and 15, "Troubleshooting SQL Server," and for more information on error logs.

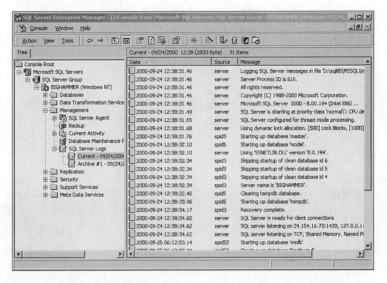

FIGURE 6.36   Error Log detail information.

SQL Server Query Analyzer

The SQL Server Query Analyzer executes and analyzes queries. To open the SQL Server Query Analyzer, double-click the Query Analyzer icon in the Microsoft SQL Server group (see Figure 6.37). The Connect to SQL Server dialog box appears (see Figure 6.38). Select the appropriate connection mode and server and click the OK button. Upon successfully connecting to SQL Server, the Query dialog box appears (see Figure 6.39). From this dialog box, you can issue Transact SQL statements, view results, and analyze query performance and optimization plans.

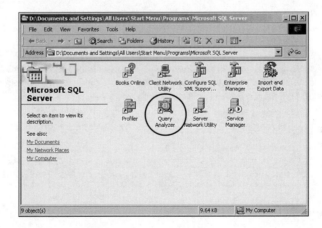

FIGURE 6.37   The Query Analyzer icon.

FIGURE 6.38   The Connect to SQL Server dialog box.

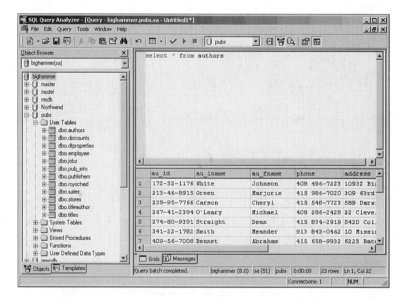

FIGURE 6.39   The Query dialog box.

TIP

From the Query dialog box, you can concurrently run multiple SQL statements against the server. Click the New Query toolbar button in the Query dialog box. This action opens a new connection to SQL Server, which can be used to issue a new query while maintaining previous connections. This feature enables you to switch connections while queries are being processed. Because the processing takes place on the server and not on the client, your machine is free to continue with other tasks.

Also from the Query dialog box, you can run an individual Transact SQL statement by high-lighting just the text and clicking the Execute Query toolbar button (see Figure 6.40).

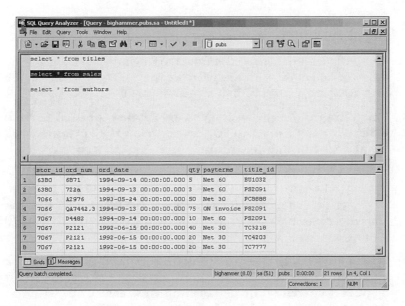

FIGURE 6.40   Executing only the highlighted text.

Starting and Stopping the Distributed Transaction Coordinator (DTC)

To start or stop the Distributed Transaction Coordinator (DTC), open the SQL Server Service Manager. Select the Distributed Transaction Coordinator. From this prompt, you can stop and start the DTC service.

FIGURE 6.41   The Distributed Transaction Coordinator.

FAQ

Following are some of the common questions asked by DBAs about the SQL Server Enterprise Management Process:

Q Does deleting a registered server from the Enterprise Manager actually delete SQL Server from the machine?

A No, when you delete SQL Server from the Enterprise Manager, you are only removing Enterprise Manager's reference to SQL Server. To add the reference back, register the server with the Enterprise Manager.

Q I'm getting the error message "Login failed for user 'username'" when I try to connect to SQL Server from the Enterprise Manager. What does this message mean?

A Usually it means that the login/password combination is invalid. From within the Enterprise Manager, right-mouse click on the server and select the Edit SQL Server Registration properties menu option. The Registered SQL Server Properties dialog box appears. From this dialog box, you can change the login/password combination.

Q Whenever I try to start or stop SQL Server from the Enterprise Manager, I get the following error message: "An error 5 (Access is denied) occurred while performing this service operation on the MSSQLServer service." I'm logged in as sa. Why am I getting this message?

A This message appears when someone is not a member of the Windows 2000 Domain Admins group or the Windows 2000 Administrators group. Although you are the administrator for SQL Server, you are not designated as an administrator of the Windows 2000 machine that runs SQL Server. You must be a Windows 2000 administrator to start or stop a service. To resolve the problem, have your account added to the Windows 2000 Domain Admins group or the Windows 2000 Administrators group.

Q Can I copy the MMC settings to another machine?

A Yes, MMC settings are portable. Select the Save As menu option from the Console menu in the Microsoft Management Console dialog box to save the current MMC settings. To open the previously saved settings, select the Open menu option from the Console menu in the Microsoft Management Console dialog box.

Summary

As you can see, the graphical interface provided by the SQL Server Enterprise Manager simplifies the tasks required to manage SQL Server. However, to manage a production environment, a DBA must know more than how to right-click an object. A DBA must be knowledgeable about the various components of SQL Server, how they interact, and how to effectively manage the system.

7

Configuring and Tuning SQL Server

by Mark Spenik

IN THIS CHAPTER

- Configuring SQL Server
- SQL Server 2000 Self-Tuning Features
- Configuration Parameters
- Advanced Configuration Parameters
- Configuration FAQ

Y ou now have SQL Server installed and running. Maybe you are about to roll out your first production database and your boss is breathing down your neck asking, "Mister (or Madam) DBA, have you tuned and optimized the server?" You tell your boss no, but tuning and optimizing SQL Server was next on your list. You bring up the SQL Enterprise Manager. You stare at the Enterprise Manager configuration screen and ask yourself, "So, which knobs do I turn?" How about very few (maybe none), which in many organizations will be the case! Remember the goal of SQL Server 2000 is to be a self-tuning database that requires very little tuning or tweaking to get the best performance from the database engine. SQL Server 2000 removes the server tuning conditions required by the DBA and puts the tuning back into the application developer's hands. The tuning required is minimal!

This chapter covers how to modify SQL Server's configuration parameters. Each configuration parameter is examined for functionality and its effect on SQL Server performance and tuning. With SQL Server 2000, many of the key performance-oriented configuration parameters such as memory allocation are dynamic and self-tuning, requiring no DBA intervention. Microsoft has excelled at producing in SQL Server 2000 a RDBMS that is simpler to configure and maintain.

SQL SERVER TUNING OR APPLICATION TUNING?

As you start to tune SQL Server, keep in mind that other factors such as the hardware configuration chosen for the database, the network the database clients and SQL Server belong to, and the overall size and structure of your databases also affect the performance of the database server.

I have a friend who used to work for a Fortune 500 company that was bringing several SQL Servers online. He had spent some time tuning SQL Server and everything was up and running quite smoothly. As the days went on, the organization started to experience problems with a particular application running progressively slower. Upper management thought the problem must be a SQL Server configuration problem. My friend tried to explain to them that the problem was not a SQL Server tuning issue but an application issue. He explained how they had done everything right: researched and purchased a very fast RAID 5 machine, tuned Windows NT Server, and then used SQL Server tools to properly configure SQL Server.

Management didn't buy it, so they brought in another consulting firm with a highly certified and expensive specialist. The specialist examined the SQL Server and did not change any configuration parameters because they were all reasonably set. So the hired guns left without fixing anything and upper management was left scratching their heads. I stopped by to see if I could help them out, and as it turned out, their problem was a failure to issue a simple command that needed to be executed on three of their tables. (UPDATE STATISTICS, what else?)

The moral of the story is that many things affect the overall performance of SQL Server. Performance issues start from square one when you research and purchase the machine and set up Windows NT or Windows 2000 Server. Too often, the real problems are not understood, so people think tuning SQL Server is the answer. SQL Server 2000 has all but eliminated the need for tuning and configuring the database server. The auto-tuning features of SQL Server 2000 enable the server to use the available resources on the machine optimally but do not prevent problems resulting from poor database and application design or a poor hardware platform selection. It is important to understand the value and limitations of tuning SQL Server. Oh yeah, SQL Server 2000 can also automatically execute the UPDATE STATISTICS command!

Configuring SQL Server

Before discussing the many different configuration parameters, you must learn how to modify SQL Server parameters using the Enterprise Manager. Start up the Enterprise Manager and perform the following steps:

1. From the Enterprise Manager, select a SQL Server by clicking it. Right-click and from the pop-out menu, select Properties; the SQL Server Properties dialog appears (see Figure 7.1).

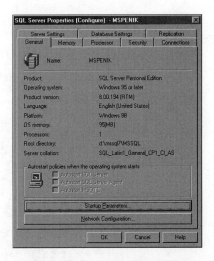

FIGURE 7.1   The SQL Server Properties dialog box—General tab.

The General tab of the SQL Server Properties dialog box displays information about the machine, the operating system, memory, processors, SQL Server root directory, and the SQL Server version and product type (that is, Enterprise, Personal, Standard, or Developer). You can also set SQL Server startup parameters and network parameters as well as the Auto-start option for SQL Server, MSDTC, and the SQL Server agent.

2. Click the Memory tab in the SQL Server Properties dialog box (see Figure 7.2).

The Memory tab enables you to set the SQL Server memory configuration parameter. The default setting is to dynamically configure memory. However, you can fix the amount of memory used by SQL Server by selecting the Use a Fixed Memory Size radio button and using the slider control to adjust the memory setting. The configuration parameter Min memory per query can be set by changing the value displayed in the Minimum Query Memory text box. You can view the running values used for the memory setting by selecting the Running Values radio button shown in Figure 7.2. To reserve physical memory for SQL server, check the Reserve Physical Memory for SQL Server check box shown in Figure 7.2.

3. Click the Processor tab in the SQL Server Properties dialog box (see Figure 7.3).

The Processor tab enables you to configure several options relating to SMP systems such as which processors can execute SQL Server. The Processor tab can be used to configure the following SQL Server configuration parameters: max worker threads, priority boost, lightweight pooling and cost threshold for parallelism (note: the SMP options are not available on a Windows 9x machine). To view the running values being used, select the Running Values radio button, shown in Figure 7.3.

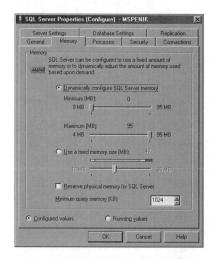

FIGURE 7.2   The Memory tab in the SQL Server Properties dialog box.

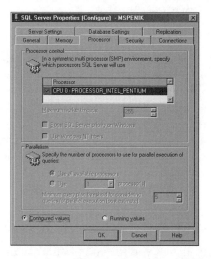

FIGURE 7.3   The Processor tab in the SQL Server Properties dialog box.

4. Click the Connections tab in the SQL Server Properties dialog box (see Figure 7.4).

The Connections tab enables you to configure options relating to user connections, such as the number of concurrent connections. The Connections tab can be used to configure the following SQL Server configuration parameters: remote access, remote query timeout, remote proc trans, user connections, and user options. To view the running values being used, select the Running Values radio button, shown in Figure 7.4.

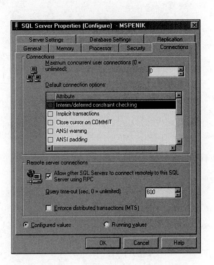

FIGURE 7.4   The Connections tab in the SQL Server Properties dialog box.

5. Click the Server Settings tab in the SQL Server Properties dialog box (see Figure 7.5).

   The Server Settings tab enables you to configure the following SQL Server configuration parameters: allow updates, default language, query governor cost limit, two digit year support, and nested triggers. To view the running values being used, select the Running Values radio button, shown in Figure 7.5.

6. Click the Database Settings tab in SQL Server Properties dialog box (see Figure 7.6).

   The Database Settings tab enables you to configure the following SQL Server configuration parameters: fill factor, default data and log file directories for new databases, and recovery interval. To view the running values being used, select the Running Values radio button, shown in Figure 7.6.

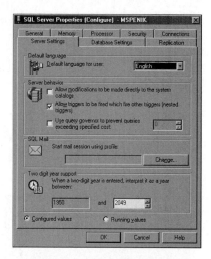

FIGURE 7.5   The Server Settings tab in the SQL Server Properties dialog box.

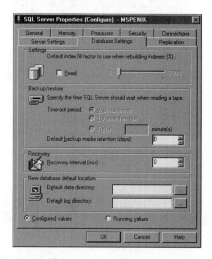

FIGURE 7.6   The Database Settings tab in the SQL Server Properties dialog box.

You can also change system configuration parameters using the system stored procedure sp_configure, which has the following syntax:

```
sp_configure [configuration_name [, configuration_value]]
```

In this syntax, *configuration_name* is the configuration parameter name you want to change and *configuration_value* is the new value for the configuration parameter.

SQL Server configuration values are stored in the system table sysconfigures. If you use sp_configure to modify an option, you must use the RECONFIGURE command to make the change take effect. RECONFIGURE has the following syntax:

RECONFIGURE [WITH OVERRIDE]

The WITH OVERRIDE parameter is required only when you set the allow updates configuration parameter to 1. This provides an added security check to make sure that you really want to modify allow updates. The output of sp_configure is shown in Listing 7.1.

LISTING 7.1   sp_configure Output with Show Advanced Options

name	minimum	maximum	config_value	run_value
affinity mask	0	2147483647	0	0
allow updates	0	1	0	0
awe enabled	0	1	0	0
c2 audit mode	0	1	0	0
cost threshold for parallelism	0	32767	5	5
cursor threshold	-1	2147483647	-1	-1
default full-text language	0	2147483647	1033	1033
default language	0	9999	0	0
fill factor (%)	0	100	0	0
index create memory (KB)	704	2147483647	0	0
lightweight pooling	0	1	0	0
locks	5000	2147483647	0	0
max degree of parallelism	0	32	0	0
max server memory (MB)	4	2147483647	2147483647	2147483647
max text repl size (B)	0	2147483647	65536	65536
max worker threads	32	32767	255	255
media retention	0	365	0	0
min memory per query (KB)	512	2147483647	1024	1024
min server memory (MB)	0	2147483647	0	0
nested triggers	0	1	1	1
network packet size (B)	512	65536	4096	4096
open objects	0	2147483647	0	0
priority boost	0	1	0	0
query governor cost limit	0	2147483647	0	0

LISTING 7.1   Continued

query wait (s)	-1	2147483647	-1	-1
recovery interval (min)	0	32767	0	0
remote access	0	1	1	1
remote login timeout (s)	0	2147483647	20	20
remote proc trans	0	1	0	0
remote query timeout (s)	0	2147483647	600	600
scan for startup procs	0	1	0	0
set working set size	0	1	0	0
show advanced options	0	1	1	1
two digit year cutoff	1753	9999	2049	2049
user connections	0	32767	0	0
user options	0	32767	0	0

NOTE

What is the difference between the Running column and the Current column? Most of the time, the two values are the same. As you start to change and modify SQL Server configurations, however, the Current column reflects the changes you have made. These changes do not become the running value until you execute the Reconfigure command. (For some configuration variables, you have to shut down and restart the server before the parameter changes take effect.)

Certain configuration parameters can take effect without restarting SQL Server. These configuration parameters are referred to as *dynamic configuration variables* and are as follows:

- allow updates

- cursor threshold

- cost threshold for parallelism

- default language

- default full-text language

- index create memory

- max degree of parallelism

- max server memory

- max text repl size

- min memory per query

- min server memory

- max worker threads

- network packet size

- query governor cost limit

- query wait

- recovery interval

- remote login timeout

- remote proc trans

- remote query timeout

- show advanced options

- two digit year cutoff

- user_option

- using nested triggers

SQL Server 2000 Self-Tuning Features

One goal of the Microsoft SQL Server team was to create a product that for the majority of installations would be self-tuning and would require very limited changes to configuration parameters to obtain optimum performance. In previous versions of SQL Server, two key DBA tuning areas that were frequently not set correctly and could impact system performance were SQL Server memory allocation and read aheads. With SQL Server 7.0, both features became dynamic and no longer require DBA intervention. Both of these features are available as well in SQL Server 2000 and are discussed in more detail in the next section. One other key area changed in SQL Server 7.0 and enhanced in SQL Server 2000 is locking; it is discussed in more detail in Chapter 20, "Multiuser Considerations."

Memory

In general, SQL Server loves memory; that is, adding more memory can enhance the performance of your SQL Server system by keeping data pages loaded in memory. SQL Server 2000 has an auto-tuning memory feature, first released in SQL Server 7.0, which allows SQL Server to dynamically increase or decrease memory utilization based on the overall system memory requirements. SQL Server 2000 is also much smarter about how memory is used and is able to use more memory for queries than previous versions. So how does SQL Server use memory?

First, a certain amount of memory is allocated for SQL Server overhead, which includes the size of the SQL Server executable. The amount of SQL Server static overhead is not affected in any way by configuration parameters.

SQL Server then allocates memory for various configuration options, such as locks and open databases. (For example, each lock used in SQL Server requires 96 bytes of memory.) Other subsystems such as the Log Manager request memory for their log caches. The remaining memory is then used for a single buffer cache, which hosts the procedure cache and data cache. The procedure cache stores the most recently used stored procedures, execution plans, and query trees, and the data cache stores the most recently used data and index pages. As you increase the amount of SQL Server memory, the size of the buffer cache increases, boosting performance because SQL Server can retrieve more information from memory without performing disk I/O to retrieve the information. SQL Server 2000 attempts to keep between 4MB and 10MB of free memory in the system. With SQL Server 2000, the auto-tuning memory feature uses as much memory as required by SQL Server. If another application, such as Microsoft Exchange, is started up and the amount of page/faults increases or the free memory falls below 4MB, SQL Server automatically decreases the amount of memory on the NT system it uses, thus freeing up memory for the new application. If SQL Server begins a query that requires additional memory and the free memory in the system exceeds 4MB, SQL Server adds the additional memory to the buffer cache. Dynamic memory also works when running multiple instances of SQL Server 2000. Each instance of SQL Server 2000 will use the dynamic memory allocation algorithms to share the system memory. SQL Server requires some event or task to occur to have it add memory to the buffer cache; when the server is idle, it will not add memory to the buffer cache.

NOTE

The `tempdb` in Ram option, available in Version 6.5, is no longer available with SQL Server 7.0 or 2000.

It is highly recommended that you use the dynamic memory allocation feature provided by SQL Server 2000 to ensure that the memory on your system is being used effectively. However, if you want to set the amount of memory required by SQL Server, thus preallocating the full amount of memory regardless of the server load, you can set the SQL Server 2000 memory configuration parameters `min server memory` and `max server memory`. You might want to consider presetting the memory in situations where SQL Server is on a dedicated box using a single instance of SQL Server and using dynamic memory allocation is not necessary or in situations where you want to make sure that SQL Server is allocated a certain amount of memory at all times; for example, systems with frequent user fluctuations running several other Microsoft Backoffice applications.

Monitoring Memory

This section offers some tips to help you monitor memory use for your SQL Server. The primary tools are the SQL Performance Monitor counters. To determine whether you have enough or too much memory, use the Performance Monitor and watch the counters listed in Table 7.1. Of course if you are using the dynamic memory allocation feature, you can still use these techniques to determine if the server you are using has enough memory to work with SQL Server and any other services.

TABLE 7.1   Performance Monitor Counter for Tuning SQL Server Memory

Performance Monitor Object	Counter
Memory	Page Faults/sec
SQLServer:Memory Manager	Lock Memory
SQLServer:Memory Manager	Connection Memory
SQLServer:Memory Manager	SQL Cache Memory
SQLServer:Cache Manager	Ad Hoc SQL Plans
SQLServer:Cache Manager	Prepared SQL Plans
SQLServer:Cache Manager	Procedure Plans
SQLServer:Buffer Manager	Checkpoint pages/sec
SQLServer:Buffer Manager	Page Reads/sec
SQLServer:Buffer Manager	Page Writes/sec
SQLServer:Buffer Manager	Buffer Cache Hit Ratio

The first step—and one of the most important steps when trying to tune SQL Server for memory—is to make sure that you are running your typical processes and workloads on SQL Server while you are using the Performance Monitor. The idea behind tuning SQL Server for memory is to keep a high cache-hit ratio (that is, data being retrieved is in the cache), low physical I/O (disk I/O is low because data pages are in memory), and no page faults (a page fault occurs when not enough memory has been allocated to Windows NT, causing Windows NT to rely heavily on virtual memory). If your cache-hit ratio is below 85%–90%, your SQL Server might benefit from increased memory. If you are continuously experiencing page faults, you have allocated too much memory to SQL Server and not enough to Windows NT. The problem can be corrected by reducing the amount of memory allocated to SQL Server or by adding more physical memory to be used by Windows NT.

Asynchronous Read Ahead

SQL Server 6.x shipped with a feature called *Parallel Data Scan*, also referred to as *Asynchronous Read Ahead*. The read-ahead technology (RA for short) decreases the time required to perform logical sequential data reads, which translates to improved performance for table scans, index creation, DBCC commands, UPDATE STATISTICS, and covered queries. The idea behind the parallel data scan is simple. Using separate threads, SQL Server reads extents (8 data pages or 64KB) into memory before the thread running the query needs the extent. When the extent is needed to satisfy the query, the data pages are already in the memory cache thanks to the read ahead. The read ahead features of SQL Server 6.5 could be finely tuned with several configuration parameters and a good DBA. Unlike SQL Server 6.5, read aheads no longer needs to be configured and has been tightly integrated with the query processor. The query processor tells the RA exactly what it needs. RA now understands logical page I/O versus physical I/O and works on heaps as well as clustered indexes.

Configuration Parameters

The following sections examine each of the SQL Server configuration parameters. The configuration parameters are in alphabetical order, except in special cases when the parameters have already been discussed, such as the memory configuration parameters. Additionally, the advanced options are reviewed separately from the standard options.

> **NOTE**
>
> For each SQL Server 2000 configuration parameter, the Minimum, Maximum, and Default values are listed in table format as well as the dynamic variable status.

allow updates

If the value of allow updates is set to 1, the SQL Server system tables can be modified. But *do not set this configuration value to 1* unless told to do so by Microsoft Technical Support.

CAUTION

Directly updating system tables is risky business and could prevent your SQL Server from running.

If you need to update system tables, use the system stored procedures; after all, that is what they are for. If you need to turn on this option, start SQL Server in single-user mode (command-line option -m) to prevent any other users from accidentally modifying the system tables.

> **Minimum:** 0
>
> **Maximum:** 1
>
> **Default:** 0
>
> **Dynamic Variable:** Yes

NOTE

Stored procedures created to modify system tables while the allow updates option is on can always modify the system tables, even after the allow updates option is turned off.

default language

The default language option determines the number of the language used to display system messages.

> **Minimum:** 0
>
> **Maximum:** 9,999
>
> **Default:** Varies (US English = 0)
>
> **Dynamic Variable:** Yes

max text repl size

This option specifies the maximum amount of data that can be written to a replicated text or image column.

> **Minimum:** 0
>
> **Maximum:** 2,147,483,647
>
> **Default:** 65,536
>
> **Dynamic Variable:** Yes

nested triggers

When the `nested triggers` option is set to 1, the action of a trigger can fire another trigger, which can in turn fire another trigger and this can continue up to 32 levels of nesting. When this option is set to 0, calling a trigger from another trigger is prohibited. A trigger will not call itself over and over unless the `RECURSIVE_TRIGGERS` database option is set.

> **Minimum:** 0
>
> **Maximum:** 1
>
> **Default:** 1
>
> **Dynamic Variable:** Yes

remote access

The `remote access` option controls the logins from remote SQL Servers. When set to 1, users from remote SQL Servers have access to the server.

> **Minimum:** 0
>
> **Maximum:** 1
>
> **Default:** 1
>
> **Dynamic Variable:** No

remote login timeout

The `remote login timeout` option specifies the number of seconds to wait before returning from a remote login attempt. The default of 0 specifies an infinite timeout value. This parameter effects connections made to linked servers using distributed queries.

> **Minimum:** 0
>
> **Maximum:** 2,147,483,647
>
> **Default:** 20
>
> **Dynamic Variable:** Yes

remote query timeout

The `remote query timeout` option specifies the number of seconds to wait before timing out as a result of a remote query (be it a remote stored procedure or distributed query). The default of 0 specifies an infinite timeout value.

Minimum: 0

Maximum: 2,147,483,647

Default: 6000

Dynamic Variable: Yes

remote proc trans

When set to 1, the `remote proc trans` option provides a DTC distributed transaction that protects the ACID properties of transactions.

Minimum: 0

Maximum: 1

Default: 0

Dynamic Variable: Yes

show advanced options

The `show advanced options` option displays the advanced configuration options when using the SQL Server Enterprise Manager or the `sp_configure` system stored procedure. Set this value to 1 to display the advanced options.

Minimum: 0

Maximum: 1

Default: 1

Dynamic Variable: Yes

two digit year cutoff

The `show advanced options` option displays the advanced configuration options when using the SQL Server Enterprise Manager or the `sp_configure` system stored procedure. Set this value to 1 to display the advanced options.

Minimum: 1,753

Maximum: 9,999

Default: 2,049

Dynamic Variable: Yes

user_option

The user_option option enables you to set global default options for all users. Using this parameter, you can control implicit transactions, ANSI warnings, ANSI NULLs, ANSI defaults, the distinction between a single quote and a double quote, and several other options. The options set take effect during the user's login session; the user can override them by using the SET statement.

> **Minimum:** 0
>
> **Maximum:** 4,095
>
> **Default:** 0
>
> **Dynamic Variable:** Yes

Advanced Configuration Parameters

> **CAUTION**
>
> The following configuration parameters are considered advanced and can be seen only by turning on the show advanced options configuration option. I highly suggest leaving them alone. Microsoft has done a good job setting the default values, and you can easily hinder the performance of your SQL Server by incorrectly setting one of the advanced configuration options. If you do modify them, make sure that you fully understand the option and the overall impact of your changes!

affinity mask

The affinity mask option enables you to associate a thread to a processor and specify which processors SQL Server can use.

> **Minimum:** 0
>
> **Maximum:** 2,147,483,647
>
> **Default:** 0
>
> **Dynamic Variable:** No

awe enabled

The awe enabled option allows you to use the Microsoft Windows 2000 Address Windows Extensions to address up to 64GB of memory. This option is only available with the Enterprise Edition and Developer Edition of SQL Server. When awe is set,

SQL Server can address close to 8 gigabytes of memory on Windows Advanced Server and close to 64 gigabytes of memory when using the Windows Datacenter.

Minimum: 0

Maximum: 1

Default: 0

Dynamic Variable: No

C2 Audit Mode

The C2 Audit Mode option, if set to 1, turns on C2 audit mode and logs all statement and object access, successful and unsuccessful, to a log file located in the \mssql\data directory. When the log file reaches 200MB, the current log file is closed and a new log file is started. The log files will be created until the option is turned off. Note that using C2 audit mode will impact system performance.

Minimum: 0

Maximum: 1

Default: 0

Dynamic Variable: No

cost threshold for parallelism

The cost threshold for parallelism option is used only on systems with multiple processors. The option enables you to set the threshold for which a parallel plan is created and executed by SQL Server. The cost is the estimated amount of time in seconds required to complete the plan in a serial fashion. If the query exceeds the parameter setting, a parallel plan will be used. In general, longer queries benefit from the execution of a parallel plan and shorter queries benefit from a serial plan; so don't set the parameter too low.

Minimum: 0

Maximum: 32,767

Default: 5

Dynamic Variable: Yes

cursor threshold

The cursor threshold option determines how the keyset for a cursor is generated. If the option is set to -1, all cursor keysets are generated synchronously (good for small cursor sets). If the option is set to 0, all cursor keysets are generated asynchronously. Otherwise, the query optimizer compares the number of expected rows in the cursor set; if the number of expected rows exceeds the `cursor threshold` configuration variable, the keyset is built asynchronously.

> **Minimum:** −1
>
> **Maximum:** 2,147,483,647
>
> **Default:** −1
>
> **Dynamic Variable:** Yes

default full-text language

The `default full-text language` option is used by full text searches and allows you to specify a language for the full text search. It defaults to the language of the server.

> **Minimum:** 0
>
> **Maximum:** 2,147,483,647
>
> **Default:** 1,033
>
> **Dynamic Variable:** Yes

fill factor

The `fill factor` option specifies how densely packed you want your index and data pages to be while creating an index. The default is 0, which leaves room on the nonleaf pages but makes the leaf pages 100% full. Use a low `fill factor` value to spread data over more pages. For more information on using `fill factor`, see Chapter 18, "Understanding Indexes."

> **Minimum:** 0
>
> **Maximum:** 100
>
> **Default:** 0
>
> **Dynamic Variable:** No

NOTE

The `fill factor` option is not maintained by SQL Server after index creation and is only maintained when the index is built.

---

index create memory

The `index create memory` option controls the amount of memory (in kilobytes) used by creating an index to sort the data during the index creation. The default value of `0` indicates that SQL Server will automatically configure the value.

> **Minimum:** 704
>
> **Maximum:** 2,147,483,647
>
> **Default:** 0
>
> **Dynamic Variable:** Yes

lightweight pooling

The `lightweight pooling` configuration option is primarily for SMP environments. By setting the option to 1, SQL Server thread scheduling switches to fiber mode scheduling, which can reduce excessive context switches that sometimes occur in an SMP environment (See Chapter 16, Architecture Features," for more information.)

> **Minimum:** 0
>
> **Maximum:** 1
>
> **Default:** 0
>
> **Dynamic Variable:** Yes

locks

The `locks` configuration variable sets the number of available locks. By default, SQL Server uses dynamic lock allocation (a setting of zero). Initially, 2% of the memory allocated to SQL Server is used for `locks` using the dynamic setting. Each lock consumes about 96 bytes of memory. The dynamic locking allocation is the recommended configuration. However, you can override dynamic lock allocation by presetting the number of locks. If you preset the number of locks and run out of them, increase the value.

> **Minimum:** 5,000
>
> **Maximum:** 214,748,364
>
> **Default:** 0
>
> **Dynamic Variable:** No

max degree of parallelism

The `max degree of parallelism` option is only valid for systems with multiple processors. This parameter enables you to determine the number of threads used to execute a parallel plan. The default of `0` uses the number of CPUs.

Minimum: 0

Maximum: 32

Default: 0

Dynamic Variable: Yes

max server memory

Use the `max server memory` configuration parameter to prevent SQL Server from using more than a certain amount of memory. You can also use this parameter with the `min server memory` parameter to disable dynamic memory allocation and force SQL Server to use a specified amount of memory. To use a fixed amount of memory, set the `max server memory` parameter to the same value as the `min server memory` parameter.

Minimum: 4

Maximum: 2,147,483,647

Default: 2,147,483,647

Dynamic Variable: Yes

max worker threads

Worker threads are used by SQL Server for things such as checkpoints, users, and network support. The `max worker threads` configuration parameter sets the maximum number of worker threads SQL Server can use. If the configured value is greater than the number of concurrent user connections, each user connection has its own thread; otherwise, the user shares a pool of worker threads.

Minimum: 32

Maximum: 32,767

Default: 255

Dynamic Variable: No

media retention

The `media retention` option sets the number of days you want to retain backup media before overwriting it with a new backup. If you attempt to overwrite the media before the number of retention days has expired, you get a warning message.

Minimum: 0

Maximum: 365

Default: 0

Dynamic Variable: No

min memory per query

The `min memory per query` parameter enables you to specify the minimum amount of memory used to execute a query. Increasing this value can boost the performance of queries that have sorting or hashing operations.

Minimum: 0

Maximum: 2,147,483,647

Default: 1,024

Dynamic Variable: Yes

min server memory

Use the `min server memory` configuration parameter to force SQL Server to use at least a certain amount of memory. You can also use this parameter with the `max server memory` parameter to disable dynamic memory allocation and force SQL Server to use a specified amount of memory. To use a fixed amount of memory, set the `max server memory` parameter to the same value as the `min server memory` parameter.

Minimum: 0

Maximum: 2,147,483,647

Default: 0

Dynamic Variable: Yes

network packet size

If you have a network that supports a large packet size, you can increase the network performance with SQL Server by increasing the packet size. The default of 4,096 bytes is a welcome change to the anemic 512-byte packet size used in versions prior to version 6.5. For most applications, the default packet size of 4,096 is sufficient, so be careful when changing this parameter and verify that you actually do get the performance gain expected.

Minimum: 512

Maximum: 65,536

Default: 4,096

Dynamic Variable: Yes

open objects

The open objects option specifies the maximum number of database objects that can be open at one time on SQL Server. Database objects are stored procedures, views, tables, rules, defaults, and triggers. In SQL Server 2000, open objects is dynamically configured. However, if you receive a warning stating that the number of open objects is too low, you can manually set the value to solve the problem. Each open object consumes about 276 bytes of memory.

Minimum: 0

Maximum: 2,147,483,647

Default: 0

Dynamic Variable: No

priority boost

If the priority boost configuration value is set to 1, SQL Server runs as a higher priority on the Windows NT server.

Minimum: 0

Maximum: 1

Default: 0

Dynamic Variable: No

CAUTION

Even if you have a dedicated machine for SQL Server, do not boost the priority of SQL Server. It runs fine as a regular Windows NT Service; boosting the priority can cause some unexpected problems when you try to bring down SQL Server or when you try to use other NT tools on the server. This parameter should only be set for SMP machines dedicated to SQL Server.

---

query governor cost limit

The `query governor cost limit` enables you to specify the maximum amount of time in seconds a query can run on the current server. The default value of 0 turns off the governor.

Minimum: 0

Maximum: 2,147,483,647

Default: 0

Dynamic Variable: Yes

query wait

The `query wait` option sets the amount of time in seconds that SQL Server will wait before timing out a long-running query (that is, if the query does not finish running in this amount of time, SQL Server will halt the query because of a timeout). With a value of -1, the timeout value is computed at 25 times the estimated cost of the query.

Minimum: 0

Maximum: 2,147,483,647

Default: –1

Dynamic Variable: Yes

recovery interval

SQL Server uses the `recovery interval` option, the database Truncate Log on Checkpoint setting, and the amount of database activity to determine when a checkpoint should be performed to write the "dirty pages" (modified pages not yet flushed to disk). The `recovery interval` option specified is not the amount of time between SQL Server checkpoints; it is the maximum amount of time per database that SQL Server needs to recover the database in the event of a system failure. SQL Server 2000 automatically configures this parameter and attempts to require less than a minute per database for an automatic recovery and a checkpoint process every minute. Setting the value higher reduces the number of checkpoints SQL Server performs reducing disk I/O; however the trade-off is longer time to recover the database after a system crash. The values for the recovery interval are in minutes.

Minimum: 0

Maximum: 32,767

Default: 0

Dynamic Variable: Yes

scan for startup procs

The `scan for startup procs` parameter determines whether SQL Server scans for stored procedures to execute when starting up the server. The default value of `0` is not to scan and execute startup stored procedures.

Minimum: 0

Maximum: 1

Default: 0

Dynamic Variable: No

set working set size

If the value of the `set working set size` option is set to `1` when SQL Server starts, Windows NT locks all the memory in the `memory` configuration parameters `min server memory` and `max server memory`. By locking the memory, Windows NT does not swap SQL Server pages out of memory even if the server is idle and another process needs the memory. Setting this option can potentially provide an increase in performance but must be used with caution because it could also have the reverse effect. You can disable the creation of the memory working set by setting the option to `0`. When this option is disabled, SQL Server asks the Cache Manager for memory as needed up to the value in the `memory` configuration parameters if they are set. If you are using dynamic memory, do not turn on this option.

Minimum: 0

Maximum: 1

Default: 0

Dynamic Variable: No

user connections

The `user connections` option specifies the maximum number of simultaneous user connections allowed on SQL Server. In SQL Server 2000, user connections are automatically and dynamically configured when set to a default value of `0`. If you have 50 users logged in to the system, you have 50 user connections; if someone else logs in, you automatically get another connection up to the maximum number of connections allowed (Select `@@max_connections`). If the maximum number is exceeded, you get an error and are unable to establish the new connection until one becomes available. Be careful about setting this parameter too high because each user connection takes up approximately 12KB + (3 * Network Packet Size) of memory overhead, regardless of whether the connection is used.

Minimum: 0

Maximum: 32,767

Default: 0

Dynamic Variable: No

Configuration FAQ

The following are some frequently asked questions for configuring SQL Server:

Q I'm running a batch operation that consists of lots of queries and transactions. I'm trying to improve the performance and I'm thinking about changing several configuration parameters. Is this a good starting point?

A As stated earlier, SQL Server 2000 comes out of the box tuned and ready to go. (Although users of SMP machines might want to modify some parameters after installing.) The best place to start tuning is to look at the application and examine the query plans being used. If you are confident that the application is in good order, use the performance monitor while the batch executes to determine if you have a bottleneck in the processor, memory, or disk I/O. If a bottleneck exists, modify SQL Server configuration parameters or add additional hardware.

Q I was messing around and set several SQL Server configuration parameters. Now I'm unable to start SQL Server. What do I do?

A You have probably overallocated a resource (for example, memory) that prevents SQL Server from starting. To restart SQL Server with a minimum configuration add -f to the SQLServr.EXE startup command line. Then use sp_configure or the Enterprise Manager to reset your default configuration.

Summary

The answer to the question, "Which knobs do I turn?" is "Not many!" The nice thing about SQL Server 2000 is that it provides optimal SQL Server performance for most database installations right out of the box. The majority of possible tuning parameters deal with machines that have multiple processors and the capability to run a parallel query. SQL Server 2000 limits the amount of tuning required by the DBA. Keep in mind that for the best possible performance, tuning is a many-phase process. It includes the hardware, the installation of the operating system, the installation and tuning of SQL Server, and the overall design of the databases and applications.

This chapter examined all the SQL Server configuration parameters. Following are some of the more important points to remember about tuning and configuring SQL Server:

- Let SQL Server manage the memory configuration for you by using the dynamic memory allocation feature of SQL Server 2000.

- When you tune SQL Server using the Performance Monitor, make sure that the SQL Server is running against the expected real-world workload.

- Understand the impact of changing configuration parameters before modifying them.

8

Managing Databases

by Orryn Sledge

IN THIS CHAPTER

- A Database Primer
- Database Basics
- Additional Database Information
- Filegroups
- Database FAQ

It is important to understand how to manage a database in SQL Server. Every object and its corresponding data revolves around the database. If a database isn't properly managed, it can result in system downtime, countless headaches, and loss of data.

A Database Primer

The following sections discuss the fundamental terminology and concepts necessary to manage a SQL Server database.

What Is a Database?

A *database* is an organized collection of data (see Figure 8.1). This collection of data is logically structured and systematically maintained. SQL Server extends the concept of a database by allowing you to create and store other types of objects, such as stored procedures, triggers, views, and other objects that interact with your data.

What Is the Transaction Log?

The *transaction log* is the history of data modifications to a database (see Figure 8.2). Whenever you create a database, SQL Server automatically creates a corresponding database transaction log. SQL Server uses the transaction log to ensure transaction completeness and to incrementally restore data changes (see Chapter 10, "Backup and Recovery," for more information on restoring the transaction log).

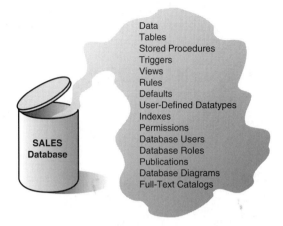

FIGURE 8.1 A database.

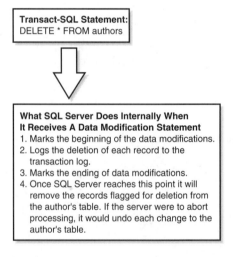

FIGURE 8.2 A transaction.

The capability to guarantee transaction completeness helps separate SQL Server from less well-equipped RDBMS software. To SQL Server, virtually every data modification must have a starting point and an ending point. If the ending point isn't reached, SQL Server automatically reverses any changes that were made. Suppose that the power to the server goes out midway through a process that is deleting all the rows from a table. When SQL Server restarts, it automatically restores all the rows that had been deleted, thus returning the table to its original state before the delete process was run. Through the use of the transaction log, SQL Server can guarantee that all the work was done or that none of the work was done.

SQL Server automatically uses a *write-ahead* type of transaction log. This means that changes to the database are first written to the transaction log and then they are written to the database. Examples of database changes written to the transaction log include data modified through the UPDATE, INSERT, and DELETE SQL commands; any type of object creation; and any security changes.

SQL Server automatically marks the starting point and ending point whenever you execute a command that performs data modifications. For greater control, you can define the starting point and ending point for a group of data modifications. This is often done when more than one set of data modifications occurs within a unit of work.

For example, if a user transfers $1,000 from checking to savings, you can use a user-defined transaction to ensure that the checking account was debited and the savings account was credited. If the transaction did not complete, the checking and savings accounts return to their original states (their states before the transaction began).

To specify the beginning of a user-defined transaction, use the following statement:

```
BEGIN TRANsaction [transaction_name]
```

To specify the end of a user-defined transaction, use the following statement:

```
COMMIT TRANsaction [transaction_name]
```

To roll back any changes made within a user-defined transaction, use the following statement:

```
ROLLBACK TRANsaction [transaction_name | savepoint_name]
```

The transaction log is the log operating system file (default extension of .LDF). Keep in mind that every database has at least one transaction log.

How Databases and Operating System Datafiles Interact

Every database in SQL Server must use at least one data operating system file and one log operating system file. Depending on your needs, you can create your entire database on one data operating system file and one log operating system file or on multiple data operating system files and/or multiple log operating system files (see Figure 8.3).

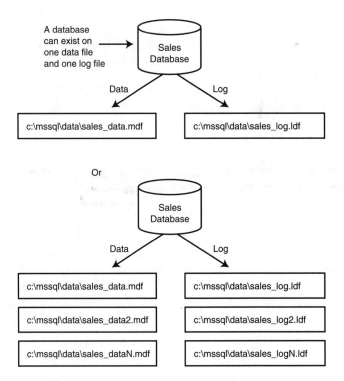

FIGURE 8.3   Database and operating system file interaction.

Database Basics

The following sections provide step-by-step instructions for managing a database.

Creating a Database

Before you can create tables and start to manage your data, you must create a database. Follow these steps to create a new database:

1. From the SQL Server Enterprise Manager, click the plus (+) sign next to the server that will contain the database.

2. Right-click the Databases folder. From the right-mouse menu, select the New Database menu option. The Database Properties dialog box appears (see Figure 8.4).

FIGURE 8.4   Creating a database with Enterprise Manager—General tab.

3. Select the General tab and enter a name for the database. Enter a collation name if necessary. (Leave the Collation Name field alone if you are not sure about this setting.)

NOTE

Database names can contain up to 128 characters. I recommend being consistent when naming a database (for example, use all uppercase or lowercase characters). Don't forget that you might often need to type the database name in a SQL statement—this might make you think twice about using all 128 characters! Try to make the name meaningful and relatively short.

4. Select the Data Files tab (see Figure 8.5). From this tab, enter the filename, location, and initial size.

TIP

If you have a high-end server with separate drives and separate asynchronous disk controllers, I recommend placing the database file and log file on separate hard drives. This can dramatically improve performance.

5. Select the Automatically Grow File option if you want to have SQL Server automatically grow the database file on an as-needed basis. If this option is selected, you can also enter the File Growth and Maximum File Size settings.

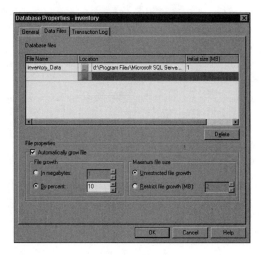

FIGURE 8.5   Creating a database with Enterprise Manager—Data Files tab.

TIP

I recommend using the Automatically Grow File option in conjunction with specifying a maximum file size. This helps enable the database to grow in space, but keeps it from consuming the entire hard drive.

When using the Automatically Grow File option, I also recommend pre-sizing the database files if possible. This reduces the need for SQL Server to continuously grow the database until it reaches the proper size. Having SQL Server grow the database does introduce some overhead (approximately 5%). Although the overhead is small, the database has to work to keep up with the requests to grow the database. When SQL Server is growing the database, locks must be held until the operation is complete. In a high-traffic database, this delay might be noticeable.

---

6. Select the Transaction Log tab.

7. From the Transaction Log Files portion of the Transaction Log tab, enter the filename, location, and initial size for the transaction log.

8. Select the Automatically Grow File option if you want to have SQL Server automatically grow the log file on an as-needed basis. If this option is selected, you can also enter the File Growth and Maximum File Size settings.

NOTE

The minimum size of a database is 1MB. The maximum size of a database is 1,048,516 terabytes. The minimum size of a log is 1MB.

---

9. Choose OK to create the database.

TIP
_____
Always back up the `master` database after you create a new database. Doing so makes it easier to recover your database should the `master` database become damaged (see Chapter 10, "Backup and Recovery" for more information about backing up the `master` database).

NOTE
_____
The `sa` and members of the `sysadmin` (System Administrators) or `dbcreator` (Database Creators) roles are the only users who can create a database, unless the CREATE DATABASE statement permission is granted to other users (see Chapter 9, "Managing SQL Server Users and Security," for more information about managing statement permissions).

Listing 8.1 shows the Transact-SQL command to create a database.

LISTING 8.1   Creating a Database
_____
```
CREATE DATABASE database_name
[ ON
    [ < filespec > [ ,...n ] ]
    [ , < filegroup > [ ,...n ] ]
]
[ LOG ON { < filespec > [ ,...n ] } ]
[ COLLATE collation_name ]
[ FOR LOAD | FOR ATTACH ]

< filespec > ::=
[ PRIMARY ]
( [ NAME = logical_file_name , ]
    FILENAME = 'os_file_name'
    [ , SIZE = size ]
    [ , MAXSIZE = { max_size | UNLIMITED } ]
    [ , FILEGROWTH = growth_increment ] ) [ ,...n ]
< filegroup > ::=
FILEGROUP filegroup_name < filespec > [ ,...n ]
```
_____

NOTE
_____
Do not store data or transaction files on compressed drives. Only store files on FAT or NTFS volumes. Using compressed drives can cause database stability and performance issues.

Table 8.1 shows the operating system files and corresponding extensions.

TABLE 8.1   Operating System Files

Operating System File Type	Use	Default Extension
Primary	This file type is the starting point for each database, and it also holds pointers to other files used by the database. Each database has one primary data file.	.MDF
Secondary	This file type contains data that do not reside on the primary file type. Depending on the database configuration, a database might have zero, one, or more secondary data files.	.NDF
Log	This file type contains the log for the database. Every database has at least one log file. Databases can also have more than one log file.	.LDF

After you create a database, review the following checklist:

❏ Do you need to set any database options? See the topic "Setting Database Options" later in this chapter for more information.

❏ Did you backup the master database? See Chapter 10 for more information.

❏ Did you document the configuration of the database? Use the output from sp_helpdb to document the database. Having a documented database can be useful for disaster recovery.

❏ Are you planning on backing up the database? If so, you might want to go ahead and implement your database backup strategy. See Chapter 10 for more information.

❏ Are you planning on backing up the database log? If so, you might want to go ahead and implement your log backup strategy. See Chapter 10 for more information. If you are not planning on backing up the database log, go ahead and set the database recovery model to SIMPLE. This will prevent the database log from filling up over time.

RAID AND STRIPING DATA ACROSS DISKS

In SQL Server (or any other database server), one of the most likely bottlenecks is the disk I/O from clients reading and writing from different tables or different databases simultaneously.

Suppose that you have a PC configured as a server. It has a fast processor and a large amount of memory, but you bought a single 12GB hard drive with a single disk controller to store all your database information. Because you have only one disk drive, any database files and transaction logs you create physically reside on the single hard drive. What happens when users start inserting and retrieving data simultaneously? SQL Server has more than enough memory and the processor is fast enough to handle the request, but what about the single disk drive and disk controller?

A bottleneck will quickly form as I/O requests queue up to the single disk. An old SQL Server trick has been to use a smart disk controller card or disk array; rather than use a single 12GB hard drive, use four 3GB hard drives. Database files and transaction logs can then be created on different physical hard drives. Although this arrangement is a better solution than a single hard drive, it still has some deficiencies. Databases are spread over multiple SQL Server data files, but the hot data everyone is after might be on a single drive, causing disk I/O bottlenecks similar to those on a single drive. The NT operating system and advanced hardware systems have created a solution to address this problem: hardware or software *disk striping*.

Figure 8.6 is a conceptual diagram of disk striping for a drive labeled J. Drive J drive looks like a single physical drive to the SQL Server DBA who is creating data and transaction log files. Logically, a striped drive is a single drive, but, physically, the logical drive spans many different disk drives. A striped disk is made up of a special file system called a *striped set*. All the disks in the disk array that make up the logical drive are part of the striped set. Data on each of the drives is divided into equal blocks and is spread over all the drives. By spreading the file system over several disk drives, disk I/O performance is improved because the disk I/O is spread over multiple drives. The balancing of the I/O is transparent to the DBA, who no longer has to worry about spreading out file I/O.

Disk striping is also referred to as *RAID 0* (Redundant Array of Inexpensive Disks). RAID level 0 is the fastest RAID configuration. The level of fault tolerance is measured in levels 0 through 5, with 0 providing no fault tolerance. If a single disk fails in a RAID 0 system, none of the data in the stripe set can be accessed. Windows NT provides software-level disk striping. Disk striping can also be handled by special hardware disk arrays.

Lately, RAID level 10 (1+0) has been popular on expensive and proprietary hardware systems. RAID 10 is mirroring with striping. RAID 10 provides the best read/write performance on any RAID systems, but it is expensive since it uses twice as many disks. Also, it provides excellent fault tolerance since the data is mirrored across the various disks.

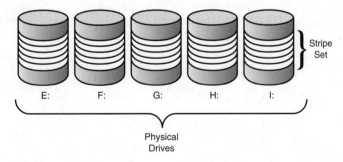

FIGURE 8.6   Disk striping.

A RAID 0 system has no fault tolerance; the entire file system can be rendered useless if a single drive fails. RAID 1 is also known as *disk mirroring*. In a RAID 1 configuration, data written to a primary disk is also written to a mirrored disk. RAID 2 uses disk striping along with error correction. RAID 3 and RAID 4 also use disk striping and error correction and vary in their degrees of effectiveness and disk space requirements. A RAID 5 system has the maximum fault tolerance: a single disk can fail and the system continues to function. A backup drive can be placed in the disk array so that the lost data file or log file can be re-created on the new drive by the RAID system. RAID 5 technology can be implemented using Windows NT disk striping with parity or as a hardware-based solution.

Hardware-based disk striping (RAID configurations) outperforms Windows NT software disk striping. NT's implementation is accomplished through software and requires system processor resources. The disadvantage of hardware striping solutions is cost. RAID systems can be quite expensive, depending on the level of fault tolerance you select.

Viewing Information About a Database

After you create a database, you can view information such as general information, file space allocation and usage, log space allocation and usage, table and index space usage, and a database diagram. Follow these steps to view information about a specific database:

1. From the SQL Server Enterprise Manager, click the plus (+) sign next to the server that contains the database you want to view.

2. Click the plus (+) sign next to the Databases folder. This opens the Databases folder.

3. Left-click the database in which you want to view information.

4. The corresponding database information appears in the Taskpad portion of the SQL Server Enterprise Manager (see Figure 8.7). (Note: the Taskpad must be active; to activate, select Taskpad from the View menu.)

You can use the following Transact-SQL command to view information about a database:

```
sp_helpdb [dbname]
```

Setting Database Options

Each database in SQL Server has its own database options. Follow these steps to set database options:

1. From the SQL Server Enterprise Manager, click the plus (+) sign next to the server that contains the database you want to view or set options for.

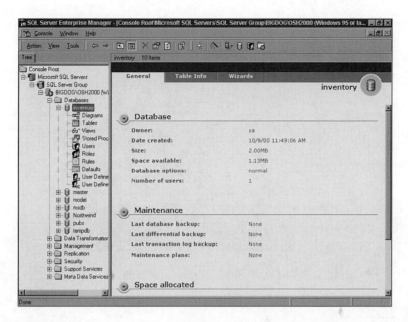

FIGURE 8.7   Database information in the Taskpad pane of Enterprise Manager.

2. Click the plus (+) sign next to the Databases folder. This opens the Databases folder.

3. Right-click the database in which you want to set the database option. From the right-mouse menu, select the Properties menu option. The Properties dialog box appears.

4. From the Properties dialog box, select the Options tab (see Figure 8.8). From this tab, select or deselect the appropriate options.

5. Click OK to save your changes.

TIP

When you change database options, the changes take effect immediately. You do not have to restart the server for the option to take effect.

The following sections describe each of the database options available on this tab.

FIGURE 8.8   Setting database options on the Options tab.

Restrict Access
Default setting: FALSE

This feature has two options:

- Members of db_owner, dbcreator, or sysadmin: When this option is set to TRUE, only members of these groups can access the database. Use this option if you want to keep everyone except these members out of the database.

- Single User: When this option is set to TRUE, only one user at a time (including the system administrator) can be in the database.

Read-only
Default setting: FALSE

When the Read-only option is set to TRUE, the contents of the database can be viewed but not modified.

Recovery Model
Default setting: Simple for Personal Edition and Desktop Edition. Full Recovery for the other versions.

NOTE
_____

SQL Server 2000's Simple recovery mode is nearly identical to setting Truncate Log on Checkpoint = TRUE in SQL Server 7.0.
_____

Recovery Model determines the speed and size of transaction log backups. The following is a brief overview of each setting (see Chapter 10 for more details).

- `Simple`—The database is recoverable up to the last backup, but does not include the transaction log. This setting is not recommended for production environments because it provides the lowest level of data protection.

- `Bulk-Logged`—This provides better performance than `Full` for certain operations (`SELECT INTO`, `bcp`, `BULK INSERT`, `CREATE INDEX`, `WRITETEXT`, and `UPDATE-TEXT`), but provides a lower level of data protection than `Full`.

- `Full`—The database is recoverable up to a specific point-of-failure or point-in-time. This setting provides the highest level of data protection.

CAUTION

If you do not back up your transaction log frequently, you should use the `Simple` recovery mode. If you use one of the other modes and fail to back up the transaction log on a continuous basis, the log will grow until it consumes all your available disk space or until it reaches the maximum specified log size.

`ANSI NULL Default`
Default setting: FALSE

If `NULL` or `NOT NULL` is not explicitly stated during column creation, SQL Server uses this option to determine the `NULL` or `NOT NULL` characteristic for the column.

NOTE

The `ANSI NULL Default` option was named `Columns Null by Default` in previous versions of SQL Server.

The following examples explain the impact of setting the `ANSI NULL Default` option.

Example A:

```
ANSI Null Default = FALSE
CREATE TABLE sales (sales_id int)
```

Result: The column sales_id is defined as `NOT NULL`.

Example B:

```
ANSI Null Default = TRUE
CREATE TABLE sales (sales_id int)
```

Result: The column sales_id is defined as NULL.

NOTE

Explicitly specifying a column as NULL or NOT NULL with the CREATE TABLE command over-rides the ANSI NULL Default option.

Auto Close

Default setting: FALSE on Windows NT version and TRUE on Windows 9x version.

When the Auto Close option is set to TRUE, the database is automatically closed when users are not in the database. This option is designed to reduce database resources and enables the physical database files to be copied and mailed.

The drawback of setting Auto Close to TRUE is the overhead associated with opening and closing the database. Therefore, this option is not recommended for databases that are constantly in use.

CAUTION

I recommend setting autoclose = FALSE for databases that are constantly in use. Setting autoclose = TRUE will create additional overhead associated with opening and closing the database files.

Recursive Triggers

Default setting: FALSE

If this option is TRUE, a trigger can recursively call itself. The following is an example of recursion: Table T1 has a trigger that modifies data in table T2; T2 modifies data in T1, which in turns fires the T1 trigger again. As another example, table T1 has a trigger that modifies data in T1. This causes the trigger in table T1 to fire again.

CAUTION

Look out for endless recursion! As with any programming language, recursion must be care-fully controlled. If it is not properly implemented, recursion can lead to endless looping. To prevent those runaway triggers, SQL Server has limited the maximum number of recursive levels to 32.

Auto Shrink
Default setting: FALSE

When the Auto Shrink option is set to TRUE, the database and log files automatically shrink, thus reducing hard disk space.

CAUTION

autoshrink = TRUE might degrade performance. The locking associated with reducing the size of the database can lead to blocking and consume server resources. Therefore, I do not recommend leaving this option on with a high-transaction database. If you need to shrink the database, I recommend temporarily turning this option on and then turning it off after the database has been shrunk. An alternative to autoshrink is the DBCC SHRINKDATABASE command.

Auto Update Statistics
Default setting: TRUE

When the Auto Update Statistics option is set to TRUE, index statistics are automatically updated.

Auto Create Statistics
Default setting: TRUE

When the Auto Create Statistics option is set to TRUE, index statistics are automatically created.

Torn Page Detection
Default setting: TRUE

When the Torn Page Detection option is set to TRUE, SQL Server automatically detects torn pages. A torn page contains incomplete data modifications. A torn page can occur when SQL Server has been abnormally terminated (for example, during a power failure) while in the process of updating a database page. If a torn page is detected, the database must be restored from a backup.

NOTE

To prevent torn pages, configure your server with the following:

- Disk cache with a battery backup
- Uninterrupted Power Supply (UPS)

Use Quoted Identifiers
Default setting: FALSE

When the Use Quoted Identifiers option is set to TRUE, object names within double quotes do not have to adhere to Transact-SQL naming conventions. For example, the following statement is valid when this option is TRUE ("primary" and "date" are SQL Server reserved words):

```
CREATE TABLE "primary" ("date" datetime)
```

Compatibility Level
This setting enables you to specify the database compatibility setting: 6.0, 6.5, 7.0, or 8.0. Use this feature when you migrate a database to SQL Server 2000 and you need to preserve the characteristics of a previous version of SQL Server.

Other Database Options
Several additional database options are not accessible through the Options tab of the database Properties dialog box. You can use the following Transact-SQL command to set database options:

```
sp_dboption [dbname, optname, {TRUE | FALSE}]
```

> **NOTE**
>
> Other database options are not discussed in this chapter (for example: merge publish, offline, published, subscribed, and so on). SQL Server typically controls these database options. Therefore, I do not recommend using sp_dboption to change options not discussed in this chapter.

Concat NULL Yields NULL
Default setting: FALSE

When the Concat NULL Yields NULL option is set to TRUE, concatenation of a NULL and a non-NULL value results in a NULL. When this option equals FALSE, the NULL value is treated as an empty (zero length) string. Listing 8.2 is an example of this option.

LISTING 8.2 The Concat NULL Yields NULL Option

```
/* ------------------- */
/* query with option ON */
/* ------------------- */
sp_dboption pubs,'concat null yields null',true
go
```

LISTING 8.2   Continued

```
declare @x varchar(11)
select @x = null
select @x
select 'pubs' + @x


/* ------------------ */
-- result:
/* ------------------ */
NULL


/* ------------------ */
/* query with option OFF*/
/* ------------------ */
sp_dboption pubs,'concat null yields null',false
go
declare @x varchar(11)
select @x = null
select @x
select 'pubs' + @x


/* ------------------ */
-- result:
/* ------------------ */
pubs
```

Cursor Close on Commit
Default setting: FALSE

When the Cursor Close on Commit option is set to TRUE, all open cursors are auto-matically closed when data is committed. This is in compliance with SQL-92 ANSI standards.

Default to Local Cursor
Default setting: FALSE

When the Default to Local Cursor option is set to TRUE, cursors that do not explicitly contain the GLOBAL scope keyword default to LOCAL. When the Default to Local Cursor option is set to FALSE, cursors that do not explicitly contain the LOCAL or GLOBAL scope keywords default to GLOBAL. (See Chapter 22, "Using Stored Procedures and Cursors," for more information on LOCAL and GLOBAL cursors.)

Subscribed
Default setting: FALSE

When the Subscribed option is set to TRUE, it permits the database to be subscribed for replication (see Chapters 27, 28, and 29 for more information on replication). It does not perform the subscription; it only allows it to be subscribed to.

When this option is set to FALSE, it prevents the database from being subscribed. Set this option to FALSE unless you want this to be a subscribed database.

Expanding the Database and Log Size

You can easily expand the size of a database and its log after it has been created. SQL Server offers two approaches to increasing the size of a database. Before proceeding, you should review which approach best suits your needs.

Approach 1: Have SQL Server Automatically Expand the Database and Log

A database and its log can be configured to automatically expand on an as-needed basis. This eliminates the need to manually resize the database.

To have the database and log automatically expand in size, select the Automatically Grow File option (see Figures 8.9 and 8.10) from the Properties dialog box. File growth settings, such as In Megabytes or By Percent, can also be set when the Automatically Grow File option is on.

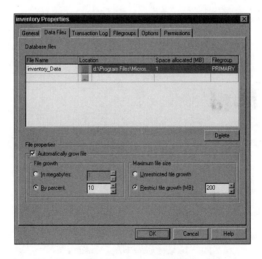

FIGURE 8.9   Automatically Grow File Option—Data Files tab.

FIGURE 8.10   Automatically Grow File Option—Transaction Log tab.

Approach 2: Manually Expand the Database and Log

The second way you can expand the database and log is to manually increase the size of the file(s) in use. Perform the following steps to manually increase the size of the file(s) in use.

1. From the SQL Server Enterprise Manager, click the plus (+) sign next to the server that contains the database you want to view or set options for.

2. Click the plus (+) sign next to the Databases folder. This opens the Databases folder.

3. Right-click the database. From the right-mouse menu, select the Properties menu option. The Properties dialog box appears.

4. From the Properties dialog box, select the Data Files or Transaction Log tab. From either tab, specify the file size in the Space Allocated portion of the dialog box (see Figure 8.11).

5. Click OK to save your changes.

Another way to increase the size of the database or log is to assign a new file. By assigning a new file, you are supplying a new physical file for the database or log. This is useful when a database or log needs to span multiple hard drives. Perform the following steps to manually assign a new file.

1. From the SQL Server Enterprise Manager, click the plus (+) sign next to the server that contains the database you want to view or set options for.

FIGURE 8.11   Increasing database size.

2. Click the plus (+) sign next to the Databases folder. This opens the Databases folder.

3. Right-click the database in which you want to set the database option. From the right-mouse menu, select the Properties menu option. The Properties dialog box appears.

4. From the Properties dialog box, select the Data Files or Transaction Log tab. From either tab, enter one or more additional filenames (see Figure 8.12).

5. Click OK to save your changes.

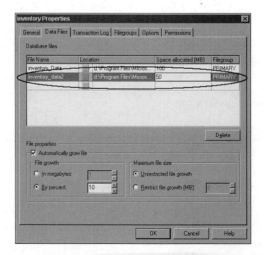

FIGURE 8.12   Assigning new files to an existing database or log.

You can also use the Transact-SQL command in Listing 8.3 to expand a database or log:

LISTING 8.3   Expanding a Database or Log

```
ALTER DATABASE database
{ ADD FILE < filespec > [ ,...n ] [ TO FILEGROUP filegroup_name ]
| ADD LOG FILE < filespec > [ ,...n ]
| REMOVE FILE logical_file_name
| ADD FILEGROUP filegroup_name
| REMOVE FILEGROUP filegroup_name
| MODIFY FILE < filespec >
| MODIFY NAME = new_dbname
| MODIFY FILEGROUP
➥ filegroup_name {filegroup_property | NAME = new_filegroup_name }
| SET < optionspec > [ ,...n ] [ WITH < termination > ]
| COLLATE < collation_name >
}
<filespec> ::=
 ( NAME = logical_file_name
    [ , NEWNAME = new_logical_name ]
    [ , FILENAME = 'os_file_name' ]
    [ , SIZE = size ]
    [ , MAXSIZE = { max_size | UNLIMITED } ]
    [ , FILEGROWTH = growth_increment ] )
<optionspec> ::=
    < state_option >
    | < cursor_option >
    | < auto_option >
    | < sql_option >
    | < recovery_option >
    < state_option > ::=
        { SINGLE_USER | RESTRICTED_USER | MULTI_USER }
        | { OFFLINE | ONLINE }
        | { READ_ONLY | READ_WRITE }
    < termination > ::=
        ROLLBACK AFTER integer [ SECONDS ]
        | ROLLBACK IMMEDIATE
        | NO_WAIT
    < cursor_option > ::=
        CURSOR_CLOSE_ON_COMMIT { ON | OFF }
        | CURSOR_DEFAULT { LOCAL | GLOBAL }
    < auto_option > ::=
```

LISTING 8.3   Continued

```
        AUTO_CLOSE { ON | OFF }
        | AUTO_CREATE_STATISTICS { ON | OFF }
        | AUTO_SHRINK { ON | OFF }
        | AUTO_UPDATE_STATISTICS { ON | OFF }
    < sql_option > ::=
        ANSI_NULL_DEFAULT { ON | OFF }
        | ANSI_NULLS { ON | OFF }
        | ANSI_PADDING { ON | OFF }
        | ANSI_WARNINGS { ON | OFF }
        | ARITHABORT { ON | OFF }
        | CONCAT_NULL_YIELDS_NULL { ON | OFF }
        | NUMERIC_ROUNDABORT { ON | OFF }
        | QUOTED_IDENTIFIER { ON | OFF }
        | RECURSIVE_TRIGGERS { ON | OFF }
    < recovery_option > ::=
        RECOVERY { FULL | BULK_LOGGED | SIMPLE }
        | TORN_PAGE_DETECTION { ON | OFF }
```

Shrinking a Database and Log

By shrinking a database and log, you decrease the amount of space allocated to the database and log. SQL Server can automatically shrink the size of a database, or you can manually shrink the database.

To have SQL Server automatically shrink a database and log, set the database option autoshrink to TRUE (see the topic "Setting Database Options" earlier in this chapter for more information on autoshrink). The following is an example of setting the autoshrink database option for the pubs database.

```
sp_dboption 'pubs', 'autoshrink', TRUE
```

To manually shrink a database and log, follow these steps:

1. From the SQL Server Enterprise Manager, click the plus (+) sign next to the server that contains the database you want to view or set options for.

2. Click the plus (+) sign next to the Databases folder. This opens the Databases folder.

3. Right-click the database that you want to shrink. From the right-mouse menu, select the All Tasks menu option. From the All Tasks menu option, select the Shrink Database menu option. The Shrink Database dialog box appears (see Figure 8.13).

4. From the Shrink Database dialog box, select the Shrink settings and click the OK button.

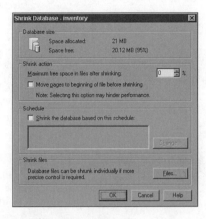

FIGURE 8.13 The Shrink Database dialog box.

You can also use the following Transact-SQL command to shrink a database:

```
DBCC SHRINKDATABASE ( database_name [, target_percent]
➡ [, {NOTRUNCATE | TRUNCATEONLY}])
```

NOTE

Starting with SQL Server 2000, the request to shrink the database or file is processed immediately. (In version 7.0, there was a delay.) When shrinking the transaction log, you should truncate the transaction log prior to shrinking it (see Chapter 10 for details on truncating the transaction log).

Renaming a Database

You can rename any database after it has been created. Only the sa or members of the sysadmin role can rename a database. Follow these steps to rename a database:

1. Set the database you are going to rename to Single User mode. (Refer to the section "Setting Database Options" earlier in this chapter for more information about single-user mode.)

2. From the Microsoft SQL Server Query Analyzer, access the Query dialog box and enter the following syntax:

```
sp_renamedb oldname, newname
```

3. Run the query.

4. Reset the database to multiuser mode.

The following is an example of renaming a database.

```
use master
go
sp_dboption pubs,'single user',true
go
-- change db name
sp_renamedb 'pubs','pubs_db'
go
-- change it back to its original name
sp_renamedb 'pubs_db','pubs'
go
sp_dboption pubs,'single user',false
go
```

CAUTION

When renaming a database, watch out for SQL statements that explicitly refer to the database name; for example, SELECT * FROM *pubs*..authors. If you rename the pubs database to pub_db, you must remember to change the statement to SELECT * FROM pubs_db..authors. Some common areas in which you should look for database references are views, stored procedures, triggers, BCP scripts, and embedded SQL commands in applications.

Deleting a Database

When you delete a database, you physically remove the database and its associated operating system files. This also destroys all objects contained within the database. Only the sa, members of the sysadmin role, and database owner can delete a database. Follow these steps to delete a database:

1. From the SQL Server Enterprise Manager, click the plus (+) sign next to the server that contains the database you want to view or set options for.

2. Click the plus (+) sign next to the Databases folder. This opens the Databases folder.

3. Right-click the database that you want to delete. From the right-mouse menu, select the Delete menu option (see Figure 8.14).

4. At the Delete Database prompt, select Yes to delete the database.

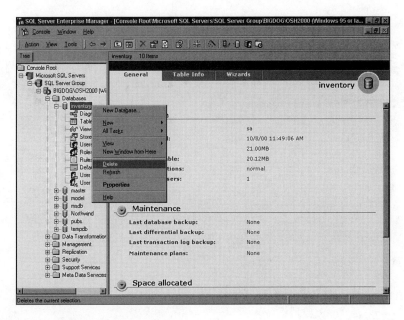

FIGURE 8.14   Deleting a database.

You can use the following Transact-SQL command to delete a database:

```
DROP DATABASE database_name [, database_name...]
```

CAUTION

You cannot delete a database if any of the following are true:

- The database is being restored

- The database is in use

- The database contains objects that are published for replication

NOTE

Deleting a database also removes the database files and log files associated with the database. Therefore, you do not need to manually delete these files from the operating system.

TIP

Always back up the master database after you drop a database. Doing so makes it easier to recover your database should the master database become damaged (see Chapter 10, "Backup and Recovery" for more information about backing up the master database).

Moving Database Files

The Detach and Attach methods enable you to move and/or copy database files. Detaching a database removes the database from SQL Server, but does not remove the database files from the operating system. Attaching a database creates a new database that references the data stored in the existing data and log files.

Use the following Transact-SQL command to attach a database:

sp_attach_db [@dbname =] *'dbname'*,

[@filename1 =] *'filename1'*

[[, ...@filename16 =] *'filename'*]

Use the following Transact-SQL command to detach a database:

sp_detach_db [@dbname =] *'dbname'*

[, [@skipchecks =] *'skipchecks'*]

The following is an example of how to move the pubs database from c:\mssql\data to c:\mydatabases. (In the real world, you probably would never move the pubs database to another directory. However, this example can be applied to situations such as moving a database to another server or to another hard drive.)

1. From the Microsoft SQL Server Query Analyzer, access the Query dialog box and enter the following syntax:

   exec sp_detach_db pubs,true

2. Run the query.

3. Move the operating system files associated with the database. You can use the Cut and Paste facility found in the Microsoft Windows Explorer product. You will always have at least two files: .MDF and .LDF. Depending on the database configuration, you might have multiple .MDF and .LDF files, and you may also have .NDF files associated with the database. For this example, the pubs database was moved by cutting and pasting pubs.mdf and pubs_log.ldf to a directory named c:\mydatabases. You can also copy the files to a different directory or drive on the same computer or to another computer.

TIP

Use sp_helpdb to list the files associated with a database.

---

4. From the Microsoft SQL Server Query Analyzer, access the Query dialog box and enter the following syntax:

```
EXEC sp_attach_db @dbname = 'pubs',
@filename1 = 'c:\mydatabases\pubs.mdf',
@filename2 = 'c:\mydatabases\pubs_log.ldf'
```

5. Run the query, and the pubs database now resides in the c:\mydatabases directory.

To copy the pubs database to another database named pubs2, perform the following steps:

1. Copy the operating system files associated with the database. This is similar to step 3 of the preceding example, except that the pubs database is copied to another directory instead of being cut and pasted.

2. Rename the operating system files so that they are not duplicates of the pubs operating system files. For this example, pubs.mdf was renamed pubs2.mdf, and pubs_log.ldf was renamed pubs2_log.ldf from within Explorer.

3. From the Microsoft SQL Server Query Analyzer, access the Query dialog box and enter the following syntax:

```
EXEC sp_attach_db @dbname = 'pubs2',
@filename1 = 'c:\mydatabases\pubs2.mdf',
@filename2 = 'c:\mydatabases\pubs2_log.ldf'
```

4. Run the query, and the pubs2 database is created with the files that reside in the c:\mydatabases directory.

NOTE

You can choose from several different methods to move and copy a database. In addition to using the Detach and Attach facilities, you can back up and restore a database by using the Copy Database Wizard, or you can use DTS.

Additional Database Information

The following sections list tips and tricks that can help improve the management of databases. These tips can simplify database maintenance and improve database recoverability.

Tip 1: Document the Database

Always document the configuration of the database after it has been modified. This is in addition to backing up the master database. The easiest way to document the configuration of a database is to use the sp_helpdb command. You should save the output from the command to a text file (preferably somewhere other than the server's hard drive).

Tip 2: Take Advantage of the model Database

Use the model database to simplify object creation. The model database enables you to define a template for the creation of new databases. When you create a new database, SQL Server copies the contents of the model database into the newly created database. This makes a handy mechanism for copying frequently used database options and objects into a new database. Anything you want automatically copied into a new database should be placed in the model.

> **TIP**
>
> Perform the following steps to view the model database and other system databases from the Enterprise Manager:
>
> 1. Right-click the server. From the right-mouse menu, select the Edit SQL Server Registration Properties menu option. The Registered SQL Server Properties dialog box appears.
> 2. From the Registered SQL Server Properties dialog box, select the Show System Databases and System Objects option.
> 3. Click the OK button to save the change.

> **NOTE**
>
> The model database is automatically created when you install SQL Server. It cannot be deleted.
>
> Changes to the model database do not impact existing databases. The model database is used only when creating new databases.

The following are common types of objects and settings that can be stored in the model database:

- Frequently used user-defined datatypes, rules, and defaults.
- Database options. Any database option you set in the model database is copied into a new database. For example, if you always set Recovery Model = Bulk-Logged, go ahead and set it in the model database.

- Any tables, views, or stored procedures that you always add to a new database can be placed in the model database.

- Database size. If you expand the model database (the default size is 1MB), its new size becomes the minimum size for any new database.

CAUTION

Be careful when you increase the size of the model database. Whenever SQL Server creates a new database, it copies the contents of the model database into the new database. Therefore, the new database cannot be smaller than the model database.

Filegroups

Filegroups allow database files and objects to be logically grouped together. Tables, indexes, text datatypes, ntext datatypes, and image datatypes can be placed on specific filegroups (see Figure 8.15). By spreading database I/O across hard drives, filegroups provide the potential to improve database performance. Filegroups can also simplify administrative tasks such as backing up a filegroup or adding new files to new disks.

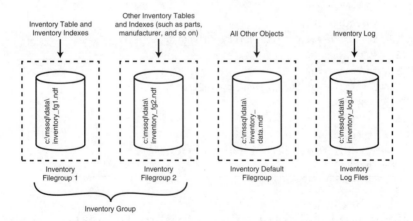

FIGURE 8.15   Filegroups.

NOTE

If you are considering implementing filegroups, you should consider implementing hardware with RAID technology. A high quality RAID system can often deliver performance gains similar to filegroups, and with fewer hassles. To successfully implement filegroups, you need detailed knowledge of table and index usage. If the knowledge used to implement filegroups changes over time, you will need to modify your filegroups. A RAID implementation does not require detailed table and index knowledge.

If you have worked with Oracle, you will find filegroups to be similar to Oracle's implementation of table spaces.

The following topics discuss how to implement and manage filegroups.

Implementing a Filegroup During Database Creation

To implement a filegroup during database creation, use the FILEGROUP filegroup_name <filespec> [,...n] clause of the CREATE DATABASE command.

Listing 8.4 is an example of creating a database named inventory with a filegroup named inventorygrp that contains two files: inventory_fg1 and inventory_fg2.

LISTING 8.4   Creating a Database Named inventory

```
CREATE DATABASE inventory
ON PRIMARY
( NAME = inventory_data,
  FILENAME = 'c:\mssql\data\inventory_data.mdf',
  SIZE = 1MB ),
FILEGROUP inventorygrp
( NAME = inventory_fg1,
  FILENAME = 'c:\mssql\data\inventory_fg1.ndf',
  SIZE = 1MB ),
( NAME = inventory_fg2,
  FILENAME = 'c:\mssql\data\inventory_fg2.ndf',
  SIZE = 1MB)
LOG ON
( NAME = inventory_log,
  FILENAME = 'c:\mssql\data\inventory_log.ldf',
  SIZE = 1MB)
```

Implementing a Filegroup for an Existing Database

To implement a filegroup for an existing database, use the ALTER DATABASE command with the ADD FILEGROUP keywords to create a filegroup:

```
ALTER DATABASE database
ADD FILEGROUP filegroup_name
```

In this statement, *database* is the name of the database you are going to use; *file-group_name* is the name of the filegroup you are going to create. (The database must already exist. For more information, see the section "Creating a Database" earlier in this chapter.)

To create a filegroup named `inventorygrp` using the `inventory` database, use the following command:

```
ALTER DATABASE inventory
ADD FILEGROUP inventorygrp
```

Adding Secondary Data Files to the Filegroup

In Listing 8.5, the `ALTER DATABASE` command is used with the `ADD FILE` and `TO FILEGROUP` keywords to create the secondary data files that will be used by the file-group.

LISTING 8.5   Creating Secondary Data Files

```
ALTER DATABASE database
ADD FILE <filespec>
TO FILEGROUP filegroup_name
<filespec> ::=
  (NAME = 'logical_file_name',
   FILENAME = 'os_file_name'
  [, SIZE = size]
  [, MAXSIZE = { max_size | UNLIMITED } ]
  [, FILEGROWTH = growth_increment] )
```

In this statement, *database* is the name of the database you are going to use; *file-spec* contains the information used to create the secondary data files; *filegroup_name* is the name of the filegroup to use. (The filegroup must already exist.)

Use the command in Listing 8.6 to add two secondary files to the `inventorygrp` file-group in the `inventory` database.

LISTING 8.6   Creating Secondary Data Files

```
ALTER DATABASE inventory
ADD FILE
(NAME = inventory_fg1,
FILENAME = 'c:\mssql\data\inventory_fg1.ndf',
SIZE = 1MB),
```

LISTING 8.6   Continued

```
(NAME = inventory_fg2,
FILENAME = 'c:\mssql\data\inventory_fg2.ndf',
SIZE = 1MB)
TO FILEGROUP inventorygrp
```

Place an Object on the Filegroup

The following types of objects can be placed on a filegroup.

- Table
- Index
- Text datatypes
- Ntext datatypes
- Image datatypes

Use the CREATE TABLE command with the ON filegroup_name option to create a table on a filegroup:

```
CREATE TABLE [database.[owner].]table_name
( <column_definition>
)
[ON filegroup_name| DEFAULT} ]
[TEXTIMAGE_ON {filegroup | DEFAULT} ]
```

To create the inventory table on the inventorygrp filegroup, use the following command:

```
CREATE TABLE inventory
(inventory_id integer primary key,
inventory_amount money,
inventory_qty integer,
inventory_location varchar(35))
ON inventorygrp
```

Creating an Index on a Filegroup

Use the CREATE INDEX command with the ON *filegroup_name* option to create an index on a filegroup:

```
CREATE [UNIQUE] [CLUSTERED | NONCLUSTERED]
INDEX index_name ON table (column [, ...n])
...
[ON filegroup_name]
```

For example, to create an index on the `inventorygrp` filegroup for the `inventory` table, use the following command:

```
CREATE INDEX inventory_location_idx
ON inventory(inventory_location)
ON inventorygrp
```

Viewing Information About a Filegroup

To view information about a filegroup, follow these steps:

1. From the SQL Server Enterprise Manager, click the plus (+) sign next to the server that contains the database you want to view or set options for.

2. Click the plus (+) sign next to the Databases folder to open the Databases folder.

3. Right-click the database in which you want to view filegroup information. From the right-mouse menu, select the Properties menu option. The Properties dialog appears.

4. From the Properties dialog box, select the Filegroups tab. The filegroup information is displayed (see Figure 8.16).

FIGURE 8.16   Filegroup information.

The Transact-SQL command can also be used to view filegroup information:

```
sp_helpfilegroup [@filegroupname =] 'name'
```

where the optional parameter @filegroupname specifies the filegroup name.

The following are examples.

Example 1:

```
use inventory
go
sp_helpfilegroup
```

Sample output:

```
groupname           groupid filecount
------------------- ------- ---------
inventorygrp        2       2
PRIMARY             1       1
```

Example 2:

```
use inventory
go
sp_helpfilegroup inventorygrp
```

Sample output:

```
groupname                groupid filecount
------------------------ ------- -----------
inventorygrp             2       2
```

```
file_in_group fileid filename                                size    maxsize   growth
------------- ------ --------------------------------------- ------- --------- -------
inventory_fg1 3      c:\mssql\data\inventory_fg1.ndf 1024 KB Unlimited 10%
inventory_fg2 4      c:\mssql\data\inventory_fg2.ndf 1024 KB Unlimited 10%
```

Database FAQ

The following section lists some of the common questions asked by DBAs about SQL Server database management.

Q Can the transaction log be disabled?

A No, you cannot disable the transaction log. This question is commonly asked when the log is not part of someone's backup strategy. Consequently, many people would rather not periodically backup the transaction log. Unfortunately, you can't avoid having transactions written to the log. But you *can* have the transaction log truncated automatically in SQL Server; set the database recovery model to `Simple` (see the section "Setting Database Options" earlier in this chapter for more information about `Simple` recovery).

Q Can I read the transaction log or use the transaction log for auditing purposes?

A SQL Server does not provide an interface to read the transaction log. However, third party vendors have developed systems to read the log. For more information, contact Lumigent Technologies about its Log Explorer product (www.lumigent.com).

Q What does the following error message mean?

```
Server: Msg 9002, Level 17, State 2
The log file for database 'database_name' is full.
Back up the transaction log for the database
to free up some log space.
```

A Whenever you fill up the transaction log or run out of disk space for the transaction log, you receive the error message shown. To resolve the error you must back up the transaction log with the no_log option or increase free space on the hard drive that contains the transaction log. (Note: Increasing hard drive space only works if the transaction log auto-grow option is on.)

To help avoid this error, do one of the following:

- **Increase the free space on the hard drive until the problem goes away:** Although this is the simplest solution, it might not be the most effective solution. If you do not properly manage your transactions, you can fill up the transaction log regardless of how space has been allocated to it.

- **Increase the frequency of the log backup:** Doing so might reduce the frequency of the error or prevent it from occurring.

- **Set the database recovery model to `Simple`:** This option automatically truncates the inactive portion of the log when the log is 70% full. Only use this option if you are not backing up the transaction log; this option *is not* recommended for production databases!

Q What does the following error message mean?

```
Server: Msg 1105, Level 17, State 2
Could not allocate space for object 'object_name'
in database 'database_name' because the 'PRIMARY'
filegroup is full.
```

A This error message is notifying you that the data portion of the database has run out of storage space. Perform the following tasks to resolve this error message.

- If the database auto-grow option is on, increase hard drive free space. If the option is off, you must manually expand the database files (see the topic "Expanding the Database and Log Size" earlier in this chapter for more information).

- Remove unused tables.

- Remove unnecessary indexes.

Summary

Basic database management techniques combined with supplemental tips provide you with the skills to intelligently manage a database. Remember that intelligent database management is the key to keeping your database up and running. Following are some important notes to remember when managing databases:

- Use the SQL Server Enterprise Manager or Transact-SQL commands to manage databases. For ease-of-use, the Enterprise Manager is generally preferred over Transact-SQL commands.

- Every database in SQL Server has a transaction log.

- SQL Server uses the transaction log to ensure transaction completeness and to incrementally restore data changes.

- Virtually all changes to the database are first written to the transaction log and then to the database.

- Every database in SQL Server must use at least one data file and one log file.

- The sa and members of the sysadmin or dbcreate roles are the only users who can create a database unless the statement permission is granted to another user.

- Watch out when the database recovery model is set to `Simple`. When this option is set, it might impact your backup strategy.

- Use the `sp_helpdb` command to document important database information.

- Databases and logs can automatically grow and contract in size on an as-needed basis.

- Use filegroups to logically group database objects (tables, indexes, text, ntext, and image datatypes) and/or partition database I/O across different hard drives.

9

Managing SQL Server Users and Security

by Orryn Sledge

IN THIS CHAPTER

- Introduction
- An Overview of SQL Server's Security Model
- Managing Logins
- Managing Server Roles
- Managing Database Access and Database Roles
- Viewing and Modifying Login Information
- Removing Logins
- Changing a Password
- Managing SQL Server Security
- Beyond Security Basics: Suggested Strategies
- Managing SQL Server Users and Security FAQ

Introduction

This chapter discusses how to create and manage user accounts. It also discusses how to implement and manage security. I think that you will find SQL Server's account management model and security model easy to use and understand. SQL Server provides built-in security and data protection. Its security features are trustworthy and relatively easy to administer. By taking advantage of SQL Server's security features, you can create a secure database that prevents unauthorized access and allows data modification to occur in a controlled and orderly manner.

TIP

The following is a listing of guidelines and resources to help you secure SQL Server:

- Stay current with Microsoft's security updates and patches by visiting the following site: `http://www.microsoft.com/sql/techinfo/adminis-tration/2000/security.asp`

- Do not publicly expose port 1433 over the Internet. Install SQL Server behind your firewall or set-up a VPN solution if you must externally access SQL Server.

- If you are serious about hardening SQL Server, take a look at a product such as ISS's Database Scanner (`www.iss.net`) or PentaSafe's (`www.pentasafe.com`) VigilEnt Security Agent for SQL Server. These products automate the process of security settings, intruders, and analyzing detailed reporting, which fixes security vulnerabilities.

An Overview of SQL Server's Security Model

SQL Server's security model comprises the following components:

- SQL Server login
- Database user
- guest user
- Permissions
- Roles

SQL Server Login

The SQL Server login model supports two security modes:

- Windows Authentication
- SQL Server and Windows (Mixed Mode)

CAUTION

By default, the sa account is not password protected! After installing SQL Server, I recommend immediately changing the sa password.

Windows Authentication

Windows Authentication takes advantage of Windows 2000 user security and account mechanisms. This security mode allows SQL Server to share the username and password used for Windows 2000 and allows the user to bypass the SQL Server login process. Users with a valid Windows 2000 account can log in to SQL Server without supplying a username and password.

Some benefits of Windows Authentication are as follows:

- A user does not have to remember a separate password and username.
- When the password changes in Windows 2000, the user does not have to change the password in SQL Server.

How does Windows Authentication work? When a user accesses SQL Server, SQL Server obtains the user and password information from the user's Windows 2000 network security attributes. These attributes are established when the user logs in to Windows 2000. If the user has been granted access to SQL Server, the user is automatically logged in to SQL Server. Using Windows Authentication allows you to take advantage of Windows 2000 features such as password aging and login auditing.

Windows Authentication requires more hands-on experience with Windows 2000 or working closely with the Windows 2000 system administrator when setting up user accounts and groups. Setting up Windows Authentication requires a few more steps than setting up SQL Server Authentication, but the benefits outweigh the additional configuration steps.

TIP

With Windows Authentication, I recommend placing users into Windows 2000 groups and adding the Windows 2000 group login to SQL Server. This powerful feature allows you to group your users at the domain level and apply permissions at the SQL Server level. For example, a group named sales could exist in the domain. A new login based on the sales group could be added to SQL Server. When a new Windows 2000 account is created, the Windows 2000 administrator can add the new account to the group named sales. The SQL Server DBA can apply the appropriate role(s) and permissions to the sales group. The new Windows 2000 login automatically contains the necessary permissions to log into SQL Server because the sales group was previously granted a login. This strategy makes it easy for new users to be added to the system.

SQL Server and Windows Security (Mixed Mode)

In *mixed mode* security, both *Windows Authentication* and SQL Server Authentication are enabled. When using SQL Server Authentication, an individual logging in to SQL Server must supply a username and a password that SQL Server validates against a system table. When using *Windows Authentication* (see the earlier section *"Windows Authentication"* for more information), users can log in to SQL Server without being prompted for a login ID and password.

NOTE

Did you ever wonder where logins are stored in SQL Server? They are stored in the master..syslogins table.

Database User

The *database user* concept defines the database(s) that an individual can access. After an individual has successfully logged in to SQL Server, either through Windows Authentication or SQL Server Authentication, SQL Server determines whether the user is a valid user for the database he is accessing. Regardless of the security mode, a user must be permitted to access the database. If the user is not permitted in the database, SQL Server returns an error message.

The only exception to the database user concept is the guest user. See the next section for more information on the guest user.

guest **User**

A special username, guest, can be added to a database to allow anyone with a valid SQL Server login to access the database. The guest username is a member of the public role. After the guest user has been added to a database, any individual with a valid SQL Server login—regardless of security mode—can access the database as the guest user. A guest user works as follows:

1. SQL Server checks to see whether the login ID has a valid username or alias assigned. If so, SQL Server grants the user access to the database as the username or aliases. If not, go to step 2.

2. SQL Server checks to see whether a guest username exists. If so, the login ID is granted access to the database as guest. If the guest account does not exist, SQL Server denies access to the database.

NOTE

The guest user always has an uid of 2.

A guest user is added to the master database and the pubs database when the system is installed. SQL Server prevents you from dropping the guest user from the master database accidentally. If you removed guest from the master database, only the sa user could log in to SQL Server! When users log in to SQL Server, they have access to the master database as the guest user. (Don't worry, the guest user has very few permissions in the master database.)

To prevent guest access in any database other than master, drop the guest account from the corresponding database.

Permissions

A *permission* allows someone to do something within a database. There are two types of permissions: object and statement. *Object permissions* control who can access and manipulate data in tables and views and who can run stored procedures. *Statement permissions* control who can drop and create objects within a database.

SQL Server uses the commands GRANT, REVOKE, and DENY to manage permissions.

- GRANT—When you GRANT a permission to an object, you allow someone to perform an action against the object (for example, SELECT, UPDATE, INSERT, DELETE, or EXECUTE). When you GRANT permission to a statement, you allow someone to run the statement (for example, CREATE TABLE).

- REVOKE—When you REVOKE a permission from an object, you prevent someone from performing an action against the object (for example, SELECT, UPDATE, INSERT, DELETE, or EXECUTE). When you REVOKE permission from a statement, you take away a user's ability to run the statement (for example, CREATE TABLE).

- DENY—When you DENY a permission from an object, you explicitly prevent someone from using the permission (for example, SELECT, UPDATE, INSERT, DELETE, or EXECUTE), whereas REVOKE actually removes the permission.

Object Permissions

Object permissions control access to objects within SQL Server. You can grant and revoke permissions to tables, table columns, views, and stored procedures through the Enterprise Manager or through system procedures. A user who wants to perform an action against an object must have the appropriate permission. For example, when a user wants to SELECT * FROM table1, she must have SELECT permission for the table. Table 9.2 summarizes the types of object permissions.

TABLE 9.2   Summary of Object Permissions

Object Type	Possible Actions
table	SELECT, UPDATE, DELETE, INSERT, REFERENCE
column	SELECT, UPDATE
view	SELECT, UPDATE, INSERT, DELETE
stored procedure	EXECUTE

Statement Permissions

Statement permissions control who can perform administrative actions such as creating or backing up a database. Only the sa, members of the sysadmin role, or database owner can administer statement permissions. I advise prudence in granting access to statement permissions such as CREATE DATABASE, BACKUP DATABASE, and BACKUP LOG. Usually, the best approach is to let the sa, a member of the sysadmin role, or the database owner manage these statements. Following is a list of statement permissions that can be granted or revoked:

- CREATE DATABASE—Creates a database. This permission can be granted only by the sa and only to users in the master database.

- CREATE DEFAULT—Creates a default value for a table column.

- CREATE PROCEDURE—Creates a stored procedure.

- CREATE RULE—Creates a table column rule.

- CREATE TABLE—Creates a table.

- CREATE VIEW—Creates a view.

- BACKUP DATABASE—Backs up the database.

- BACKUP TRANSACTION—Backs up the transaction log.

Roles

Roles provide a logical way to group users with permissions. The following are the types of roles found in SQL Server:

- Server roles
- Database roles

Server Roles

Server roles provide levels of access to server operations and tasks. If an individual is placed in a certain role, he can perform the function permitted by the role. For example, an individual who is member of the sysadmin role can perform any type of action in SQL Server.

Server roles are predefined and are serverwide. These roles are not database specific and cannot be customized.

Table 9.3 provides a listing and explanation for each type of server role.

TABLE 9.3   Server Roles

Server Role	Description
sysadmin	Able to do anything in SQL Server
serveradmin	Able to modify SQL Server settings and shut down SQL Server
setupadmin	Able to install replication and control extended stored procedures
securityadmin	Able to control server logins and create database permissions
processadmin	Able to control SQL Server processes
dbcreator	Able to create and modify databases
diskadmin	Able to manage disk files
bulkadmin	Able to execute bulk insert statements

Database Roles

Database roles provide the assignment of a set of database-specific permissions to an individual or a group of users. Database roles can be assigned to Windows Authenticated logins or SQL Server Authenticated logins. Roles that are assigned to Windows Authenticated logins can be assigned to Window 2000 users and groups. Roles can also be nested so that a hierarchical group of permissions can be assigned to logins.

Database roles are database specific. SQL Server provides three types of roles:

- Predefined database roles
- User-defined database roles
- Implicit roles

Predefined Database Roles   Predefined database roles are standard SQL Server database roles. Each database in SQL Server has these roles. Predefined database roles make it easy to delegate responsibility. For example, a developer might be assigned the db_ddladmin role in a development database. This role would allow a developer to create and drop objects (tables, stored procedures, views, and so on) on an as-needed basis.

Predefined database roles are database specific and cannot be customized. Table 9.4 provides a description of each predefined database role.

TABLE 9.4   Predefined Database Roles

Database Role	Description
db_owner	Has complete access to all objects within the database, can drop and re-create objects, and has the capability to assign object permissions to other users. It can modify database settings and perform database maintenance tasks. This role encompasses all functionality listed in the other predefined database roles.
db_accessadmin	Controls access to the database by adding or removing *Windows Authentication* users and SQL Server users.
db_datareader	Has complete access to SELECT data from any table in the database. This role does not grant INSERT, DELETE, or UPDATE permissions on any table in the database.
db_datawriter	Can perform INSERT, DELETE, or UPDATE statements on any table in the database. This role does not grant SELECT permission on any table in the database.
db_ddladmin	Has the capability to create, modify, and drop objects in the database.
db_securityadmin	Performs security management within the database. This role manages statement and object permissions and roles within the database.
db_backupoperator	Has the capability to back up the database.
db_denydatareader	Denies SELECT permission on all tables in the database. However, this role does allow users to modify existing table schemas. It does not allow them to create or drop existing tables.
db_denydatawriter	Denies data modification statements (INSERT, DELETE, or UPDATE) from being performed against any tables in the databases
public	Every database user is a member of the public role. A user automatically becomes part of the public role when she is permitted access to the database.

NOTE

When everyone in a database needs the same permission to the same object, use the public role. When you grant or revoke a permission to the public role, everyone feels the effect. Using the public role is often an easy way to streamline security administration.

User-Defined Roles   User-defined roles allow the grouping of users to a particular security function. User-defined roles are database specific, whereas server roles are server specific.

Several features of user-defined roles are listed as follows:

- Role security is user-defined so that flexible security models can be implemented.

- Users can participate in multiple user-defined roles in the same database, whereas in previous versions users could only belong to one group other than the `public` group.

- NT Authenticated logins and SQL Server Authenticated logins can participate in user-defined roles.

- Roles can be nested, thus creating a hierarchy of security relationships.

NOTE

Role members must be known to the database already. Therefore, Window Authenticated logins or SQL Server Authenticated logins must be permitted in the database prior to assigning the login to a database-specific role.

The following are types of user-defined database roles:

- Standard role

- Application role

Standard Role   The standard role provides a database-specific method for creating user-defined roles that are used to enforce and manage security. The standard role is conceptually similar to database groups, which were found in previous versions of SQL Server, but provides additional functionality.

A common use of a standard role is to group users logically according to their security level. For example, most applications have several types of security levels. The following security levels apply to this example:

- Power user—Can do anything within the database. This group of users is typically granted `SELECT/INSERT/DELETE/UPDATE` permissions for all the tables in the database.

- Normal user—Can modify certain types of data. This group of users is typically granted `SELECT/INSERT/DELETE/UPDATE` permissions for certain tables and `SELECT` permissions for the remaining tables.

- Bonehead user—Is not allowed to modify anything. These users are boneheads, and the DBA is worried that they are going to mess up things! This group of users is typically granted only SELECT access to the data.

Applying the preceding scenario to SQL Server's implementation of roles could result in the mapping of users to roles shown in Table 9.5.

TABLE 9.5   Sample Role Mapping

User Type	Sample Role
Power user	db_datareader and db_datawriter; these predefined database roles allow users to query and modify all tables in the database.
Standard user	standard_user role; this user-defined database role is created by the DBA. It typically contains a mix of SELECT/INSERT/DELETE/UPDATE permissions.
Bonehead user	db_datareader role; this predefined database role allows users to perform only SELECT queries in the database.

Application Role   The application role is a special type of role that allows a user to take on the characteristics of a role. When a user takes on an application role, he takes on a new role and temporarily forgoes all other assigned database-specific permissions. You are probably asking, "Why would I want a user to take on a new role?" The answer is that when an application role is active, the user can perform database querying and processing in a very controlled manner. When the role is not active, the user is limited to his standard database permissions.

The following points define differences between application roles and standard roles:

- Application roles can be password protected, whereas user-defined standard roles cannot. If the application role is password protected, a password must be supplied to activate the role.

- Both application roles and standard roles are user defined and database specific.

- Users are not directly assigned to application roles. Instead, users activate the role within a specific database.

A good use of the application role is whenever you have an environment in which users query and modify data through a controlled interface and *ad hoc* querying. A typical example would be an HR module that allows users to manage employee information. Users of the HR module probably need SELECT/INSERT/DELETE/UPDATE permissions to view and change employee information. But what happens when a user begins to implement Microsoft Access to perform *ad hoc* querying and reporting? A great feature of Microsoft Access is the capability to directly modify data from within its grids. This feature can be a big headache for DBAs because a user can make a data modification directly from Microsoft Access. This change could potentially bypass any logic and controls that are built in to the application to manage the employee data.

Here's where application roles fit in. Instead of granting SELECT/INSERT/DELETE/UPDATE permissions directly to the users of the application, grant the SELECT/INSERT/DELETE/UPDATE permissions to an application role. Next, add logic to the application to activate the application role through the sp_setapp-role system procedure. When the role is active, the users will be able to perform data modification and query operations on the employee table. When the role is not active, the users will not be able to query or modify data through Microsoft Access because the application role is not active. If the users do not know about the application role and do not know the application role's password, they will not be able to activate the role when performing *ad hoc* reporting.

TIP

I recommend taking advantage of application roles. Stop writing custom security routines such as shadow logins! Application roles solve the problem of users needing permissions to modify data through an application and DBAs wanting to prevent data modifications through external tools such as Microsoft Access and Microsoft Query.

NOTE

The following are notes about application roles. The database that contains the role must be in use prior to activating the role. To activate a database from a query window, specify USE *databasename*.

To deactivate an application role, the connection to SQL Server must be broken. There is not a facility to reset an active application role.

You cannot activate an application role within a user-defined transaction or from a stored procedure.

The following is the Transact-SQL command to activate an application role:

```
sp_setapprole [@rolename =] 'name' ,
➥ [@password =] {Encrypt N 'password'} | 'password'
[,[@encrypt =] 'encrypt_style']
```

Managing Logins

Perform the following steps to manage SQL Server logins.

NOTE

If you plan to use Windows Authentication, the Windows 2000 user or Windows 2000 group must exist prior to adding the Windows 2000 user or Windows 2000 group to SQL Server. Use Windows 2000 administration tools to create users and groups.

If you plan to use SQL Server Authentication, SQL Server's authentication mode must be configured to SQL Server and Windows. If you plan to use only Windows Authentication and you want to prevent users from using SQL Server Authentication, SQL Server's authentication mode must be configured to Windows only.

To change the authentication mode setting, use the SQL Server Enterprise Manager. Right-click the server and select Properties from the right-mouse menu to open the SQL Server Properties dialog box. From the dialog box, select the Security tab; then select the appropriate authentication mode.

1. From the SQL Server Enterprise Manager, click the plus (+) sign next to the server that will contain the login.

2. Click the plus (+) sign next to the Security folder.

3. Right-click the Logins icon. From the right-mouse menu, select the New Login menu option. The SQL Server Login Properties—New Login dialog box appears.

4. Enter the login name (see Figure 9.1).

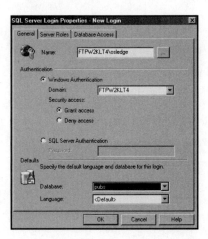

FIGURE 9.1   SQL Server Login Properties—New Login dialog box.

NOTE

If you are using Windows Authentication, the login name must be the same as the login name in the Windows 2000 Domain. Otherwise, an error occurs when the login is created.

5. Select the authentication mode. If you are using Windows Authentication, select the Windows Authentication radio button and the Domain name. If you are using SQL Server Authentication, select the SQL Server authentication radio button and enter a password for the login.

NOTE

A password is optional with SQL Server Authentication. If the optional password issue concerns you, use Windows Authentication, which is integrated with Windows 2000 Security. Through Windows 2000 Security, you can specify a minimum password length and force password aging.

6. Specify the Default Database and Default Language for the login.

NOTE

I recommend specifying a default database that is not the master database. This approach can help prevent users from accidentally creating tables or other objects in the master database. Additionally, it automatically places the user in the proper database when he or she uses the SQL Server Query Analyzer or another similar tool to log in to SQL Server.

7. Click the OK button to create the login.

The following are the corresponding Transact-SQL commands to manage logins:

```
sp_grantlogin [@loginame =] 'login'
sp_revokelogin [@loginame =] 'login'
sp_denylogin [@loginame =] 'login'
sp_addlogin [@loginame =] 'login' [,[@passwd =] 'password']
➥ [,[@defdb =] 'database'] [,[@deflanguage =] 'language']
➥ [,[@sid =] 'sid'] [,[@encryptopt =] 'encryption_option']
sp_helplogins [[@LoginNamePattern =] 'login']
```

NOTE

SQL Server 2000 provides a Security Wizard that walks the user through login creation and permissions assignment. However, the wizard does not support modifications to existing logins and permissions.

Managing Server Roles

Perform the following steps to grant a server role:

1. From the SQL Server Enterprise Manager, click the plus (+) sign next to the server that contains the login.

2. Click the plus (+) sign next to the Security folder.

3. Left-click the Logins icon. A list of logins appears in the Result pane.

4. Right-click the name in the Result pane. From the right-mouse menu, select the Properties menu option. The SQL Server Login Properties dialog box appears.

5. From the SQL Server Login Properties dialog box, click the Server Roles tab (see Figure 9.2).

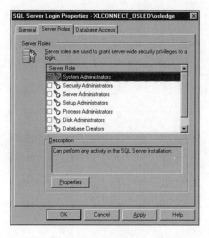

FIGURE 9.2   The SQL Server Login Properties dialog box—Server Roles tab.

6. Left-click the corresponding server role (refer to Table 9.3 for a detailed explanation of each server role).

NOTE

Clicking the Properties button displays the Server Role Properties dialog box, which contains a list of users currently assigned to the selected Server Role (see Figure 9.3). Clicking the Permissions tab displays the commands associated with the corresponding server role (see Figure 9.4).

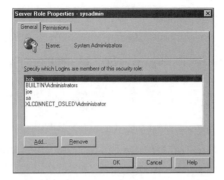

FIGURE 9.3 The Server Role Properties dialog box—General tab.

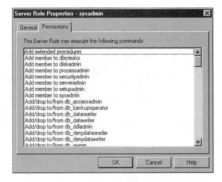

FIGURE 9.4 The Server Role Properties dialog box—Permissions tab.

7. Click the OK button to grant the server role.

The corresponding Transact-SQL commands to manage server roles are as follows:

```
sp_addsrvrolemember [@loginame =] 'login' [,[@rolename =] 'role']
sp_dropsrvrolemember [@loginame =] 'login' [,[@rolename =] 'role']
sp_helpsrvrolemember [[@srvrolename =] 'role']
sp_srvrolepermission [[@srvrolename =] 'role']
```

Managing Database Access and Database Roles

Perform the following steps to grant database access and database roles:

1. From the SQL Server Enterprise Manager, click the plus (+) sign next to the server that contains the login.

2. Click the plus (+) sign next to the Security folder.

3. Left-click the Logins icon. A list of logins appears in the Result pane.

4. Right-click the name in the Result pane. From the right-mouse menu, select the Properties menu option. The SQL Server Login Properties dialog box appears.

5. From the SQL Server Login Properties dialog box, click the Database Access tab (see Figure 9.5).

FIGURE 9.5   The SQL Server Login Properties dialog box—Database Access tab.

6. Left-click a Permit check box. This permits the login to access the database.

NOTE

If a login is not permitted access to a database, the login will not be able to perform any type of operation in the database. Logins are an effective security tool to keep users out of selected databases. The only exception to this rule is the guest user (see the section titled "guest User" for more information).

7. Left-click a Permit in Database Role check box to add the login to a database role (refer to Table 9.4 for a detailed explanation of each database role).

NOTE

Clicking the Properties button displays the Database Role Properties dialog box, which contains a list of users currently assigned to the selected Database Role (see Figure 9.6). If you are viewing a user-defined role or the public role, the Permissions button is enabled. Clicking the Permissions button displays the permissions associated with the corresponding database role (see Figure 9.7).

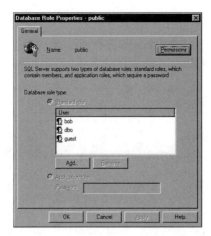

FIGURE 9.6   The Database Role Properties dialog box.

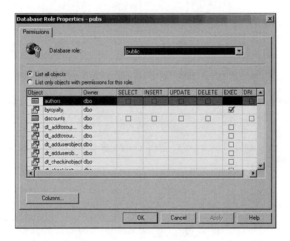

FIGURE 9.7   The Database Role Properties dialog box—Permissions.

    8. Click the OK button to grant the database role.

The corresponding Transact-SQL commands to manage database access and database roles are as follows:

```
sp_grantdbaccess [@loginame =] 'login' [,[@name_in_db =] 'name_in_db' [OUTPUT]]
sp_revokedbaccess {[@name_in_db =] 'name'}
sp_helpuser [[@name_in_db =] 'security_account']
```

```
sp_addrole [@rolename =] 'role' [,[@ownername =] 'owner']
sp_droprole [@rolename =] 'role'
sp_helprole  [[@rolename =] 'role']


sp_addapprole [@rolename =] 'role', [@password =] 'password'
sp_dropapprole [@rolename =] 'role'
sp_setapprole [@rolename =] 'name' ,
[@password =] {Encrypt N 'password'} | 'password'
[,[@encrypt =] 'encrypt_style']


sp_helprolemember [[@rolename =] 'role']
sp_addrolemember [@rolename =] 'role', [@membername =] 'security_account'
sp_helpdbfixedrole [[@rolename =] 'role']
sp_dbfixedrolepermission  [[@rolename =] 'role']
```

Viewing and Modifying Login Information

Perform the following steps to view login information:

1. From the SQL Server Enterprise Manager, click the plus (+) sign next to the server that contains the login.

2. Click the plus (+) sign next to the Security folder.

3. Left-click the Logins icon. A list of logins appears in the Result pane.

4. Right-click the name in the Result pane. From the right-mouse menu, select the Properties menu option. The SQL Server Login Properties dialog box appears. From this dialog box, you can view and modify login information.

The corresponding Transact-SQL commands to view login information are as follows:

```
sp_helplogins [[@LoginNamePattern =] 'login']
sp_helprotect  [[@name =] 'object_statement']
[,[@username =] 'security_account']
[,[@grantorname =] 'grantor'] [,[@permissionarea =] 'type']
```

Removing Logins

Perform the following steps to modify login information:

1. From the SQL Server Enterprise Manager, click the plus (+) sign next to the server that contains the login.

2. Click the plus (+) sign next to the Security folder.

3. Left-click the Logins icon. A list of logins appears in the Result pane.

4. Right-click the name in the Result pane. From the right-mouse menu, select the Delete menu option.

5. Select Yes from the delete confirmation dialog box. This step deletes the user from SQL Server.

NOTE

You cannot delete a login that is an object owner. You must drop the object(s) owned by the login or change the owner of the object(s). To change an object's owner, use the `sp_changeobjectowner` system procedure. The following is the `sp_changeobjectowner` syntax.

```
sp_changeobjectowner [@objname =] 'object', [@newowner =] 'owner'
```

Use the following query to generate a list of logins and the objects they own.

```
select 'login name' = b.name, 'object name ' = a.name
from sysobjects a, master..syslogins b
where a.uid = b.suid
order by 1,2
```

The corresponding Transact-SQL command to remove a login is as follows:

```
sp_droplogin [@loginame =] 'login'
```

Changing a Password

Perform the following steps to change a login password:

1. From the SQL Server Enterprise Manager, click the plus (+) sign next to the server that contains the login.

2. Click the plus (+) sign next to the Security folder.

3. Left-click the Logins icon. A list of logins appears in the Result pane.

4. Right-click the name in the Result pane. From the right-mouse menu, select the Properties menu option. The SQL Server Login Properties dialog box appears.

5. Enter the new password.

6. Click the OK button to save the password. The Confirm Password dialog box appears.

7. In the Confirm Password dialog box, enter the password again to confirm the change.

8. Click the OK button to save the password.

NOTE

This topic of changing passwords is relevant only to logins that use SQL Server Authentication. If the login uses Windows Authentication, the password must be changed through Windows 2000.

The corresponding Transact-SQL command to change a password is as follows:

```
sp_password  [[@old =] 'old_password',]
➥ {[@new =] 'new_password'} [,[@loginame =] 'login']
```

LOGIN GOTCHAS

The following information can help you avoid login headaches!

- Removing a Windows 2000 user or group from a Windows Domain does not drop the corresponding SQL Server login. Whenever you are using Windows Authentication and you remove a user or group from a Windows Domain, the corresponding SQL Server login becomes orphaned (see the next paragraph for more information on orphaned logins). A record remains in the `master..syslogins` table after the Windows user or group has been removed from the Windows Domain. I recommend removing the login from SQL Server prior to removing the Windows login. An alternative to removing the Windows login is to disable the account in the Windows Domain. This approach is useful if an employee quits and then gets rehired.

- An orphaned login might prevent a login from being re-created. If a login is orphaned, and you try to re-create a login with the same name, you will receive an error message because the login still exists in the `master..syslogins` table. To remove the login, use the Enterprise Manager. Follow the instructions discussed in the "Removing Logins" section. After the login has been removed from SQL Server, the login can be re-created.

- Detaching a database and moving it to a different machine can also cause problems if the database has logins that point to the local Windows group. The login will appear to be there, but it will not work because the GUIDs are different, even though the group name is the name. To work around this problem, script out the logins on the source machine and drop/re-create the logins on the target machine.

    - You cannot restore permissions to a removed user by adding the login or group back to the Windows Domain. The reason is that the new login or group contains a security access identifier (SID) that is different from the login that was deleted. SQL Server uses the SID to track permissions. If this scenario occurs, you must manually re-create the corresponding permissions.

Managing SQL Server Security

SQL Server provides built-in security and data protection. Its security features are trustworthy and relatively easy to administer. By taking advantage of SQL Server's security features, you can create a secure database that prevents unauthorized access and allows data modification to occur in a controlled and orderly manner.

Levels of Security

The term *security* is a broad term that carries different meanings depending on how it is applied. It can be applied to the following levels (see Figure 9.8):

- **Operating system**—To connect to the server, a user typically must go through some type of operating system login routine that validates system access.

- **SQL server**—To connect to SQL Server, the user must have a valid SQL server user login.

- **Database**—To access a database within SQL Server, the user must have been granted permission to the database.

- **Object (table, view, or stored procedure)**—To access an object within a database, the user must be granted permission to the object.

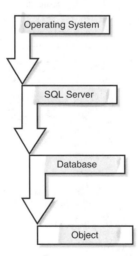

FIGURE 9.8   The four levels of security.

When dealing with security, you spend most of your time working at the database and object level. Therefore, the remainder of this chapter concentrates on database and object security.

Security Hierarchy

SQL Server's security mechanism is hierarchical. Four types of users exist within the hierarchy: the system administrator, database owners, database object owners, and other users of the database (see Figure 9.9).

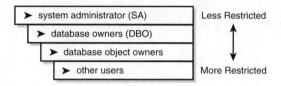

FIGURE 9.9   Security hierarchy.

System Administrator

The *system administrator (login ID sa)* and members of the sysadmin role are considered to be "the almighty ones" who have unrestricted access to SQL Server. They have the ability to execute any SQL command. The sa and members of the sysadmin role can also grant permissions to other users.

Database Owners (DBO)

The *database owner (DBO)* is the user who created the database or has had ownership assigned to him. The DBO has complete access to all objects within his database and can assign object permissions to other users.

> **TIP**
>
> To determine the owner of a database, issue the following command from the Query Analyzer: sp_helpdb [*database name*].

Database Object Owners

The person who creates the database object is considered the owner of the object and is called the *database object owner.* SQL Server assumes that if you have the necessary permission to create the object, you are automatically given all permissions to that object (SELECT, UPDATE, INSERT, DELETE, REFERENCE, and EXECUTE).

> **TIP**
>
> To determine the owner of an object within a database, issue the following command from the Query Analyzer: sp_help [*object name*].
>
> To simplify object access, the DBO or system administrator should create all objects within the database. This approach automatically makes the DBO the database object owner.

Other Users

Other users must be granted object permissions (SELECT, UPDATE, INSERT, DELETE, REFERENCE, and EXECUTE) to operate within the database. The system administrator can also grant statement permissions to other users so that they can create and drop objects within the database.

Granting and Revoking Object Permissions

Perform the following steps to grant and revoke object permissions (see the "Object Permissions" section earlier in the chapter for more information).

1. From the SQL Server Enterprise Manager, click the plus (+) sign next to the server that contains the database objects.

2. Left-click the Databases folder.

3. Left-click the corresponding database.

4. Left-click the icon of the object to grant a permission: Tables, Views, or Stored Procedures. This populates the Result pane with the corresponding objects.

5. Right-click the object in the Result pane to grant a permission. From the right-mouse menu, select the All Tasks menu option. From the All Tasks menu option, select Manage Permissions. The Object Properties dialog box appears (see Figure 9.10).

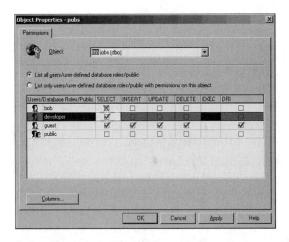

FIGURE 9.10   Granting and revoking object permissions.

6. From the Object Properties dialog box, select the appropriate check box to grant SELECT, INSERT, UPDATE, DELETE, EXEC, or DRI object permissions. A check appears if the permission is granted. Deselect the appropriate check box to

revoke object permissions. To deny a permission, click the appropriate check box until a red X appears.

7. Click the OK button to commit any changes that have been made.

TIP

Perform the following to grant permissions to multiple objects at once:

1. From the SQL Server Enterprise Manager, click the plus (+) sign next to the server that contains the database objects.

2. Left-click the Databases folder.

3. Left-click the corresponding database.

4. Left-click the Users or Roles icon. This populates the Result pane with the corresponding information.

5. Right-click a name in the Result pane. From the right-mouse menu, select the Properties option. The corresponding Database User Properties or Database Role Properties dialog box appears.

6. Click the Permissions button. A second Database User Properties or Database Role Properties dialog box appears. From this dialog box, you can assign permissions to multiple objects.

The corresponding Transact-SQL commands to manage object permissions are as follows:

```
GRANT
    { ALL [ PRIVILEGES ] | permission [ ,...n ] }
    {
        [ ( column [ ,...n ] ) ] ON { table | view }
        | ON { table | view } [ ( column [ ,...n ] ) ]
        | ON { stored_procedure | extended_procedure }
        | ON { user_defined_function }
    }
TO security_account [ ,...n ]
[ WITH GRANT OPTION ]
[ AS { group | role } ]

REVOKE [ GRANT OPTION FOR ]
    { ALL [ PRIVILEGES ] | permission [ ,...n ] }
    {
        [ ( column [ ,...n ] ) ] ON { table | view }
        | ON { table | view } [ ( column [ ,...n ] ) ]
        | ON { stored_procedure | extended_procedure }
```

```
        | ON { user_defined_function }
    }
{ TO | FROM }
    security_account [ ,...n ]
[ CASCADE ]
[ AS { group | role } ]
```

NOTE

To specify column level permissions, list the column name(s) after the table name. The following is an example of granting column-level permissions:

```
grant select on authors (au_lname, au_fname) to bob
```

When bob tries to query the authors table, he is limited to the au_lname and au_fname columns. If he tries to query other columns in the table, he will receive an error message.

CAUTION

Be careful when granting a permission to a user with the WITH GRANT OPTION. This option allows the user to grant the permission to another user. Therefore, a user can assign permissions without the DBA's knowledge.

For example, the following statement grants the SELECT permission for the authors table to mary:

```
GRANT SELECT ON authors to mary WITH GRANT OPTION
```

User mary can, in turn, grant the SELECT permission to user sam:

```
GRANT SELECT ON authors to sam
```

User sam is now granted the SELECT permission for the authors table.

Tips for Managing Object Permissions

Use the following tips to help manage object permissions:

- Object and statement permissions take effect immediately. A user does not have to log out and log back in to SQL Server for the change to take effect.

- Permissions are object specific; therefore, each object (table, view, or stored procedure) must be assigned the appropriate permission.

- By default, the sa and members of the sysadmin role automatically have all permissions for all objects; therefore, you do not need to assign permissions to the sa or sysadmin role.

- If you are logged in as sa or a member of the sysadmin role or the database owner, you can use SETUSER to impersonate another user within the system. Using SETUSER is an easy way to test changes without having to log out and log back in. Also, you do not have to know the password of the user you are trying to impersonate. Look at the following syntax:

```
SETUSER ['username' [WITH NORESET]]
```

This command works with SQL Server Authentication and Windows Authentication. The following are examples:

```
--SQL Server Authentication
setuser 'osledge'
--Windows Authentication
setuser 'xlconnect_osled\osledge'
```

If the WITH NORESET parameter *is not* specified, you can issue the SETUSER statement without any parameters to revert to the profile of the logged-in user. If the WITH NORESET parameter *is* specified, you can reopen the database (USE *database_name*) to revert to the profile of the logged-in user.

If you forget who you are impersonating, you can use the user_name() function to determine the active user profile, as in the following syntax:

```
SELECT user_name()
```

NOTE

Microsoft has stated that future versions of SQL Server might not support the SETUSER statement. I'm not sure why Microsoft is planning on dropping the statement, but I do not recommend using the statement in stored procedures or inside applications. It is still okay to use the SETUSER statement in the Query Analyzer to test permissions.

- Be sure to save an object's permissions before you drop and re-create a table, view, or stored procedure. All permissions to the object are removed when it is dropped, and SQL Server does not prompt you to save permissions to the object. An easy way to save the permissions of an object is to use the Generate SQL Scripts feature of SQL Server. To generate SQL scripts, right-click the object in the Result pane of the Enterprise Manager; from the right mouse menu, select the All Tasks menu option and then select the Generate SQL Scripts menu option. From the Generate SQL Scripts dialog box, select the Options tab. From the Options tab, select the Script Object-Level Permissions check box and generate the script. After you re-create the object, you can apply the script to restore permissions.

Granting and Revoking Statement Permissions

Perform the following steps to grant and revoke statement permissions (see the "Statement Permissions" section earlier in this chapter for more information).

1. From the SQL Server Enterprise Manager, click the plus (+) sign next to the server that contains the database.

2. Left-click the Databases folder.

3. Right-click the database in which you want to grant a statement permission. From the right-mouse menu, select the Properties menu option. The Properties dialog box appears.

4. From the Properties dialog box, select the Permissions tab (see Figure 9.11).

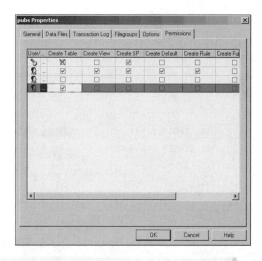

FIGURE 9.11   Granting and revoking statement permissions.

5. From the Permissions tab, select the appropriate check box to grant CREATE TABLE, CREATE VIEW, CREATE PROCEDURE, CREATE DEFAULT, CREATE RULE, BACKUP DATABASE, or BACKUP LOG statement permissions. A check will appear if the permission is granted. Deselect the appropriate check box to revoke the permission. To deny a permission, click the appropriate check box until a red X appears.

6. Click the OK button to commit any changes that you made.

NOTE

The CREATE DB permission can be granted only by the sa or by a member of the sysadmin role and only to users in the master database.

The corresponding Transact-SQL commands to manage statement permissions are as follows:

```
GRANT {ALL | statement[,...n]}
TO security_account[,...n]


REVOKE {ALL | statement[,...n]}
FROM security_account[,...n]


sp_helprotect [[@name =] 'object_statement']
[,[@username =] 'security_account']
➡ [,[@grantorname =] 'grantor'] [,[@permissionarea =] 'type']
```

WINDOWS 2000 AND KERBEROS

If you are running Windows 2000, you can take advantage of Kerberos security support. Kerberos offers stronger security and better performance than the *NT LAN Manager (NTLM)* implementation found in Windows NT 4.0.

Additionally, SQL Server 2000 takes advantage of the account delegation capabilities found in Kerberos. This enables a client's security credentials to be passed to a remote server running a distributed query. Also, it is important to note that Kerberos is not enabled by default and the account delegation capabilities have to be turned on.

Beyond Security Basics: Suggested Strategies

In addition to object and statement permissions, you can combine various components within SQL Server to facilitate administration and provide improved security. Following is a list of suggested security strategies:

- Role-based security management
- Views for data security
- Stored procedures for data security
- Triggers for audit trails

Role-Based Security Management

In the corporate environment, users often work in groups. People in these groups require similar permissions to the database. Whenever multiple users require similar permissions, you should use role-based security. With role-based security, you reduce the number of GRANT, REVOKE, and DENY statements that must be maintained.

Before diving headfirst into role-based security management, you should keep in mind the following points:

- When everyone in a database needs the same permission to the same object, use the public role. When you grant or revoke a permission to the public role, everyone feels the effect. The public role provides an easy way to streamline security administration.

- Try to avoid deep nesting of roles. Nesting of roles is a nice feature in that it allows a role to be a member of another role. However, when using deep nesting this feature might result in a performance decrease.

Views for Data Security

Views help control data security for the following reasons:

- A view can limit the amount of data a user can see and modify. To the user, a view looks and acts like a real table, even though she might be working with a subset of the data. Behind the scenes, a view is a virtual table that defines the presentation and manipulation of the actual table(s).

- A user only needs permissions to the view, not to the table(s) that make up the view.

Using Views for Column-Level Security

Often you use a view when a user needs access to a table but, for security reasons, you want to restrict access to certain columns (such as salary data) within the table. By using a view, you can easily restrict access to sensitive data.

Syntax:

```
CREATE VIEW view_name [(column [,...n])] [WITH ENCRYPTION]
AS select_statement [WITH CHECK OPTION]
```

For example, to prohibit access to the employee_ssn, salary, last_updated_by, and last_update_datetime columns in the employee table, use the following syntax:

```
CREATE VIEW  employee_view AS
SELECT name, address, city, state, zip
FROM employee
```

The following listing shows the schema for the employee table:

```
employee_ssn char (9)
name char (35)
address char (35)
```

```
city char (35)
state char (35)
zip char (35)
salary money
last_updated_by char (50)
last_update_datetime datetime
```

When the user issues `SELECT * FROM employee_view`, she gets back only the following columns:

```
name
address
city
state
zip
```

To users, the view looks like a real table except that they never see the `employee_ssn`, `salary`, `last_updated_by`, and `last_update_datetime` columns. Users can't modify what they can't see.

Using Views for Row-Level and Column-Level Security

A simple way to implement row-level security is to add a `WHERE` clause to the `CREATE VIEW` statement. For example, use the following syntax to create a view that limits column and row access:

```
CREATE VIEW employee_view_by_state AS
SELECT name, address, city, state, zip
FROM employee
WHERE state = 'VA' OR state = 'MA'
```

When users issue this statement, they see only the employees with a state code of VA or MA:

```
SELECT * FROM employee_view_by_state
```

> **TIP**
>
> To further ensure data security and to prevent typing errors, you can add the `WITH CHECK OPTION` to the `CREATE VIEW` statement.
>
> The `WITH CHECK OPTION` prevents users from inserting rows or updating columns that do not conform to the `WHERE` clause, as in the following example:
>
> ```
> CREATE VIEW  employee_view_by_state AS
> SELECT name, address, city, state, zip
> FROM employee
> ```

```
WHERE state = 'VA' OR state = 'MA'
WITH CHECK OPTION
```

With this view, users can only add rows with a VA or MA state code; they can only update a state code to MA or VA. If users try to change the state code to something other than VA or MA, they receive the following message:

```
Msg 550, Level 16, State 2
The attempted insert or update failed because the target view
➥ either specifies WITH CHECK OPTION or
➥ spans a view which specifies WITH CHECK OPTION
➥ and one or more rows resulting from the operation did
➥ not qualify under the CHECK OPTION constraint.
Command has been aborted.
```

How Views and Permissions Work Together

When you grant object permissions to a view, you do not have to grant permissions to the underlying tables in the view. Therefore, users can SELECT employee data from the employee view, even though they do not have SELECT permission for the employee table. This feature can simplify administration when the view consists of multiple tables.

TIP

You might be wondering, "Why not use column-level permissions to prevent access to the employee_ssn, salary, last_updated_by, and last_update_datetime columns?" Good question! Both views and column-level permissions can prevent users from accessing restricted columns.

The reason for using a view rather than column-level security is that the view allows a user to issue the SELECT * statement without receiving error messages while still providing column-level security. Consider the following examples:

Example A

John's SELECT permission has been revoked from the employee_ssn column in the employee table. When John issues SELECT * FROM employee, he receives the following error message:

```
Msg 230, Level 14, State 1
SELECT permission denied on column employee_ssn
➥ of object employee, database xxx, owner dbo
```

To avoid the error message, John must explicitly name each column in the SELECT statement.

Example B

A view has been developed for John to use. The view does not include the employee_ssn column. John can issue a SELECT * statement against the view, and he will see only the columns specified in the view. He does not receive any error messages.

Stored Procedures for Data Security

The advantage of using stored procedures to access and modify data is that users need only EXECUTE permission to run a stored procedure; they do not need access to the tables and views that make up the stored procedure. This approach alleviates the headache of assigning permissions to all underlying tables and views referenced within a stored procedure. The following syntax is an example of a stored procedure that returns all rows in the employee table:

```
CREATE PROCEDURE usp_employee AS
SELECT * FROM employee
```

To run the procedure, the user needs only EXECUTE permission for usp_employee. The user does *not* need the SELECT permission for the employee table.

GOING TO EXTREMES (BUT IT MIGHT BE WORTH IT!)

You can really clamp down on end-user data modifications by implementing stored procedures to handle *all* data modifications. To implement this strategy, you must design your applications to use only stored procedures and not embedded SQL to handle data modifications. Next, you must revoke all UPDATE, DELETE, and INSERT (and maybe even SELECT) privileges to *all* tables and views in the database. End users are now denied access whenever they try to modify data. This approach requires extensive use of stored procedures, careful planning, and tight coordination between the application developers and the DBA.

Triggers for Audit Trails

Triggers are made up of Transact-SQL statements that automatically execute when a table is modified through INSERT, UPDATE, or DELETE statements. Because a trigger is automatically executed, it can be a useful facility for auditing data changes. Additionally, you do not have to grant a user the privilege to execute a trigger.

An often-used type of trigger is one that tracks who made the last change to a table and when the change occurred. To track this information, use the following syntax:

```
CREATE TRIGGER iutrg_employee ON dbo.employee
FOR INSERT,UPDATE
AS
UPDATE employee
SET employee.last_updated_by = USER_NAME(),
employee.last_update_datetime = GETDATE()
FROM inserted,employee
WHERE inserted.employee_ssn = employee.employee_ssn
```

Whenever an INSERT or UPDATE statement is run against the employee table in this example, the column last_updated_by is set to the name of the user who made the change and the column `last_update_datetime` is set to the time the change was made.

Managing SQL Server Users and Security FAQ

This section contains some of the common questions DBAs ask about SQL Server users and security.

Q When should Windows Authentication be used?

A Windows Authentication should be used when you do not want users going through a separate login process with SQL Server. Windows Authentication does not require users to maintain separate passwords for SQL Server. Additionally, Windows Authentication can map domain groups to SQL Server and force minimum password lengths and aging.

Q When should SQL Server Authentication be used?

A SQL Server Authentication should be used when users are connecting from clients that do not provide Windows Authentication (such as Web clients or UNIX clients). SQL Server Authentication is also simpler to implement and troubleshoot than Windows Authentication. SQL Server Authentication is also appropriate for applications that automatically log the user in to the system or that always use the same login.

Q When a Windows login or group is removed from the Windows Domain, does the corresponding login in SQL Server also get removed?

A No! When a Windows login or group is removed from Windows 2000, the corresponding login is not deleted from SQL Server. This creates orphaned logins. See the sidebar titled "Login Gotchas" in this chapter for more information on orphaned logins.

Q Does Windows Authentication require a trusted protocol (such as named pipes or multiprotocol) as in previous versions of SQL Server?

A No. SQL Server's protocols—named pipes, multiprotocol, and TCP/IP—automatically support trusted connections. Therefore, you usually do not have to change any client settings (as in previous versions) to implement Windows Authentication.

Q How can I generate a security audit trail with SQL Server?

A You can use SQL Server Profiler to generate a detailed log of all activity that is taking place on the server. Keep in mind that the SQL Server Profiler can generate a lot of information, and it must be running to generate an audit trail. Therefore, I recommend using the SQL Server Profiler on an as-needed basis, rather than on a full-time basis, to generate audit trails.

Triggers can be implemented to generate audit trails on a table-by-table basis. The advantage of using a trigger is that you can record the before and after image of the data and track who made the modification and/or when it was made. The disadvantage of using a trigger is that you must hand-code this functionality.

Q Are statement permissions (found in SQL Server 6.x) considered a thing of the past?

A No, statement permissions are still available. However, server roles and database roles can provide similar functionality and might be easier to implement.

Q Are Windows 2000 administrators automatically administrators of SQL Server?

A Yes. Windows 2000 administrators are automatically SQL Server administrators. Additionally, the following Windows groups are SQL Server administrators: Administrators, Domain Administrators.

Q I forgot the sa password. Is there any way to retrieve it?

A You cannot retrieve a lost password. However, you can reset the sa password by logging in to SQL Server with the Windows administrator account. (Windows 2000 administrators are automatically SQL Server administrators.)

RESETTING THE SA PASSWORD

Perform the following to reset the sa password:

1. Log in to Windows 2000 with an account that contains Windows 2000 administrative privileges.

2. Use the SQL Server Query Analyzer to connect to SQL Server. When connecting to SQL Server, select Windows Authentication at the login prompt.

3. Execute the following command to reset the sa password:

```
sp_password null, 'newpassword', 'sa'
```

Q If I add a login to SQL Server and do not permit the login access to a database (let's say pubs), the new login can query information in the database from the Query Analyzer. Why?

A The answer resides in the guest account (see the section "guest User" in this chapter for more information). If the guest account exists in the database and the login is not mapped to the database, SQL Server automatically uses the guest account. Therefore the logged in user inherits the permissions assigned to the guest user. You can delete the guest account from all databases except master. Keep in mind that when you create a new database, the guest account is automatically added to the new database. (This is true even after the guest account has been deleted from the model database.)

Summary

The following are the key points on managing SQL Server logins and security:

- SQL Server supports two authentication models: Windows Authentication and SQL Server Authentication. Windows Authentication is directly integrated with Windows 2000.

- The guest user might exist in a database. SQL Server uses the guest login when a login is not mapped to a database. The guest user is a member of the public database role.

- SQL Server supports several types of roles: server roles, database roles, and application roles.

- Server roles are serverwide and cannot be customized.

- SQL Server provides two types of database roles: predefined roles and user-defined roles.

- Predefined database roles are database specific and cannot be customized.

- Every database user is automatically a member of the public database role.

- SQL Server provides two types of user-defined roles: standard role and application role.

- User-defined database roles are database specific and can be customized.

- Application roles are database specific, customizable, and can be password protected. Application roles must be activated and do not contain users.

- GRANT, REVOKE, and DENY are Transact-SQL commands used to manage object and statement permissions.

- Views, triggers, and stored procedures can be used as additional security measures.

PART IV

Database Backup and Recovery

IN THIS PART

10 Backup and Recovery

10

Backup and Recovery

by Mark Spenik and Orryn Sledge

Backups are copies of SQL Server databases or transaction logs used to restore a database if the database becomes corrupt or is lost in a catastrophic event. The task of backing up and protecting the data is probably the number one job responsibility of the DBA. In many organizations, the sole responsibilities of the DBA are backup and database maintenance.

Restore is the process of recovering a damaged, corrupted, or missing database. Being able to restore a database when several disk drives crash or a table or database becomes corrupted is when good DBAs earn their keep. Remember that your ability to restore a database depends on proper planning and testing.

SQL Server 2000 has made many improvements and enhancements to the backup and restore processes. In this chapter, you learn about the different methods available for backing up SQL Server databases and transaction logs as well as how to use those methods to restore databases. Even more important, you learn how to create a backup and restore strategy.

BETTER SAFE THAN SORRY!

Okay, if you have read the previous editions of the *SQL Server DBA Survival Guide*, you're probably thinking, "Hey I've read this story before." And, of course, you are right! During the five years since the first edition of the book was published, I have run into many corrupted databases and rescued many organizations. But, I still think this story goes a long way toward enlightening you on how it does not take a disk drive crash or database corruption to require a complete database restore. By the way, I still talk to Don from time to time and yes, he still is "The Man" when it comes to SQL Server development.

IN THIS CHAPTER

- SQL Server 2000 Backups—Simplified with Recovery Models (But Few Changes Under the Covers)

- What Is a File/Filegroup Backup?

- Creating a Backup Device

- Performing Database, Transaction Log, Differential, and File/Filegroup Backups

- Understanding Log Truncation Options

- Backup Wizard

- Using Multiple Backup Devices (Striped Backups) and Media Sets

- Full Recovery Model and Bulk Logged Recovery Model—Using Database Complete Backups and Transaction Log Backups to Restore a Database

- Performing a Database Restore

- Restoring the master Database

- Interactive Example of Losing and Restoring a Database

- Creating a Backup Schedule

- Backup and Restore FAQ

I learned the value of having a good set of database backups the hard way. Several years ago, while working on a Sybase 4.2 UNIX system, I was hired as a contractor to help out an organization with several large Sybase databases. They had recently lost several key MIS employees and were shorthanded.

I was working with a gentleman I'll refer to as Don "The Man," one of the few really good jack-of-all-trades (UNIX system administrator, Sybase DBA, and Client/Server developer) individuals who I have met. I had been at the organization for only two days; Don and I were busy trying to get a clean set of backups for the database and the UNIX system. The nightly UNIX backup had failed for the previous two days, and the database backups were going slowly because several databases were flagged with errors during *DBCC (database consistency check).*

We were working with Sybase tech support to correct the database problems. Don was preparing one of the larger databases for a backup when I heard him exclaim, "Oh no! I can't believe I did that. I can't believe what I just did. We are doomed!"

It turned out that Don had entered a SQL statement incorrectly, which had started one large transaction that was deleting all the rows of a table with about four million rows! I said, "No problem. We'll just restore from a database backup." It was then that Don informed me that the only database backup was 30 days old and outdated! What could we do?

Because Don had blocked the delete within a single transaction, we killed the server before it could complete the operation and commit the transaction. The server took a while to come back up as several thousand transactions were rolled back. We then verified the table row count from some numbers taken earlier in the day to verify that no data had been lost (information was always added to the table, but never updated).

At this point, Don and I realized that we needed backups—***now***. We stayed late that night verifying previous backup tapes which we found could not be read because of media problems. We continued to work early into the morning and created a whole new set of UNIX system backups and database backups.

The moral of the story is "backups are serious business!" Too often, I have heard someone say, "The nightly backup did not run; not sure why, but I'll run it again tonight." Big mistake. Remember that you don't know the hour, day, or minute when the disk drive will give up, the building will be hit by a natural disaster, or someone like Don will issue a SQL command that will ruin the production database! If you don't have a good backup, you will find yourself trying to explain to your boss how you lost a day's worth of data because the nightly backup did not work and you did nothing about it that morning.

SQL Server 2000 Backups—Simplified with Recovery Models (But Few Changes Under the Covers)

For those of you who have used previous versions of SQL Server and are curious about how your current backup and restore plans will change with SQL Server 2000, you will be happy to hear that you might not have to change any of your current backup and restore plans! SQL Server 2000 database restore still consists of database backups associated with transaction log backups. But the new recovery models introduced in SQL Server 2000 makes it easier for non-DBAs to successfully restore databases and for DBAs to understand exactly how their databases are protected against data loss. SQL Server 2000 still provides functionality and capabilities introduced in Version 7.0, such as a differential database backups and file/filegroup backups. SQL Server 6.x DBAs will want to re-examine their current procedures and determine if the new functionality can be used to speed up their backup and restore time or reduce the potential loss of data. Before discussing the different types of backups available in SQL Server 2000, let's review the recovery models introduced in SQL Server 2000.

Recovery Models

In previous versions of SQL Server, one of the most difficult things for a DBA to understand was how to properly set up backup and recovery procedures that would meet their data loss and recovery requirements when recovering the database. I found that many DBAs had good backup and recovery procedures in place but did not fully understand their exposure (or lack of exposure) to lost data in the event of having to recover a database from a backup. It was not uncommon for me to talk to DBAs who thought they had lost data exposure of up to 30 minutes when actually they were set up to have up-to-the-point-of-failure recovery.

I also found situations where the DBAs thought they had up to the point of failure recovery and in reality, would have lost an entire day's worth of data. SQL Server 2000 addresses this problem by creating three different recovery models, which allow a DBA or non-DBA to easily determine their exposure to lost data based on the model selected as well as help them determine the type of backup to use. The recovery model is a property of a SQL Server 2000 database, which can be set via the database property dialog box (discussed in Chapter 8, "Managing Databases"). By selecting the recovery model, the database and transaction log take on different behaviors to accommodate the selected recovery model. The three recovery models are as follows:

- Simple Recovery
- Full Recovery
- Bulk-Logged Recovery

Simple Recovery

In the simple recovery model, a database can be restored to the point of the last backup. The simple recovery model supports high performance bulk loading of data such as SELECT INTO and BCP (Bulk Copy Program) because these operations are not logged. You cannot do a point in time recovery, and very minimum transaction log space is required because the database option `trunc. log on chkpt.` is set. As the name implies, the simple recovery model is the easiest of the recovery models from which to manage and recover a restore. Your exposure to lost data will be the time span between backups.

Full Recovery

In the full recovery model, a database can be restored up to the point of failure. Point in time recovery is supported as well as recovery to a named transaction. In full recovery mode, bulk import operations such as `SELECT INTO` or `BCP` are treated as logged operations and therefore can be fully or partially recovered.

Bulk-Logged Recovery

In the bulk-logged recovery model, a database can be restored up to the point of failure. Bulk import operations such as `SELECT INTO` and `BCP` are only minimally logged, which provides high performance for bulk loading operations but prevents point in time recovery.

Before deciding how you select the proper recovery model for your database, let's look at the different types of database backups available in SQL Server 2000, which are as follows:

- Full Database
- Differential
- Transaction Log
- File/Filegroups

What Is a Database Backup?

Think of a database backup as a full backup of a database. When you perform a database backup, SQL Server copies all user-defined objects, system tables, and data. SQL Server 7.0 and 2000 use a fuzzy backup algorithm that allows SQL Server to back up a database that, when restored, is in the state the database was in at the time the backup completed (that is, the `BACKUP` command completes). This differs from SQL Server versions 6.x and 4.21 that restored a database to the state of the database at the start of the backup. When a database `BACKUP DATABASE` command is issued, SQL Server writes data extents to the backup even if the pages are being modified during the backup. The transaction log is copied as part of the backup. When the database is restored, the data extents are copied and the transaction log is used to roll transactions forward or back. Therefore, when the backup completes, the database is in the same state that it was in when the backup completed.

TIP

You can back up a database or transaction log while the database is in use, with a few exceptions. You cannot back up a database while database files are being created or deleted or the database is being shrunk (manual or automatic). Depending on the device(s) and the server being used, you might notice a decrease in performance during a backup process, so consider performing backups during nonpeak hours.

What Is a Differential Backup?

A differential database backup is an incremental database backup. It is an incremental database backup because only data that has changed since the last database backup is copied, resulting in a smaller and faster backup compared to a full database backup. Similar to a full database backup, the differential database backup uses fuzzy backup algorithms so that the database is restored to the point when the BACKUP command completed. A differential backup does not provide up to the point of failure recovery but the ability to recover the database up to the time the differential database BACKUP command completed.

What Is a Transaction Log Backup?

In previous editions of this book, a transaction log backup was described as a SQL Server incremental backup. But SQL Server 2000 truly has an incremental database backup; the differential backup that copies any data changed since the last backup. You can still think of a transaction log backup as an incremental database backup that provides up to the point of failure recovery or point in time recovery. The transaction log backup contains all the completed transactions performed since the last database, differential, or transaction log backup. (For more information on transaction logs, see Chapter 8.) New to SQL Server 2000 is the ability of a transaction log to log bulk load statements such as BCP or BULK INSERT for recovery purposes which is discussed in more detail later in this chapter under "Recovery Models." A transaction log backup performs the following operations:

- Copies the inactive part of the transaction log to the backup device
- Truncates (clears and frees up space) the inactive part of the transaction log

The inactive part of the transaction log contains all the completed transactions up to, but on the same page as, the earliest outstanding transaction or the earliest transaction that has not been moved to the distribution database and is marked for replication.

TIP

Performing a full database backup does not clear out the inactive part of the transaction log. If you perform only database backups, eventually your transaction log fills up and you are unable to perform any transactions in the database (no INSERT, UPDATE, or DELETE actions) until you back up the transaction log. You have to perform transaction log backups to clear out the inactive part of the transaction log, even if you rely on full database backups.

What Is a File/Filegroup Backup?

If you have limited time in which to perform a database backup and you cannot perform the backup using a full database backup, differential backup, or transaction log backup, SQL Server 2000 offers the option of performing a File/Filegroup backup. Files or filegroups can be backed up individually or together. Restoring a complete database from a File/Filegroup backup is a little trickier than a regular SQL Server backup/restore. Tables or indexes that span multiple filegroups need to have the files and filegroups with spanning objects backed up together. Fortunately, if you attempt to back up an object with spanning file/filegroups, SQL Server tells you that the missing file/filegroups must also be backed up. To properly restore using file/filegroups requires the use of transaction log backups.

Although other forms of database backups and restores are simpler and easier to restore from, having the file/filegroup option definitely helps some IS shops with large databases and limited backup times. File/Filegroups recovery can be useful when only one drive goes down and you only need to recover the file/filegroups located on that drive. A file/filegroup recovery can be performed using file/filegroup backups or full database backups; and, in both cases, the transaction logs since the backup (if data has changed). Additionally, the file/filegroup option might be more comfortable for Windows 2000 administrators acting as DBAs to use. If you feel like you need to use this type of backup, here is an example of how file and filegroup backups are done.

Suppose that you have a very large database spread across three different filegroups. Because of time constraints, you decide that you cannot perform a complete or differential backup. Instead, you decide to back up one filegroup a day and perform a transaction log backup daily. One filegroup is backed up daily. (Each filegroup is backed up once every three days.) A transaction log backup is performed daily. To properly restore the database if you lose all the filegroups requires a backup of each filegroup as well as transaction log backups from the oldest filegroup backup to the most recent.

> **NOTE**
>
> File and Filegroups can be restored from a full database backup as well as a File/Filegroup backup. If SQL Server detects that no modifications were made while the file/filegroup was backed up, you do not need to use a transaction log backup.

Selecting the Right Recovery Model for Your Database

When selecting the right recovery models for a database, you have to weigh the different trade-offs associated with each model and the requirements for your database. So, how do you determine which database model is right for you? Let's start with the following questions:

1. Do you need up to the point of failure recovery capability (that is, you cannot afford to lose any data or transactions that have occurred between backups)?

   If you answered yes, go to question 2. If you answered no, you can use the Simple Recovery model. On the plus side, using the Simple Recovery model will provide you with the simplest SQL Server backup and recovery model available and high performance bulk loading operations. On the minus side, there is the possibility of losing data modifications. Your exposure to losing data modifications/additions will be the time span between backups. You will need to perform either full or differential backups at a frequency that meets your minimal data loss requirements. If you find that you must perform frequent backups and they hinder your system's performance, you might want to evaluate one of the other recovery models and use transaction log backups during peak usage.

2. Do you need point in time recovery?

   If you answered no to this question, go to question 3. If you answered yes, you need to use the Full Recovery Model. The Full Recovery Model provides you with the ability to recover up to the point of failure as well as perform point in time recovery.

> **NOTE**
>
> The full recovery and bulk-logged recovery models give you up to point of failure recovery if the log files are intact. If you lose the log file, you lose the ability to recover up to the point of recovery and you would only be able to recover up to the last transaction log backup. For this reason, you should place the logs on redundant hardware configurations such as RAID 1 (mirrored disk drives) to limit the potential to lose your log file.

3. Does the database require lots of bulk loading operations such as BCP or SELECT INTO? If so, do you want to maximize the performance of the bulk loading operations?

If you answered yes to both these questions, you should select the bulk-logged recovery model. On the plus side, you will be able to perform up to the point of failure recovery and you will have high performance bulk loading operations. On the minus side, you will not have point in time recovery.

If you answered no to both questions, you should pick the Full Recovery Model, which will give you full recovery capabilities, including up-to-the-point-of-failure recovery and point in time recovery. In the Full Recovery Model, bulk loading operations are slower than in the two other recovery models because all bulk load operations are logged in the Full Recovery Model.

Creating a Backup Device

Before backing up a database, you need to create a backup device to copy the database, transaction log, or file/filegroup. The backup devices can be tapes, disk files, or a network drive. When a disk backup device is allocated, no storage space is allocated until the database backup is performed. Tape drives must be connected to the machine running SQL Server. SQL Server cannot use a tape drive on a remote machine.

NOTE

Network drives use the *Universal Naming Convention (UNC)*, which is \\Servername\Sharename\Path\File, or a locally mapped network drive can be used. Make sure that the user account used by SQL Server has the proper permissions to access the backup file and directory.

To create a backup device using the Enterprise Manager, select the server that you want to add the backup device to and then perform the following steps:

1. Select the Management folder and then select the Backup icon. Right-click the icon. A shortcut menu appears.

2. Select New Backup Device from the shortcut menu to display the Backup Device Properties—New Device dialog box (see Figure 10.1).

   The following list describes the different parameters in the New Backup Device dialog box (see Figure 10.1):

   Name—The SQL Server logical name for the backup device. The rules and limitations for a backup device name are the same as those for database devices.

   Filename—This parameter applies only if the backup device being created is a hard disk file. The location is the path and filename of the hard disk. (Tip: The location for a backup device can be on a network drive.)

Tape Drive name—This parameter applies only if the backup device being created is a tape drive that is installed on the database server.

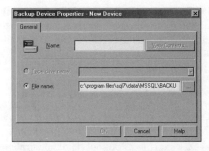

FIGURE 10.1   Backup Device Properties—New Device dialog box.

3. Enter the required information, described in the following options, and click the OK button to create the backup device.

Adding a backup device with SQL Server Manager is the same as executing the stored procedure sp_addumpdevice, which has the following parameters:

```
sp_addumpdevice Type, 'Logical_Name',
'Physical_Name'
[,controller_type | devstatus = {noskip | skip}]
```

The Type parameter specifies the type of device and can be 'disk', 'tape', or 'pipe'. Logical Name is the logical name of the dump device. Physical Name is the physical path and name of the dump device.

Use the controller_type parameter or the devstatus parameter although neither is required. The controller_type parameter can be set to 2 for a disk, 5 for tape, and 6 for a pipe. Set devstatus to skip or noskip. These parameters determine whether SQL Server tries to read ANSI labels before performing a backup.

When a backup device is added, SQL Server makes an entry in the sysdevices table.

Performing Database, Transaction Log, Differential, and File/File Group Backups

SQL Server 2000 eases the pain of the backup process by providing a common interface for backups. Whether you are performing a database backup, differential backup, File/Filegroup backup, or transaction log backup, the same steps are followed. Examine the steps required to perform a database backup or transaction log backup using the SQL Server Enterprise Manager.

TIP

Because of many different storage and engine changes made in SQL Server 7.0 and 2000, it is not necessary to run DBCC's commands before performing a database backup. However, if you are a DBA from the SQL Server 6.x school, you can still execute the commands for peace of mind. For SQL Server 2000, the only command required is the DBCC command CHECKDB. CHECKDB performs all the necessary database consistency checks. If you use CHECKDB, you no longer have to perform the other DBCC commands required in previous versions: NEWALLOC (or CHECKALLOC) and CHECKCATALOG.

Personally, I still think I'll use the DBCC command CHECKDB at least once a week before doing backups. A database backed up with errors has the same errors on a restored database and, in some severe cases, could prevent a successful restoration of the database. SQL Server 2000 has improved the CHECKDB by doing away with the shared table locks and instead using a schema lock that blocks DDL statements but not data modifications statements which occurred in previous versions of SQL Server. Even with the new locking scheme, I would recommend performing DBCC during off hours.

From the SQL Enterprise Manager, select Tools and then select Backup Database. The Database Backup dialog box appears (see Figure 10.2).

Figure 10.2   The Database Backup dialog box—General tab.

The Steps to Perform a Backup

To back up a database, transaction log, or file/filegroup, follow these steps:

1. From the Database Backup dialog box—General tab, select a database to back up by selecting the database name in the combo box.

2. Enter the name for the database backup in the Name text box and a description of the database backup in the Description text box, as shown in Figure 10.2. This information can be viewed later using the SQL Enterprise manager or Transact SQL.

3. Select the type of backup to perform by selecting a radio button in the backup section on the Database Backup dialog box—General tab (refer to Figure 10.2). The available options are as follows:

   Database—Complete

   Database—Differential

   Transaction Log

   File and Filegroup

4. Select the backup device or backup devices by clicking the Add button. The Select Backup Destination dialog box, shown in Figure 10.3, appears. Select a current backup device by selecting the backup device radio button and then selecting the backup device from the combo box. To back up to a file, select the filename radio button and provide a filepath and name. After you have selected the backup device, click the OK button.

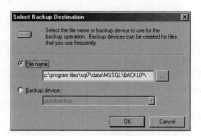

FIGURE 10.3   The Select Backup Destination dialog box.

5. To write over an existing backup on the selected device, select the Overwrite Existing Media option. To append to the current media, check the Append to Media option.

6. To schedule the backup for later use, check the Schedule box. Checking the Schedule box executes the backup on the default date, which is every week on Sundays at 12:00 a.m. To change the schedule time of the backup, click the button to the right of the default time, and the Edit Schedule dialog box, shown in Figure 10.4, appears.

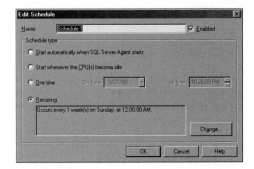

FIGURE 10.4   The Edit Schedule dialog box.

7. Enter a name for the scheduled job in the Name text box or accept the default name Schedule1.

TIP

Use a descriptive name for the scheduled backup. Using a descriptive name makes it easier to identify the backup later in the Windows 2000 event log or in the SQL Server Scheduled job history log.

8. Select when you want the scheduled backup to occur. For the backup to occur when the SQL Server Agents starts up, select Start Automatically when SQL Server Agent Starts. To execute during a CPU idle cycle, select Start Whenever the CPU(s) Become Idle. For the job to occur one time only, select the One Time radio button, and then set the date and time you want the backup to occur. To set up a recurring backup, select the Recurring radio button. To schedule the recurring backup, click the Change button; the Edit Recurring Job dialog box appears (see Figure 10.5).

Using the Edit Recurring Job Schedule dialog box, you can easily schedule the backup to occur daily, weekly, or monthly on a given day or time. (The Task Schedule dialog box is covered in detail in Chapter 12, "Automating Database Administration Tasks.")

NOTE

Be careful about scheduling backup jobs that append to a disk device every day or weekly. I recently had someone from a client company ask me what had happened to the 40GB of free disk space that was on his company's database server. I checked the server and it turned out that the client's DBA had scheduled 20+ database backup jobs and all 20 jobs appended backups to the backup device files. About five months worth of backups were appended to the devices, which were consuming over 36GB!

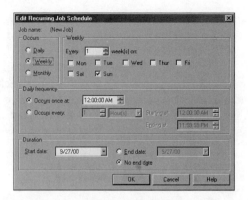

FIGURE 10.5   The Edit Recurring Job Schedule dialog box.

9. After you choose when you want the backup to occur, click OK to schedule the backup.

    The success or failure of the scheduled job can be viewed from the SQL Server Agent—Jobs using the SQL Enterprise (see Chapter 12).

10. To set additional options, select the Options tab in the Server Backup dialog box. The Options tab is shown in Figure 10.6.

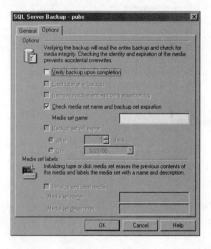

FIGURE 10.6   The Server Backup dialog box—Options tab.

11. To check integrity of the backup media (so that SQL Server reads the entire backup to verify that the media can be read) check the Verify Backup upon Completion check box. To Eject a tape upon completion of the backup, check

the Eject Tape after Backup check box. To remove the inactive transactions from the transaction log (that is, truncate the transaction log), which also will free up space in the transaction log, check the Remove Inactive Entries from the transaction log check box. To check the selected media set and backup set for expiration (that is, if device can be overwritten) check the Check Media Set Name and Backup Set Expiration check box. If you select the Backup Set Will Expire check box, set one of the following check boxes to determine at what time an existing backup device tape or file can be overwritten with new information:

- **Expires after**—Sets the number of days before the tape or file can be overwritten

- **Expires on**—Sets the date on which the tape or file can be overwritten

---

TIP

Use the Expires On or the Expires After options to protect your backups from being accidentally overwritten.

---

12. To start the database, transaction log, or file/filegroup backup, click the OK button in the Database Backup dialog box. The Backup Progress dialog box is displayed. The Backup Progress dialog box uses a progress indicator to display the progression of the backup. To cancel a backup in progress, click the Cancel button. When the backup is complete, the Backup Progress Completion dialog box is displayed. If you selected Verify Backup Upon Completion Option, a dialog box is displayed letting you know that the backup media has been verified.

The Transact SQL command used to back up the database is the BACKUP DATABASE command, which has the following format for a database:

```
BACKUP DATABASE {database_name | @database_name_var}
TO <backup_device> [, ...n]
[WITH
[BLOCKSIZE = {blocksize | @blocksize_variable}]
[[,] DESCRIPTION = {text | @text_variable}]
[[,] DIFFERENTIAL]
[[,] EXPIREDATE = {date | @date_var}
| RETAINDAYS = {days | @days_var}]
[[,] PASSWORD = {password | @password_var}]
[[,] FORMAT | NOFORMAT]
[[,] {INIT | NOINIT}]
```

```
[[,] MEDIADESCRIPTION = {text | @text_variable}]
[[,] MEDIANAME = {media_name | @media_name_variable}]
[],] MEDIANPASSWORD = {mediapassword | @mediapassword_var}]
[[,] [NAME = {backup_set_name | @backup_set_name_var}]
[[,] {NOSKIP | SKIP}]
[[,] {NOUNLOAD | UNLOAD}]
[[,] [RESTART]
[[,] STATS [= percentage]]
```

To back up a transaction log, use the following Transact SQL:

```
BACKUP LOG {database_name | @database_name_var}
[WITH
{ NO_LOG | TRUNCATE_ONLY }
TO <backup_device> [, …n]
[WITH
[BLOCKSIZE = {blocksize | @blocksize_variable}]
[[,] DESCRIPTION = {text | @text_variable}]
[[,] EXPIREDATE = {date | @date_var}
| RETAINDAYS = {days | @days_var}]
[[,] PASSWORD = {password | @password_var}]
[[,] FORMAT | NOFORMAT]
[[,] {INIT | NOINIT}]
[[,] MEDIADESCRIPTION = {text | @text_variable}]
[[,] MEDIANAME = {media_name | @media_name_variable}]
[],] MEDIANPASSWORD = {mediapassword | @mediapassword_var}]
[[,] [NAME = {backup_set_name | @backup_set_name_var}]
[[,] NO_TRUNCATE]
[[,] {NOSKIP | SKIP}]
[[,] {NOUNLOAD | UNLOAD}]
[[,] [RESTART]
[[,] STATS [= percentage]]]}
```

To back up a file/filegroup, use the Transact SQL:

```
BACKUP DATABASE {database_name | @database_name_var}
<file_or_filegroup> [, ...m]
TO <backup_device> [, ...n]
[WITH
[BLOCKSIZE = {blocksize | @blocksize_variable}]
[[,] DESCRIPTION = {text | @text_variable}]
[[,] EXPIREDATE = {date | @date_var}
| RETAINDAYS = {days | @days_var}]
```

```
[[,] PASSWORD = {password | @password_var}]
[[,] FORMAT | NOFORMAT]
[[,] {INIT | NOINIT}]
[[,] MEDIADESCRIPTION = {text | @text_variable}]
[[,] MEDIANAME = {media_name | @media_name_variable}]
[],] MEDIANPASSWORD = {mediapassword | @mediapassword_var}]
[[,] [NAME = {backup_set_name | @backup_set_name_var}]
[[,] {NOSKIP | SKIP}]
[[,] {NOUNLOAD | UNLOAD}]
[[,] [RESTART]
[[, ] STATS [= percentage]]
]
```

And file or filegroup has the following format:

```
<file_or_filegroup> :: =
{
FILE = {logical_file_name | @logical_file_name_var}
|
FILEGROUP = {logical_filegroup_name | @logical_filegroup_name_var}
}
```

For all three backup commands, backup_device has the following format:

```
{backup_device_name | @backup_device_namevar}
| {DISK | TAPE | PIPE} =
{'temp_dump_device' | @temp_dump_device_var}}
[VOLUME = {volid | @volid_var}]
```

The optional parameters INIT and NOINIT, available with tape devices, are available for other backup devices. Use the INIT option to overwrite the information stored on the dump device. Use NOINIT to append the information. Remember that the capability to overwrite a device also depends on the expiration and retention dates set for the backup device.

TEMPORARY BACKUP DEVICES

SQL Server 2000 enables you to create and use temporary backup devices when backing up databases or transaction logs. A *temporary backup device* is a backup device that is created at the time of the BACKUP command and has not been added to the system table sysdevices with the system-stored procedure sp_addumpdevice. To back up a database to a temporary backup device, you must specify the type of media the backup device is on (use the options DISK, TAPE, or PIPE) and then specify the complete path and filename. In the case of PIPE, you must specify the name of the named pipe used in the client application. You can also use variables to create a temporary backup device. Look at some examples using temporary devices.

Example: Dump the `master` database to a temporary disk backup device called `tdump_master.dat`, located in the directory `C:\MSSQL\BACKUP`.

Using the path and filename as follows:

```
BACKUP DATABASE master
to DISK='C:\MSSQL7\BACKUP\tdump_master.dat'
```

Using a variable as follows:

```
Declare @temp_dump varchar(255)
Select @temp_dump = 'C:\MSSQL7\BACKUP\tdump_master.dat'
BACKUP DATABASE master
to DISK = @temp_dump
```

Understanding Log Truncation Options

The different backup log truncation options are often overlooked by new DBAs. Quite frequently new DBAs do not know the options exist, or if they do know about the options, they don't know how or when to use them. The following sections explain each of the options in detail and when to use them.

TRUNCATE_ONLY

The `TRUNCATE_ONLY` option removes the inactive part of the transaction log (truncates) without backing up (copying) the log to a backup device. You do not have to specify a backup device when using `TRUNCATE_ONLY` because the log is not copied. For example, the syntax to back up the `master` database transaction log with the `TRUNCATE_ONLY` option is as follows:

```
Backup Log master
WITH TRUNCATE_ONLY
```

CAUTION

Always perform a database backup (complete or differential) before using the `TRUNCATE_ONLY` option. If you use the `TRUNCATE_ONLY` option without a database backup, you cannot restore the completed transactions in the inactive part of the transaction log at the time the `BACKUP LOG` with `TRUNCATE_ONLY` command was issued.

NO_LOG

When a BACKUP LOG command is issued with the NO_LOG option, SQL Server truncates the inactive part of the transaction log without logging the BACKUP LOG
command.

> **CAUTION**
>
> After using the NO_LOG option, always perform a full database backup; otherwise, the changes
> that had been in the transaction log when the log was truncated with the NO_LOG option
> aren't restorable.

Use the NO_LOG option only when the transaction log is completely full. When the
log fills up completely, you cannot truncate the transaction log by executing a
normal BACKUP LOG command. This occurs because SQL Server attempts to log the
BACKUP LOG command and no room is left in the transaction log. Similar to the
TRUNCATE_ONLY option, the NO_LOG option does not require a backup device because
the log is not copied to a device.

> **TIP**
>
> Microsoft SQL Server 2000 now enables you to grow the transaction log without having to
> specify a maximum size. This capability should go a long way in preventing the problems that
> a full transaction log caused previous users. Automatically growing the transaction log also
> takes away the burden of estimating the correct size of the transaction log. In previous
> versions, if you overestimated, you wasted disk space. If you underestimated, you were busy
> running commands to truncate a full log and constantly resizing the log.

NO_TRUNCATE

Use the NO_TRUNCATE option when the database you are trying to access is corrupted
and you are about to restore the database. To use NO_TRUNCATE, the following must be
true:

- The transaction log must reside on a device separate from the database.
- The master database must not be corrupted.

> **SQL 7.0 PRIMARY DATA FILE PROBLEM CORRECTED!**
>
> The requirements for NO_TRUNCATE are different in SQL Server 2000 than in SQL Server 7.0,
> which is good news because it's the way it should be (that is, the same as SQL Server 6.5). In
> SQL Server 2000, as long as the transaction log file is intact, you can use the NO_TRUNCATE
> option. SQL Server 7.0 requires that the log file and the primary data file (file with database
> system tables) must be intact to use NO_TRUNCATE.

The NO_TRUNCATE option writes all the transaction log entries from the time of the last transaction backup to the point of the database corruption. You can then restore the transaction log backup as the last backup in the restore process for up-to-the-millisecond data restore.

TIP

Become familiar with the NO_TRUNCATE option. I have met many DBAs who were unfamiliar with the option or were not sure when to use it.

Backup Wizard

SQL Server 2000 goes a long way in enabling a casual user to perform standard DBA tasks successfully using wizards. Of course, there is a wizard that enables you to perform a backup. To use the Backup Wizard, perform the following:

1. From the SQL Enterprise Manager main menu, select Tools and the Wizards option.

2. The Select Wizard dialog box appears. Click on the + sign next to Management to expand the list of management wizards. Select the Backup Wizard and click OK. The Create Database Backup Wizard dialog box, shown in Figure 10.7, appears.

FIGURE 10.7   The Create Database Backup Wizard dialog box.

3. Click the Next button; the Select Database to Backup dialog box, shown in Figure 10.8, appears. Select the database to back up in the combo box and click the Next button.

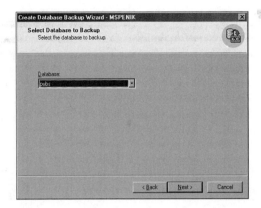

FIGURE 10.8   Select Database to Backup—Create Database Backup Wizard dialog box.

4. The Type Name and Description for Backup dialog box, shown in Figure 10.9, appears. Enter the name you want to use to refer to the backup. You can also enter a description to provide you with more information. Click the Next button.

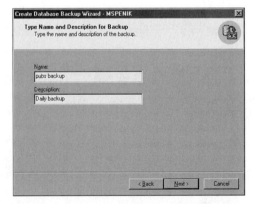

FIGURE 10.9   The Type Name and Description for Backup—Create Database Backup Wizard dialog box.

5. The Select Type of Backup dialog box, shown in Figure 10.10, appears. Select the type of backup you want to perform by clicking the appropriate radio button. Click the Next button to continue.

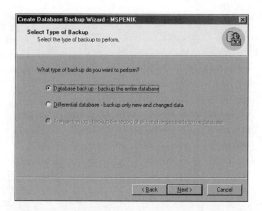

FIGURE 10.10   The Select Type of Backup—Create Database Backup Wizard dialog box.

6. The Select Backup Destination and Action dialog box, shown in Figure 10.11, appears. Select the location of the backup file to create or check the Backup device radio button to select the backup device where you want to back up the chosen database. Check one of the radio buttons to either append to the selected device or overwrite the selected device. To verify that the backup is valid and can be read, check the Read and Verify the Integrity of the Backup After Backup check box. Click the Next button to continue.

NOTE

If you choose to overwrite the existing media, upon clicking the Next button, you will be prompted with a dialog box that allows you to initialize the media set as well, which erases all previous content on the media set.

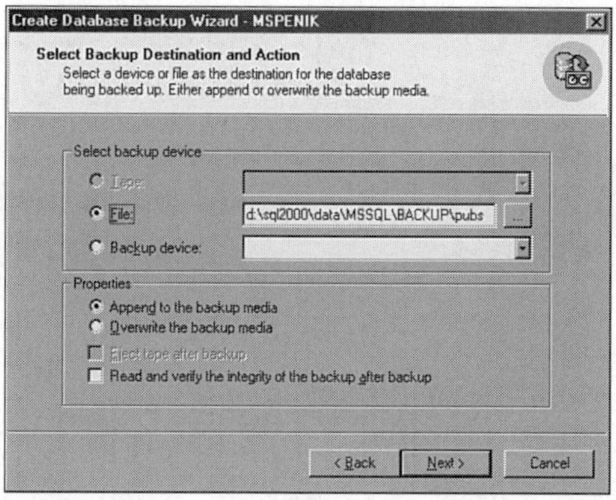

FIGURE 10.11   The Select Destination and Action—Create Database Backup Wizard dialog box.

7. The Backup Verification and Scheduling dialog box, shown in Figure 10.12, appears. This dialog box enables you to make sure that the device selected for the backup has expired and can be overwritten. Also you can assign a media set name to the backup as well as schedule the backup. After you have made your selections, click the Next button to continue.

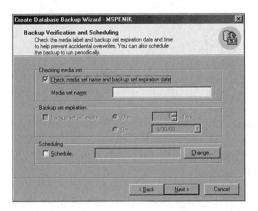

FIGURE 10.12   The Backup Verification and Scheduling—Create Database Backup Wizard dialog box.

8. The Display Selected Options dialog box, shown in Figure 10.13, appears. This dialog box displays the current selections you have made. If you want to make changes, click the Back button to walk backward through the wizard and make modifications. To perform the backup, click the Finish button. The Backup Progress dialog box appears as well as a Verification dialog box if the Verify Backup option was selected.

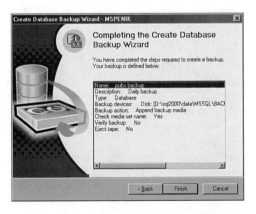

FIGURE 10.13   The Display Selected Options—Create Database Backup Wizard dialog box.

Using Multiple Backup Devices (Striped Backups) and Media Sets

SQL Server 6.x added the capability to perform backups to multiple backup devices called *parallel striped backups*. SQL Server 2000 continues and enhances the capability, but now refers to it as using multiple backup devices. Using multiple backup devices lessens the amount of time required to back up a database, filegroup, or transaction log by reading/writing to backup devices simultaneously. For example, if it takes you three hours to perform a database backup on a single tape drive, you can add two more tape drives and cut the backup time to about an hour. An example of a multiple device backup is shown in Figure 10.14.

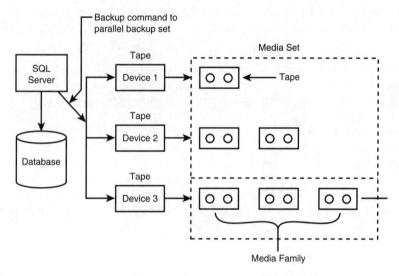

FIGURE 10.14   An example of using multiple devices in a media set.

The database, file/filegroup, or transaction log can be backed up to multiple devices of the same media (tape or disk) called the *media set*. The media participating in the media set has to be the same type (that is, disk or tape) but can be of different size, speed, and storage space. In the case of tapes, if one tape runs out, the backup continues on the remaining tapes until the tape can be removed and a new tape added. Throughout the backup process, synchronization is performed across all media and requires that all media be operational. If a tape should run out during the synchronization process, the backup halts on the other tapes until the tape is replaced and the synchronization can be performed. If a database or transaction log is backed up to multiple backup devices, it must also be restored from multiple devices.

SQL Server 2000 can use from 2 to 32 backup devices in a multiple device backup. You can perform a multiple device backup with SQL Server Enterprise Manager using the Backup dialog box or the Backup Wizard by selecting more than one backup device to copy the database. To perform a multiple device backup to multiple devices using the BACKUP DATABASE command, list the backup devices separated by commas. For example, to back up the master database to three backup disk devices called backup1, backup2, and backup3, the syntax is as follows:

```
Backup DATABASE master
to backup1, backup2, backup3
```

When restoring a database, using multiple devices requires that all the devices be used to restore the database in the case of disk files. If you used tapes, you can restore the database using fewer tape drives and loading the tapes as prompted.

Earlier, it was mentioned that the multiple devices used in a backup were called a media set. A media set is all the media used in a single backup. A media set could consist of a single disk file or 100 backup tapes. A media family is all the media used during a backup on a specific backup device. For example, suppose that you back up a database to two backup devices (that is, tape drives) Tape0 and Tape1. The backup requires a total of 20 tapes. Because Tape0 uses larger capacity tapes, six tapes are used on Tape0 and 14 tapes on Tape1. The six tapes used on Tape0 are a media family. The first tape used is referred to as the initial media, and the remaining tapes are called the continuation media. (Note: Only tape media can have continuation media.) The initial media is stamped with a sequence number of 1, the next tape 2 and so on. So in our example, the media set consists of two backup devices, which translates to two media families and a total of 20 tapes. The media families break down as six tapes in the Tape0 media family and 14 tapes in the Tape1 media family.

Full Recovery Model and Bulk Logged Recovery Model— Using Database Complete Backups and Transaction Log Backups to Restore a Database

The Full Recovery model and Bulk Logged Recovery model rely on using database backups in conjunction with transaction log backups to achieve up to the point of time recovery. It is important as a DBA to understand how to use database backups and transaction log backups to restore a database with up-to-the millisecond information. Let's walk through a database restore using the following example (see Figure 10.15).

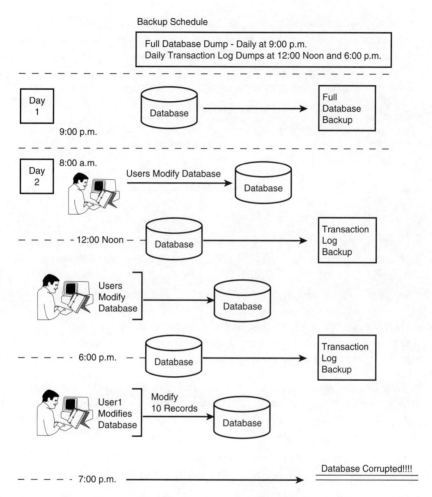

Backup Schedule

Full Database Dump - Daily at 9:00 p.m.
Daily Transaction Log Dumps at 12:00 Noon and 6:00 p.m.

FIGURE 10.15 An example of database and transaction log backups.

Using the example in Figure 10.15, the backup schedule for a database is as follows:

- Full database backup performed daily at 9:00 p.m.

- Transaction log backups performed daily at 12:00 (noon) and 6:00 p.m.

The backup schedule was set up this way because the majority of the people working on the database go to lunch at noon and go home for the evening before 6:00 p.m., so the backups occur during nonpeak hours. Of course, this not a requirement. SQL Server 2000 can perform database backups and transaction log backups while people are working with the database. SQL Server 2000 backups are more efficient than previous versions. Therefore, the performance hit of backups is not as great as it was say with 6.x. The two transaction log backups and the daily full database backup meet the user's restore needs as far as minimizing possible data loss. Follow through Figure 10.15 starting with Day 1.

Day 1: Full Database Backup Occurs

Day 1 is the starting point for this example. All you are concerned about is that at 9:00 p.m. on Day 1, SQL Server successfully performs a full database backup.

Day 2: Database Modified, Database Corrupted

Between 8:00 a.m. and 11:59 a.m., the database users log on to the database and make minor modifications and changes to the data stored in the database.

Between 12:00 noon and 12:59 p.m., many of the database users are at lunch, although some continue to work. The SQL Agent kicks off the scheduled transaction log backup. The transaction log of the database is backed up to a backup device, saving all the changes made to the data since the last full backup at 9:00 p.m. the previous evening.

Between 1:00 p.m. and 5:59 p.m., the database users continue to make minor modifications to the data in the database. By 6:00 p.m., the majority of the users have logged off the database and are on their way home.

Between 6:00 p.m. and 6:59 p.m., the SQL Agent starts the evening transaction log backup, saving all the committed transactions made to the database before the previous transaction log backup at noon. Shortly after the transaction log backup completes, User 1 modifies ten records on the database.

At 7:00 p.m., the database becomes corrupted and users are no longer able to access the database. The DBA is called in to remedy the problem. Now what?

Using the Backups to Restore the Database

Later in this chapter, the commands and detailed requirements to restore a corrupted database are discussed in detail. But the basic restore process of using a complete database backup and transaction logs is part of this example. So getting back to the example, the database has become corrupted, so where do you start the restore process?

Problem Resolution

The first thing to do is to evaluate the situation. What is wrong with the database? Well, you should do a couple of things to try and determine what is wrong with the database. A good starting point is to look at the error log and see what types of error messages appear when SQL Server tries to activate the database during startup or when users actually began to get database error messages. After you have viewed the error log and evaluated the situation, if any error numbers are displayed, you can search for the error number on SQL Server Books Online for possible resolution. You can also use a SQL Server 2000 function called `databaseproperty`. The `database-property` function returns `True` (1) or `False` (0) about a database and particular database property. For example, one such property is `IsShutDown`, which is set if SQL Server is unable to open a database's files during startup. To check if the `IsShutDown` status has been set on a database called Finance, you would enter the following in a query window:

```
Select databaseproperty('Finance','IsShutDown')
```

If a 1 is returned, the database is in Shutdown mode and the problem can be resolved by fixing the database files and log files and then restarting the computer. Some of the property names are as follows:

- `IsEmergencyMode`
- `IsShutDown`
- `IsSuspect`
- `IsInLoad`
- `IsInRecovery`

For a complete list of possible properties with the `databaseproperty` function, look up the `databaseproperty` function on SQL Server Books Online. You can also try and view the database in the Enterprise manager. If the database is corrupted or damaged, the database will appear gray in the Enterprise Manager with the text *Suspect* alongside the database icon. Now let's go back to the example.

Using the Backups to Restore the Database

After evaluating the situation, it is determined that the database is unable to load because the disk drive that the primary data file is located on has burned up. You have the drive swapped out and now it's time to begin the restore process.

Because the log file is intact, the first thing to do is to back up the transaction log with the `NO_TRUNCATE` option to restore the modifications made by user 1 after the last transaction log backup was performed. Now it's time to start to recover the database. Unlike 6.x versions of SQL Server, you do not need to drop the database before restoring it because you can overwrite the existing suspect database. However, you can still drop the database via the Enterprise Manager by selecting the database and right-clicking and selecting Delete or by using the DROP DATABASE command. The syntax for the DROP DATABASE command is as follows:

DROP DATABASE dbname[,dbname1,dbname2,…,N]

For example, to drop the database Finance, enter the following:

DROP DATABASE Finance

NOTE

DROP DATABASE can be used to remove a database that is marked suspect (or anything else except OFFLINE). The DROP DATABASE command in SQL Server 2000 also removes the files used to create the database (three cheers!!!!).

For this example, you do not need to drop the database, so it's time to start restoring the database from your backups. To re-create the database, you must load a full database backup. So you load the database backup performed on Day 1 at 9:00 p.m. and tell it to overwrite the existing database. The database now exists in the exact same state as the corrupted database on Day 1 at 9:00 p.m. How do you get back the work that was done on Day 2? You use the incremental database backups (that is, the transaction log backups).

Transaction log backups are sequenced and must be loaded in the correct order. You load the first transaction log backup that was made at 12:00 noon on Day 2. Loading a transaction log (also referred to as *applying the transaction log*) causes the transactions in the transaction log to re-execute. When the transaction log has completed, the database is now in the exact state the database was in as of 12:00 noon on Day 2.

To regain the 12:00 noon until 6:00 p.m. transactions, you load the second transaction log backup performed at 6:00 p.m. on Day 2. After the second transaction log successfully loads, the database is in the same state as the original database at 6:00 p.m. on Day 2. But what about the ten records modified by User 1 after the transaction log backup completed but before the database was corrupted? If the database and transaction log were on the same device or you forgot to run the BACKUP LOG with the NO_TRUNCATE command, those modified records are lost because you do not have a transaction log backup or a full database backup with the modifications in them. User 1 would have to go back and update the records manually. However, because you had the database and transaction log on separate devices and you executed the BACKUP LOG with the NO_TRUNCATE command, you load the transaction log backup produced by the NO_TRUNCATE backup command. The database is back in the same state (including the ten modified records) as the original database just before it became corrupted. You now know how transaction logs and database backups are used to restore a database.

Restore Example—Reality Check

In the previous example, the database backup and transaction log backups were loaded one at a time and in the exact order from oldest to newest. Obviously, this would be a lot of work in a production environment with a weekly full database backup and transaction logs backed up every half hour. Don't worry. The step-by-step process used in the previous example was done to help you understand the relationships between complete backups and transaction log backups in the database restore process. In the real world, if you are using the SQL Enterprise Manager, you would only have to perform the restore operation once. SQL Server would then automatically apply all the transaction logs associated with the complete database backup. This is demonstrated in the next section.

Using Differential Backups to Speed Up the Restore Time

The previous example of a database backup and restore scenario followed the pattern of full database backups with transaction log backups as the incremental backups. You can speed up your restore time by using full database backups, differential backups, and transaction log backups. To do so, you would plan your full backups on a regular basis, maybe weekly, every three days, and so on. You would then plan differential backups in between (for example, daily). Transaction log backups would then be performed frequently (based on your requirements) just as they are in the backup and restore scenario described earlier (the difference being that the transaction log backups would be associated with the differential backups performed). Instead of three days worth of transactions logs being applied during the restore process (if the log was backed up hourly, around 72 logs would need to be applied), you have at most a single days worth of transaction logs.

Performing a Database Restore

In the previous section, you learned how to use database backups and transaction logs to get up to the point of disaster restore. This section covers the necessary steps and commands to restore a SQL Server database using SQL Server backups.

> **NOTE**
>
> The database being restored cannot be in use while you are trying to restore it.

To restore a corrupted, suspect, damaged, missing, or moving database, perform the following:

1. From the SQL Enterprise Manager, select Tools and then select Restore Database. The Restore Database dialog box appears (see Figure 10.16).

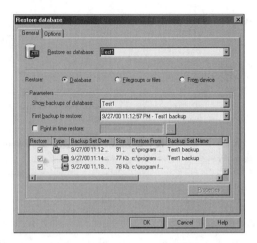

FIGURE 10.16   The Restore Database dialog box—General tab.

2. Use the Restore as Database combo box to select the database to restore to.

3. To select the type of database backup to perform, select the appropriate backup type radio button in the Restore label shown in Figure 10.16.

4. In the Parameters frame, shown in Figure 10.16, use the Show backups of database drop-down combo box to select a database that will display recent backups of the database. If backups have been performed on the selected database, the First Backup to Restore combo box is populated. Select the backup you want to restore from the First Backup to Restore combo box. The default is the Most Recent Backup. The grid shown in Figure 10.16 displays the type of backups (Complete, Differential, Transaction Logs) associated with the backup selected in the combo box. Each database backup type is reflected with a different icon, and differential database backups and transaction log backups have a line that connects them with their associated complete database backup. Check Point In Time Restore to select a particular point and time on the selected backup to halt the restore process. Point In Time Restore is useful for situations when a user might have executed a SQL command that wipes out lots of data and you need to restore to the time prior to him executing the command. Point In Time Restore is only available in the Full Recovery model.

5. To set additional restore options, click the Options tab, shown in Figure 10.17.

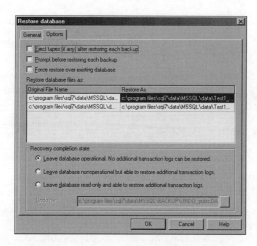

FIGURE 10.17   The Restore Database dialog box—Options tab.

6. The Options tab enables you to set the following options:

   Eject Tapes (if any) After Restoring Each Backup—Automatically ejects the tape from the tape drive when the selected backup completes.

   Prompt Before Restoring Each Backup—Select this option to have SQL Server prompt you after a backup is successfully loaded and prior to loading the next backup. For example, if you select to load a complete database backup, a differential database backup, and a transaction log backup, you receive a prompt after the full backup completes and after the differential backup completes. You can press Cancel at any of the prompts to halt the restore.

   Force Restore over Existing Database—Automatically writes over the existing database files when selected.

   Restore Database Files as—The grid shown in Figure 10.17 shows the backup file physical name in the Backup Physical Name column. You can change the path and location of the file during the restore process by editing the Restore As column shown in the grid.

   Recovery Completion State Frame—Contains several options that enable you to leave the database in certain states after the restore process completes. The default, Leave Database Operational, completes the entire restore process including applying any transactions in the transaction logs loaded and rolling back all incomplete transactions. With this option selected, the restore is complete, and the database is ready for use. The Leave Database Non-Operational, But Able To Restore Additional Transaction Logs option leaves the database in an unusable state and does not process transactions logs loaded. Use this option when you are restoring a database and are unable to load all the logs at once or with the database backup. In this scenario, when the last transaction log is loaded, check the Leave Databases Operational option. The Leave Database Read-Only and Able To Restore Additional Transaction Logs option is used for standby servers. It can also be used to enable you to check the status of a database. For example, suppose that a user deleted or changed some records but is not exactly sure of what time the change occured. You could query after each transaction log loads and find out when the problem occurred and then restore the database again and not apply the last log.

7. After you have selected the backup and set any options, click the OK button shown in Figure 10.17 to restore the database. A Completion dialog box is displayed when the database is successfully restored.

The Transact SQL command used to restore a database, the RESTORE command, has the following format for a database:

```
RESTORE DATABASE {database_name | @database_name_var}
[FROM <backup_device> [, ... n]]
[WITH
[RESTRICTED_USER]
[[,] FILE = file_number]
[[,] PASSWORD = {password | @password_var}]
[[,] MEDIANAME = {media_name | @media_name_variable}]
[[,MEDIAPASSWORD = {media_password | @media_password_var}]
[[,] MOVE 'logical_file_name' TO 'operating_system_file_name']
[,…p]
[[,] KEEP_REPLICATION ]
[[,] {NORECOVERY| RECOVERY | STANDBY = undo_file_name}]
[[,{NOREWIND | REWIND}]
[[,] {NOUNLOAD | UNLOAD}]
[[,] REPLACE]
[[,] RESTART]
[[,] STATS [= percentage]]]
```

To restore a transaction log, use the following Transact SQL:

```
RESTORE LOG {database_name | @database_name_var}
[FROM <backup_device> [, ...n]]
[WITH
```

```
[RESTRICTED_USER]
[[,] FILE = file_number]
[[,] PASSWORD = {password | @password_var}]
[[,] MOVE 'logical_file_name' TO 'operating_system_file_name']
[,...p]
[[,] MEDIANAME = {media_name | @media_name_variable}]
[[,MEDIAPASSWORD = {media_password | @media_password_var}]
[[,] KEEP_REPLICATION]
[[,] {NORECOVERY | RECOVERY | STANDBY = undo_file_name}]
[[,] {NOREWIND | REWIND }]
[[,] {NOUNLOAD | UNLOAD}]
[[,] RESTART]
[[,] STATS [= percentage]]
[[,] STOPAT = {date_time | @date_time_var} | [,]
STOPATMARK='mark_name' [After datetime]
          | [,]STOPBEFOREMARK = 'mark_name' [AFTER datetime]]]
```

To restore a file/filegroup, use the following Transact SQL:

```
RESTORE DATABASE {database_name | @database_name_var}
<file_or_filegroup> [, ...m]
[FROM <backup_device> [, ...n]]
[WITH
[RESTRICTED_USER]
[[,] FILE = file_number]
[[,] PASSWORD = {password | @password_var}]
[[,] MEDIANAME = {media_name | @media_name_variable}]
[[,MEDIAPASSWORD = {media_password | @media_password_var}]
[[,] MOVE 'logical_file_name' TO 'operating_system_file_name']
[,...p]
[[,] NORECOVERY]
[[,] {NOREWIND | REWIND}]
[[,] {NOUNLOAD | UNLOAD}]
[[,] REPLACE]
[[,] RESTART]
[[,] STATS [= percentage]]]
```

Restoring the master Database

You have probably guessed by now that the master database is definitely not just another database and is required to allow SQL Server to start, stop, and run as a service. The master database stores all the information about the users and databases on your system. Restoring the master database can be performed one of two ways. If you are able to start SQL Server and you find out that the `master` database is damaged, you can restore the database from a previous backup just as you would with a regular user database. If you have performed any operations that made modifications to the `master` database after the backup was performed, you might have to perform the operations again, for example, in the case of adding or deleting logins. If you have added a database since the backup was made, you can attach the database files or load from a backup.

If SQL Server does not start, you need to execute the Rebuild Master Utility to restore the `master` database.

NOTE

The procedure to restore the `master` database has steadily improved over the last few releases. The SQL Server 2000 version has greatly simplified the process.

To rebuild the `master` database, use the Rebuild Master database utility, `rebuildm.EXE` located in the BINN directory of the SQL Server 2000-root directory (see Figure 10.18).

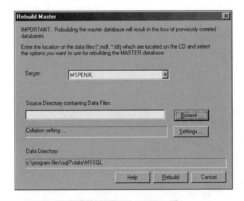

FIGURE 10.18   The Rebuild Master database utility.

To rebuild the `master` database, perform the following steps:

1. Before you can execute the Rebuild Master Utility, you must shut down SQL Server. Use the SQL Service Manager to shutdown SQL Server.

2. Execute the `rebuildm.EXE` located in the BINN directory of the SQL Server 2000 root directory.

3. Use the Browse button to select the source directory from which SQL Server was installed. The source directory is the DATA directory on the SQL Server CD-ROM or a network path for network installations.

4. Click the Settings button, shown in Figure 10.18, to modify the collation setting.

5. Click the Restore button to rebuild the master database.

After you have rebuilt the master database, you need to load your most recent backup of the master database. If all the other databases are still available and are not lost or damaged because of drive failure, you will be up and running. If you lost other databases, you need to restore them from backups. If you added databases since you made your current backup, you can perform a SQL Server 2000 function that reattaches the files to recreate the database.

Reattaching Database Files

SQL Server 2000 enables you to detach the database data and log files from a server and reattach them to the same server or another server. When database files are detached, the database is dropped from the SQL Server, but the files themselves remain intact enabling you to move them to another machine or reattach them on the same server later. This is an awesome feature that makes moving databases or rebuilding the master database less traumatic than it previously was and saves time in both processes. To detach a database, issue the following Transact SQL command:

```
sp_detach_db [@dbname =] 'dbname'
[, [@skipchecks =] 'skipchecks']
```

Where dbname is the database name and skipchecks, when set to True, performs and updates statistics on all the tables in the database before reattaching the files. For example,

```
sp_detach_db TestRestore, True
```

To reattach the database using Transact SQL, use the following command:

```
sp_attach_db [@dbname =] 'dbname',
[@filename1 = ] 'filename1'
[[, ...@filename16 = ] 'filename']
```

The following example reattaches the database TestRestore:

```
sp_attach_db TestRestore,'e:\MSSQL7\data\testrestore_data.mdf',
➥'e:\\MSSQL7\data\testrestore_log.ldf'
```

You can also attach a database via the Enterprise Manager by selecting the Databases folder, right-click, select All Tasks and then select Attach Database. The Attach Database dialog box, shown in Figure 10.19, is displayed.

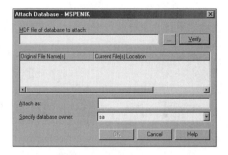

FIGURE 10.19　Attach Database dialog box.

To detach a database via the Enterprise Manager, select the database you want to detach, right-click, select All Tasks and then select Detach Database.

Interactive Example of Losing and Restoring a Database

Database backup and restores are the most important tasks performed by a DBA. As such, it is very important to be prepared for the day that you must perform your first real-world backup and restore procedure to restore critical user data. To help you along, walk through an actual backup and restore of a database. This exercise is similar to the restore process described in the previous section and simulates an actual backup and restore that you might perform some day!

CAUTION

The following exercise is one that I have been doing for several years in various DBA workshops and training sessions performed at Trilogy Consulting. The exercise is meant to be interactive, so it requires access to SQL Server. Parts of the exercise require shutting down SQL Server and deleting a file. *DO NOT PERFORM THIS EXERCISE ON A PRODUCTION SQL SERVER.* Your best bet is to perform this exercise on your workstation using your own personal copy of SQL Server. Shutting down a production server and deleting files can cost you your job as well as cause your company to lose valuable information! *DO NOT PERFORM THIS EXERCISE ON A SQL SERVER WITH USERS OR INFORMATION BEING USED BY YOU OR OTHERS.*

This exercise is designed to help you understand how to properly perform a SQL Server backup/restore and the relationship of database backups with transaction log backups during the restore process. For this exercise, you will perform the following:

1. Create a database.

2. Create a table.

3. Create a backup device.

4. Add rows to the table (perform transactions).

5. Back up the database.

6. Add more rows to the table.

7. Back up the transaction log.

8. Add more rows to the table.

9. Shut down SQL Server.

10. Delete the database data file.

11. Restart SQL Server.

12. Restore and test the database.

Start the Enterprise Manager, bring up a query window, and perform the following steps.

Step 1: Create a Database

Bring up a SQL Server Query Analyzer by selecting Tools and SQL Server Query Analyzer from the SQL Enterprise Manager. In the query window, enter the following text:

```
Create Database TestRestore
go
sp_dboption 'TestRestore','trunc. log on chkpt.',false
```

Press Ctrl+E to execute the script. You have now created a database called TestRestore. The files used by the database are located in the SQL Server default directory. The standard default directory is drive:\MSSQL\DATA.

Step 2: Create a Table

Create a table called *test* that will be used to check the success of your restore process. Change the current database in the SQL Server Query Analyzer window by selecting TestRestore in the database combo box. Enter the following syntax in the Query Analyzer window and press Ctrl+E to execute the script:

```
create table test(id int NOT NULL,
   date_entered datetime NOT NULL)
```

Step 3: Create a Backup Device

Add a backup device to back up the TestRestore database. The backup device will be named TestRestore_BackUp.

> **NOTE**
>
> Make sure that the selected database in the combo box in the Query Analyzer window is
> `TestRestore` through Step 8.

Enter the following syntax in the Query Analyzer window and press Ctrl+E to
execute the script. Note: For the third parameter, use the root directory of your SQL
Server installation with a filename of `TstRBack.dat`:

```
sp_addumpdevice 'disk','TestRestore_Backup','C:\MSSQL\BACKUP\TstRBack.dat'
```

Step 4: Add Rows to the Table

In this step, you add several rows into the Test table. Each row will be sequentially
numbered and date and time stamped so that you can validate the information after
the restore process is completed. Enter the following syntax in the Query Analyzer
window and press Ctrl+E to execute the script:

```
Insert Test
Values(1,getdate())
Insert Test
Values(2,getdate())
Insert Test
Values(3,getdate())
Insert Test
Values(4,getdate())
```

To verify that the information is in the table, execute the following SQL statement in
the Query Analyzer window:

```
Select * from test
```

The query should return information similar to Listing 10.1. However, the dates
returned will be different. (They will reflect the date and time the `Insert` statements
were executed.)

LISTING 10.1   Test Table Query Results

```
id          date_entered
----------- --------------------------
1           2002-07-13 21:10:41.487
2           2002-07-13 21:10:41.520
3           2002-07-13 21:10:41.520
4           2002-07-13 21:10:41.523
```

Step 5: Back Up the TestRestore Database

Back up the database TestRestore to the backup device TestRestore_Backup. To back up the database, use the Enterprise Manager, the Backup Database Wizard described earlier in the chapter, or execute the following command with the Query Analyzer:

```
backup database TestRestore to TestRestore_Backup
```

Step 6: Add More Rows to the Table

Insert two more rows in the table test by executing the following script in the Query Analyzer window:

```
Insert Test
Values(5,getdate())
Insert Test
Values(6,getdate())
```

Step 7: Back Up the Transaction Log

Back up the TestRestore transaction log to the backup device TestRestore_Backup. To back up the transaction log, use the Enterprise Manager, the Backup Database Wizard described earlier in the chapter, or execute the following command with the Query Analyzer:

```
BACKUP LOG TestRestore to TestRestore_Backup
```

Step 8: Add More Rows to the Table

Insert two more rows in the table test by executing the following script in the Query Analyzer window:

```
Insert Test
Values(7,getdate())
Insert Test
Values(8,getdate())
```

Checkpoint: Backup Part of Exercise Completed

You have now completed the first part of the exercise! So, recap what you have accomplished so far and what will be accomplished in the remaining steps. First, you created a new database called TestRestore. Next, you created a file group to store user tables and added a single table called Test. You inserted four rows of data into the table, IDs 1–4 and backed them up using a SQL Server full database backup. You then inserted two rows with IDs 5 and 6 and performed a transaction log backup to back them up. Finally, two additional rows were inserted, IDs 7 and 8, and not backed up. So we have created a scenario that is found frequently in the real world. The DBA has a database backup and one or more transaction log backups, and users have added information since the last transaction log backup was performed. Now take this one step further by causing a media failure and then using the backups to restore the database.

Step 9: Shut Down SQL Server

Using the SQL Service Manager, click the red light to stop SQL Server. Make sure that others are not using the server!

Step 10: Delete the Database Data File

CAUTION

This step requires you to delete a database file. Make sure that you delete the proper file. *DO NOT PERFORM THIS EXERCISE ON A PRODUCTION SQL SERVER.* Your best bet is to perform this exercise on your workstation using your own personal copy of SQL Server. Deleting the wrong file can cost you your job as well as cause your company to lose valuable information! *DO NOT PERFORM THIS EXERCISE ON A SQL SERVER WITH USERS OR INFORMATION BEING USED BY YOU OR OTHERS.*

Delete the primary data file for the TestRestore database, TestRestore.mdf. The data file is located off of the SQL Server root directory in the subdirectory data.

Step 11: Restart SQL Server

Using the SQL Service Manager, click the green light to start SQL Server. Log on to SQL Server using the Enterprise Manager.

Step 12: Restore the Database TestRestore

Of course, you know that the database TestRestore has a problem; after all, you deleted the data file! However, look at some of the different SQL Server facilities available to you to detect a problem with a database. If the database status is unknown or suspect, it appears gray in the database folder of the SQL Server Enterprise Manager. View the current error log. Notice that several error messages exist when SQL Server tries to open the TestRestore database. Try the following databaseproperty function in a query window:

```
Select databaseproperty('TestRestore','IsShutDown')
```

The function returns a 1, indicating that the database is in a Shutdown mode, which means that the database had problems during startup.

Now begin the restore process.

12-a Restore Transactions in the Transaction Log

When you are having problems with a database, the transaction log is intact, you don't have Truncate Log on Checkpoint set, and you have not performed any unlogged operations, the first thing you should do is back up the completed transactions in the transaction log. In this example, backing up the transactions in the log since the last backup gives us rows seven and eight that were added after the last transaction log backup. To back up completed transactions in the log, enter the following (which will complete, but displays an error message):

```
BACKUP LOG TestRestore
to TestRestore_Backup
With NO_TRUNCATE
```

12-b1 Restore the Database and Transaction Logs

Use the Enterprise Manager to restore the database. (For detailed steps, see "Performing a Database Restore" section earlier in this chapter.) Select the TestRestore database in the Database combo box on the General tab of the Restore Database dialog box. Select the Restore Database radio button on the General tab of the Restore Database dialog box. Go to the Options tab of the Restore Database dialog box and check the Force restore over existing database option. This will overwrite the existing transaction log file. Click the OK button to restore the database and transaction logs. From a query window, execute the following SQL statement in the TestRestore database:

```
Select * from Test
```

Rows one through eight appear. Congratulations! You have successfully restored a database!

12-b2 Restore Database and Transaction Logs: Option 2

This option is more academic than real world. In this option, you restore the database without the transactions logs by unchecking the Transaction Logs Restore check boxes in the list of recent backups on the General tab of the Restore Database dialog box. Execute the following query:

```
Select * from Test
```

This validates that rows one through four appear. You then restore each transaction log (the database is automatically selected each time), one at a time. Note that in order to do this you must specify the Leave Database Read-Only and Able To Restore Additional Transactions Logs options. Also, when using the SQL Enterprise Manager, you are forced to include the full backup when loading the transaction logs (as well as previous logs). After doing the first log, execute the `Select * from Test` query and rows one through six appear. When you select the final transaction log (a full restore) rows one through eight appear. Selecting one at a time and then viewing the information after each restore helps many beginners understand the relationship between database backups and transaction log backups.

Creating a Backup Schedule

You know *how* to schedule backups of transaction logs and databases, but *when* should you back them up? To answer that question, you are going to create two separate categories: Category 1 consists of actions performed in a database that warrant an immediate database backup. Category 2 consists of scheduling backups that meet your restore needs.

Category 1: Actions that Warrant Dumping a Database

In general, you are aware that you should perform database backups on a timely schedule. Backups should also be performed after certain actions occur in a database to ensure full and easy restores.

User Databases

After you perform certain actions on a user database, you should back up the database as soon as possible to guarantee the restore of your changes in a timely fashion. For example, perform a database backup in the following cases:

- After the database is created

- After performing large or timely data imports

- After you make substantial database modifications (new triggers, stored procedures, tables, and so on)

- After you create a large index (doing so can speed up the restore process because SQL Server does not have to rebuild the index during restore)

The master Database

Of course, the master database has its own set of rules for when it should be backed up. Remember that keeping a healthy master database is a high priority. Therefore, backing up the master database regularly is a must. The master database should be backed up when changes are made to system tables. A list of the commands that modify the system tables can be found in the SQL Server documentation. Here is a short list of some of those commands:

- `ALTER DATABASE`
- `CREATE DATABASE`
- `sp_addlogin`
- `sp_droplogin`

Because many of you use the SQL Enterprise Manager to perform your database administrative tasks, you might be unaware of the SQL Server commands and system-stored procedures being executed. In SQL Enterprise Manager lingo, back up the `master` database after you have done the following:

- Added or removed databases
- Altered the size of a database
- Added system login IDs
- Modified system configuration parameters

`msdb`

Because the `msdb` database stores all the information about jobs and schedules, you should back up the database after creating jobs or schedules to prevent having to re-create them in the event of a lost database.

Category 2: Scheduled Database Backups

Unfortunately, there is no exact formula to tell you when you should backup your databases. Why? Because each database has its own backup requirements. For example, in the backup and restore example you stepped through earlier in this chapter, transaction log backups were performed twice a day. It was acceptable to lose a half a day's work if the example SQL Server suddenly lost the database's transaction log. Many organizations cannot afford to lose any data and require up to the point of disaster restore.

As another example, maybe you are in a development environment in which a bimonthly database backup is all that is required.

Your backup strategy should enable you to restore any of your databases within an acceptable amount of time and for an acceptable data loss limit for each database. Before any further discussion of backup strategies, remember that it is just as important to perform routine database and table maintenance as it is to properly back up your databases. (Database maintenance plans are discussed in more detail in Chapter 11, "Developing a SQL Server Maintenance Plan.")

In general, you can find more information on setting up appropriate backup schedules in the documentation that ships with SQL Server or the white papers found on Microsoft's Web site. Review a few questions and suggestions that you can use to help you set up a proper backup plan.

NOTE

In my opinion, a backup plan and a restore plan are the same. To test and verify your backup plan, you must use the database backups to restore your SQL Server databases; thus, the two go hand in hand.

System Databases

Having up-to-date, valid database backups can save you a lot of time, especially if you need to restore a system database (such as the `master` database). You need to back up the model database only if and when you make changes to it. Take special care with the `master` database; consider mirroring the `master` device for added protection. It is recommended that you back up the following system databases (at the minimum) daily:

- `master`

- `msdb`

- `model`

- distribution database (for distribution replication servers)

How Often Should I Back Up the Transaction Log and Database?

If the database and the transaction log both became corrupted, how many transactions can you afford to lose? How many transactions are performed in an hour? A day? You must ask and answer these questions and more to determine how often you should dump the transaction log and database. Try to perform your database and transaction log dumps during nonpeak hours.

Also, keep in mind what is required to restore a database using full database dumps and transaction logs. For example, if you perform transaction log dumps (incremental backups) six times a day and a full database backup every five days, what do you have to do to restore the database? Depending on when the database became corrupted, you stand the possibility of having to load a full database backup and 0 to 30 transaction log dumps. Is this acceptable? Get the picture? If you have a database that is not updated very often, performing a biweekly transaction log dump and a weekly database dump might meet your requirements.

How Do I Manage the Backups?

How are you going to manage the various database and transaction log dumps on tapes or dump files, and how long are you going to keep your backups? Believe me, this is a problem in organizations with several databases. Organization is the key here. Come up with consistent naming conventions and a filing system for your backups. You will want to keep old backups around for several weeks or months. Organization makes it easy to find dumps that are several weeks or months old. Also, don't forget to keep a backup offsite just in case something catastrophic happens to your place of employment.

How Long Will It Take to Restore the Database?

If your database becomes corrupted, how long will it take to restore the database? Is the restore time acceptable? If you find that the restore time is not acceptable, you might have to consider hot backups. A *hot backup* is a term given to a system that uses specialized hardware to mirror the main database server; the hot backup can be used immediately if the main database server goes down. SQL Server 2000 provides a mechanism to support fallback restore when two computers share the same hard drive. If one computer fails, the other computer takes over. The bottom line is that by using a hot backup or fallback restore configuration, you decrease the chance of experiencing downtime. SQL Server also allows you to create standby servers (see the FAQ at the end of this chapter).

In What Other Ways Is the Database Protected?

It never hurts to have more than one level of data protection for very sensitive data. For example, is the database on a hardware device that is mirrored or does it reside on a RAID 5 drive configuration? It's always a good idea to mirror your transaction logs and master database. Is the SQL Server shut down weekly and the SQL Server directory and database devices backed up to tape by a system administrator? Always know what other restore options are available to you, just in case your well-constructed backup and restore plan fails.

Log Shipping Overview

SQL Server 2000 and 7.0 provide a utility called Log Shipping. The purpose of the log shipping utility is to automatically copy and apply the log from database A to database B (see Figure 10.20) . The source and target databases can be on the same server or separate servers.

The Log Shipping tool takes the changes in the source database and automatically applies them to the target database. Changes can include: data changes, schema changes, permission changes, stored procedure changes, and so on. This is different than replication, in that replication is exclusively focused on synchronizing data.

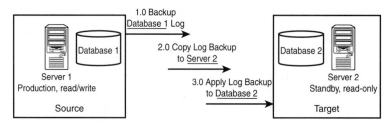

FIGURE 10.20   The Log Shipping overview.

Common uses of log shipping are

- `Warm-Standby Server`—Log shipping is a low-cost solution that enables you to create a standby server without having to incur the expensive of clustering.

- `Reporting Server`—Log shipping can automatically synchronize data between servers. This enables you to offload reporting, or other query intensive types of operations, to another server.

Log Shipping Requirements

The following is a listing of requirements for log shipping:

- **`Enterprise or Developer Edition`**—Log shipping is included only with the Enterprise and Developer editions of SQL Server. If you are running the Standard or Personal edition of SQL Server you are out of luck.

TIP

Run the following query to determine the version of SQL Server in-use.

`select @@version`

Read the last line returned from the query. It will tell you if you are running Enterprise, Standard, Developer, or the Personal edition of SQL Server 2000.

- **`Database Recovery Model must be set to Full or Bulk-Logged`**—Log shipping will not work if your database mode is set to Simple. To determine the mode, go to the properties of the database, and click on the Options tab.

- **`Existing transaction log backup jobs must be disabled`**—If you are currently running a log backup job on the source database, you must disable the job. Be sure to look for 3rd party software that performs a log backup behind the scenes.

- **Exclusive database access**—When the log is applied to the target database, SQL Server must have exclusive access to the database. You should let log shipping terminate any open connections, otherwise the process will fail.

TIP

The following article is a great source of information when setting up log shipping or trying to troubleshoot a log shipping problem.

`http://support.microsoft.com/default.aspx?scid=kb;en-us;q314515`

Title: INF: Frequently Asked Questions - SQL Server 2000 - Log Shipping

Microsoft Knowledge Base Article - Q314515

Setting-Up Log Shipping

To set-up log shipping, use the SQL Server Enterprise Manager and follow these steps:

NOTE

You must first create a network folder for the transaction log backups and this folder must be shared. You must grant the READ and CHANGE permissions. Grant these permissions to the account used by the SQL Server service and the SQL Server Agent service. If you are running pass-through security, grant the permissions on the local Windows NT account.

---

1. From the Database folder, select the source database. Right-click the source database. From the right click menu, select All Tasks. From the All Tasks menu, select Maintenance Plan. The Database Maintenance Plan Wizard appears.

2. Click the Next button to proceed. The Select Databases window appears. From this window, select the database and the Ship the transactions logs to other SQL Servers (log shipping) check box (see Figure 10.21) .

TIP

If the check box to enable log shipping is disabled, you have either selected a database that has its recovery model set to simple or you have selected multiple databases. If the recovery model is set to simple, change the database recover model to full or bulk-logged. If you have selected multiple databases, restart the process and select only one database.

---

3. Continue to click the Next button until the Specify the Transaction Log Share window appears. Enter the network share (see Figure 10.22).

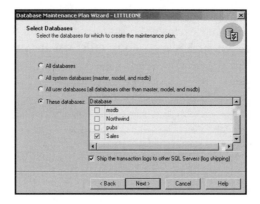

FIGURE 10.21   Select Database/Enable Log Shipping.

TIP

Do not leave the network share blank! Doing so will cause the process to fail.

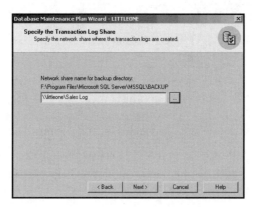

FIGURE 10.22   Specify network share.

4. Click Next to continue. The Specify the Log Shipping Destinations window appears. From this window, click the Add button. The Add Destination Database window appears. From this window, enter the following information (see Figure 10.23): server name, transaction log destination directory, destination database information, database load state, and allow database to assume primary role. Click the OK button to continue. The Specify the Log Shipping Destinations window re-appears (see Figure 10.24) .

TIP

I recommend using the following settings for the Add Destination Database window.

Create and initialize new database or Use existing database (no initialization): Use the create and initialize new database option if the target database does not already exist. The log shipping tool automatically creates the target database by backing up and restoring the source database.

Database Load State: Use the standby mode option if you want the target database to be in a read-only mode. This will enables you to view data and object changes on-the-fly. This setting should also be used if you want to use the database for read-only reporting purposes. If you set the load state to no recovery mode, the database will remain in a loading state and you will be unable to view the contents.

Terminate users in database: Use this setting when you want SQL Server to kill any connections in the target database. This is important because log shipping will fail if there are open connections in the target database.

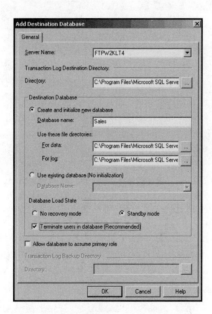

FIGURE 10.23   Add destination database.

5. Click Next to continue. The Initialize the Destination Databases window appears (see Figure 10.25). Click the desired radio button: Perform a full database backup now or Use most recent backup file.

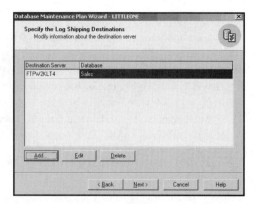

FIGURE 10.24   Specify log shipping destination.

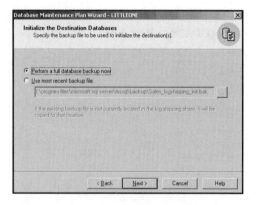

FIGURE 10.25   Initialize destination databases.

6. Click Next to continue. The Log Shipping Schedules window appears (see Figure 10.26). Enter the schedule, copy/load frequency, load delay, and file retention period.

NOTE

The settings to use in the Log Shipping Schedules window are dependant depend on the purpose of your implementation. For example, if you are planning on using log shipping to create a warm standby server, you will want to use a short time interval (for example, every 5 minutes). If you are planning on using log shipping to create a reporting server, the duration should be longer (for example, every 12 hours). When using log shipping to manage a reporting server, you need to keep in mind that the log shipping tool requires exclusive database access. If you have a short time interval, your reporting applications will be continuously terminated by SQL Server when the log is applied.

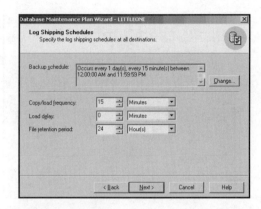

FIGURE 10.26   Log shipping schedule.

7. Click Next to continue. The Log Shipping Thresholds window appears (see Figure 10.27). Enter the backup alert threshold and out-of-sync alert threshold.

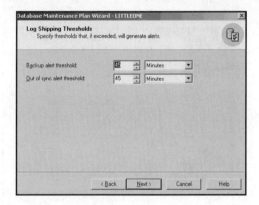

FIGURE 10.27   Log shipping thresholds.

8. Click Next to continue. The Specify the Log Shipping Monitor Server Information window appears (see Figure 10.28). Enter the server name and authentication type.

NOTE

If you select SQL Server authentication in the Specify the Log Shipping Monitor Server Information window, the Log Shipping tool will automatically create the log_shipping_monitor_probe account if it does not already exist. If this account already exists, and you have forgotten the password, use the Enterprise Manager to reset the password.

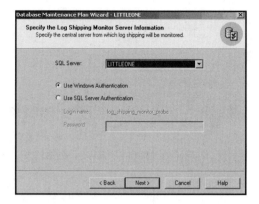

FIGURE 10.28   Log Shipping Monitor Server.

9. Continue to click the Next button until the Completing the Database
   Maintenance Plan Wizard window appears. Click the Finish button. Each task
   executes and the corresponding status appears (see Figure 10.29).

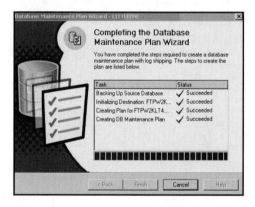

FIGURE 10.29   Task completion.

Modifying and Removing Log Shipping

To modify log shipping, use the SQL Server Enterprise Manager and follow these
steps:

1. From the Management folder, click Database Maintenance. Double-click the
   plan name. The Database Maintenance Plan window appears. Click the Log
   Shipping tab.

2. From the Log Shipping tab (see Figure 10.30), you can add/edit/delete destination server settings.

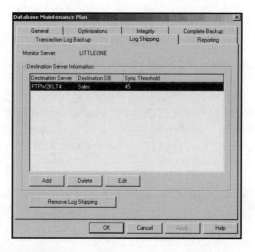

FIGURE 10.30   Log Shipping Tab.

TIP

If you want to delete the log shipping process, click the Remove Log Shipping button on the Log Shipping Tab. This removes the log shipping jobs. However, it will not remove the maintenance plan. To delete the maintenance plan, go back to the Database Maintenance Plan and delete the plan.

3. From the Transaction Log Backup tab (see Figure 10.31), you can modify the transaction log backup settings.

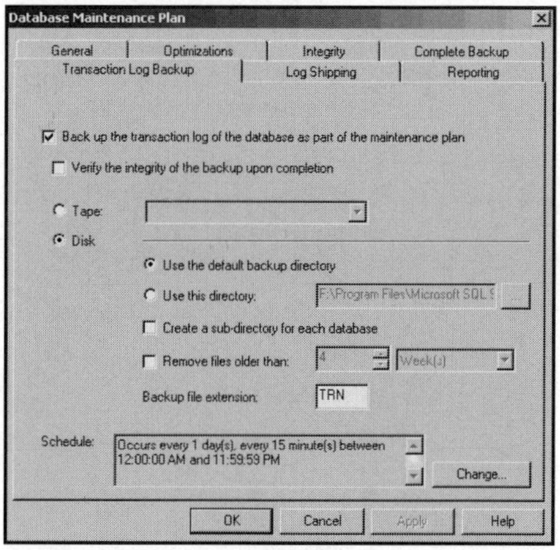

FIGURE 10.31   Transaction Log Backup Tab.

Monitoring and Troubleshooting Log Shipping

The following explains how to monitor and troubleshoot log shipping:

- Log Shipping Monitor: To run the log shipping monitor, go to the Log Shipping Monitor folder (under the Management folder). The Log Shipping Monitor alerts you to out-of-sync conditions (see Figure 10.32 for an example). Double-click the Log Shipping Pair for additional information (see Figure 10.33). You can also right-click the log shipping pair to view backup history and view copy/restore history. You can often use this information to troubleshoot log shipping problems.

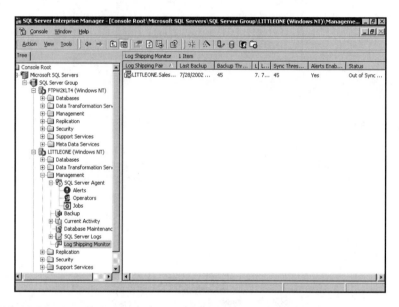

FIGURE 10.32   Log Shipping Monitor—Out of sync example.

- View Jobs: The log shipping monitor creates several jobs on the source and target server (see Figures 10.34 and 10.35). When troubleshooting log shipping jobs, look at the history for troubleshooting information.

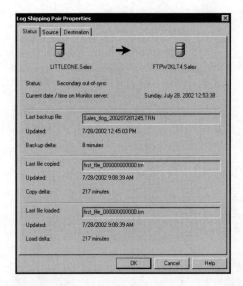

FIGURE 10.33   Log shipping pair.

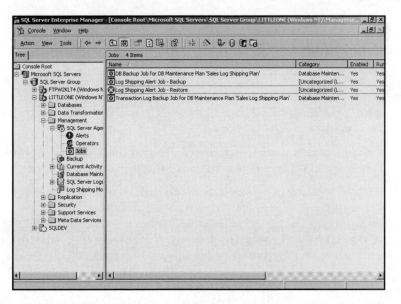

FIGURE 10.34   Log Shipping Jobs—Source server.

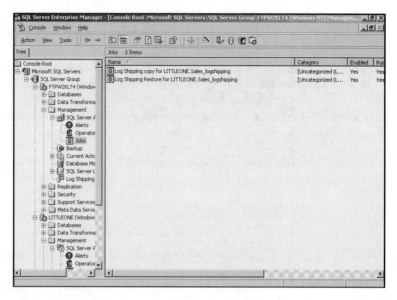

FIGURE 10.35   Log Shipping Jobs—Target server.

Backup and Restore FAQ

Q Can I load a 6.x or 7.0 database backup into SQL Server 2000?

A You cannot load SQL Server 6.x databases using backup and restore. You must use the SQL Server 2000 upgrade utility. You can load a SQL Server 7.0 database backup into SQL Server 2000.

Q I have a single tape drive, and I need to back up SQL Server and the Windows 2000 box using an automated process. How can I do this?

A Without purchasing a third-party product that backs up both SQL Server and Windows 2000, you can back up a database to a disk file backup device and then copy the backup device to tape, just like a regular Windows 2000 file. When you need to restore the database, copy the file from tape back to disk and then use SQL Server Enterprise Manager to restore the database.

Q How can I move a database?

A You can use database backups to move a database, you can use the database copy wizard, or you can copy and reattach the files that make up the database. Make sure that the two servers share the same character set, sort order, and Unicode locale.

Q How can I see what's on a backup device (disk or tape)?

A You can graphically view what backups are on a current backup device by double-clicking on the backup device in the Enterprise Manager and then clicking the View Contents button on the Backup device properties page. You can also use the Transact SQL command RESTORE HEADERONLY and specify the backup device you want to view.

Q Can I create a standby server using SQL Server backup and restore?

A Creating a standby server using backup and restore is simple. On the standby server load, use full database backups with the RESTORE STANDBY clause. Load transaction logs from the primary server to the standby server using the RESTORE STANDBY clause. If the primary server fails, use the BACKUP LOG with the NO_TRUNCATE clause on the primary server database. Load the transaction log on the standby server with the RESTORE STANDBY clause. Then execute the RESTORE DATABASE with the RECOVERY clause. The standby server can be used in Read-only mode while the primary server is fully functional, and of course, you have to keep the standby server up-to-date with backups from the primary server. If you are running the Enterprise Edition of SQL Server, you can use log shipping to maintain a standby server.

Q What is log shipping?

A The Enterprise Edition of SQL Server 2000 contains functionality called log shipping. Log shipping enables a SQL Server to send and restore transactions logs to another SQL Server on a periodic basis. Sending and restoring transaction logs via log shipping make it simple for you to maintain a backup or standby server.

Q I have a very large database and would like to verify that I can read the backup tapes without actually restoring the database. How do I accomplish this?

A To verify your backups without actually restoring the database, use the RESTORE VERIFYONLY command, which reads and verifies that the backup set is complete. It does not check the data structures on the disk, so you should also perform a DBCC CHECKDB on your databases to verify the integrity of the data and the data structures.

Q What happened to the database options trunc. log on chkpt. and select into/bulkcopy?

A The database options still exist and are set automatically when you select a recovery model from the Enterprise Manager. You can still set them manually by using the sp_dboption system-stored procedure.

Q What is a named transaction?

A SQL Server 2000 allows you to assign a name to a particular transaction via the `BEGIN TRANSACTION`. You can then use point in time recovery to recover to a particular mark. Using named transactions does consume additional transaction log space as well as adds a row to the `logmarkhistory` table in the `msdb` database.

Q What's the best advice you can give a new DBA for backup and restore?

A After you have created a backup plan, don't stop there. Make sure that you test your backup plan by actually restoring the databases. When you are done testing, test your restore plan again. When the day comes and a database fails, you should feel very comfortable and confident in your ability to restore the database. The bottom line is, test and practice your backup and restore plans. With SQL Server 2000 running on Windows 9x/XP as well as Windows 2000 Server, you should have no problem finding a machine on which to practice.

Summary

Maintaining a good set of database backups and knowing how to use them to recover a database is one of the most important responsibilities of a DBA. Use the ideas and suggestions in this chapter to help build your own backup and recovery plan.

- SQL Server 2000 has three different recovery models—simple, bulk logged, and full.

- Database backups can be complete backups, which are full backups of the data and database objects, or differential database backups, which are just the data that has changed.

- Transaction log backups are incremental backups that reflect the changes in the database since the previous transaction log backup or database backup.

- Users can still implement the database during backups.

- Use the header information on backup devices or the Enterprise Manager to display important information about the currently stored backups.

- You can append backups to disk backup devices as well as tape backup devices.

- Review the section in this chapter about the `BACKUP LOG` options: `TRUNCATE_ONLY`, `NO_LOG`, and `NO_TRUNCATE`.

- To decrease the amount of time required for database backups, use a media set with multiple devices.

- Backups can be reliably and easily scheduled from the SQL Enterprise Manager.

- Create a backup and restore plan to protect your databases. Make sure that you test and practice the plan.

- Back up the `master` database daily.

PART V

SQL Database Maintenance

IN THIS PART

11 Developing a SQL Server Maintenance Plan

12 Automating Database Administration Tasks

Developing a SQL Server Maintenance Plan

IN THIS CHAPTER

- Areas of Maintenance
- Maintenance Checklist
- Maintenance FAQ

by Orryn Sledge

Developing a SQL Server maintenance plan is a proactive approach that can help minimize system downtime. SQL Server 2000 has greatly simplified database maintenance, however, I still like to compare SQL Server to a car. Both require preventive maintenance and periodic tune-ups. To help you keep SQL Server motoring along, this chapter discusses the types of maintenance that should be performed by a DBA. To learn how to automate several of the tasks discussed in this chapter, see Chapter 12, "Automating Database Administration Tasks."

NOTE

Starting with SQL Server 7.0, the product became significantly better than previous versions in automatically administering and adjusting engine parameters. Parameters, such as lock management, memory management, user connections, tempdb sizing, database sizing, and log sizing are automatically managed by SQL Server. (Note: The autogrow setting must be on for databases and logs to automatically resize on-the-fly.) These changes simplify, but do not eliminate, the need for maintenance.

Areas of Maintenance

As a DBA, you should be concerned with five broad areas of maintenance:

- SQL Server maintenance
- Database maintenance

- Table/object maintenance

- Job maintenance

- Windows maintenance

SQL Server Maintenance

The following list summarizes the types of maintenance that should be performed at the SQL Server database engine level:

- Monitor error logs

- Record configuration information

- Manage logins

Monitor Error Logs

As a DBA, you should frequently review SQL Server's error log. When you review the error log, look for messages that do not appear under normal circumstances. Unfortunately, the error log contains more than error messages. It also contains statements about the status of events, copyright information, and so on. This means that you have to know what to look for when you scan the error log. A good starting point is to look for the following keywords:

- `error`

- `failed`

- `table corrupt`

- `level 16`

- `level 17`

- `level 21`

- `Severity: 16`

- `Severity: 17`

- `Severity: 21`

NOTE

You can view the SQL Server's error log from the SQL Server Enterprise Manager or from a text editor.

To view the SQL Server error log from the SQL Server Enterprise Manager, select a server from the server group, click the plus (+) sign next to the server that contains the SQL Server error logs, click the plus (+) sign next to the Management folder, and click the plus (+) sign next to the SQL Server Logs icon. From the Result pane, double-click an error log to view its contents (see Figure 11.1).

To view the current error log with a text editor, open the file `C:\Program Files\Microsoft SQL Server\MSSQL\LOG`. You also can view the last six versions of the error log by opening the corresponding file (`errorlog.1`, `errorlog.2`, and so on).

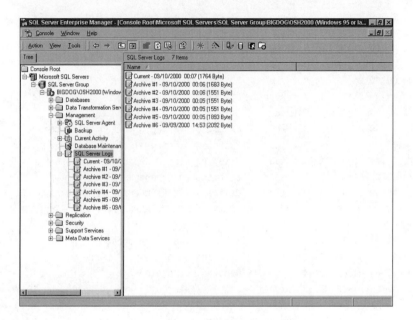

FIGURE 11.1   The SQL Server error log Result pane.

The following listing shows a sample error log. The item in bold is an example of an error a DBA might want to investigate. This example illustrates what happens if the log device does not exist for a given database.

```
2000-09-09 21:32:30.14 server    Microsoft SQL Server
➡ 2000 - 8.00.534 (Intel X86)
    Nov 19 2001 13:23:50
    Copyright (c) 1988-2000 Microsoft Corporation
    Personal Edition on Windows NT 5.0 (Build 2195: Service Pack 2)
2000-09-09 21:32:30.15 server    Copyright (C) 1988-2000 Microsoft Corporation.
2000-09-09 21:32:30.15 server    All rights reserved.
2000-09-09 21:32:30.15 server    Server Process ID is 2088.
2000-09-09 21:32:30.15 server    Logging SQL Server messages in file
➡ 'd:\Program Files\Microsoft SQL Server\MSSQL$OS2000\log\ERRORLOG'.
```

```
2000-09-09 21:32:30.18 server    SQL Server is starting at priority class
➥ 'normal'(1 CPU detected).
2000-09-09 21:32:30.32 server    SQL Server configured for thread
➥ mode processing.
2000-09-09 21:32:30.33 server    Using dynamic lock allocation.
➥ [500] Lock Blocks, [1000] Lock Owner Blocks.
2000-09-09 21:32:30.44 spid3     Starting up database 'master'.
2000-09-09 21:32:30.77 server    Using 'SSNETLIB.DLL' version '8.0.194'.
2000-09-09 21:32:30.98 spid5     Starting up database 'model'.
2000-09-09 21:32:31.00 server    SQL server listening on TCP,
➥ Shared Memory, Named Pipes.
2000-09-09 21:32:31.00 server    SQL server listening on 127.0.0.1:1794.
2000-09-09 21:32:31.00 server    SQL Server is ready for client connections
2000-09-09 21:32:31.12 spid3     Server name is 'WHOSLEGEW\OS2000'.
2000-09-09 21:32:31.12 spid3     Skipping startup of clean database id 4
2000-09-09 21:32:31.12 spid3     Skipping startup of clean database id 5
2000-09-09 21:32:31.12 spid3     Skipping startup of clean database id 6
2000-09-09 21:32:31.12 spid3     Starting up database 'sales'.
```
2000-09-09 21:32:31.29 spid3   Device activation error. The physical file name
➥ **'d:\Program Files\Microsoft SQL Server\MSSQL$OS2000\data\sales_log.LDF'**
➥ **may be incorrect.**
```
2000-09-09 21:32:31.41 spid5     Clearing tempdb database.
2000-09-09 21:32:32.87 spid5     Starting up database 'tempdb'.
2000-09-09 21:32:33.14 spid3     Recovery complete.
2000-09-09 21:32:45.38 spid51    Using 'xpstar.dll' version '2000.80.194'
➥ to execute extended stored procedure 'sp_MSgetversion'.
2000-09-09 21:32:45.53 spid51    Starting up database 'msdb'.
2000-09-09 21:32:49.08 spid51    Starting up database 'Northwind'.
2000-09-09 21:32:49.34 spid51    Starting up database 'pubs'.
```

TIP

Use the Windows FINDSTR.EXE utility to search for text patterns in the error logs. (For the UNIX folks, FINDSTR.EXE is Windows equivalent of GREP.) This utility can help automate the process of scanning the log for errors. The following example shows how to scan the error log for the keyword error.

```
findstr /i /n /c:"error" errorlog
```

The following is sample output:

```
9:2000-09-09 21:32:30.15 server    Logging SQL Server messages in
➥ file 'd:\Program Files\Microsoft SQL Server\MSSQL$OS2000\log\ERRORLOG'
24:2000-09-09 21:32:31.29 spid3    Device activation error.
➥ The physical file name
```

```
➥ 'd:\Program Files\Microsoft SQL Server\
➥ MSSQL$OS2000\data\sales_log.LDF'
➥ maybe incorrect.
32:2000-09-09 21:38:38.77 spid51
➥ Error: 15457, Severity: 0, State: 1
35:2000-09-09 21:41:11.63 spid52
➥ Error: 15457, Severity: 0, State: 1
```

Record Configuration Information

When you are unable to start SQL Server, server configuration information can help Microsoft's technical support group get you back up and running.

Use the system procedure sp_configure to generate a list of configuration information, as in the following example:

```
exec sp_configure
```

The following is the output:

name	minimum	maximum	config_value	run_value
affinity mask	0	2147483647	0	0
allow updates	0	1	0	0
awe enabled	0	1	0	0
c2 audit mode	0	1	0	0
cost threshold for parallelism	0	32767	5	5
cursor threshold	-1	2147483647	-1	-1
default full-text language	0	2147483647	1033	1033
default language	0	9999	0	0
fill factor (%)	0	100	0	0
index create memory (KB)	704	2147483647	0	0
lightweight pooling	0	1	0	0
locks	5000	2147483647	0	0
max degree of parallelism	0	32	0	0
max server memory (MB)	4	2147483647	2147483647	2147483647
max text repl size (B)	0	2147483647	65536	65536
max worker threads	32	32767	255	255
media retention	0	365	0	0
min memory per query (KB)	512	2147483647	1024	1024
min server memory (MB)	0	2147483647	0	0
nested triggers	0	1	1	1
network packet size (B)	512	65536	4096	4096
open objects	0	2147483647	0	0

priority boost	0	1	0	0
query governor cost limit	0	2147483647	0	0
query wait (s)	-1	2147483647	-1	-1
recovery interval (min)	0	32767	0	0
remote access	0	1	1	1
remote login timeout (s)	0	2147483647	20	20
remote proc trans	0	1	0	0
remote query timeout (s)	0	2147483647	600	600
scan for startup procs	0	1	0	0
set working set size	0	1	0	0
show advanced options	0	1	1	1
two digit year cutoff	1753	9999	2049	2049
user connections	0	32767	0	0
user options	0	32767	0	0

TIP

Use the SQL Server Agent to schedule a job that automatically runs sp_configure. When you create the job step, you can capture the output from sp_configure to a text file.

To save the output from a job step, select the Advanced tab from the New Job Step Properties dialog box and enter an output path and filename. I also recommend using the Append to File feature, found on the Advanced tab of the New Job Step Properties dialog box, so that a history of configuration settings can be logged (see Figure 11.2).

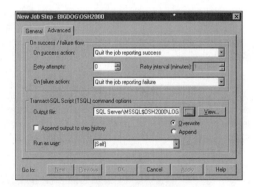

FIGURE 11.2   Advanced tab, New Job Step Properties.

Manage Logins

As a DBA, you should periodically review who has access to your SQL Server. In large organizations, people frequently change jobs. This means that you might have several SQL Server accounts that are not actively being used. You should deactivate these accounts to prevent unauthorized access to SQL Server. If you are using Windows Authentication, you can force password aging and password minimum lengths through Windows security.

Database Maintenance

The following list summarizes the types of maintenance that should be performed at the database level:

- Back up your database and transaction log
- Test your backup and recovery strategy
- Audit database access

NOTE

Several of the tasks discussed in this chapter can be automated through the Database Maintenance Plan Wizard included with SQL Server 2000. For more information about the Database Maintenance Wizard, see Chapter 12.

Back Up Your Database and Transaction Log

To ensure database recovery, it is essential to frequently back up the database and transaction log. Create a backup strategy that meets your needs and then periodically review this strategy to ensure that it continues to satisfy your backup requirements (see Chapter 10, "Backup and Recovery," for more information).

Test Your Backup/Recovery Strategy

Many DBAs back up SQL Server on a frequent basis, but only the good DBAs actually test their backup strategy by simulating database recovery. You should frequently test the integrity of your backups by actually performing a database recovery (see Chapter 10 for more information). Try to cover all the scenarios: dead server, lost drives, corrupt database, and so on. Do not put yourself in the position of having to be the one to tell the CEO that your backup strategy didn't work.

TIP

An easy way to validate your backup strategy is to create a database with a different name. For example, if I wanted to test my backup/restoration strategy for the pubs database, I would back up the pubs database, create a pubs2 database (or some other database name), and restore the pubs backup to pubs2. If the restoration is successful, I have validated my backup strategy.

Audit Database Access

You should periodically perform a review of who has access to your production databases and what type of rights they possess. Doing so can prevent unauthorized access
to production data.

Table/Object Maintenance

The following list summarizes the types of maintenance that should be performed at
the table/object level:

- Monitor the record count

- Audit object permissions

Monitor Record Count

In a transaction-oriented environment, it might be necessary to establish a limit on
the number of records that should exist in your tables. When the limit is exceeded,
the records should be archived from the table. Doing so can ensure a consistent
performance level.

Audit Object Permissions

Periodically review the types of permissions (SELECT, INSERT, UPDATE, DELETE, and
EXECUTE) that each user has to your production data. Doing so can help prevent
security violations.

Job Maintenance

Regularly scheduled jobs should be reviewed for success or failure. Quite often, jobs
are created and implemented, but never monitored. Do not wait until it is too late to
find out that your backup job did not successfully run! The following are items of
maintenance and review for jobs. (See Chapter 12 for more information about jobs.)

- **Job status**—Monitor the success or failure of each job.

- **Schedule**—Review the schedule and frequency of the job. Schedules often
  need to be modified due to changing business needs.

- **Duration**—Review the time it takes to run the job. Load balancing and tuning
  might be required for jobs that are taking too long to run.

- **Output**—Review the output from the job.

TIP

SQL Server Agent logs errors to the file `c:\program files\Microsoft sql server\instance
name\log\sqlagent.out`.

To view the SQL Server Agent Error Log from the SQL Server Enterprise Manager, select a server from the server group, click the plus (+) sign next to the server that contains the SQL Server Agent Error Logs, click the plus (+) sign next to the Management folder, right-click the SQL Server Agent icon, and from the right-click menu, select the Display Error Log option. The SQL Server Agent Error Log window appears. From this window, view the contents of the SQL Server Agent Error Log (see Figure 11.3).

This file also can be viewed with a text editor. You can view the last nine versions of the SQL Server Agent log as well by opening the corresponding file (`sqlagent.1`, `sqlagent.2`, and so on).

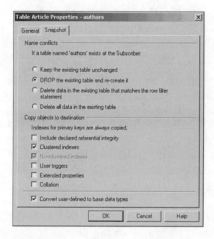

FIGURE 11.3   SQL Server Agent Error Log.

Windows Maintenance

The following list summarizes the types of maintenance that should be performed at the operating system level:

- Monitor the Windows event log
- Keep the Emergency Repair disk current and backup the registry
- Run disk defragmentation utilities
- Monitor available disk space
- Monitor CPU and memory usage

Monitor the Windows Event Log

When it comes to monitoring the event log, you should look for two types of errors: *system errors* and *application errors*.

System errors are hardware and operating system specific. Examples include network errors, hardware problems, and driver errors.

Application errors are those errors associated with the application as well as certain types of SQL Server errors. Examples include connection errors, abnormal termination errors, and database failure errors.

Keep the Emergency Repair Disk Current and Back Up the Registry

Whenever hardware and software configurations change, you should update the Emergency Repair disk. For Windows 2000, use the Backup utility. For Windows NT 4.0, use RDISK.EXE to keep your Emergency Repair disk current. When you create an Emergency Repair Disk, it will also backup the registry.

Run Disk Defragmentation Utilities

Periodically, you should run disk defragmentation utilities on your server's hard disks. A high degree of hard disk fragmentation can lead to decreased hard disk performance. With Windows 2000, you can use the built-in Disk Defragmenter program. With version 4.0 of Windows NT, a NTFS drive must be checked with a third-party product or a FAT drive can be checked with SCANDISK.EXE.

Monitor Available Disk Space

It's a good idea to have at least 50% of the server's hard disk space not in use. This leaves enough free space for database and log growth, database dumps, DTS imports/exports, BCP imports/exports, script generation, and so on.

Monitor CPU and Memory Usage

The easiest way to monitor CPU and memory usage is to use the Performance Monitor (for more information on using the Performance Monitor, refer to Chapter 24, "Monitoring SQL Server"). If you see sustained spikes in CPU usage, it might be time to upgrade your CPU or redistribute the workload. Also, keep an eye on memory usage and the number of free bytes. Insufficient memory leads to a high number of page faults, which degrades performance.

Maintenance Checklist

Here's a checklist of items for maintenance:

Frequency of Execution	Task
Daily	
❑	Monitor error logs
❑	Back up database and transaction log
❑	Monitor jobs
❑	Monitor the Windows event log
❑	Monitor CPU and memory usage
Weekly	
❑	Monitor available disk space
Monthly	
❑	Test your backup strategy
❑	Monitor record count
❑	Manage logins
❑	Audit database access
❑	Audit object permissions
As Needed	
❑	Keep the Emergency Repair disk current and back up the registry
❑	Run disk defragmentation utilities

Maintenance FAQ

The following are some of the common questions asked by DBAs about SQL Server maintenance:

Q Who in my organization should be tasked with managing the SQL Server maintenance plan?

A If your organization has a designated DBA, he should probably be responsible for the maintenance plan. If not, the LAN manager is probably the next best person. Regardless of who is responsible for the maintenance plan, it is important that the someone is the owner of this plan. SQL Server 2000 still requires day-to-day monitoring.

Q Are there any third-party tools that can help automate the maintenance plan?

A Yes, most backup products include add-ins that can manage the backup and dbcc portion of the maintenance plan. There are also third-party products that can automatically read Windows event viewer and forward alerts. However, I've found that these products still require some level of day-to-day monitoring.

Summary

Several types of tasks are required to maintain SQL Server. Many of these tasks can be automated through SQL Server's scheduler and Alert Manager. The next chapter, "Automating Database Administration Tasks," discusses how to automate common DBA tasks.

12

Automating Database Administration Tasks

by Orryn Sledge

IN THIS CHAPTER

- Introduction
- SQL Server Agent
- Database Maintenance Plan Wizard
- Automating Database Administration Tasks FAQ

Introduction

Virtually every organization can reduce administrative effort by automating common DBA tasks. SQL Server 2000 provides several tools that can help automate common tasks: Job Scheduler, Alert Manager, and Database Maintenance Plan Wizard. These tools are integrated with SQL Server Agent. Together, these tools and SQL Server Agent can automate common tasks and, when taken to the next level, can provide proactive database management.

SQL Server Agent

SQL Server Agent is an easy-to-use and robust task scheduler and alert manager. It includes several useful features, such as history logs and the capability to email or page an operator when an event occurs.

SQL Server Agent has the following components:

- Jobs
- Alerts

Jobs

Jobs are typically used to schedule and automate tasks. SQL Server Agent can automate many types of jobs, including the following:

- **Backups**—Automatic database backups should be an integral part of everyone's production systems. SQL Server Agent can automatically back up a database at a preset interval. See Chapter 10, "Backup and Recovery," for more information on automatically backing up the database.

- **Scheduled database maintenance**—Database maintenance commands, such as DBCC checkdb, can be scheduled to run during off hours.

- **Data warehouse import and export routines**—Many companies import data into SQL Server and export data to other non-SQL Server systems within the organization. Jobs that are built using the Data Transformation Service (DTS) and run from the SQL Server Agent are great for automating the transfer of information.

Creating and Managing Jobs

Now that you know the types of jobs that can be automated, here's a simple example that actually schedules a job. For this example, assume that you want to schedule a stored procedure that removes any sales data more than seven days old. In addition, you want the procedure to run on a nightly basis at 3:00 a.m., and you want to be notified by email that the procedure successfully ran.

The following is a sample procedure:

```
CREATE PROCEDURE del_remove_old_data AS
/* remove transactions that are 7 or more days old */
DELETE
FROM sales
WHERE DATEDIFF(dd,ord_date,getdate()) > = 7
```

> **NOTE**
>
> The SQL Server Agent service must be running for the Job Scheduler to work. To determine whether SQL Server Agent is running, check the SQL Server Agent status indicator in the Task Tray or from the SQL Server Enterprise Manager.

To schedule the del_remove_old_data stored procedure, follow these steps:

1. From the SQL Server Enterprise Manager, click the plus (+) sign next to the server that will execute the job.

2. Click the plus (+) sign next to the Management folder.

3. Click the plus (+) sign next to the SQL Server Agent.

4. Right-click the Jobs icon. From the right mouse menu, select the New Job menu option. The New Job Properties dialog box appears (see Figure 12.1).

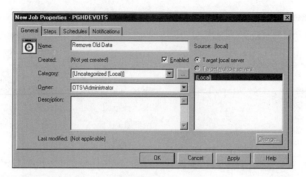

FIGURE 12.1   The New Job Properties dialog box.

5. From the New Job Properties dialog box, select the General tab. From the General tab, enter a name for the job. Names can be up to 128 characters long. This example uses Remove Old Data for the name.

6. Select the Steps tab. From the Steps tab, click the New button. The New Job Step dialog box appears.

7. From the New Job Step dialog box (see Figure 12.2), enter the following information:

   • **Step Name**—The name of the step. This example uses Call Delete Procedure for the Step Name.

   • **Type**—The type of step. This example uses TSQL as the type. The following table describes the purpose of each job type.

Active Script	Runs a script built in Visual Basic or JScript. See the "Active Scripting Jobs" section later in the chapter for more information on Active Scripting.
Operating System Command (CmdExec)	Executes a .BAT, .EXE, or .CMD file. Examples include BCP.EXE, ISQL.EXE, and CUSTOM.BAT.
Replication Distributor	Used with replication. Enables you to define replication distribution commands. This type of job is usually managed by SQL Server and is not part of user-defined jobs.
Replication Transaction-Log Reader	Used with replication. Enables you to define replication log reader commands. This type of job is usually managed by SQL Server and is not part of user-defined jobs.

Replication Merge	Used with replication. Enables you to define replication merge commands. This type of job is usually managed by SQL Server and is not part of user-defined jobs.
Replication Snapshot	Used with replication. Enables you to define replication snapshot commands. This type of job is usually managed by SQL Server and is not part of user-defined jobs.
Replication Transact-SQL Script (TSQL)	Executes Transact-SQL statements. Examples include `TRUNCATE TABLE authors`, `UPDATE authors SET au_id = 100`, `EXEC usp_my_proc`, and so on.

- **Database**—The name of the database. This option is enabled only when the type of task is TSQL. This example uses the pubs database.

NOTE

Certain commands are database specific, whereas others can be run from any database. Commands such as `INSERT`, `DELETE`, `UPDATE`, `SELECT`, and `EXECUTE` must be run from the corresponding database. Commands such as `BACKUP DATABASE`, `BACKUP LOG`, `DBCC CHECKDB`, and system procedures that reside in the master database (such as `sp_addlogin`, and `sp_configure`) can be run from any database.

- **Command**—The command to run. This example uses `exec del_remove_old_data` to run the stored procedure that removes expired sales data.

TIP

Practically anything can be scheduled through the SQL Server Job Scheduler. It isn't just for scheduling backups and DBCC commands. Jobs such as nightly report generation and data summarization are some of the other uses of the Job Scheduler.

8. Click the Advanced tab (see Figure 12.3) to enter the following optional information:

- **On Success Action**—This option defines the action to take after the job has successfully run. Table 12.1 shows valid actions for this command. This example uses the Quit the Job Reporting Success option.

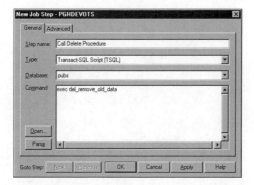

FIGURE 12.2   The New Job Step dialog box.

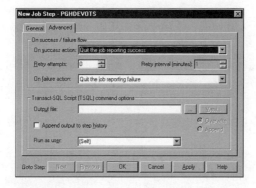

FIGURE 12.3   The New Job Step dialog box, Advanced tab.

NOTE

The On Success Action and the On Failure Action options are important when creating jobs with multiple steps. These options control flow logic. For example, a job might comprise the following four steps: import data from an external system, summarize data, export data to another system, and generate reports. If a step fails to run successfully, the On Failure Action option determines the next action to be taken. For example, if a job fails because the import step failed, the On Failure Action option could be set to Quit the Job Reporting Failure. See the "Job Steps" section later in the chapter for more information.

TABLE 12.1   Step Actions

Step Action	Explanation
Quit the Job Reporting Success	Terminates the job if the step is successful. This option does not execute any additional steps in the job.
Quit the Job Reporting Failure	Terminates the job if the step fails. This option does not execute any additional steps in the job.

TABLE 12.1   Continued

Step Action	Explanation
Goto the Next Step	Instructs SQL Server Agent to go to the next step listed in the job. This option is typically used when the job comprises multiple steps that run sequentially.
Goto Step N	Instructs SQL Server Agent to skip to step *N*.

NOTE

The Goto Step N option is available only if the job contains multiple steps. This option is not visible for single-step jobs.

- **Retry Attempts and Retry Interval(minutes)**—Sets the number of retries and the retry interval for the step. The default for this option is 0 retry attempts.

- **On Failure Action**—This option defines the action to take when the job has failed. This example uses the Quit the Job Reporting Failure option.

- **Output File**—The filename to log messages.

TIP

The Output File feature of the Advanced tab is great for logging status messages, error messages, or any other type of message that the routine may generate. Additionally, the Append option allows job output to be appended.

The output file feature can also be used for basic reporting. For example, if a job has `select * from authors`, the output from the SQL statement can be written to an output file. This feature is handy for simple reports that need to be run on a regular schedule.

- **Run as User**—Specifies the username to utilize when the step is run.

    Click the OK button to continue. The New Job Properties dialog box reappears.

9. Select the Schedules tab. From this tab, click the New Schedule button to schedule the job. The New Job Schedule dialog box appears (see Figure 12.4).

10. In the New Job Schedule dialog box, enter the following information:

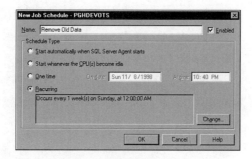

FIGURE 12.4 The New Job Schedule dialog box.

- **Name**—The name of the schedule. This example uses Remove Old Data.

- **Schedule Type**—The frequency and scheduling of the job. This example uses the Recurring feature to automatically run the task every day. Table 12.2 contains a listing of schedule types.

TABLE 12.2 Schedule Types

Schedule Type	Explanation
Start automatically when SQL Server Agent starts	Executes the job when SQL Server Agent is started. This option typically is not utilized for administrative purposes.
Start whenever the CPU(s) become idle	Executes the job when the CPU is idle. The option defaults to a sustained CPU usage below 10% and for 600 seconds. This option can be adjusted by going to the Properties dialog box of the SQL Server Agent and selecting the Advanced tab. From the Advanced tab, the Idle parameters can be set.
One Time	Executes the job one time. This option is useful when a maintenance type of job needs to be run during off-hours. For example, if a table needs a large set of its values updated, you can schedule a one-time job to execute the query. This option is also useful for scheduling long-running queries so that the workstation is not held up waiting for the query to finish running.
Recurring	Executes a job on a recurring basis. This option is typically used for backups and any other type of job that needs to run on a recurring basis.

(handwritten note: 10 minutes)

11. Click the Change button from the New Job Schedule dialog box. The Edit Recurring Job Schedule dialog box appears.

12. From the Edit Recurring Job Schedule dialog box (see Figure 12.5), enter the job's schedule.

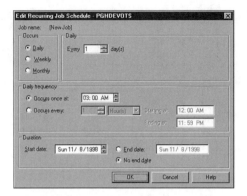

FIGURE 12.5   The Edit Recurring Job Schedule dialog box.

13. Click the OK button to return to the New Job Schedule dialog box.

14. From the New Job Schedule dialog box, click the OK button to return to the Job Properties dialog box.

NOTE

A useful feature in SQL Server 2000 is the ability to define multiple schedules for a single job. For example, a job can be defined to run on Monday at 8:00 p.m. and on Tuesday at 9:00 p.m. To define additional schedules, click the New Schedule button from the Schedules tab in the Job Properties dialog box.

15. From the New Job Properties dialog box, click the Notifications tab. From the Notifications tab (see Figure 12.6), you can specify the following actions. This example uses an email operator and writes to the Windows NT application event log. It also uses the option when the job completes for email and event log notification. This option will send an email to the operator after the job has run.

- Email operator

- Page operator

- Net send operator

- Write to Windows NT application event log

- Automatically delete job

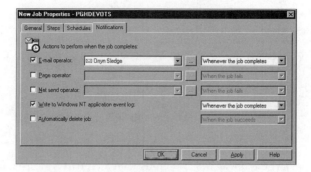

FIGURE 12.6   The Notifications tab in the Job Properties dialog box.

A FEW TIPS ON EMAIL NOTIFICATION

- To notify an operator by email, SQL Mail must be running and connected to your email service. Use the SQL Mail status indicator in the Enterprise Manager to validate that SQL Mail is successfully running.

- Use the extended stored procedure xp_sendmail to test whether your email service is properly configured, as in the following example:

  ```
  xp_sendmail 'recipient_name', 'this is a test'
  ```

- Notifications cannot email query results to an email operator. A notification can email only the following information: job run time, job duration, status, and status messages.

A FEW TIPS ON NET SEND NOTIFICATION

- A net send message can be sent to a computername, username, or messaging name. For more information on the Net Send command, type **net help send** at a command prompt.

- The messenger service must be running on Windows NT for a net send notification to work. To determine whether the messenger service is running, open Control Panel, double-click the Services applet, and select the Messenger service. The Status setting displays the condition of the messenger service.

16. Click the OK button to save the job.

After a job has been created, it is a good idea to test the job by manually executing it. Follow these steps to manually execute the job:

1. From the SQL Server Enterprise Manager, click the plus (+) sign next to the server that will execute the job.

2. Click the plus (+) sign next to the Management folder.

3. Click the plus (+) sign next to the SQL Server Agent.

4. Click the Jobs icon. A list of jobs appears in the result pane.

5. Right-click the job that was previously created (this example uses the job Remove Old Data). From the right mouse menu, select the Start Job option. The job starts immediately.

6. Right-click the job. From the right mouse menu, select the Refresh Job option. This step updates the status of the job. (Note: Status information is *not* refreshed automatically.)

7. Review the Last Run Status column in the result pane (see Figure 12.7) to determine whether the job ran successfully. For this example, you also can see that this job was successfully executed by reviewing the email message and the Windows NT event log (see Figures 12.8 and 12.9).

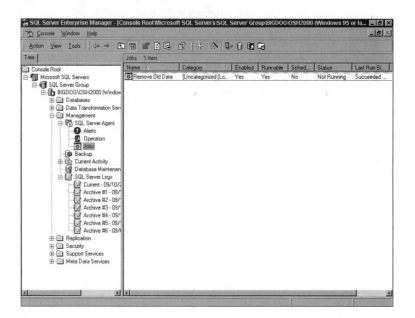

FIGURE 12.7 Last run status.

FIGURE 12.8 Email notification.

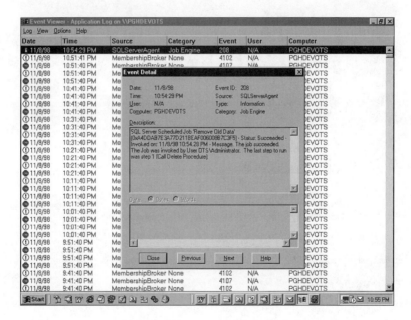

FIGURE 12.9 Event log notification.

Job Steps

Job steps control flow logic such as the following: If job 1 successfully completes, run job 2; otherwise, skip job 2 and run job 3. A more realistic example of job steps is the loading of data into a data warehouse. Figure 12.10 graphically represents an example of the steps involved in loading a data warehouse on a scheduled basis.

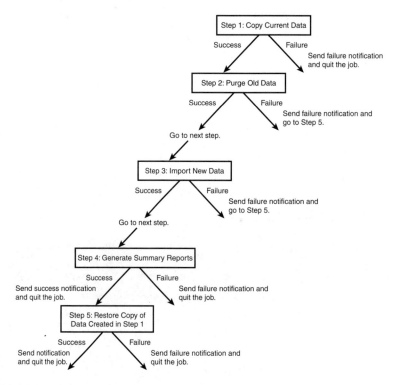

FIGURE 12.10 Job step diagram.

As you can see, a step can be dependent upon the success or failure of another step. If a step fails, a corresponding routine is called to handle failure.

A job step can be defined to take one of the following actions:

- Quit the job
- Go to the next step
- Go to step N

Figure 12.11 provides sample job steps that manage the process defined in Figure 12.10.

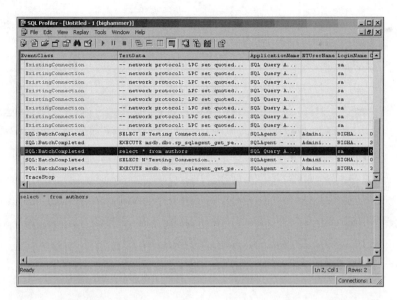

FIGURE 12.11   Sample job steps.

See the section "Creating and Managing Jobs" earlier in this chapter for information on implementing job steps.

Active Scripting Jobs

Active Scripting Jobs is new with SQL Server 2000. This feature allows you to extend a job through scripting. Active scripts can be written in VBScript or JScript.

A simple example of an active script job is one that generates a schema for all the tables in the pubs database. The following script generates the tables (this example uses VBScript with SQL DMO; see Chapter 26, "Using SQL-DMO," for more information on SQL DMO).

```
Set objServer = CreateObject("SQLDMO.SQLServer")objServer.Connect
➥".","sa"For Each objTable in objServer.Databases("pubs").Tables
➥  objTable.Script, "c:\temp\" & objTable.Name & ".
➥sql"NextobjServer.Disconnect
Set objServer = nothing
```

To schedule an active script, perform the following steps:

1. Follow steps 1 through 4 in the "Creating and Managing Jobs" section. After step 4, the New Job Properties dialog box appears.

2. From the Edit Job Step dialog box (see Figure 12.12), enter the following information:

   - **Step Name**—The name of the step. This example uses generate schema for the Step Name option.

   - **Type**—The type of step. This example uses Active Script.

   - **Language**—The type of language. This example uses Visual Basic Script.

   - **Command**—The code that is executed.

3. Click the OK button to save the job step.

4. Enter any additional information such as scheduling and notification.

5. Run the job. This will generate the schema scripts to c:\temp. Each table will have a corresponding .SQL file. Figure 12.13 contains an example of the output from this example.

NOTE

A great feature of active scripting is that it can use objects created in other languages. For example, an object can be created in Visual Basic (or another language that creates ActiveX objects) and be implemented in VBScript or JScript.

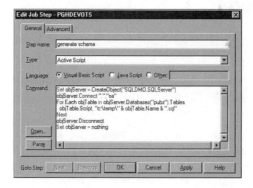

FIGURE 12.12   Active scripting example.

Extending Jobs

In the "Creating and Managing Jobs" section, you learned how to schedule a job and how to email an operator when the job is complete. The current section builds on what you learned earlier. For this example, assume that you want to schedule the same job, but you want the email message to contain the number of rows deleted by the stored procedure.

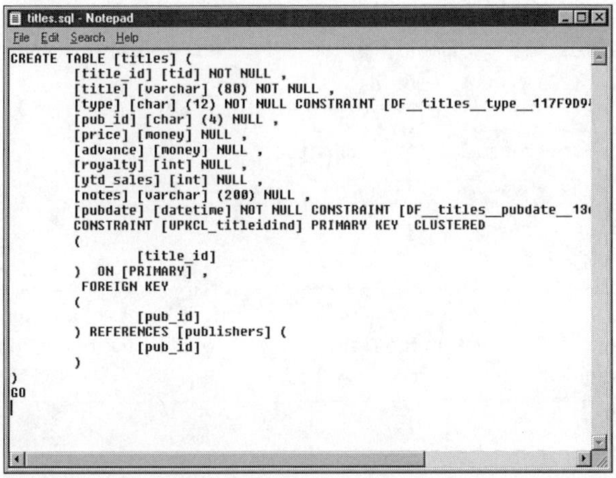

FIGURE 12.13 Sample output from the active script example.

No problem! However, you *do* have to shift the email notification logic to the stored procedure rather than leave it with the Job Scheduler. The Job Scheduler can only send a success or failure email message; the scheduler cannot return the number of rows deleted, updated, and so on.

To send an email message that contains the number of rows deleted, you must make a few modifications to the del_remove_old_data stored procedure. The procedure is enhanced by calling the xp_sendmail extended stored procedure. The xp_sendmail command enables you to email a message that contains the number of rows deleted.

The following stored procedure contains the necessary modifications:

```
CREATE PROCEDURE del_remove_old_data AS
declare @rows_deleted int
declare @e_mail_message varchar(255)

/* remove transactions that are 7 or more days old */
DELETE
FROM transaction_control
WHERE DATEDIFF(dd,transaction_date,getdate()) > = 7

/* store number of rows deleted to a variable */
SELECT @rows_deleted = @@rowcount
```

```
/* build message */
SELECT @e_mail_message = 'Numbers of rows removed by del_remove_old_data = ' +
 CONVERT(varchar(20),@rows_deleted)

/* e-mail the results back to the operator */
EXEC master..xp_sendmail 'orryn sledge',  @e_mail_message
```

> **NOTE**
>
> The sample procedure references a fictitious table named `transaction_control`. This table is used to illustrate the concept. In the real world, you could apply this example to any table that is purged or achieved on a scheduled basis.

> **NOTE**
>
> Whenever you call an extended stored procedure, you should include the master database in the statement (as in `master..xp_sendmail`). Otherwise, you must be in the master database to run an extended stored procedure.

When the Job Scheduler executes the `del_remove_old_data` stored procedure, the number of rows deleted is included in the email message (see Figure 12.14).

FIGURE 12.14   An email message stating the number of rows deleted.

Alerts

The *Alert Manager* enables you to define alerts that are executed automatically on the occurrence of an event. When the alert is executed, an operator can be notified by email or pager. An alert also can execute additional jobs, such as calling another Transact-SQL command or calling an external program in the form of a .BAT, .EXE, or .CMD file. These features enable a DBA to be more proactive to conditions that require attention.

With the Alert Manager, you can create three types of alerts: event alerts, performance condition alerts, and custom alerts.

Following are examples of event alerts:

- Database out of space
- SQL Server was abnormally terminated
- Database is corrupted
- Table is corrupted

Following are examples of performance condition alerts:

- Transaction log almost full
- Number of merge conflicts exceeds an user-defined threshold

Following are examples of custom alerts:

- Low inventory
- Aborted download

Event Alerts

Now that you have an understanding of the different types of alerts that can be managed, this section runs through a simple example of how to configure the Alert Manager for an event alert. For this example, assume that you want to define an alert that notifies an operator by email when the log file for the pubs database is full.

NOTE

SQL Server Agent must be running for the Alert Manager to work.

To create a sample alert that notifies an operator through email, follow these steps:

1. From the SQL Server Enterprise Manager, click the plus (+) sign next to the server that will execute the job.

2. Click the plus (+) sign next to the Management folder.

3. Click the plus (+) sign next to the SQL Server Agent.

4. Right-click the Alert icon. From the right mouse menu, select the New Alert option. The New Alert Properties dialog box appears.

5. From the New Job Properties dialog box, select the General tab. From the General tab (see Figure 12.15), enter the following information:

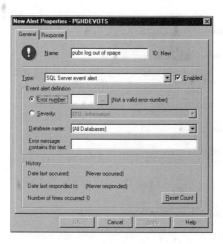

FIGURE 12.15   The New Job Properties dialog box—event alert example.

- **Name**—User-defined alert name. This example uses `pubs log out of space`.

- **Type**—The type of alert. This example uses SQL Server event alert.

- **Event Alert Definition**—The error number or severity of the alert. Additionally, a specific database and error message text can be defined.

6. To enable an event alert definition for a specific error number, click the Error Number radio button. Next, click the Manage Error Messages button next to the Error Number field in the Event Alert Definition section of the New Alert Properties dialog box. The Manage SQL Server Messages dialog box appears (see Figure 12.16).

7. From the Manage SQL Server Messages dialog box, you can find, add, delete, and edit error messages. For example, the following message is returned when the pubs log is full:

```
Server: Msg 9002, Level 17, State 2
The log file for database 'pubs' is full. Back up the transaction
➥log for the database to free up some log space.
```

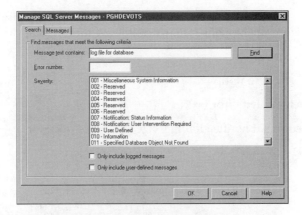

FIGURE 12.16   Manage SQL Server Messages dialog box.

To find the corresponding error number for an error message, enter the following in the Message Text Contains section of the dialog box:

```
log file for database
```

Click the Find button to list all matching error messages (see Figure 12.17).

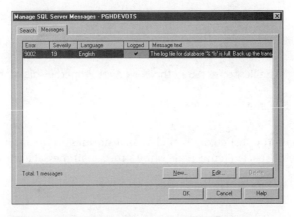

FIGURE 12.17   Finding an error message.

8. You want to base your alert on error number 9002. Highlight the row that contains error number 9002 and click the OK button. The New Alert Properties dialog box reappears, showing the selected error number.

9. Select the database name. For this example, use the pubs database.

10. From the New Alert Properties dialog box, select the Response tab (see Figure 12.18). From the Response tab, the following information can be entered:

    - Execute job

    - Operator to notify

    - Include alert error text in

    - Additional notification message to send to operator

    - Delay between responses for a recurring alert

FIGURE 12.18   The Response tab in the New Alert Properties dialog box.

11. Click the OK button to save the new alert.

Congratulations! You just created an alert that notifies an operator when the pubs database is out of space. Figure 12.19 shows the email message the operator receives in this of case.

NOTE

SQL Server ships with several demo alerts. To view, modify, or enable these alerts from the Enterprise Manager, go to the Alerts section of the SQL Server Agent folder.

FIGURE 12.19   The email notification sent to the operator when the *pubs* database log is out of space.

Performance Condition Alerts

Any type of alert that can be created in the Performance Monitor can be implemented as a performance condition alert through the Alert Manager. A performance condition alert can be automatically triggered when a condition goes above or falls below a predefined threshold. In turn, the alert can perform an action such as emailing or paging an operator or executing a job. Performance condition alerts are typically used to proactively prevent problems. For example, if a database's transaction log is rapidly filling up, a performance condition alert can notify SQL Server to execute a job such as backing up the transaction log.

To illustrate how performance condition alerts are processed, the following steps build an alert that notifies an operator when the pubs transaction log is more than 70% full. The performance condition alert also backs up the transaction log.

1. From the SQL Server Enterprise Manager, click the plus (+) sign next to the server that will execute the performance condition alert.

2. Click the plus (+) sign next to the Management folder.

3. Click the plus (+) sign next to the SQL Server Agent.

4. Right-click the Alert icon. From the right mouse menu, select the New Alert option. The New Alert Properties dialog box appears.

5. From the New Alert Properties dialog box, select the General tab. From the General tab, enter the following information (see Figure 12.20).

- **Name**—User-defined alert name. This example uses `pubs transaction log almost full`.

- **Type**—The type of alert. This example uses SQL Server performance condition alert.

- **Object**—The Windows NT Performance Monitor object. This example uses SQLServer:Databases.

- **Counter**—The Windows NT Performance Monitor counter. This example uses Percent Log Used.

- **Instance**—The instance of the counter specified. When working with the Percent Log Used counter, the instance is the database log tracked by the counter. This example uses pubs.

- **Alert if counter**—The threshold for the condition. Alerts can occur if they are below, equal to, or above a specified value. This example uses rises above.

- **Value**—The threshold limit for the alert. This example uses `70` to specify a value above 70%.

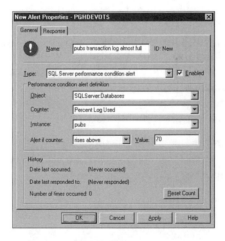

FIGURE 12.20   The New Alert Properties dialog box—performance condition alert example.

6. From the New Alert Properties dialog box, select the Response tab. The purpose of this tab is to specify the action that will take place when the alert is triggered. For this example, we want the following two actions to take place:

   - Execute a job that automatically backs up the transaction log. By backing up the transaction log at the 70% full interval, we increase the amount of free space available to the transaction log.

- Notify an operator by email. When the log is 70% full, an operator will be notified via email that the log exceeded the threshold defined for the alert and that the log was automatically backed up.

From the Response tab, select the Execute Job check box. From the Execute Job pick list, select the (New Job) option. The New Job Properties dialog box appears.

7. From the New Job Properties dialog box, enter the name of the job. This example uses `backup pubs transaction log` (see Figure 12.21). Click the Steps tab.

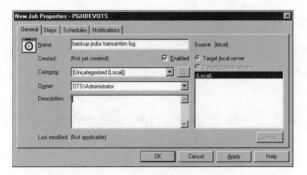

FIGURE 12.21   The General tab on the New Job Properties dialog box.

8. From the Steps tab of the New Job Properties dialog box, click the New button. The New Job Step dialog box appears.

9. From the New Job Step dialog box, enter the following information (see Figure 12.22).

- **Step name**—The name of the step. This example uses `backup transaction log`.

- **Type**—The step type. This examples uses Transact-SQL Script (TSQL).

- **Database**—The name of the database from which the job step is run. This example uses pubs.

- **Command**—The command to execute. This example uses the following command to back up the pubs transaction log to a backup file named `D:\Program Files\Microsoft SQL Server\MSSQL$OS2000\BACKUP \pubs_log_backup.bak`:

```
backup log pubs to DISK =
'D:\Program Files\Microsoft SQL Server\MSSQL$OS2000\BACKUP
\pubs_log_backup.bak'
```

Click the OK button. The New Job Properties dialog box reappears.

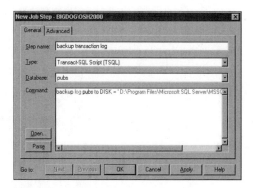

FIGURE 12.22   New Job Step dialog box.

   10. From the New Job Properties dialog box, click the OK button. The New Alert
       Properties dialog box reappears with the name of the job created in the previ-
       ous step (see Figure 12.23).

FIGURE 12.23   New Job Properties dialog box—Response tab with job information.

   11. To notify an operator by email, click the email check box for the name of the
       operator. For this example, Orryn Sledge is selected to receive email
       notification.

This step completes the performance condition alert example. Figure 12.24 shows
the completed performance condition alert. Figure 12.25 shows the email message
an operator would receive when this alert is triggered.

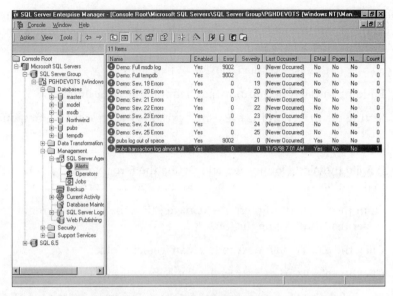

FIGURE 12.24   Completed performance condition alert.

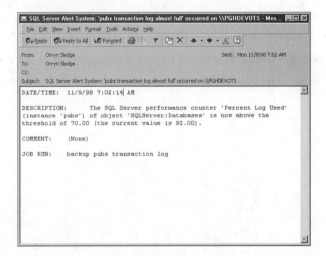

FIGURE 12.25   Sample email message when the alert is triggered.

Custom Alerts

In addition to handling SQL Server errors and thresholds, you can use the Alert Manager to alert operators to predefined conditions. Suppose that you own a used car dealership and you want to be alerted by email whenever the number of cars on the lot is below 20.

Assume that the number of cars on your lot can be determined by counting the number of records in a table named cars. Also assume that each time a car is sold, it is deleted from the cars table.

The creation of this type of alert consists of two steps:

1. Building the alert notification and defining the error number

2. Setting the trigger on the event that executes the error that corresponds to the alert

Step 1: Build the Alert Notification and Define the Error Number   Follow these steps to define a custom error number and message that corresponds to the alert:

1. From the SQL Server Enterprise Manager, click the plus (+) sign next to the server that will execute the job.

2. Click the plus (+) sign next to the Management folder.

3. Click the plus (+) sign next to the SQL Server Agent.

4. Right-click the Alert icon. From the right mouse menu, select the New Alert option. The New Alert Properties dialog box appears.

5. From the New Job Properties dialog box, select the General tab. From the General tab (see Figure 12.26), enter the following information:

    • **Name**—User-defined alert name. This example uses cars on hand < 20.

    • **Type**—The type of alert. This example uses SQL Server event alert.

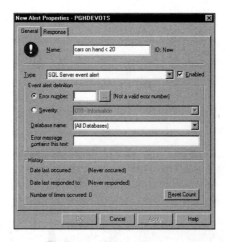

FIGURE 12.26   Custom alert example.

6. Left-click the Error Number radio button. Click the Manage Error Messages button next to the Error Number field. The Manage SQL Server Messages dialog box appears.

7. From the Manage SQL Server Messages dialog box, select the Messages tab and click the New button. The New SQL Server Message dialog box appears (see Figure 12.27).

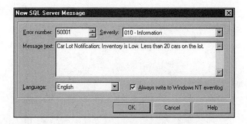

FIGURE 12.27   The New SQL Server Message dialog box.

8. From the New SQL Server Message dialog box, enter the following information:

   • **Error Number**—This example uses `50001` for an error number.

   • **Message Text**—This example uses `Car Lot Notification: Inventory is Low. Less than 20 cars on the lot.`

   • **Always Write to Windows NT Eventlog**—Select this option to write the alert to the Windows NT Eventlog; otherwise, the Alert Manager cannot recognize the event.

9. Click the OK button to save the alert. The Manage SQL Server Messages dialog box reappears.

10. From the Manage SQL Server Messages dialog box, click the OK button. The New Alert Properties dialog box reappears with the error number from step 8.

11. Select the Response tab from the New Alert Properties dialog box. From this tab, enter an operator to notify and a notification message (see Figure 12.28).

12. Click the OK button to save the alert.

Step 2: Set Up the Event That Executes the Error   Every time a car is sold, assume that it is deleted from the cars table. This arrangement enables you to use a trigger that checks whether the number of cars on hand is below 20. (Remember that triggers are automatically executed when a DELETE, UPDATE, or INSERT event occurs.)

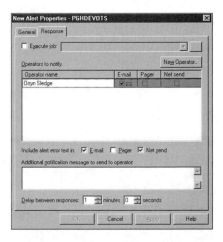

FIGURE 12.28 The Response tab in the New Alert Properties dialog box.

NOTE

The following is the table schema used for this example:

```
create table cars
(car_id int identity primary key,
car_description varchar(35))
```

The following code creates a trigger that automatically issues error number 50001 when fewer than 20 cars are on the lot. In turn, the SQL Server Agent detects error 50001 and automatically sends an email message to the operator.

```
/* DELETE Trigger Example */
CREATE TRIGGER trg_delete_cars ON dbo.cars
FOR DELETE
AS
/* declare variables */
declare @car_count int

/* count the number of cars on hand */
SELECT @car_count = COUNT(*)
FROM cars

/* If quantity is less than < 20 */
/* issue error 50001 (user defined error message).  This will */
/* fire an alert which will notify an operator */
```

```
IF @car_count < 20
  BEGIN
    /* RAISERROR parameter explanation: */
    /* 50001 = low inventory message */
    /* 16 = severity level (miscellaneous user error) */
    /* -1 = error state */
    RAISERROR(50001,16,-1)
  END
```

Now the low inventory alert is automatically executed whenever the number of cars on hand falls below 20. Figure 12.29 shows the email message that an operator receives when this alert is triggered.

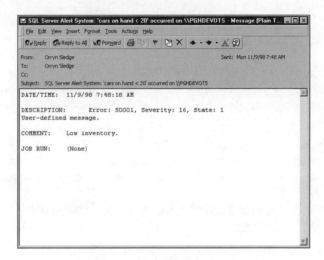

FIGURE 12.29   The low inventory email message.

Database Maintenance Plan Wizard

The Database Maintenance Plan Wizard automates many of the common jobs a DBA normally performs. Before this wizard was developed, many DBA jobs were script based. With this wizard, however, you can now graphically automate backups, DBCC commands, and other administrative functions. A nice feature of the Database Maintenance Plan Wizard is that it can email results to an operator.

The following steps explain how to use the Database Maintenance Plan Wizard:

1. From the SQL Server Enterprise Manager, click the Run a Wizard toolbar button. The Select Wizard dialog box appears (see Figure 12.30).

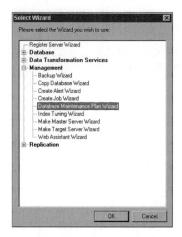

FIGURE 12.30   The Select Wizard dialog box.

2. From the Select Wizard dialog box, Click the plus (+) sign next to the Management topic. Click the Database Maintenance Plan Wizard and click the OK button. The Database Maintenance Plan Wizard appears.

3. From the Database Maintenance Plan Wizard dialog box, click the Next button to continue with this operation. The Select Databases dialog box appears. Select the appropriate database (see Figure 12.31) and click the Next button to continue. The Update Data Optimization Information dialog box appears.

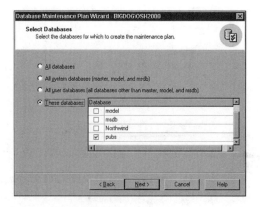

FIGURE 12.31   The Select Databases dialog box.

NOTE

Do not forget to include the following system databases when using the Database Maintenance Plan Wizard to automate backups and DBCC jobs: `master`, `model`, `msdb`, and `distribution` (you do not need to include `tempdb` in your backup plan). These system databases are actual databases, just as the `pubs` database or any other database used to store information is a database. It is just as important to back up these databases as it is for any other database.

4. From the Update Data Optimization Information dialog box (see Figure 12.32), select the appropriate responses for the following: Reorganize Data and Index Pages, Update Statistics Used by Query Optimizer, Removed Unused Space from Database Files, and Schedule options. Following are explanations of the Data Optimization options:

   - **Reorganize Data and Index Pages**—Selecting this option is the equivalent of using the `DBCC DBREINDEX` command (see Appendix C, "SQL Server Resources," for more information on `DBCC DBREINDEX`). This option rebuilds all indexes associated with all tables in the selected database (see Chapter 18, "Understanding Indexes," and Chapter 19, "Query Optimization," for more information). Using this option might reduce page splitting and improve data modification performance. Additionally, the Reorganize Pages with the Original Amount of Free Space and Change Free Space Per Page Percentage To radio buttons control the fill factor level.

   - **Update Statistics Used by the Query Optimizer**—Selecting this option is the equivalent of using the `UPDATE STATISTICS` command (see Chapters 18 and 19 for more information).

   - **Remove Unused Space from Database Files**—Selecting this will shrink the database files to the specified size. Selecting this option is the equivalent of using the `DBCC SHRINKDATABSE` command (see Appendix B, "DBCC Commands," for more information).

5. Click the Next button to continue. The Database Integrity Check dialog box appears.

6. From the Database Integrity Check dialog box (see Figure 12.33), select the appropriate Check Database Integrity, Perform Tests Before Doing Backups, Schedule options. Explanations of the Data Integrity Check options follow:

   - **Check Database Integrity**—This option checks all data pages and tables in the database for database errors. If the Include Indexes radio button is selected, it is the equivalent of using `DBCC CHECKDB` (see Appendix B for more information on `DBCC CHECKDB`). If the Exclude

Indexes radio button is selected, it is the equivalent of using DBCC
CHECKDB with the NOINDEX option.

- **Perform Tests Before Doing Backups**—Executes the checks before
running the backup.

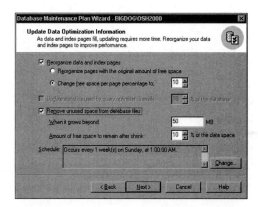

FIGURE 12.32   Update Data Optimization Information dialog box.

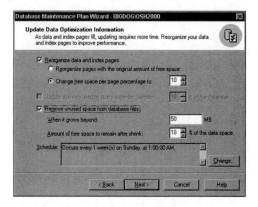

FIGURE 12.33   Database Integrity Check dialog box.

NOTE

The Database Integrity Check option checks text, ntext (Unicode data), and image types.
Prior to version 7.0, SQL Server required a separate process to check these datatypes.

7. Click the Next button to continue. The Specify the Database Backup Plan
dialog box appears.

8. From the Specify the Database Backup Plan dialog box (see Figure 12.34), select the appropriate backup and scheduling options. Click the Next button to continue.

If you are storing your backup to disk, the Specify Backup Disk Directory dialog box appears (see Figure 12.35). Enter the appropriate disk backup information and click the Next button. The Specify the Transaction Log Backup Plan dialog box appears.

TIP

As a general rule, I recommend backing up all databases (don't forget master, msdb, model, and distribution) on a nightly basis. See Chapter 10 for more information.

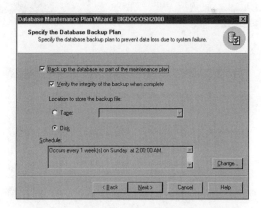

FIGURE 12.34   The Specify the Database Backup Plan dialog box.

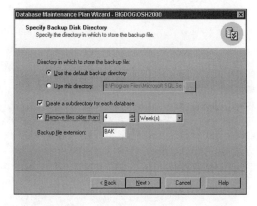

FIGURE 12.35   The Specify Backup Disk Directory dialog box.

9. From the Specify the Transaction Log Backup Plan dialog box (see Figure
   12.36), select the appropriate backup and scheduling options. Click the Next
   button to continue.

   If you are storing your transaction log backup to disk, the Specify Transaction
   Log Backup Disk Directory dialog box appears (see Figure 12.37). Enter the
   appropriate disk backup information and click the Next button to continue.

TIP

As a general rule, I recommend backing up the transaction log on a daily basis. I recommend
backing up the transaction log more frequently (several times a day, for example, every hour)
for databases that are subject to constant data modifications. The following databases do not
need their transaction log backed up: master, model, msdb, and distribution. Additionally,
any database that has the database option recovery model = simple does not need its
transaction log backed up. See Chapter 8, "Managing Databases," and Chapter 10 for more
information.

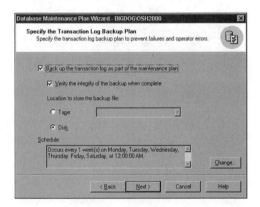

FIGURE 12.36   The Specify the Transaction Log Backup Plan dialog box.

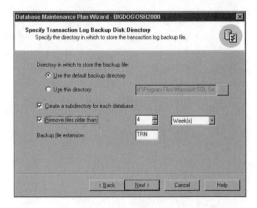

FIGURE 12.37   The Specify Transaction Log Backup Disk Directory dialog box.

10. From the Reports to Generate dialog box (see Figure 12.38), select the appropriate Write Report to a Text File in Directory and Send E-mail Report to Operator options. Click the Next button to continue. The Maintenance Plan History dialog box appears.

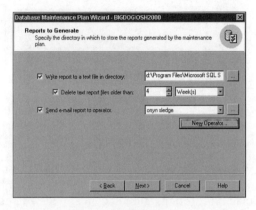

FIGURE 12.38   The Reports to Generate dialog box.

11. From the Maintenance Plan History dialog box (see Figure 12.39), select the appropriate options to record maintenance activities. Click the Next button to continue. The Completing the Database Maintenance Plan Wizard dialog box appears.

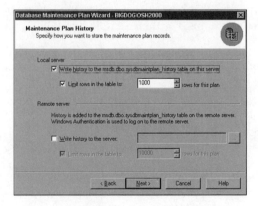

FIGURE 12.39   The Maintenance Plan History dialog box.

12. From the Completing the Database Maintenance Plan Wizard dialog box (see Figure 12.40), review the plan summary information. If the summary information is correct, click the Finish button to complete the job.

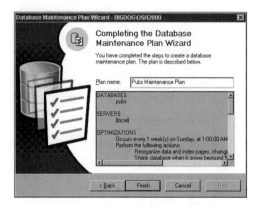

FIGURE 12.40   The Completing the Database Maintenance Plan Wizard dialog box.

Congratulations! You have completed the Database Administration Wizard job. If possible, I recommend testing the plan at this point. Doing so helps verify that your backup strategy, email notification, and job components are properly configured. Perform the following steps to run the new plan:

1. From the SQL Server Enterprise Manager, click the plus (+) sign next to the server that will execute the job.

2. Click the plus (+) sign next to the Management folder.

3. Click the plus (+) sign next to the SQL Server Agent.

4. From the expanded SQL Server Agent, click the Jobs icon. The Result pane displays a listing of jobs. For this example, the following jobs were created (see Figure 12.41):

   - DB Backup Job for DB Maintenance Plan 'Pubs Maintenance Plan'

   - Integrity Checks Job for DB Maintenance Plan 'Pubs Maintenance Plan'

   - Optimizations Job for DB Maintenance Plan 'Pubs Maintenance Plan'

   - Transaction Log Backup Job for DB Maintenance Plan 'Pubs Maintenance Plan'

5. From the right pane, right-click each job in the list. From the right mouse menu, select the Start menu option (see Figure 12.42) to start the job. Note: For this example, run the DB Backup Job before running the Transaction Log Backup Job.

6. Right-click the job to refresh the status information. When the job is complete, check the Last Run Status. If the job successfully executed, the Last Run Status is Succeeded.

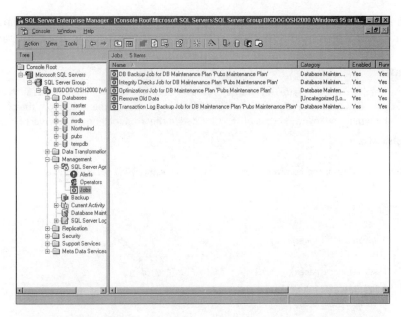

FIGURE 12.41   Listing of jobs.

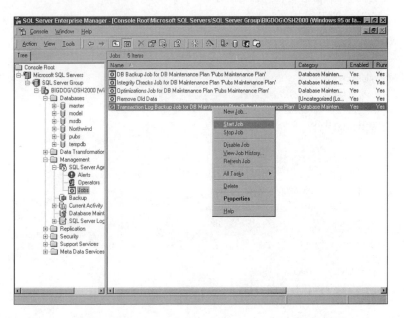

FIGURE 12.42   Starting a job.

If you need to modify the job, you can rerun the Database Maintenance Plan Wizard; or you can modify the job by double-clicking the job in the right pane.

NOTE

The Database Administrator Wizard uses `sqlmaint.exe` to execute common jobs such as backups, DBCC commands, and so on. In addition, you can run the utility from the command line by typing the following (this utility is located in the `binn` folder of SQL server):

sqlmaint.exe

Here is a listing of the command-line parameters available with `sqlmaint.exe`:

```
sqlmaint
[-?] |
  [-S server]
  [-U login_ID [-P password]]
  {
    [ -D database_name | -PlanName name | -PlanID guid ]
    [-Rpt text_file [-DelTxtRpt <time_period>] ]
    [-To operator_name]
    [-HtmlRpt html_file [-DelHtmlRpt <time_period>] ]
    [-RmUnusedSpace threshold_percent free_percent]
    [-CkDB | -CkDBNoIdx]
    [-CkAl | -CkAlNoIdx]
    [-CkTxtAl]
    [-CkCat]
    [-UpdSts]
    [-UpdOptiStats sample_percent]
    [-RebldIdx free_space]
    [-WriteHistory]
    [
      {-BkUpDB [backup_path] | -BkUpLog [backup_path] }
        {-BkUpMedia
          {DISK [ [-DelBkUps <time_period>]
             [-CrBkSubDir ] [ -UseDefDir ]]
          | TAPE
          }
        }
      [-BkUpOnlyIfClean]
      [-VrfyBackup]
    ]
  }
]
time_period> ::=
number[minutes | hours | days | weeks | months]
```

Automating Database Administration Tasks FAQ

The following section lists some commonly asked questions and answers about SQL Server 2000 tasks.

Q Does the UDPATE STATISTICS command need to be run on a frequent basis?

A No, the UPDATE STATISTICS command does not need to be run on a frequent basis. SQL Server 2000 automatically manages index statistics. If statistics are out-of-date, SQL Server will detect the problem and automatically update the statistics.

Q Does DBCC CHECKDB still need to run in version 2000?

A According to Microsoft, DBCC CHECKDB does not need to be run on a frequent basis. If you want to be overly cautious, it does not hurt anything to continue to run CHECKDB. The drawback to running CHECKDB is that object creation and modification statements (for example, adding a new column to an existing table) cannot be processed when CHECKDB is running. CHECKDB places shared locks on the objects in the database. These shared locks force object creation and modification statements to wait until CHECKDB is complete.

Q Which database contains job, alert, and operator information?

A The MSDB database contains job, alert, and operator information. The following tables store information used by jobs, alerts, and operators: sysjobs, sysjob-schedules, sysalerts, and sysoperators.

Q Are there any commands that the Database Maintenance Plan Wizard does not include that should be part of a scheduled maintenance plan?

A Yes, the wizard does not include the DBCC CHECKFILEGROUP command (see Appendix C for more information). This command should be scheduled if the database contains file groups.

Q What are multiserver jobs?

A Multiserver jobs are jobs that can be built once and run on multiple servers. This feature is great for DBAs! For example, a backup job can be created on one server and automatically run on other servers.

Summary

The following are the key points to keep in mind when you want to automate database administration tasks.

- SQL Server Agent must be running so that alerts and jobs can be processed.

- Use the Job Scheduler to automate common DBA jobs such as backing up a database, backing up a transaction log, running DBCC commands, and importing/exporting data.

- Jobs can contain one or more steps and can have step dependencies.

- Jobs can contain Transact-SQL commands, VBScript, JScript, and scripts built in other languages.

- Jobs can execute external .BAT, .EXE, and .CMD files.

- Use the Alert Manager to automatically notify an operator of problems, such as a database errors or user-defined error messages.

- The Job Scheduler, Alert Manager, and Database Maintenance Plan Wizard can notify an operator through email or a pager.

PART VI

Importing and
Exporting Data

IN THIS PART

13 Data Transformation Services

14 Using BCP and Bulk Insert

13

Data Transformation Services

by Mark Spenik

IN THIS CHAPTER

- DTS and the Data Warehouse
- DTS and OLE DB/ODBC
- The DTS Framework
- Using the DTS Wizard
- Using the DTS Designer
- What Are Workflow and Batch Processing?
- Using DTS Packages
- Data Transformation Services FAQ

Just about everyone who has interacted with SQL Server in the past has had to either import data into or export data out of it. This task has proven to be cumbersome and complex. BCP, SQL server's tried-and-true command-line data pump has probably caused a headache or two for most DBAs. Whenever the need arises to import a large amount of information, most people once again look to the help files to figure out how to construct the dreaded format file or try and find a developer to write some custom Visual Basic code and stored procedures to import and transform the data.

Those days are over: SQL Server 7.0 introduced the *Data Transformation Services (DTS)* that has been enhanced in SQL 2000. DTS is a set of tools and interfaces that make it simple to import, export, and transform information from any source to any destination that supports OLE DB. This means that you can load and extract not only SQL Server data, but also Oracle, DB2, Informix, text files, or any data source for which you have OLE DB or ODBC drivers. DTS can be thought of as a generic data pump that happens to work with SQL Server very well. Its functionality and robustness are a far cry from the feature set of the limited BCP. Some new features added to SQL Server 2000 include new custom tasks, global variables between packages, and a multiphase data pump.

In this chapter, we discuss the components that make up the DTS framework and how to use DTS for workflow, as well as look at some DTS examples.

DTS and the Data Warehouse

Most new database projects follow the same pattern. We are developing this new system to take the place of an older one. We currently have a decade or so of information stored in system A. When we go live with system B, we need to leave all our previously collected information intact. So, a fair amount of time is spent designing the database schema and taking into account that we will need to preserve the information as it exists now. A plan of action usually develops for how to extract, transform, move, and finally load this information from system A to system B. The data load is usually done once, and the old machine (whatever it might be) is then turned off and sold for scrap. Because this is usually done only once, the requirements for this conversion process could be less robust: "Just get it there" might be the main idea. Speed and ease of use rarely play a part in the design of a one-time import.

In contrast, data warehousing involves continuously and periodically loading information from one or many heterogeneous data sources. The load should be expected to be efficient and accurate, but not take an extremely large amount of time. It could be as simple as a direct copy of the information, or it could involve complicated validations or summarization. Getting data into a warehouse or smaller data marts usually involve the following steps:

1. Connecting to the external data sources directly

2. Selecting or extracting the desired information

3. Performing any transformations, filling in missing values, aggregating data, and so on

4. Moving the data from the source machine to the destination system

5. Loading the data into the destination tables

DTS provides all these required features, as well as the ability to schedule these operations regularly and share the information about these operations with other tools by storing them in the Microsoft Meta Data Services (repository).

DTS and OLE DB/ODBC

The DTS framework is built solidly around Microsoft's OLE DB, which is a set of APIs that provide a common interface to many types of heterogeneous data sources. In conjunction with OLE DB, DTS can help you communicate with any data source for which you have either an OLE DB or ODBC driver. SQL 2000 provides native OLE DB drivers for SQL Server, Oracle, Excel, Access, ASCII text files, DTS Packages, and ODBC data sources. ODBC drivers are widely available for most data sources.

By integrating OLE DB with ODBC, Microsoft has positioned DTS as an open tool for importing or exporting data across an organization.

> **NOTE**
>
> DTS is so flexible that the data source and data destination do not have to include SQL Server. You could use DTS to extract data from a DB2 database to an Oracle database. I actually worked with a company that purchased SQL Server just to use DTS because it was much cheaper then other competing data transformation products.

Text files still remain one of the most widely used transit mechanisms for data to and from various systems. SQL Server 2000 provides you with OLE DB Drivers that allow you to import and export text files. So, if you can get your data into a text file, you can usually move it from any database system regardless of the driver support. Later in this chapter, you will see what features are available in DTS that help with managing text file imports and exports.

The DTS Framework

DTS introduces a set of new database objects and tools to help with the movement of information from place to place. Simple wizards provide the typical question-and-answer approach to importing or exporting data. The DTS Designer gives more knowledgeable users the ability to create more complex transformations that utilize many tables and advanced workflow techniques. DTS provides you the access to the underlying transformation engine via COM objects. This allows you to build complete import, export, or transformation applications using any Component Object Model (COM) enabled environment such as Visual Basic, a Windows scripting host, or Active Server Pages. You can also save DTS packages as Visual Basic code to incorporate in your Visual Basic programs.

DTS provides the following services:

- The Import and Export Wizards allow you to build simple table imports, exports, or transforms quickly and easily.

- The DTS Designer allows you to build more advanced transformations that incorporate multiple tables and sophisticated workflow operations.

- DTS COM objects are extensible components for integrating DTS functionality into external programs or scripts.

The services provide access to a set of underlying objects that complete the DTS framework. The top-level encompassing object is called a *package*. Within a DTS package are connections, steps, tasks, and global variables. The DTS Data Pump is the real workhorse of the framework: This is where the bulk of the information is transferred. Let's look at each of these DTS objects in detail.

Packages

Packages are self-contained definitions of the tasks that need to be performed as part of a transformation. You can create a package by using any of the three services described in the preceding section. A package can be stored as a file in the operating system, Visual Basic file, shared in the Microsoft Meta Data Services (Repository) or within the msdb database on the server. You can access the packages that are stored in the latter two places by selecting the Data Transformation Services folder from the Enterprise Manager as illustrated in Figure 13.1.

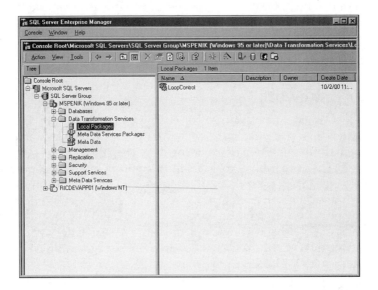

FIGURE 13.1   The Data Transformation Services folder.

You can execute packages directly from Enterprise Manager, from the command line, from a custom application, from another package, or from a script. Security can be assigned on a per-package basis to ensure that only the desired individuals do certain operations.

Each package can contain multiple steps. One step might be to import a product line table. After the successful completion of that step, we might want to import the product table or run some additional SQL scripts to validate the information. If the previous step had failed, we might have wanted to alert the database operator via a simple email message. These operations can be executed conditionally based on previous steps. These features of the DTS package contribute to robust workflow functionality. DTS packages can execute other DTS packages, and DTS packages can be executed asynchronously.

The following DTS package operations are available to you from within the Enterprise Manager:

- Generating new packages using the DTS Wizard

- Creating a new package from scratch using the DTS Designer

- Viewing, editing, and executing packages stored in the local server or the Microsoft Meta Data Services

- Loading packages stored in the file system into the DTS Designer

Connections

Connections store the information about the source and destination data stores—either actual database systems or flat files. The connection object contains data such as security credentials, file locations, and data formats. Connections are shared or pooled in order to operate efficiently during the transformation operations.

Tasks

Tasks are the operations that need to be performed within the package. A task can be

ActiveX script	SQL script
Transfer SQL objects	Bulk insert
Win32 executable	Fata driven query
Mail message	Database transformation
Execute package	Transfer error messages
Transfer master stored procedures	Transfer jobs
Transfer logins	Transfer databases
Dynamic properties	File transfer protocol
Message queue	

The following are some examples of tasks:

- **ActiveX scripts**—A script that instantiates an ActiveX server that opens a database and dumps records to a text file for import by another step in the package.

- **SQL scripts**—A simple or complex piece of T-SQL script that, for example, truncates a table prior to the import or performs a backup of the current table before a new import.

- **Transfer SQL Server Objects**—Allows you to copy schema objects such as tables, views, constraints, or indexes from a source server to a destination.

- **Bulk Insert**—The fastest method for importing text files into SQL Server. This speed comes at a price, no data validations or transformations might be performed. This feature is essentially a graphical version of bcp.

- **Execute Process**—An external process that can be executed as part of the package. This could, for example, run another DTS package.

- **Data Driven Query**—An advanced type of task where each data row needs to be sent to parameterized stored procedures for processing. A data driven query might be used to process incremental updates of a table into a data mart.

- **Send Mail**—A mail message to an operator that the weekly load of the customer table executed successfully.

- **Transform**—A set of procedural logic that needs to be performed on each row as it travels from the source to the destination. This can be as simple as a straight copy from source to destination, or it can involve a mapping from the characters M and F to the descriptions Male and Female.

- **Dynamic Properties**—Used to obtain values from outside the DTS package such as ini files, data files, DTS package global variable, and a query or environment variable.

- **Execute Package**—Allows you to run another DTS package.

- **File Transfer Protocol**—Allows you to copy files or directories using FTP.

- **Message Queue**—Allows you to use Microsoft Message queuing between DTS packages.

Steps

The object that coordinates the flow and execution of tasks is the DTS *Step* object. The Step object can be associated with a single task or no task. Step object's have *precedence constraints,* which determine the order in which a DTS task executes based on the outcome of other tasks. Step objects can have multiple precedence constraints. A precedence constraint has a source step (starting point) and a destination step (ending point). Each precedence constraint is represented by one of the following values:

- On Success—Executes a destination step only if the source step succeeds.

- On Failure—Executes a destination step only if the source step fails.

- On Completion—Executes the destination step regardless of success or failure.

A task will not execute unless all the conditions of the precedence constraints have been met. A task that does not have any precedence constraints can execute immediately up to the number of available threads for the package.

The DTS Data Pump

The DTS multiphase Data Pump is a COM component that is the real workhorse that performs the movements of the source data to the destination. It provides an extensible, scriptable interface for which complex data validation and transformations can be built. Transformations can incorporate any ActiveX scripting engine, such as VBScript, JScript, or PerlScript. These reusable scripts can combine multiple source columns into a single destination column. The Data Pump scripting facilities can invoke the services of any COM object that supports automation, such as ActiveX Data Objects (ADO).

Using the DTS Wizard

DTS supplies two wizards that allow a user to interactively define the tasks for a package: the Import Wizard and the Export Wizard. As with the other wizards in SQL 2000, you access the Import and Export Wizards by selecting Tools, Wizards. Alternatively, you can launch the wizards by right-clicking Data Transformations Packages and selecting New Import or New Export.

> **NOTE**
>
> The Import and Export Wizards are essentially the same, except for some textual elements. You are not restricted to either the source being SQL Server during an export or the destination being SQL Server on the import. Whenever you need to move data from one place to the other, you can select either option, import or export. Throughout the rest of the chapter, we refer to both of these wizards as the *DTS Wizard*. See Figure 13.2.

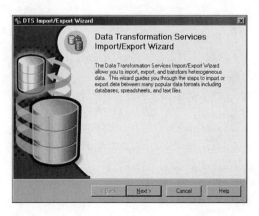

FIGURE 13.2   The DTS Wizard.

The DTS Wizard essentially helps the user build a package of simple steps based on Data Pump tasks. These tasks move information from any OLE DB or ODBC source to a destination. The number of steps it generates depends on the options that are selected and the number of tables transformed. For example, if the destination table did not previously exist, a separate SQL script step is created that automatically generates the table. Other subsequent steps actually move the data if the table creation step was a success.

The first phase of the wizard helps you define the connection to the source data. Next, you define the connection to the destination data and any transformations that need to take place between the two. Finally you are able to run the package, save it for later use, and even schedule it to run automatically.

A DTS Wizard Example

The following sections illustrate how to use the DTS Wizard to import a customer table that was previously dumped to text file from the authors table located in the SQL Server 2000 pubs database. The text file can be found on the CD that ships with book (newauthors.txt) or you can use the DTS Wizard to export the authors table to a text file. Each step of the wizard is described in detail in order for you to understand all the options.

Step 1: Making the Source Connection

When you start the wizard the first time, you are prompted for the data source. This is where the transformation will originate. In this example, we are using a text file on the hard drive. Select the Text OLE DB provider, and then enter the physical location for the file shown in Figure 13.3.

FIGURE 13.3   Selecting a data source in the DTS Wizard.

Each OLE DB provider operates differently and contains individual requirements. For example, if you were importing from an Oracle database, you would be prompted for a server name, login, and password. Some OLE DB providers support custom settings, in which case you can tweak these options by clicking the button labeled Advanced.

If the data source were a database containing multiple record sources, you would then be prompted to select one. You can choose to copy an entire table or the results of a SQL query, such as queries involving joins of multiple tables. Alternatively, you can choose to build a query using the Query Builder within the wizards. This allows users who are inexperienced with the SQL language to construct queries with familiar drag-and-drop operations.

Step 2: Determining File Format

The next wizard step relates to the text file data source. Here you find options regarding the format of the text file itself. You can select delimited or fixed field lengths. Also, there are options for the file type, record delimiter, and text qualifier. These are common format requirements of data in text files. A preview of the file contents is displayed near the bottom of the wizard to aid in the selection of these options as displayed in Figure 13.4.

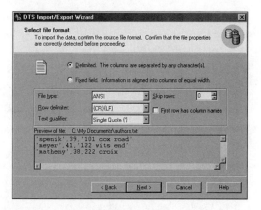

FIGURE 13.4   The DTS Wizard file format options.

Our text file does not have column names on the first row of the file: It uses a carriage return and line feeds separating each row, as well as text columns that are qualified by a single quote. We select these options and move on to the next step.

Step 3: Choosing the Column Delimiter

Step 3 involves options only required for the delimited text file data source. Here, you can select the character that separates columns in the file records. The most common options are provided; an entry field to provide a custom separator is also available. Figure 13.5 displays the column delimiter step.

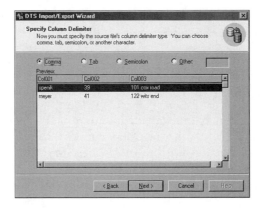

FIGURE 13.5   Selecting a column delimiter with the DTS Wizard.

Our example uses a comma separator. Suppose you used a separator that was not one of the radio button selections (for example, a single space). To use a space character as a separator, you simply type in a space in the field labeled Other, and the information in the file is then parsed to display the columns, using the delimiter you have chosen.

Step 4: Establishing the Destination Connection

At this wizard step, we are able to define the destination for the transfer. We are importing into SQL Server 2000, so we choose the SQL Server OLE DB provider. The requirements for this provider are displayed in Figure 13.6.

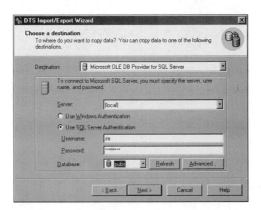

FIGURE 13.6   Choosing a destination in the DTS Wizard.

The server, username, and password are required to establish a connection to SQL Server. Also, the wizard needs to know what type of authentication scheme it should use to connect. The wizard needs to read schema information from the destination database, so these parameters are required for the wizard to proceed any further.

After the login credentials have been validated, a list of databases that the username has access to is displayed in the Database combo box. Select the database that will be the destination for your information.

TIP

If your destination database does not currently exist, you need not stop the wizard to create it. From the database drop-down, select the <new> option. Then, you will be prompted for a database name and initial sizes for the data and log. The database is created for you without interrupting the wizard.

The destination for this example is a database that is called pubs on the local server.

Step 5: Selecting Source and Destination Tables

This step allows you to select the source and the destination tables that receive the data. If the source were a database, such as SQL Server, Oracle, or Access, multiple tables would be listed here and you would select the desired ones to be copied or transformed. However, our source is a text file containing only one table, so this step is easy. The destination for this example is a table, called author1 in the pubs database, that is created during the import. This can be seen in Figure 13.7.

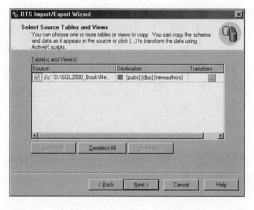

FIGURE 13.7   Mapping source to destination tables with the DTS Wizard.

If a simple copy is all that were required, we could proceed to the next step. But instead of a simple copy, we will perform a slight transformation on this table.

The author1 table in our text file has a column for the number of books in thousands sold. Before adding to the database, we want to convert the number to reflect the actual number, so we want to multiply by thousands. We will use a small bit of VBScript in a custom transformation to accomplish this.

Each table can have its own transformations applied to it. You will notice a small button to the right of each destination table in the list. This button will launch the Transform dialog box.

Step 6: Column Mappings and Transformations

The Transform dialog box allows you to specify which source columns map to which destination columns. It also allows you to select what operations are done to the destination table prior to the use of the data pump. The following options are supported on the destination table:

- **Create Destination Table**—If this option is selected, you can modify the CREATE TABLE statement to further customize the destination table without leaving the wizard. You can also choose to drop the table if it currently exists. Each of these options creates separate package steps.

- **Delete Rows in Destination Table**—This option generates a package step that truncates the table prior to performing the data pump task.

- **Append Rows to Destination Table**—This option creates no other tasks or steps besides the data pump task. This is the default.

For this example, the appropriate options are selected, as displayed in Figure 13.8.

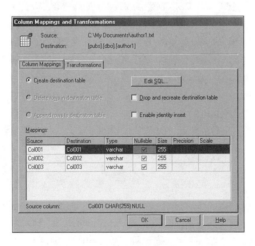

FIGURE 13.8   Column mappings in the DTS Wizard.

Below these options is a grid showing the default mappings of columns from the source to the destination. It is here that the user can ignore any source columns not required in the destination. Also, valid data conversion can be performed, such as converting a varchar(255) to a varchar(50).

We are planning to do our mappings with some ActiveX script, so we need to take a quick trip over to the Transformation tab to find more options, as shown in Figure 13.9.

FIGURE 13.9   Transformations in the DTS Wizard.

The default option for the wizard is to copy all mapped columns to the destination. The DTS Wizard generates a transformation script that handles this automatically. If your transformation requires anything outside the realm of a straight copy of data values (as ours does), you need to modify the ActiveX script here. From this page, you select the script engine that you want to use (for example, VBScript). There is also a button for selecting advanced options about how the Data Pump should handle data type conversions.

The script that this example uses is typical of some of the simple operations that can be accomplished with the VBScript language. Listing 13.1 is the script used to transform the Customer table.

LISTING 13.1   Customer Transform Script

```
'***********************************************************************
'  Visual Basic Transformation Script for customer table
'  Perform copy of most fields, and divide Contact name into
'     first name and last name columns'*********************************


'***********************************************************************
'  Visual Basic Transformation Script
```

LISTING 13.1   Continued

```
'  Copy each source column to the
'  destination column
'***********************************************************************

Function Main()
    DTSDestination("Col001") = DTSSource("Col001")
    DTSDestination("Col002") = DTSSource("Col002") * 1000
    DTSDestination("Col003") = DTSSource("Col003")
    Main = DTSTransformStat_OK
End Function
```

The source and destination are represented in script as two different collections of data. You can access the elements of the collection with the *collectionName*("*elementName*") syntax. Thus, the second field from the source text file is represented by the term DTSSource("Col002").

The bulk of the script is occupied with straight copies from source fields to the destination columns. It is not until we get down to the second column that any real interesting work is done.

The script in Listing 13.1 multiplies the value by 1000 before placing it in the database.

Step 7: Package Actions

On the next wizard page, displayed in Figure 13.10, you can select optional actions related to the current package. You can select to run the package now, and you can also choose to have the wizard publish the destination tables for replication.

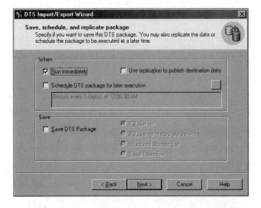

FIGURE 13.10   Running, saving, and scheduling transformations with the DTS Wizard.

If this is not a one-time import or export, you might want to run it again at another time. To accomplish this, select the option to save the resulting package to SQL Server.

After it is saved, this DTS package can be manually run later or scheduled to run at reoccurring intervals, similar to any other SQL Agent job. For more information on running and scheduling DTS packages, see the section "Running Packages from the Command Line" later in this chapter.

> **TIP**
>
> It is also convenient to use the wizard to interactively generate the basis of the package. After this is done, you can add more in-depth steps or tasks using the DTS Designer. De-select the Run Task option and select the Save option. After the package is saved, right-click the package and select Design Package. This launches the DTS Designer.

Step 8: Saving a Package

Using this wizard step, you can provide a name, a description, an owner password, and a location for the DTS package. It is always a good idea to be descriptive in your naming of database objects and DTS packages.

The Owner Password field allows you to secure this package. A secure package can only be viewed or modified if this password is provided. Secure packages can also be given an operator password, which enables you to execute the package, but still limits viewing or changing the package steps or tasks to only the owner. If you do not specify a password, the package remains open for any users to view, modify, or execute.

The last section of this page deals with the storage location for this package. You can choose to save the package locally or in the local storage of another SQL Server. The local DTS packages are held in the msdb database. You must choose the appropriate authentication scheme and provide a username and password for the destination server. Figure 13.11 illustrates this wizard step.

Step 9: Package Execution

A summary of the tasks to be performed is then presented. Pressing the Finish button causes the selected actions to be executed. If you are running the package now, a screen similar to that in Figure 13.12 is displayed.

Each package step attempts to execute in a logical order (that is, table creation precedes table loading). As each step completes (or fails), its status is displayed. If a step involving the transfer of data completes successfully, a record count is displayed within the Status column, as shown in the three customer records in the example.

FIGURE 13.11   The Save Package options in the DTS Wizard.

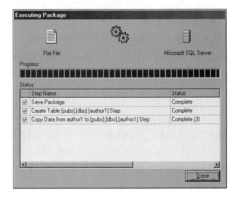

FIGURE 13.12   Running the package with the DTS Wizard.

If an error occurs during the execution of any step, you can view the error by double-clicking the individual step. Because later steps might be dependent on previous ones, early step failures can halt the execution of the package.

Using the DTS Designer

The DTS Designer is a graphical workspace for building sophisticated import, export, or transformation operations. Whereas the DTS Wizard is designed to handle most of your simple import or export needs, the DTS Designer picks up where the wizard leaves off by allowing you to define all your own tasks and set precedence constraints on the steps between these tasks.

You arrange source and destination data sources, along with other execution objects, in a fashion similar to a typical flowchart. Arrows connect these objects and form the tasks and steps of the package. These arrows provide the package with directional flow or conditional logic.

Creating a DTS Package and Adding Simple Workflow

To create a DTS package from the Microsoft SQL Server Enterprise Manager, perform the following:

1. Select the Data Transformation Services folder in the Enterprise Manager using a single mouse-click.

2. Right-click and select New Package from the pop-up menu; the DTS Designer, shown in Figure 13.13, appears.

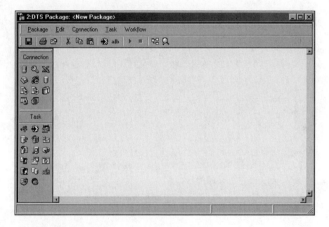

FIGURE 13.13   The DTS Designer.

The icons below the Task label, shown in Figure 13.13, are the available DTS tasks, which are discussed in detail in the Using DTS for Workflow white paper. The icons below the Data label, shown in Figure 13.13, are the available DTS connection objects. To add DTS tasks and simple workflow to the package, perform the following:

1. Add an ActiveX Script Task, by double-clicking the icon located in the upper-left corner below the Task label shown in Figure 13.13.

2. The ActiveX Script Task Properties dialog box appears. You can use the ActiveX Script Task Properties dialog box to write script to perform various functions. Click the OK button.

3. Repeat Steps 1–2 to add a second Active Script Task to the DTS Designer.

4. To add workflow to the package, select any one of the ActiveX Script Task objects with a single mouse click.

5. Press the Ctrl key and select the other task with a single mouse click.

6. Release the Ctrl key, right-click, and select Workflow from the pop-up menu.

7. Select the On Success option from the pop-up menu. A green arrow is drawn between the two tasks. You have now added simple point and click workflow.

The environment of the package designer is optimized for quickly producing highly robust DTS applications. To the left sits a tool palette of data source and destination connection objects.

NOTE

The few icons on the toolbox under the data section are not the only types of connections supported by the designer. The complete ranges of OLE DB or ODBC data sources are supported. The most common data types are displayed as quick-connect tool buttons. Each connection type opens a property dialog where you can pick from the entire list of available data sources.

Below the data source/destination palette sits a group of tasks elements that were listed earlier in this chapter. These elements represent custom tasks for the package

The toolbar near the top houses a set of commonly used operations for saving, running, and printing the package, as well as buttons for adding arrows to represent workflow steps and data movement tasks. There are also tools associated with viewing and arranging the objects in the current package. The big benefit of the DTS Designer is to allow a DBA or Developer to drag and drop objects on the palette, set workflow properties, and add script or code to perform necessary tasks. Using the DTS Designer, you can perform complex data warehousing imports and exports from various data sources. You can also use DTS to perform workflow and batch processing. Before looking at using DTS for workflow, let's examine some of the tasks and how they are used.

Execute Process Task

The execute process task allows you to execute a program (i.e. executable) from within a DTS package. Using the execute process task is simple and involves a few points and clicks. When you select an execute process task from the Task toolbar shown in Figure 13.13, the Execute Process Task Properties dialog box, shown in Figure 13.14 is displayed.

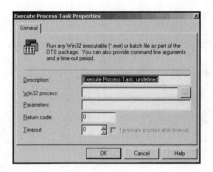

FIGURE 13.14   The Execute Process Properties dialog box.

To assign an application to the task, input the executable name in the Win32 process text box shown in Figure 13.14 or click on the Browse button to the right of the text box. For this example, open a new DTS package and add a Execute Process task, enter **calc.exe** in the Win32 process text box (which is the Windows calculator). You can provide command-line parameters to the application by adding them to the Parameters text box shown in Figure 13.14. Enter the value you want to return after the process has executed successfully by filling in the Return code text box. The Timeout text box allows you to set the amount of time the process can execute before a timeout occurs. The default value of 0 indicates no timeout. If you assign a timeout value to the task, you also have the option of checking the Terminate Process After Timeout box, which will terminate the application if the timeout value is exceeded. Run the package by clicking the green execute arrow on the DTS Designer toolbar. The Windows calculator will appear. Experiment with the timeout and terminate process after timeout features to see how they work.

Dynamic Properties Task

The dynamic properties task allows you to retrieve values from external resources .ini files, global variables, data files environment variables, such as or even a query. You can use the dynamic properties task to retrieve information at runtime to use within the DTS package. The dynamic properties task is also easy to use. When you add a dynamic properties task to a package the Dynamic Task Properties Task Properties dialog box, shown in Figure 13.15 appears.

FIGURE 13.15   The Dynamic Properties Task Properties dialog box.

The dynamic properties task can be used to retrieve multiple values and then assign them to values within the package to be used later. Let's do a quick example of assigning an environmental variable to a DTS package global variable. Create a new DTS package and perform the following:

1. Right mouse click inside the DTS package, a pop-up menu appears: Select Package Properties. The Package Properties dialog box appears.

   Select the Global Variables tab, shown in Figure 13.16.

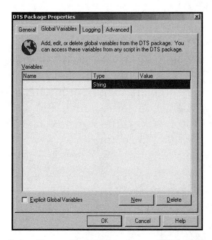

FIGURE 13.16   DTS Package Properties dialog box—Global Variables Tab.

In the Name column, enter **ComputerName**, in the Type filed select String and leave the Value field blank. Click OK.

Add a Dynamic Properties Task to the package. The Dynamic Task Properties Task Properties dialog box, shown in Figure 13.15 appears.

Click the Add button, the Dynamic Properties Task: Package Properties dialog box, shown in Figure 13.17 appears.

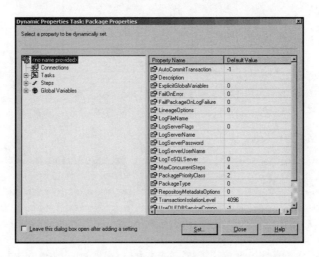

FIGURE 13.17   Dynamic Properties Task: Package Properties dialog box.

Expand the Global Variables folder, shown in the left panel in Figure 13.17. Select ComputerName.

In the grid to the right, ComputerName is filled in the Property Name column. Double-click the Default Value column and the Add/Edit Assignment dialog box, shown in Figure 13.18 appears.

Using the Source drop-down box, shown in Figure 13.18, select Environment Variable.

Using the Variable drop down box, select COMPUTERNAME. Click OK. Click OK on the Dynamic Properties Task Properties dialog box.

You have now used a dynamic properties task to retrieve and store an environment variable in a global variable. To view the global variable you need to add another task to the project, the ActiveX script task.

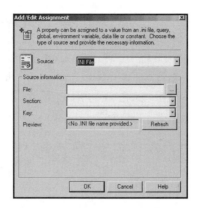

FIGURE 13.18   The Add/Edit Assignment dialog box.

ActiveX Script Task

The ActiveX script task allows you to custom program DTS packages by writing ActiveX script that's executed at runtime as part of the package process. You can use ActiveX script for workflow (shown later in the book) or to perform custom tasks that can't be performed with SQL or with Windows executables. ActiveX script tasks have access to the DTS package object model and all the tasks contained, including the task and step objects. This makes ActiveX script task very powerful. The downside to ActiveX script task is it is not complied code but interpreted runtime code so using lots of ActiveX script in a repetitive manner such as row-by-row operations can degrade package performance. Let's use an ActiveX task to view the global variable added by the dynamic properties task in the previous section. Add an ActiveX script task to the package. Double-click the ActiveX task in the DTS Designer to bring up the Script window. The Script window contains a default function called Main. Add the lines of code in bold to the Main function, which calls the Visual Basic script function that displays a Windows message box with the Computer Name environment variable stored in the DTS Package global variable ComputerName.

```
Function Main()
    MsgBox DTSGlobalVariables("ComputerName").Value
    Main = DTSTaskExecResult_Success
End Function
```

Once you add the code, save your changes and then click the start button to test the package. A message box displaying the computer name appears.

Execute SQL Task

The Execute SQL task can be used to execute SQL statements or other database objects such as stored procedures or functions against a data source. The execute SQL task must be assigned to a database connection object. The database connection object does not have to be SQL Server, it can be Oracle, Excel, Microsoft Access, or any database if you have an ODBC or OLE DB driver. When you add an Execute SQL task, the Execute SQL Task properties dialog box, shown in Figure 13.19, appears.

The Existing connection drop-down box, shown in Figure 13.19, assigns the execute SQL task to an existing connection. The command timeout value is the amount of time the SQL command is allowed to execute before a timeout occurs. Just like the execute process task, the default value of 0 means no timeout. The SQL statement text box, shown in Figure 13.19, accepts any valid SQL statement that can be executed against the existing database connection. The SQL statement can be a single SQL statement, a SQL statement with parameters, a series of SQL statements, or a stored procedure (if the connection supports stored procedures). You can enter the SQL statement directly into the SQL Statement text box or you can build the SQL statement using the Build Query button shown in Figure 13.19, which brings up a graphical query builder. You can check to make sure the SQL statement(s) are valid by clicking the Parse Query button. You can also set the SQL text box by loading SQL statements from files using the Browse button shown in Figure 13.19.

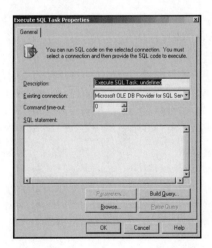

FIGURE 13.19 The Execute SQL task Properties dialog box.

FTP Task

The FTP (File Transfer Protocol) task allows you to send and receive files over the Internet or an intranet using FTP. This task is quite useful because SQL Server is used in many Internet-based and intranet-based applications. You can use other DTS tasks to import and export data to flat files and the FTP task to send or retrieve these files from remote sites using ftp. The File Transfer Protocol Task Properties dialog box is shown in Figure 13.20.

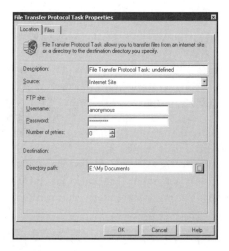

FIGURE 13.20   The File Transfer Protocol Task Properties dialog box—Location Tab.

The FTP Task Properties dialog box contains two tabs: the Location Tab, shown in Figure 13.20 and the Files Tab, shown in Figure 13.21. Use the Location Tab to set up the parameters used to transfer the site. The Source combo box shown in Figure 13.20 allows you to specify the source of the file transfer—either an Internet site or a directory. Place the address of the ftp site in the FTP Site text box shown in Figure 13.20, as well as the user account and password information in the Username and Password text boxes. To specify the number of retries, set the Number of retires box shown in Figure 13.20. The Directory Path text box allows you to set the destination directory for the files that are copied. To specify the files you want to copy, use the Files tab shown in Figure 13.21. You can select files from the Source side and move them to the destination. To overwrite an existing file, check the Overwrite checkbox, shown in Figure 13.21.

You can also set the files to be copied at runtime using a Dynamic Data Properties task or with an ActiveX Script Task that uses the FTP object task and the property "SourceFilename." If you are having problems getting the FTP task to connect to your FTP site. Use ftp.exe to debug and figure out the proper settings to use. Once you get ftp.exe to transfer files, you can use the same parameters to set up the FTP DTS task object.

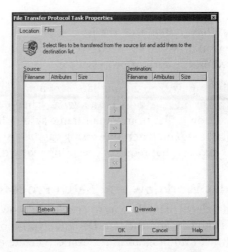

FIGURE 13.21   The File Transfer Protocol Task Properties dialog box—Files Tab.

Execute Package Task

The Execute Package task allows you to execute another DTS package and pass information to that package using DTS package global variables. The Execute Package task is quite useful for reusing different DTS packages as part of a larger workflow process. For example, suppose you create a package that loads in a data file and merges the data with your data. You also have a package that exports a file once a week to another office and finally you have a package that executes once a week to perform many different server tuning features like selectively recreating clustered indexes or updating database statistics. Suddenly a requirement comes up to perform all three functions every Sunday morning. Instead of re-creating each package in one large package, you can create a DTS package that executes each of the existing packages.

What Are Workflow and Batch Processing?

Workflow is defined as executing a series of steps (that is, work) and having the ability to take different paths (that is, actions) based on the outcome of the steps. Workflow processing contains three important elements called the three S's. The three S's are

- **Status**—Where is the process now?
- **Stages**—Where has it been?
- **State**—Where is it going?

Essentially, the three S's describe the key elements that make up workflow processing. To build workflow into a process, the process needs to maintain a status so that we can determine what the task is currently doing. To have workflow, you must have more than one stage (that is, step) that the process is to execute. As a process (that is, task) completes, the workflow process needs to be able to determine what is the next stage to execute based on the current process state.

Batch processing is allowing work to accumulate over a period of time and then processing the work all at once, usually on a regular schedule. An example of batch processing would be loading files from a mainframe system into Microsoft's SQL Server every night at 11:00 p.m. Batch processing can be a simple import and export process or a complex process that requires executing many different tasks and steps.

How DTS Provides Workflow and Batch Processing Capabilities

DTS provides several objects that allow us to create workflow and batch processing solutions. Using these objects and the DTS Designer, you can create workflow solutions that contain little or no programming. You can create more advanced workflow solutions using ActiveX script and DTS objects, which will be demonstrated in several examples.

Before going into an overview of how to create workflow solutions with DTS, you might be asking yourself, "Does using DTS for workflow and batch processing work?" I have a lot of happy DTS customers who would tell you that the answer is yes! Several clients who I have worked with over the past five years had developed applications/processes to load files, run stored procedures, export files, launch applications, and notify someone when the process broke down or completed. The solutions varied from Unix scripts to Microsoft Visual Basic programs. The bottom line is a lot of work was done to automate every day business processes. All the custom solutions worked fine but suffered from a variety of problems, including ease of maintenance and overly complex task-to-task communications. I was able to go into many of these customers and redo these automated processes using DTS in a lot less time (days instead of weeks) with a solution that is easier to maintain, less complex, and in some cases implemented without writing a single line of code.

DTS provides package level and task level properties that allow you to perform more advanced workflow and batch processing. Let's take a look at the DTS package properties and workflow properties that can be used to create more advanced workflow and batch processing solutions.

DTS Package Properties

To view the DTS Package Properties dialog box, open a DTS package or create a new package using the DTS Designer. While inside the DTS Designer, click on whitespace in the package and then right-click and select Package Properties. The DTS Package Properties dialog box, shown in Figure 13.22, appears.

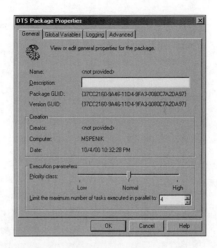

FIGURE 13.22   The DTS Package Properties dialog box—General tab.

The DTS Package Properties dialog box allows you to set or view properties for the package, such as global variables or the package name. The properties we are interested in can be found in the Execution parameters frame located on the General tab of the DTS Package Properties dialog box, shown in Figure 13.22. The first property of interest is the Priority class property, which can be modified by using the slider bar shown in Figure 13.22. The Priority class property allows you to change the WIN32 thread priority under which the task executes. The possible choices are Low, Normal, and High. The default value is Normal, which is the recommended setting for most packages. If you have a package that consumes a lot of I/O resources, such as CPU time or disk time and is not of a critical nature, you might want to set the class priority lower to allow other mission-critical processes to take over while the package is running.

The Limit the Maximum Number of Tasks Executed in Parallel toggle control allows you to control the number of possible threads that a package can use and sets the package property `MaxConcurrentSteps` to the selected number. The `MaxConcurrentSteps` property determines the maximum number of threads used to execute parallel steps. Steps that have no precedence constraints or have constraints independent of one another can execute concurrently up to the maximum number of threads. So if you have 10 parallel steps, and the Limit the Maximum Number of Tasks Executed in Parallel property is set to four, four of the steps would start concurrently. After a step completes, another parallel step begins to execute up to the maximum number of threads. On an *SMP (Symmetric Multi-Processor)* computer, you might be able to boost the performance of the overall package execution time by increasing the number of threads that the package can run in parallel. If you decide to increase or decrease the number of threads, execute several time trials to make sure that you are getting the expected and desired result. Setting the number of threads to High can hurt performance and can actually decrease the package execution time. Keep in mind that this property is for packages that have several parallel step objects. Also, connections can only be used by one task at a time. In some cases, to get parallel instead of serial processing, you might have to set up separate connections for the tasks to use.

To help you determine the status of packages that have executed, click the Logging tab shown in Figure 13.22, and the Logging tab of the DTS Package Properties dialog box is shown in Figure 13.23.

You can have the package and steps status saved to the msdb database by clicking the Log Package Execution to SQL Server check box shown in Figure 13.23. To have error information for the package and steps written to a file, provide an error file path and filename with extension in the Error File text box shown in Figure 13.23. To have the package stop execution if the first step fails, check the Fail Package on First Error check box shown in Figure 13.23. If you are running on Windows NT 4.0 or Windows 2000, check the Write Completion Status to Event Log check box to write the package completion status to the event log (grayed out in Windows 9x).

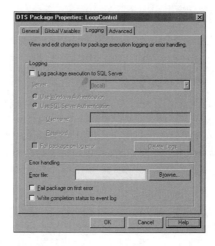

FIGURE 13.23   The DTS Package Properties dialog box—Logging tab.

Individual Task Workflow Properties

You can further tune the behavior of a DTS package by setting individual workflow properties on a DTS task. The individual task properties can be set by performing the following steps in the DTS Designer:

1. Select a task by performing a single-click on a task in the DTS Designer.

2. Right-click to bring up a pop-up menu.

3. Select Workflow and then Workflow properties to bring up the Workflow Properties dialog box.

To see the workflow properties, click the Options tab of the Workflow Properties dialog box, shown in Figure 13.24.

FIGURE 13.24   The Workflow Properties dialog box—Options tab.

Let's examine some of the properties that can be used in a workflow situation. Similar to a DTS package, you can set the Windows NT priority level that a individual task executes under from Low to High by using the Task Priority slider control shown in Figure 13.24.

Another property you can set is the Close Connection on Completion property. By default, DTS keeps connections open after they are used until the entire package completes. In some circumstances, you might want to close the connection prior to the package completing. For example, suppose that you want to archive information into a database and then detach the database files. In order to detach the database files, you have to make sure that no users are logged in to the database in order to detach the database. You might also want to close some connections when dealing with a system of low memory resources or a package that uses hundreds of connections.

The Execute on Main Package Thread property allows you to specify that the task is executed on the main DTS package thread. This property is useful if you want to debug multiple ActiveX script tasks in a package. To debug multiple ActiveX script tasks, set this property for each task you want to debug. For performance reasons, you should avoid setting this property except when debugging. Some OLE DB data providers are not free threaded and require this property to be set (check the documentation for your OLE DB provider).

TIP

To debug ActiveX script executing in a DTS package, you need to have the Microsoft script debugger installed on the machine where the package is executing. The script debugger is installed with Visual InterDev 6.0, Windows 2000, or the Microsoft Windows NT 4.0 Option pack. After you have the script debugger installed, add a STOP statement in the ActiveX script you want to debug. When DTS reaches the STOP statement, you will enter break mode in the script debugger, and then you can step through the ActiveX script. You will also enter break mode if a script error occurs or an object raises an error while the package is executing.

However, from a workflow point of view, the most useful and interesting property on the DTS Task Workflow Properties dialog box Option Tab is the Use ActiveX Script option shown in Figure 13.24. To add workflow script or edit existing workflow script, check the Use ActiveX Script property and click the Properties button, shown in Figure 13.24. The Workflow ActiveX Script Properties dialog box, shown in Figure 13.25, appears.

FIGURE 13.25   The Workflow ActiveX Script Properties dialog box.

The Workflow ActiveX Script Properties dialog box is very similar to the standard ActiveX Script Task Properties dialog box, which allows you to edit script for an ActiveX script task. You use the script window to add and edit script that is executed at runtime. The Workflow ActiveX Script property differs from the ActiveX Script Task property in that the workflow script is executed before the ActiveX Script Task property code, which allows us to perform more advanced workflow processing than the simple point-and-click workflow available with the DTS designer.

Using the Workflow ActiveX Script Property for Loop Control and Conditions

By using the ActiveX script workflow property, you can create simple loop control that allows you to repeat or execute steps when certain conditions are met. Let's examine simple loop control in more detail by looking at the following example called Loop Control. This example is contained on the CD-ROM that comes with the book. Perform the following steps to open the package (file—loopcontrol.dts) in the DTS Designer:

1. In the Enterprise Manager, select the Data Transformation Services folder

2. Right-click, and a pop-up menu appears.

3. From the pop-up menu, select Open Package.

4. An Open File dialog box appears. Select the sample .DTS package located on the CD (loopcontrol.dts) and click Open. The open package is shown in Figure 13.26.

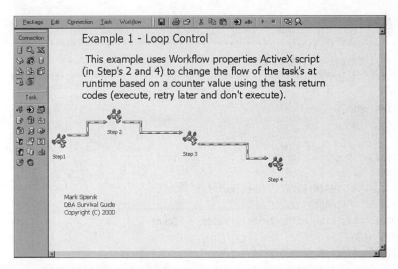

FIGURE 13.26   DTS Example—Loop Control.

The Loop Control example contains a series of ActiveX Script tasks, named step 1 through step 4, that execute serially. With the normal point-and-click workflow provided by the DTS designer, each task would execute one time and in sequential order. However, by using the ActiveX Script Workflow property and adding some script, this example will cause steps 1, 2, and 3 to execute multiple times and step 4 will not execute until a certain condition is met. Each ActiveX script task contains VB Script, which displays a message box that indicates the name of the step executing and, in some cases, the event. For example, the code in ActiveX script step 1 is shown in Listing 13.2.

LISTING 13.2   ActiveX Script Task Code for Step 1

```
Function Main()
   Msgbox "Step 1 - Executed"
   Main = DTSTaskExecResult_Success
End Function
```

The statement `Main=DTSTaskExecResult_Success` sets the return code for the ActiveX
Script task function `Main` to success, which signals a success or, on completion, a
precedence constraint to execute the next step. The other valid ActiveX script return
code is `DTSTaskExecResult_Failure`, which indicates that the step failed to execute
successfully and would cause a success precedence constraint not to execute the next
step and a failure or completion precedence constraint to execute the next step. The
code in steps 1 through 4 is similar to Listing 13.2 with only minor modifications to
the message box text. The workflow code is contained in the Workflow ActiveX
Script properties of step 2 and step 4. The code for the step 2 task Workflow ActiveX
Script property is shown in Listing 13.3.

LISTING 13.3   Code for Step 2 Workflow ActiveX Script Property

```
'***********************************************************************
'   Visual Basic ActiveX Script
'***********************************************************************

Function Main()
Dim iCount,oPkg

    MsgBox "WorkFlow Script Step 2 - Executing"
    'Bump Value
    iCount = DTSGlobalVariables("retries").Value
    iCount = iCount + 1
    DTSGlobalVariables("retries").Value = iCount

    If iCount <= 2 then
        'By setting property to retry - we execute the Waiting step
        MsgBox "Execute Step 1 Next Instead of Step 2"
          Set oPkg = DTSGlobalVariables.Parent
oPkg.Steps("DTSStep_DTSActiveScriptTask_4").ExecutionStatus
➡ =DTSStepExecStat_Waiting
                        Main = DTSStepScriptResult_DontExecuteTask
    ElseIf iCount = 3 then
        MsgBox "Retry Step 2 Next"
         Main = DTSStepScriptResult_RetryLater
    Else
```

LISTING 13.3 Continued

```
      'Now Step 2 will Execute
      MsgBox "Execute Step 2 Next"
      Main = DTSStepScriptResult_ExecuteTask
   End If

End Function
```

The code uses a global variable called `retries` to determine whether to execute step 1 again, execute step 2, or retry step 2. Listing 13.3 is overriding the point-and-click precedence constraints added by the DTS Designer, allowing you to determine which step should run next based on a runtime condition other than task completion status (in this case, the global variable—`retries`). To change execution control requires one or two steps, depending on the execution code returned by the Workflow ActiveX script. Using the execution code, you can retry a task, not execute a task or redirect to another task. The following codes are valid return codes for ActiveX script objects associated with a step:

- `DTSStepScriptResult_DontExecuteTask`—Don't execute the task.

- `DTSStepScriptResult_RetryLater`—Retry the step later.

- `DTSStepScriptResult_Execute Task`—Execute the task.

Listing 13.3 uses an example of each of the previous return codes. When the global variable `retries` equals 3, the Retry Later code is used and the workflow properties script for step 2 is re-executed. When `retries` is greater than 3, the Execute the Task code is returned, and step 2 executes. The Don't Execute Task status is used to redirect to another task. When using the retry or execute return code, all you need to do is set the proper return code. For example, the following code returns an execute task status in a function called `Main`:

```
Main = DTSStepScriptResult_Execute Task
```

Redirecting execution to another step requires two steps. First set the execution status of the step you want to execute next to `waiting`, and then return the don't execute status in the ActiveX Workflow Script property. The task execution status code is a set of codes that can have the following values:

- `DTSStepExecStat_Waiting`—Step is waiting to execute.

- `DTSStepExecStat_Completed`—Step has completed.

- `DTSStepExecStat_InProgress`—Step is currently executing.

- `DTSStepExecStat_Inactive`—Step execution is inactive.

However, before you can set the task status to `waiting`, you need to get the proper task object to set the object's `ExecutionStatus` property. When you are working with DTS packages and you want to change a property or use a method of any DTS object at runtime, such as the SQL statement being executed, an exported data's filename, or the execution status of a task, you need to get the current Package object and then use the DTS object hierarchy to obtain the object you want to modify. To get the Package object, execute the following code:

```
Set oPkg = DTSGlobalVariables.Parent
```

This code sets the local variable `oPkg` to the current package. When you have the current package object, you can use the Package object's collections: Connections, Tasks, Steps, and Global variables to access objects in the package. (Note: A *collection* is an array of objects, so the Connections collection contains all the Connection objects used in the package.)

TIP

I have been doing many different demos of DTS and its capabilities, and the question that comes up most frequently is, "How do you figure out which object and property to use?" My answer is that when programming with the DTS object model, your two best resources are SQL Server 2000 Books Online and the Script Debugger. The SQL Server 2000 Books Online, DTS Reference book contains the DTS model hierarchy as well as detail on each object, collection, property, and method. Using the DTS Reference book, you can determine the proper object and how to obtain the object. The Script Debugger can be used to place an ActiveX Script task in debug mode and then use debugger features like the locals window to help you figure out how different object properties are used. SQL Server 2000 does provide an Object browser in DTS that is also helpful.

In our Loop Control example, the code in Listing 13.4 sets step 1's execution status to `waiting` and sets the Workflow ActiveX Script property return code to `DTSStepScriptResult_DontExecuteTask`.

LISTING 13.4   Setting Execution Status to Waiting

```
Set oPkg = DTSGlobalVariables.Parent
oPkg.Steps("DTSStep_DTSActiveScriptTask_4").ExecutionStatus=DTSStepExecStat_Waiting
Main = DTSStepScriptResult_DontExecuteTask
```

These two actions will override the DTS Designer precedence constraints and instead of executing step 2, step 1 will execute (for example, we have looped back). The Loop Control example shows how to perform loop control using global variables and execution status codes to determine which step executes and when. Using these techniques, you can solve difficult workflow problems.

Let's examine an export problem where you have records for different states, and each state wants you to create an export text file with just their records. The process has to be flexible enough to handle adding new states or removing states without changing the code. Example 2, the `ExampleBatchExport`, solves the problem using the authors table in the pubs database. Instead of creating a transaction file for each branch office, Example 2 creates a separate file for each state that contains only authors for that state. The `ExampleBatchExport` package is shown in the DTS Designer in Figure 13.27.

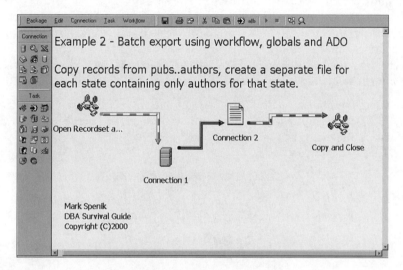

FIGURE 13.27 `ExampleBatchExport` DTS Package.

The `ExampleBatchExport` consists of two connection objects: one for SQL Server and one for a flat file. The example also contains a data transformation task and two ActiveX Script tasks. Let's examine how this package is used to solve our problem.

To export data from SQL Server to a flat file, two DTS Connection objects are used and a data transformation object is used to pull the data from the SQL Server connection and write it to the flat file connection. The SQL statement used by the data transformation task is as follows:

```
select [authors].[au_id],[authors].[au_lname], [authors].[au_fname]from [authors]
where [authors].[state]=?
```

Using a ? as part of the query string is a new feature of SQL Server 2000, support for parameterized queries. Using the connection objects with the data transformation object solves the problem of exporting the data. The real challenge with this problem is how to

- Change the WHERE clause on the SQL statement used by the data transformation task object.

- Get a list of states from the database.

- Change the export filename.

- Repeat the steps for each state After the SQL statement and filename have been changed.

Let's take a look how each of the problems are solved.

Changing the WHERE Clause of the SQL Statement

Changing the SQL statement WHERE clause in SQL Server 2000 is much simpler than in SQL Server 7.0. You can now change the WHERE clause using a parameterized query and a global variable. With SQL Server 7.0, you needed to figure out the proper DTS object model hierarchy. To make a parameterized query and add a global variable, perform the following from the DTS Designer:

1. Select the transformation (line between the two connections shown in Figure 13.27), right-mouse click, and then select Properties. The Transform Data Task Properties dialog box appears, shown in Figure 13.28.

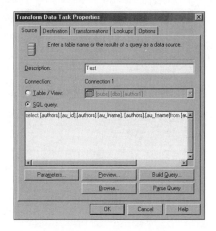

FIGURE 13.28   The Transform Data Task Properties dialog box.

2. If you used a ? in your WHERE clause, skip to step number 3. If you did not use a ? in the WHERE clause, modify the hard-coded condition to a ?: This creates a parameter.

3. Click the Parameters button, shown in Figure 13.29. The Parameter Mapping dialog box, shown in Figure 13.29, appears.

FIGURE 13.29   Parameter Mapping dialog box.

4. Using the Parameter Mapping dialog box, assign the parameters in your query string to a global variable. If you need to create a global variable, click the Create Global Variables button. All you need to do now to change the WHERE clause at runtime is to set the global variable.

The code to change the SQL statement (by setting the global variable) is placed in the data transformation's task Workflow ActiveX Script property so that the WHERE clause is changed prior to the transformation executing.

Get a List of States from the Database

To get a list of states from the authors table, the following SQL statement is used:

```
Select distinct(state) from pubs..authors
```

Microsoft's *ActiveX Data Objects (ADO)* are used to open a recordset of distinct states in the authors table. This approach allows new states to be added without having to change or modify the code. The ADO recordset object is stored as a global variable so that it is available to the other tasks in the package. We could have also used DTS Lookup objects to run the SQL statement.

NOTE

Before you can open the ADO recordset, you will need to modify the connection string located in the ActiveX Script Task labeled Open a Recordset to reflect the actual password and server name.

Changing the Exported Filename

Changing the export filename is quite simple, get the file connection object and modify the DataSource property. Changing the export filename occurs as part of the data transformation's Workflow ActiveX Script property, shown in Listing 13.5, which contains all the code for the data transformation's Workflow ActiveX Script property code.

LISTING 13.5   Data Transformation's Workflow ActiveX Script Property Code

```
'************************************************************************
'   Visual Basic ActiveX Script
'************************************************************************
Function Main()
Dim oPackage, oTask, oPumpTask
Dim oRS, strSQL
Dim oConn,strNewName

'Get the Global recordset
Set oRS = DTSGlobalVariables("rsState").Value
If Not oRS.EOF AND Not oRS.BOF Then

    'Change the value of the file name on the connection
    Set oPackage = DTSGlobalVariables.parent
    Set oConn = oPackage.Connections(2)
    strNewName = oConn.DataSource
    strNewName = Left(strNewName, _
        (Len(strNewName) - (Len(strNewName) - InStrRev(strNewName,"\"))))
    strNewName = strNewName & "pubs" & oRS(0) & ".txt"
    oConn.DataSource = strNewName

    'Set global variable with state from the recordset
    DTSGlobalVariables("State") = oRS(0)

End If
'Clean Up
Set oPumpTask = Nothing
Set oTask = Nothing
Set oPackage = Nothing
Set oConn = Nothing

Main = DTSTaskExecResult_Success
End Function
```

Repeat the Steps

To repeat the data transformation step and close down the connections after all the states have been exported requires using the same techniques used in the Loop Control example. The Workflow ActiveX Script property of the Copy and Close ActiveX task is used to redirect the process back to the data transformation task until every state in the list has been processed. After the list is complete, the Copy and Close task is allowed to execute.

Using DTS Packages

You can view existing packages from the Data Transformation Services folder of the Enterprise Manager. The DTS packages can be stored in the local msdb database or in the Microsoft Repository.

> **NOTE**
>
> The advantage to storing the packages in the Repository is that objects contained in these packages, such as ActiveX scripts and data transformations, can be accessed from other tools that support the Registry components. Also, by storing DTS packages in the Repository, you can take advantage of data lineage, which helps you keep track of a data element's transformations from the source system to its final destination.

You can view the packages contained in these two locations by selecting that icon from the DTS folder in the Enterprise Manager tree. Double-clicking any of these packages opens it in the DTS Designer. You can access other packages stored in the file system by choosing the Open Package task from the DTS folder. If permission to access this package is provided, the DTS Designer loads the package.

Running Packages from the Command Line

You can use the Enterprise Manager to run DTS packages, and you can also run packages with the command-line utility dtsrun. This tool allows you to execute, delete, and overwrite packages that are stored on the local SQL server, in the Repository, or in files. The syntax for the dtsrun utility is

```
dtsrun /S<servername> /U<user name> /P<password> /N<package name>
```

DTS Package Performance

DTS is a very powerful tool for both importing and exporting data and for doing simple workflow applications. However, DTS performance can become an issue if you have to do lots of database look ups, use lots of ActiveX script during transformations, or you have very large datasets to import. When importing large datasets into SQL Server that require no data transformations, you will greatly decrease the load time by using BULK INSERT statement or BCP instead of the Data Transformation task. It is also faster to use BCP to export from SQL Server to a flat file then to use the DTS Data Transformation task. If you are importing large datasets into SQL Server using a DTS data transformation task and you are unhappy with the package execution time you may consider using the BULK INSERT statement to load the information in to a SQL Server holding table and then write a stored procedure to transform the data and move it to its final SQL Server destination. You can also improve the performance of Data Transformation tasks that use lots of ActiveX script during the transformation by saving the package as a Visual Basic 6.0 module and compiling the package. Most data transformations into SQL Server will be generated using the DTS Import/Export Wizard so they don't typically take a long time to createOnce you have created the package, if you find that the load and transformation time to SQL Server does not meet your requirements, you may have to look at other means such as BULK INSERT and stored procedures to achieve faster load times, but you still can use DTS to tie together the task.

Data Transformation Services FAQ

This section lists some commonly asked questions and answers about SQL Server 2000 DTS.

Q Is DTS used only for data warehousing duties?

A No, as shown in this chapter, DTS provides functionality for transferring data and schema from various sources to destinations, as well as the ability to perform batch processing and workflow.

Q Is DTS only good for importing or exporting data from or to SQL Server?

A No. DTS allows you to transfer data to or from any source or destination that you have OLE DB or ODBC drivers for. This comes in handy when you need to move information between two systems that do not have compatible import/export facilities. However, when using DTS in environments that do not have SQL Server and are using SQL Server to use DTS for workflow or importing and exporting data, you must still purchase and install a copy of SQL Server.

Q Can I still use bcp to import or export data?

A Yes, bcp still exists as the command-line tool. The Bulk Import task from the DTS Designer provides a graphical way to import data at top speed. Also, bcp format files are supported with the Bulk Import task.

Q Can I execute packages serially; that is, create a package that calls another package?

A Yes. You can create a package that calls another package with an Execute Package Task. Alternatively, you can run packages together as separate steps of a SQL Server Agent job.

Q Using the DTS Wizard, can I specify a normalized source to be transferred to multiple destinations?

A No. The DTS Wizard will only allow one source and one destination. Using the DTS Designer will allow you to send the data to multiple destinations.

Q What types of operations can I accomplish in ActiveX scripting during transformations?

A Any operations supported by the scripting engines, such as instantiating other components with `CreateObject()`, accessing Active Data Objects (ADO), or calling built-in SQL server components.

Q How can I summarize or even skip rows when I am transforming information in a source table to a destination table?

A Incorporated into every transformation task is the ability to generate a query of the source data. An extensive Query Designer is provided to graphically construct and validate the query. You could use the query to selectively restrict the output. Alternatively, you could write an ActiveX script that conditionally instructs the Data Pump to skip rows based on some logic that you provide.

Q In the DTS Designer, the Tasks menu provides an option for Registering Custom Tasks. How are custom tasks generated?

A When you reach a point where the particular operation cannot be implemented within the confines of the DTS Designer, you might need a custom task. Custom tasks can be created using the DTS COM interfaces in an external development environment such as Visual Basic, Visual C++, or Visual J++.

Q In SQL Server 2000, can I save a DTS package as a Visual Basic file?

A One of the save options for DTS is as a Visual Basic 6.0 file. This allows you to use the package as a compiled program for a runtime performance boost or to easily integrate it into a Visual Basic application. To save a package as a Visual Basic 6.0 file, from the DTS Designer menu select Package and then Save As, the Save DTS Package dialog box, shown in Figure 13.30 appears. Select Visual Basic File in the Location combo box shown in Figure 13.30. The DTS package will be save as a Visual Basic 6.0 .BAS module that can be compiled using Visual Basic 6.0.

FIGURE 13.30   The Save DTS Package dialog box.

Summary

DTS helps SQL Server 2000 users reach a new level of simplicity. The possibilities are vast and difficult to imagine in the context of one chapter. However, you should now have an understanding of how DTS can make it easy to move information in and out of other data sources (especially SQL Server).

We have shown that the DTS package is a self-contained element that can be executed, scheduled, and shared. You have seen that the DTS Wizard can help you get up-to-speed quickly by developing packages for simple imports and exports. You have also been introduced to the power of the DTS Designer for complex workflow-oriented transformation application. Also, COM-based interfaces allow you to create highly customized imports, exports, and transformations from other development environments.

By using DTS, an organization can access data that can be distributed in a variety of formats. DTS is built around a strong OLE DB foundation, which lends itself to providing access to a wide variety of database systems. With this newly gained access, knowledge workers can gather information for data warehouses and data marts on a regular and timely basis.

14

Using BCP and BULK INSERT

Orryn Sledge

IN THIS CHAPTER

- BCP
- BCP Syntax
- Permissions Required to Run BCP
- Character Mode Versus Native Mode
- Interactive BCP
- Sample BCP Scripts
- Modes of Operation
- BCP and Enforcement of Triggers, Rules, Defaults, Constraints, and Unique Indexes
- Common BCP Traps
- BCP Tips
- BULK INSERT
- BCP FAQ

You can use various methods to import and export SQL Server data. Almost all systems require some type of data transfer. BCP is the utility provided by SQL Server to transfer data. BULK INSERT was introduced in version 7.0. It provides an import-only Transact-SQL statement that is the fastest way to load data into SQL Server. This chapter discusses the BCP utility in detail and provides an overview of the BULK INSERT statement.

IMPORTANT NOTE

Starting with version 7.0, you no longer have to use BCP to import and export SQL Server data. Both SQL Server 2000 and 7.0 provide Data Transformation Services (DTS), which simplify the process of importing and exporting data.

I recommend using DTS for the majority of import and export operations (see Chapter 13, "Data Transformation Services," for more information). Features of DTS include a graphical interface, import and export support for a variety of data sources, and the ability to transform data via rules and scripts.

The main reasons to continue running BCP are as follows:

- Backward compatibility.
- Performance—BCP with its optimization hints enabled (TABLOCK, ORDER, and so on) runs faster than DTS.
- It's hard to teach an old dog new tricks; several DBAs (including myself) spent years mastering BCP's quirks and frustrating syntax!

You will find that BCP has not radically changed over the years. However, several small changes to BCP improve its performance and functionality. To those DBAs already familiar with BCP, I recommend that you browse the remainder of the chapter for notes and tips about the current version of BCP.

CAUTION

Be careful when using BCP to import data from 6.x to SQL Server 2000. In particular, if the table uses date (datetime or smalldatetime) or money data types you must use the -V (60|65) option or use the 6.x version of BCP. Version SQL Server 2000 of BCP uses ODBC, whereas previous versions used DB-Library. ODBC treats date and money data types differently from DB-Library.

I also recommend reviewing any BCP export routines that were upgraded from 6.x to SQL Server 2000. Again, the date and money data types are formatted differently upon export. If left untouched, you will find that date information will appear in the ODBC format (yyyy-mm-dd hh:mm:ss), which is significantly different from the DB-Library format (mmm dd yyy hh:mm(AM/PM)). You will also find that money data appears in the ODBC format (no commas, and four digits after the decimal), which is also significantly different from the DB-Library format (commas and two digits after the decimal). Routines that read fixed-length exports will probably choke on the new format. To avoid the export problem, use the –V (60|65) option or use the 6.x version of BCP.

BCP

BCP stands for *Bulk Copy Program*. It is a tool SQL Server provides to import and export data. Data can be either *native mode* (SQL Server specific), *character mode* (ASCII text), or Unicode. ASCII text data is commonly used to share data between SQL Server and other systems.

IS IT LOVE OR HATE?

As a DBA, you will probably have a love/hate relationship with BCP. BCP is limited in scope and lacks common file formats, but it does provide excellent performance.

For those new to SQL Server, the following list provides some insight into BCP. These are the reasons why I like BCP:

- **Performance**—BCP is one the fastest raw data loaders around. I have seen BCP turn in impressive performance numbers as compared to other import/export products.

- **Minimal overhead**—Because BCP is command-line based, it requires a nominal amount of memory to run as compared to today's memory-intensive GUI applications. This leaves memory for other tasks.

Now for the drawbacks of BCP. These are the reasons why I hate BCP:

- **Unforgiving syntax**—BCP's switches are case and order sensitive. This is because BCP's origins stem from Sybase and the UNIX world, where commands are case sensitive.

- **Minimal file support**—Basically, the choices are ASCII text, native SQL Server format, Unicode, or nothing at all. Do not try to load an Excel spreadsheet or an Access database directly into SQL Server; it will never work. (Note: You can now use DTS to perform this function; see Chapter 13 for more information.)

- **Inadequate error messages**—BCP's error messages are minimal and too generic. It would be nice if Microsoft would enhance BCP's error messages to be more informative and specific.

As you can see, BCP is far from perfect, but it does provide some valuable import and export functionality. Keeping this in mind, the remainder of this chapter provides you with some useful tips and tricks to make your life easier when you use BCP.

BCP Syntax

Use the following syntax to perform BCP operations:

```
bcp [[database_name.]owner.]table_name | "query"
➡ {in | out | format | queryout} datafile
[switch1 parameter1] [switch2]
...
[switch10 parameter10]
...
```

in which the following are the parameters:

database_name	Name of the database being accessed. Database name is optional; if the database name is omitted, the user's default database is used.
owner	Owner of the table or view being accessed.

TIP

Use the .. symbol to specify ownership. The .. syntax is more generic than specifying an owner (for example, pubs..authors instead of pubs.dbo.authors).

table_name	Name of the table or view being accessed.

TIP

Use the # or ## symbol to copy a temporary table.

query	SQL statement that generates a resultset. Enclose the query within double quotation marks. queryout must also be specified.
in | out | format | queryout	Direction of data transfer where in means import and out means export. queryout is used when exporting the output from a SQL query or stored procedure. format specifies the creation of a format file based on the -n, -c, -w, or -V (60|65) switches.
	The format setting also requires the use of the -f switch.

| *datafile* | The name of the data file for an import or the name of the file to be created during an export. A path can be included with this statement, such as c:\mssql\binn\authors.txt. |
| *switch1, parameter1* and so on | Choose the switch and its parameter (if one is required) from Table 14.1. |

TABLE 14.1 BCP Switches and Their Parameters

Parameter	Explanation
-m *maxerrors*	Maximum number of errors that can occur before the BCP operation is terminated. Each failed insert counts as one error. Default value is 10.
-f *formatfile*	The name of the format file used to import or export data. A path can be included with this statement, such as c:\mssql\binn\authors.fmt.
-e *errfile*	The name of the error file to store BCP error messages and unsuccessfully transferred rows. A path can be included with this statement, such as c:\mssql\binn\authors.err.

TIP

Error files are useful for pinpointing BCP errors during unattended operations such as nightly data imports.

| -F *firstrow* | The number of the first row to copy. |
| -L *lastrow* | The number of the last row to copy. |

TIP

The -F and -L switches are useful when copying portions of data. For example, to export the first 1,000 records from a table, use the following syntax: -F 1 -L 1000.

| -b *batchsize* | The number of rows transferred in a batch. The default setting is the number of rows in the data file. |

TIP

Microsoft recommends against using the -b option in conjunction with the -h ROWS_PER_BATCH = bb option.

| -n | Native data mode. Native data is SQL Server specific. Native data mode does not prompt the user for field information. |

TABLE 14.1   Continued

Parameter	Explanation
-c	Character data mode. Character data (ASCII) can be transferred to and from SQL Server tables and other non-SQL Server products. Character mode does not prompt the user for field information. By default, fields are tab delimited, and rows are newline delimited.

TIP

Character data mode is usually easier to work with than native data mode. If you have a problem with character mode, you can open the text file with a text editor to view and/or modify the data.

Parameter	Explanation
-w	Unicode data mode.
-N	Native export for non-character data and Unicode character export for character data provide better performance than the -w option.
-V (60|65|70)	Specifies the file format version.

TIP

Use this option when using BCP to import files generated from SQL Server 6.x. This switch is necessary when transferring date (datetime or smalldatetime) and money data types between SQL Server 2000 and previous versions of SQL Server.

Parameter	Explanation
-q	Uses quoted identifiers.
-C code page	Code page in use by the file being imported. Code page needs to be specified only if the file contains char, varchar, or text data types and the data contains values greater than 127 or less than 32. The following is a list of valid code pages.
	ACP—ANSI/Microsoft Windows.
	OEM-—Default code page.
	RAW-—No conversion between code pages.
	<value>—Specific code page number, such as 850.
-t field_term	Field terminator. See Table 14.2 for BCP terminators.
-r row_term	Row terminator. See Table 14.2 for BCP terminators.
-i inputfile	File to redirect input. This switch generally is not used.
-o outputfile	File to redirect BCP output.

TIP

Use the -o switch to log BCP output during unattended BCP operation. This creates a useful trail of BCP output that can be used to monitor and diagnose BCP performance and execution.

TABLE 14.1   Continued

Parameter	Explanation
-a *packet_size*	The number of bytes contained in a network packet. The default value for Windows 2000 Server and clients is 4096.

TIP

Depending on your network architecture, you might be able to improve BCP performance by increasing the packet size. Try setting the packet size between 4096 and 8192 bytes. Use the statistics returned by BCP (the clock time and rows per second) to help tailor this setting.

-E	Used when you import data into a table that contains an identity data type and you want to populate the column with values from the data file. If this switch is omitted, SQL Server automatically populates the identity column and ignores the field's corresponding data values in the import file. The following example shows how the -E switch impacts data imports: Sample table structure: id int identity(1,1) descr char(15) Sample data file: 5 xxx 6 yyy 7 zzz BCP syntax WITHOUT the -E switch: bcp sales..table2 in table2.txt -c -U sa -P Results: id descr ---------- ---------------------------------- 1 xxx 2 yyy 3 zzz Notice the values in the id column. SQL Server populated the id column with an automatically incremented data value. It ignored the values 5,6,7 in the data file. The following is BCP syntax with the -E switch: bcp sales..table2 in table2.txt -c -E -U sa -P Results: id descr

TABLE 14.1   Continued

Parameter	Explanation
	- - - - - - - - - - - - - - - - - - - - - -
	5 xxx
	6 yyy
	7 zzz

With the -E switch, the values in the text file were observed, and SQL Server did *not* automatically generate a set of data values for the id column.

TIP

Use the -E switch to preserve data values when you are unloading and reloading data in a table that contains an identity datatype. Otherwise, SQL Server automatically populates the identity column with its own set of values.

-U *login_id*	SQL Server login ID.
-P *password*	SQL Server password. If the *password* is omitted, BCP prompts you for a password.

NOTE

If you are using integrated security or your SQL Server login does not have a password, BCP still prompts you for a password. To bypass BCP's prompt, use the -P switch without a password, as in the following example:

```
BCP pubs..authors in authors.txt -U sa -P
```

-S *servername*	The name of the server that contains the database and table you are working with. The -S *servername* switch is required if you are using BCP from a remote client on a network.
-v	Displays the version of BCP in use.
-T	Uses a trusted connection to connect to SQL Server.
-k	Preserves null values found in the data file. If this switch is omitted, SQL Server will apply default values if they exist.
-R	Instructs SQL Server to copy currency, date, and time data based on the regional format of the locale setting of the client machine. Regional settings are ignored by default.
-h *load hints*	Notifies SQL Server to use hints to help improve import performance. The following is a list of valid hints: ORDER (*column_list*)where *column_list* = {*column* [ASC | DESC] [,*n*]}—Use this option if your data is presorted and the sort column(s) match the clustered index in the corresponding table. By presorting the data, the clustered index can be updated more quickly.

TABLE 14.1   Continued

Parameter	Explanation
	ROWS_PER_BATCH = *value*—Number of rows per batch. Higher values might result in faster load times.
	KILOBYTES_PER_BATCH = *value*—Number of kilobytes per batch. Higher values might result in faster load times.
	TABLOCK-—Specifies that a table lock is used when loading data.

TIP

This option can significantly improve import performance.

CHECK_CONSTRAINTS-—Specifies that table constraints are observed when importing data. This can decrease import performance. This option is off by default.

The following is an example of BCP hints:

```
bcp customer..customer in customer.n -n -T
-hTABLOCK,ORDER(customer_id),
➥ROWS_PER_BATCH=67000
```

NOTE

With BCP, you can use - or / to preface a switch. For example, the following two statements are equivalent:

```
bcp pubs..sales out sales.out /c /Usa /P
bcp pubs..sales out sales.out -c -Usa -P
```

Table 14.2 shows a list of BCP terminator types.

TABLE 14.2   Valid BCP Terminators

Terminator Type	Syntax
Tab	\t
New line	\n
Carriage return	\r
Backslash	\\
NULL terminator	\0
User-defined terminator	Character (^, %, *, and so on)

Permissions Required to Run BCP

No permissions are required to run the BCP command-line utility. However, to use BCP to copy data into a table, the user must be granted INSERT permission to the target table. To export data from a table, the user must be granted SELECT permission for the source table.

Character Mode Versus Native Mode

BCP can import or export data in a character file format or native file format. *Character mode* is plain old ASCII text. Use the -c switch or a format file to specify character mode. *Native mode* uses special formatting characters internal to SQL Server to represent data. Use native mode only when you are transferring data between SQL Server tables. Use the -n switch to specify native mode. Following is sample output from character mode BCP:

```
bcp pubs..jobs out jobs.txt -c -U sa -P

1       New Hire - Job not specified    10      10
2       Chief Executive Officer         200     250
3       Business Operations Manager     175     225
```

> **TIP**
>
> Character mode is usually easier to work with than native mode because you can view the contents of a character mode data file with a standard text editor.

Interactive BCP

Interactive BCP is used to selectively import or export data. Interactive mode is automatically activated when the following switches are *not* included in the BCP statement:

- -n (native format)
- -N (native format for non-character data and Unicode native format for character data)
- -c (character format)
- -f (format file)
- -w (Unicode native format)

Through the use of interactive prompts, you can tailor BCP to your import and export specifications. Interactive BCP prompts you for four pieces of information:

- File storage type
- Prefix length

- Field length

- Field and row terminator

The following are sample interactive BCP prompts:

```
Enter the file storage type of field discounttype [char]:
Enter prefix-length of field discounttype [0]:
Enter length of field discounttype [40]:
Enter field terminator [none]:
```

> **TIP**
>
> When importing data, you can skip a column by entering 0 for prefix length, 0 for length, and no terminator. You cannot skip a column when exporting data.

At the end of an interactive BCP session, you receive the following prompt:

```
Do you want to save this format information in a file? [Y/n]
Host filename [bcp.fmt]:
```

If you answer *yes* at this prompt, your interactive responses are saved to a format file. This enables you to later specify the -f switch (format file) to automatically reuse the information from your interactive BCP session.

File Storage Type

The *file storage type* specifies the data types used to read from and write to data files. Table 14.3 lists valid file storage types.

> **TIP**
>
> When working with ASCII files, set all file storage types to char, regardless of the table's data types. This is the only way you can load ASCII data into SQL Server using BCP.

TABLE 14.3   File Storage Types

char	image	smallint
varchar	datetime	tinyint
nchar	smalldatetime	money
nvarchar	decimal	smallmoney
text	numeric	bit
ntext	float	uniqueidentifier
binary	real	timestamp
varbinary	int	

Prefix Length

SQL Server uses the *prefix length* to store compacted data. When working in native mode, accept the default values whenever possible.

TIP

When working with fixed-width ASCII data, set the prefix length to 0.

Field Length

The *field length* specifies the number of bytes required to store a SQL Server data type. Use default field lengths whenever possible; otherwise, data truncation or overflow errors can occur. Table 14.4 lists default field lengths.

TABLE 14.4   Default Field Lengths

Data Type	Length in Bytes
binary	Column length + 1
bit	1
char	Column length
datetime	24
decimal	41
float	30
image	0
int	12
money	30
nchar	2 times column length
ntext	0
numeric	41
nvarchar	2 times column length
real	30
smalldatetime	24
smallint	7
smallmoney	30
text	0
timestamp	17
tinyint	5
uniqueidentifier	37
varbinary	2 times column length + 1
varchar	Column length

TIP

When importing and exporting ASCII fixed-width data files, you might need to modify the field length to match your import/export specification. For example, to export a char(15) column as a 25-byte piece of data, specify a field length of 25. This pads the data length to 25 bytes.

Field Terminator

The *field terminator* prompt controls how field data is delimited (separated). The default delimiter is no terminator. See Table 14.5 for valid field terminators.

TIP

The last field in a table acts as a row terminator. To separate rows with a newline delimiter, specify \n at the field terminator prompt.

NOTE

At the BCP command line, you can also use the -t (field terminator) and -r (row terminator) switches to specify terminators.

TABLE 14.5   Valid Field Terminators

Terminator Type	Syntax
Tab	\t
Newline	\n
Carriage return	\r
Backslash	\\
NULL terminator	\0
User-defined terminator	Character (^, %, *, and so on)

Format Files

A *format file* is a template for BCP to use when you import or export data. With this template, you can define how BCP should transfer your data.

The easiest way to create a format file is to initiate an interactive BCP session. Interactive mode is initiated when you do *not* specify one of the following switches:

- -n (native format)

- -N (native format for non-character data and Unicode native format for character data)

- -c (character format)

- -f (format file)

- -w (Unicode native format)

At the end of your interactive session, you see the following prompt:

```
Do you want to save this format information in a file? [Y/n] y
Host filename [bcp.fmt]:sample.fmt
```

At this prompt, enter a filename to save the format information. SQL Server then creates a format file, which is really an ASCII text file (see Figure 14.1). You can make modifications to an existing format file by using a standard text editor.

TIP

Use the FMT extension when saving format files to simplify file identification.

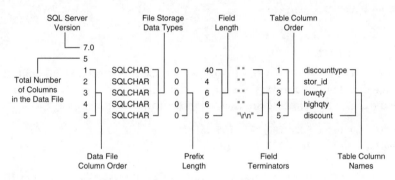

FIGURE 14.1   A sample format file.

After you have saved the format file, you can reuse the format file by specifying the -f (format file) switch, as in the following example:

```
bcp sales..discounts in discount.txt -f sample.fmt -U sa -P
```

NOTE

If a table has a corresponding format file, any column modification to the table must be reflected in the format file. For example, if you drop a column from a table, you must also remove the column from the format file.

Sample BCP Scripts

This section describes how to use BCP to perform typical import and export routines. The examples discussed in this section use the pubs..discounts table.

The following is the structure of the discounts table:

```
discounttype varchar (40)
stor_id varchar
lowqty smallint
highqty smallint
discount decimal(4, 2)
```

The following is discounts table data:

```
discounttype                                stor_id lowqty highqty discount
------------------------------------------- ------- ------ ------- --------
Initial Customer                            (null)  (null) (null)  10.50
Volume Discount                             (null)  100    1000    6.70
Customer Discount                           8042    (null) (null)  5.00
```

Simple Import

This example uses the -c switch to load a data file that contains tab-delimited fields and newline-delimited rows. For this example, the import data is contained in a file named disc.txt. Following are the contents of the sample import file:

```
Preferred Customer 6380 200 800  5.5
Valued Customer    7896 100 1000 8.5
```

The following syntax shows how to import the contents of the disc.txt file into the discounts table:

```
bcp pubs..discounts in disc.txt -c -U sa -P
```

Simple Export

This example uses the -c switch to export data to a file with tab-delimited fields and newline-delimited rows. The following syntax shows how to export the contents of the discounts table to the discount.out file:

```
bcp pubs..discounts out discount.out -c -U sa -P
```

Following is the output:

```
Initial Customer                                         10.50
Volume Discount                     100    1000   6.70
Customer Discount                   8042                 5.00
```

Comma-Delimited Import

This example imports a data file that contains comma-delimited fields and newline-delimited rows. The -t switch specifies a comma delimiter; the -r\n switch specifies a newline row delimiter. For this example, the import data is contained in a file named disc2.txt. Following are the contents of the sample import file:

```
Preferred Customer,6380,200,800,5.5
Valued Customer,7896,100,1000,8.5
```

The following syntax shows how to import the contents of the disc2.txt file into the discounts table:

```
bcp pubs..discounts in disc2.txt -c -t, -r\n -U sa -P
```

Comma-Delimited Export

This example exports the discounts table to a file with comma-delimited fields and newline row delimiters. The following syntax shows how to export the contents of the discounts table to the disc3.txt file:

```
bcp pubs..discounts out disc3.txt -c -t, -r\n -U sa -P
```

Following is the output:

```
Initial Customer,,,,10.50
Volume Discount,,100,1000,6.70
Customer Discount,8042,,,5.00
```

Fixed-Length Import

This example uses a fixed-length ASCII text file named disc4.txt. Table 14.6 shows the layout of the text file.

TABLE 14.6 File Layout of disc4.txt

Column Name	File Length	File Position
discounttype	40	1–39
stor_id	4	40–43
lowqty	6	44–49
highqty	6	50–55
discount	5	56–60

The following is sample data from disc4.txt:

```
12345678901234567890123456789012345678901234567890123456789012345678901234567890
Preferred Customer                      6380200  800   5.5
Valued Customer                         7896100  1000  8.5
```

For fixed-length data transfers, SQL Server needs to know the field positions in the data file. An easy way to do this is to use interactive BCP. To begin interactive BCP, use the following command.

```
bcp pubs..discounts in disc4.txt -U sa -P
```

For the first two prompts, you can accept the default values because they match the layout in the data file. For the third, fourth, and fifth prompts (see the highlighted text in Figure 14.2), you have to override the default prompts.

> **NOTE**
>
> When importing fixed-length ASCII data, *always* use char for the file storage type and 0 for the prefix length.

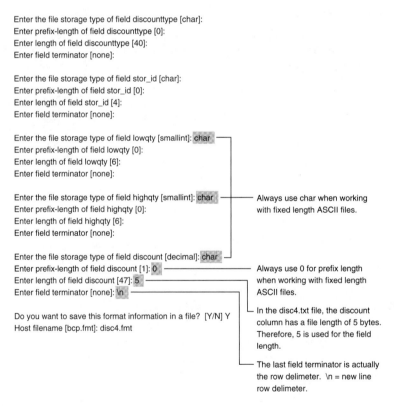

FIGURE 14.2   Interactive BCP responses.

Fixed-Length Export

Suppose that you need to export the `discounts` table in a fixed-length file format and the format must follow the specification used in the previous example. No problem—you can reuse the format file you created in the previous example (see Figure 14.3).

The following syntax shows how to export the contents of the `discounts` table to the `disc4.out` file:

```
bcp pubs..discounts out disc4.out -c -f disc4.fmt -U sa -P
```

```
7.0
5
1      SQLCHAR    0    40    " "      1    discounttype
2      SQLCHAR    0    4     " "      2    stor_id
3      SQLCHAR    0    6     " "      3    lowqty
4      SQLCHAR    0    6     " "      4    highqty
5      SQLCHAR    0    5     "\r\n"   5    discount
```

FIGURE 14.3   The `disc4.fmt` format file.

Skipped Fields on Import

Suppose that you want to skip the columns `stor_id`, `lowqty`, and `highqty` when you load the `disc4.txt` ASCII file. To do this, you must modify the format file. To skip a column, enter **0** for the table column order (see Figure 14.4).

```
7.0
5
1      SQLCHAR    0    40    " "      1    discounttype
2      SQLCHAR    0    4     " "      0    stor_id
3      SQLCHAR    0    6     " "      0 ⌐  lowqty
4      SQLCHAR    0    6     " "      0 |  highqty
5      SQLCHAR    0    5     "\r\n"   5    discount
```

A 0 indicates
that the column
should be skipped

FIGURE 14.4   The format file used to skip columns.

After you modify your format file, you can use the following BCP syntax to load the data:

```
bcp pubs..discounts in disc4.txt -c -f disc4.fmt -U sa -P
```

Skipped Fields on Export

BCP does not allow you to skip a column in a table during an export. However, you can trick BCP into skipping a column by creating a view that only references the columns you want to export, thus skipping unwanted columns. Then use BCP to export the data from the view.

The following syntax shows how to export only the discounttype and discount columns from the discounts table:

```
create view discounts_view as
select output = convert(char(40),discounttype) + convert(char(5),discount)
from discounts
```

Next, create a format file that contains one column (see Figure 14.5). Only one column is listed in the format file because the view concatenates the discounttype and discount columns.

```
7.0
1
1       SQLCHAR      0      45       "\r\n"      1      output
```

FIGURE 14.5   The format file used to export data from a view.

Finally, use BCP to export the data from the view:

```
bcp pubs..discounts_view out discview.txt -f discview.fmt -U sa -P
```

The following is sample output:

```
Initial Customer                         10.50
Volume Discount                           6.70
Customer Discount                         5.00
```

Modes of Operation

When importing data, BCP has two modes of operation: fast mode and slow mode. As you probably guessed, the fast mode runs faster than the slow mode. The performance difference is caused by the logging of transactions. Fast mode bypasses the transaction log; slow mode posts all data inserts to the transaction log.

> **NOTE**
>
> You need to be concerned with fast and slow mode BCP only when you import data. BCP does not use a fast or slow mode when you export data.
>
> When you run BCP, SQL Server automatically decides which BCP mode to run. There is no BCP switch that enables you to toggle between fast and slow modes.

Achieving Fast Mode BCP

In SQL Server 2000, several factors determine whether BCP can run in fast mode: SELECT INTO/BULKCOPY and indexes. For BCP to run in fast mode, the following four conditions must be true:

- The database option SELECT INTO/BULKCOPY must equal TRUE.

- Indexes must not exist on the target table.

- Triggers must not exist on the target table.

- The target table must not be replicated.

If any of these conditions are FALSE, BCP runs in slow mode (see Figure 14.6).

Why You Should Be Concerned with Which BCP Mode Is Running

You might be asking yourself, "Why not always run the BCP in fast mode?" The answer is based on the following two factors:

- Backup strategy

- Window of opportunity

Backup Strategy

To run the fast mode of BCP, you must have the SELECT INTO/BULKCOPY option set to TRUE. By setting this option to TRUE, you might be sacrificing data recovery for BCP performance. When SELECT INTO/BULKCOPY is set to TRUE, you cannot back up the transaction log for a database. Instead, you can only back up the entire database. This means that you will be unable to use the transaction log to provide up-to-the-minute data recovery.

Window of Opportunity

Fast mode BCP requires that the target table not contain any indexes. This means that you must consider the downtime involved with dropping the indexes and/or triggers, loading the data, and re-creating the indexes and/or triggers. For a table that requires 24-hour data access, it is not feasible to drop and re-create indexes.

TIP

To significantly reduce the time required to create a clustered index, have your import data presorted on the fields that make up your clustered index. Then use the WITH SORTED_DATA option to create the clustered index, as in the following example:

```
CREATE CLUSTERED INDEX pk_idx ON table1 (id) WITH SORTED_DATA
```

The WITH SORTED_DATA option bypasses the physical data sort step normally used to create a clustered index.

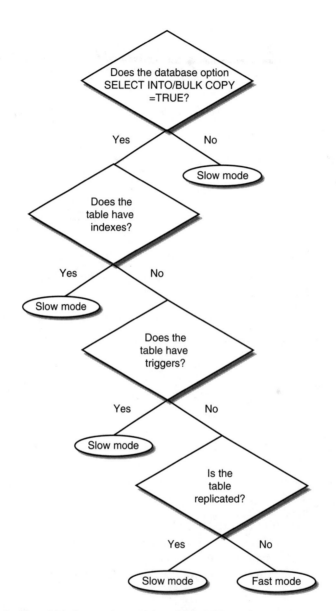

FIGURE 14.6   How SQL Server determines which BCP mode to run.

Table 14.7 helps clarify the differences between the two modes.

TABLE 14.7   Fast BCP Versus Slow BCP

Fast Mode	Slow Mode
PROS	
Fast! Operations are not logged. Don't have to worry about filling up the transaction log.	Maximum recoverability.
CONS	
Zero recoverability. Must back up the database after using BCP. Cannot back up the transaction log. Indexes must be rebuilt after loading the data.	Slow! Every insert is written to the transaction log. Can easily fill up the transaction log during large data imports, thus complicating the import process.

NOTE

BCP does not display the mode in use (fast or slow). To get BCP to run in fast mode, you need to know the rules of fast mode BCP!

BCP and Enforcement of Triggers, Rules, Defaults, Constraints, and Unique Indexes

When using BCP to import data into a SQL Server table, it is important that you understand how triggers, rules, defaults, constraints, and unique indexes are enforced. Many people forget that certain types of objects are bypassed when using BCP to import data. Table 14.8 summarizes which objects are enforced when BCP is used to import data.

TABLE 14.8   Enforcement of Objects

Object	Enforced?
Default	Yes
Unique index/unique constraints	Yes
Primary key and foreign key constraints	Yes
Check constraint	No*
Rule	No
Trigger	No

By default, constraints are not enforced. However, in SQL Server 2000, you can enable constraint checking by using the CHECK_CONSTRAINTS hint.

CAUTION

Do not forget that triggers, check constraints (unless the CHECK_CONSTRAINTS hint is enabled), and rules are not enforced when using BCP. To prevent data integrity problems, load your data into a work table and run it through a validation routine similar to the validation defined in your triggers, constraints, and table rules. When you are satisfied that the data meets your integrity requirements, transfer the data to your target table.

NOTE

Defaults are not enforced if the -k option is specified when importing data.

Common BCP Traps

Be on the lookout for the following traps. They always seem to be lurking out there.

- **Invalid dates**—When importing data, a data file that contains dates represented as 00/00/00 and 000000 will fail. These are invalid SQL Server date formats. This problem often arises when data is transferred from a mainframe system to SQL Server. You must adhere to SQL Server date formats when importing date information into datetime columns.

- **Space-filled dates**—When importing spaces into a datetime column, SQL Server defaults the column to 1/1/1900. This is probably not what you want! To avoid this problem, do not pad the column with any data; just follow the column with a delimiter. SQL Server sets the data column to NULL, which is presumably more in line with what you expected.

- **Improper delimiter**—Do not use a delimiter that exists in your data, or you will have problems. For example, if the first and last names are stored as one field and a user must enter **Smith, Mike**, do not use a comma delimiter. For this example, use a tab or another type of delimiter.

BCP Tips

Use the following tips to help simplify data imports and exports:

- **Use BCP hints to improve performance**—The following hints can significantly improve BCP performance:

Hint	Purpose
TABLOCK	Implements a table-level lock for the duration of the import. During informal testing of this option, BCP load times have decreased as much as 400%!
ORDER (`column_list`) where [ASC | DESC] [,`n`]}	Use this option if your data `column_list` = {column is presorted, and the sort column(s) match the clustered index in the corresponding table. By presorting the data, the clustered index can be updated more quickly.

- **Load from local files**—BCP runs faster when importing a file on the local machine, as opposed to importing a file over the network. Loading locally can improve BCP performance by a magnitude of 2–3 times.

- **Use parallel loading to improve performance**—By running BCP in parallel on multiple machines, you can greatly decrease the time required to import data files.

- **Use views to export data**—Views allow increased flexibility to filter and physically arrange your data. For example, to export only the date portion of a datetime column, use a view and the CONVERT function.

- **Sample table**:

  ```
  emp_id char(3)
  hire_date datetime
  ```

- **Sample view**:

  ```
  CREATE VIEW date_example_view AS
  SELECT emp_id,convert(char(12),hire_date,1)
  FROM sample_table
  ```

- **Sample BCP statement**:

  ```
  bcp sales..date_example_view out sample.out -c -Usa -P
  ```

NOTE

Refer to the CONVERT function in SQL Server's Books Online for other date formats.

- **Echo BCP output and errors to a text file**—To capture BCP's output, use the -o switch. To capture BCP's error messages, use the -e switch.

- **Automate data imports and exports**—An easy way to automate this process is to create a stored procedure that calls BCP and then runs any additional processes. The advantage of creating a single stored procedure to run your import process is that you can schedule it through SQL Server Agent. The following syntax is an example of a stored procedure that calls BCP to load data into the system and then executes summary procedures against the data:

```
CREATE PROCEDURE usp_load_example AS
/* flush out work table */
truncate table table1

/* BCP in data */
exec master..xp_cmdshell "bcp sales..table1 in table1.txt -c -Usa -P"

/* run summary procedures */
exec usp_summary1
exec usp_summaryN
```

CAUTION

Do not use xp_cmdshell to call BCP from within a user-defined transaction in a stored procedure. Doing so can lead to endless blocking!

TIP

Do you ever have to export or import data for all the tables in a database? To perform this task, you could manually create BCP scripts, but that can be tedious and time-consuming, especially if you must use BCP to copy data from numerous tables in the database. An alternative to manually creating the scripts is building a SQL statement that automatically generates the BCP syntax. Suppose that you need to export data from all the tables in the pubs database. To generate the BCP syntax, create a query that references the sysobjects table (each database in SQL Server has a sysobjects table and a corresponding record for each object in the database). In the WHERE clause of the query, specify type = 'U' (this clause only returns user tables). The following is a sample query used to generate the BCP syntax (the -c switch is used in this example to export the data in a tab-delimited character format):

```
select 'bcp pubs..' + name + ' out ' + name + '.txt' + '
➡ -c -Usa -P -Stfnserver'
        from pubs..sysobjects
        where type ='U'
        order by name
```

Following is the output from the query:

```
bcp pubs..authors out authors.txt -c -Usa -Ppassword -Stfnserver
bcp pubs..discounts out discounts.txt -c -Usa -Ppassword -Stfnserver
bcp pubs..employee out employee.txt -c -Usa -Ppassword -Stfnserver
bcp pubs..jobs out jobs.txt -c -Usa -Ppassword -Stfnserver
bcp pubs..pub_info out pub_info.txt -c -Usa -Ppassword -Stfnserver
bcp pubs..publishers out publishers.txt -c -Usa -Ppassword -Stfnserver
bcp pubs..roysched out roysched.txt -c -Usa -Ppassword -Stfnserver
bcp pubs..sales out sales.txt -c -Usa -Ppassword -Stfnserver
bcp pubs..stores out stores.txt -c -Usa -Ppassword -Stfnserver
bcp pubs..titleauthor out titleauthor.txt -c -Usa -Ppassword -Stfnserver
bcp pubs..titles out titles.txt -c -Usa -Ppassword -Stfnserver
```

Now that you have the proper BCP syntax, you can save the output from the query to a .BAT file and automatically run the file from the command line. As you see, the combination of SQL Server syntax with information from the system tables can simplify common DBA chores.

BULK INSERT

BULK INSERT is an import-only Transact-SQL statement that is similar in syntax and operation to BCP. BULK INSERT is faster than BCP and DTS, thus making it very appealing for those operations that require maximum performance.

Use the following syntax to perform BULK INSERT operations:

```
BULK INSERT [['database_name'.]['owner'].]{'table_name' FROM data_file}
[WITH
([switch1 parameter1] [switch2]
...
[switch10 parameter10]
...)
```

where the following are the parameters:

database_name	Name of the database being accessed. Database name is optional; if the database name is omitted, the user's default database is used.
owner	Owner of the table or view being accessed.
table_name	Name of the table or view being accessed.
datafile	The name of the data file for an import or the name of the file to be created during an export. A path can be included with this statement, such as c:\mssql\binn\authors.txt.
switch1, parameter1 and so on	Choose the switch and its parameter (if one is required) from Table 14.9.

TABLE 14.9   BULK INSERT Switches and Their Parameters

Parameter	Explanation
BATCHSIZE = *batch size*	The number of rows transferred in a batch. The default setting is the number of rows in the data file.
CHECK_CONSTRAINTS	Specifies that table constraints are observed when importing data. This can decrease import performance. By default, this option is off.
CODEPAGE = *code page*	Code page in use by the file being imported. Code page only needs to be specified if the file contains char, varchar, or text data types, and the data contains values greater than 127 or less than 32. The following is a list of valid code pages: ACP—ANSI/Microsoft Windows OEM—Default code page RAW—No conversion between code pages <value>—A specific code page number, such as 850
DATAFILETYPE = *'filetype'*	The type of file to import. The following is a list of valid file types: char—Character data mode. By default, fields are tab delimited, and rows are newline delimited. This is the default DATAFILETYPE. native—Native data mode. Use this option when importing data that was exporting via BCP and the -n switch (native mode export). widechar—Unicode data mode. widenative—Native import for non-character data and Unicode import for character data, provides better performance than the widechar option.
FIELDTERMINATOR = *'field_terminator'*	Field terminator. See Table 14.2 for terminators.
FIRSTROW = *first_row*	The number of the first row to copy.
FIRE_TRIGGERS	Notifies SQL Server to execute insert triggers during the bulk insert. By default, this setting is false.
FORMATFILE = *'format_file'*	The name of the format file used to import or export data. A path can be included with this statement, such as c:\mssql\binn\authors.fmt.
KEEPIDENTITY	Used when importing data into a table that contains an identity data type and you want to populate the column with values from the data file. If this switch is omitted, SQL Server automatically populates the identity column and ignores the field's corresponding data values in the import file. If this switch is included, the values from the data file are observed.

TABLE 14.9 Continued

Parameter	Explanation
KILOBYTES_PER_BATCH = *kilobytes_per_batch*	Number of kilobytes per batch. Higher values might result in faster load times.
KEEPNULLS	Preserves NULL values found in the data file. If this switch is omitted, SQL Server applies default values if they exist.
LASTROW = *last_row*	The number of the last row to copy.
MAXERRORS = *max_errors*	Maximum number of errors that can occur before the operation is terminated. Each failed insert counts as one error. Default value is 10.
ORDER (*column_list*) where *column_list* = {*column* [ASC | DESC] [,*n*]}	Use this option if your data is presorted and the sort column(s) match the clustered index in the corresponding table. By presorting the data, the clustered index can be updated quicker.
ROWS_PER_BATCH =U *rows_per_batch*	Number of rows per batch. Higher values might result in faster load times.
ROWTERMINATOR = '*row_terminator*'	Row terminator (see Table 14.2 for terminators).
TABLOCK	Specifies that a table lock is used when loading data.

TIP

This option can significantly improve import performance.

TIP

As I previously mentioned, BULK INSERT is very similar to BCP. Therefore, the BCP examples discussed in this chapter (format files, field terminators, row terminators, tips, and so on) can be directly applied to BULK INSERT.

The following are BULK INSERT examples:

```
/* simple character data import */
bulk insert customer from  'c:\temp\bcptest\customer.txt'
/* simple native data import */
bulk insert customer from  'c:\temp\bcptest\customer.n'
➥ with (DATAFILETYPE = 'native')

/* high performance character data import
   with ORDER and TABLOCK options */
bulk insert customer from  'c:\temp\bcptest\customer.txt'
➥ with (ORDER(customer_id),TABLOCK)
```

BCP FAQ

The following section lists some of the common questions asked by DBAs about BCP:

Q How can I use BCP to import data from a 6.x version of SQL Server? Whenever I use BCP to import the data, I get various ODBC errors.

A Use the -V (60|65) option when importing data from a 6.x version of SQL Server. The SQL Server 2000 version of BCP uses ODBC to interface with SQL Server, whereas previous versions used DB-Library. ODBC treats data types differently from DB-Library.

Q When should I use BCP instead of DTS?

A The main reason to use BCP is performance. BCP can import and export data faster than DTS. If performance is not an issue, I recommend using DTS. DTS is easier to use and is more flexible than BCP.

Q Which file formats are supported by BCP?

A BCP supports the following formats: ASCII text, native, and Unicode. Use DTS to import and export other file formats.

Q Can BCP export the result returned by a query? What about exporting the contents of a stored procedure?

A Yes, instead of specifying a table name, specify a query and use the queryout option. The following is an example of using BCP to export the output from a query to a text file.

```
bcp "select * from pubs..authors order by au_lname"
➥ queryout authors.txt -c -Usa -P -Spghdev3
```

The following is an example of using BCP to export the output from a stored procedure to a text file.

```
bcp "exec sp_who" queryout sp_who.txt -c -Usa -P -Spghdev3
```

Summary

The following is BCP and BULK INSERT summary information:

- BCP and BULK INSERT use three file types to transfer data: character mode, native mode, and Unicode. Character mode is ASCII text, and native mode is a SQL Server file type. Character mode is usually easier to work with.

- When working with fixed-length ASCII files, always use the char data type and 0 prefix length.

- To skip a column in interactive BCP, enter 0 prefix length, 0 length, and no terminator.

- When importing data, BCP has two modes of operation: fast and slow. Fast mode bypasses the transaction log; slow mode posts all data inserts to the transaction log.

- To achieve fast mode BCP, set the database option SELECT INTO/BULKCOPY to TRUE, drop the indexes on the target table, drop any triggers on the table, and do not have the table participate in replication.

- Your ability to continuously run fast mode BCP depends on the backup and data access requirements in your production environment.

- Check constraints, rules, and triggers are not enforced when using BCP and BULK INSERT, unless the CHECK_CONSTRAINTS hint is enabled. The CHECK_CONSTRAINTS hint specifies that table constraints are enforced when running BCP and BULK INSERT.

- When importing data into a date column, spaces in a data file convert to 1/1/1900.

- The TABLOCK and ORDER hints can significantly improve BCP and BULK INSERT performance.

PART VII

Troubleshooting

IN THIS PART

15 Troubleshooting SQL Server

15

Troubleshooting SQL Server

by Mark Spenik

So far, each chapter in this book has covered common problems and resolutions. This chapter steps back and focuses on how SQL Server alerts you to possible problems with databases, objects, or the server; how to find more information about the problem; how to fix the problem; and how to get help in determining and fixing your problem. Quite frequently DBAs are confronted with helping to troubleshoot and tune poorly performing applications. For example, a user may be complaining about a report taking too much time to run. If other users have very few complaints and your monitoring shows that the processor, disk I/O, and memory are all fine more than likely you will find the problem in the queries running the report. Troubleshooting a poorly performing application is covered in the following:

- Chapter 18, "Understand Indexes"

- Chapter 19, "Query Optimization"

- Chapter 20, "Multiuser Issues"

- Chapter 22, "Using Stored Procedures and Cursors"

- Chapter 24, "Monitoring SQL Server"

They cover important application performance issues as well as introduce tools to monitor applications. This chapter looks at troubleshooting problems with SQL Server, interrupting error messages, and other various problems that might occur. Start by taking a look at SQL Server error messages.

IN THIS CHAPTER

- SQL Error Messages

- Using the Error Message Number to Resolve the Error

- Deciphering the Error Log

- Using the Event Viewer

- Killing a Process

- Viewing Detailed Process Activity

- Using DBCC and Trace Statements to Troubleshoot

- Troubleshooting Applications

- Other Sources of Help and Information

- Troubleshooting FAQ

SQL Error Messages

If you run a query and accidentally make a mistake by entering a table that does not exist in the database, what happens? SQL Server returns an error message. Actually, SQL Server reacts to all errors in the same manner, whether those errors are generated by users, databases, objects, or the system. SQL Server returns a formatted error message and/or writes the error message to the error log and/or event log. Here is a quick example that executes a SQL statement to update a nonexistent table in the pubs database. The SQL statement for the example is as follows:

```
UPDATE new_authors
Set author1 = "Spenik",
author2 = "Sledge",
title="Microsoft SQL Server DBA Survival Guide"
```

When the statement is executed, the following error message is returned:

```
Server: Msg 208, Level 16, State 1, Line 1
Invalid object name 'new_authors'.
```

The preceding error message demonstrates the standard message format for error messages returned by SQL Server. Examine the format of a standard SQL Server error message.

> **TIP**
>
> The first thing presented in the error message is the message number, severity level, state, and line number. To most users, these numbers are just garbage to be ignored, so they skip down to the message and try to resolve the problem. In reality, the error message number is very useful for obtaining more error information. You can use the severity levels to help find errors that need to be handled. When tracking a problem, always write down all the error information, including the message number, severity level, and state. In many cases, these will be of more assistance than the actual message.

Error Message Number

Each error message displayed by SQL Server has an associated error message number that uniquely identifies the type of error.

> **TIP**
>
> You can define your own error messages. User-defined error message numbers must be greater than 50,000 and less than 2,147,483,647. You can use the system stored procedure sp_addmessage to add the error message to the system table sysmessages. From a trigger or stored procedure, you can use the RAISERROR statement to report a user-defined error

message to the client and SQL Server. You can also use the Transact SQL function `FormatMessage` to construct an error message to send to a client from an existing error message in the `sysmessages` table.

Error Severity

The error severity levels provide a quick reference about the nature of the error. The severity levels range from 0 to 25.

0 to 10	Messages with a severity level of 0 to 10 are informational messages and not actual errors.
11 to 16	Severity levels 11 to 16 are generated as a result of user problems and can be fixed by the user. For example, the error message returned in the invalid update query, used earlier, had a severity level of 16.
17	Severity level 17 indicates that SQL Server has run out of a configurable resource, such as locks. Severity error 17 can be corrected by the DBA, and in some cases, by the database owner.
18	Severity level 18 messages indicate nonfatal internal software problems.
19	Severity level 19 indicates that a nonconfigurable resource limit has been exceeded.

NOTE

Severity errors 19 through 25 are fatal errors and can only be used via `RAISERROR` by members of the fixed database role sysadmin with the `log option` required. Severity 0–18 can be used by all users. When a fatal error occurs (20–25), the running process that generated the error is terminated (nonfatal errors continue processing). For error severity levels 20 and greater, the client connection to SQL Server is terminated.

20	Severity level 20 indicates a problem with a statement issued by the current process.
21	Severity level 21 indicates that SQL Server has encountered a problem that affects all the processes in a database.
22	Severity level 22 means a table or index has been damaged. To try to determine the extent of the problem, stop and restart SQL Server. If the problem is in the cache and not on the disk, the restart corrects the problem. Otherwise, use DBCC to determine the extent of the damage and the required action to take.

23	Severity level 23 indicates a suspect database. To determine the extent of the damage and the proper action to take, use the DBCC commands.
24	Severity level 24 indicates a hardware problem.
25	Severity level 25 indicates some type of system error.

State Number

The error state number is an integer value between 1 and 127; it represents information about the source that issued the error (such as the error can be called from more then one place).

Error Message

The error message is a description of the error that occurred. The error messages are stored in the sysmessages system table. Figure 15.1 shows a query result of the sysmessages table.

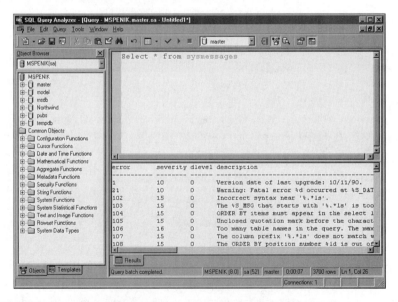

FIGURE 15.1   Query results of sysmessage using the Query Analyzer.

TIP

To use the SQL Enterprise Manager to view error messages or search for error messages, select a server and right-click. Select All Tasks and Manage SQL Server Messages, and the SQL Server Message dialog box appears. Using the dialog box, you can search for error messages by error number or key words.

Using the Error Message Number to Resolve the Error

Earlier in this chapter, you learned that, by using the error message number, you could quickly retrieve detailed information about the error and possible ways to resolve the error. How, you might ask? Books Online!

INFORMATION AT YOUR FINGERTIPS

Isn't technology great? I believe that to really appreciate Microsoft's Books Online, you have to have been a Sybase DBA from the 4.2 UNIX days. When an error would occur that displayed the error number, you jotted down the error number and then tried to locate the error messages and the troubleshooting guide. Of course, the book was never in the same place. And if you had my luck, when you found the book, the error number was never in the book—it always fell within the "reserved" section or something similar. Microsoft first gave us Books Online in SQL Server 6.0, and it continues to improve the overall content and usefulness of the product. New DBAs, who start with SQL Server 2000, will truly be spoiled by Microsoft's Books Online. By the way, always, always install the Books Online to your hard drive; it's well worth the 10MB or so of disk space.

When you installed SQL Server, you should have included the Books Online utility shown in Figure 15.2.

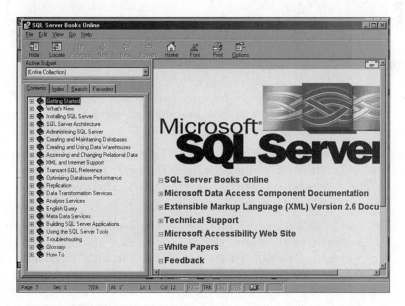

FIGURE 15.2   The SQL Server Books Online dialog box.

To see how to use Books Online to find more information on the error message number displayed during the invalid query example (error message number 208), follow these steps:

1. From the Windows NT or Windows 9*x* Start menu, select the SQL Server 2000 program group and select Books Online. The SQL Server Books Online dialog box, shown in Figure 15.2, appears. From the SQL Server Books Online dialog box, click the Search Tab, shown in Figure 15.3.

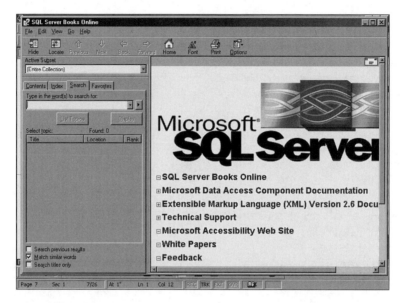

FIGURE 15.3   The Search tab.

2. The Search tab enables you to quickly search Books Online for specific information. In the Query combo box, type the error message number: **208**. In the Topic Area To Search frame, select the Search Titles Only check box.

3. To run the search, click the List Topics button. The query runs, searching for 208 in the title of any of the book topics. If one or more items are found, they are displayed in a query results frame in the SQL Server Books Online dialog box (see Figure 15.4).

4. To view the document(s) found in the search, double-click the item or select the item and click the Display button. The detailed information for the error message number, including a detailed explanation and the action to take, is displayed in the document. You can even print the document! Just think, no more trying to locate a troubleshooting or error message book! No more flipping through pages searching for error messages; if the error number is not in the book, you know immediately! When getting multiple documents back for an error message query, select the document title Error Error_Number. For example, the document title Error 208 displays detailed information on error 208. The detailed information found for error number 208 is displayed in

Figure 15.5. After you have displayed the error number document, read through the document for an explanation of the error and then follow the directions in the Action section of the document to correct the error.

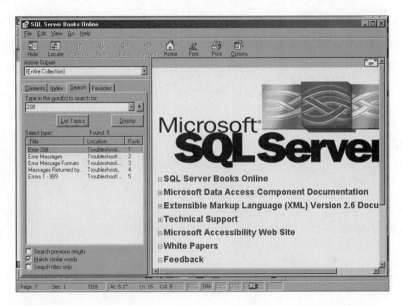

FIGURE 15.4   Query results frame in the SQL Server Books Online dialog box.

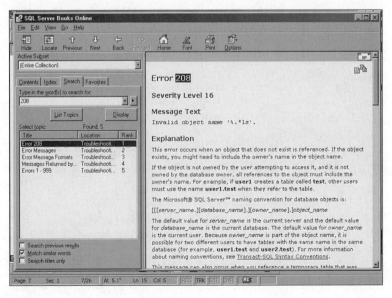

FIGURE 15.5   The Books Online description of error message 208.

Deciphering the Error Log

The error log is a standard text file that holds SQL Server information and error messages. The error log is used both in Windows NT systems as well as Windows 9*x* systems. The error log can provide meaningful information to help you track down problems or to alert you to potential or existing problems. SQL Server maintains the current error log and a default value of six previous error log files. SQL Server 2000 allows you to configure the number of previous log files to maintain before reusing them. The current error log filename is ERRORLOG; the previous error log files, referred to as *archived error logs*, are named ERRORLOG.1 (most recent) to ERRORLOG.6 (the oldest). The default location of the error log file is in the \LOG directory off the SQL Server home directory, which is under Program Files\Microsoft SQL Server\Instance Name. The following is an example of a SQL Server error log:

```
2000-09-01 21:49:31.08 server    Microsoft SQL Server  2000 - 8.00.100
➥(Intel X86)
     Apr 18 2000 01:19:00
     Copyright (c) 1988-2000 Microsoft Corporation
     Personal Edition on Windows 4.10 (Build 1998:  )


2000-09-01 21:49:31.10 server    Copyright (C) 1988-2000 Microsoft Corporation.
2000-09-01 21:49:31.10 server    All rights reserved.
2000-09-01 21:49:31.10 server    Server Process ID is -676985.
2000-09-01 21:49:31.10 server    Logging SQL Server messages in file
➥'d:\mssql7\data\MSSQL\log\ERRORLOG'.
2000-09-01 21:49:31.33 server    SQL Server is starting at priority class
➥'normal'(1 CPU detected).
2000-09-01 21:49:32.01 server    User Mode Scheduler configured for thread
➥ processing
2000-09-01 21:49:32.12 server    Using dynamic lock allocation.
➥ [500] Lock Blocks, [1000] Lock Owner Blocks
2000-09-01 21:49:32.53 spid3     Starting up database 'master'.
2000-09-01 21:49:34.15 spid3     0 transactions rolled back in
➥ database 'master' (1).
2000-09-01 21:49:34.22 spid3     Recovery is checkpointing database 'master' (1)
2000-09-01 21:49:34.70 server    Using 'SSNETLIB.DLL' version '8.0.100'.
2000-09-01 21:49:34.95 spid3     Server name is 'MSPENIK'.
2000-09-01 21:49:35.14 spid7     Starting up database 'msdb'.
2000-09-01 21:49:35.33 spid8     Starting up database 'pubs'.
2000-09-01 21:49:36.00 server    SQL server listening on TCP port 1433,
➥ Shared Memory.
2000-09-01 21:49:37.02 spid5     Clearing tempdb database.
2000-09-01 21:49:40.11 spid5     Starting up database 'tempdb'.
```

```
2000-09-01 21:49:40.61 spid3      Recovery complete.
2000-09-01 21:50:53.58 spid51     Using 'xpstar.dll' version '2000.80.100'
➥ to execute extended stored procedure 'sp_MSgetversion'.
```

The error log output includes the time and date the message was logged, the source of the message, and the description of the error message. If an error occurs, the log contains the error message number and description.

TIP

Spend some time looking at and understanding the messages in the error log, especially the proper startup sequence messages. When and if your SQL Server begins to have problems, you will be able to quickly decipher abnormal events or messages in your error log. The archive files come in handy here as well because you can use them as a reference for when things were running fine.

You can view the error log using the SQL Server Enterprise Manager. To use the Enterprise Manager, simply expand the error log tree located in the management folder on the server you want to view, expand the SQL Server Logs icon, and then select the error log you want to see. The error log is loaded into the right frame of the SQL Server Enterprise Manager as shown in Figure 15.6.

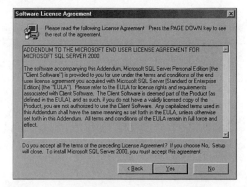

FIGURE 15.6   The server error log displayed in the SQL Server Enterprise Manager.

The error log can be a useful source of information in certain problems. For example, if SQL Server immediately shuts down after startup or when clients lose network connections, the error log provides you with valuable information to debug the problem. If you are unable to connect to SQL Server with the Enterprise Manager, you can use the Windows Notepad application to open and view the error log.

Using the Event Viewer

SQL Server also logs information and error messages to the Windows NT event log. NT uses the event log NT as a repository for the operating system and applications to log informational and error messages. The Windows NT Event Viewer is located in the Windows NT Administrative Tools group. The advantage of using the Event Viewer over the error log is that errors are easy to spot because NT highlights all error messages with a red stop sign; it highlights information messages with a blue exclamation mark (see Figure 15.7).

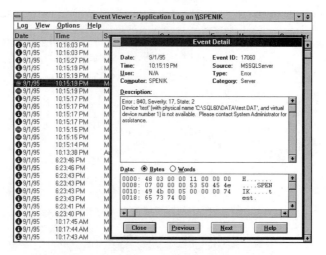

FIGURE 15.7   The Windows NT Event Viewer, showing the application event log.

To view the detailed error message description, severity level, and state, double-click the line item. An Event Details dialog box appears. The Event Viewer also provides a search utility that enables you to search for specific types of events in the event log. For example, you can search for all the error messages in the event log.

> **NOTE**
>
> Of course, the Windows NT event log is only available with SQL Server 2000 running on NT and Windows 2000 platforms and is not available with Windows 9x.

Killing a Process

A SQL Server *user process* is a task or request made to SQL Server by a user. Occasionally, you might be required to halt (stop) a user process before it completes. Perhaps the user has incorrectly formatted a query or launched a massive transaction that will take hours to complete and has blocked out other users from necessary table information. Whatever the case might be, you can bet that sooner or later someone will ask you to stop her process or someone else will complain about not getting back any information. The proper terminology for halting a process is called *killing a process*, which sounds much more severe than just halting or stopping the process. When you kill a process, you completely remove the process from SQL Server. You can kill a distributed transaction in SQL Server 2000.

TIP

The number one reason to kill a process is interference with other users' processing. (That is, the rogue process prevents them from getting to the required information by "blocking" them out, as in exclusive table locks, for a lengthy transaction.)

SQL Server assigns each task a unique identity number called a spid (system process ID). To view the currently running processes and their spids, issue the system stored procedure sp_who, which has the following format:

```
sp_who [login id | 'spid']
```

In this syntax, `login_id` is the specific user login ID for which you want to report activity and `spid` is a specific process ID for which you want to report activity.

Issuing the sp_who command with no parameters displays a report on all the current processes on SQL Server, as in the following example:

spid	ecid	status	loginame	hostname	blk	dbname	cmd
1	0	background	sa		0	NULL	LAZY WRITER
2	0	sleeping	sa		0	NULL	LOG WRITER
3	0	background	sa		0	master	SIGNAL HANDLER
4	0	background	sa		0	NULL	LOCK MONITOR
5	0	background	sa		0	master	TASK MANAGER
6	0	sleeping	sa		0	NULL	CHECKPOINT SLEEP
7	0	background	sa		0	master	TASK MANAGER
8	0	background	sa		0	master	TASK MANAGER
9	0	background	sa		0	master	TASK MANAGER
51	0	sleeping	sa		0	master	AWAITING COMMAND
52	0	runnable	sa		0	master	SELECT
53	0	sleeping	sa		0	master	AWAITING COMMAND

To kill a process, use the KILL command, which has the following syntax:

```
KILL {spid | UOW} [With STATUSONLY]
```

In this syntax, *spid* is the system process ID of the process you want to terminate. UOW stands for *Unit of Work* and refers to a distributed transaction you want to halt. The uow is a character string that can be obtained via the DTC monitor, error log, or syslockinfo table. The WITH STATUSONLY argument can be used to obtain information about a spid or uow that is being rolled back.

You can kill only one spid at a time, and the statement cannot be reversed. After you have issued the command, the process *will* be killed. If the command being killed has a lot of work to roll back, it might take some time for the process to shut down. To kill spid number 52 shown in the previous sample, you issue the following command:

```
kill 52
```

> **NOTE**
>
> In presystem 10 versions of Sybase and pre-Windows NT versions of Microsoft SQL Server, the KILL command did not always work. If the spid was a sleeping process, the only way to kill the process was to shut down the server. The inability to kill a process with the KILL statement was a kind of joke among DBAs; the processes were nicknamed *zombies*. A zombie process was a serious problem when a process really did need to be shut down and the KILL command was ineffective. Microsoft corrected the problem in SQL Server for Windows NT 4.21. In some cases with Microsoft SQL Server, you might be unable to or should not attempt to kill a process. In such cases, you must shut down the server. For instance, you cannot kill your own process, system processes, or processes that are executing an extended stored procedure. You should also avoid killing the following processes:
>
> - Awaiting Command
> - Select
> - Signal Handler
> - Checkpoint Sleep
> - Lazy Writer
> - Lock Monitor

You also can kill a process using the SQL Server Enterprise Manager by performing the following steps:

1. After you select a server, expand the Management folder and expand the Current Activity icon with a single click. Select the Process Info icon; all the current processes running on SQL Server as well as the spids of the processes are displayed in the right frame of the Enterprise Manager, shown in Figure 15.8.

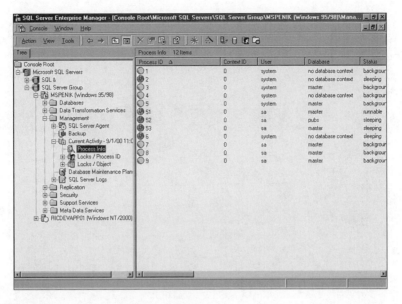

FIGURE 15.8 The Current Activity dialog box.

2. To kill a process, select the process you want to terminate with a single mouse click, and then right-click and select the Kill Process option. A dialog box appears asking if you want to terminate the process. Click Yes to terminate the selected process.

Viewing Detailed Process Activity

The day will come when your phone is ringing off the hook because suddenly the system is slow or a user has been waiting a very long time for a report to complete. With SQL Server 2000, you can easily view the current activity of the system using the Current Activity dialog box (refer to Figure 15.8). To view detailed information on an executing process, select the process in which you wish to view the information from the current activity view (refer to Fig 15.8) with a single mouse click, and then right-click and select the Properties option. The Process Information dialog box of the Current Activity dialog box appears (see Figure 15.9).

The Process Information dialog box allows you to view the last command executed by a process or the resource usage of the process (CPU and disk usage).

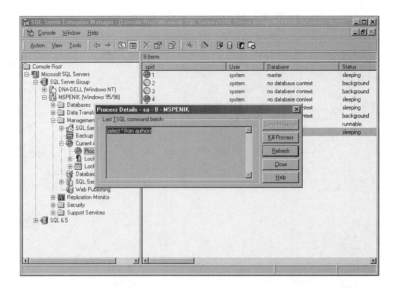

FIGURE 15.9   The Process Information dialog box.

Using DBCC and Trace Statements to Troubleshoot

DBCC stands for *Database Consistency Checker*. DBCC consists of a series of
commands that perform a variety of functions on databases and database objects.
DBCC commands are used to perform database and database object maintenance but
also can be used to find errors—and in some cases, fix them. SQL Server also
provides a series of trace flags that can be used to provide additional information
about SQL Server such as the estimated and actual cost of a sort (trace flag 326). To
turn a trace flag on for a single user connection, use the following syntax:

```
DBCC TRACEON(FLAG_NUMBER)
```

For example, the following syntax would turn on trace flag 326:

```
DBCC TRACEON(326)
```

To turn off a trace flag, use the following syntax:

```
DBCC TRACEOFF(FLAG_NUMBER)
```

To turn off trace flag 326, you would issue the following command:

```
DBCC TRACEOFF(326)
```

To turn a trace flag on for all connections, use the SQL Server startup command-line option -T followed by the trace flag number. You can add startup command-line options using the Enterprise Manager or by starting the server from the command line. For useful trace flag settings, see the "Troubleshooting FAQ" section later in this chapter.

NOTE

DBCC commands are detailed in Appendix B, "DBCC Commands." It is highly recommended that you read and reread Appendix B. Understanding when and how to use DBCC can save you a lot of headaches. In previous versions of SQL Server, DBCC was required for maintenance as well. In SQL Server 2000, the maintenance aspect of DBCC has diminished, but it is still useful for troubleshooting and in some cases correcting database problems.

So how do you use DBCC to track errors? For starters, you can examine the output of your DBCC maintenance commands for standard SQL Server error messages. If you find an error message in a DBCC output, treat the error message like any other SQL Server error message and use Books Online or technical support to resolve the error. When you call technical support or find the error number in Books Online, one or many of the resolution steps might be to execute DBCC command(s) to resolve the problem.

Become familiar with DBCC commands. Use the correct DBCC options (if any) to fix a problem in your database when instructed to do so.

FOLLOW THE CLUES

The following story is a story I have used in the previous editions, but I still think it rings true. It also brings to light a frustration many readers have expressed about the lack of documentation, articles, or information about problems encountered at your sites. As the story shows, a lot can happen, especially unexpected things that are hard to document.

One night, while working late to help a group fix an SQL Server problem, I was reminded of a very important tip when troubleshooting SQL Server problems: *Follow the clues. Do not speculate first.* The reason I was reminded of this tip is that, when I arrived on the scene, everyone involved was ready to blame the problem on the new release of SQL Server that they had upgraded to two weeks earlier. (The upgrade was from release 4.21 to release 6.0—and I performed the upgrade.) When I looked over the error log and the general state of the system, I quickly ruled out the upgrade.

The problem they were having was running a new stored procedure that pulled in information from a mainframe flat file and massaged and reformatted the data to be output to another flat file to feed the mainframe. Whenever the stored procedure ran, the transaction log filled up before the process could complete. They had expanded the log several times, and still the stored procedure could not run to completion. One important fact to mention is that the procedure had been tested with 500 rows on versions 4.21 and 6.0, but now they were attempting to run 16,000 rows.

One problem I spotted and fixed immediately with DBCC commands was that the transaction log's size was invalid and would not respond correctly to `TRANSACTION WITH NO_LOG` command. After the transaction log problem was corrected, I set up a threshold to back up the log when it was 80% full. Still, the procedure would not run. When I examined the stored procedure, I found nothing unusual. A transaction was started and then the 16,000 rows were copied to four tables. This organization had several stored procedures that performed the same operation, and nothing looked unusual with the stored procedure. Again the cry of "Maybe it's version 6.0—let's try 4.21" was echoed.

Because there was no evidence to suggest that it was a version 6.0 problem, we tried the procedure again. This time, we monitored the server from the version 4.21 Object Manager using `sp_who`, `sp_lock`, and `DBCC SQLPERF(LOGSPACE)` to track what was going on. It was not long before we noticed that the `spid` executing the stored procedure seemed to be stuck on an `UPDATE` statement. That seemed odd because the only `UPDATE` occurred outside of the transaction and had already occurred. Again moans about the upgrade or the corrupted transaction log rose across the room. They came from everyone except the developer, who quietly stated, "I bet there is an update trigger on the table I'm inserting into." Well, she was right. Not only was there an update trigger, but also the SQL statement was incorrectly copying 16,000 rows into a table with an update trigger when only 39 rows should have been copied. The problem was quickly solved.

The moral of this story is that troubleshooting can be difficult and often consists of more than one clue (such as an upgrade, a corrupted transaction log, and a new process). Try not to jump to conclusions. Solve each problem, one at a time, and if something does not make sense, keep searching for the real reason the process fails so that you can fix it. It is very easy to go down the wrong road. Oh, by the way, beware of triggers on tables when troubleshooting a developer process. They are easy to forget and, in some cases, might be the unexpected root of the problem!

Table/Index Fragmentation

Table/Index fragmentation occurs on tables that have a lot of insert/update/delete activity. Because the table is modified over time, pages begin to fill, possibly causing page splits on clustered indexes. As pages split, the newly added pages might use disk space that is not contiguous; this hurts performance because contiguous pages are a form of sequential I/O that is faster (about twice as fast) than nonsequential I/O. The fullness of each data page can also vary (that is, pages are not full) under heavy data modifications. You can defragment the table by executing DBCC `DBREINDEX` on the tables clustered index, which packs each page with the fill factor amount of data and reorders the information on contiguous data pages. You can also drop and re-create the index. However, using the `DBREINDEX` command is faster than dropping and re-creating the index(es). Not only does rebuilding an index improve performance when you read the table, but it also can increase the available database space. Rebuilding a clustered index on a very large table can take a fair amount of time. SQL Server 2000 provides the DBCC `SHOWCONTIG` command, which enables you to determine how fragmented a table or index is (that is, whether or not you need to rebuild it). The SHOWCONTIG option has the following format:

```
DBCC SHOWCONTIG (table id, [index id])
```

In this syntax, *table id* and *index id* are the IDs of the object found in the sysobjects table of the database. For example, the following is the command line and output from a DBCC SHOWCONTIG command performed on the authors table in the pubs database:

```
DBCC SHOWCONTIG scanning 'authors' table...
Table: 'authors' (117575457); index ID: 1, database ID: 5
TABLE level scan performed.
- Pages Scanned...............................: 1
- Extents Scanned.............................: 1
- Extent Switches.............................: 0
- Avg. Pages per Extent.......................: 1.0
- Scan Density [Best Count:Actual Count].......: 100.00% [1:1]
- Logical Scan Fragmentation ..................: 0.00%
- Extent Scan Fragmentation ...................: 0.00%
- Avg. Bytes Free per Page....................: 6008.0
- Avg. Page Density (full)....................: 25.77%- DBCC execution completed.
If DBCC printed error messages, see your System Administrator.
```

To determine if you need to rebuild the index because of excessive index page splits, look at the Scan Density value displayed by DBCC SHOWCONTIG. The Scan Density value should be at or near 100%. If it is significantly below 100%, rebuild the index.

TIP

For those of you wondering how to find the table ID using sysobjects, the query used for the authors table is shown here. Remember: To get a table ID for a specific table, you must be in the database when you query sysobjects or make a direct reference to the database such as database..sysobjects. The query (executed from the master database) is as follows:

```
select id from pubs..sysobjects where name = 'authors'
```

Better yet, use the Transact SQL function, object_id as follows:

```
Select object_id('authors')
```

Troubleshooting Applications

SQL Server 2000 comes with many different utilities to help you debug your applications and get the best performance. The SQL Server Profiler (previously SQL Trace) enables you to monitor SQL Server while your applications are executing in a production or test environment. You can use the SQL Server Profiler to look at different events, objects, Transact-SQL statements, locking, and errors. You can save the traces to a file to replay on the server (or a different server). This ability is useful when tuning a server and application or in situations when an event occurs that causes your server or application to behave in an undesirable manner. You can read more about the SQL Server Profiler in Chapter 24.

The SQL Server Query Analyzer provides more SHOWPLAN detail about the query being executed, allowing you to make better decisions about tuning the query. Another feature to help you tune applications is the SQL Server Index Tuning Wizard, which can read a trace from the SQL Server Profiler as well as a query from the SQL Server Query Analyzer, and make recommendations on how to index the tables to get better performance. You can learn more about these utilities in Chapter 18 and Chapter 19.

Other Sources of Help and Information

In SQL Server 2000, Microsoft has done a good job of providing useful and valuable information in Books Online. However, as a DBA, it is important for you to know that there are many other good sources of information for Microsoft SQL Server (such as this book). What happens when the problem is beyond the scope of published resources? The following sections discuss some of the options available to you.

Technical Support

When you run across a problem not covered in this book or one of a very critical and urgent nature, it's time to get in touch with your tech support company. If you have purchased SQL Server, you have also (hopefully) purchased a support agreement with Microsoft or with a Microsoft Solution Provider to help you in an emergency. If not, Microsoft can still provide help (for a per-incident charge). In general, Microsoft's support contracts and agreements are less expensive than those of some of the other RDBMS companies. A Microsoft Solution Provider is an independent organization that provides consulting and integration services for Microsoft products and also can provide support. Before calling tech support, be sure to have all the information required to start an incident report. You should have the following information:

- Hardware platform
- Version of Windows NT
- Version of SQL Server (you can get this from the error log or by using the @@Version global variable)

- Complete error message (number, level, state, and description)

- Type of environment (production or development)

- Urgency of problem resolution

- Description and scenario of the problem and the cause

SQL Server 2000 provides a utility called `sqldiag` that will collect this information for you besides lots and lots of additional information to supply to tech support. For more information, see the "Troubleshooting FAQ" section in this chapter.

> **TIP**
>
> If the problem is one that can be reproduced using SQL commands or a sequence of events, have this information written down so that the tech support person can duplicate the results. Even better than writing it down, you can use the SQL Server 2000 extended stored procedure `xp_trace_setqueryhistory` to create a trace file of the last 100 queries executed. You can also use `xp_trace_flushqueryhistory` to include exceptions that occur as well.

Microsoft TechNet and Microsoft Developer Network

Before there was SQL Server Books Online, there was Microsoft TechNet. Microsoft TechNet is a monthly CD subscription that provides a wealth of information about Microsoft products. TechNet provides product white papers, release notes, current patches and drivers, and a knowledge base of product information and problem resolution. TechNet is fairly inexpensive for a yearly subscription of 12 monthly CDs packed with information. To find out more about TechNet, visit its Web site at `http://www.microsoft.com/technet`.

> **TIP**
>
> TechNet is my second line of defense. If I can't resolve the problem based on my knowledge and Books Online, I check TechNet for information on the problem. Do yourself a favor and subscribe!

The advantage of TechNet is that it is a monthly CD, so problem resolution not available when SQL Server 2000 shipped can be placed in the TechNet knowledge base for your immediate use. TechNet's search facility is similar to the Books Online search facility (or vice versa because TechNet was here first), as shown in Figure 15.10. As with Books Online, you can perform searches on error numbers or keywords and get a list of articles that contain the keyword or error number.

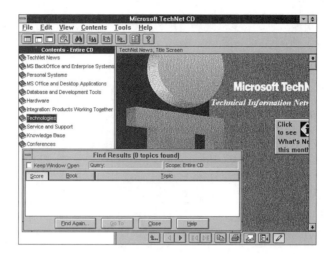

FIGURE 15.10   Microsoft TechNet.

Microsoft Developer Network is also a very useful source of highly technical information on SQL Server. You can subscribe to MSDN like TechNet, and you can also view MSDN online at `http://www.msdn.microsoft.com`.

The Internet

To obtain interactive support without using tech support, try one of the many Internet sites or newsgroups offered by Microsoft for SQL Server. The newsgroup for SQL Server can be found at `http://www.msdn.Microsoft.com`. Microsoft's Web page for SQL Server is `http://www.Microsoft.com/SQL`. Using the online services, you can search for existing messages that deal with problems you are experiencing, or you can post messages asking for help from your peers. The online services seem to be very useful. Many individuals have their problems resolved on the online services, but most of these problems are of a noncritical nature because turnaround time for a posted question is an unknown.

User Groups

SQL Server user groups can provide a forum in which you can discuss problems or issues with your local peers. They also tend to enlighten you on current products and future releases.

Using the Performance Monitor for Trend Analysis

Frequently problems arise because DBAs are caught off guard and run out of system resources such as disk space, processing power or memory. For example, a DBA may not realize that a particular database (maybe one of 100 he is managing) is growing at an alarming rate due to heavy transaction load. Or perhaps your company is adding new employees on a monthly basis to use your SQL Server systems and suddenly one day you realize that the processors on the machine are pegged constantly above 90 percent. Maybe you do a great job monitoring your system resources and you are always looking for ways to improve the performance of your SQL Server and databases and one such way would be to properly size tempDB and your database transaction logs to prevent them from constantly resizing during peak periods or batch processes. So how can a DBA prevent resource problems from catching him off guard or get additional information to help them tune his databases and servers? One tool available to the DBA is the Windows performance monitor. In Chapter 24 "Monitoring SQL Server," using the performance monitor and the counters to track are described in detail. However, this section differs by showing you how to capture the log information into a file to import into a database for further analysis and capacity planning. For example, using the performance monitor a DBA can capture Windows counters and SQL counters (for example, processor utilization, SQL Server Cache hit ratio are all examples of counters) to a log file. The log file can be imported into a database to be used for trend analysis and performance analysis. You can save the information in a database for several weeks, months, or even years. Having historical data will allow you to view the data and look for trends, such as increasing processor utilization or increasing disk space usage. You can also use the information to find out extremes, such as the largest size reached by tempDB (data and log file) by performing simple SQL queries. Because the data is stored in a database, you can use tools like Microsoft Excel or Crystal reports to review and analyze the data.

Generating a Log File with the Performance Monitor

The performance monitor ships with all versions of Windows except Windows 9x. The performance monitor can be found in the Administrative Tools folder located in the Control Panel. To generate a log using the performance monitor do the following:

1. From the Administrative Tools folder, double-click the Performance Monitor icon. The Performance Monitor dialog box, shown in Figure 15.11 appears.

2. Select the Performance Logs and Alerts folder in the left pane, shown in Figure 15.11.

3. Select Counter Logs, in the right pane, shown in Figure 15.11, and right-mouse click to bring up a pop-up window. Select New Log Settings from the pop-up menu and the New Log Settings dialog box shown in Figure 15.12 appears.

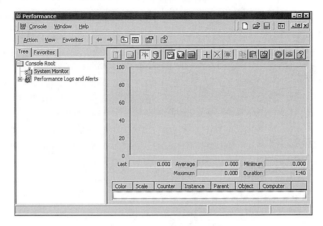

FIGURE 15.11   Performance Monitor dialog box.

FIGURE 15.12   New Log Settings dialog box.

4. Enter the name of log file you want to capture and click the OK button shown in Figure 15.12.

5. The Counter Log Properties dialog box, shown in Figure 15.13 appears. The General tab shown in Figure 15.13, allows you to Add counters to monitor and capture the data.

FIGURE 15.13   Counter Log Properties dialog box.

6. Click the Add button, shown in Figure 15.13 and the Select Counter dialog box shown in Figure 15.14 appears.

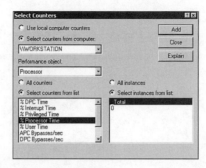

FIGURE 15.14   Select Counter dialog box.

Using the Select Counter dialog box, you can select the counters you want to monitor and log to the file. You use the Select Computer drop-down box, shown in Figure 15.14 to select the computer you want to monitor. To pick a counter, first you must select the Performance Object from the Performance Object drop down box shown in Figure 15.14. Performance objects are things such as Processor, SQL Server Databases, and Memory. After you select an object, the associated counters will appear in the counters list box shown in Figure 15.14. Select the counters you want to monitor and click Add. If you are not sure what a particular counter is or monitors click on the Explain button for additional detail about the counter. You can add several counters by selecting the counter and clicking the Add button. When you are done adding counters, click the Close button shown in Figure 15.14.

7. After you have added a counter and clicked closed, you are taken back to the Counter Log Properties dialog box with the Interval text box and the Unit combo box enabled as shown in Figure 15.15.

Use the Interval text box and the Units combo box to set the time period over which the data is sampled. You can sample in seconds, minutes, hours, and days. To start monitoring and save the output to a file, click the OK button shown in Figure 15.15.

You can also make use of the other tabs on the Counter Log Properties dialog box to set log file properties or schedule the log to sample over a specified period. The Counter Log Properties dialog box Log Files tab is shown in Figure 15.16.

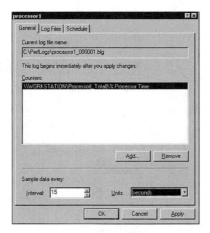

FIGURE 15.15   Counter Log Properties dialog bx—General Tab.

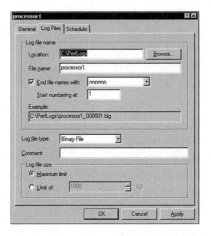

FIGURE 15.16   Counter Log Properties dialog box—Log Files Tab.

You can use the Counter Log properties dialog box to set different file properties, such as the file location and name. You can also set the Log file type, for example binary or CSV (that is, comma delimited). Binary files allow you to open the files with the Performance Monitor and play back the results. For easy data analysis and importing into a database, select the CSV format, which can easily be read by Microsoft Access or SQL Server DTS. The Counter Log Properties Schedule tab shown in Figure 15.17, allows you to schedule the start and stop periods for the counters to be monitored and logged. To see which counters you should monitor go to Chapter 24 "Monitoring SQL Server".

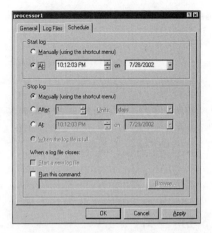

FIGURE 15.17   Counter Log Properties dialog box—Schedule Tab.

Troubleshooting FAQ

The following section lists some commonly asked questions and answers about SQL Server 2000 troubleshooting.

> **Q I have heard that an open transaction can block a user from a table because of an exclusive lock and prevent the transaction log from truncating completely. How can I check SQL Server for an open transaction?**

> **A** An open transaction can be a problem when a user is running an extremely long process that starts one large transaction, thus locking users out of the system until the transaction is committed or rolled back. Or someone has issued a Begin Transaction statement by issuing a COMMIT or ROLLBACK. To find an open transaction, use the DBCC command with OPENTRAN. The syntax is as follows:

```
DBCC OPENTRAN [('database_name' or 'database_id')]
[With TABLERESULTS or NO_INFOMSGS]
```

> **Q What are some useful trace statements to find out additional dead locking information?**

> **A** To find out what types of locks are being acquired and released during a session, use trace flag 1200. To track down additional locking information for deadlocks, set trace flags 1204 and 1205. Using these trace flags provides you with information about the types of locks and the commands being executed at the time of the deadlock.

Q How can I send trace information to the error log?

A Use the trace flag 3605.

Q How can I send trace information to my screen?

A Use trace flag 3604.

Q I'm having trouble starting my SQL Server because of a startup stored procedure I added. How can I disable the startup stored procedure from executing so I can start SQL Server?

A You can disable startup stored procedures from executing by using Trace flag 4022. Set the flag by adding it to the SQL Server startup parameters (or command line) using the -T option.

Q I'm having trouble installing SQL Server. What do I do?

A Look in Chapters 4, "Planning an Installation or Upgrade," and 5, "Installing or Upgrading SQL Server," for additional information on installing and upgrading SQL Server. Additionally, look in the SQL Server Install directory at the files with an extension of .OUT. These are output files for the installation process and contain success and error messages that can be used to help you troubleshoot an installation problem.

Q I need to call tech support. Is there any easy way to gather all the information they might need about my server and my SQL Server?

A SQL Server provides a utility called `sqldiag` that captures information about SQL Server and the environment such as Registry information; diagnostic reports (System report, Drivers report, Memory report, and so forth); output from several system stored procedures (`sp_who`, `sp_lock`, `sp_configure`, `sp_helpdb`, `xp_msver`, `sp_helpextendedproc`, and `sysprocesses`); and lots of other information. `sqldiag` is a command line utility that has the following format:

```
Sqldiag [-?] | [-I instance name] | [[-U user id] [-P password] | [-E]]
➡ | [-O file] [-X][-M][-C]
```

In which ? displays the information. -I is the instance name, -U is the SQL Server login ID, -P the password, -E uses the trusted connection, -O is the output file, X is excludes error logs, -M performs the DBCC stack dump, and -C provides cluster information.

Q Are any good monthly publications helpful for troubleshooting SQL Server problems?

A A column of useful SQL Server information—be it troubleshooting, tips, or tricks—is found in the monthly magazine, *Windows NT Magazine* by Duke Publishing (`http://www.winntmag.com`). The column is the SQL Server Source by Karen Watterson and Brian Moran. Duke Publishing also publishes a magazine dedicated to SQL Server called *SQL Server Magazine*, and the Web site is `http://www.sqlmag.com`.

Summary

You should now know where to search for SQL Server error messages as well as understand the format and meaning of SQL Server error messages. This chapter provides the foundation for your understanding how to interpret and research the error messages you receive during routine maintenance. Another important point in this chapter is that to be a good DBA, you need to stay informed. You can get involved in your local SQL Server user group or spend a few hours a week on the Web, or interacting with your peers and learning more about SQL Server. In Chapter 11, "Developing a SQL Server Maintenance Plan," and Chapter 12, "Automating Database Administration Tasks," you learned how to perform preventive maintenance on your SQL Server to limit the amount of time you spend troubleshooting. Here are some of the important points to review when you troubleshoot SQL Server:

- SQL Server displays error messages in the following format: `Msg #, Level #, State #, Description`.

- If an error occurs, write down the entire message, not just part of it.

- Use Books Online and the Microsoft TechNet search facilities to help resolve problems.

- Make it a point to understand the SQL Server error log.

- Check the Windows NT event log for errors by using the Event Viewer search facility.

- Stop user processes with the `KILL` command.

- Use DBCC and trace flags to help troubleshoot problems.

- For application troubleshooting, take advantage of SQL Server 2000's index tuning wizard, the SQL Server Profiler.

- Stay informed by taking advantage of user groups and online services such as the Internet.

PART VIII

Architecture and Database Design

IN THIS PART

16 Architecture Features

17 Database Design Issues

16

Architecture Features

by Mark Spenik

IN THIS CHAPTER

- SQL Server Thread Scheduling

- Disk I/O and Data Management

- Multiple Database Instances

- Federated Database Servers

- Other Enhancements

SQL Server 7.0 was a major rewrite of previous versions of SQL Server and is the foundation for SQL Server 2000 along with some enhancements such as XML, multiple instances, and federated database servers. This chapter focuses on some of the SQL Server internals that have not been discussed in detail in previous chapters. Most of these features changed very little from SQL Server 7.0 to SQL Server 2000, but the changes compared between previous versions and SQL Server 7.0 and SQL Server 2000 are stark. To highlight the improved architecture for reliability and scalability with SQL Server 2000 (and 7.0), this chapter will look back at the previous SQL Server 6.x versions and how things such as thread scheduling and disk storage worked and how the changes to SQL Server 7.0 and SQL Server 2000 internals have made SQL Server 2000 the most scalable and reliable version of SQL Server ever. Why bother learning about what SQL Server does behind the scenes? Besides making you look good at technical interviews, it provides you with insight into improving database performance during database design (such as page layout and effective use of file groups), as well as determining the proper hardware server configuration. This chapter examines the following areas:

- Thread Scheduling

- Disk Storage Changes

- Multiple instances of SQL Server

- Federated Database Servers

- Locking Enhancements

- Read Ahead Improvements

SQL Server Thread Scheduling

One of the improvements made in SQL Server 7.0 and SQL Server 2000 is how SQL Server threads are managed and scheduled. Before you learn about the changes made to thread scheduling, the following sections cover some basic terms used when talking about threads and thread scheduling.

What Is a Thread?

When working with Windows NT, Windows 2000, Windows XP, and Windows 9x, the term *thread* comes up quite frequently. So what exactly is a thread? Simply put, a thread is executing code, and each Windows application has at least a single thread of execution. A multithreaded application, such as SQL Server, has the capability to have more than one thread of execution.

The term *executing code* does not mean much in the real-world, so let's look at an example of using threads in SQL Server. Suppose you start a long running query— one thread—and then you start another query—a second thread. The second query executes without waiting for the first query to complete. This is an example of multi-threading and multitasking.

Operating systems such as Windows 2000, Windows XP, Windows NT, and Windows 9x are multithreaded and multitasking systems because they provide the system services required to allow multiple threads and tasks to execute. With a single CPU system, two threads cannot truly run simultaneously on the same processor. So Windows 2000, Windows NT, and Windows 9x allow the second thread to execute while the first thread is executing an action that does not use the CPU—such as a disk read or write.

In a preemptive multitasking operating system, a thread yields the processor to another thread when it is waiting for a system resource or for a non-CPU event (such as a disk operation). The operating system can also preempt the process if an interrupt occurs such as a higher priority thread requesting CPU time. This gives the appearance of simultaneous execution because the threads execute without waiting for the other threads to complete.

Threads can execute with different privileges or modes. A Windows NT thread executes in Kernel mode, which grants the thread access to system hardware and memory. A thread that executes in User mode (such as an application) can gain access to system hardware and services by calling the operating system.

What Is a Context Switch?

Windows 2000, NT, XP, and Windows 9x are preemptive multithreaded operating systems. The term *preemptive* means that the operating system can stop the current executing thread to allow another thread to execute if the current thread does not yield the processor in a certain amount of time. This time period is called a *time quantum*. Preemptive operating systems do not require the application to yield the CPU. Preempting an executing thread prevents an application from hogging the processor and allows other threads to execute.

The process of halting an executing thread and saving all the context information of a thread so that another thread can execute is called a *context switch*. A context switch can occur by way of an interrupt or a time quantum expiration. When the context switch occurs, the operating system saves information about the executing thread (such as stack pointer and register values). The saved information allows the operating system to restart the thread at its execution point prior to the context switch during the next time quantum.

What Is SMP?

SMP stands for *symmetric multiprocessor* and refers to servers with more than one processor. Windows NT and SQL Server support SMP systems. An SMP system allows Windows NT to execute threads on more than one processor so that threads can truly execute simultaneously. SQL Server can perform special operations on SMP systems. One such special operation is a *parallel query*, which is a complex query broken up into parts and executed across multiple processors.

SQL Server 6.x Thread Scheduling

To understand how SQL Server 2000 thread scheduling has improved, take a quick look at how SQL Server 6.x performed thread scheduling. SQL Server 6.x did not have a separate thread scheduler. Instead, 6.x took advantage of Windows NT thread scheduling services by allowing NT to schedule and synchronize the threads across processors. SQL Server 6.x maintains a pool of worker threads that translate to one thread per user until the max worker thread pool size is met. This approach works well but is not as scalable on SMP systems because excessive context-switches can become expensive (in time), and SQL Server 6.x has very little control over when its threads are preempted (switched out).

SQL Server 2000 Thread Scheduling

SQL Server 2000 thread scheduling defaults to using Windows NT thread scheduling like previous versions of SQL Server 6.x. SQL Server 2000 also contains another option of thread management called *lightweight pooling*, which uses a User Mode Scheduler (UMS) and Windows NT fibers. *Fibers* are lightweight user-mode threads. Fibers run on top of Windows NT threads but cannot be preempted. Fibers can be used by setting the system configuration parameter lightweight pooling to 1 (see Chapter 7, "Configuring and Tuning SQL Server," for more information).

The UMS controls the scheduling of SQL Server threads, as well as when the threads are switched out. In fiber mode, SQL Server 2000 still uses a pool of worker threads. One worker thread is used per CPU, and each user connection is assigned a thread up to the maximum number of worker threads. By allowing the UMS to schedule threads and to use fibers instead of native threads, SQL Server 2000 reduces the number of context switches, reduces the amount of system resources used, and controls preemption. Most SQL Server systems will achieve the best performance when using the default thread scheduling mode, which allows the operating system to schedule the threads across various processors. However, if you are on a SMP machine with four or more processors that is experiencing extensive context switching, you may be able to improve system performance by switching to fiber mode scheduling. As always if you decide to change the thread scheduling mode, make sure to benchmark the system before and after to make sure the change has the desired effect anticipated. To determine the context switches, use the Windows performance monitor and select the performance object system and then select the counter Context/Switches/sec.

Disk I/O and Data Management

SQL Server 7.0 made several improvements that are part of SQL Server 2000 to support very large databases. Several of these improvements involved changes to the underlying data storage structures, including data page size and the use of files and file groups instead of devices. Let's takes a closer look at some of these changes and how the changes help improve large database support.

Page Size

SQL Server 6.x uses a 2KB data page or a 16KB extent (8 pages in an extent). The maximum width of a single row of data in SQL Server 6.x is 1962 bytes and the maximum size of a varchar column is 255 bytes. The limitation of 1962 bytes per row and the 255-byte limit to varchars have personally caused me much grief over the years. SQL Server 7.0 introduced a new data page with a size of 8KB or a 64KB extent which is also the page size for SQL Server 2000. Microsoft decided to change the data page size to read in larger amounts of data as well as to take advantage of modern-day disk controllers. The larger data page has increased the maximum row width of a single row of data to 8060 bytes and the maximum size of a varchar column to 8000 bytes!

Concurrency issues (locking and blocking) because of a larger page size are no longer a problem because SQL Server 2000 supports row-level locking on all types of data modifications (for example INSERT, UPDATE, and DELETE). SQL Server 2000 also improves how Text and Image datatypes are retrieved and stored. In SQL Server 6.5, Text and Image datatypes use a linked list data structure, which is costly in CPU time for data retrieval. SQL Server 2000 uses a b-tree structure that is simpler and requires less I/O.

NOTE

The increased page size also offers better performance for the SQL Server cache and Cache Manager.

File Groups

With SQL Server 6.x, as drive systems become more sophisticated with RAID configurations that use disk striping (like RAID 5), the use of segments by a DBA become less and less important for your average database. The RAID disk striping is used to spread the disk I/O across several physical drives. However, for very large tables or databases, the SQL Server 6.x segment is used to pull a table or index to a specific logical or physical drive in an attempt to improve performance. Segments have the following shortcomings:

- They are difficult to manage.

- Tables and indexes are mapped to the segment, not to databases.

- DBAs are limited to 32 segments per database.

Another problem with segments is shown in Figure 16.1.

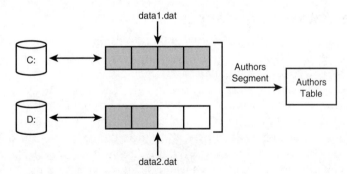

Note: Shaded area indicates used disk space

FIGURE 16.1   SQL Server 6.x segment fill.

In Figure 16.1, the authors table is placed on four different segments. Each segment represents a physical hard drive or a different RAID set. With SQL Server 6.x, only one drive or set is used at a time. When the drive or set fills up, the data is stored on the next drive. In this type of environment, you cannot take advantage of the multiple segments (drives or stripe sets) assigned to the object.

SQL Server 7.0 and SQL Server 2000 have replaced both devices and segments with the file and file group concept (discussed in detail in Chapter 8, "Managing Databases"). Files and file groups simplify the management of databases and disk management as well as provide you the flexibility to move specific objects to a select drive or drives. Figure 16.2 shows how SQL Server 2000 file groups give you the flexibility of segments to place objects as well as to evenly partition the data across the multiple files (drives or RAID sets) in a file group. As you can see in Figure 16.2, unlike Figure 16.1, the drives are used evenly throughout the storage of the object and are not filled one at a time.

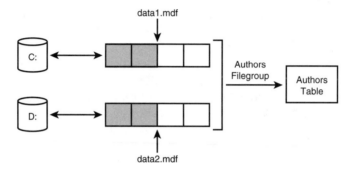

Note: Shaded area indicates used disk space

FIGURE 16.2   SQL Server 2000 file group fill.

Multiple Database Instances

A big enhancement new to SQL Server 2000 is the ability to run multiple instances of the SQL Server 2000 database engine on the same computer. Each instance has its own databases (system and user databases), memory pool, SQL Server Agent services, SQL Server services, network connections, registry keys associated with the SQL Server Agent, SQL Server services, or RDBMS engine, and different names. Only one copy of the client utilities is installed and can be used by the multiple instances. Applications connecting to the different instances connect using the different names assigned to each instance. In many ways, it is similar to using SQL Server 6.5 or SQL Server 7.0 on different computers. Oracle has had this feature for several years (however, Oracle can run one database per instance; SQL Server can manage multiple databases per instance). Multiple instances are very useful when sharing a computer with other companies (that is, ISP environment) or other groups within a corporation; and you want each group or company to manage their own instances of SQL Server without any possible access to the other groups' databases or users. Multiple instances are also useful in a development or test environment by creating a second instance of SQL Server for testing or staging.

Federated Database Servers

At the Windows 2000 launch, Microsoft made a surprise announcement. Using Windows 2000 and SQL Server 2000, they had blown away all the time performance based TPC-C benchmarks! Microsoft had always placed in the top spots on the Price/Performance benchmark, which rewards high transactions at a low cost. But Microsoft had not been able to place SQL Server 6.5 or SQL Server 7.0 in the top 10 TPC-C marks, which exclude cost and are based solely on performance. The top 10 lists have been owned by UNIX based systems running Oracle, DB2, or Sybase. However, Windows 2000 and SQL Server 2000 changed all that by taking the top two positions at the time of the Windows 2000 launch. SQL Server 2000 has improved on its top marks and now holds many of the top positions for both performance and price performance.

> **NOTE**
>
> To view the most up-to-date TPC-C benchmarks, visit `http://www.tpc.org`.

How did Microsoft achieve such stunning results with SQL Server 2000 in the TPC-C benchmark? Federated database servers! A federated database server allows a database to be split across multiple independent servers. When an application uses a federated database, the appearance from the application's standpoint is that it is working with a single server and a single database. In reality, the database is spread out across multiple independent servers. This is achieved using a partitioned view. A partitioned view allows a developer to split a table across multiple servers. Using a `UNION ALL` statement and properly partitioning the data across the servers enables a developer to create an application that is very scalable. So for a Web-based application, if the site traffic increases and the database server becomes the bottleneck, another server or multiple servers can be added to the federation to decrease the bottleneck.

From a DBA standpoint, a federated database server does not require any special setup by a DBA. Each database server participating in the "federation" is an independent SQL Server. The data partitioning is done via the design of the view and distribution of the data, which will require a very good understanding of the SQL statements that are being executed against the database. DBAs will need to make sure that the backup and recoveries being performed by the "federation" allows them to be in synch.

Other Enhancements

SQL Server 7.0 made several changes and modifications to 6.x read aheads and locking management which have been continued in SQL Server 2000. These changes improve the overall performance and concurrency of both SQL Server 7.0 and SQL Server 2000.

Read-Ahead Logic

Read-ahead logic was introduced in SQL Server 6.5. The purpose of read aheads is to read data pages from the hard drive into memory (cache) before an executing query requests the data page. Read aheads tend to benefit queries that are retrieving sequential type or range information. The 6.5 read-ahead logic does the page retrieval job quite well, retrieving 16KB extents into memory prior to a query requesting them. In 6.5, read aheads are triggered using several configuration parameters that track the number of cache hit misses. When the cache hit or miss threshold is reached, read-ahead threads are invoked to retrieve the pages. The problem with 6.5 read-ahead logic is that it's difficult to tune, and the read-ahead logic doesn't work with the query processor. SQL Server 2000 read-ahead logic requires no tuning and works hand in hand with the query processor to retrieve only data pages required by the query processor.

Locking Enhancements

SQL Server 6.5 introduced dynamic locking strategy for data inserts. The dynamic locking strategy allows SQL Server to determine whether to use a page, table, or row-level lock for data modifications. SQL Server 2000 supports the dynamic locking strategy for all forms of data modifications (INSERTS, UPDATES, and DELETES). The dynamic locking strategy uses the fastest possible locking strategy while providing concurrency. The query processor determines whether to use a page lock, table lock, or row-level lock. When possible, page or table level locks are used, which are faster and more efficient than row-level locks. However, if row-level locking is required, the lock manager uses row-level locks. The lock manager can even deescalate page locks to row-level locks. The best thing about the SQL Server dynamic locking strategy is that it does not require any tuning! SQL Server manages and maintains all the locking for you!

Summary

SQL Server 2000 has many internal changes that help boost its performance and scalability beyond SQL Server 6.5. SQL Server 2000 has added functionality such as federated database servers that allow it to scale out to levels unachievable by SQL Server 7.0. Some of the key changes are as follows:

- SQL Server 2000 can use NT threads or lightweight threads called fibers.

- SQL Server 2000 uses an 8KB data page and a 64KB extent (8 pages).

- SQL Server supports multiple instances.

- SQL Server 2000 allows you to create federated database servers to create scalable applications.

- SQL Server 2000 supports row-level locking for data modification operations.

17

Database Design Issues

by Orryn Sledge

A properly designed database can increase data integrity and simplify data maintenance. To help you better understand how to design a database, the following concepts are discussed in this chapter:

- Problems that can arise from an improperly designed database

- How to correctly design a database

- How to take a properly designed database a step backwards in order to improve performance

IN THIS CHAPTER

- Problems that Can Arise from an Improperly Designed Database

- Normalization

- Denormalization

- FAQ

Problems that Can Arise from an Improperly Designed Database

The following problems can occur because of an improperly designed database:

- Redundant data

- Limited data tracking

- Inconsistent data

- Update anomalies

- Delete anomalies

- Insert anomalies

Redundant Data

As you can see in the sample table in Figure 17.1, several names and descriptions are continuously repeated. This increases the amount of physical storage required to track training data.

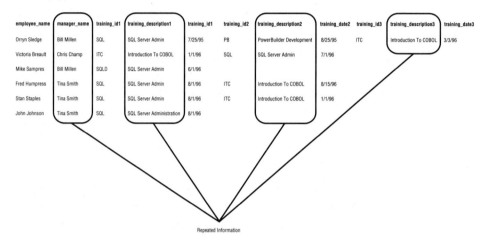

FIGURE 17.1   Redundant data.

Limited Data Tracking

The table design in Figure 17.2 is limited to tracking three training courses per employee. Additional columns must be added to the table if you want to track more than three classes.

					This table allows a maximum of 3 training courses to be tracked.					
employee_name	manager_name	training_id1	training_description1	training_data 1	training_id2	training_description2	training_date2	training_id3	training_description3	training_date3
Orryn Sledge	Bill Millen	SQL	SQL Server Admin	7/25/95	PB	PowerBuilder Development	8/25/95	ITC	Introduction To COBOL	3/3/96
Victoria Breault	Chris Champ	ITC	Introduction To COBOL	1/1/96	SQL	SQL Server Admin	7/1/96			
Mike Sampres	Bill Millen	SQLD	SQL Server Admin	6/1/96						
Fred Humpress	Tina Smith	SQL	SQL Server Admin	8/1/96	ITC	Introduction To COBOL	8/15/96			
Stan Staples	Tina Smith	SQL	SQL Server Admin	8/1/96	ITC	Introduction To COBOL	1/1/96			
John Johnson	Tina Smith	SQL	SQL Server Administration	8/1/96						

FIGURE 17.2   Limited data tracking.

Inconsistent Data

Consider the likelihood of a training class being misspelled when a new record is added to the employee_training table (see Figure 17.3). As more records are added to the table, the potential for inconsistent data from typing errors increases.

employee_name	manager_name	training_id1	training_description1	training_date1	training_id2	training_description2	training_date2	training_id3	training_description3	training_date3
Orryn Sledge	Bill Millen	SQL	SQL Server Admin	7/25/95	PB	PowerBuilder Development	8/25/95	ITC	Introduction To COBOL	3/3/96
Victoria Breault	Chris Champ	ITC	Introduction To COBOL	1/1/96	SQL	SQL Server Admin	7/1/96			
Mike Sampres	Bill Millen	SQLD	SQL Server Admin	6/1/96						
Fred Humpress	Tina Smith	SQL	SQL Server Admin	8/1/96	ITC	Introduction To COBOL	8/15/96			
Stan Staples	Tina Smith	SQL	SQL Server Admin	8/1/96	ITC	Introduction To COBOL	1/1/96			
John Johnson	Tina Smith	SQL	SQL Server Administration	8/1/96						

Are these two different training classes or is this a data entry error?

FIGURE 17.3 Inconsistent data.

Update Anomalies

Suppose that you just realized that the *SQL Server Admin* class should be named *SQL Server Administration* (see Figure 17.4). To change the class name, you must update it in five different places. Wouldn't it be easier if you could change the name in one place and have it automatically reflected throughout the application?

employee_name	manager_name	training_id1	training_description1	training_date1	training_id2	training_description2	training_date2	training_id3	training_description3	training_date3
Orryn Sledge	Bill Millen	SQL	(1) SQL Server Admin incorrect	7/25/95	PB	PowerBuilder Development	8/25/95	ITC	Introduction To COBOL	3/3/96
Victoria Breault	Chris Champ	ITC	Introduction To COBOL	1/1/96	SQL	(5) SQL Server Admin incorrect	7/1/96			
Mike Sampres	Bill Millen	SQLD	(2) SQL Server Admin incorrect	6/1/96						
Fred Humpress	Tina Smith	SQL	(3) SQL Server Admin incorrect	8/1/96	ITC	Introduction To COBOL	8/15/96			
Stan Staples	Tina Smith	SQL	(4) SQL Server Admin incorrect	8/1/96	ITC	Introduction To COBOL	1/1/96			
John Johnson	Tina Smith	SQL	SQL Server Administration correct	8/1/96						

You just realized that "SQL Server Admin" should be "SQL Server Administration."
To change the class name you will need to update it in 5 different places.

FIGURE 17.4 Update anomalies.

Delete Anomalies

Suppose that you are no longer interested in tracking the *Introduction to COBOL* training class, so you delete matching records (see Figure 17.5). But wait...you just realized that you deleted other important information. The removal of more than one type of information from a table is considered a *delete anomaly*.

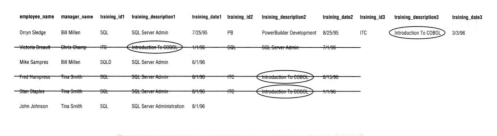

employee_name	manager_name	training_id1	training_description1	training_date1	training_id2	training_description2	training_date2	training_id3	training_description3	training_date3
Orryn Sledge	Bill Millen	SQL	SQL Server Admin	7/25/95	PB	PowerBuilder Development	8/25/95	ITC	Introduction To COBOL	3/3/96
Victoria Breault	Chris Champ	ITC	Introduction To COBOL	1/1/96	SQL	SQL Server Admin	7/1/96			
Mike Sampres	Bill Millen	SQLD	SQL Server Admin	6/1/96						
Fred Humpress	Tina Smith	SQL	SQL Server Admin	8/1/96	ITC	Introduction To COBOL	8/15/96			
Stan Staples	Tina Smith	SQL	SQL Server Admin	8/1/96	ITC	Introduction To COBOL	1/1/96			
John Johnson	Tina Smith	SQL	SQL Server Administration	8/1/96						

You are no longer interested in tracking the "Introduction To COBOL" training class so you delete matching records. But wait . . . you just realized that you deleted other important information.

FIGURE 17.5   Delete anomalies.

Insert Anomalies

Suppose that you want to track a new training course titled *Database Design* and you designate the code DD for training_id1. What values will you use for employee_name and manager_name when you insert the record into the sample table (see Figure 17.6)? Do you leave the values blank? Do you insert a special code such as unknown for employee_name and manager_name?

employee_name	manager_name	training_id1	training_description1	training_date1	training_id2	training_description2	training_date2	training_id3	training_description3	training_date3
Orryn Sledge	Bill Millen	SQL	SQL Server Admin	7/25/95	PB	PowerBuilder Development	8/25/95	ITC	Introduction To COBOL	3/3/96
Victoria Breault	Chris Champ	ITC	Introduction To COBOL	1/1/96	SQL	SQL Server Admin	7/1/96			
Mike Sampres	Bill Millen	SQLD	SQL Server Admin	6/1/96						
Fred Humpress	Tina Smith	SQL	SQL Server Admin	8/1/96	ITC	Introduction To COBOL	8/15/96			
Stan Staples	Tina Smith	SQL	SQL Server Admin	8/1/96	ITC	Introduction To COBOL	1/1/96			
John Johnson	Tina Smith	SQL	SQL Server Administration	8/1/96						
? ?	? ?	DD	Database Design							

You want to track a new training course called "Database Design." Where do you insert the record?

FIGURE 17.6   Insert anomalies.

Normalization

Normalization is a set of standard rules that tests the soundness of database design. It can help prevent the problems described in the first part of this chapter. By applying these standard rules, you can pinpoint design flaws that might jeopardize data integrity and complicate data maintenance.

How to Normalize a Database

There are three standard normalization rules. After a design successfully passes a rule, it is said to be in # normal form (where the # represents *1st*, *2nd*, or *3rd*). Rules are cumulative. For example, for a design to be in 3rd normal form, it must satisfy the requirements of the 3rd normal form as well as the requirements for 2nd and 1st normal forms.

Technically speaking, there are other types of normalization rules beyond 3rd normal form. However, for most database designs, the first three normal forms are sufficient. You will seldom need to apply the other types of normalization. Therefore, this section concentrates only on the 1st, 2nd, and 3rd normal forms of database design.

- **1st normal form**—No repeating groups.

- **2nd normal form**—No nonkey attributes depend on a portion of the primary key.

- **3rd normal form**—No attributes depend on other nonkey attributes.

Now that you know the rules regarding normalization, apply them to a sample application.

For this application example, suppose that you are tracking training classes taken by each employee. Figure 17.7 contains a denormalized listing of the data tracked by this application. Each employee might have taken *0* or *N* (zero or many) classes.

employee_id	char(5)
employee_name	char(35)
employee_address	char(35)
employee_city	char(35)
employee_state	char(2)
employee_zip	char(11)
manager_id	char(5)
manager_name	char(35)
training_id1	char(5)
training_description1	char(25)
training_date1	datetime
training_id2	char(5)
training_description2	char(25)
training_date2	datetime
training_id3	char(5)
training_description3	char(25)
training_date3	datetime

FIGURE 17.7 A denormalized database design.

1st Normal Form

Look at the `training_id`, `training_description`, and `training_date` attributes in
Figure 17.8. See how they are repeated? This violates the concept of 1st normal form:
no repeating groups.

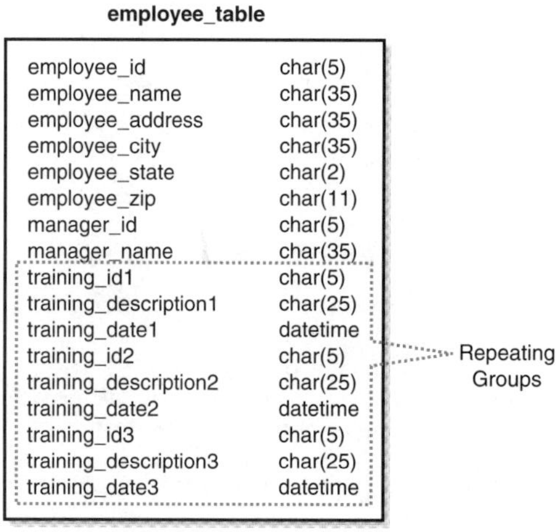

employee_table

employee_id	char(5)
employee_name	char(35)
employee_address	char(35)
employee_city	char(35)
employee_state	char(2)
employee_zip	char(11)
manager_id	char(5)
manager_name	char(35)
training_id1	char(5)
training_description1	char(25)
training_date1	datetime
training_id2	char(5)
training_description2	char(25)
training_date2	datetime
training_id3	char(5)
training_description3	char(25)
training_date3	datetime

Repeating Groups

FIGURE 17.8   Repeating groups.

Move the training information into a separate table called `employee_training` and
create a relationship between the `employee` table and the `employee_training` table.
Now the table design meets the requirements of 1st normal form (see Figure 17.9).

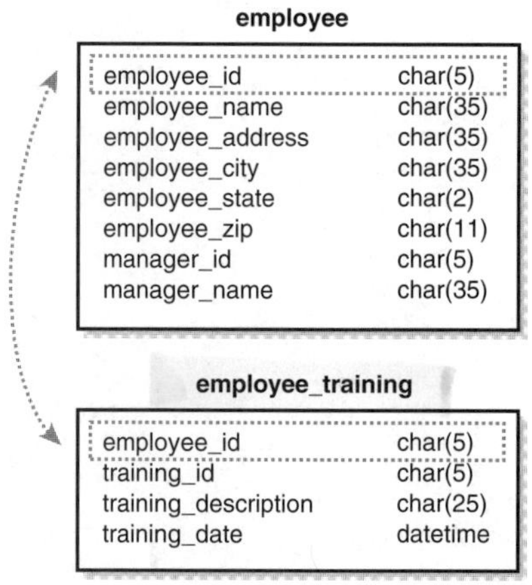

employee

employee_id	char(5)
employee_name	char(35)
employee_address	char(35)
employee_city	char(35)
employee_state	char(2)
employee_zip	char(11)
manager_id	char(5)
manager_name	char(35)

employee_training

employee_id	char(5)
training_id	char(5)
training_description	char(25)
training_date	datetime

FIGURE 17.9   Tables that meet 1st normal form.

2nd Normal Form

In Figure 17.10, notice how the `training_description` attribute depends only on the `training_id` attribute and not on the `employee_id` attribute in the `employee_training` table. This violates 2nd normal form: no nonkey attributes depend on a portion of the primary key. (The primary key for this table is `employee_id` + `training_id`.) This rule is applied only to entities that have compound primary keys (a primary key consisting of more than one attribute).

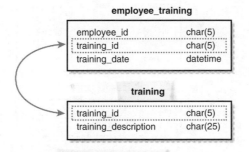

employee_training

employee_id	char(5)
training_id	char(5)
training_description	char(25)
training_date	datetime

training_description is dependent upon
training_id *not* employee_id

FIGURE 17.10   A nonkey attribute depends on a portion of the primary key.

Move the `training_description` attribute into a separate table called `training`. Relate the `training` table to the `employee_training` table through the `training_id` attribute. Now the design satisfies 2nd normal form (see Figure 17.11).

employee_training

employee_id	char(5)
training_id	char(5)
training_date	datetime

training

| training_id | char(5) |
| training_description | char(25) |

FIGURE 17.11   Tables that meet 2nd normal form.

3rd Normal Form

Look at the `manager_name` attribute for the `employee` table in Figure 17.12. The primary key for the `employee` table is the `employee_id` attribute. Does the `manager_name` attribute depend on the `employee_id` attribute? No! This violates 3rd normal form: No attributes can depend on other nonkey attributes.

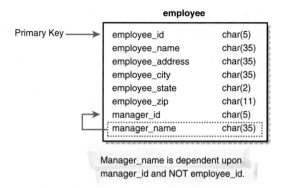

FIGURE 17.12   An attribute depends on a nonkey attribute.

Move the `manager_name` attribute into a separate table called `manager`. The `manager` table can be related to the `employee` table through the `manager_id` attribute. By making this change, the design meets the requirements of 3rd normal form (see Figure 17.13).

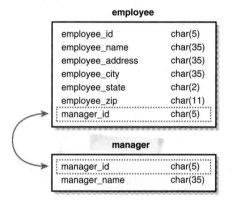

FIGURE 17.13   Tables that meet 3rd normal form.

Now you have completed the normalization process (see Figure 17.14). This process helped isolate design flaws that would have lead to an awkward and inefficient database design.

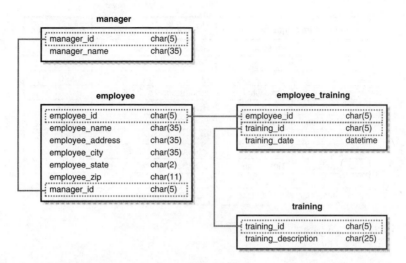

FIGURE 17.14   A normalized database design.

Denormalization

Denormalization means that you are purposely designing your database so that it is *not* in 3rd normal form. This is done to maximize performance or to simplify end-user reporting. Whenever you denormalize a database, you must be willing to forego the benefits gained from the 3rd normal form.

> **NOTE**
>
> I recommend that you start your initial database design in 3rd normal form. If you find that performance problems exist, selectively step back to 2nd or 1st normal form. Keep in mind that when you denormalize a database, you do so for a specific set of application require-ments. Future requirements may not need or benefit from past denormalization decisions. Only denormalize when you have to.

Performance

A database design in 3rd normal form might require more table joins to process a query than a design in 2nd or 1st normal form. These additional table joins can be expensive in terms of CPU and disk I/O.

Suppose that you need a report that lists the training classes taken by each employee (see Figure 17.15).

employee name	manager name	training description	training date
Orryn Sledge	Bill Millen	SQL Server Admin	7/25/95
		PowerBuilder Development	8/25/95
		Introduction To COBOL	3/3/96
Victoria Breault	Chris Champ	Introduction To COBOL	1/1/96
		SQL Server Admin	7/1/96
Mike Sampres	Bill Millen	SQL Server Admin	6/1/96
Fred Humpress	Tina Smith	SQL Server Admin	8/1/96
		Introduction To COBOL	8/15/96
Stan Staples	Tina Smith	SQL Server Admin	8/1/96
		Introduction To COBOL	1/1/96
John Johnson	Tina Smith	SQL Server Admin	8/1/96

FIGURE 17.15   A sample report.

NOTE

The examples used in this section are overly simplistic; however, they *do* explain how multi-table joins can complicate data processing.

To retrieve the data from your fully normalized database, you create the following query, which is a sample query for a fully normalized database:

```
SELECT a.employee_name, d.manager_name, c.training_description,b.training_date
FROM employee a, employee_training b, training c, manager d
WHERE a.emp_id = b.emp_id
 AND b.training_id = c. training_id
 AND a.manager_id = d.manager_id
```

As you can see, this simple report requires four tables to be joined. Assume that each table contains one million rows. Can you imagine the work involved to join four tables, each containing one million rows? You can be assured that performance will suffer.

To maximize performance, you sometimes have to step back to 2nd or 1st normal form. If you denormalized your data into a single table, you can use the following query, which is a sample query for a denormalized database:

```
SELECT employee_name, manager_name, training_description, training_date
FROM training_summary
```

Ad Hoc Reporting

Another reason to denormalize a database is to simplify ad-hoc reporting. Ad hoc reporting is the unstructured reporting and querying performed by end users. End users are often confused when they have to join a significant number of tables. To avoid the confusion, DBAs can create a special set of tables designed for ad hoc reporting. If the data is used for reporting and not online processing, you can avoid some of the problems associated with a denormalized design.

> **TIP**
>
> Views can sometimes be used as an alternative to denormalization. Views can present your data in a denormalized manner, which can simplify ad hoc reporting.

Denormalization Techniques

Following is brief summary of the various techniques you can use to denormalize a database:

- **Duplicate data**—Duplicate data can reduce the number of joins required to process a query, thus reducing CPU and disk I/O usage.

- **Summary data**—Summary data can provide improved query performance by reducing or eliminating the steps required to summarize your data.

- **Horizontal partitioning**—Horizontal partitioning is the splitting of a table into two separate tables at the record level, thus reducing the number of rows per table (see Figure 17.16).

- **Vertical partitioning**—Vertical partitioning is the splitting of a table into two separate tables at the column level, thus reducing the number of columns per table (see Figure 17.17).

id	name	favorite_food	favorite_color	shoe_size
111-11-1111	Orryn Sledge	Pizza	Blue	9.5
222-22-2222	Victoria Breault	Ice Cream	Peach	6.0
333-33-3333	Mike Sampres	Pizza	Silver	9.0
444-44-4444	Fred Humpress	Fish	Red	10.0
555-55-5555	Stan Staples	Meat	Red	8.0
666-66-6666	John Johnson	Poultry	Black	9.0
777-77-7777	Mary Douglous	Pizza	White	6.0
888-88-8888	Jack Johnson	Pizza	Blue	10.0
999-99-9999	Jan Smithe	Pizza	Blue	10.0

With horizontal partitioning, a table is split into two tables at the row level. Usually, the split occurs at a predefined key value.

id	name	favorite_food	favorite_color	shoe_size
111-11-1111	Orryn Sledge	Pizza	Blue	9.5
222-22-2222	Victoria Breault	Ice Cream	Peach	6.0
333-33-3333	Mike Sampres	Pizza	Silver	9.0
444-44-4444	Fred Humpress	Fish	Red	10.0
555-55-5555	Stan Staples	Meat	Red	8.0

id	name	favorite_food	favorite_color	shoe_size
666-66-6666	John Johnson	Poultry	Black	9.0
777-77-7777	Mary Douglous	Pizza	White	6.0
888-88-8888	Jack Johnson	Pizza	Blue	10.0
999-99-9999	Jan Smithe	Pizza	Blue	10.0

FIGURE 17.16   Horizontal partitioning.

id	name	favorite_food	favorite_color	shoe size
111-11-1111	Orryn Sledge	Pizza	Blue	9.5
222-22-2222	Victoria Breault	Ice Cream	Peach	6.0
333-33-3333	Mike Sampres	Pizza	Silver	9.0
444-44-4444	Fred Humpress	Fish	Red	10.0
555-55-5555	Stan Staples	Meat	Red	8.0
666-66-6666	John Johnson	Poultry	Black	9.0
777-77-7777	Mary Douglous	Pizza	White	6.0
888-88-8888	Jack Johnson	Pizza	Blue	10.0
999-99-9999	Jan Smithe	Pizza	Blue	10.0

With vertical partitioning, a table is split into two separate tables and joined by a common key.

id	name
111-11-1111	Orryn Sledge
222-22-2222	Victoria Breault
333-33-3333	Mike Sampres
444-44-4444	Fred Humpress
555-55-5555	Stan Staples
666-66-6666	John Johnson
777-77-7777	Mary Douglous
888-88-8888	Jack Johnson
999-99-9999	Jan Smithe

id	favorite_food	favorite_color	shoe size
111-11-1111	Pizza	Blue	9.5
222-22-2222	Ice Cream	Peach	6.0
333-33-3333	Pizza	Silver	9.0
444-44-4444	Fish	Red	10.0
555-55-5555	Meat	Red	8.0
666-66-6666	Poultry	Black	9.0
777-77-7777	Pizza	White	6.0
888-88-8888	Pizza	Blue	10.0
999-99-9999	Pizza	Blue	10.0

FIGURE 17.17   Vertical partitioning.

FAQ

Listed in the following are some of the common questions asked by DBAs about database design:

Q Should an identity column be used as a primary key?

A As a general rule, use an identity column (an identity is an auto-incrementing number) as the primary key of a table. The following are the benefits of using an identity as the primary key.

- **Guaranteed to be unique**—SQL Server automatically generates the identity value and it is guaranteed to be unique in a multiuser environment. A person's Social Security number is often used as the primary key of a table. Did you know that Social Security numbers are not truly unique? In the past, the U.S. government has issued duplicate Social Security numbers! Instead of using a Social Security number as the primary key, you might want to consider using an identity.

- **Avoids compound keys**—An identity column removes the need to create compound keys. (A compound key is a primary key that contains two or more columns.) This simplifies joins between tables and creates a more compact index. Both of these factors can provide improved performance over compound keys.

Q Does SQL Server 2000 provide any datamodeling tools?

A SQL Server 2000 provides database diagrams for datamodeling. The database diagrams are somewhat limited in functionality when compared to third-party tools such as DataArchitect and ErWin.

Summary

Important notes to remember when designing databases are

- The following are the three forms of normalization:

  - **1st normal form**—No repeating groups.

  - **2nd normal form**—No nonkey attributes depend on a portion of the primary key.

  - **3rd normal form**—No attributes depend on other nonkey attributes.

- Strive for 3rd normal form to maximize data consistency and minimize update anomalies.

- When a significant number of tables must be joined to process a query, you might want to selectively denormalize the database to improve performance.

PART IX

Performance and Tuning

IN THIS PART

18 Understanding Indexes

19 Query Optimization

20 Multiuser Issues

18

Understanding Indexes

by Mark Spenik

IN THIS CHAPTER

- General Principle Behind Indexes
- Structure of SQL Server Indexes
- Data Modification and Index Performance Considerations
- How to Create Indexes
- Other Index Operations
- Suggested Index Strategies
- Letting SQL Server Help with Index Selection
- Index FAQ

You might wonder what a chapter on indexes and index selection is doing in a book about database administration. For a DBA, it is important to understand how SQL Server uses indexes and how they can be used to enhance performance. For example, developers always come to the DBA seeking words of wisdom and advice for slow applications or queries. Not only will index tuning knowledge elevate you in their eyes, but also a working knowledge of indexes will help you with space management. Also, every DBA should be aware of another SQL Server 2000 index bonus—using a clustered index to move a frequently used table to a specific file or filegroup located on a separate physical disk drive to increase application performance.

This chapter gives you a very basic understanding of an index, the type of structures used by indexes, and how to use the various utilities provided to you by SQL Server to help you select the proper indexes for your company's applications.

To get started, you need to know what an index is. An *index* is a separate, physical database structure created on a table or view that facilitates faster data retrieval when you search on an indexed column. SQL Server also uses indexes to enforce uniqueness on a row or column in a table or view, to physically order the data or to spread out the data across multiple filegroups to boost performance.

General Principle Behind Indexes

Take a high-level look at how indexing can help speed up data retrieval. Figure 18.1 shows a single table called School Employee that lists the name and occupation of each employee in the school.

School Employee

row	name	occupation
1	John	Janitor
2	David	Principal
3	Adam	Bus Driver
4	Gary	Teacher
5	Lisa	Janitor
6	Chris	Teacher
7	Debbie	Guidance Counselor
8	Denise	Assistant Principal
9	Bryan	Janitor

FIGURE 18.1   The `School Employee` table.

Using the table shown in Figure 18.1, what would you do if you wanted to select the names of all the people in the `School Employee` table who were janitors? You would have to read every row in the table and display only the names where the occupation in the row is `Janitor`. The process of reading every row or record in a table to satisfy a query is called a *table scan*. Now add an index to the Occupation column. Figure 18.2 shows the index on the Occupation column of the `School Employee` table.

School Employee

row	name	occupation
1	John	Janitor
2	David	Principal
3	Adam	Bus Driver
4	Gary	Teacher
5	Lisa	Janitor
6	Chris	Teacher
7	Debbie	Guidance Counselor
8	Denise	Assistant Principal
9	Bryan	Janitor

FIGURE 18.2   An index on the Occupation column of the `School Employee` table.

The type of index shown in Figure 18.2 contains a pointer to the data. Using the index shown in Figure 18.2, walk through the same query to find the names of all employees who are janitors. Rather than performing a table scan on the `School Employee` table, you read the first row of the index and check the occupation until you find `Janitor`. When a row contains `Janitor`, you use the value in the row pointer column to find the exact row number in the `School Employee` table of a `Janitor`. You continue to read the index as long as the occupation is `Janitor`.

When the occupation is no longer `Janitor`, you stop reading the index. Pretty simple, right?

Apply to SQL Server this little bit of knowledge of tables and indexes just described. For starters, SQL Server stores data and index information on a page (see Figure 18.3).

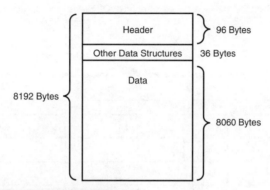

FIGURE 18.3   The SQL Server page format.

A page is 8192 bytes (8KB) in size with a 96-byte header. Additional space is used for other data structures such as row offset information, but the majority of the page, 8060 bytes, can be used to store data (that is, table or index information). So, in SQL Server 2000 (and SQL Server 7.0), the maximum width of a single row (not including text and image data) is 8060 bytes. Previous versions (4.21 and 6.x) of SQL Server could store only 1962 bytes per row.

TIP

SQL Server allocates space for tables and indexes eight pages at a time—a grouping called an *extent*. When the extent is filled, another extent (eight pages) is allocated. Remember this tip if you take the Microsoft SQL Server certification test. The odds are that you will be asked a question on index and table space allocation and the name of the allocation unit. The exception to extent allocation is when indexes are created on very small tables or views. SQL Server allocates a single page at a time. After eight pages are allocated, future page allocation is done in extents.

Suppose that the `School Employee` table, used earlier, contained other information, such as the employee's home address, phone number, spouse's name, education, and number of years of service. The size of a single row of information for the `School Employee` table would be around 2000 bytes; the maximum size of the Occupation column is 25 bytes. Using these row and column sizes and placing the `School`

`Employee` table (shown in Figure 18.1) and the index (shown in Figure 18.2) on SQL Server data pages produces Figure 18.4.

NOTE

The layouts of the table information and index information on the SQL Server pages shown in Figure 18.4 are not the actual index and table layouts used by SQL Server. They are used here to help you understand the general idea behind SQL Server pages, table scans, and indexes.

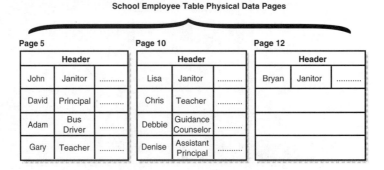

School Employee Table Physical Data Pages

Page 5				Page 10				Page 12		
Header				Header				Header		
John	Janitor	....		Lisa	Janitor	....		Bryan	Janitor	....
David	Principal	....		Chris	Teacher	....				
Adam	Bus Driver	....		Debbie	Guidance Counselor	....				
Gary	Teacher	....		Denise	Assistant Principal	....				

School Employee Occupation Index Physical Data Pages

Page 35

Header	
Assitant Principal	Page 10, Row 4
Bus Driver	Page 5, Row 3
Guidance Counselor	Page 10, Row 3
Janitor	Page 5, Row 1
Janitor	Page 10, Row 1
Janitor	Page 12, Row 1
Principal	Page 5, Row 2
Teacher	Page 5, Row 4
Teacher	Page 10, Row 2

FIGURE 18.4   The `School Employee` table and index on SQL Server data pages.

Using the diagram shown in Figure 18.4, how would SQL Server find all the employee names whose occupation is `Assistant Principal` without the index? First, SQL Server would read data page 5 and search each record for an employee with an occupation equal to `Assistant Principal`. No records are found on the first page. SQL Server reads the second data page (page 10), searches each record, and displays the fourth record. Because SQL Server has no way of knowing how many records there are with the occupation of `Assistant Principal`, SQL Server reads and searches the third and final page, page 12.

What happened? SQL Server performed a table scan, reading all the data pages. In this example, a table scan did not seem all that bad because SQL Server only had to read three data pages. But what if the School Employee table had 1,000 times more records for a total of 9,000 records (a small amount for SQL Server)? SQL Server would have to read 3,000 data pages to find all the Assistant Principals; even if only one employee was an Assistant Principal, and that record was located on the first data page.

Walk through the same query using the index. First, SQL Server reads the index page and begins to search for Assistant Principal. The first row read is Assistant Principal. SQL Server then checks the pointer, which tells SQL Server that the record is located on data page 10, row 4. SQL Server reads data page 10, goes to the fourth row, and displays the name. The row number of the page is called a RID, which stands for *Row Identifier*. RIDs do not change unless the row is deleted and then reinserted. If a row is deleted, the RID can be reused.

The next row in the index page is checked; because the occupation is not Assistant Principal, SQL Server stops. The number of pages read using the index is two pages as opposed to the three pages read in the table scan example.

What about the Janitor query used earlier? Performing a table scan requires SQL Server to read all three data pages. Using the index requires SQL Server to read all three data pages plus the index page, for a total of four data pages—one more than a table scan! In some cases, a table scan might be faster than using the index. It's the job of the SQL Server query optimizer to determine which index to select and when to perform a table scan.

TIP

You will read recommendations in this book about keeping indexes small and the row width of a table small for maximum performance. All too often, the reasoning behind small row and index width is left out. It boils down to data pages and how many data pages SQL Server has to read to fulfill a query.

Suppose that you have a table with 5,000,000 rows; the size of a row (with overhead bytes) is 1250 bytes or maximum row width (8060 bytes / 1250 bytes = 6)—six records per data page. The number of data pages required for all 5,000,000 records is (5,000,000 / 6 = 833,333) 833,333. SQL Server pages or 104,166 extents (eight pages in an extent).

Suppose that you look at your overall table design and decide that you can shrink the size of the maximum row width just over 10% so that seven rather than six records fit on a data page. The number of data pages is reduced by almost 120,000 pages (or 15,000 extents)! A SQL Server page used for an index is the same. Indexing a 20-character field (with overhead) and a 6-byte field (with overhead), for example, is the difference between 100 keys per page versus 336 keys per page.

The larger index requires SQL Server to read three times as many pages to access the same number of keys. (This does not take into account the added B-Tree levels caused by a larger index key!) Select the proper data types and sizes when creating your tables. One last bit of advice is normalize your tables and select smart indexes.

Structure of SQL Server Indexes

SQL Server maintains indexes with a B-Tree structure (see Figure 18.5). B-Trees are multilevel, self-maintaining structures.

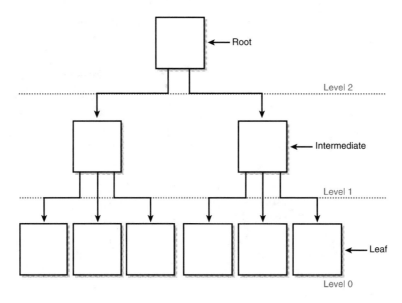

FIGURE 18.5   The B-Tree structure.

A B-Tree structure consists of a top level, called the *root*; a bottom level, called the *leaf* (always level 0); and zero to many intermediate levels (the B-Tree in Figure 18.5 has one intermediate level). In SQL Server terms, each square shown in Figure 18.5 represents an index page (or data page). The greater the number of levels in your index, the more index pages you must read to retrieve the records you are searching for. (That is, performance degrades as the number of levels increases.) SQL Server maintains two different types of indexes: a clustered index and a nonclustered index.

TIP

The levels of the B-Tree can point to possible performance problems or poor index selection. A B-Tree with a large number of levels requires more time to find rows because each level adds more data pages that must be read to get to the leaf pages.

You can reduce the number of B-Tree levels by reducing the width of the indexed columns, which increases the number of index keys per page.

Clustered Index

A *clustered index* is a B-Tree structure where level 0, the leaf, contains the actual data pages of the table and the data is physically stored in the logical order of the index.

Figure 18.6 shows a clustered index on the Name column in the School Employee table. Notice that the data pages are the leaf pages of the clustered index and that the data is stored in logical order on the data pages.

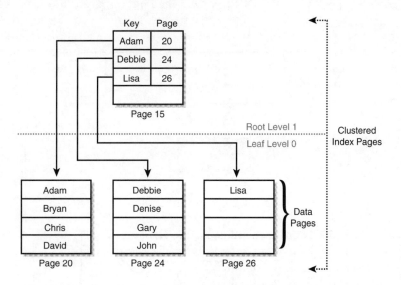

FIGURE 18.6   A clustered index on the Name column of the School Employee table.

SQL Server index pages contain a page header followed by index rows. The index rows contain the key value and a pointer to an index page or the data row (leaf level of a clustered index). Index pages are further linked together using a doubly linked list.

Nonclustered Index

With a nonclustered index, the leaf-level pages contain row locators to the data pages and rows, not the actual data (as does the clustered index). A nonclustered index does not reorder the physical data pages of the table. Therefore, creating a nonclustered index does not require the large amounts of free disk space associated with creating a clustered index. Figure 18.7 shows a nonclustered index on the School Employee table. Notice that the data in the data pages is not in the order of the index key, but a random order because it uses heap storage. In SQL Server 6.5, heap storage was always at the end of the data page and could cause hot spots on tables without clustered indexes. SQL Server 2000 changed the way heap storage works and no longer stores at the bottom of the data page, thus removing a potential hot spot for tables without clustered indexes. Also, note that the nonclustered index adds one more level by always arriving at the leaf and then having to read the data page. If the table has a clustered index on the table, the row indicator is the clustered index of the table. SQL Server will then use the clustered index to find the data page. Because SQL Server 2000 uses the clustered index key for the row indicator of a nonclustered index, you must choose your clustered indexes carefully and limit the key size for optimum performance. If the table does not contain a clustered index, the row locator is a Row ID, or RID, which is built using the file ID, page number, and row number on the page.

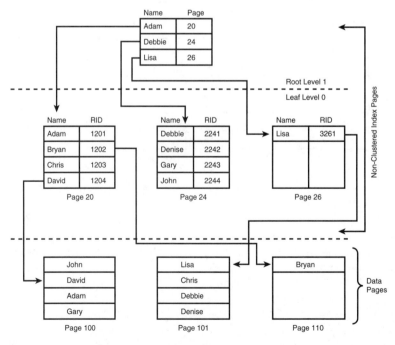

FIGURE 18.7   A nonclustered index on the Name column of the School Employee table.

NOTE

You can have up to 249 nonclustered indexes on a table; although you would *never* want to create anywhere near 249 indexes on a single table. A large number of indexes on a single table affects the performance of other operations, such as UPDATE, DELETE, and INSERT. An index cannot exceed 900 bytes in width or 16 columns. Again, you would *never* want an index that is 900 bytes in width. Remember to use narrow-width indexes to maximize the number of index keys on a data page. This improves performance by requiring less disk I/O to scan the index. In previous versions of SQL Server, we recommended that you try not to exceed four columns when creating indexes. However, with SQL Server 2000, this rule is no longer true. Microsoft has made many significant improvements in index management, memory use, and disk I/O. Keep in mind that indexes with smaller key sizes will outperform indexes with larger key sizes instead of concerning yourself with the number of columns in the index. A table can have both clustered and nonclustered indexes. Because you are allowed to have only a single clustered index on a table, you can meet your other indexing needs with nonclustered indexes. Try not to over-index; in many cases, a clustered index and two to six nonclustered indexes is more than sufficient (except in data warehouse situations). Also, when creating a clustered index, keep key size to a minimum because the clustered index key will be used as the row identifier for nonclustered indexes.

Data Modification and Index Performance Considerations

It is widely known that an index can help speed data retrievals; from time to time, you might hear someone say that indexes slow down other operations, such as inserts, updates, and deletes, which is true. It has been mentioned that B-Tree data structures are, for the most part, self-maintaining data structures. As rows are added, deleted, or updated, the indexes also are updated to reflect the changes, requiring extra I/O to update the index pages.

SQL Server 7 introduced several performance improvements, also available in SQL Server 2000, to greatly reduce the disk I/O required to maintain indexes. One feature worth noting is that nonclustered indexes no longer have to be updated when a clustered index page splits. What is an index page split? Remember, data added to a clustered index is inserted into the correct physical and logical order in the table, and other rows can be moved up or down, depending on where the data is placed, causing additional disk I/O to maintain the index. Over time, as a page grows, a new record might be added that requires the page to be split because the page is full. Thus, records are moved to a new page. In previous versions of SQL Server, the nonclustered index also had to be updated to reflect the rows on the new page. This disk I/O has been totally eliminated from SQL Server 2000, by using the clustered index key value for nonclustered indexes for tables with a clustered index instead of the physical page number. Page splits still occur in SQL Server 7 and 2000 and can affect performance in other ways. For additional information, see the FAQ for this chapter on why Fill Factor is important.

In general, you should not worry about the time required to maintain indexes during inserts, deletes, and updates unless you are in a heavy transaction environment. Be aware that extra time is required to update the indexes during data modification and that performance can become an issue if you over-index a table. On tables that are frequently modified, try to restrict the tables to a clustered index and no more than three or four nonclustered indexes. Tables involved in heavy transaction processing should be restricted to from zero to three indexes. If you find the need to index beyond these numbers, run some benchmark tests to check for performance degradation. Don't forget to use the Index Tuning Wizard to help you make your index selections.

How to Create Indexes

You can create an index using the SQL Server 2000 Index Wizard, TRANSACT-SQL, or via the Enterprise Manager.

NOTE

You cannot create an index on the following data types:

bit

text

image

New for SQL Server 2000 is index creation on a view and a computed column.

Using the SQL Enterprise Manager, select a server and then click the Wizards icon from the toolbar. The Wizard Selection dialog box appears. Expand the Database options by clicking on the + sign. Then follow these steps to create an index (the following example uses the pubs database):

1. Select the Create Index Wizard from the Wizard Selection dialog box. The Create Index Wizard Welcome dialog box appears (see Figure 18.8).

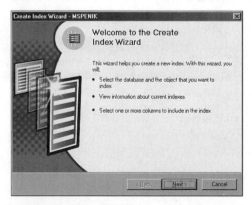

FIGURE 18.8   The Create Index Wizard Welcome dialog box.

2. Click the Next button. The Select Database and Table dialog box appears (see Figure 18.9). Using the combo boxes, select the database and the table to which you want to add the index. Click the Next button.

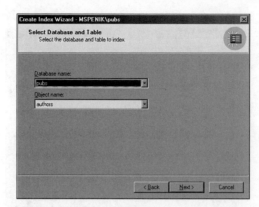

FIGURE 18.9   The Create Index Wizard Database and Select Database and Table dialog box.

3. If indexes already exist on the table, you will see the Current Index Information dialog box shown in Figure 18.10.

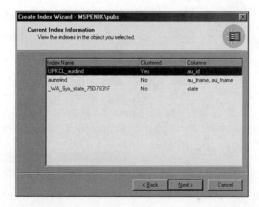

FIGURE 18.10   The Create Index Wizard Current Index Information dialog box.

If no indexes exist, the wizard skips this step and goes to step 4.

4. Check the columns you want to include in your index. The Index Wizard enables you to select only columns that have valid index data types. Notice in Figure 18.11, the red x for the table column contract, which consists of an

invalid index data type. Check the Sort Order (DESC) if you would like the sort direction of the index to be created in descending order: The default is ascending order. Being able to select the sort order of an index is new to SQL Server 2000.

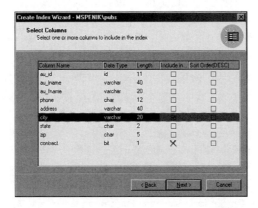

FIGURE 18.11   The Create Index Wizard Column Select Columns dialog box.

After you select the column(s) for your index, click the Next button. The Specify Index Option dialog box appears (see Figure 18.12).

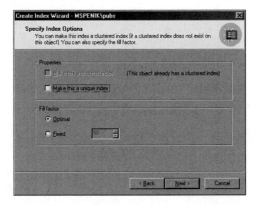

FIGURE 18.12   The Create Index Wizard Specify Index Option dialog box.

5. The Index Option dialog box options are as follows:

- **The Clustered check box**—When the Make This a Clustered Index check box is selected, a clustered index with the selected columns is created on the table. If a clustered index already exists on the table, this option is not available. Remember that you can have only one clustered index per table. When this option is not selected, a nonclustered index is created.

- **The Unique Keys check box**—The Make This a Unique Index option creates an index that enforces uniqueness on the indexed column(s). Use the Unique Keys option when uniqueness is an attribute of the data (for example, the primary key of the table).

CAUTION

If you try to create a unique index on a column with duplicate data, the index creation will fail. You must remove the duplicate data entries to build the index.

- **The Fill Factor frame**—The Fill Factor specifies how densely packed you want your index and data pages when creating an index. The default (Optimal) is 0, which leaves room on the nonleaf pages with the leaf pages 100% full. A high Fill Factor value increases performance for queries because the index pages are packed, reducing the number of index levels (that is, the number of pages to read when traversing an index). The trade-off is the increase in time when performing INSERT and UPDATE statements caused by page splitting. Use high Fill Factor values for static tables or tables that are not modified frequently. Specify a low Fill Factor value to spread data over more pages. A low Fill Factor value is good for tables involved with many UPDATE and INSERT transactions—the chance of a page split occurring is reduced because of the initial number of rows per page being reduced, thus leaving more empty space on the data page for additional records. The penalty for a low Fill Factor is a decrease in query performance because the number of index levels is increased, requiring more data pages to be read when querying the table. *Note:* The default value of 0 is a special case and is not considered a low Fill Factor value because the leaf pages are filled to 100 percent capacity and some space is left on the index pages). The default Fill Factor value used by your SQL Server can be configured using sp_configure or the Enterprise Manager.

NOTE

The Fill Factor value is not maintained by SQL Server after index creation; it is maintained only when the index is built.

After you select the options you want for the index, click the Next button. The Completing the Create Index Wizard dialog box appears (see Figure 18.13).

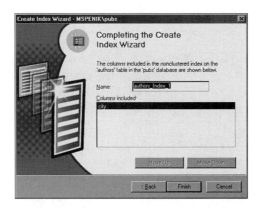

FIGURE 18.13   The Create Index Wizard Completing the Create Index Wizard dialog box.

   6. Enter a name for the index in the Index Name text box. Use a meaningful naming convention for indexes and stick with it. For example, you can prefix indexes with *cidx* for a clustered index and *idx* for a nonclustered index. If the index is on the primary key table, add *pk*. If the index is a foreign key, add *fk*. Then use the column names to remind yourself which columns make up the index. For example, for a clustered index on the primary key column of the authors table, au_id in the pubs database, the index would be named cidx_pk_au_id. The maximum number of characters you can use for an index is 30. Use the Move Up or Move Down buttons to change the order of the columns in the index. When you are done, click the Finish button to build the index. A dialog box is displayed, telling you of the success or failure of your index creation.

When an index is created, a row is placed in the sysindexes database system table. Index creation time has been improved on multiprocessor machines when using the Enterprise or Developer editions. When an index is created on an SMP machine using one of these versions of SQL Server, the data scan and sort is performed on multiple processors. The number of processors used can be tuned by setting the SQL Server configuration parameter *max degree of parallelism*.

TIP

Always build a clustered index before building a nonclustered index. When a clustered index is built, all nonclustered indexes currently on the table are rebuilt, so more time is required to build the clustered index. You also can build an index on a temporary table.

The Transact SQL statement used to create an index is the CREATE INDEX command, which has the following syntax:

```
CREATE [UNIQUE] [CLUSTERED | NONCLUSTERED] INDEX index_name
ON table_name | view_name (column_name [ASC | DESC] [, column_name]...)
[WITH [PAD_INDEX,][[,]FILLFACTOR = x][[,] IGNORE_DUP_KEY][[,]DROP_EXISTING]
[[,]STATISTICS_NORECOMPUTE] [[,]SORT_IN_TEMPDB]
[ON filegroup]
```

Some of the CREATE INDEX options were discussed in the section of this chapter covering the Create Index Wizard Index Options dialog box (see Figure 18.12). The remaining options are as follows:

- PAD_INDEX—The PAD_INDEX option specifies the amount of space to leave open on each interior node. By default, the number of items is never less than two on an interior page. The PAD_INDEX option works in conjunction with the FILLFACTOR option and uses the FILLFACTOR percentage.

- IGNORE_DUP_KEY—The IGNORE_DUP_KEY option does not enable you to create a unique index with duplicate values, but if an attempt is made to insert a duplicate row, the duplicate row is ignored and an informational message is displayed. If the INSERT or UPDATE is part of a transaction, the transaction continues instead of rolling back on a duplicate key error. This option exists in SQL Server 2000 for backward compatibility and is only supported for INSERT statements.

- DROP_EXISTING—This option is for clustered indexes only and affects the nonclustered indexes on the table. When DROP_EXISTING is used on an index creation statement, the clustered index is dropped and rebuilt. The nonclustered indexes are modified only after the index is re-created. Without this option, the nonclustered indexes would also be updated when the clustered index is dropped.

- STATISTICS_NORECOMPUTE—The STATISTICS_NORECOMPUTE option turns off auto updating of the index statistical information, requiring you to perform an UPDATE STATISTICS command manually.

- SORT_IN_TEMPDB—The intermediate resultset to create the index will be built in tempdb.

NOTE

SQL Server 2000 provides another method to create indexes called *constraints*. A constraint is added to a table during the table creation and can be used to maintain referential integrity. The primary key constraint places a unique index, clustered or nonclustered, on the columns defined as the `primary key`. You cannot drop a constraint index with the SQL Enterprise Manager (using the Manage Index dialog box). To remove a constraint, you must use the `ALTER TABLE` command. Here's the good news if you use SQL Server 2000: You can use the DBCC `DBREINDEX` statement to dynamically rebuild indexes without having to drop and re-create the index or constraint.

Other Index Operations

Following is a quick review of other index operations you can perform using Transact SQL and/or the Enterprise Manager.

Indexes on Views and Computed Columns

SQL Server 2000 allows you to create indexes on computed columns and views. This new feature can improve the performance when performing queries against complex views or on computed columns. If a user queries a non-indexed view, SQL Server dynamically builds the resultset, which can be time-consuming. If an index is created on a view, SQL Server stores the resultset of the view in the database, improving query times because the resultset is no longer created dynamically. Modifications made to the tables in the view are also reflected in the index (even after index creation). In order to create an index on a view, you must first create a unique clustered index on the view. After you create a unique clustered index, you can create nonclustered indexes on the view. Other restrictions for a view are as follows:

- The following Set options must be set `ON` when creating the view or modifying the data in the tables in the view—`ANSI_NULLS`, `ARITHABORT`, `CONCAT_NULL_YIELDS_NULL`, `QUOTED_IDENTIFIER`, `ANSI_PADDING`, and `ANSI_WARNING`. The option `NUMERIC_ROUNDABORT` must be set to `OFF`.

- The Select statement defining the view cannot contain `TOP`, `DISTINCT`, `UNION`, `COMPUTE`, and `HAVING` keywords.

- No subqueries allowed.

- No outer joins allowed.

- No views allowed on the select statement.

- Whoever creates the index must be the table(s) owner.

Viewing Indexes on Tables in a Database

In SQL Server 2000, you can view all the tables in a database, as well as the existing indexes on the tables, the number of rows in the tables, and the amount of disk space being used by each table and index using the Enterprise Manager. To view the table and index information, perform the following:

1. From the Enterprise Manager, select the database you want to view the information by clicking the database in the databases folder (for the following steps, the Northwind sample database is used). Database information is loaded into the right frame of the Enterprise Manager.

2. Select the Table Info tab located in the right frame. The Table and Indexes tab is displayed, shown in Figure 18.14.

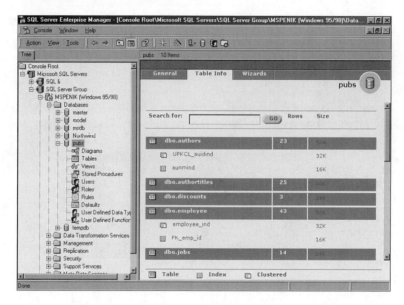

FIGURE 18.14   The Database Information Tables and Indexes dialog box.

The Table and Indexes tab displays all the tables and indexes associated with the tables in the selected database, as well as the amount of disk space being used by the table and indexes, and the total number of rows for each table. You can use the Transact SQL commands `sp_help_index` and `sp_statistics` to view index information for an associated table.

Renaming, Adding, or Deleting an Index

This section covers how to add, remove, and rename an index by using the Enterprise Manager. Before examining how to perform these tasks with the Enterprise Manager, here are the Transact SQL statements to delete (remove) an index and rename an index. To remove an index with Transact SQL, use the Transact SQL command `DROP INDEX`, which has the following format:

```
DROP INDEX [owner.]table_name.index_name | view_name.index_name
[, [owner.]table_name.index_name...]
```

To rename an index with Transact SQL, use the SQL Server system stored procedure sp_rename, which has the following syntax:

```
sp_rename objname, newname [, COLUMN | INDEX ]
```

To use the Enterprise Manager to perform index adding, renaming, or deleting, perform the following (Note: the following uses the Northwind database):

1. Select the database from the databases folder in the Enterprise Manager.

2. Collapse the database to view the database objects by clicking the + sign located to the left of the database name.

3. Select the table to index.

4. Right-click to display a pop-up menu. Select All Tasks, and Manage Indexes. The Manage Indexes dialog box, shown in Figure 18.15, appears.

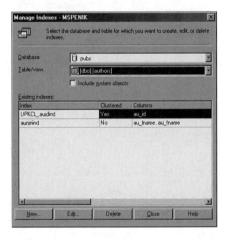

FIGURE 18.15   The Manage Indexes dialog box.

To delete an index, select the index you want to remove in the grid and click the Delete button shown in Figure 18.15.

To add a new index, click the New button shown in Figure 18.15. Add the columns that make up the index in the Column Name grid. Give the index a name by entering the name in the Index name text box. Select the File group to place the index using the Index File group combo box. You can then set the fill factor, unique property, clustered index, create as an index or constraint, and check to not automatically update statistics by checking appropriate check boxes or radio buttons. Click the Close button shown in Figure 18.15 to save the index.

To modify an index, double-click on the index you want to modify in the grid shown in Figure 18.15. The Edit Existing Index dialog box, shown in Figure 18.16, appears.

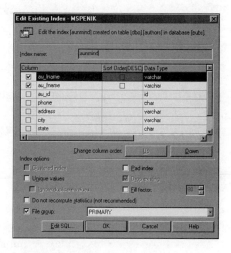

FIGURE 18.16   Edit Existing Index dialog box.

To add columns, check the columns you want to add or uncheck columns you want to remove. To make other changes check or uncheck the appropriate check boxes and click OK to save your changes.

Suggested Index Strategies

Index selection is based on the design of the tables and the queries that are executed against the tables. Before you create indexes, make sure that the indexed columns are part of a query or are being placed on the table for other reasons, such as preventing duplicate data. The following sections suggest some indexing strategies.

What to Index

The following list shows criteria you can use to help determine which columns will make good indexes:

- Columns used in table joins
- Columns used in range queries
- Columns used in order by queries

- Columns used in group by queries
- Columns used in aggregate functions

What Not to Index

The following list shows cases in which columns or indexes should not be used or should be used sparingly:

- Tables with a small number of rows
- Columns with poor selectivity (that is, with a wide range of values)
- Columns that are very large in width (try to limit indexes to columns less than 25 bytes in size)
- Tables with heavy transaction loads (lots of inserts and deletes) but very few decision-support operations
- Columns not used in queries

Clustered or Nonclustered Index

As you know, you can have only one clustered index per table. Following are some situations in which a clustered index works well:

- Columns used in range queries
- Columns used in order by or group by queries
- Columns used in table joins
- Queries returning large result sets

Nonclustered indexes work well in the following situations:

- Columns used in aggregate functions
- Foreign keys
- Queries returning small resultsets
- When using the DBCC DBREINDEX statement to dynamically rebuild nonclustered indexes, the requested index can be rebuilt without rebuilding all the other indexes on a table. When a clustered index is rebuilt, all the nonclustered indexes are also rebuilt. (Note: With DBCC DBREINDEX, you don't have to drop and re-create the index or constraint.)

- Information frequently accessed by a specific column in table joins or order by or group by queries.

- Primary keys that are sequential surrogate keys (identity columns, sequence numbers).

Letting SQL Server Help with Index Selection

One of the goals of the SQL Server team was to make SQL Server an easy tool for maintaining and using databases. Index selection has always been a problem because of the knowledge required to tune a query. In addition, one must know how and when to override the query optimizer. SQL Server 2000 provides several tools to help the DBA take the guesswork out of index creation. The most effective tool is the SQL Server Index Tuning Wizard. The SQL Server Index Tuning Wizard analyzes real workloads captured by the SQL Server profiler. The SQL Server Index Tuning Wizard tests the various SQL statements found in the profiler workload and creates what if indexes. The wizard then checks the what if indexes with the Query Processor to determine the cost of the index. The wizard then makes the best index recommendations based on the workload. The suggested indexes can be created immediately or scheduled. Like all SQL Server wizards, the Index Tuning Wizard is simple to use and can be found under the Enterprise Manager's Wizards dialog box.

Capturing a SQL Server profiler workload is discussed in detail in Chapter 24, "Monitoring SQL Server." The real power of the Index Tuning Wizard from a DBA standpoint is that you do not need to know anything about the application, how the application is used, or the data structure of the database. The SQL Server profiler captures the SQL statements being performed during actual workloads for the Index Tuning Wizard to analyze—enabling the DBA to do an expert index-tuning job quickly. An important point to make is that to get the most from the tuning wizard, you should capture actual workloads.

Index FAQ

The following section contains several frequently asked questions and answers about indexes.

Q How can I view the index selectivity (density) of an indexed column?

A The index selectivity can be viewed by using the Transact SQL Statement DBCC SHOW_STATISTICS. DBCC SHOW_STATISTICS displays the average key length of an index, the index density, and the distribution steps.

Q What are composite indexes?

A Composite indexes are indexes created with two or more columns. (The maximum number of columns for an index is 16.) SQL Server 2000 keeps distribution page and histogram statistics on the columns that make up the index. Try not to get carried away by creating composite indexes with a large number of columns. (I try to keep them under four columns.) Too many columns affect performance and make the index key large, increasing the size of the index and requiring you to scan more data pages to read the index keys.

Q Can SQL Server use more than one index in a single query?

A In SQL Server 2000, the query optimizer can use multiple indexes to retrieve the information.

Q What is index covering?

A Index covering is a term used to explain a situation in which all the columns returned by a query and all the columns in the WHERE clause are the key columns in a single nonclustered index (that is, a composite index). SQL Server does not have to read the data pages to satisfy the query; instead, it returns the values on the leaf page of the index, which can boost speed significantly on tables where the table row size is much larger than the index key size. Keep in mind that over indexing a table can hurt data modification performance.

Q Can SQL Server use index covering with indexes that are not composite indexes?

A SQL Server 2000 can use single column indexes to cover a query! This is an outstanding new feature because the main problem of composite indexes with index covering is having to create composite indexes that covered various query scenarios. Now by creating several single column indexes on columns that are frequently returned, joined, or filtered, you can get the benefits of covered queries. Again keep in mind that over indexing a table can hurt data modification performance.

Q Can users access a table while an index is being created?

A The table on which the index is being created is locked during index creation. Creating indexes on very large tables or creating clustered indexes (which might reorder the data pages) can take some time to complete. You cannot access the table until the index creation is complete. Try to create clustered indexes and very large nonclustered indexes during nonpeak hours.

Q What is the best way to drop and re-create an index?

A The fastest way to drop and re-create a clustered or nonclustered index with SQL Server 2000 is to use the DBCC REINDEX command.

Q Do I still have to perform an UPDATE STATISTICS with SQL Server 2000?

A SQL Server 2000 will automatically update statistical information for you as a background task that can be disabled. If you disable this feature, you will need to manually issue the UPDATE STATISTICS command. If you have the Auto Update Statistics feature enabled, you might still want to execute the UPDATE STATISTICS command after importing or updating large amounts of information.

Q Why are the Index FillFactor and PAD_INDEX options important?

A FillFactor and PAD_INDEX are important for several reasons. For example, you can use them to maintain contiguous disk space. When SQL Server creates an index using FillFactor and PAD_INDEX, the space allocated for the indexes is contiguous disk space. So when a user queries against the index, sequential disk I/O is being used to traverse the index B-Tree. Over time, as index pages split, the new pages added as a result of the split are no longer contiguous, thus resulting in non-sequential reads (which are slower). The real trick is trying to determine the right combination of FillFactor and PAD_INDEX that will put as many index keys on a page while leaving enough room to avoid page splits. Tables that rarely change can use a FillFactor of 100 to completely fill the page and maximize query time. However, if you add a record to a table with full index pages, you immediately get a page split.

Q How do I keep distribution statistics on a non-indexed column (or columns)?

A Use the Create Statistics command to create statistics (histogram and density information) on a column or set of columns without creating an index (this also counts as one of the 249 allowed nonclustered indexes). If the database has the Auto Create Statistics turned on, when queries are executed with non-indexed columns in the where clause, SQL Server will issue a create statistics command on the column and table. These autogenerated statistics have a index name that begins with an _.

Q Should I always index a table?

A You should not index tables that have very few rows in them. When a table consists of only a few data pages, it might be faster for SQL Server to perform a table scan rather than walk through an index.

Q What is the best advice I can give someone on indexes?

A Try to keep the index key values small. This provides you with lots of rows per data page, which reduces disk I/O. For tables with clustered indexes, it is important to choose small key values because the clustered index key value is stored as the row identifier of nonclustered indexes.

Q When should I choose the `SORT_IN_TEMPDB` option in the `CREATE INDEX` command?

A If you have `tempdb` on a very fast drive system or on a drive system different from the table and index being created, you can improve performance using the `SORT_IN_TEMPDB` option on the `CREATE INDEX` command. When this option is used, the intermediate resultset used to create the index is generated in `tempdb`. The trade-off is this requires more disk space than a regular index create but is faster if the database is on a drive or set of drives different from `tempdb`.

Summary

It is important that you understand the basic ideas behind SQL Server indexes. In the next chapter, you build on the basic concepts of this chapter and learn about the Query Processor. If you understand indexes, the Query Processor, and the tools SQL Server provides to help you select the proper indexes, you will be able to provide valuable support to developers. Following are some important points to remember about SQL Server indexes:

- SQL Server maintains indexes with a B-Tree structure.

- In a clustered index, the leaf contains the actual data pages of the table, and the data is physically stored in the logical order of the index.

- The SQL Server query optimizer can use more than one index to resolve a query.

- SQL Server 2000 can maintain distribution statistics on non-indexed columns.

- SQL Server 2000 can automatically update statistics for indexes.

- Composite indexes are indexes created with two or more columns.

- Indexes can be created on views and computed columns.

- Use the Index Tuning Wizard to help you select the proper indexes for you databases.

- Select indexes carefully.

19

Query Optimization

by Orryn Sledge

IN THIS CHAPTER

- What's a Query Optimizer?
- What Are Statistics?
- Basic Query Optimization Suggestions
- Tools to Help Optimize a Query
- Reading Showplans
- Overriding the Optimizer
- Other Tuning Tricks
- Query Optimization FAQ

Query optimization involves understanding SQL Server's optimizer, query optimization tools, and proper indexing techniques. With this knowledge, you can write queries that run faster, build better indexes, and resolve performance problems.

What's a Query Optimizer?

A query optimizer is a process that generates the "optimal" execution path for a query. The optimal execution path is the path that offers the best performance. Before the query is run, the optimizer assigns a cost based on CPU and disk I/O usage for different execution paths. The optimizer then uses the least expensive execution path to process the query. See Figure 19.1 for examples of execution paths.

The advantage of the query optimizer is that it relieves users from the tedious process of having to decide how their SQL statements should be constructed to use indexes and in what order the data should be accessed. The query optimizer enables users to build SQL statements that *automatically* take advantage of indexes and *automatically* determine the optimal order to process table joins.

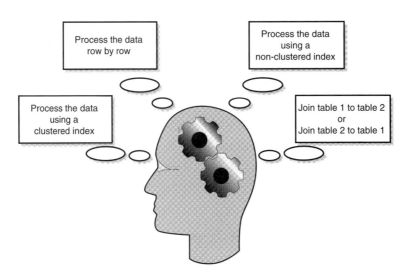

FIGURE 19.1   Examples of execution paths.

NOTE

SQL Server 2000 uses an *intelligent* cost-based optimizer that has significantly improved over the years. In previous editions of this book, I stated that a DBA "should not be misled by the word *intelligent,* and I have yet to meet a query optimizer that is more intelligent than a good DBA."

The changes Microsoft has made to the query optimizer is causing me to eat some of my own words! The optimizer employs techniques such as automatic statistic gathering, enhanced execution strategies, and multi-index operations. These techniques reduce the amount of time spent tuning a query.

However, I still feel that the query optimizer can never understand all the nuances and intricacies of your query and data. I recommend that you try to understand how the optimizer works and how you can finesse it into delivering a better performance.

What Are Statistics?

Whenever you create an index, SQL Server creates a set of statistics about the data contained within the index. The query optimizer uses these statistics to determine whether it should use the index to help process the query.

SQL Server 2000 automatically maintains statistic information. This is a great feature! Previous versions of SQL Server required that the UPDATE STATISTICS command be run on a frequent basis. If the UPDATE STATISTICS command was not frequently run, statistics could become stale. In turn, this would cause the optimizer to ignore useful indexes.

Starting with SQL Server 7.0, the query optimizer automatically detects that statistics are out of date and automatically regenerates the statistics. This eliminates the problem with the optimizer ignoring useful indexes. As if this isn't amazing enough, statistic generation occurs almost instantly (on average, 1 second)! This amazing feat is accomplished through a data-sampling algorithm.

By default, auto-update statistics are automatically turned on for all tables. Should you need to modify or view this setting, use the sp_autostats system stored procedure. This command also displays when the statistics were last updated. The following is the syntax:

```
sp_autostats [@tblname =] 'table_name'
[, [@flagc =] 'stats_flag']
[, [@indname =] 'index_name']
```

Sample query:

```
sp_autostats authors
```

The following is sample output:

```
Global statistics settings for [pubs]:
  Automatic update statistics: ON
  Automatic create statistics: ON


Settings for table [authors]


Index Name                        AUTOSTATS Last Updated
--------------------------------- --------- ---------------------------
authors.UPKCL_auidind             ON        2000-10-30 16:27:06.987
authors.aunmind                   ON        2000-10-30 16:27:07.017
```

For those hardcore DBAs, use the DBCC SHOW_STATISTICS command to probe deep into the statistics gathered by SQL Server. The following is the syntax:

```
DBCC SHOW_STATISTICS (table_name,
 index_name or collection)
```

Sample query:

```
dbcc show_statistics(authors,aunmind)
```

The following is sample output:

```
Statistics for INDEX 'aunmind'.
Updated              Rows    Rows Sampled  Steps  Density   Average key length
-------------------- ------- ------------- ------ --------- --------------------
Aug  6 2000  1:34AM  23      23            22     0.0       24.52174

(1 row(s) affected)


All density              Average Length           Columns
------------------------ ------------------------ -----------------------------
-------------------------------------------------------------------------------
-------------------------------------------------------------------------------
4.5454547E-2             7.3913045                au_lname
4.3478262E-2             13.52174                 au_lname, au_fname
4.3478262E-2             24.52174                 au_lname, au_fname, au_id

(3 row(s) affected)


RANGE_HI_KEY       RANGE_ROWS      EQ_ROWS      DISTINCT_RANGE_ROWS   AVG_RANGE_ROWS
----------------   -------------   ----------   -------------------   --------------
Bennet             0.0             1.0          0                     0.0
Blotchet-Halls     0.0             1.0          0                     0.0
Carson             0.0             1.0          0                     0.0
DeFrance           0.0             1.0          0                     0.0
del Castillo       0.0             1.0          0                     0.0
Dull               0.0             1.0          0                     0.0
Green              0.0             1.0          0                     0.0
Greene             0.0             1.0          0                     0.0
Gringlesby         0.0             1.0          0                     0.0
Hunter             0.0             1.0          0                     0.0
Karsen             0.0             1.0          0                     0.0
Locksley           0.0             1.0          0                     0.0
MacFeather         0.0             1.0          0                     0.0
McBadden           0.0             1.0          0                     0.0
O'Leary            0.0             1.0          0                     0.0
Panteley           0.0             1.0          0                     0.0
Ringer             0.0             2.0          0                     0.0
Smith              0.0             1.0          0                     0.0
Straight           0.0             1.0          0                     0.0
Stringer           0.0             1.0          0                     0.0
White              0.0             1.0          0                     0.0
Yokomoto           0.0             1.0          0                     0.0

(22 row(s) affected)
```

Basic Query Optimization Suggestions

The following list of suggestions concentrates on the basics of query optimization. It is best to start with the basics when trying to improve query performance. Quite often, a minor modification to a query yields a substantial gain in performance.

- **Target queries that run slowly and frequently.** By simply adding an index, you can often see a dramatic improvement in query performance.

- **Understand your data.** To use optimization tricks, you must understand your query and how it relates to your data. Otherwise, your lack of knowledge might hamper your ability to effectively rewrite a query.

- **Record statistics about the existing query.** Before you begin to optimize a query, record a showplan (see "Showplan and Reading Showplans" later in this chapter, for more information) and I/O statistics. This provides you with a benchmark against which you can measure the success of your revisions.

- **Start with the basics.** Look for the obvious when you start to optimize a query. Do useful indexes exist? Are triggers being executed when the query is run? Does the query reference a view? Does the query use nonsearch arguments?

- **Understand the output from a showplan.** It is important to understand what is relevant and what is not when evaluating a showplan.

- **Throw conventional wisdom out the window.** Sometimes, you have to break the rules to optimize a query. Your ability to extract maximum query performance is a mix between art and science. What works on one query might not work on another query. Therefore, you occasionally have to go against conventional wisdom to maximize performance.

Tools to Help Optimize a Query

The following tools can be used to help optimize a query:

- Index Tuning Wizard

- SQL Server Profiler

- Showplan

- Statistics I/O

- Stats Time tool

Index Tuning Wizard

The Index Tuning Wizard analyzes a query and makes index recommendations. (See Chapter 18, "Understanding Indexes," for more information.) It's like having a DBA on your staff who never sleeps and never asks for a raise!

New and experienced DBAs should look at the Index Tuning Wizard. Overall, the Index Tuning Wizard does a good job of recommending indexes. However, the wizard should be used as a starting point for query optimization and not as the ending point. The wizard is not always 100% correct. For example, it will occasionally make a mistake by not recommending an index or by recommending a suboptimal index.

To use the Index Tuning Wizard, enter a Transact-SQL statement in the Query dialog box. From the Query menu, select the Index Tuning Wizard menu option. After the query is analyzed, the index recommendations are displayed in the Query Analyzer Index Analysis dialog box (see Figure 19.2). Click the Accept button to apply the index. If the analyzer decided that additional indexes were not necessary, the No indexes were recommended message will appear in the Results portion of the SQL Server Query Analyzer dialog box.

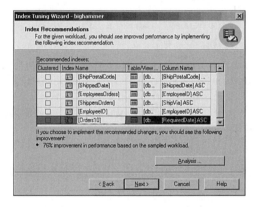

FIGURE 19.2 Index recommendations.

Consider the following query that is run from the Northwind database:

```
select *
from orders
where RequiredDate = '05/18/1998'
```

If you look at the showplan and statistic I/O before using the Index Tuning Wizard, you can establish a benchmark to see if the recommendation by the Index Tuning Wizard is correct.

Showplan output:

```
StmtText
-----------------------------------------------------------
|--Clustered Index Scan(OBJECT:([Northwind].[dbo].[Orders].[PK_Orders]),
WHERE:([Orders].[RequiredDate]=Convert([@1])))
```

Statistics I/O output:

```
Table 'Orders'. Scan count 1, logical reads 22,
  physical reads 0, read-ahead reads 0.
```

The following is the index recommended and implemented by the Index Tuning Wizard:

```
USE Northwind
CREATE NONCLUSTERED INDEX [orders0]
  ON [dbo].[orders]([requireddate])
```

Next, look at the showplan and statistic I/O after using the Index Tuning Wizard. The following is the revised SHOWPLAN output after implementing the index recommendation:

```
StmtText
-----------------------------------------------------------
  |--Bookmark Lookup(BOOKMARK:([Bmk1000]), OBJECT:([Northwind].[dbo].[Orders]))
    |--Index Seek(OBJECT:([Northwind].[dbo].[Orders].[orders0]),
        SEEK:([Orders].[RequiredDate]=Convert([@1])) ORDERED FORWARD)
```

Revised Statistics I/O output:

```
Table 'Orders'. Scan count 1, logical reads 8,
  physical reads 2, read-ahead reads 0.
```

If you compare the SHOWPLAN output, you will notice that the query optimizer has utilized the new index created by the Index Tuning Wizard. If you compare the statistics I/O output, you will notice that the number of logical reads (the number of pages read from the data cache) dropped significantly. It went from 22 logical reads to 8 logical reads and 2 physical reads. If the orders table had thousands of records, you would have noticed a huge decrease in the time required to run the query. As you can see, the Index Tuning Wizard is pretty darn smart!

TIP

I recommend running the Index Tuning Wizard several times against the same query until the `No indexes were suggested` message appears. This is especially important when optimizing a query that contains multiple tables. Failure to do so might cause the wizard to skip tables, and thus the wizard will be unable to recommend other useful indexes.

NOTE

When a new index is added to a table, additional overhead is required to process data modification queries because the index page must be updated in addition to the data page. This will increase index page I/O. I recommend performing a balancing act when adding indexes. In an environment where transaction throughput is important (especially `INSERT` operations), I advise against an index-everything strategy. In a data-warehouse environment, where the majority of activity is `SELECT` type of operations, increasing the number of indexes on a table probably doesn't hurt anything.

SQL Server Profiler

The SQL Server Profiler is a great tool for finding slow running queries and bottlenecks. (See Chapter 24, "Monitoring SQL Server," for more information on SQL Server Profiler.) For example, you can run a trace that captures all SQL Server query activity. This information can be loaded into the Index Tuning Wizard. The Index Tuning Wizard can analyze the trace information and suggest the appropriate indexes.

The next detailed example uses SQL Server Profiler in conjunction with the Index Tuning Wizard. Perform the following steps to create sample data:

1. Start the Query Analyzer by double-clicking the Query Analyzer icon in the Microsoft SQL Server program group. The Connect to SQL Server dialog box appears.

2. From the Connect to SQL Server dialog box, enter the necessary connection information and click the OK button to connect to SQL Server. The SQL Server Query Analyzer dialog box appears.

3. From the SQL Server Query Analyzer dialog box, enter the following syntax (see Figure 19.3). This syntax creates a table and populates it with data from the `master..sysmessages` table. Note: The `INSERT` statement in this example is executed four times; this was necessary to create a large recordset to work with.

```
use pubs
go
create table sample_table
```

```
(error int not null,
severity smallint not null,
dlevel smallint not null)
go
declare @nLoopCounter int
select @nLoopCounter = 1
while @nLoopCounter <=4
 begin
  insert into sample_table
   select error, severity,dlevel
   from master..sysmessages
  select @nLoopCounter = @nLoopCounter + 1
 end
go
```

4. Execute the previous statement.

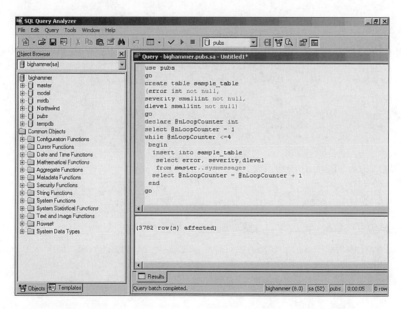

FIGURE 19.3   Sample data.

Perform the following steps to start the trace:

1. Start the SQL Server Profiler by double-clicking the Profiler icon in the Microsoft SQL Server program group. The SQL Server Profiler dialog box appears.

2. From the File menu, select the New menu option. From the New menu option, select the Trace menu option. The Connect to SQL Server dialog box appears. Enter the corresponding information and click connect. The Trace Properties dialog box appears.

3. At the Trace Properties dialog box, enter the following information: trace name, template type, and save to settings (see Figure 19.4). For this example, the output is captured to a file.

4. Click the Run button to begin the trace.

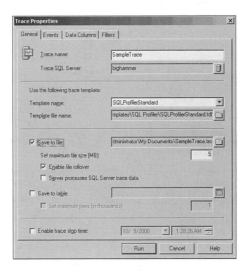

FIGURE 19.4   Trace Properties.

Perform the following steps to create sample trace data:

1. Switch back to the SQL Server Query Analyzer.

2. From the SQL Server Query Analyzer dialog box, enter the following query (see Figure 19.5):

```
select *
from sample_table
where error = 102
```

3. Execute the previous statement.

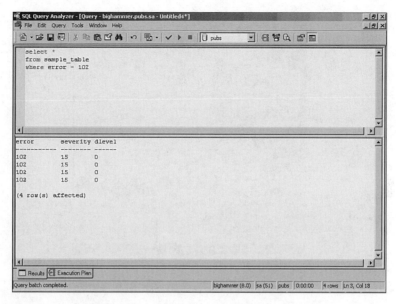

FIGURE 19.5   Sample query.

Perform the following steps to stop the trace:

1. Switch back to the SQL Server Profiler.

2. From the File menu, select the Stop Traces menu option. The Stop Selected Traces dialog box appears. Click the OK button to stop the trace.

Perform the following steps to run the Index Tuning Wizard:

1. From the Tools menu of the SQL Server Profiler, select the Index Tuning Wizard menu option. The Index Tuning Wizard dialog box appears (see Figure 19.6). Click the Next button to continue. The Select Server and Database screen appears.

2. From the Select Server and Database screen of the Index Tuning Wizard, enter the following information: server, database, and the optimization type (see Figure 19.7). Click the Next button to continue. The Specify Workload screen appears.

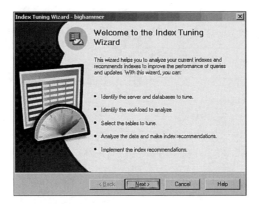

FIGURE 19.6   The Index Tuning Wizard.

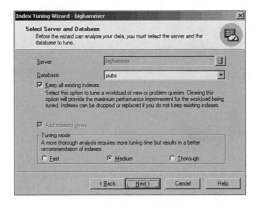

FIGURE 19.7   The Select Server and Database screen.

3. From the Specify Workload screen of the Index Tuning Wizard, select the workload type. For this example, select my workload file radio button (see Figure 19.8).

4. If you would like to enter advanced options such as index tuning parameters, click the Advanced Options button (see Figure 19.9). Enter the corresponding information and click the OK button. Click the Next button to continue. The Select Tables to Tune screen appears.

5. From the Select Tables to Tune screen of the Index Tuning Wizard, select the tables to tune (see Figure 19.10). Click the Next button to continue. The Index Recommendations screen appears.

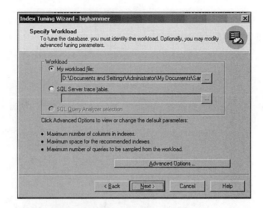

FIGURE 19.8   The Specify Workload screen.

FIGURE 19.9   The Advanced Options screen.

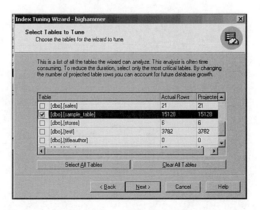

FIGURE 19.10   The Select Tables to Tune screen.

6. From the Index Recommendations screen of the Index Tuning Wizard, you can approve or reject the index suggestions (see Figure 19.11). Click the Next button to continue. The Schedule Index Update Job screen appears.

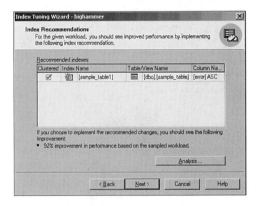

FIGURE 19.11   The Index Recommendations screen.

7. From the Schedule Index Update Job screen of the Index Tuning Wizard, select the appropriate method to implement the indexes. For this example, the Execute recommendations now option is selected (see Figure 19.12). This option tells the wizard to immediately create the recommended indexes. Click the Next button to continue. The Completing the Index Tuning Wizard screen appears.

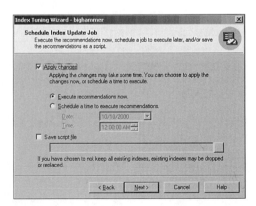

FIGURE 19.12   The Schedule Index Update Job screen.

8. From the Completing the Index Tuning Wizard screen of the Index Tuning Wizard, click the Finish button to implement the recommendations (see Figure 19.13). After the wizard implements the indexes, a message box appears notifying that the indexes have been successfully implemented.

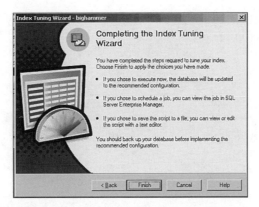

FIGURE 19.13   The Completing the Index Tuning Wizard screen.

TIP

I recommend periodically using the SQL Server Profiler to gather workload data and using the Index Tuning Wizard to analyze the workload data. This is a great way to maximize performance, especially if your database is continuously evolving.

Showplan

A *showplan* provides insight about how SQL Server is going to process a SQL statement. Over the years, showplan information has been made easier to understand, but its output can still be somewhat cryptic and based on technical jargon. However, if you know how to interpret its cryptic output, it can be useful for tuning queries.

The following are the different types of showplans:

- Graphical showplan
- Text-based showplan

Graphical Showplan

To generate a graphical showplan, open the Query Analyzer. Enter a Transact-SQL statement in the Query dialog box. From the Query menu, select the Display Estimated Execution Plan menu option.

The graphical showplan appears in the SQL Execution Plan portion of the Query dialog box (see Figure 19.14).

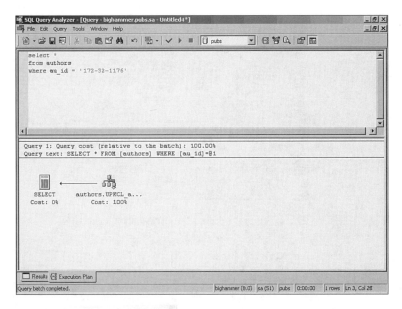

FIGURE 19.14   A graphical showplan.

TIP

The graphical showplan window has several great right-mouse click features. For example, right-click a showplan icon and you can manage indexes, create/update statistics, and create missing statistics. Right-click the background of the graphical showplan window and you can adjust the zoom factor.

Text-Based Showplan

An alternative to the graphical showplan is the text-based showplan. The text-based showplan is useful if you need to email someone the query plan or if you prefer to work in a text based environment.

There are two types of text-based showplans: SET SHOWPLAN_TEXT and SET SHOW-PLAN_ALL. SET SHOWPLAN_ALL is the more detailed version. To execute a text-based showplan, enter SET SHOWPLAN_TEXT or SET SHOWPLAN_ALL in a query window and execute a query.

The following is the syntax for text-based showplans:

```
SET SHOWPLAN_TEXT {ON | OFF}
SET SHOWPLAN_ALL {ON | OFF}
```

The following is an example SET `SHOWPLAN_TEXT`:

Sample query:

```
SET SHOWPLAN_TEXT ON
go
select * from authors
where au_id = '267-41-2394'
go
```

Sample Output:

```
StmtText
- - - - - - - - - - - - - - - - - - - - - - - - - - - - - - - - - - - - - - - - - - - - - - - - - -
select * from authors
where au_id = '267-41-2394'

(1 row(s) affected)

StmtText
- - - - - - - - - - - - - - - - - - - - - - - - - - - - - - - - - - - - - - - - - - - - - - - - - -
  |--Clustered Index Seek
    (OBJECT:([pubs].[dbo].[authors].[UPKCL_auidind]),
      SEEK:([authors].[au_id]=[@1]) ORDERED)
```

Statistics I/O

Statistics I/O is useful in determining the amount of I/O that will occur to process a query. The less I/O you have, the faster your query will run. When tuning queries, try to minimize the amount of I/O used by the query. SQL Server uses statistics I/O to help determine the optimal query execution path.

Statistics I/O provides four types of I/O measurements: *scan count*, *logical reads*, *physical reads*, and *read-ahead reads*. The following list explains the four types of I/O measurements:

- *scan count* is the number of scans required to process the query.

- *logical reads* is the number of pages accessed in cache to process the query.

- *physical reads* is the number of pages accessed from disk to process the query.

- *read-ahead reads* is the number of pages loaded into cache to process the query.

> **NOTE**
>
> Each time a query is run, the data used to process the query might become loaded into the
> data cache. This can reduce the number of *physical reads* required to process the query
> when it is run again. You can detect whether the data is loaded into the data cache by moni-
> toring the *logical reads* and *physical reads* for a query. If *physical reads* is less than
> *logical reads*, some or all the data was in the data cache.

To generate statistics I/O, enter a Transact-SQL statement in the Query dialog box. From the Query menu, select the Current Connection Properties menu option. Select the Set Statistics IO option from the Query Flags page of the Query Options dialog box (see Figure 19.15).

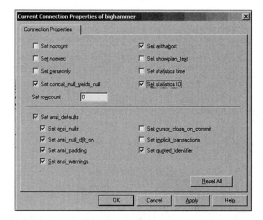

FIGURE 19.15   Setting the Set Statistics I/O query option.

After you execute your query, the output from the statistics I/O appears in the results window (see Figure 19.16).

> **NOTE**
>
> We gained the graphical showplan in 7.0 but we lost the graphical statistics I/O feature!
> Previous versions were displayed in nice graphs with statistics I/O information. Hey Microsoft,
> maybe we could have the graphical statistics I/O feature back in a future release?

Statistics Time Tool

The Statistics Time tool displays the time required by SQL Server to parse, compile, and execute a query.

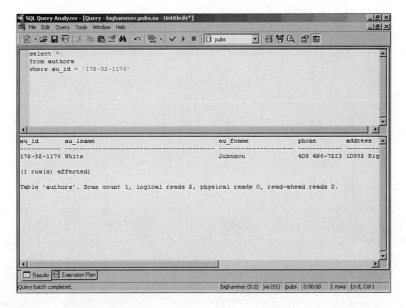

FIGURE 19.16   Statistics I/O.

To use the Statistics Time option, enter a Transact-SQL statement in the Query dialog box. From the Query menu, select the Current Connection Options menu option. Select the Set Statistics Time option from the Query Flags page of the Query Option dialog box (see Figure 19.17).

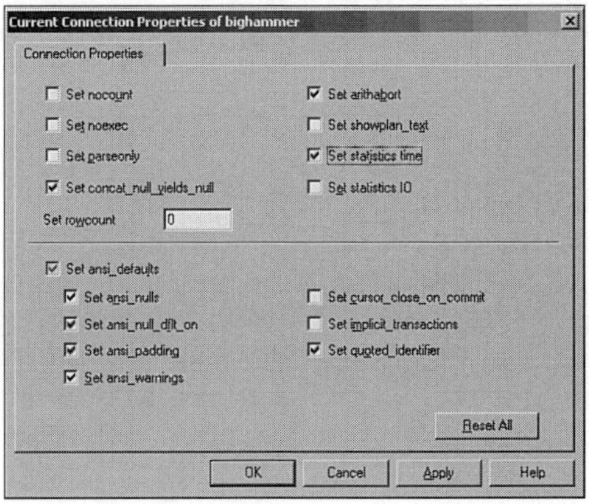

FIGURE 19.17   Setting the Set Statistics Time query option.

TIP

You might see a performance improvement when moving queries that contain lengthy parse and compile times to stored procedures. This is because of the stored procedure being precompiled.

Reading Showplans

The showplan provides insight about how SQL Server is going to process a SQL statement. If you know what to look for in a showplan, the information it provides can be useful for tuning queries.

Those new to SQL Server should not be dismayed by the jargon used in the showplan. For example, the showplan uses words such as STREAM AGGREGATE. This is just a fancy way of saying that the query contains an aggregate function, such as AVG(), COUNT(), MAX(), MIN(), or SUM(). After you get past the lingo used by the showplan, you will find it a useful tool for optimizing queries.

Instead of looking at every possible output from the showplan, look for table scans in the showplan on tables that contain a large number of records. (Note: It is okay to have a table scan on a table that contains a small number of records.) Generally, a query containing a WHERE clause and generating a table scan is a good query to optimize. The table scan is probably slowing down your query because each row in the table is processed, which can lead to unnecessary I/O. To avoid a table scan, try to build a useful index that matches the WHERE clause.

The following example shows the difference in showplans for a retrieval based on a table scan and a retrieval that uses an index. The first listing shows the showplan for a table without an index:

```
Table:
CREATE TABLE sales
          (sales_id int not null,
          descr char(50) null)
Primary Key: sales_id (for this example assume
               that the primary key has not been created)
Indexes: None
Row Count: 1,000,000
Query:
SELECT * FROM sales
          WHERE sales_id = 450
Showplan:
  |--Table Scan(customer..sales, WHERE:(sales.sales_id=[@1]))
```

Now consider the inefficiencies involved with a table scan. The user wants only one row returned from the table, but the server had to process *every row* in the table (see Figure 19.18).

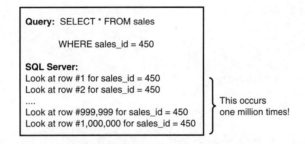

FIGURE 19.18   A table scan on a 1,000,000-row table.

To prevent the table scan in this example, create a clustered index on the column sales_id. By creating the index, the optimizer can generate a showplan that directly accesses the data without having to look at each row of data (see Figure 19.19). This will significantly improve performance. The following is the showplan with the clustered index.

```
Index:
CREATE UNIQUE CLUSTERED INDEX sales_cdx ON sales(sales_id)
Showplan:
 |--Clustered Index Seek(customer..sales.sales_cdx,
      SEEK:(sales.sales_id=[@1]) ORDERED)
```

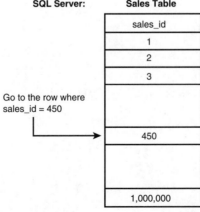

FIGURE 19.19   Using a clustered index to find data on a 1,000,000-row table.

A DISCUSSION ABOUT COMPOSITE INDEXES

A *composite index* is an index made up of more than one column. The rules regarding composite index optimization sometimes cause confusion. The source of the confusion stems from when SQL Server can take advantage of the index and when it cannot use the index.

Following is the structure of a table that is used for this discussion:

```
/* Table */
CREATE TABLE table1
          (col1 int not null,
          col2 int not null,
          col3 int not null,
          description char(50) null)
/* Implementation of the index */
create index col1_col2_col3_idx
  on table1(col1,col2,col3)
Number of rows:
1000
```

When working with a large table, the optimizer takes advantage of the composite index when one of the following is true:

- All columns in the index are referenced in the WHERE clause and contain useful search arguments.
- The first column in the index is referenced in the WHERE clause with a useful search argument.

For example, the following queries can take advantage of the composite index:

```
SELECT *
          FROM table1
          WHERE col1 = 100
          and col2 = 250
          and col3 = 179


SELECT *
          FROM table1
          WHERE col1 = 100
          and col2 = 250


SELECT *
          FROM table1
          WHERE col1 = 100


SELECT *
          FROM table1
          WHERE col1 = 100
          and col3 = 250
```

The following queries *cannot* take advantage of the composite index:

```
SELECT *
        FROM table1
        WHERE col2 = 100
        and col3 = 250

SELECT *
        FROM table1
        WHERE col2 = 100

SELECT *
        FROM table1
        WHERE col3 = 100
```

Overriding the Optimizer

Use the following features to override the optimizer:

- Index hints
- The SET FORCEPLAN ON command

Index Hints

By using an index hint, you can force the optimizer to use an index or force it not to choose an index. You usually want to let the optimizer determine how to process the query. However, it might be beneficial to override the optimizer if you find that it is not taking advantage of useful indexes. The syntax used to override the optimizer is as follows:

```
SELECT ...
FROM [table_name] (optimizer_hint)
```

In this syntax, `optimizer_hint` has the following format:

```
(INDEX(index_name|index_id}))
```

In this format, `index_name` is any valid name of an existing index on the table and `index_id` is the corresponding index ID.

The following is an example of forcing the optimizer to use a particular index:

```
select * from customer (INDEX(customer_last_idx))
where last_name like 'jacks%'
order by last_name
```

TIP

I recommend using index hints with prudence. Only in cases where SQL Server is choosing a less-than-optimal execution plan should the optimizer be overridden.

For example, I've seen queries that contain wildcards and will occasionally generate table scans. When testing SQL Server, I discovered that the following query was running slowly on my sample database, which has over 100,000 customer records.

```
Sample query:
select * from customer
where last_name like 'jacks%'
order by last_name
```

I was surprised to see that a table scan was generated because the following index existed:

```
create index customer_last_idx on customer(last_name)
```

I added an index hint, and the query ran significantly faster. The following is the query with the index hint:

```
select * from customer (INDEX(customer_last_idx))
where last_name like 'jacks%'
order by last_name
```

The previous index hint reduced the number of logical scans by 300 percent, which shows that even the query optimizer can occasionally make mistakes!

The SET FORCEPLAN ON Command

The SET FORCEPLAN ON command forces the optimizer to join tables based on the order specified in the FROM clause. Normally, you want to let the optimizer determine the order in which to join tables; however, if you think that the optimizer is selecting an inefficient join order, you can use SET FORCEPLAN ON to force the join order.

When forcing SQL Server to use a predefined join order, you usually want the table with the fewest number of qualifying rows to come first in the FROM clause (or the table with the least amount of I/O, if you are dealing with a very wide or a very narrow table). The table with the second lowest number of qualifying rows should be next in the FROM clause, and so on.

CAUTION

Use the SET FORCEPLAN ON option as a last resort. You usually want to let the optimizer determine the order in which to process tables.

The following example shows how SET FORCEPLAN ON can impact query optimization:

```
SET FORCEPLAN ON
select *
from  titleauthor , authors
where titleauthor.au_id = authors.au_id
SET FORCEPLAN OFF
```

The following is showplan output with SET FORCEPLAN ON:

```
|--Nested Loops(Inner Join)
      |--Clustered Index Scan
            (OBJECT:([pubs].[dbo].[titleauthor].[UPKCL_taind]))
      |--Clustered Index Seek
            (OBJECT:([pubs].[dbo].[authors].[UPKCL_auidind]),
                  SEEK:([authors].[au_id]=[titleauthor].[au_id]) ORDERED)
```

Notice that, with SET FORCEPLAN ON, the optimizer processes the titleauthor table before processing the authors table.

If FORCEPLAN is not utilized, the query optimizer generates the following syntax:

```
|--Nested Loops(Inner Join)
      |--Clustered Index Scan
            (OBJECT:([pubs].[dbo].[authors].[UPKCL_auidind]))
      |--Clustered Index Seek
            (OBJECT:([pubs].[dbo].[titleauthor].[UPKCL_taind]),
                  SEEK:([titleauthor].[au_id]=[authors].[au_id]) ORDERED)
```

TIP

Whenever you use SET FORCEPLAN ON, be sure that you turn it off by issuing SET FORCEPLAN OFF. The feature remains in effect for your current connection until the connection is broken or until it is explicitly turned off.

Other Tuning Tricks

Whenever you try to optimize a query, you should be on the lookout for obstructions that can lead to poor performance. The following sections discuss common causes of poor query performance.

Are You Trying to Tune an UPDATE, DELETE, or INSERT Query?

If you are trying to tune an UPDATE, DELETE, or INSERT query, does the table have a trigger? The query might be okay, but the trigger might need improvement. An easy way to determine whether the trigger is the bottleneck is to drop the trigger and rerun the query. If query performance improves, you should tune the trigger.

Does the Query Reference a View?

If the query references a view, you should test the view to determine whether it is optimized. An easy way to test whether the view is optimized is to run a showplan on the view. Also, SQL Server 2000 introduced the concept of indexed views. An indexed view enables you to create an index on a view. This can further improve performance.

Are the Datatypes Mismatched?

If you are joining on columns of different datatypes, the optimizer might not be able to implement useful indexes. Instead, it might have to choose a table scan to process the query, as in the following example:

```
Table:
CREATE TABLE table1
(col1 char(10) not null)
Index: CREATE INDEX col1_idx ON table1(col1)
Row Count: 1000
Table:
CREATE TABLE table2
(col1 integer not null)
Index: CREATE INDEX col1_idx ON table2(col1)
Row Count: 1000
Query:
SELECT *
FROM table1, table2
WHERE table1.col1 = convert(char(10),table2.col1)
and table1.col1 = '100'
```

This query results in a table scan on `table2` because you are joining a `char(10)` column to an `integer` column with the `convert()` function. Internally, SQL Server must convert these values to process the query, which results in a table scan. To avoid this problem, maintain consistency within your database design.

Does the Query Use a Nonsearch Argument?

Nonsearch arguments force the optimizer to process the query with a table scan. This is because the search value is unknown until runtime.

The following are some common examples of queries that use nonsearch arguments and how to convert them to search arguments that can take advantage of an index:

```
Table:
CREATE TABLE table1
(col1 int not null)
Index: CREATE UNIQUE CLUSTERED INDEX col1_idx ON table1(col1)
Row Count: 1000 rows
```

A nonsearch argument query is as follows:

```
select *
from table1
where col1 * 10 = 100
```

A search argument query is as follows:

```
select *
from table1
where col1 = 100/10
```

A nonsearch argument query is as follows:

```
select *
from table1
where convert(char(8),col1) =  '10'
```

A search argument query is as follows:

```
select *
from table1
where col1 =  convert(int,'10')
```

> **TIP**
>
> One way to help reduce the use of a nonsearch argument is to keep the table column on the left side of the equation and to keep the search criteria on the right side of the equation.

Query Optimization FAQ

Some of the common questions asked by DBAs about SQL Server Query Optimization are as follows:

Q Does UPDATE STATISTICS need be run on a frequent basis?

A UPDATE STATISTICS does not need to be run on a frequent basis because the query optimizer automatically notices that statistics are out of date and automatically rebuilds the statistics. This is significantly different from previous versions, which required that the UPDATE STATISTICS command run on a frequent basis. It does not hurt anything to run UPDATE STATISTICS, but you might not gain anything. In certain rare occurrences, you might need to run UPDATE STATISTICS if you feel that you are getting a poor query optimization plan or if the data is changing rapidly and you need up-to-the-minute statistics.

Q Is automatic updating of statistics always enabled?

A By default, automatic updating of statistics is always enabled regardless of the database backward compatibility setting (6.0, 6.5, 7.0, and 8.0). If you need to turn off automatic updating of statistics, use the sp_autostats system procedure.

Q How can I tell when SQL Server last updated an index's statistics?

A Use the sp_autostats system procedure. This procedure will tell you the time of the last update and the automatic update setting.

Q Does a query have to be coded a certain way for it to run in parallel on multiple processors?

A SQL Server automatically decides when a query will run in parallel. This is unlike other database products that require special tuning and syntax to make a query run in parallel. The only requirement for a parallel query is that the machine must have multiple processors. Queries cannot run in parallel on single processor machines.

Summary

The following are some important notes to remember when working with the query optimizer:

- SQL Server's query optimizer has been significantly improved from previous versions. New optimization techniques result in faster query response times.

- Query optimization is part science, part luck. What works on one query might not work on another query. Try different techniques until you get the performance you expect.

- Use the Index Tuning Wizard, Showplan, Statistics I/O, Stats Time, and SQL Profiler tools to help tune a query.

- If you want to maximize OLTP performance, do everything you can to prevent a table scan on a large table.

A good DBA knows how the SQL Server optimizer works. This knowledge enables the DBA to turn an agonizingly slow query into a fast query. Consequently, knowledge of the optimizer can keep the DBA from creating needless indexes that are never used by the system. The next chapter discusses multiuser considerations.

20

Multiuser Issues

by Orryn Sledge

IN THIS CHAPTER

- Locks
- Multiuser Configuration Options
- Multiuser FAQ

How many times have you seen an application that works with a single user but when multiple users access the application, all sorts of performance and data problems occur? When these types of problems arise, it usually is up to the DBA to fix them. You have probably heard that SQL Server is a high-performance database capable of handling thousands of users. That is a true statement. But to extract maximum performance and data consistency in a multi-user environment, you must understand how SQL Server manages transactions. Otherwise, performance and data consistency will suffer. To help you avoid these problems, the topics discussed in this chapter explain how to design multiuser databases that maximize transaction throughput while maintaining data consistency.

Locks

SQL Server uses *locks* to maintain data consistency in a multiuser environment. SQL Server automatically handles locking behavior, and starting with SQL Server 7.0, locking automatically escalates and de-escalates on an as-needed basis.

To help understand why locks are important, look at the banking example shown in Figure 20.1. Suppose that you decide to transfer $100 from checking to savings. Your bank decides to run a report that shows your combined balance for checking and savings. What happens if the report is run while the transfer is in progress? Would the report show a balance of $200 or $100?

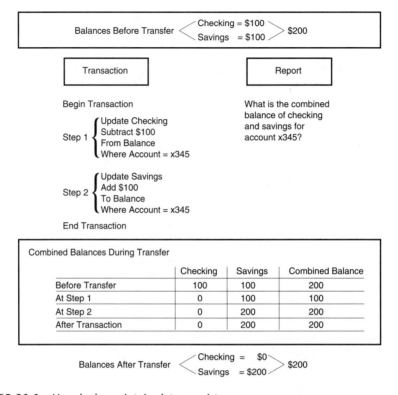

FIGURE 20.1   How locks maintain data consistency.

The answer resides in how SQL Server uses locks to maintain data consistency. When the transaction is initiated, SQL Server places a lock on the checking account information and on the savings account information. These locks force other users to wait until the locks are released before they can access the data. This prevents users from reading incomplete or pending changes. Therefore, when the transaction is complete, the report is allowed to access the account data, thus reporting the correct balance of $200.

> **NOTE**
>
> When pending changes can be read by a transaction, it is known as a *dirty read*. SQL Server's default transaction isolation level prevents dirty reads.

Without locks, the report might have shown a balance of $100, which is incorrect. For example, if the report read the data after the $100 was subtracted from checking but before it was added to savings, the report would show a combined balance of $100.

Understanding SQL Server's Locking Behavior

If locks are automatically handled by SQL Server you might wonder, "Why are we having this discussion?" The answer is *blocking* and *deadlocks*. Whenever multiple users try to access or modify the same data, the potential for blocking and deadlocks increases.

By understanding SQL Server's locking behavior, you can decrease the likelihood of blocking and deadlocks.

Some of the variables that can impact the frequency of blocking and deadlocks are as follows:

- Transaction management
- Query implementation
- Number of records modified or read by a query
- Number of users concurrently accessing the data
- Indexing scheme
- Table design
- Hardware configuration

Blocking

Blocking occurs when a process must wait for another process to complete. The process must wait because the resources it needs are exclusively used by another process. A blocked process resumes operation after the other process releases the resources.

For this example, assume that the bank decides to eliminate the monthly service charge for all existing customers (see Figure 20.2). Therefore, the DBA sets the service_charge to $0.00 for all accounts. Not being a good DBA, he runs this transaction during prime hours. This forces transactions 2, 3, and 4 to wait until transaction 1 is complete. The waiting transactions are considered to be *blocked* by transaction 1.

When blocking occurs, it looks like your machine is frozen. What has happened is that SQL Server has put your process in a holding queue. The process remains in the queue until it can acquire the resources it needs to complete its tasks.

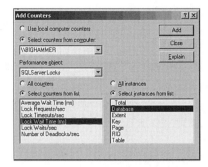

FIGURE 20.2   A blocking example.

BLOCKING PROBLEMS

I once was thrown into a project that involved converting a mainframe application to SQL Server. Management was eager to convert the application quickly. They did not want any time spent on table design or index strategy. I tried to explain to them that their existing database design could lead to blocking.

The day that application went into production was a prime example of how blocking can impact a system. Whenever certain components of the application were run, the transaction-processing component of the application would halt because of blocking.

The reason the blocking was so severe was because of poor table design and index strategy. The main table used by the application was not properly normalized, thus making it very wide. Very wide tables can substantially slow processing throughput. Additionally, the table lacked any useful indexes. The combination of these factors is a sure-fire way to generate massive blocking.

After management realized what had happened, they were willing to allocate the resources to go back and redesign the table schema and reevaluate the index strategy. After the redesign, the blocking problem ceased, and the application could be used without impacting the transaction processing aspect of the application.

Deadlock

Deadlock occurs when two users have locks on separate objects and each user is trying to lock the other user's objects. SQL Server automatically detects and breaks the deadlock. It terminates the process that has used the least amount of CPU utilization. This enables the other user's transaction to continue processing. The terminated transaction is automatically rolled back and an error code 1205 is issued.

Figure 20.3 shows an example of a deadlock. Assume that transaction 1 and transaction 2 begin at the exact same time. By default, SQL Server automatically places exclusive locks on data being updated. This causes transaction 1 to wait for transaction 2 to complete—but transaction 2 has to wait for transaction 1 to complete.

This is classic deadlock. To resolve the deadlock, SQL Server automatically terminates one of the transactions.

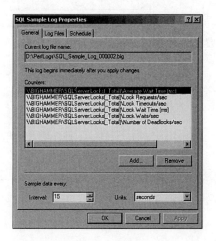

FIGURE 20.3 An example of deadlock.

Physical Locks

Now that you know why it is important to understand SQL Server's locking behavior, we'll get into the nuts and bolts of locking.

Any transaction that reads or modifies data (SELECT, INSERT, DELETE, UPDATE, CREATE INDEX, and so on) generates some type of lock. The degree of locking is determined by the following two questions:

- Is the data being modified or read?

- How many rows are being accessed or modified?

To answer these questions, you must look at the three levels of physical locks: row, page, and table.

Row Lock

A *row-level lock* is a lock on a row of data page or index lock. Prior to version 7.0, previous versions of SQL Server were limited to page-level locking.

Figure 20.4 illustrates row-level locking. The advantage of row-level locking is that it improves multi-user data access. The disadvantage of row-level locking is that it increases overhead. Therefore, SQL Server automatically determines when to utilize row-level locking and when it is more efficient to escalate a lock to a page-level lock.

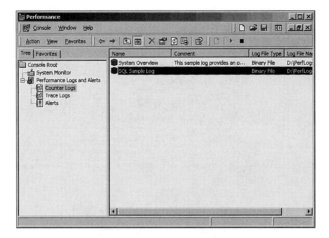

FIGURE 20.4   Row-level locking.

Page Lock

A *page lock* is a lock on an 8KB data page. Whenever feasible, SQL Server attempts to use a page lock rather than a table lock. Page locks are preferred over table locks because they are less likely to block other processes. Figure 20.5 illustrates page-level locking.

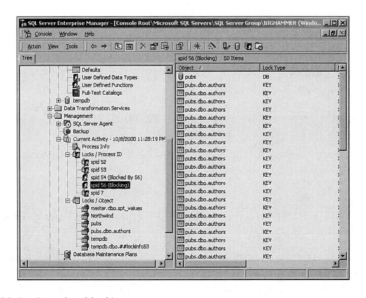

FIGURE 20.5   Page-level locking.

Table Lock

A *table lock* occurs when the entire table (data and indexes) is locked. When this happens, SQL Server has detected that it is faster to process the transaction by locking the table rather than incurring the overhead of locking numerous pages. Figure 20.6 illustrates table-level locking.

The drawback of table locking is that it increases the likelihood of blocking. When other transactions try to access or modify information in a locked table, they must wait for the table lock to be released before proceeding.

FIGURE 20.6   Table lock.

Lock Methods

In addition to managing physical locks, SQL Server's lock manager also manages lock methods. The following are the different lock methods used by SQL Server.

- **Shared**—A shared lock is used for read transactions (typically SELECT statements). If a row, page, or table is marked as shared, other transactions can still read the data. A shared lock must be released before an exclusive lock can be acquired. Shared locks are released after the data has been read.

- **Update**—When an UPDATE or DELETE statement is initially processed, SQL Server places update locks on the row, page, or table being read. It then escalates the update locks to exclusive locks before it modifies the data. Only one transaction at a time can receive an update lock. If other transactions are also requesting update locks, the lock manager will make the other transactions wait until the update lock is released.

- **Exclusive**—An exclusive lock is used for write transactions (typically INSERT, UPDATE, or DELETE statements). Other transactions must wait for the exclusive lock to be released before they can read or write information.

- **Intent**—An intent lock occurs when SQL Server has the intention of acquiring a shared or exclusive resource. SQL Server uses intent locks to keep other transactions from placing exclusive locks on the resource in which it is currently processing. Intent share, intent exclusive, and share with intent exclusive are the three types of intent locks.

- **Schema**—Schema locks come in two flavors—schema stability and schema modification. A schema stability lock occurs when SQL Server needs to prevent a table or index from being modified. A schema modification lock occurs when someone is actually modifying the table or index schema.

TIP

Typically, read statements acquire shared locks and data modification statements acquire exclusive locks. The following are a couple of tips that can help with locking:

- `sp_indexoption`—This procedure can control the granularity of index locking.
- `SET LOCK_TIMEOUT`—This is a user definable lock timeout setting implemented to specify (in milliseconds) how long a blocked process will wait before timing out. The default setting is no timeout. The global variable `@@lock_timeout` displays the current lock timeout setting.

Viewing Locks and Blocking

Now that you know something about locks and blocking, let's talk about how to view them in SQL Server. The following are the different methods used to view locks and blocking. Several of the methods provide overlapping functionality, so choose the method that you are most comfortable with.

- System procedures
- SQL Server Enterprise Manager
- Performance Monitor
- SQL Server Profiler
- Trace flags

System Procedures

The system procedures `sp_lock` and `sp_who` provide information about locks and blocking. The system procedure `sp_lock` displays the status of locks for all processes or the information about locks for a particular process.

The following is the syntax for `sp_lock`.

```
sp_lock [[@spid1 =] 'spid1'] [,[@spid2 =] 'spid2']
```

Use the SQL Server Query Analyzer to run the `sp_lock` system procedure. The following is sample output from `sp_lock`.

spid	dbid	ObjId	IndId	Type	Resource	Mode	Status
1	1	0	0	DB		S	GRANT
6	1	0	0	DB		S	GRANT
7	5	0	0	DB		S	GRANT
7	5	341576255	1	PAG	1:106	IX	GRANT
7	5	341576255	3	PAG	1:139	IX	GRANT
7	5	341576255	1	PAG	1:137	IX	GRANT
7	5	341576255	0	TAB		IX	GRANT
7	5	341576255	2	KEY	(d597a25250d8)	X	GRANT
7	5	341576255	1	KEY	(d597a25250d8)	X	GRANT
..							
8	5	0	0	DB		S	GRANT
8	5	341576255	1	PAG	1:106	IS	GRANT
8	5	341576255	0	TAB		IS	GRANT
8	5	341576255	1	KEY	(d9b61289d4f0)	S	WAIT
9	1	0	0	DB		S	GRANT
9	2	0	0	DB		S	GRANT
9	5	0	0	DB		S	GRANT
9	1	117575457	0	TAB		IS	GRANT

When running sp_lock, I usually look for a status = WAIT. If you see status = WAIT, this is bad in a transaction-oriented environment! This means that a process is waiting for another process to complete. Possible causes are long running queries that are not optimized and poor transaction management.

The sp_who system procedure displays information about users and their processes.

The following is the syntax for sp_who:

```
sp_who [[@login_name =] 'login']
```

Use the SQL Server Query Analyzer to run the sp_who system procedure. The following is sample output from sp_who:

spid	status	loginame	hostname	blk	dbname	cmd
..						
7	sleeping	sa	PGHDEV3	0	pubs	AWAITING COMMAND
8	sleeping	sa	PGHDEV3	7	pubs	SELECT
9	runnable	sa	PGHDEV3	0	pubs	DELETE

When running sp_who, I usually look at the blk column and the cmd column. If the blk column has a value > 0, it indicates that the process is blocked by the number represented in the `blk` column. The `cmd` column displays the command that the process is currently running.

TIP

Use the `DBCC INPUTBUFFER(spid)` command to gather detailed information about a process. For example, `sp_who` and `sp_lock` both display process IDs. The process ID returned by either system procedure can be used with `DBCC INPUTBUFFER` to return detailed information about the process, such as the SQL command currently running.

NOTE

Two undocumented system procedures in version 7.0 can also be used to diagnose blocking and locking activity. Table 20.1 provides a brief summary of each procedure.

TABLE 20.1   Undocumented System Procedures

System Procedure	Purpose	Notes
sp_who2	Useful for viewing process and blocking information. Similar to sp_who, except that it is easier to read and it includes the following additional information: CPUTime, DiskIO, LastBatch, and ProgramName.	
sp_blockcnt	Returns a count of blocked users.	Useful for quickly determining whether blocking exists.

SQL Server Enterprise Manager

Follow these steps to view locks and blocking from the Enterprise Manager:

1. From the SQL Server Enterprise Manager, click the plus (+) sign next to the server.

2. Click the plus (+) sign next to the Management folder.

3. Click the plus (+) sign next to the Current Activity icon.

4. To view blocking, click the Locks/Process ID icon. The result pane contains a listing of current processes (see Figure 20.7). Processes containing a red

exclamation mark indicate the source of the blocking. Processes containing a
red square indicate a blocked process.

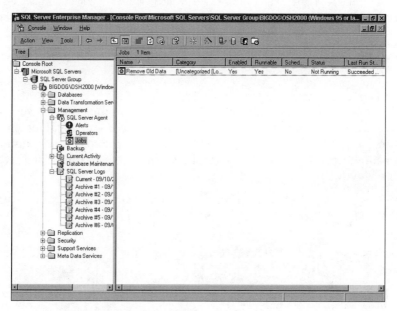

FIGURE 20.7   Locks/process ID information.

5. To view locks, click the Locks/Object icon. The result pane contains a listing of
objects with locks. Left-click an object to view lock information (see Figure 20.8).

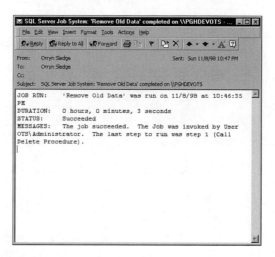

FIGURE 20.8   Locks/object information.

NOTE

I think it is easier to use the system procedures sp_who and sp_lock to diagnose blocking (see the "System Procedures" section for more information), instead of using the Enterprise Manager. The reason it is easier to use is that when severe blocking occurs, the Enterprise Manager can be slow to respond. Also, the output from the system procedures can be printed and saved to a text file.

Performance Monitor

The Performance Monitor can graphically track lock information. The SQL Server:Locks object and the SQL Server:Memory Manager are useful for graphically tracking locking. The Log feature of the Performance Monitor is useful for logging information over various time intervals. These time intervals can be analyzed for locking activity.

See Figures 20.9 and 20.10 for Performance Monitor Lock Counters, and see Figure 20.11 for a Performance Monitor lock graph sample.

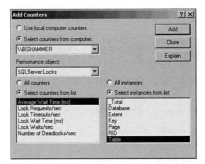

FIGURE 20.9 Performance Monitor SQL Server:Locks object counters.

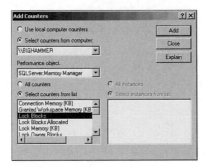

FIGURE 20.10 Performance Monitor SQL Server:Memory Manager object counters.

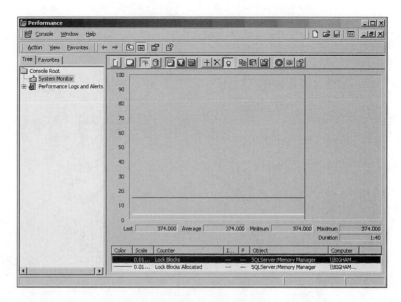

FIGURE 20.11   Performance Monitor lock graph sample.

SQL Server Profiler

The SQL Server Profiler can trace a variety of locking details. These details can be stored to a file or table for analysis. A feature of SQL Server Profiler is that the trace can be replayed. This is great for diagnosing and troubleshooting locking issues.

Table 20.2 lists the types of locking events that the SQL Server Profiler can trace.

TABLE 20.2   SQL Server Locking Events

Event	Event Description
Lock:Deadlock	Tracks deadlocks and related process information.
Lock:Deadlock Chain	Tracks the events that lead to the deadlock.

See Figure 20.12 for SQL Server Profiler Lock events (see Chapter 24, "Monitoring SQL Server," for more information on SQL Server Profiler).

Trace Flags

The trace flags displayed in Table 20.3 provide extended insight into SQL Server's locking behavior and deadlocks.

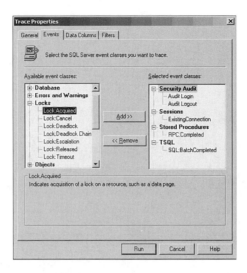

FIGURE 20.12   SQL Server Profiler lock events.

TABLE 20.3   Useful Trace Flags

Trace Flag	Output
1200	Displays the process ID and types of locks being requested.
1204	Displays the locks in use with a deadlock and the command involved in the deadlock.
1205	Displays information about the commands used during a deadlock.

TIP

The trace flag 1200 can be useful for tracking locking behavior. The easiest way to use the trace flag is to use the DBCC traceon() function. You also must turn on trace flag 3604 to echo trace information to the client workstation, as in the following example:

```
DBCC traceon(3604)
DBCC traceon(1200)
UPDATE t_1
  SET c_1 = 0
```

The following is sample output from DBCC trace flag 1200:

```
Process 55 acquiring IX lock on TAB: 5:1301579675 []
➥ (class bit2000000 ref1) result: OK
Process 55 acquiring IU lock on PAG: 5:1:181
➥ (class bit0 ref1) result: OK
Process 55 acquiring U lock on RID: 5:1:181:0
➥ (class bit0 ref1) result: OK
```

```
Process 55 acquiring IX lock on PAG: 5:1:181
➥ (class bit2000000 ref1) result: OK
Process 55 acquiring X lock on RID: 5:1:181:0
➥ (class bit2000000 ref1) result: OK
Process 55 releasing lock reference on RID: 5:1:181:0
Process 55 releasing lock reference on PAG: 5:1:181
Process 55 releasing lock reference on RID: 5:1:181:0
```

Tips to Help Minimize Locking and Prevent Deadlocks

Try using the tips in the following sections to resolve locking problems. These tips can help minimize locking problems and prevent deadlocks.

Tip 1: Create Indexes for UPDATE/DELETE Statements That Contain WHERE Clauses

Whenever you issue an UPDATE or DELETE statement that does *not* use an index, an exclusive table lock is used to process the transaction. The exclusive table lock might block other transactions.

To reduce the chance of an exclusive table lock, specify a WHERE clause that takes advantage of an existing index. This might enable SQL Server to use row- and page-level locks instead of an exclusive table lock.

Tip 2: Convert a Large INSERT Statement into a Single INSERT Statement Within a Loop

Inserting a large number of rows into a table might result in an exclusive table lock. For example, INSERT INTO table2 SELECT * FROM table1 will result in an exclusive table lock on table2 that will prevent others from accessing data in table2. To avoid this problem, convert the INSERT statement into an INSERT statement within a loop. For example, the following code opens a cursor and then initiates a loop that fetches the data from table1 into a variable and then inserts the contents of the variable into table2. This approach decreases the likelihood of blocking because it generates locks when the INSERT is issued and the lock is immediately released after the INSERT is processed. The drawback of this approach is that it runs slower than a batch INSERT.

```
declare @col1 varchar(11)
declare sample_cursor cursor
 for select col1 from table1
open sample_cursor
fetch next from sample_cursor into @col1
while @@fetch_status = 0
 begin
 insert into table2 values (@col1)
```

```
fetch next from sample_cursor into @col1
end
deallocate sample_cursor
```

Tip 3: Avoid Using HOLDLOCK

HOLDLOCK is one of the keywords that almost every developer new to SQL Server has tried to use. Quite often, the developer uses HOLDLOCK without fully understanding the ramifications behind it.

When HOLDLOCK is used with a SELECT statement, all shared locks (remember that shared locks are acquired whenever a SELECT is issued) remain in effect until the transaction is *complete*. This means additional locking overhead, which degrades performance and increases the likelihood of blocking or deadlocks. When the HOLD-LOCK command is not used, SQL Server releases the shared locks as soon as possible rather than waiting for the transaction to complete.

What usually happens is that developers use the HOLDLOCK command, thinking that they can temporarily prevent other users from reading the same data. What they do not realize is that HOLDLOCK only generates shared locks, not exclusive locks. Because the locks are shared, other users can still read the same data values.

Tip 4: Keep Transactions Short

Long-running transactions—especially data modification transactions—increase the likelihood of blocking and deadlocks. Whenever possible, try to keep the length of a transaction to a minimum. Following are suggestions to help decrease the length of a transaction:

- **Break long running transactions into multiple shorter running transactions**—Whenever you can reduce the duration of a lock, you can reduce the possibility of blocking. For this example, assume that table t_2 has 100 records with a sequential ID going from 1 to 100. (The number 100 is used to illustrate this example: A more realistic number would be 100,000 or more records.) The following is a long-running transaction:

```
INSERT INTO t_1
SELECT * FROM t_2
```

  You can rewrite this long-running transaction into two shorter running transactions, reducing the duration of locks in use:

```
INSERT INTO t_1
SELECT * FROM t_2
WHERE t_2.id <= 50
INSERT INTO t_1
SELECT * FROM t_2
WHERE t_2.id > 50
```

- **Minimize nonclustered indexes**—Avoid unnecessary nonclustered indexes. Each index adds more overhead that must be maintained whenever a record is inserted or deleted, or whenever an indexed column is modified. This can decrease throughput.

- **Reduce the number of columns per table**—An INSERT processes faster on a narrow table (a table with few columns) than it can on a wide table (a table with many columns). The reduction of the overall width of a table enables more rows to exist on a page. This means that fewer pages must be accessed to process the transaction, thus shortening transaction times.

Tip 5: Understand Transactions

Two common misunderstandings in using transactions are nested transactions and user interaction within a transaction.

Nested Transactions   Look at the approach taken in Figure 20.13. Do you see any problems with the code?

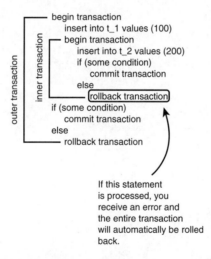

FIGURE 20.13   A nested transaction: The common (incorrect) approach.

The problem is with the rollback statement for the inner transaction. If the inner transaction is rolled back, you receive an error message, and both INSERT transactions are automatically rolled back by SQL Server, as in the following error message:

```
The commit transaction request has no corresponding BEGIN TRANSACTION.
```

To avoid the error message, use the SAVE TRANSACTION statement (see Figure 20.14).

NOTE

The COMMIT TRANSACTION statement must be issued after the ROLLBACK TRANSACTION INNER_TRANS statement.

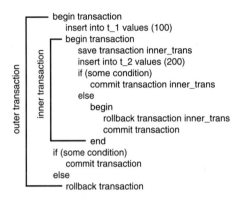

FIGURE 20.14   A nested transaction: The correct approach.

Now look at Figure 20.15. If the outer transaction is rolled back, do you think the inner transaction will also be rolled back? The answer is *yes*. SQL Server always rolls back the inner transaction when the outer transaction is rolled back, even though the inner transaction has been committed. This is how SQL Server handles nested transactions.

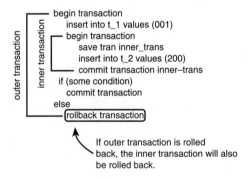

FIGURE 20.15   The way in which SQL Server handles nested transactions.

NOTE

In my experience as a DBA, the way SQL Server handles nested transactions is often contrary to what developers expect. Developers usually expect the inner transaction *not* to be rolled back because it has been committed. Make sure that your developers understand how SQL Server handles nested transactions.

Whenever you nest a transaction, all locks are held for the duration of the transaction (see Figure 20.16). This means that when the inner transaction is committed, its locks are not released until the outer transaction is committed. Be on the lookout for nested transactions; it increases the likelihood of blocking or deadlocks.

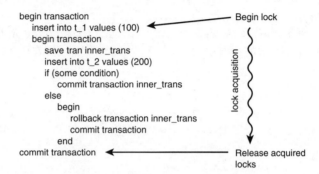

FIGURE 20.16   The way locks are held within a nested transaction.

User Interaction Within a Transaction   Keeping a watchful eye on transaction implementation can help ward off blocking. Consider the example in Figure 20.17. This situation virtually guarantees blocking in a multiuser environment. Always avoid user interaction within a transaction.

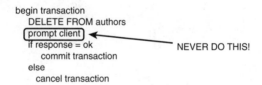

FIGURE 20.17   User interaction within a transaction.

You should rewrite the transaction to prompt the user first; based on the user's response, you can then perform the DELETE (see Figure 20.18). Transactions should always be managed in a single batch.

FIGURE 20.18   The transaction rewritten to avoid user interaction.

Tip 6: Run Transactions That Modify Large Amounts of Data During Off-Hours

You should process CREATE CLUSTERED INDEX and mass UPDATE/DELETE/INSERT statements during off-hours. These types of transactions require exclusive table locks and can be resource intensive.

Tip 7: Add More Memory to Your Server

By adding more memory to your server, you increase the amount of data that can remain in cache. This improves transaction performance, which reduces resource contention.

Tip 8: Know How to Safely Increment an ID

Most applications require some type of auto-incrementing ID to be used as a key field. Before a new record is inserted into the table, the application must get the next available ID.

The easiest way to create an auto-incrementing ID is to use the identity property. This data type has been optimized for performance and eliminates the need to have a separate table to track the next available ID.

If you cannot use the identity property (for example, when you need complete control over the counter values), you can use the following stored procedure to return the next ID. Because the update statement is within a transaction, the risk of two users receiving the same ID is eliminated.

Sample table that holds the next ID value is as follows:

```
/* table that contains NEXT ID value */
create table t_1 (id integer not null)
go
/* insert single record to set the SEED value */
insert into t_1 (id) values (0)
go
```

The following stored procedure returns the next id:

```
CREATE PROCEDURE usp_next_id AS
declare @next_id integer
begin transaction
 update t_1
 set id = id + 1
 select @next_id = id from t_1
commit transaction
RETURN @next_id
```

The following is an example of how to use the usp_next_id stored procedure:

```
declare @next_id integer
exec @next_id = usp_next_id
select @next_id
```

Tip 9: Use Cursor Options That Minimize Locking

When using a cursor that is read-only, use the READ_ONLY cursor option. When using a cursor that provides update or delete capability, use the OPTIMISTIC cursor option instead of the DYNAMIC or SCROLL LOCKS cursor options. The OPTIMISTIC cursor option will not place locks on data when it is read into the cursor (see Chapter 22, "Using Stored Procedures and Cursors," for more information on cursors).

Multiuser Configuration Options

SQL Server has several configuration options that allow you to tailor locking and other multiuser considerations. These options provide maximum control for multiuser access.

Transaction Isolation Level

With SQL Server, you can configure the transaction isolation level for a connection. A transaction isolation level remains in effect for the life of the connection unless the value is modified or the connection is broken.

To set the transaction isolation level, use the SET TRANSACTION ISOLATION LEVEL command, as in the following syntax. For an explanation of the differences among transaction isolation levels, see Tables 20.4 and 20.5.

```
SET TRANSACTION ISOLATION LEVEL {READ COMMITTED
➥ | READ UNCOMMITTED | REPEATABLE READ | SERIALIZABLE}
```

TABLE 20.4   Transaction Isolation Levels

Setting	Purpose
READ COMMITTED	SQL Server's default transaction isolation level. Prevents dirty reads; nonrepeatable reads might occur with this setting.
READ UNCOMMITTED	Minimizes locking by issuing locks only for UPDATE commands. Using this setting might result in dirty reads, phantom values, and nonrepeatable reads. In terms of performance, this setting is the most efficient option.
REPEATABLE READ	Prevents dirty reads and nonrepeatable reads by locking the data while it is being read. This prevents others from updating the data until the transaction is complete.
SERIALIZABLE	Prevents dirty reads, phantom values, and nonrepeatable reads. In terms of performance, this setting is the least efficient option.

TABLE 20.5   Transaction Isolation Matrix

Isolation Level	Blocking Risk	Prevents Dirty Reads	Prevents Nonrepeatable Reads	Prevents Phantom Reads
READ UNCOMMITTED	Lowest	No	No	No
READ COMMITTED*	Lower	Yes	No	No
REPEATABLE READ	Higher	Yes	Yes	No
SERIALIZABLE	Highest	Yes	Yes	Yes

*indicates default isolation level

NOTE

Explicit locking, such as NOLOCK, will override transaction isolation levels. See the section "Explicit Locking" for more information.

You can use the command DBCC USEROPTIONS to display the current transaction isolation level.

TRANSACTION ISOLATION ISSUES AND TIPS

The READ UNCOMMITTED transaction isolation level does not place locks on data when it is being read. This is different from the default transaction isolation level READ COMMITTED, which will place shared locks on data as it is being read. If you need a quick fix to blocking problems, this setting might solve your problems. With this transaction isolation level, locks will only be placed on the data when it is being modified.

Keep in mind that dirty reads, phantom values, and nonrepeatable reads can occur with this isolation level. For some applications, these drawbacks are outweighed by the multiuser access that can be gained by switching to this isolation level.

However, I would recommend using this isolation level only if you are experiencing blocking problems and you have unsuccessfully tried tuning your queries.

The following is the syntax for READ UNCOMMITTED isolation level:

```
SET TRANSACTION ISOLATION LEVEL READ UNCOMMITTED
```

At the other end of the transaction spectrum is the SERIALIZABLE transaction isolation level. This transaction level places range locks on the data until the transaction is complete. This prevents other users from modifying and adding records in the data being processed. This increases the likelihood of blocking and increases locking overhead.

Explicit Locking

With SELECT, INSERT, DELETE, and UPDATE statements, you can override SQL Server's default locking behavior. To specify the locking behavior, use the keywords listed in Table 20.6.

NOTE

It is recommended that you do not override the SQL Server's default locking behavior, except when absolutely necessary.

TABLE 20.6   Explicit Lock Summary

Lock	Purpose	Notes
HOLDLOCK	Forces all locks to be held for the duration of the transaction.	
NOLOCK	Turns off locking. Permits dirty reads.	
PAGLOCK	Forces page locking rather than table locking.	
READCOMMITTED	Same as setting the transaction isolation level to READ COMMITTED.	Default isolation level.
READPAST	Skips locked rows.	Transaction isolation level must be set to READ COMMITTED (SQL Server's default transaction isolation level). If you execute the same query after the locked rows are unlocked, you might receive a different resultset.
READUNCOMMITTED	Same as NOLOCK.	
REPEATABLEREAD	Same as setting the transaction isolation level to REPEATABLEREAD.	
ROWLOCK	Uses row locks instead of page or table locks.	
SERIALIZABLE	Same as HOLDLOCK.	
TABLOCK	Forces table locking rather than page locking and uses a shared lock.	
TABLOCKX	Forces table locking rather than page locking and uses an exclusive lock.	
UPDLOCK	Forces an update lock to be issued rather than a shared lock. This type of lock ensures consistency when you intend to read data and then perform an update based on the values you just read.	

The following syntax controls explicit locking.

- SELECT

    Explicit lock syntax:

    ```
    SELECT select_list
    FROM table list WITH [(HOLDLOCK | NOLOCK | PAGLOCK |
      READCOMMITTED | READPAST | READUNCOMMITTED |
      REPEATABLEREAD | ROWLOCK | SERIALIZABLE |
      TABLOCK | TABLOCKX |UPDLOCK)]
    ```

    Explicit lock example:

    ```
    SELECT * FROM AUTHORS WITH (ROWLOCK)
      WHERE au_id <= '555-55-5555'
    ```

- INSERT

    Explicit lock syntax:

    ```
    INSERT <table_or_view> (column_list) WITH [(HOLDLOCK | NOLOCK | PAGLOCK |
      READCOMMITTED | READPAST | READUNCOMMITTED |
       REPEATABLEREAD | ROWLOCK | SERIALIZABLE |
       TABLOCK | TABLOCKX |UPDLOCK)]
    VALUES (values list)
    ```

    Explicit lock example:

    ```
    INSERT authors WITH (ROWLOCK)
      (au_id,au_lname,au_fname,phone,contract)
      VALUES ('111-22-1111','Sledge','Orryn','555-555-5555',0)
    ```

- UPDATE

    Explicit lock syntax:

    ```
    UPDATE <table_or_view> WITH [(HOLDLOCK | NOLOCK | PAGLOCK |
      READCOMMITTED | READPAST | READUNCOMMITTED |
      REPEATABLEREAD | ROWLOCK | SERIALIZABLE |
      TABLOCK | TABLOCKX |UPDLOCK)]
    SET column = value
    ```

    Explicit lock example:

    ```
    UPDATE authors WITH (ROWLOCK)
      SET phone = '412-963-0505'
      WHERE au_id = '111-22-1111'
    ```

- DELETE

Explicit lock syntax:

```
DELETE <table_or_view> WITH [(HOLDLOCK | NOLOCK | PAGLOCK |
  READCOMMITTED | READPAST | READUNCOMMITTED |
  REPEATABLEREAD | ROWLOCK | SERIALIZABLE |
  TABLOCK | TABLOCKX |UPDLOCK)]
```

Explicit lock example:

```
DELETE authors WITH (ROWLOCK)
  WHERE au_id = '111-22-1111'
```

Multiuser FAQ

Some of the common questions asked by DBAs about multiuser issues are as follows:

Q Does the lock manager inspect the number of records in a table when deciding the type of lock to implement?

A No, the lock manager utilizes information such as the number of records accessed or modified by the query, the density of the rows per page, and the number of users concurrently accessing the table.

Additionally, the lock manager looks to see whether the table has a primary key. When processing an UPDATE or DELETE statement, the lock manager must utilize a table lock instead of a row- or page-level lock if the table does not contain a primary key.

Q When should the default transaction isolation not be used?

A The default transaction isolation level should be changed when you need to increase multiuser concurrency control or decrease locking. I generally recommend changing the default transaction isolation level (READ COMMITTED) to REPEATABLE READ or SERIALIZABLE only when you need to prevent nonrepeatable reads or phantom reads. Keep in mind that going to REPEATABLE READ or SERIALIZABLE will increase locking and might lead to multiuser access problems. I also recommend changing the default transaction isolation level to READ UNCOMMMITTED only after optimizing your table's indexes. READ UNCOMMMITTED will significantly reduce locking activity; thus potentially improving multiuser access, but will result in dirty reads.

Q Does row-level locking eliminate blocking?

A No, row-level locking does not eliminate blocking. However, it reduces the likelihood of blocking by locking only a row of information on a data or index page, as opposed to previous versions that locked the entire page.

Q Is row-level locking always better than page-level locking?

A The answer depends on the amount of data being read or modified by a query. Generally speaking, SQL Server will utilize row-level locking when a relatively few number of records are being read or modified. If a substantial number of records are being modified, SQL Server will utilize page or table locking. For example, consider a table that has one million records and an UPDATE query that modifies every record in the table. If SQL Server only utilized row-level locking, it would have to make one million calls to the lock manager. Obviously, this would not be very efficient. Therefore, SQL Server uses dynamic locking that considers information such as the number of locks required, the number of calls to the lock manager, and other information. For this example, it is more efficient for SQL Server to process the query with a table lock instead of a row or page lock.

Summary

Following are important notes to remember when addressing multiuser issues in SQL Server:

- Locks are used to maintain data consistency in a multiuser environment.

- Excessive locking can lead to blocking.

- Blocking occurs when a process must wait for another process to complete.

- Deadlock occurs when two users have locks on separate objects and each user is trying to lock the other user's objects.

- Use the Enterprise Manager, Performance Monitor, SQL Server Profiler, system procedures (sp_who, sp_lock), and trace flags to diagnose blocking and locking issues.

- Almost every SQL operation against a table results in some sort of lock.

- Row and page locks are generally preferred to table locks because they are less likely to cause blocking.

- Read statements acquire shared locks; data modification statements acquire exclusive locks.

- Row locks can escalate to page locks, and page locks can escalate to table locks. When this occurs, it is more efficient for SQL Server to process the transaction with the higher level type of lock.

- Always avoid user interaction within a transaction.

PART X

Transact-SQL

IN THIS PART

21 SQL Essentials

22 Using Stored Procedures and Cursors

21

SQL Essentials

by Mark Spenik

This chapter is an overview of *SQL (Structured Query Language)*, the ANSI-standard relational database language used for managing objects, data, and security. Microsoft SQL Server has an enhanced version of ANSI SQL called *Transact SQL* or *T-SQL* for short. The primary difference between T-SQL and ANSI SQL is in functions (like date and time or system functions) and the programming syntax used in writing stored procedures. This chapter discusses basic ANSI SQL statements and commands to get you started accessing and manipulating your data. You learn how to retrieve, add, update, and delete the data in the tables in your database. You also review two ways to create new tables.

All the examples in this chapter reference tables found in the pubs database that comes with SQL Server. Figure 21.1 outlines the structure of the following pubs tables authors, titleauthor, and titles used in the examples.

IN THIS CHAPTER

- An Overview of Basic SQL Statements
- SELECT
- INSERT
- UPDATE
- DELETE
- CREATE TABLE
- SELECT...INTO
- Distributed Queries

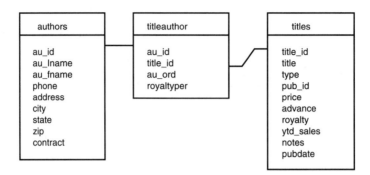

FIGURE 21.1   Structure of the authors, titleauthor, and titles tables in the pubs database.

An Overview of Basic SQL Statements

The number of different types of SQL statements you can execute is tremendous. Using SQL, you can perform tasks such as a simple table query, creating tables, executing stored procedures and even assigning user rights. This primer will focus on retrieving, updating, and reporting on data from client applications. For this purpose, the most important SQL statements you need to know are SELECT, INSERT, UPDATE, DELETE, CREATE...TABLE, and SELECT...INTO. A brief description of these commands is shown in Table 21.1.

TABLE 21.1   Important SQL Statements

Command	Description
SELECT	Retrieves columns and rows from a table or tables
INSERT	Adds rows to a table
UPDATE	Updates columns in existing rows in a table
DELETE	Deletes rows from a table
CREATE...TABLE	Creates a new table based on the specified table schema
SELECT...INTO	Creates a new table based on rows and columns output by a SELECT statement

These commands are pretty simple, but they can be qualified to perform a number of complex functions as you will see in the following examples.

SELECT

The SELECT statement specifies the columns of data you want to retrieve, where the columns are stored, what criteria the returned data must meet, and the sort order to be applied to the data. A SELECT statement can further group rows of data and assign retrieval criteria at the group level. The components of the SELECT statement are described in Table 21.2.

TABLE 21.2   Components of a SQL SELECT Statement

Component	Description
SELECT	Specifies the columns of data to be retrieved
FROM	Specifies the table/s from which to retrieve rows
WHERE	Specifies criteria for which returned data must meet
GROUP BY	For aggregate queries, specifies the returned column/s by which the data is to be grouped
HAVING	For aggregate queries, specifies criteria for which the aggregate value returned must meet
ORDER BY	Specifies the sort order of the returned rows

A Simple SELECT Statement

The following example queries several columns in the authors table:

```
SELECT au_id, au_lname, au_fname, state, zip, contract
FROM authors
```

The results of this simple query (shown in Figure 21.2) reveal that the data in the selected columns was returned for each row that exists in the authors table.

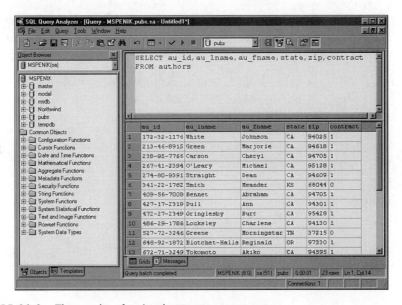

FIGURE 21.2   The results of a simple SELECT statement.

Adding the WHERE Clause

Using the same basic SELECT statement, you can narrow the results by adding a WHERE clause. Suppose you only want to know the names of authors located in the state of California. In the following example, only those records whose state column has a value of 'CA' are returned (see Figure 21.3).

```
SELECT au_id, au_lname, au_fname, state, zip, contract
FROM authors
WHERE state = 'CA'
```

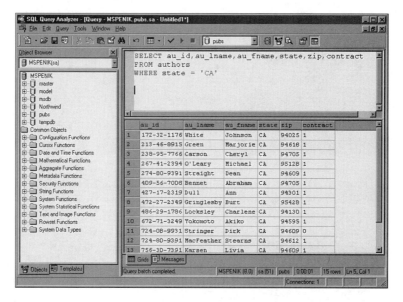

FIGURE 21.3   The results of a simple SELECT statement demonstrating the WHERE clause.

Your WHERE clause can use several columns as criteria for row retrieval. If you wanted only those rows whose contract value was zero, you would use a logical AND, as in the following example:

```
SELECT au_id, au_lname, au_fname, state, zip, contract
FROM authors
WHERE state = 'CA' AND contract = 0
```

You can also have the query return rows for authors in any state except California. The way to indicate inequality in SQL is to combine a less than and greater than sign (<>).

```
SELECT au_id, au_lname, au_fname, state, zip, contract
FROM authors
WHERE state <> 'CA'
```

The WHERE clause can use different comparison operators for checking field values. Table 21.3 lists and describes these operators.

TABLE 21.3   WHERE Clause Comparison Operators

Operator	Description
=	Is equal to
>	Is greater than
<	Is less than
>=	Is greater than or equal to
<=	Is less than or equal to
< >	Is not equal to
IN	Is in a specified list of values or in the results of a specified subquery
BETWEEN...AND	Is between two values
LIKE	Contains the same pattern as a specified string. The pattern being compared is a string that contains one or more wildcard characters. You should refer to SQL Server help for a list of these operators.

In addition to a variety of comparison operators, the columns included in the WHERE clause can be checked using the AND and OR logical operators. If the AND operator is used, both conditions on either side of the AND must be met for a row to be returned. The OR operator requires that at least one of the conditions be met.

Adding the ORDER BY Clause

You can take the simple query one step further and sort the results by author last name (au_lname). To do this, add an ORDER BY clause.

```
SELECT au_id, au_lname, au_fname, state, zip, contract
FROM authors
WHERE state = 'CA'
ORDER BY au_lname
```

The resulting rows are returned in ascending alphabetical order by the author's last name as shown in Figure 21.4.

FIGURE 21.4   The results of a simple SELECT statement demonstrating the ORDER BY clause.

You can also sort the records in a field in descending order using the keyword DESC. Suppose that you want to first sort the records in descending order by contract and then in ascending order by author last name. An example is shown in the following SQL statement:

```
SELECT au_id, au_lname, au_fname, state, zip, contract
FROM authors
WHERE state = 'CA'
ORDER BY contract DESC, au_lname
```

NOTE

Microsoft SQL Server offers several sort orders (that is collation setting), the default being Dictionary Order, Case-insensitive. The sort order is defined during SQL Server installation and cannot be overridden later. Sort orders are important because they determine how a query will be processed and how data is ordered. For example, a sort order that is not case sensitive treats a lowercase a the same as a capital A. Therefore, if you asked to see all the people with the last name Smith, you would get all the records with a last name of Smith whether it was Smith, smith, or SMITH. A case-sensitive sort order would return Smith only, so this does affect the records that are processed by your SQL statements.

Using the WHERE Clause to Join Tables

You have seen several ways to use SQL SELECT statements to look at the data in the authors table by specifying columns to return, assigning retrieval criteria, and sorting the results. However in the real world, will you only want to look at data from a single table at a time? Most likely, the answer is no. The data in the authors table has relationships with data in other tables in the pubs database. For example, what if you wanted to know which titles were written by these authors? The authors table alone won't tell you this. You must search the cross-reference table, titleauthor, which links (for example, joins) authors to titles by the columns au_id and title_id. Unfortunately, this isn't enough. Most people don't recognize authors or titles by IDs or codes; they know them by names. Because the names of the authors are located in the table authors, (the titles are located in the table titles, and the relationships between the two are located in titleauthor,) you need to tie together these three tables in a single SELECT statement. You can do this using the WHERE clause:

```
SELECT authors.au_lname, authors.au_fname, titles.title
FROM authors, titleauthor, titles
WHERE
  authors.au_id = titleauthor.au_id AND
  titleauthor.title_id = titles.title_id
ORDER BY authors.au_lname, authors.au_fname, titles.title
```

The resulting list of authors and their titles is shown in Figure 21.5. Note the way the column names are referenced in this statement. When retrieving data from multiple tables in a single SQL statement, you must preface column names that appear in more than one of the tables in the FROM clause with their associated table names to avoid an ambiguity error.

Using the Join Operator to Join Tables

Another way to join tables is using the join operator. This is the ANSI standard method for joining tables and it uses the following syntax:

```
SELECT column1, column2, column3
FROM table1 join operator table2
ON join criteria
```

The join operator indicates how rows should be returned from the joined tables. The ON clause acts like a WHERE clause, indicating which fields in the joined table should be compared for equality. Table 21.4 describes the different join operators.

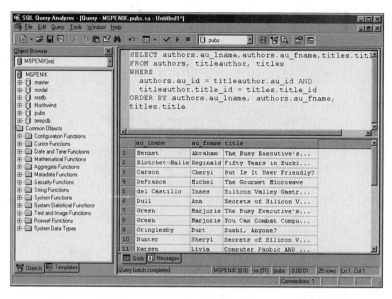

FIGURE 21.5   The results of a SELECT statement demonstrating the use of the WHERE clause in joining tables.

TABLE 21.4   Table Join Operators

Join Operator	Description
CROSS JOIN	Returns each row from the first table joined with each row from the second table, resulting in a returned number of rows equal to the product of the two tables' rowcounts.
INNER JOIN	Returns all rows from each table that meet the WHERE clause search criteria and where there is a match on the joined fields in the ON clause.
LEFT [OUTER] JOIN	Returns all rows from the table on the left side of the join that meet the WHERE clause search criteria and only those from the right side of the join where there is a match on the joined fields in the ON clause.
RIGHT [OUTER] JOIN	Returns all rows from the table on the right side of the join that meet the WHERE clause search criteria and only those from the left side of the join where there is a match on the joined fields in the ON clause.
FULL [OUTER] JOIN	Returns all rows from each table that meet the WHERE clause search criteria and where there is no match on the joined fields in the ON clause.

Using the join operator, the SQL statement in the previous example would be written as follows:

```
SELECT authors.au_lname, authors.au_fname, titles.title
FROM (authors INNER JOIN titleauthor
```

```
      ON authors.au_id = titleauthor.au_id) INNER JOIN titles
      ON titleauthor.title_id = titles.title_id
ORDER BY authors.au_lname, authors.au_fname, titles.title
```

One use for an outer join would be if you wanted a list of all authors and, if each author wrote a book, the title_id of that book (through an outer join with titleauthor). If she did not write a book, you would still be able to see the author's name listed, but the title_id would be returned as NULL.

Aggregate Functions in SQL Statements

Aggregate functions return summary values for specified columns or expressions in the form of sum totals, number of records, averages, and so on. The aggregate function might return a single value for all rows represented by the query. If a GROUP BY clause has been added to the SQL statement, such summary values are calculated at each level of grouping. Table 21.5 lists the aggregate functions you can use. Note that the StDev and Var functions are not available in SQL Server.

TABLE 21.5   Aggregate Functions

Aggregate Function	Description
Avg	Returns the average of all values in the columns by taking their sum and dividing by the count.
Count	Returns the number of non-null values in the specified column or expression. If the expression is an asterisk (for example, count(*)), the result is the number of rows in the query.
Min	Returns the minimum value in the specified column or expression.
Max	Returns the maximum value in the specified column or expression.
Sum	Returns the sum of values in the specified column or expression.

The following statement illustrates the use of the count function on the entire titles table with no grouping.

```
SELECT count(title) 'titles'
FROM titles
```

The result is the total number of title records in the titles table as shown in Figure 21.6.

NOTE

You can use an alias to return a different name for a column or assign a name to a column that returns an expression (and, therefore, has no name). Three ways to assign an alias to a column are as follows:

```
SELECT count(title) AS titles FROM titles
SELECT count(title) 'titles' FROM titles
SELECT 'titles' = count(title) FROM titles
```

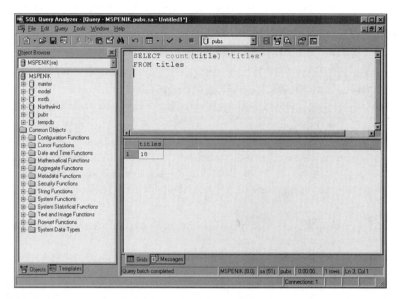

FIGURE 21.6   An example of the aggregate count function on the titles table.

Use of the GROUP BY Clause

Suppose you want to group all like rows in the query result by the values of one or more columns. You can group these results by specifying those columns in a GROUP BY clause. If more than one column is specified, the rows are grouped first by the first column and then within those groups by the second column and so on.

In the following example, the GROUP BY clause is combined with an aggregate function to show how that function is applied to the values within each distinct group. Notice that, contrary to the previous example, each group of authors has its own title count, rather than the count being performed on an entire table.

```
SELECT authors.au_lname, authors.au_fname, count(titles.title) 'titles'
FROM authors, titleauthor, titles
WHERE
   authors.au_id = titleauthor.au_id AND
   titleauthor.title_id = titles.title_id
GROUP BY authors.au_lname, authors.au_fname
```

With the results shown in Figure 21.7, you can determine how many books each author wrote.

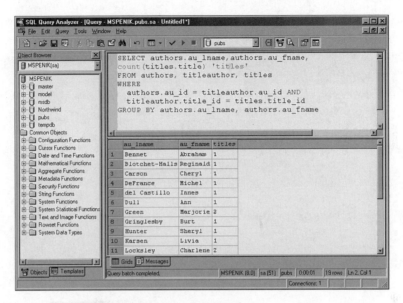

FIGURE 21.7 An example of a GROUP BY query.

NOTE

At this point, you are familiar with the use of table names prefacing column names in order to avoid ambiguity in multi-table queries. You might also have begun to notice that this can result in lengthy SQL statements. Using a table alias, you can shorten your SQL statement and make it easier to both read and type. As with the previous column alias examples, the table alias is simply the use of a new name to represent the actual table name. Aliases are often used to shorten the SQL statement and to enhance the readability of the WHERE clause, so the table names are usually replaced by an alias of a single character. Once you alias a table, you must always use the alias when referring to the table in the SQL statement. Look at the preceding SQL example; here aliases replace table names:

```
SELECT a.au_lname, a.au_fname, count(c.title) 'titles'
FROM authors a, titleauthor b, titles c
WHERE
  a.au_id = b.au_id and
  b.title_id = c.title_id
GROUP BY a.au_lname, a.au_fname
```

Use of the HAVING Clause

Like the WHERE clause, the HAVING clause is used for specifying criteria for data to be returned in a query. The difference lies in the level at which the criteria is checked. The WHERE clause uses criteria to restrict rows of data returned by a query. The GROUP BY clause then forms the returned rows into groups and calculates any aggregate values. The criteria in the HAVING clause is then used to restrict groups of rows according to the group level data.

In the following example, the HAVING clause is used to return the names of only those authors who have written more than one book.

```
SELECT a.au_lname, a.au_fname, count(c.title) 'titles'
FROM authors a, titleauthor b, titles c
WHERE
    a.au_id = b.au_id and
    b.title_id = c.title_id
GROUP BY a.au_lname, a.au_fname
HAVING count(c.title) > 1
```

Figure 21.8 shows that only those authors with more than one book are returned by the query.

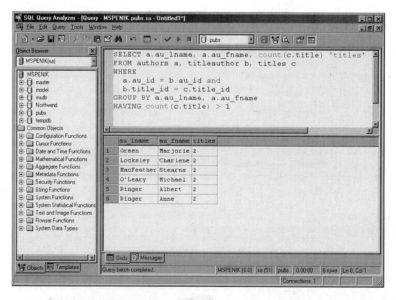

FIGURE 21.8   The use of the HAVING clause.

INSERT

The INSERT statement is used to add rows of data to a table. The INSERT statement specifies the table to which rows are to be added, the columns in which the data is to be stored, the source of the data being added, and the data itself. The components of the INSERT statement are described in Table 21.6.

TABLE 21.6 Components of a SQL INSERT Statement

Component	Description
INSERT INTO	Specifies the table to which rows are to be added.
column list	Specifies columns in which to add the data. (It is only necessary to provide a column list when not all the table's columns are to have data added and if you are inserting all the columns in a different order.) If left blank, the column list can be understood to be every column in the table, in the order in which they appear in the table structure.
VALUES (value list)	Specifies the values to be filled in the respective columns in the column list. (For example, the first value in the value list will be assigned to the first column in the column list and so on.)
SELECT	The SELECT statement that returns rows to be added to the table.

Note that either a value list or a SELECT statement (not both) is used to provide the data to be added.

Use of the INSERT Statement with a Value List

This example shows the use of the value list to add a row to the titles table, providing values for each column in the table. Note that with a value list, you can insert only a single row into the table:

```
INSERT INTO titles
VALUES
  ('SM1234', 'The Small Business Tax Guide', 'business',
  '1389', 15.99, 3000, 10, 0,
  'Tax guide for owners of small businesses', '1/1/1997')
```

You can also specify which columns to fill in the INSERT clause:

```
INSERT INTO titles (title_id, title)
VALUES ('SM5678', 'The Small Business Marketing Guide')
```

A couple of reasons for not specifying all values would be that you do not know those values and want any possible default values to be added or you have a field defined with a default or sequence number. Note, however, that if there are no default values for the omitted columns and the structure of the table to which you are adding the row requires that an omitted column be filled, you will get an error.

In the first example shown, you might have noticed that the list of columns in the INSERT clause was omitted. This is the equivalent of listing all columns in the table in the order in which they appear in the table structure. This saves you some typing time. However, it is usually better to include the column list so that if fields are reordered or added to the table at a later date, the SQL statement need not be altered to reflect the structure change.

Use of the INSERT Statement with a SELECT Statement

The following example shows the use of the SELECT statement to add one or more rows of data to the titles table. Assume that the newtitles table is a temporary working table that holds new title information. From this table, you want to add all titles whose processing date is NULL.

```
INSERT INTO titles
( title_id, title, type, pub_id, price, advance, royalty, ytd_sales,
➥notes, pubdate )
SELECT
  title_id, title, type, pub_id, price, advance, royalty, ytd_sales,
➥notes, pubdate
FROM newtitles
WHERE procdate IS NULL
```

NOTE

The INSERT INTO...SELECT statement can be interpreted as a two-part query. That is, the SELECT portion of the statement actually is performed by itself as step one of the statement. The resulting set of rows is then given to the INSERT INTO portion of the statement (step two of the statement). For this reason, there is no ambiguity between the identical column lists in these two distinct portions of the SQL statement. Therefore, it is not necessary to preface the column names with the table names to distinguish those in the destination table from those in the source table.

UPDATE

The UPDATE statement is used to modify column values in existing rows in a table. The UPDATE statement specifies the table to be updated, the columns to update, the new values to assign those columns, and criteria for the rows to updated. Table 21.7 describes the components of an UPDATE statement.

TABLE 21.7 Components of an SQL UPDATE Statement

Component	Description
UPDATE	Specifies the table to be updated
SET	Specifies columns to update and the new values to assign to those columns
FROM	Specifies the tables to include in the UPDATE statement
WHERE	Specifies the criteria to determine which rows' columns are to be updated

Setting Columns to a Fixed Value with UPDATE Statement

In some cases, you might want to update columns in a table with a fixed value for every row in the table. For example, assume that you want to update the processing date to January 1, 1997 for each row in the newtitles table (see the previous example), which currently has a processing date of NULL:

```
UPDATE newtitles
SET procdate = '1/1/1997'
WHERE procdate IS NULL
```

Setting a Column Value Based on Existing Column Values

Suppose you want to increase the price of each book in the titles table by 10% of the current price. It would be difficult to update the table with fixed values (as in the previous example) because all books need to be updated to different prices; that could take all day. A better way to perform this update is to use the existing price as a base for the updated price. Just as you can assign a fixed value to a column, you can assign the results of an expression as shown in the following statement:

```
UPDATE titles
SET price = price * 1.10
```

Therefore, without knowing the value of any of the prices in the titles table, you can successfully increase their values by 10% in one easy UPDATE statement.

Setting a Column Based on Values in a Joined Table

Now, say that you want to update the publisher associated with all titles written by a specific author. The author information is nowhere to be found in the titles table. You can only get that information by joining the titles table with the titleauthor table. To do this, add a FROM clause to the UPDATE statement. This FROM clause works the same way as the FROM clause in a SELECT statement. The UPDATE clause indicates the table to be updated, whereas the FROM clause indicates the source of the data with which to update that table. In the following example, the pub_id column is updated to '1389' for all titles associated with au_id '998-72-3567':

```
UPDATE titles
SET pub_id = '1389'
FROM titles a, titleauthor b
WHERE
  a.title_id = b.title_id AND
  b.au_id = '998-72-3567'
```

DELETE

The DELETE statement enables you to remove rows from tables. This statement specifies the table from which rows are to be deleted and criteria for the rows to deleted. Table 21.8 describes the components of a DELETE statement

TABLE 21.8   Components of a SQL DELETE Statement

Component	Description
DELETE FROM	Specifies the table from which to delete rows
WHERE	Specifies the criteria that determines which rows are to be deleted

Using DELETE to Delete All Rows from a Table

To delete all rows from a table, you need only specify the name of the table from which to delete those rows. The following example shows how to delete all rows from the titles table:

```
DELETE FROM titles
```

NOTE

SQL Server offers another method for removing all rows from a table called the TRUNCATE TABLE statement. It acts like a DELETE statement without a WHERE clause, with a couple of notable exceptions. The DELETE statement deletes rows from a table one row at a time, logging each deletion as a transaction that can be rolled back. The TRUNCATE TABLE statement, on the other hand, removes entire pages of data from a table and does not log individual row deletions. Rows removed from a table with a TRUNCATE TABLE statement cannot be recovered. The other important note is that delete triggers associated with a table will not be fired when that table is truncated. Why would you use a TRUNCATE TABLE statement? Speed! The TRUNCATE TABLE statement performs the task of removing all rows from a table much faster than a DELETE statement. Just keep in mind that it will always remove all the rows from a table and these rows are *not* recoverable.

Sometimes you will not want to wipe out all the rows in a table. Assume that you want to delete only a specific title from the titles table.

Using DELETE to Delete Specific Rows from a Table

To delete specific rows from a table, you add the familiar WHERE clause. As you might expect, only those rows that meet the criteria of the WHERE clause are deleted. The following snippet removes only the title 'Silicon Valley Gastronomic Treats' whose title_id is 'MC2222'.

```
DELETE FROM titles
WHERE title_id = 'MC2222'
```

Using a Subquery to Delete Rows Based on Values in a Different Table

Say that the DELETE statement criteria is based on a value in another table. For example, what if you wanted to delete all titles from the titles table that do not have an author. Because a title's author information is not stored in the titles table, you must search the titleauthor table to determine whether any authors exist for that title.

To do this, you need to use a subquery. That is, you use the results of a nested select query as the criteria for the outer delete query. In the following statement, the subquery (shown in parentheses) is a complete SQL statement in and of itself. It returns a resultset of each title_id found in the titleauthors table. The outer delete query uses this set of title_ids as the criteria for rows to be deleted.

```
DELETE FROM titles
WHERE title_id <>
( SELECT title_id FROM titleauthor)
```

NOTE

Because you can only compare a single column from the outer query to the set of values returned by the nested subquery, your subquery should return only one column. Furthermore, that column's datatype should be compatible with the datatype of the column being compared in the outer query.

CREATE TABLE

The CREATE TABLE statement enables you to create a new table in the database. However, the database should already be established by the DBA. Sometimes you need to access the data in such a way that a SELECT statement would not effectively produce the desired results. An example might be that the set of data you need must be accessed and processed one row at a time through a cursor. Another example is a resultset that would require table joins so complex that the query takes a very long time to run. In such cases, it is useful to have an empty table structured the way you want the resultset structured so that you can fill in phases by using a cursor or a combination of INSERT and UPDATE statements. Table 21.9 describes the components of a CREATE TABLE statement

TABLE 21.9   Components of a CREATE TABLE Statement

Component	Description
CREATE TABLE	Specifies the table to be created
column list	Specifies the columns of the new table and their attributes

Using CREATE TABLE to Create the authors Table

To create a new table using the CREATE TABLE statement, specify the table you want to create and the columns that will configure the table. The following statement creates the newauthors table as it is currently structured in the pubs database on SQL Server:

```
CREATE TABLE newauthors
( au_id id NOT NULL ,
  au_lname varchar (40) NOT NULL ,
  au_fname varchar (20) NOT NULL ,
  phone char (12) NOT NULL ,
  address varchar (40) NULL ,
  city varchar (20) NULL ,
  state char (2) NULL ,
  zip char (5) NULL ,
  contract bit NOT NULL )
```

Table 21.10 lists the possible datatypes you can assign to columns in the CREATE TABLE statement.

TABLE 21.10   CREATE TABLE Datatypes

Type of Data	Datatypes
binary	binary, varbinary
character	char, varchar
date and time	datetime, smalldatetime
exact numeric	decimal, numeric
approximate numeric	float, real
integer	int, smallint, tinyint

TABLE 21.10   Continued

Type of Data	Datatypes
monetary	money, smallmoney
special	bit, timestamp
text and image	text, image

SELECT...INTO

The SELECT...INTO statement is another way you can create a new table. This method differs from the CREATE TABLE method in that the structure of the table to create is not explicitly stated, rather it is determined by the results of a SELECT statement. Table 21.11 lists the components of the SELECT...INTO statement.

TABLE 21.11   Components of a SELECT...INTO Statement

Component	Description
SELECT INTO	Specifies the table to be created.
column list	Specifies the columns of the new table and their attributes.

Using SELECT...INTO to Create a New authortitles Table

Suppose you want to store the results of a SELECT statement in a table for use later in your application or in a report. The SELECT...INTO statement enables you to do just that. You simply need to add the INTO clause to a standard SELECT statement. In the following example, you use the SELECT statement from an earlier example, which displayed author names and the titles of books that they wrote, to create a new table called authortitles:

```
SELECT a.au_lname, a.au_fname, c.title
INTO authortitles
FROM authors a, titleauthor b, titles c
WHERE
  a.au_id = b.au_id and
  b.title_id = c.title_id
ORDER BY a.au_lname, a.au_fname, c.title
```

Now, if you select all rows from the authortitles table, you get the same results as you got in the SELECT statement, as shown in Figure 21.9.

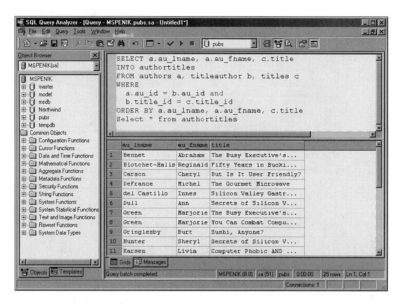

FIGURE 21.9   The results of using SELECT...INTO to create the authortitles table.

Distributed Queries

Distributed queries allow SQL Server users to retrieve and manipulate data located in other data sources (that is, other databases, files, spreadsheets, and so on) using T-SQL. To the user, it appears as if these data sources are just another SQL Server table. The capability of a RDBMS to retrieve and manipulate other data sources as if it were a native table of the RDBMS is not a new idea. Several vendors such as Oracle and Sybase have had gateway products available for several years. However, as with many things in Microsoft SQL Server 2000, distributed queries ship free with the product and allow you to connect to any data source for which you have a valid OLE DB Driver. Because Microsoft includes an OLE DB driver for ODBC, you can connect to any data source for which you have an ODBC driver! Here are few ideas of how you can use distributed queries:

- Manipulate non-relational data sources using T-SQL

- Create real-time reports that span multiple data sources without importing and exporting data

- Create stored procedures that easily utilize data from remote data sources (that is, temp tables, variables, cursors)

- Closely integrate various data sources with a straightforward T-SQL approach

- Execute pass through queries to execute as much as possible on remote servers

Distributed Query Restrictions

Okay, so distributed queries are part of the SQL Server product and allow you to access various data sources as if they were native SQL Server objects. What's the catch? Well, some restrictions that exist for all remote data sources are listed as follows:

- You cannot perform a SELECT INTO where the table being populated is a remote table.

- Several restrictions on large object data types (that is, text, image, and so on) such as no ORDER BY clause if a large object column is contained in the select list, or you cannot use the IS NULL or IS NOT NULL function on a large object column.

- GROUP BY ALL is not allowed.

- WRITETEXT, READTEXT, and UPDATETEXT statements are not allowed.

- You cannot include DDL (Data Definition Language) statements in a distributed query.

- Only STATIC and INSENSITIVE cursors are supported. Depending on the OLE DB provider, the KEYSET cursor might be supported.

What about performance, transactions, and data type conversions? The answer is going to vary depending on the OLE DB provider (or ODBC driver) and the data source you are using with distributed queries. For example, I have been impressed with performance and functionality provided when using distributed queries with Oracle databases and not satisfied with the performance and restrictions I encountered when using distributed queries with DBase files. If you are using an OLE DB provider provided with SQL Server 2000, you can check Books On-Line for the restrictions and features supported by the OLE DB provider. The following OLE DB providers ship with SQL Server 2000:

- Jet
- Oracle
- SQL Server
- ODBC

If you are using another provider or an ODBC driver, you can check the Internet for information or the specific provider documentation to determine the level of support. However, in this situation, I have found it is much easier to just add the server with the OLE DB provider or ODBC driver in question and execute various distributed queries against the data source to see if the functionality I need is supported and if the performance is acceptable.

Adding a Linked Server

Before you can execute a distributed query, you must add the data source as a SQL Server linked server. A linked server is a SQL Server object that contains the required information for accessing the data source and provides you with a mechanism to access the data source via T-SQL. A linked server can be added using the system stored procedure sp_addlinkedserver, which has the following syntax:

```
sp_addlinkedserver [@server][, @srvproduct][, @provider][, @datasrc][,
@location][, @provstr][, @catalog]
```

where

```
@server = Name of the linked server being created
@srvproduct = OLE DB data source product name
@provider = OLE DB provider programmatic identifier (PROGID)
@datasrc = Data source name interpreted by the OLE DB provider
@location = Database location expected by the OLE DB provider
@provstr = Connection string information required by the OLE DB provider
@catalog = Catalog name used when making a connection
```

THE REAL CHALLENGE WITH DISTRIBUTED QUERIES

Microsoft has made distributed queries easy to use and available to many different data sources. However, the availability to so many different data sources can also be your biggest challenge. Trying to decipher what a particular data source and OLE DB provider might require when trying to set up a linked server can be difficult. Fortunately, Books On-Line contains many different examples of setting up linked servers. (Look under the definition and description of sp_addlinkedserver for examples.) However, if you are using a data source that is not covered in the examples, you might find yourself struggling to properly set up and access the data source. In the case of some ODBC drivers, setting up the linked server is easy, but figuring out the proper syntax to access the data source can be challenging.

You can also add a linked server using the Enterprise Manager as follows:

1. From the Enterprise Manager, expand the Security folder.

2. Select Linked Servers, right-click and select New Linked Server. The Linked Server Properties—New Linked Server dialog box, shown in Figure 21.10, appears.

3. Add the proper values and click the OK button.

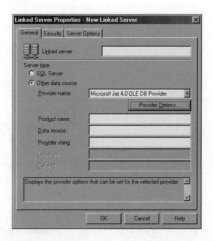

FIGURE 21.10   Linked Server Properties—New Linked Server dialog box.

For this book, I have created two data sources to use for the following examples: a Microsoft Access database called sqlsol1.mdb that contains a single table called titles, and a Microsoft Excel spreadsheet called sqlsol2.xls that contains a single table called titleauthor. Both tables are from the Microsoft SQL Server pubs database and were exported to the different data sources to demonstrate distributed queries. The following examples can be found on the Web site. To add the Microsoft Access database, we will use the OLE DB provider for Jet and sp_addlinkserver (Note: this example uses named parameters) as follows with the SQL Server Query Analyzer:

```
EXEC sp_addlinkedserver
@server = 'AccessTitles',
@provider = 'Microsoft.Jet.OLEDB.4.0',
@srvproduct = 'OLE DB Provider for Jet',
@datasrc = 'd:\distrq\sqlsol1.mdb'
```

> **NOTE**
>
> The parameter @datasrc will vary depending on where you put the Access database on your computer.

For the Microsoft Excel spreadsheet, we will also use the OLE DB provider for Jet, which can also be used with text files. To add the linked server, enter the following (Note: this example does not use named parameters):

```
EXEC sp_addlinkedserver 'ExcelTitleAuthor', 'Jet 4.0',
'Microsoft.Jet.OLEDB.4.0',
'd:\distrq\sqlsol2.xls',
NULL,
'Excel 5.0'
```

Logon IDs

When a user executes a distributed query, the local SQL Server logs on to the remote server using a logon ID and password to connect to the remote server. The remote server is responsible for managing the security and object access granted to the user logon. You have many different options for setting distributed query logon mappings. The default logon mapping is for the SQL Server to log on to the remote server using the current logon user credentials. You can also map all users to a specific account, require no user credentials, or allow only a specific SQL Server account to access the linked server. If the linked server supports Windows NT Authentication mode, account delegation on the client and server, and the provider supports Windows NT Authentication mode, you can also use the Windows NT security credentials to log on to the linked server. To change the default logon mapping, use the system stored procedure sp_addlinkedsrvlogin, which has the following format:

```
sp_addlinkedsrvlogin linked_server_name, useself,

local_login, rmtuser, rmt_password
```

where

```
linked_server_name is the name of the linked server.
useself is a varchar(8) that can be set to true or false.  When set to
true SQL Server authenticated logins use their own credentials to connect to
the linked server, if set to false use the user name and password supplied.
local_login can be used to specify that only a particular SQL Server login
or NT user that can access the linked server.  The default is NULL which
allows all logins access to the linked server.
rmtuser is the user name to use to connect to the linked server.  If set to NULL
and rmt_password is set to NULL, no login or password is used.
rmt_password is the password used to connect to the linked server.
```

You can also modify the logon information using the Linked Server Properties dialog box shown in Figure 21.11.

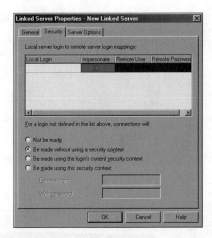

FIGURE 21.11 Linked Server Properties dialog box—Security tab.

The following example uses the `sp_addlinkedsrvlogin` stored procedure to connect all local logins to a single username and password:

```
exec sp_addlinkedsrvlogin 'MySQL', 'false', NULL, 'user1','password'
```

Let's add security for our two linked servers. We will set up the security to perform no authentication checking on the two distributed resources. To modify the security setting for the two linked server examples, enter the following:

```
exec sp_addlinkedsrvlogin 'AccessTitles', 'false'
exec sp_addlinkedsrvlogin 'ExcelTitleAuthor', 'false'
```

One way to quickly test if your linked server has been added correctly is to use the Enterprise Manager to view the linked server tables. To view a linked server's table using the Enterprise Manager, perform the following:

1. From the Enterprise Manager, click on the Security folder.

2. Expand the Linked Servers icon by clicking on the + sign.

3. A list of linked servers is displayed. Select a linked server by clicking on the + sign located next to the linked server name.

4. To view the tables associated with the linked server, click on the Tables icon.

If you have set up your linked server properly, you will see the tables in the linked server in the right frame of the Enterprise Manager as shown in Figure 21.12.

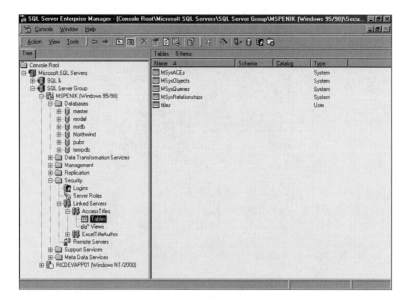

FIGURE 21.12   Viewing tables associated with a linked server.

Retrieving Data from a Linked Server

To work with linked servers, SQL Server uses a four-part naming convention that has the following format:

```
linked_server.catalog.schema.object
```

Where `linked_server` is the linked server name in SQL Server, `catalog` is the catalog that contains the object, `schema` is the schema in the catalog that contains the object, and `object` is the name of the object you want to reference. How does this translate to the real word with linked servers? Again it varies with the data source and the OLE DB provider. For example, with a SQL Server linked server named `MyPubs` that points to the `pubs` database, to retrieve records from the `authors` table, you would enter the following:

Select * From MyPubs.pubs.dbo.authors

In the case of a SQL Server linked server, the catalog is the database name, the schema is the owner and the object you are referencing. For an Oracle linked server, there is no catalog. The schema is the owner's username, and the object name is the table or view you are referencing. For example, with an Oracle linked server called `MyOracle` and a table called `employees` that is owned by the user `SCOTT`, to retrieve all the records, you would enter the following:

Select * From MyOracle..SCOTT.employees

For Microsoft Access and Microsoft Excel, there is no catalog or schema, just the linked server name and the object name. For example, to retrieve all the records from the Access database linked server we added earlier, you would write the following:

```
Select * from AccessTitles...Titles
```

To help you determine the proper four-part name, you can use the system stored procedure sp_linkedservers. sp_linkedservers returns a list of all the linked servers as well as the catalog associated with each linked server.

Examples

The first example demonstrates the power and ease of use of distributed queries to return real-time information from multiple data sources. The example creates a view that uses the two linked servers created earlier in this chapter. The view returns information from three different data sources: Microsoft Access, Microsoft Excel, and Microsoft SQL Server. A view is used so that a user could access the information without using the four-part naming convention for the linked servers involved in the query. (Note: to create this view, make sure that you are in the pubs database.) The view is as follows:

```
CREATE VIEW dbabook_titleview
AS
select title, au_ord, au_lname, price, ytd_sales, pub_id
from authors a, AccessTitles...titles b, ExcelTitleAuthor...titleauthor c
where a.au_id = c.au_id
AND b.title_id = c.title_id
```

To retrieve records from the view, execute the following command in the Query Analyzer:

```
Select * from dbabook_titleview
```

You can see that we are able to retrieve and join records from multiple data sources using T-SQL. The next example updates a column in an Excel spreadsheet using T-SQL. If you open the spreadsheet in Excel, you will see that the second and third rows contain an author ID of 213-46-8915 and a royalty percentage of 40. Using T-SQL we will update the royalty percentage to 100 for these two rows. If you have ever tried to modify a cell in Excel using Visual Basic or Visual Basic for applications, you know it takes quite a few lines of code. Using linked servers, you use a single UPDATE statement, as follows:

```
UPDATE ExcelTitleAuthor...titleauthor
Set royaltyper = 100
Where au_id = '213-46-8915'
```

Linked Servers Pass Through Queries

You can perform a pass through query in which SQL Server will not parse the query string and pass it directly to the linked server's OLE DB provider. In order to perform a pass through query, the OLE DB provider must support the OLE DB COMMAND object. If your provider supports the COMMAND object, you can use the OPENQUERY function to issue a pass through SQL statement. Pass through queries can only be read only statements (that is SELECT). The syntax for OPENQUERY is as follows:

```
OPENQUERY(linked_server_name,'SQL Statement')
```

For example, the following is a pass through query to the Access database added earlier in this chapter as a linked server:

```
select * from OpenQuery(AccessTitles,'Select * from titles;')
```

Summary

This chapter provides you with the basic tools for performing the most common SQL commands. You have learned how to retrieve rows in many different formats using the SELECT statement as well as how to add, update, and delete rows in tables using the INSERT, UPDATE, and DELETE statements, respectively. You have also learned how to create a new table using either the CREATE TABLE or SELECT...INTO statements. You should take the time to try out the commands described here until you feel you have a good understanding of how they work and review the examples found in SQL Server Books On-Line as well or buy other books from SAMS publishing that focus on SQL. You should also become familiar with as many of SQL Server's built-in functions as possible. Such functions enable you to broaden the scope of SQL statements that you can create.

Distributed queries allow you to use T-SQL to access non-SQL Server data sources. Setting up linked servers to use for distributed queries is a straightforward and simple task. The challenge with distributed queries is the vast number of data sources supported and the subtle differences and restrictions that pop up, depending on the OLE DB provider and the data source you use. However, despite the subtle issues or minor restrictions that might occur, distributed queries is a powerful technology built in SQL Server 2000 that will allow you to solve complex problems of data sharing or real-time data modifications in a low transaction environment using T-SQL.

22

Using Stored Procedures and Cursors

by Orryn Sledge

D oes the topic of stored procedures fall into the realm of developers or DBAs? Knowledge of stored procedures is required for DBAs and developers alike. As a DBA, you use stored procedures frequently. Microsoft supplies many stored procedures that you use to perform database and system maintenance. You will also find that you are frequently required to write your own stored procedures to perform specific DBA tasks for your organization or to help a group of developers solve a complex business problem.

What Is a Stored Procedure?

A *stored procedure* is a series of precompiled SQL statements and control-of-flow language statements. Stored procedures can enhance standard SQL by enabling you to use parameters, make decisions, declare variables, and return information. You can think of a stored procedure as a program or function that is stored as a database object on SQL Server. When a stored procedure is executed, the stored procedure runs on SQL Server—not on the client issuing the request. A stored procedure can be a simple SQL statement such as this one:

```
Select * from authors
```

A stored procedure can also be a series of complex SQL statements and control-of-flow language statements that apply a complex business rule or task to a series of tables in the database.

IN THIS CHAPTER

- What Is a Stored Procedure?
- Stored Procedure Pros and Cons
- How to Create a Stored Procedure
- How to Modify a Stored Procedure
- Control-of-Flow Language
- Parameters Used with Stored Procedures
- Commonly Used Global Variables
- How to Debug a Stored Procedure
- What Is a Cursor?
- Creating a Cursor
- Putting It All Together
- Stored Procedure and Cursor FAQ

NOTE

The following are a couple of technical notes on stored procedures:

- Names and identifiers can be a maximum of 128 characters.

- You can have a maximum of 1,024 parameters per stored procedure.

- Maximum size of a stored procedure is equal to the batch size (batch size = 128 * Network Packet Size [Note: the default network packet size is 4096]).

- Stored procedures support up to 32 levels of nesting. Previous versions were limited to 16 levels of nesting.

Stored Procedure Pros and Cons

Before further defining a stored procedure, here are some of the pros and cons of using stored procedures:

Stored Procedure Pros:

- Stored procedures enable you to perform complex operations that cannot be performed with straight SQL.

- Stored procedures offer a substantial performance gain over standard SQL statements because the SQL statements in a stored procedure are precompiled. An execution plan is prepared after the stored procedure executes the first time. After the execution plan is created and stored in the procedure cache, subsequent execution of the stored procedure is much faster than equivalent SQL statements.

- Stored procedures can be used as a security mechanism. For example, if you have many tables or views you do not want users to access directly, you can revoke all access to the underlying tables and create a stored procedure granting the users EXECUTE privileges on the stored procedure. The users can then access the tables by executing the stored procedure.

Stored Procedure Cons:

- It can be difficult to implement complex logic with a stored procedure. The problem stems from Transact-SQL not providing sophisticated programming constructs.

- Stored procedures can be difficult to manage. When dealing with development projects or special administrative needs, the number of stored procedures can increase dramatically. Trying to remember what each stored procedure does and what other procedures use the stored procedure can become a problem.

TIP

One successful method I have used to keep track of stored procedures is to produce a catalog of stored procedures using a Windows help file. Find a utility that enables you to easily create Windows help files. Create a help file to catalog all your stored procedures. Include the name of the procedure, a description of the procedure, a list and description of procedures, tables, or views that the procedure accesses, and other procedures called. As you add, modify, and delete stored procedures, keep the help file up to date. The help files are easy to distribute and have very good search utilities. However, this approach requires the cooperation of anyone who creates or modifies stored procedures on your system to keep the help file up to date.

Another recommendation is to store your stored procedures as text files in a version control system such as Microsoft Visual SourceSafe. Although it is not integrated with SQL Server, it does provide good version control capabilities, such as rollback, and automatically highlights differences between versions.

To take advantage of SourceSafe, you will need to store your stored procedures as text files inside SourceSafe. Every time you change a stored procedure, you will need to recompile the procedure and save the changes back to the file in SourceSafe.

How to Create a Stored Procedure

To create a stored procedure, use the Create Procedure statement, which has the following syntax:

```
Create PROCEDURE [owner.]procedure_name [;number][(@parameter1 data_type
➥ [VARYING] [=default] [OUTPUT] [,@parameter2]...
➥[@parameter1024])] [{FOR REPLICATION} |
➥{WITH RECOMPILE} [{[WITH]|[,]}ENCRYPTION]] As SQL Statements
```

TIP

Use the Stored Procedure Wizard found in Enterprise Manager to create INSERT, DELETE, UPDATE statements for a stored procedure. To access the wizard, click the Run a Wizard toolbar button. Next select Database, Create Stored Procedure Wizard to initiate the wizard.

In this syntax, *procedure name* is the name of the stored procedure. Stored procedure names conform to the standard SQL Server naming conventions. The maximum size of a procedure name is 128 characters.

You can also create a local temporary stored procedure by adding # to the beginning of the procedure name. A local temporary stored procedure can be used only by the connection that created the stored procedure; it is dropped when the connection ends. You can create a global temporary stored procedure by adding ## to the beginning of the stored procedure name. A global temporary stored procedure can be implemented by all user connections and is dropped at the end of the last session using the procedure. Suggested stored procedure naming conventions are found in Appendix A, "Naming Conventions."

Also in this syntax, *number* is an optional integer that can be used to group stored procedures with the same name so that they can be dropped with a single drop statement. *Parameter* allows parameters to be passed into the stored procedure. Parameters are optional; a stored procedure can have up to 1,024 parameters. The text FOR REPLICATION marks a stored procedure for use only by the replication process.

NOTE

When you use the Create Procedure statement, you can type the statement Create Procedure as in the following example:

```
Create Procedure usp_test
```

Alternatively, you can use the shortcut statement Create Proc as in the following example:

```
Create Proc usp_test
```

When the WITH RECOMPILE option is used, the query plan of the stored procedure is not kept in the procedure cache. A new query plan is generated every time the procedure is executed. You cannot use the FOR REPLICATION and WITH RECOMPILE options together.

SOLVING THE WITH RECOMPILE MYTH

The WITH RECOMPILE option is a highly misunderstood option. I have heard things like, "Why would you ever use that? When you use the WITH RECOMPILE option with a stored procedure, you lose the advantage of a compiled query plan. You might as well use straight SQL!" Did you ever think that ignorance is bliss and no wonder your system is slow?

When using the WITH RECOMPILE statement, you lose the benefit of a compiled query plan. However, the stored procedure is still faster than straight SQL because the SQL text has already been parsed and a query tree has been constructed. Even more important, in cases when you use the WITH RECOMPILE option, you lose the small amount of time it takes to create the query plan as opposed to using an incorrect query plan that might cost minutes or hours.

When do you use the WITH RECOMPILE option? When you are passing into stored procedure parameters that differ greatly in data distribution, these different parameters would cause the query optimizer to create different query plans. Also consider using the WITH RECOMPILE option if you pass parameters into a stored procedure, and the time to execute the stored procedure is inconsistent. You can force a stored procedure to recompile the next time it is executed by executing the system stored procedure sp_recompile on a table or view referenced in the stored procedure.

The WITH ENCRYPTION option encrypts the text of the stored procedure so that users cannot query the text of the procedure. Use this option only when necessary.

SQL Statements are the SQL statements or control-of-flow language statements that make up the stored procedure.

Now look at some simple examples of creating stored procedures in the pubs database. The following example creates a stored procedure called usp_show_authors that selects all the columns and rows from the authors table:

```
Create Procedure usp_show_authors
as
Select * from authors
```

The next example creates a stored procedure called usp_Texas_Publisher that selects all the publisher's names from the publishers table using the WITH ENCRYPTION option:

```
Create Proc usp_Texas_Publisher WITH ENCRYPTION
as
Select pub_name
From publishers
Where state = 'TX'
```

> **TIP**
>
> Stored procedures are created in the database from which the Create Procedure command is executed; the exception is temporary stored procedures, which are created in the tempdb database.

Use the Microsoft SQL Server Query Analyzer tool to enter the procedure name and click the green arrow to execute the stored procedure. If the stored procedure is not the first statement, use the EXECUTE statement as follows:

```
execute procedure name
```

Here is a shortcut and commonly used format:

```
exec procedure name
```

> **NOTE**
>
> To make your stored procedures easier to read and maintain, add a header to the start of your stored procedure. Following are two examples of headers you can use in your stored procedures.

Example header style 1:

```
Create Procedure usp_proc_name as
/****************************************************************************
** Name:
**
** Description:
**
** Parameters:
**
** Returns: 0 - Success
**          -1 - Error
**
** Other Outputs: Populates the table xxxx for Access reports.
**
** History:
**     Mark A. Spenik KSCS, 9/16/00   Initial Release.
**
****************************************************************************/
```

Example header style 2:

```
Create Procedure usp_proc_name as
/*-------------------------------------------------------------

Procedure Name

-------------------------------------------------------------
Description:

Called By:

Parameters:

Status Returns:

Other Outputs:

Example: <show an example of calling the stored procedure>
-------------------------------------------------------------
History:
-------------------------------------------------------------*/
```

TIP

SQL Server 2000 has finally caught up to other database products by enabling you to create user-defined functions (UDFs).

A scaler UDF enables you to create a function and use it inside a SELECT statement. The following is an example:

```
use pubs
go
CREATE FUNCTION myCalc
/*
 purpose: simple UDF example that takes an integer parameter and
    multiplies it by 2
*/
    (@value int)
RETURNS int
AS
BEGIN
    RETURN ( @value * 2)
END
go

/* call the UDF */
SELECT mySampleCalc = pubs.dbo.myCalc(12)

/* sample output */
mySampleCalc
------------
24
```

NOTE

To learn more about UDFs, I recommend installing the sample UDF functions that ship with SQL Server 2000. To install the samples, perform the following:

1. During the SQL Server installation, select Custom as the setup type.
2. Under the Components section, select Code Samples.

This will install a self-extracting file named `misc.exe` to the following directory: `C:\Program Files\Microsoft SQL Server\80\Tools\Devtools\Samples\Misc`. From explorer, double-click the `misc.exe` and this will create the sample files.

How to Modify a Stored Procedure

Use the ALTER PROCEDURE command to modify the contents of an existing stored procedure. This command preserves any security (EXECUTE permissions) that have been applied to the stored procedure. The following is the ALTER PROCEDURE syntax.

```
Alter PROCEDURE [owner.]procedure_name [;number]
➥[(@parameter1 data_type [=default] [OUTPUT]
➥[,@parameter2]...[@parameter1024])] [{FOR REPLICATION} |
{WITH RECOMPILE} [{[WITH]|[,]}ENCRYPTION]] As SQL Statements
```

See the topic titled "How to Create a Stored Procedure" in this chapter for detailed parameter information.

> **TIP**
>
> The ALTER PROCEDURE command simplifies your life by preserving a stored procedure's security whenever you need to make a modification to a stored procedure. Prior to version 7.0, you had to drop and re-create the procedure in order to make modifications. This meant that you had to re-apply the security to the procedure after it was re-created. It was easy to forget to apply the security back to the stored procedure. Even worse, it was easy to forget that you had to export the stored procedure's security prior to dropping the procedure! Fortunately, these issues are things of the past.

Control-of-Flow Language

Before getting into some of the finer points of stored procedures (such as using parameters or returning values), it is important to cover a very important topic: control-of-flow language. Control-of-flow language gives your stored procedures added capabilities not found in standard Transact-SQL. Using control-of-flow language, you can make use of standard programming techniques such as performing loops or conditional processing on variables.

> **TIP**
>
> Want to learn how to write good stored procedures? The first requirement is to learn SQL and the many additional Transact-SQL features. The next step is to become familiar with the different control-of-flow statements and their uses. Learn these fundamentals, and you are on your way to writing good stored procedures.

These control-of-flow language statements are quickly reviewed in the following sections:

- GOTO label

- BEGIN...END

- IF...ELSE

- WAITFOR

- return

- while

- break

- continue

Additionally, these Transact-SQL extensions are reviewed in the following sections:

- DECLARE statement

- PRINT statement

- RAISERROR

The DECLARE Statement

Using the DECLARE statement, you can create variables with standard SQL Server data types. Variables defined with the DECLARE statement *must* begin with the @ symbol. You can declare more than one variable in a DECLARE statement by using commas to separate the variables. The syntax for DECLARE is as follows:

```
Declare @variable1 datatype [,@variable2 datatype ...]
```

The following example creates three variables of different data types:

```
Declare @count int, @current_date datetime
Declare @My_Message varchar(255)
```

NOTE

To initialize or set the value of a variable you create with the DECLARE statement, use the keyword SELECT. For example, the following statement sets the value of the variable @count to 100:

```
Select @count = 100
```

The following example sets the variable @count to the total number of rows in the authors table located in the pubs database:

```
Select @count = count(*)
from pubs..authors
```

The GOTO Statement

The GOTO statement performs the same function it performs in many different programming languages such as C and Visual Basic. GOTO jumps the execution of the stored procedure to the associated label. The syntax for GOTO is as follows:

```
GOTO label
```

In the following example, the GOTO statement jumps over (skips) the SELECT statement and executes the UPDATE statement:

```
GOTO do_update
SELECT * from authors


do_update:


UPDATE authors
set au_lname = 'Spenik'
Where state = 'VA'
```

> **NOTE**
>
> When defining a label, the label name must end in a colon. When using the GOTO statement, refer to the label name but do not include the colon.

The BEGIN...END Statement

BEGIN and END statements are considered block statements because they group a series of SQL statements and control-of-flow language into a single entity. BEGIN and END are often used with IF...ELSE blocks. The syntax for BEGIN and END is as follows:

```
BEGIN
    {SQL Statements | statement block}
END
```

The IF...ELSE Statement

The IF and ELSE statements enable you to check for conditions and execute SQL statements based on the condition. The IF statement checks expressions that return a TRUE or FALSE value (Boolean expressions). If the value returned is TRUE, the block of statements or the single statement that follows the IF statement is executed. If the value returned is FALSE, the optional ELSE statement is executed. The syntax for the IF...ELSE statement is as follows:

```
IF Boolean Expression
   {SQL statement | Statement Block}
[ELSE [Boolean Expression]
   {SQL statement | Statement Block}]
```

Following is an example of `IF` and `IF...ELSE` using a single SQL statement and a statement block:

```
If @count = 0
   Select * from authors
else
   Select * from titles
if @Total != 0
begin
   Select count(*) from authors
   Select count(*) from titles
end
else
begin
   Select * from authors
   Select * from titles
end
```

The WAITFOR Statement

The `WAITFOR` statement is a delay that allows your stored procedure to wait for a specified time or until a specific time before execution continues. The syntax for the `WAITFOR` statement is as follows:

```
WAITFOR {DELAY 'time' | TIME 'time'}
```

A `WAITFOR` statement can delay for up to 24 hours. The `TIME` and `DELAY` options use the format hh:mm:ss. The following example causes a delay of 10 seconds:

```
WAITFOR DELAY '00:00:10'
```

The following example waits until 11 a.m.:

```
WAITFOR TIME '11:00:00'
```

The RETURN Statement

The `RETURN` statement causes a stored procedure to exit and return to the calling procedure or application. The syntax for `RETURN` is as follows:

```
RETURN [Integer Value]
```

You can return an integer value to the calling routine or application using the following syntax:

```
exec @status = procedure_name
```

The following example consists of two parts. The first part is a stored procedure, called usp_return, which returns an integer to the calling procedure or application. The second part is a stored procedure, called usp_call, which calls the stored procedure usp_return and checks the returned value:

```
Create Procedure usp_return
as
Declare @ret_val int

Select @ret_val = 0
Return @ret_val
go

Create Procedure usp_call
as
Declare @status int
exec @status = usp_return
if(@status = 0)
    Print 'Value returned is zero'
Go
```

When writing stored procedures, SQL Server uses the value 0 to indicate success. Negative values indicate that an error has occurred (see Table 22.1 for more information). The return values -1 to -99 are reserved for SQL Server. When you use the RETURN statement, you can return only integer values. If you want to return other datatypes, you must use an output parameter, as described later in this chapter.

Table 22.1 lists reserved return values and the corresponding explanation.

TABLE 22.1   Reserved Stored Procedure Return Values

Return Value	Explanation
0	Procedure executed successfully
-1	Object missing
-2	Datatype error occurred
-3	Process chosen as deadlock victim
-4	Permission error occurred
-5	Syntax error occurred
-6	Miscellaneous user error occurred
-7	Resource error, such as out of space, occurred

TABLE 22.1   Continued

Return Value	Explanation
-8	Nonfatal internal problem encountered
-9	System limit reached
-10	Fatal internal inconsistency occurred
-11	Fatal internal inconsistency occurred
-12	Table or index corrupted
-14	Hardware error occurred

The WHILE, BREAK, and CONTINUE Statements

The WHILE statement enables you to perform repeating conditional loops for the execution of a SQL statement or a statement block. The BREAK statement causes an exit from the WHILE loop; CONTINUE causes the WHILE loop to restart, skipping any statements that follow the CONTINUE statement. These statements have the following format:

```
WHILE Boolean Expressions
{SQL statement | statement block}
[BREAK | CONTINUE]
```

Examples of these statements can be found in the sample stored procedures shown at the end of this chapter.

The PRINT Statement

The PRINT statement enables you to return a message to the client's message handler. The message can have up to 1,024 characters. The PRINT statement has the following syntax:

```
PRINT 'any ASCII text' | @local_variable | @@FUNCTION | string_expr
```

If you print a local or global variable, the variable must be a char or varchar data type; otherwise, you have to convert the data type to a char or varchar before printing. Following are some examples using the PRINT statement:

```
Declare @msg varchar(255), @count int
Select @count = 0
Print 'Starting the procedure'
While @count < 5
Begin
   Select @count = @count + 1
   Select @msg = 'The Value of @count is ' + str(@count)
```

```
    Print @msg
end
Select @msg = 'This about wraps this procedure up.'
Select @msg = @msg + ' The value of @count is ' + str(@count)
Print @msg
```

Listing 22.1 shows the output generated from the preceding PRINT statements, executed from the Microsoft SQL Server Query Analyzer tool.

LISTING 22.1   *PRINT* Statement Output

```
Starting the procedure
The Value of @count is           1
The Value of @count is           2
The Value of @count is           3
The Value of @count is           4
The Value of @count is           5
This about wraps this procedure up. The value of @count is          5
```

> **TIP**
>
> Use PRINT statements in your stored procedures during testing to help debug the stored procedure. Use the PRINT statement like a trace statement to print out particular locations or values in the procedure.

The RAISERROR Statement

The RAISERROR statement sets a SQL Server system flag to signify that an error has occurred and sends back an error message to the client connection. The syntax for RAISERROR is as follows:

```
RAISERROR ({message_id | message_str}, severity, state [,arg1[,arg2]])
➥ [WITH (LOG or NOWAIT or SETERROR)]
```

Use the WITH LOG option to write the error message to the SQL Server error log and the Windows NT event log.

Comments

Comments in a stored procedure follow the C programming language standard or ANSI style comments. Comments begin with a /* and end with a */. Everything between the /* and the */ is considered part of the comment. Comments that begin with - - are ANSI standard comments. Use a lot of comments to make your stored procedures easy to read and maintain. Following are some examples of comments:

```
/* This is a one line comment */
/* This
   Comment
   Spans
   Several lines */
/*
** This is a comment - I think the added ** makes it easier to read.
*/
--This is an ANSI style comment.
```

Parameters Used with Stored Procedures   @~ ≡ Parameter

Parameters enable you to write flexible stored procedures by executing the SQL statements with values that are determined at runtime (not at compile time) and that can be changed at every execution. Parameters follow the same naming conventions as standard stored procedure variables. (They must begin with @.) Parameters can be input parameters or output parameters.

Input Parameters

Input parameters are used to pass values into a stored procedure. Input parameters have the following syntax:

```
Create proc Procedure_name @parm1 datatype, @paramN datatype
```

The following example defines three input parameters of different data types:

```
Create procedure usp_input @temp_name varchar(30), @total int,
➡ @current_date datetime
```

You can pass the values into a stored procedure in several ways. The standard way to pass the values is as follows:

```
exec usp_input 'Spenik & Sledge', 1000, '03/25/96'
```

When you use the preceding calling form, you must pass the values in the same order as they are declared in the stored procedure. Instead of passing in values, you can also pass in other variables (of the same data type) as follows:

```
exec usp_input @authors_name, @new_total, @my_date
```

Another way to pass parameters is by using the parameter name. When using the parameter name, you can pass the parameters in any order—but if you use the name for one parameter, you must use the parameter name for all parameters that follow. The following is a valid example of using parameter names:

```
exec usp_input @total = 1000, @temp_name = 'Spenik & Sledge',
➡ @current_date = '03/25/96'
```

The following example is *not* valid because after you start using a parameter name, all the parameters that follow must also include the name:

```
exec usp_input 'Spenik & Sledge', @total = 1000, '03/25/96'
```

Input parameters can also have default values. To assign a default value to an input parameter, use the following syntax:

```
@parameter_name datatype = default_value
```

For example

```
create proc usp_param @p1 int, @p2 int = 3, @p3 int
```

If the procedure is called without a parameter (as in the following example), the default value is used:

```
exec usp_param @p1=5, @p3=100
```

To use an input parameter in a stored procedure, reference the variable name (just like any other variable). The following example checks the value of the parameter; if the parameter is less than 0, a message is printed:

```
create procedure usp_test @p1 int
as
   if @p1 < 0
      print 'The value is less than zero'
```

TIP

Input parameters are NULL unless a non-null value is passed to the procedure or the procedure explicitly sets the parameter. If you are using stored procedures to INSERT data and the data is based on input parameters, verify that the parameters are not NULL.

Additionally, you can use the DEFAULT clause for a stored procedure parameter to explicitly set a value if a value is not passed to the procedure. This is useful when you have a stored procedure that has numerous input parameters and the parameters might or might not be set by the calling routine.

Output Parameters

Output parameters are used to return values into a variable to a calling procedure or application. The syntax to declare an output parameter is as follows:

```
Create procedure procedure_name @parameter_name datatype OUTPUT
```

The following example declares an output parameter called @p1:

```
create procedure usp_test @p1 int OUT
```

To call a procedure with an output parameter, you must declare a variable to hold the returned value. (The variable does not have to have the same name as the output parameter used in the create procedure statement.) Use the keyword out (output) as follows:

```
exec usp_test @v1 out
```

After the procedure executes, you can then use the value in the output parameter (in this example, @v1) for further processing. You can also use the parameter name with output parameters, as follows:

```
exec usp_test @p1 = @v1 out
```

The following example multiplies an input parameter by 2 and returns the string version of the result in an output parameter:

```
Create Procedure usp_Double_Value @old_value int, @new_value varchar(20) OUT
as
Declare @temp_value int
Select @temp_value = @old_value * 2
Select @new_value = convert(varchar(20), @temp_value)
```

The following example uses the procedure usp_Double_Value and prints out the results:

```
Declare @start_value int, @computed_value varchar(20)
Declare @msg varchar(50)

Select @start_value = 20
exec usp_Double_Value @start_value, @computed_value OUT
Select @msg = 'The computed value is ' + @computed_value
Print @msg
```

Listing 22.2 shows the output generated from the preceding routine when executed from the Microsoft SQL Server Query Analyzer tool.

LISTING 22.2 PRINT Statement Output

```
The computed value is 40
```

Commonly Used Global Variables

SQL Server provides several global variables you can use when writing stored procedures. A *global variable* is distinguished from a standard variable by the @@ that precedes the name. Following is a list of some of the commonly used global variables:

- @@ERROR is probably the most commonly used global variable. @@ERROR is used to check the error status of a statement executed by SQL Server. @@ERROR contains a 0 if the statement executed correctly. (Note: @@ERROR is kept by connection; the value of @@ERROR for your connection is not changed by other user's statements.)

- @@FETCH_STATUS is used to check the status of a cursor's fetch command and is discussed in detail in the section, "What Is a Cursor?," later in this chapter. (@@FETCH_STATUS is also kept per connection.)

- @@IDENTITY holds the value of the last successful identity value inserted. (@@IDENTITY is kept per connection.)

- @@ROWCOUNT holds the value for the number of rows affected by the last SQL statement. (@@ROWCOUNT is kept per connection.)

- @@SERVERNAME specifies the name of the local SQL Server.

- @@TRANCOUNT is the number of current active transactions for the current user.

- @@VERSION contains the version number of SQL Server.

How to Debug a Stored Procedure

Several different methods can be used to debug a stored procedure. The following is a listing of popular debugging methods:

- Transact-SQL Debugger

- Transact-SQL Debug Statements

- Other Debugging Tools

Transact-SQL Debugger

The following are the steps to use the Transact-SQL Debugger:

1. Open the Query Analyzer and connect to SQL Server.

2. Show the Object Browser by pressing F8.

3. Click the plus (+) sign next to the database that contains the stored procedure.

4. Click the plus (+) sign next to the Stored Procedures folder.

5. Right-click the stored procedure. From the right-mouse menu, select the Debug menu option. The Debug Procedure window will appear. Enter the necessary information and click the Execute button.

6. That's it! You're off and debugging your stored procedure.

Transact-SQL Debug Statements

The following are some Transact-SQL statements that are useful for debugging stored procedures:

- PRINT statement—The PRINT statement is useful to display the contents of string variables. Keep in mind that the PRINT statement cannot display any variable that is not a string. It can also be used to determine if a certain line of code is executed (see the topic titled "The PRINT Statement" in this chapter for more information).

- SELECT statement—The SELECT statement is also useful to display the contents of memory variables. A SELECT statement can display any type of memory variable, regardless of its data type. The following is an example of the SELECT statement displaying the contents of a memory variable.

```
declare @myvar integer
select @myvar = 100
select @myvar
```

Listing 22.3 shows the output generated from the preceding routine when executed from the Microsoft SQL Server Query Analyzer tool.

LISTING 22.3   *SELECT* Statement Output

```
-----------
100

(1 row(s) affected)
```

Other Debugging Tools

In addition to Transact-SQL, you can also use the following tools to debug stored procedures:

- SQL Server Debugger—This product ships with Microsoft Visual C++ 5.0 Enterprise Edition and Microsoft Visual Basic 5.0 Enterprise Edition. The debugging environment is similar to Microsoft's Visual Basic debugger, in that it enables you to set breakpoints and display the contents of a variable.

- ODBC tracing—When calling stored procedures from an ODBC client, it is often useful to view the parameters that the client is passing to the stored procedure. You can use the trace feature in ODBC to store SQL calls to a text file. To activate ODBC tracing, open Control Panel, select ODBC-32, select the Tracing tab, and click Start Tracing Now. Keep in mind that ODBC tracing might slow your application and might generate a large text file.

- SQL Server Profiler—This product traces SQL activity. Again, this can be useful when you are trying to trace the parameters that are passed to a stored procedure. See Chapter 24, "Monitoring SQL Server," for more information on SQL Server Profiler.

USING THE EXECUTE COMMAND TO EXECUTE STRING VARIABLES

You can use the EXECUTE statement to generate dynamic SQL statements and execute them all at runtime. When creating dynamic SQL, remember that you must have the proper access to all the objects you plan to use in the dynamic SQL statement. You are limited to generating dynamic SQL statements that do not exceed the maximum size of a char, varchar, or text data types.

On the performance side, keep in mind that dynamic SQL is parsed and compiled at the time the EXECUTE statement is issued. You can also use the INSERT INTO command and the EXECUTE statement to populate a local database table with information from a remote server using a remote stored procedure.

What Is a Cursor?

A *cursor* is a SQL resultset that enables you to perform row-oriented operations on the resultset. (This differs from standard SQL resultsets, which return all the rows in the resultset.) This means that you can process data row by row. With SQL Server's cursors, you can navigate forward and backward through the resultset. You can really exploit the power of cursors when you combine them with the EXEC command and a string variable substitution.

Cursors can be used in the following locations:

- In a control-of-flow batch
- Within a stored procedure
- Within a trigger

Creating a Cursor

Every cursor must have at least four components. The four key components *must* follow this order:

1. DECLARE the cursor
2. OPEN the cursor
3. FETCH from the cursor
4. CLOSE or DEALLOCATE the cursor

Step 1: DECLARE the Cursor

The DECLARE statement contains the user-defined name used to reference the result-set, as well as the SQL SELECT statement that generates the resultset. Think of the

DECLARE statement as a temporary table that contains a pointer to your actual data source.

DECLARE **Cursor Syntax**
The following is the SQL-92 cursor syntax:

```
DECLARE cursor_name [INSENSITIVE] [SCROLL] CURSOR
FOR select_statement
[FOR {READ ONLY | UPDATE [OF column_list]}]
```

The following is the cursor extension syntax. (Note: The syntax that follows is not SQL-92 compliant.) This syntax is similar to the cursor syntax supported by ODBC and ADO.

```
DECLARE cursor_name CURSOR
[LOCAL | GLOBAL]
[FORWARD_ONLY | SCROLL]
[STATIC | KEYSET | FAST_FORWARD | DYNAMIC]
[READ_ONLY | SCROLL_LOCKS | OPTIMISTIC]
FOR select_statement
[FOR {READ ONLY | UPDATE [OF column_list]}]
```

The following is the SQL-92 syntax explanation.

Type	Explanation
cursor_name	The cursor name.
INSENSITIVE	Specifies that changes in your data source will not be reflected in the cursor. Updates to a cursor are not allowed when this option is specified.
SCROLL	Allows the following FETCH commands to be used: PRIOR, FIRST, LAST, ABSOLUTE n, and RELATIVE n.
select_statement	A SQL SELECT statement. The following SQL commands force a cursor to be declared as INSENSITIVE: DISTINCT, UNION, GROUP BY, and/or HAVING.
READ ONLY	Prohibits updates from occurring against the cursor.
UPDATE [OF column_list]	Allows updates to be performed against the cursor. The optional clause [OF column_list] specifies which columns in the cursor can be updated.

The following is the cursor extension syntax explanation.

Type	Explanation
FORWARD_ONLY	Specifies that cursor navigation only supports the FETCH NEXT command. Use this option to minimize cursor resources and locks. This is default cursor setting.
STATIC	Specifies that the cursor does not allow modifications and that changes to base tables will not be reflected in the cursor. Use this option when the cursor will be read-only and you want to minimize cursor resources and locks.
KEYSET	Specifies that the cursor members and the cursor order is fixed. Only the keys to base tables used by the cursor are maintained by the cursor. (Note: A KEYSET cursor reverts to a STATIC cursor if the base table(s) do not contain unique indexes or primary keys.)
DYNAMIC	Specifies that changes to base tables are reflected within the cursor. Use this option to maximize data consistency. However, this option requires substantial cursor resources when compared to the KEYSET or STATIC or cursor types.
FAST_FORWARD	Designates a FORWARD_ONLY, READ_ONLY cursor. This option has been optimized for performance.
SCROLL_LOCKS	Specifies that locks are placed on the data used in the cursor result-set. The locks occur when the data is read into the cursor. This option ensures that UDPATES or DELETES to a cursor always succeed because the data is locked by the cursor. This option should probably be avoided when data concurrency is a priority.
OPTIMISTIC	Specifies that the cursor does not place locks on the data when it is read into the cursor. UDPATES or DELETES to a cursor might fail if the underlying cursor data has changed after it was read into the cursor. This option should be used when data concurrency is a priority.

NOTE

You cannot mix the SQL-92 cursor syntax and the cursor extension syntax. Also, the cursor extension syntax is not backward compatible with version 6.x of SQL Server, whereas the SQL-92 is backward compatible with SQL Server 6.x.

Example 1: Standard Cursor

```
declare pub_crsr cursor local
for
select pub_id,pub_name
from publishers
```

Example 2: Read-Only Cursor

```
declare pub_crsr cursor local
for
select pub_id,pub_name
from publishers
FOR READ ONLY
```

Example 3: Cursor That Allows Updates

```
declare pub_crsr cursor local
for
select pub_id,pub_name
from publishers
FOR UPDATE
```

Step 2: OPEN the Cursor

After you declare a cursor, you must open it. The OPEN statement should immediately follow the DECLARE statement.

OPEN Cursor Syntax

```
OPEN [GLOBAL] cursor_name
```

cursor_name is the name of the cursor to open.

Example

```
OPEN pub_crsr
```

> **NOTE**
>
> Starting with version 7.0, Microsoft added the database option default to local cursor. (A global cursor is global to the connection, whereas a local cursor is local to a batch, stored procedure, or trigger.) If the cursor declaration does not include the local or global setting, the cursor defaults to the setting specified by the default to local cursor setting. The default setting is FALSE. According to SQL Server's documentation, the default setting might change in future versions. Watch out! Be sure to include the local or global keyword when using cursors!

Step 3: FETCH from the Cursor

After the cursor has been opened, you can retrieve information from the resultset on a row-by-row basis. SQL Server provides forward-scrolling cursors *and* backward-scrolling cursors.

FETCH Syntax

```
FETCH [[NEXT | PRIOR | FIRST | LAST | ABSOLUTE n | RELATIVE n] FROM]
➥[GLOBAL] cursor_name
[INTO @variable_name1, @variable_name2, ...]
```

Term	Explanation
NEXT	Retrieves the next row
PRIOR	Retrieves the preceding row
FIRST	Retrieves the first row
LAST	Retrieves the last row
ABSOLUTE *n*	Retrieves a row based on the absolute position within the resultset
RELATIVE *n*	Retrieves a row based on the relative position within the resultset

TIP

Use negative numbers to move backward within a resultset when using the ABSOLUTE and RELATIVE arguments. When you use ABSOLUTE, the rows are counted backward from the last row in the recordset. When you use RELATIVE, the rows are counted backward from the current position in the recordset.

Term	Explanation
cursor_name	The name of cursor
INTO @*variable_name1*, @*variable_name2*, and so on	Copies the contents of a column into a variable

Example 1: Return the Next Row in the Resultset

```
fetch next from pub_crsr
```

Example 2: Return the Fifth Row in the Resultset

```
fetch absolute 5 from pub_crsr
```

Example 3: Copy the Contents of the Next Row into Host Variables

```
fetch next from pub_crsr into @pub_id,@pub_name
```

> **NOTE**
>
> The columns returned in the SELECT statement must exactly match the variables contained in the FETCH statement. For example, if the SELECT statement returns two columns of information, you must have two variables contained in the FETCH statement.

Step 4: CLOSE or DEALLOCATE the Cursor

After you finish processing the cursor, you must CLOSE or DEALLOCATE the cursor. The CLOSE statement closes the cursor but does not release the data structures used by the cursor. Use this statement if you plan to reopen the cursor for subsequent use. The DEALLOCATE statement closes the cursor and releases the data structures used by the cursor.

> **TIP**
>
> Always CLOSE or DEALLOCATE a cursor as soon as processing is complete. Cursors consume resources, such as locks, memory, and so on. If these resources are not released, performance and multiuser problems might arise.

CLOSE and DEALLOCATE Syntax

```
CLOSE [GLOBAL] cursor_name
DEALLOCATE [GLOBAL] cursor_name
cursor_name     The cursor name.
```

Example 1: Close a Cursor

```
CLOSE pub_crsr
```

Example 2: Deallocate a Cursor

```
DEALLOCATE pub_crsr
```

Positional UPDATE and DELETE

In addition to being able to retrieve data from a cursor, you can perform positional updates and deletes against the data contained in the cursor. When a modification is made to a cursor, that modification automatically cascades to the cursor's data source.

Syntax

```
UPDATE table_name
SET column_name1 = {expression1 | NULL | (select_statement)}
[, column_name2 = {expression2 | NULL | (select_statement)}...]
WHERE CURRENT OF cursor_name

DELETE FROM table_name
WHERE CURRENT OF cursor_name
```

Term	Explanation
table_name	The name of the table to UPDATE or DELETE
column_name	The name of column to UPDATE
cursor_name	The cursor name

Example 1: Update the pub_name Column in the publishers Table

This update is based on the current row position in the cursor:

```
UPDATE publishers
SET pub_name = 'XYZ publisher'
WHERE CURRENT OF pub_crsr
```

Example 2: Delete a Row in the publishers Table

This delete is based on the current row position in the cursor:

```
DELETE FROM publishers
WHERE CURRENT OF pub_crsr
```

Global Variables

The following two global variables can be used to monitor the status of a cursor: @@fetch_status and @@cursor_rows.

The @@fetch_status variable displays the status of a last FETCH command. Following are the possible values for @@fetch_status:

0—Successful fetch

-1—The fetch failed or the fetch caused the cursor to go beyond the resultset.

-2—The fetch row is missing from the data set.

The following is an example of @@fetch_status:

```
while @@fetch_status = 0
    ...do some processing
```

The @@cursor_rows variable displays the number of rows in the cursor set. Use this variable *after* the cursor has been opened. Following are the possible values for @@cursor_rows:

- -n—Cursor is currently being loaded with data. The number returned indicates the number of rows currently in the key result set; however, the number continues to increase as SQL Server processes the SELECT statement. (This is known as asynchronous processing.)

- *n*—Number of rows in the resultset.

- 0—No matching rows in the resultset.

- -1—Indicates that the cursor is dynamic and that the number of records is unknown.

Putting It All Together

Now that you know something about cursor statements, positional updates, and global variables, the following cursor examples show you how all these components fit together.

Example 1: Loop Through a Table

The following example shows how the different components of a cursor (DECLARE, OPEN, FETCH, and DEALLOCATE) are used to loop through the publishers table. The @@fetch_status global variable is referenced each time a FETCH is performed. After the record pointer reaches the end of the resultset, the @@fetch_status variable is equal to -1. This prevents the code inside the while @@fetch_status = 0 section from being executed.

```
/* suppress counts from being displayed */
SET NOCOUNT ON

/* declare a cursor that will contain the pub_id, pub_name columns */
/* from the publishers table */
declare pub_crsr cursor local
for
select pub_id,pub_name
from publishers

/* open the cursor */
open pub_crsr

/* get the first row from the cursor */
fetch next from pub_crsr
```

```
/* loop through the rows in the cursor */
while @@fetch_status = 0
begin
  /* get next row */
  fetch next from pub_crsr
end

/* close the cursor */
deallocate pub_crsr
```

And the output appears as

```
pub_id pub_name
------ ----------------------------------------
0736   New Moon Books

pub_id pub_name
------ ----------------------------------------
0877   Binnet & Hardley

pub_id pub_name
------ ----------------------------------------
1389   Algodata Infosystems

pub_id pub_name
------ ----------------------------------------
1622   Five Lakes Publishing

pub_id pub_name
------ ----------------------------------------
1756   Ramona Publishers

pub_id pub_name
------ ----------------------------------------
9901   GGG&G

pub_id pub_name
------ ----------------------------------------
9952   Scootney Books
```

```
pub_id pub_name
------ ----------------------------------------
9999   Lucerne Publishing


pub_id pub_name
------ ----------------------------------------
```

Example 2: Display Object Names and Object Types

The following example displays object names and types for all user-defined objects in the pubs database. It uses two variables (@name and @type) and conditional logic to determine object type.

```
/* suppress counts from being displayed */
SET NOCOUNT ON

/* declare variables */
declare @name sysname
declare @type char(2)

/* declare a cursor that will contain a list of object */
/* names and object types */
declare object_list cursor local
for
select name, type
from sysobjects
where type <> 'S'
order by type

/* open the cursor */
open object_list

/* get the first row from the cursor */
fetch next from object_list into @name,@type

/* loop through the rows in the cursor */
while @@fetch_status = 0
begin
  /* determine object type */
  if @type = 'C'
     select '(CHECK constraint) ' + @name
  if @type = 'D'
     select '(Default or DEFAULT constraint) ' + @name
```

```
   if @type = 'F'
      select '(FOREIGN KEY constraint) ' + @name
   if @type = 'K'
      select '(PRIMARY KEY or UNIQUE constraint) ' + @name
   if @type = 'L'
      select '(Log) ' + @name
   if @type = 'P'
      select '(Stored procedure) ' + @name
   if @type = 'R'
      select '(Rule) ' + @name
   if @type = 'RF'
      select '(Stored procedure for replication) ' + @name
   if @type = 'TR'
      select '(Trigger) ' + @name
   if @type = 'U'
      select '(User table) ' + @name
   if @type = 'V'
      select '(View) ' + @name
   if @type = 'X'
      select '(Extended stored procedure) ' + @name

  /* get next table name */
  fetch next from object_list into @name,@type
end

/* close the cursor */
deallocate object_list
```

And the output appears as

```
name                type
(CHECK constraint) CK__authors__au_id__02DC7882
(CHECK constraint) CK__authors__zip__04C4C0F4
(CHECK constraint) CK__jobs__max_lvl__2719D8F8
(CHECK constraint) CK__jobs__min_lvl__2625B4BF
(CHECK constraint) CK__publisher__pub_i__089551D8
(CHECK constraint) CK_emp_id
(Default or DEFAULT constraint) DF__authors__phone__03D09CBB
(Default or DEFAULT constraint) DF__employee__hire_d__30A34332
(Default or DEFAULT constraint) DF__employee__job_id__2BDE8E15
(Default or DEFAULT constraint) DF__employee__job_lv__2DC6D687
(Default or DEFAULT constraint) DF__employee__pub_id__2EBAFAC0
(Default or DEFAULT constraint) DF__jobs__job_desc__25319086
```

```
(Default or DEFAULT constraint) DF__publisher__count__09897611
(Default or DEFAULT constraint) DF__titles__pubdate__0F424F67
(Default or DEFAULT constraint) DF__titles__type__0D5A06F5
(FOREIGN KEY constraint) FK__discounts__stor___2160FFA2
(FOREIGN KEY constraint) FK__employee__job_id__2CD2B24E
(FOREIGN KEY constraint) FK__employee__pub_id__2FAF1EF9
(FOREIGN KEY constraint) FK__pub_info__pub_id__3567F84F
(FOREIGN KEY constraint) FK__roysched__title___1E8492F7
(FOREIGN KEY constraint) FK__sales__stor_id__1AB40213
(FOREIGN KEY constraint) FK__sales__title_id__1BA8264C
(FOREIGN KEY constraint) FK__titleauth__au_id__1312E04B
(FOREIGN KEY constraint) FK__titleauth__title__14070484
(FOREIGN KEY constraint) FK__titles__pub_id__0E4E2B2E
(PRIMARY KEY or UNIQUE constraint) PK__jobs__job_id__243D6C4D
(PRIMARY KEY or UNIQUE constraint) PK_emp_id
(PRIMARY KEY or UNIQUE constraint) UPK_storeid
(PRIMARY KEY or UNIQUE constraint) UPKCL_auidind
(PRIMARY KEY or UNIQUE constraint) UPKCL_pubind
(PRIMARY KEY or UNIQUE constraint) UPKCL_pubinfo
(PRIMARY KEY or UNIQUE constraint) UPKCL_sales
(PRIMARY KEY or UNIQUE constraint) UPKCL_taind
(PRIMARY KEY or UNIQUE constraint) UPKCL_titleidind
(Stored procedure) byroyalty
(Stored procedure) reptq1
(Stored procedure) reptq2
(Stored procedure) reptq3
(Trigger) employee_insupd
(User table) authors
(User table) discounts
(User table) employee
(User table) jobs
(User table) pub_info
(User table) publishers
(User table) roysched
(User table) sales
(User table) stores
(User table) titleauthor
(User table) titles
(View) titleview
```

Example 3: Delete Data from Various Tables in a Database

The following example combines the EXEC command with a cursor to automatically
DELETE the data in all tables that begin with word 'SAMPLE'.

```
/* set database */
use pubs
go

/* create sample tables and data */
CREATE TABLE sample1 (id int, descr varchar(10))
insert into sample1 values (1,'one')
insert into sample1 values (1,'two')

CREATE TABLE sample2 (id int, descr varchar(10))
insert into sample2 values (3,'three')
insert into sample2 values (4,'four')


/* declare variables */
declare @table_name sysname

/* declare a cursor that will contain a list of table */
/* names to be deleted. */
/* NOTE: this example deletes data from tables */
/* that begin with the word SAMPLE. */

declare delete_cursor cursor local
for select a.name
from sysobjects a
where a.type = 'U' and a.name LIKE 'sample%'
order by a.name

/* open the cursor */
open delete_cursor

/* get the first row from the cursor */
fetch next from delete_cursor into @table_name

/* loop through the rows in the cursor */
while @@fetch_status = 0
  begin
    /* issue DELETE command */
    EXEC ('DELETE ' + @table_name)
```

```
   /* get next table name */
   fetch next from delete_cursor into @table_name
 end


/* close the cursor */
deallocate delete_cursor
```

Example 4: Positional Update

The following example looks at each row in the publishers table. If the pub_id column is equal to '1389', the pub_name column is updated to 'XYZ publisher'.

```
/* suppress counts from being displayed */
SET NOCOUNT ON


/* declare variables */
declare @pub_id char(4),@pub_name varchar(40)


/* declare a cursor that will contain the pub_id, pub_name columns */
/* from the publishers table */
/* NOTE: for UPDATE clause allows position updates */
declare pub_crsr cursor local
for
select pub_id,pub_name
from publishers
for UPDATE OF pub_id,pub_name


/* open the cursor */
open pub_crsr


/* get the first row from the cursor */
fetch next from pub_crsr into @pub_id, @pub_name


/* loop through the rows in the cursor */
while @@fetch_status = 0
begin
  if @pub_id = '1389'
    update publishers
    set pub_name = 'XYZ publisher'
    where current of pub_crsr
```

```
    /* get next row */
    fetch next from pub_crsr into @pub_id, @pub_name
end

/* close the cursor */
deallocate pub_crsr
```

Example 5: Batch Run

The following stored procedure and cursor example enables you to schedule a single stored procedure with the SQL Server scheduler that in turn executes any stored procedures in a table of batch procedures. The following example was used for an organization that performed many different types of batch processing using nightly stored procedures. The stored procedures were required to run in a certain order, and the addition of new procedures was a common occurrence. Instead of constantly scheduling the procedures, this example creates a single table, Batch_Procedures, which holds the names of the stored procedures to execute during the nightly batch run. It then creates a stored procedure called usp_Batch_Run that executes each procedure in the Batch_Procedures table.

NOTE

The current limitations to this stored procedure (which you can easily modify) are as follows:

- usp_Batch_Run can execute only stored procedures in the same database as usp_Batch_Run. This limitation exists because the system table sysobjects is checked, as a security measure, to validate that the name in the Batch_Procedures table is an existing stored procedure.
- usp_Batch_Run does not support stored procedures with parameters.

The batch processing consists of one support table, one report table, and a stored procedure. The table schema for Batch_Procedures is as follows:

```
CREATE TABLE Batch_Procedures (
    priority int,
    procedure_name varchar (20),
    description varchar (255)
 )
CREATE  UNIQUE  CLUSTERED  INDEX cidx_priority ON Batch_Procedures
    ( priority )
```

For example, if you have a stored procedure named usp_rollups that is the first procedure to execute in the batch, you would add the procedure to the table Batch_Procedures as follows:

```
INSERT Batch_Procedures
Values(0,'usp_rollups','First procedure of the batch')
```

The stored procedure usp_Batch_Run opens a cursor on the Batch_Procedures table and executes each procedure in the Batch_Procedures table. The syntax for the Batch_Run procedure is as follows:

```
CREATE PROCEDURE usp_Batch_Run AS
/*-------------------------------------------------------------


usp_Batch_Run


-------------------------------------------------------------
Description: Executes all the stored procedures that are
             stored in the table Batch_Procedures. Results
             from the batch run is stored in the table
             Batch_Results.  This procedure is schedule to run
             via the task scheduler.


Parameters: None.


Status Returns: None.


Example: usp_Batch_Run
-------------------------------------------------------------
History:
Mark Spenik, SAMS - DBA Survival Guide
Sept 15, 2000
-------------------------------------------------------------*/
Declare @status int, @procedure_name varchar(20)
Declare @priority int, @description varchar(255), @id int
Declare @IsProc int

/*
** Declare a cursor to retrieve each stored procedure listed
** in the Batch_Procedures table.
*/

declare batch_run_crsr cursor local
For Select procedure_name,priority,description
from Batch_Procedures
Order By priority
```

```
/*
** Clear out the results table from the previous nights run.
*/
truncate table Batch_Results

/*
** Open the cursor to begin running the batch stored procedures.
*/
Open batch_run_crsr
if @@error != 0
   goto Batch_Error

/*
** Get the first Row
*/
fetch next from batch_run_crsr
into @procedure_name, @priority, @description

While ((@@fetch_status = 0) And (@@error = 0)
begin

   /*
   ** Make sure it's a stored procedure
   */
   select @IsProc = count(*)
   from sysobjects
   where id = object_id(@procedure_name)
   and type = 'P'

   if @IsProc > 0
   begin
      /*
      ** First log the starting time in the batch results table.
      */
      Insert Batch_Results
      Values(getdate(), NULL, @procedure_name, @description, NULL)

      /*
      ** Save identity value for the update.
      */
      Select @id = @@identity
```

```
        /*
        ** Execute the Stored Procedure
        */
        Execute @status = @procedure_name

        /*
        ** Update the results table.
        */
        UPDATE Batch_Results
            set end_time = getdate(),          status = @status
        Where id = @id
    END /* If IsProc > 0 */
    /*
    ** Get the next procedure.
    */
    fetch next from batch_run_crsr
    into @procedure_name, @priority, @description

end /* While */

close batch_run_crsr
deallocate batch_run_crsr
return 0

/*
** Simple Error Exit
*/
Batch_Error:
RAISERROR ('Error executing stored procedure usp_Batch_Run',16,-1) return -100
```

The table Batch_Results is truncated every time the stored procedure usp_Batch_Run
is executed. The Batch_Results table is used to log the status of the procedures that
are executed during the stored procedure usp_Batch_Run. You can enhance the
procedure by selecting all the rows from the Batch_Results table and use email to
notify users of the status of the batch run. The table schema for the Batch_Results
table is as follows:

```
CREATE TABLE Batch_Results (
    id int IDENTITY,
    start_time datetime,
    end_time datetime NULL,
    proc_name varchar (20)  NULL,
    msg varchar ( 255 ) NULL,
```

```
    status int NULL
)
CREATE  UNIQUE  CLUSTERED  INDEX cidx_Id ON Batch_Results
    ( id )
```

Stored Procedure and Cursor FAQ

Following are some of the common questions asked by DBAs about SQL Server stored procedures and cursors:

Q Do stored procedures really run faster than sending SQL statements directly to SQL Server?

A Yes, stored procedures run faster because they are precompiled, cached, and generate less network traffic.

Q When should I use stored procedures?

A Whenever you want to maximize performance and want to consolidate SQL code into a single program. Examples of stored procedure include INSERT, DELETE, and UPDATE stored procedures and reporting stored procedures.

Q When should I not use stored procedures?

A Stored procedures probably should not be used for *ad-hoc* querying because the parameters and the data being returned are often decided at runtime. Stored procedures work best when a predefined resultset is being returned.

Q How many call levels can a stored procedure perform?

A Stored procedures support up to 32 levels of procedure nesting, meaning that a stored procedure can call another stored procedure, which in turn can call another, until the maximum nesting level of 32 is reached. To determine the current level of nesting, use the global variable @@nestlevel.

Q Can I create temporary tables inside a stored procedure?

A You can create temporary tables and indexes on the temporary tables using a stored procedure. All temporary tables are created in the temporary database regardless of where the stored procedure executes. Any local temporary table created in a stored procedure is removed when the procedure exits.

Q Can I create a temporary table in a stored procedure and reference the temporary table from another stored procedure?

A If you create a temporary table in a stored procedure and call another stored procedure, the procedure called can use the temporary table created by the calling procedure.

Q **Can I create a temporary table inside a stored procedure, drop it, and create another temporary table with the same name?**

A You cannot create a temporary table in a stored procedure, drop it, and then try to create another temporary table with the same name.

Q **What commands cannot be executed from within a stored procedure?**

A You cannot perform the following SQL statements within a stored procedure: CREATE VIEW, CREATE DEFAULT, CREATE RULE, CREATE TRIGGER, and CREATE PROCEDURE.

Q **How can I remove a stored procedure?**

A To remove a stored procedure, use the DROP PROCEDURE command.

Q **How can I rename a stored procedure?**

A To rename a stored procedure, use the system stored procedure sp_rename.

Q **When are stored procedures automatically recompiled by SQL Server?**

A Stored procedures are recompiled when a table is dropped and re-created, when all query plans in the cache are in use, when the procedure is executed with the WITH RECOMPILE option, when an index is dropped, when the procedure is no longer in the procedure cache, or when the procedure is dropped and re-created.

Q **Should I use exact data types when creating memory variables within a stored procedures?**

A To decrease the overhead of data conversion when using input parameters within a stored procedure on a WHERE clause, make sure that the data type of the input parameter matches the column data type. The exception to this rule is a char data type column with N characters that allows NULL values. SQL Server treats this as a VARCHAR.

Q **What is a remote stored procedure?**

A A remote stored procedure is a stored procedure that is executed on a SQL Server different from your local SQL Server.

Q **Can users access tables within a stored procedure when they do not have permissions to the tables referenced within the stored procedure?**

A A user can execute a stored procedure that accesses tables, views, or other stored procedures to which the user does not have access. The owner of the stored procedure needs the proper access rights to objects used in the procedure. The stored procedure owner then grants to other users the only command permission a stored procedure has: EXECUTE.

Q How can I time how long a stored procedure takes to execute?

A To time the stored procedure and display the start and end times in hh:mm:ss:ms format, use the functions getdate() and convert as follows:

```
select convert(varchar(20), getdate(), 14) 'Start Time'
exec Procedure_name
select convert(varchar(20), getdate(), 14) 'End Time'
```

For a stored procedure that returns several rows of data, you can use the following timing routine, which displays both the start and end times at the end of the stored procedure:

```
declare @startmsg varchar(40)
declare @endmsg varchar(40)

select @startmsg = 'Start Time: ' + convert(varchar(20), getdate(), 14)
/* Execute stored procedure */
exec Procedure_name
select @endmsg = 'End Time:   ' + convert(varchar(20), getdate(), 14)


print @startmsg
print @endmsg
```

Q How can I troubleshoot complex SQL statements within a stored procedure?

A Use the Microsoft SQL Server Query Analyzer tool and break the stored procedure into parts, testing each part of the stored procedure and validating the results of each part. For example, you can determine whether your WHERE clause is correct by changing the SQL statement into SELECT count(*). You can quickly run the complex SQL statement and determine by the row count whether the WHERE clause is correct. The following example shows how to replace an UPDATE statement with SELECT count(*) to validate the WHERE clause. Here's the original code fragment:

```
UPDATE table_a
Set my_name = table_b.old_name
FROM table_a, table_b
WHERE table_a.id = table_b.id
AND table_a.birth_date IN (Select *
                           From table_c)
```

To test the WHERE clause, change the UPDATE statement to SELECT count(*) as follows:

```
Select count(*)
FROM table_a, table_b
WHERE table_a.id = table_b.id
AND table_a.birth_date IN (Select *
                                From table_c)
```

Q How can I subtract a date within a stored procedure?

A To subtract a date, use the dateadd() function with a negative number. The following example subtracts 10 days from the current day's date:

```
select dateadd(day,-10,getdate())
```

Q How can I display the error messages associated with an error number?

A Use the master..sysmessages table. The following stored procedure takes an error number as an input parameter and returns the severity and the description of the error number from the sysmessages table. (Blanks are returned for error numbers that do not exist in sysmessages.)

```
create procedure usp_Show_Error_Message @error_number int
as
Select severity "Error Severity", description "Error Message"
from master..sysmessages
where error = @error_number
```

Q How can I reduce network traffic when using stored procedures?

A You can reduce the amount of extraneous information sent back by a stored procedure (for example, the message N rows affected) by placing the following statement at the top of your stored procedure:

```
SET NOCOUNT ON
```

When you use the SET NOCOUNT ON statement, you limit the amount of extraneous information sent back to the calling process, thus reducing network traffic and increasing performance. The following example, created in the pubs database, shows how to use the statement in a stored procedure:

```
Create procedure usp_nocount
as
SET NOCOUNT ON
Select * from authors
```

Q When should I use a cursor?

A A cursor should be used when you need to perform row-oriented operations. Whenever possible, use SQL statements instead of cursors to perform an operation because cursors might require server resources such as memory and locks. Additionally, SQL statements usually run faster than cursors. However, certain types of operations can not be performed using standard SQL statements. When these types of situations arise, use cursors.

Q Should I use CLOSE or DEALLOCATE when I am done using a cursor?

A If you are not planning on reusing the cursor, you should use DEALLOCATE. This command releases all server resources used by the cursor. If you plan to reuse the cursor, use CLOSE. When you are done with the cursor, use DEALLOCATE.

Summary

As a DBA, it is important that you understand how you can use stored procedures and cursors to simplify your daily and weekly routines. If you understand what you can and cannot do with stored procedures and cursors, you can be of great benefit to your organization. Following are some important points to remember about SQL Server stored procedures:

- A stored procedure is a series of precompiled SQL statements and control-of-flow language statements.

- Stored procedures are stored on SQL Server and execute on SQL Server.

- A remote stored procedure is a stored procedure that is executed on a SQL Server different from your local SQL Server.

- Stored procedures can have input and output parameters.

- The only user command permission that can be granted or revoked for a stored procedure is the EXECUTE permission.

- When creating stored procedures, use lots of comments and headers to simplify future maintenance.

Following are some important points to remember about cursors:

- Use a cursor to perform row-oriented operations on a set of data.

- SQL Server's cursors enable you to navigate forward and backward through a resultset.

- Use the EXEC command inside a cursor to construct SQL statements at runtime.

PART XI

Advanced DBA Topics

IN THIS PART

23 SQL Server 2000 and the Internet

24 Monitoring SQL Server

25 SQL Mail

26 Using SQL-DMO

23

SQL Server 2000 and the Internet

by Kari A. Fernandez

IN THIS CHAPTER

- SQL Server 2000 Web Publishing

- SQL Server 2000 and Managing Web Assistant Jobs

- Advanced Template File Example

- XML Integration

- Retrieving XML Data

- Updating Information via XML

- SQL Server and the Web FAQ

The use of the Web to provide business solutions has exploded over the past several years and Web users have begun demanding more from those of us who provide them with information. Clients want up-to-date information fast. Companies can distribute data to the Web in several ways. Critical data can be stored on a Web page or in a database. You can edit static Web pages with new information using HTML-editing tools, such as Microsoft's FrontPage, or create a database-driven solution. A data-centric solution in SQL Server provides you with the ability to create a Web page once and automate its updates.

If you decide to automate your HTML page updates, your challenge is to implement a solution that allows you to publish HTML pages to your Web site with data presented in a scalable and manageable way. In addition, clients must be able to browse the pages quickly.

Speed in browsing is a combination of the capability of the PC requesting the Web page, the speed of the connection to the Web server, and the size of the page. Your Web page generated by the Web Assistant is created with SQL Server data, so further trips to SQL Server are not required: there are no more impediments to speed. In other words, the client doesn't have to connect to SQL Server to ask for data: the results of a query have already been provided to them in a pregenerated static page.

TIP

Graphics slow the load time of an HTML page. Always include the height and width attributes when using the HTML Image tag. The browser will then lay out the page before the images fully load. If you also use the HTML Image tag's Alternate attribute, you can specify an alternate name for the image so that the user can see what is loading.

Scalability is primarily achieved through the noninteractive queries you create and whose schedule you control. Manageability is provided through the Microsoft Management Console.

Figure 23.1 shows SQL Server 2000's model for Web-based client access to its databases. As you can see, from the Web browser, the client can request an HTML page from the Web server. In turn, the HTML page has been previously published from the SQL Server via a schedule and format stipulated by you when you ran the Web Assistant Wizard.

In this chapter, you'll see how SQL Server 2000's implementation of database-driven HTML pages is provided by the use of the all-encompassing Web Assistant Wizard. The Web Assistant Wizard provides an easy-to-use user interface for several SQL Server system and extended stored procedures. The wizard enables you to create queries that run against the SQL Server 2000 database to push data to your Web site in the form of static HTML pages. You can choose how often the Web client sees the changes in the SQL Server 2000 data by specifying how often the HTML pages are updated.

Use the SQL Server Agent if you need to manage any existing Web Assistant jobs that are scheduled to run once, or at specified intervals to update the Web page. If the Web page is updated when the SQL Server data changes, update the table's trigger directly.

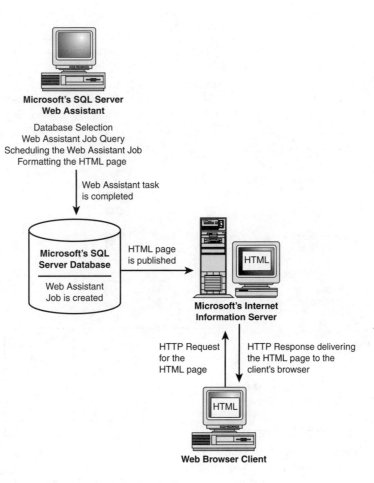

FIGURE 23.1   SQL Server 2000 and the Web.

SQL Server 2000 Web Publishing

SQL Server 2000 Web Publishing is automatically installed with Microsoft's SQL Server 2000. Knowledge of Web technologies is not necessary, although some knowledge of Transact-SQL helps. As shown in Figure 23.2, it also affords you the ability to manage existing Web Assistant Jobs easily.

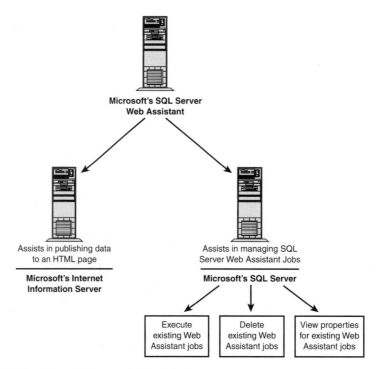

FIGURE 23.2   The SQL Server 2000 Web Assistant.

Using the Web Assistant

After opening the Enterprise Manager, you can start a Web Assistant job by selecting the Tools toolbar option and selecting Wizards from the submenu. You will find the Web Assistant Wizard under the Management category (see Figure 23.3).

The Web Assistant Wizard steps you through the process that creates a Web Assistant job. This wizard incorporates powerful scheduling options that will push data from a SQL Server 2000 database to a standard HTML page, or a predefined template file. You can decide what data is published, how often it's published, where it's published, and how it looks when it's published.

HTML pages are generated by using Transact-SQL queries, stored procedures, and extended stored procedures. You can generate an HTML page on a one-time basis, as a regularly scheduled SQL Server 2000 task, or as a result of a trigger whenever applicable data changes. If you don't have a predefined template file, the Web Assistant will create the HTML page for you after a few simple formatting questions. You can decide to return all or some of the rows from your query, as well as how many rows per page. Optionally, if you specify a template file, any directory, network, FTP, or HTTP path that is accessible from the SQL Server 2000 can be used.

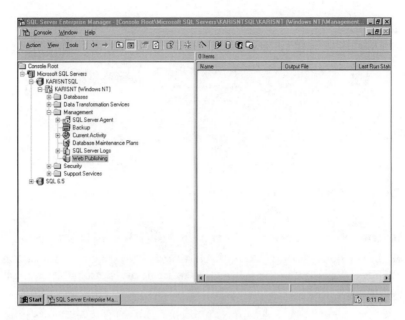

FIGURE 23.3   SQL Server 2000 Web publishing.

Web Assistant Jobs

There are four ways to execute Web Publishing jobs to create an HTML page. The first is choosing to execute the Web Assistant only once. With this option, the job can't be re-run; however, you can re-create it by saving the SQL script (an option at the end of the SQL Web Assistant Wizard) and then running it when you need to.

The second option is to run the Web Assistant on demand. With this selection, you can only re-run the job by manually re-running the stored procedure sp_runwebtask with the appropriate parameter. This selection creates a stored procedure that is executed when you run a command statement such as EXECUTE sp_runwebtask @outputfile = N'E:\DBA Survival Guide\HTML\ OnDemand.htm'.

The third option is to schedule a job to run the Web task, either only once or at schedule intervals. In this case you can re-run the Web Assistant job at any time by navigating to the Management node in the MMC and select SQL Server Agent. You will find an option called Jobs, which will be the home for all your scheduled Web Assistant job. By selecting your job, you can edit properties about the job (see Figure 23.4), or stop, start, disable, or delete the job.

Finally, you can select to update your HTML pages whenever the SQL Server data changes. You can manage this option by simply changing the SQL Server data or by updating, deleting, or running the table triggers (UPDATE, ADD, and DELETE triggers are created).

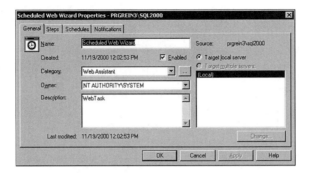

FIGURE 23.4   The SQL Server 2000 Web Assistant Job Properties screen.

Using the Web Assistant Wizard to Publish an HTML Page

You might be asking, "Where did the Web Assistant Wizard go?" It is not gone; it is better! Follow the steps later in this section to create and automatically update an HTML page you specify!

But first, because the Web Assistant is an interface for SQL Server 2000's system procedure sp_makewebtask, the name and description of the arguments will be described as each step is discussed.

This code is included to help you interpret the Web Assistant Job parameters after you create the Web task. If what you want to accomplish exceeds the capability of the wizard, you can create or edit the scripts yourself.

```
sp_makewebtask {[@outputfile =] 'outputfile'} [, [@query =] 'query']
    [, [@fixedfont =] fixedfont] [, [@bold =] bold] [, [@italic =] italic]
    [, [@colheaders =] colheaders] [, [@lastupdated =] lastupdated]
    [, [@HTMLHeader =] HTMLHeader] [, [@username =] username]
    [, [@dbname =] dbname] [, [@templatefile =] 'templatefile']
    [, [@webpagetitle =] 'webpagetitle'] [, [@resultstitle =] 'resultstitle']
    [[, [@URL =] 'URL', [@reftext =] 'reftext']
    | [, [@table_urls =] table_urls, [@url_query =] 'url_query']]
    [, [@whentype =] whentype] [, [@targetdate =] targetdate]
    [, [@targettime =] targettime] [, [@dayflags =] dayflags]
    [, [@numunits =] numunits] [, [@unittype =] unittype]
    [, [@procname =] procname ] [, [@maketask =] maketask]
    [, [@rowcnt =] rowcnt] [, [@tabborder =] tabborder]
    [, [@singlerow =] singlerow] [, [@blobfmt =] blobfmt]
    [, [@nrowsperpage =] n] [, [@datachg =] table_column_list]
```

TIP

Before using SQL Server 2000's Web Assistant Wizard, make sure that all the SQL Server 2000 databases, tables, stored procedures, and template files that you want to reference have been created. Additionally, all Windows 95 Web Assistant users must have SQL Server user accounts in the database used.

Step 1: Start SQL Server 2000's Web Assistant Wizard

From the Enterprise Manager, start the Web Assistant Wizard (refer to Figure 23.3):

- Choose the Tools toolbar option and from the submenu, select Wizards. All the wizards available in SQL Server are displayed by category. You will find the Web Assistant Wizard under the Management category.

- Choose the Wand icon in the toolbar to display all the available wizards by category. You will find the Web Assistant Wizard under the Management category.

Step 2: Select the Database

After the Web Assistant introductory screen (see Figure 23.5), select the database containing the data that you want to publish to an HTML page (see Figure 23.6).

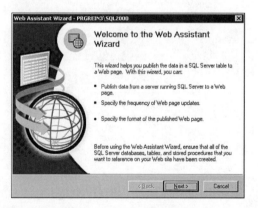

FIGURE 23.5   The Web Assistant introductory screen.

@dbname is a varchar, can be 1 to 128 characters in length, and defaults to the name of the current database.

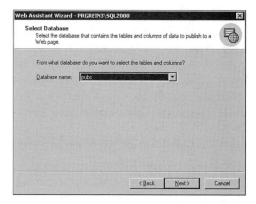

FIGURE 23.6   Selecting a database with the SQL Server 2000 Web Assistant Wizard.

Step 3: Start the New Web Assistant Job

After selecting the database, you start a New Web Assistant job (see Figure 23.7). Specify the name of the Web Assistant job and how the resultset that is published to the HTML page will be generated.

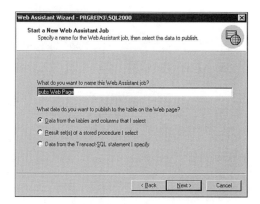

FIGURE 23.7   The Starting a New Web Assistant Job dialog box.

- @procname—is a unique varchar and can be of 1 to 128 characters in length and defaults to the name of the database and 'Web Page'. Anything over 128 characters is truncated. This name is assigned to the following:

  Stored procedures created in the database specified by the Web Assistant user (if you choose data from tables and columns or data from a SQL statement).

  SQL Server Agent jobs created when a scheduled task is used to update the HTML page.

- @query—is text with no default. This argument specifies the query to be run. If you choose data from tables and columns or data from a SQL statement, the Web Assistant builds the Transact-SQL for you. If you specify a stored procedure, an execute statement is built, including any parameters that are required for the stored procedure.

To build the query, choose from the following options:

- **Data from the Tables and Columns that I Select**—Selecting this option leads you through two additional screens. The first screen (see Figure 23.8) asks you to select the table and columns you want to publish. The next screen (see Figure 23.9) asks you to select the rows you want to publish. The default option is to select all the rows of data from the table. However, you can also select columns with certain criteria, or you can write the Transact-SQL statement yourself. With this option, you can only work with one table or view.

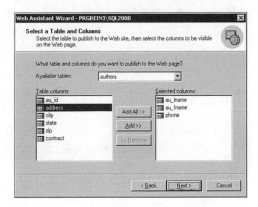

FIGURE 23.8 Selecting a table and one or all of its columns to use as the data source for the HTML page with the Web Assistant.

- **Resultset(s) of a Stored Procedure that I Select**—This option enables you to publish data based on the information returned from a stored procedure. Choose the stored procedure (see Figure 23.10) and if there are parameters necessary, the Web Assistant leads you through one additional screen (see Figure 23.11) where you specify the values for the parameter(s). With this option, multiple SELECT statements in the stored procedure result in multiple HTML tables being displayed in the output file.

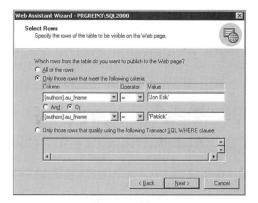

FIGURE 23.9 Selecting the rows from the table to be displayed on the HTML page with the Web Assistant.

FIGURE 23.10 Selecting the stored procedure to use as the data source for the HTML page with the Web Assistant.

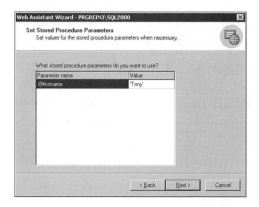

FIGURE 23.11 Specifying a stored procedure's argument(s) with the Web Assistant.

- **Data from the SQL Statement that I Specify**—This option enables you to manually enter a Transact-SQL statement as the data source for your HTML page (see Figure 23.12). Any valid SELECT statement can be used with the following clauses: FROM, WHERE, GROUP BY, HAVING, ORDER BY. With this option, multiple SELECT statements result in multiple tables being displayed in the output file.

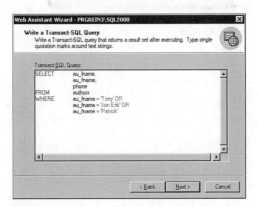

FIGURE 23.12   Entering the Transact-SQL statement to use as the data source for the HTML page with the Web Assistant.

Step 4: Schedule the Web Assistant Job

This option (see Figure 23.13) enables you to specify how often the Web page is updated. You can also choose whether to generate the HTML page just now, now and later, or just later. If you choose to generate the HTML page later, the page is created, but no data is published to the page.

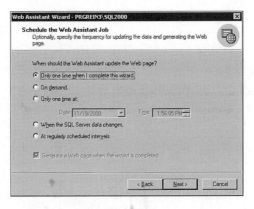

FIGURE 23.13   Scheduling the Web Assistant job.

> **CAUTION**
>
> The SQL Server Agent must be running when a Web Assistant job is scheduled to run periodically. Otherwise, generation of the HTML page will not occur.

@whentype is a tinyint and can have values of 1 to 10. The default setting is 1.

Table 23.1 shows the @whentype arguments and values.

TABLE 23.1 @whentype Argument Values of the System Procedure sp_makewebtask

When the Web Task Is Run	HTML Page Initially Created and Never Updated	HTML Page Not Initially Created and Updated Periodically	HTML Page Initially Created and Updated Periodically
After the completion of the Web Assistant Wizard	1		
On demand		5	9
Only once, on a specified date, at a specified time		2	6
When SQL Server 2000 data changes			10
On a specified day of the week		3	7
Every week, day, hour, or minute, as specified		4	8

You can select one of the following options to schedule a Web Assistant Job:

- **Only Once When I Complete the Wizard**—If you choose this option (@whentype=1), the Web task is executed immediately.

- **On Demand**—This option specifies that the HTML page is created only on request. So, the system procedure for creating the HTML page (sp_makewebtask) is created without automatic scheduling. If you choose not to generate an initial HTML page, you must later run the sp_runwebtask system procedure to create and update the HTML page (@whentype=5); otherwise an HTML will initially be created (@whentype=9). The Web task will run only when a developer executes the sp_runwebtask system procedure and it will only be deleted when a developer executes the sp_dropwebtask system procedure.

CAUTION

When running under Windows 95, an on-demand Web task can be run only by the Web task owner or the system administrator (SA).

- **Only Once, at the Following Time**—The system procedure for creating the HTML page (sp_makewebtask) is created immediately and execution of the Web task is performed as the date and time specify. If you choose not to generate an initial HTML page (@whentype=2), no page is created until the targeted date and time; otherwise an HTML page will initially be created (@whentype=6) and re-created at the targeted date and time. This Web task will be deleted automatically when the targeted date and time has passed.

  - @targetdate is required and defaults to the current date.

  - @targettime is optional and defaults to 12:00 a.m.

- **When the SQL Server 2000 Data Changes**—The system procedure for creating the HTML page (sp_makewebtask) is created immediately, and execution of the Web task is performed immediately and whenever the data in the table changes (@whentype=10). When the data changes, either the INSERT, UPDATE, or DELETE triggers are fired, which in turn runs the sp_runwebtask system procedure, which updates the HTML page. This option leads you through an additional screen (see Figure 23.14) that asks you which tables and columns (one to all) you want to monitor for changes.

  - @datachg is a required text parameter when @whentype = 10. Its value is the table and optional column names that trigger the re-creation of the HTML page when the data changes.

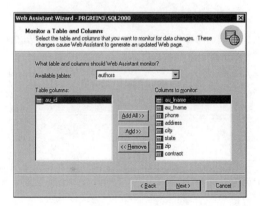

FIGURE 23.14   Specifying the tables and column(s) to monitor for changes with the Web Assistant.

CAUTION

If there are preexisting triggers on the table, the reference to the sp_runwebtask system procedure is added to the end of the trigger if that trigger was not created with WITH ENCRYPTION and the COLUMN field specification in this parameter is ignored. If there is a previously existing trigger on the table created with the WITH ENCRYPTION option, sp_makewebtask system procedure reference fails.

- **At Regularly Scheduled Intervals**—The system procedure for creating the HTML page (sp_makewebtask) is created immediately and execution of the Web task is performed periodically beginning when the date and time specify. This Web task will not be deleted automatically but runs until it is deleted with the sp_dropwebtask system procedure. This option leads you through an additional screen (see Figure 23.15) that asks when you want the page created. You can specify that the page be created periodically or on certain days of the week. You can also specify the start day and time of the HTML page creation.

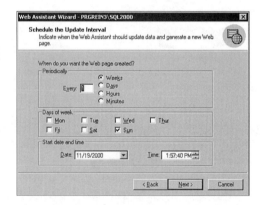

FIGURE 23.15   Scheduling the HTML page update interval with the Web Assistant.

- **Periodically**—You can specify that the HTML page is updated every week, day, hour, or minute (@unittype) at intervals (@numunits) you determine (@whentype = 4 or 8).

- @numunits—is a varchar whose values can have a length from 1 to 255 and will default to 1.

- @unittype—is a tinyint and will default to 1. A unit is either hours, days, weeks, or minutes. The values are defined in Table 23.2.

TABLE 23.2   The @unittype Argument Values for the sp_makewebtask Procedure

Unit	Value
Weeks (default)	1
Days	2
Hours	3
Minutes	4

- **Days of the Week**—You can specify that the HTML page is updated only on certain days of the week (@whentype = 3 or 7).

- @dayflags—is a tinyint that specifies which days to update the HTML page. To specify certain days, use Table 23.3 and add the values together. For example to specify Tuesday and Thursday, use @dayflags = 20.

TABLE 23.3   The @dayflags Argument Values of the System Procedure *sp_makewebtask*

Day of Week	Value
Sunday (default)	1
Monday	2
Tuesday	4
Wednesday	8
Thursday	16
Friday	32
Saturday	64

Step 5: Publish the Web Page

This option (see Figure 23.16) enables you to specify a filename for the HTML page created. You can specify a physical directory, network directory, and the HTTP or FTP path accessible from SQL Server 2000.

@outputfile is a varchar and can have a length from 1 to 255 with a default of WebPage1.htm. This is the location of the generated HTML page on the computer running SQL Server 2000.

> **TIP**
>
> The SQL Server 2000 account must have privileges to write the generated HTML document to the specified location.

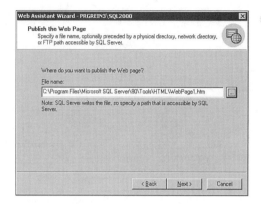

FIGURE 23.16   Publishing the HTML page with the Web Assistant.

Step 6: Format the Web Page

This option (see Figure 23.17) enables you to ask the Web Assistant to help you format an HTML page, or specify that you are using a template file. Using a template file gives you greater flexibility in the appearance of the HTML page. For example, stylesheets and additional graphics can be used on the HTML page to improve its appearance. The advanced HTML example at the end of the chapter uses a template file.

If you choose to specify a template file, the following argument is used and Steps 7, 8, and 9 will be skipped:

@templatefile is a varchar and can have a length from 1 to 255 with no default. This is the location of the template file used to generate the HTML page. The template file is used instead of HTML-type arguments that would have been found in the sp_makewebtask system procedure. Specifically, if a template file is used, the following arguments are ignored: @bold, @Colheaders, @fixfont, @HTMLHeader, @italic, @URL, lastupdated, @reftext, @singlerow, @tabborder, @table_urls, @url_query, and @webpagetitle. An example of the use of a template file is found later in this chapter.

Step 7: Specify Titles

This option (see Figure 23.18) is used when you've asked the Web Assistant for help formatting an HTML page. It enables you to enter the title of the HTML page, the header for the HTML table on the page, and specify the page size, as well as whether there is a time and date stamp on the HTML page.

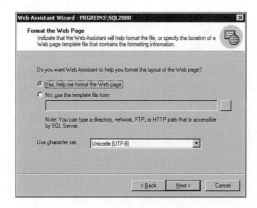

FIGURE 23.17   Formatting the HTML page with the Web Assistant.

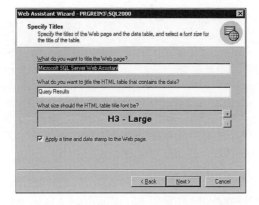

FIGURE 23.18   Specifying titles for the HTML page with the Web Assistant.

These parameters are used when you may enter titles for the HTML page generated by your Web Assistant Job:

- @webpagetitle is a varchar and can have a length from 1 to 255 with a default of Microsoft's SQL Server 2000 Web Assistant. This is the title displayed on the HTML page.

TIP

For a blank title, you can enter two spaces for the title. Another way you can change the title of the HTML page is to delete anything between the <TITLE></TITLE> HTML tags in the HTML page after it's created.

- @resultstitle is a varchar and can have a length from 1 to 255 with a default of Query Results. This is the title displayed above the results table on the HTML page.

- @HTMLHeader is a tinyint and can have values of 1 to 6 with a default of 3. This is the font of the header row in the results table. The values are defined in Table 23.4.

TABLE 23.4   @HTMLHeader Argument Values for the *sp_makewebtask* System Procedure

Value	HTML Tag
1	H1
2	H2
3 (default)	H3
4	H4
5	H5
6	H6

- @lastupdated is a tinyint and can have values of 1 or 0 with a default of 1. This argument specifies whether the HTML page will display a Last Updated: timestamp indicating the last updated date and time. The timestamp appears one line before the results table in the HTML page. The arguments are defined in Table 23.5.

TABLE 23.5   @lastupdated Argument Values for sp_makewebtask System Procedure

Value	Definition
0	No timestamp
1 (default)	The last updated date and time

Step 8: Format a Table

This option (see Figure 23.19) is used when you've asked the Web Assistant for help formatting an HTML page. It enables you to indicate how you want your results table to appear on the HTML page. You can choose to display the column names in the header row or display only the data. You also can determine whether to put borders on the results table and specify whether the font is fixed or proportional, and bold or italic.

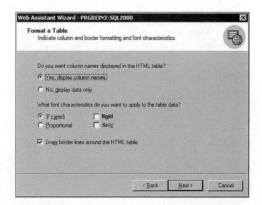

FIGURE 23.19   Formatting an HTML table with the Web Assistant.

These parameters are used when you format an HTML table for the HTML page generated by your Web Assistant Job:

- @colheader is a tinyint and can have values of 1 or 0 with a default of 1 (display column names). This argument specifies whether the HTML page will display an HTML table column header row that shows the SQL table column name.

- @fixedfont is a tinyint and can have values of 1 or 0 with a default of 1 (fixed font). This argument specifies whether the HTML table uses a default font that's a fixed or proportional font.

- @bold is a tinyint and can have values of 1 or 0 with a default of 0 (nonbold font). This argument specifies whether the HTML table will use a default font that's bold or nonbold.

- @italic is a tinyint and can have values of 1 or 0 with a default of 0 (nonitalic font). This argument specifies whether the HTML table will use a default font that's italic or nonitalic.

- @tabborder is a tinyint and can have values of 1 or 0 with a default of 0 (with a table border). This argument specifies whether the HTML table will have a border.

Step 9: Add Hyperlinks to the Web Page
This option (see Figure 23.20) is used when you've asked the Web Assistant for help formatting an HTML page. It enables you to indicate whether you'd like to add some hyperlinks, a Hypertext Transfer Protocol (HTTP) address of another HTML page or Web site, to your HTML page. You can specify one hyperlink to be displayed on your HTML page or type in a Transact-SQL statement to query a table where you've stored hyperlinks.

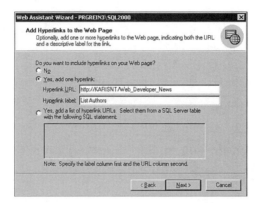

FIGURE 23.20   Adding hyperlinks to the HTML page with the Web Assistant.

These parameters are used when you add hyperlink(s) to the HTML page generated by your Web Assistant Job:

- @URL is a varchar and can have a length from 1 to 255 with no default. This argument specifies the destination of the hyperlink.

- @reftext is a varchar and can have a length from 1 to 255 with no default. This argument specifies the label for the hyperlink.

NOTE

If @URL is specified, you must also enter a label for the hyperlink. Additionally, if @URL is specified, @table_urls and @url_query must not be specified.

- @table_urls is a tinyint and can have values of 1 or 0 and has a default of 0. This argument specifies whether the hyperlink(s) displayed on the HTML page are derived from a SELECT statement executed on a SQL Server 2000 table.

- @url_query is a varchar and can have a length from 1 to 255 with no default. This argument contains the SELECT statement to create the hyperlink's destination and its label. This argument must return a resultset containing two columns. The first column is the address of a hyperlink, and the second column describes the hyperlink.

NOTE

If @table_urls = 1, @url_query must be specified. Also, if @table_urls = 1, @URL and @reftext must not be specified.

Step 10: Limit Rows

This option (see Figure 23.21) enables you to indicate whether you want to limit the total number of rows returned by SQL Server 2000. You also specify how those rows will be displayed (as one row per page or multiple rows per page).

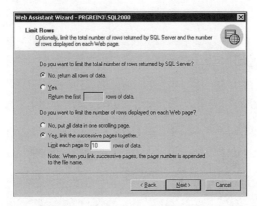

FIGURE 23.21   Limiting the number of rows in the resultset and how the rows are displayed with the Web Assistant.

These parameters are used when you limit the number of rows in the resultset that appears on the HTML page generated by your Web Assistant Job:

- @rowcnt is an int with a default of 0 (all rows). This specifies the maximum number of rows to be returned from SQL Server 2000.

- @singlerow is a tinyint and can have a value of 1 or 0 and has a default of 0 (all data on one scrolling page). With a value of 0, the resultset is displayed on one page, in one HTML table. With a value of 1, a new HTML page will be generated for every qualifying row in the resultset. Successive HTML pages are generated with a number appended to the specified output filename. When @singlerow = 1, @nrowsperpage must not be specified.

- @nrowsperpage is an int with a default of 0. With a value of 0, all results are displayed on one scrolling page. Otherwise, this argument specifies that the resultset should be displayed in multiple pages of n rows on each one. The successive pages will be linked with NEXT and PREVIOUS URLs.

Step 11: Completing the Web Assistant Wizard

This display (see Figure 23.22) shows some general information about the Web task created fby the Web Assistant Wizard. It shows the location and name of the output file, the query that generates the output file, the database the query will be run against, and the location and name of the template file, if one was specified.

You can also choose to write the Transact-SQL statement to a file for reference. This statement shows the execution of the sp_makewebtask system procedure and its arguments' values.

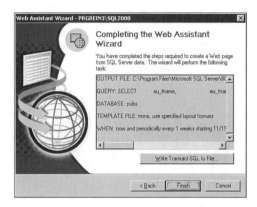

FIGURE 23.22   Completing the Web Assistant Wizard.

That's all there is to it (see Figure 23.23)! For a more in-depth look at how it all works behind the scenes, continue to the next section.

FIGURE 23.23   Finishing the Web Assistant Wizard.

Using the Web Assistant Wizard to Publish Data to a Web Page

The SQL Server 2000 Web Assistant provides a tremendous amount of automation through a graphical interface that's simple to use. However, to fully implement a Web-based solution with SQL Server 2000, you must understand how the Web Assistant automatically creates the HTML page. Here's a list and display (see Figure 23.24) of the components used by SQL Server 2000's Web Assistant:

Stored procedures	System procedures
SQL Server agent	HTML page
Triggers	

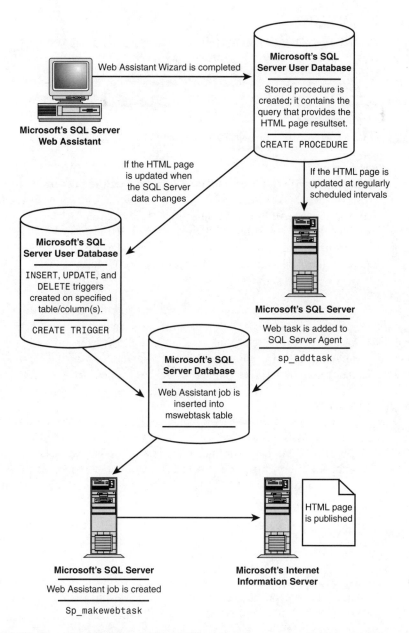

FIGURE 23.24 How the Web Assistant Wizard works.

Stored Procedures

When you start a new Web Assistant job (refer to Figure 23.5), if you choose to publish data from tables, or if you enter a Transact-SQL statement, the Web Assistant creates a stored procedure in the database you specify.

The stored procedure name is derived from the @procname argument to SQL Server 2000's sp_makewebtask system procedure.

Otherwise, the stored procedure you specified will be used.

SQL Server Agent

If you choose to schedule the Web Assistant job once or at regular intervals (refer to Figure 23.13), the SQL Server Web Assistant adds a Web task as a job for the SQL Server Agent to manage. All Web tasks are categorized as Web Assistant in Job Categories in SQL Server Agent jobs. When the scheduled task is run, sp_runwebtask is executed. For more in-depth information about managing SQL Server Agent jobs, see Chapter 6, "Enterprise Management Processes," on scheduling tasks.

Triggers

Triggers are created on the tables you specify when you choose to schedule the Web Assistant job when the SQL Server 2000 data changes (refer to Figure 23.13). The SQL Server Web Assistant creates INSERT, UPDATE, and DELETE triggers on the table and columns you have specified to monitor. When the data changes, the Web task is executed (generating a new HTML page) and the data is updated in one transaction.

System Procedures

Three SQL Server 2000 system procedures are used to manage Web Assistant jobs. The SQL Server Web Assistant Wizard executes sp_makewebtask and always produces an HTML page. This HTML page could display data immediately, or later (refer to Figure 23.13) depending on how you checked the Do Not Generate an Initial HTML Page option. Subsequent updates to the HTML page are achieved by executing sp_runwebtask.

- sp_makewebtask—Creates the Web task that produces an HTML page containing a resultset based on a specified stored procedure (created by the user or the Web Assistant Wizard).

- sp_runwebtask—Executes a previously defined Web task and generates the HTML page. The task to run is identified by the output filename, by the procedure name, or by both parameters.

- sp_deletewebtask—Deletes a previously defined Web task. The task to be deleted is identified by the output filename, by the procedure name, or by both parameters.

HTML Page

The output from the SQL Server Web Assistant Wizard is an HTML page that can be viewed in a user's Web browser. This file is static and doesn't require any further queries of the SQL Server 2000 data. If you need to modify the HTML page layout after the Web Assistant Wizard has created it, simply edit the template file if one was used, or re-run the Web Assistant Wizard if the wizard formatted your HTML page.

SQL Server 2000 and Managing Web Assistant Jobs

Remember, choosing to create your HTML page only once (at a specific time) or at regularly scheduled intervals, creates a scheduled task in SQL Server Agent.

Therefore, if you need to manage any aspect of a scheduled task created by the Web Assistant Wizard, you need to use the functionality of SQL Server Agent. From SQL Server Agent, you have the ability to create a new Web Assistant job, or start, stop, disable, get a history for, refresh, generate Transact-SQL scripts for, and delete or edit the properties for an existing Web Assistant job. For more in-depth information about managing SQL Server Agent jobs, see Chapter 12 on scheduling tasks.

Conversely, choosing to create your HTML page when the SQL Server data changes creates INSERT, UPDATE, and DELETE triggers on the table you selected. Therefore, if you need to manage any aspect of a trigger created by the Web Assistant Wizard, select Manage Triggers from the Tasks menu option after right-clicking the table you selected in the Web Assistant Wizard.

Advanced Template File Example

As previously suggested when reviewing the steps of publishing an HTML page with SQL Server 2000's Web Assistant Wizard, you can also specify a template file to use as a building block for the final HTML page. In other words, rather than publish directly to an HTML page that the SQL Server Web Assistant formats (with some direction from you), you can create a template file to be used as a model or shell for the HTML page.

This is useful because although the SQL Server Web Assistant Wizard gives you several formatting options for your HTML page, often you'll want more control over the way the HTML page appears. You might have a standard company user interface that you need to incorporate, such as a stylesheet or specific graphics you might be required to use on some pages. You might also want to try to spice up some of your Web pages with Dynamic HTML. Therefore, if you want the output of your Web Assistant job to be in anything other than an HTML table, you should use a template.

The example (see Figure 23.25) shows a Web application that can be used by Web developers to share information on standards they should be using when developing Web applications for their company. It's an intranet application, which is designed not to constrain creativity, but to ensure that Web developers create consistent Web pages (in format, flow, functionality, and look and feel), within the confines of the standards created. As shown, references that could be created include the documentation on user-interface standards. These standards could include such things as a list of stylesheets and their properties, a list of fonts and their attributes and when they should used, or a list of common graphics and how they should be used.

Developer's standards could include standards for Web page headers, the order the page is built, standards for the use of VBScript, JavaScript, Java applets, CGI script, DHTML, and so on. Internal Software Support could list the software supported by your operations department and contact numbers, or a list of software that the Web developers recommend for use as development tools and a description of their best use. Technical articles can be used as a way for Web developers to share information such as a great solution to a problem that might benefit others! If a Web developer has published a JavaScript function to the common library of functions, this is a great place to announce and describe it.

This section could also be used to give a heads up to other developers about upcoming events or technologies. Developer's resources could list developers and their area of expertise along with their contact information. So, if you needed help on a complex SQL Server stored procedure or help calling a JavaScript function in an HTML page, you would know who to call. Libraries could be used to document the contents of a Web library directory that stores common functions that all Web developers can use. It could list the functions, examples of usage syntax, any input and output parameters, and a general description of the function.

A Web application is a great place to store this documentation, which should be a living document that Web developers change as time passes.

The example shown in Figure 23.25 uses a template file to create a selection list shown in the middle of the Web browser screen. This application is built with two framesets. The first frameset builds the top two rows. When you press a navigation choice, the bottom frameset, which consists of two rows, is built. In this case, the Technical Articles choice was selected. The first row of the bottom frameset shows a selection list and is the HTML page generated from the SQL Server 2000 Web Assistant Wizard in which template file was specified. The selection list shows a list of technical articles the Web developers have published. The list is derived from a table of technical articles that stores the article ID, article title, the article's author, the date the article was posted, and the article itself.

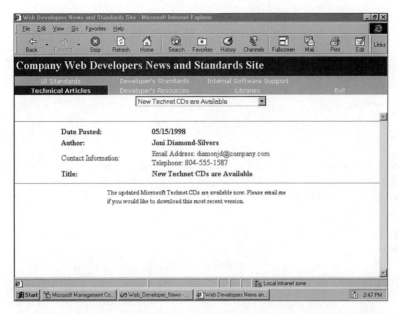

FIGURE 23.25   Example of the use of a template to generate an HTML page.

This discussion refers to the example of running the Web Assistant Wizard shown previously and highlights what you might do differently. The first difference is that in this case, the dev_articles table was chosen (refer to Figure 23.6). Then Data from the tables and columns was selected (refer to Figure 23.7). For the columns that are visible on the Web page (refer to Figure 23.8), two table columns were chosen: the article ID key field, and the article title. You could choose to return all the rows as seen in this example (refer to Figure 23.9), but again you could restrict what is shown on the HTML page by entering your own criteria or choosing a stored procedure.

For the schedule of the Web Assistant job (refer to Figure 23.13), the HTML page will be generated every time the data changes, so that whenever a Web developer posts an article, a new page is generated. This forces UPDATE, DELETE, and INSERT triggers to be created on the dev_articles table. This example shows that all of the table's columns will be monitored (refer to Figure 23.14). Because, in this case, the SQL Server and Web server are physically located together, a file directory path was specified to indicate where to publish the page (refer to Figure 23.16). If they are not located together, you can type any network, FTP, or HTTP path accessible from SQL Server. Another solution is to store the Web pages and template files in a file directory on the SQL Server and to create a virtual reference to this directory on the Web server. That way you can use the virtual reference in your Web site to access the pages. In this case, your Web server needs to have access to the SQL Server network file directory.

When formatting the Web page (refer to Figure 23.17), a template file was indicated. Again, a file directory path was specified to indicate where to get the template file. For this example, the steps that Figures 23.18, 23.19, and 23.20 illustrate were skipped. As in the first example, the rows returned or displayed on the HTML page can be limited. In this example, all rows are returned and all data is placed on one scrolling page.

For your information, Listing 23.1 shows the Web task executed by SQL Server 2000.

LISTING 23.1   Transact-SQL that Creates the Web Task

```
EXECUTE sp_makewebtask
@outputfile = 'C:\InetPub\wwwroot\Web_Developer_News\
➡content\articles\Article_Tech_Choices.htm',
@query='SELECT article_ID, title FROM Dev_Articles',
@templatefile=
'C:\InetPub\wwwroot\Web_Developer_News\ Templates\Article_template.tpl',
@dbname='Web_Developer_News',
@whentype=10,
@datachg='TABLE=Dev_Articles COLUMN=article_ID,title',

@procname=''Web_Developer_News Web Page'
```

Listing 23.2 shows the code for the template file used to generate the HTML page.

LISTING 23.2   Articles Listing Template File

```
'*********************************************************************
'    PROGRAMMER:      Kari Fernandez
'    PAGE NAME:       Article_Template.tpl
'    SITE NAME:       Web Developer's News and Standards Site
'    DESCRIPTION:     Template that builds a drop-down
'                     box of Articles submitted by
'                     Web Developers.
'
'    INPUT Parameters:
'    Name             Description
'-------------------------------------------------------------------
'    OUTPUT Parameters:
'      Name           Description
'-------------------------------------------------------------------
'
```

LISTING 23.2   Continued

```
'    SPECIAL CONSIDERATIONS:          None
'
'    PROCESSING RESTRICTIONS:         None
'
'    PREREQUISTITES:                  None
'
'    INITIATED:
'
'    Modification:
'      Date            Programmer      Description
'      --------        ----------      --------
'      11/2000 (KAF)                   Original Implementation
'
'***********************************************************************
</comment>
<HEAD>
<TITLE>Web Developers and Standards Combo Box Template</TITLE>
<SCRIPT LANGUAGE="JAVASCRIPT">
<!--
function BuildURL(s)
{
// This function allows the user to select a record in the combo box
// which triggers an http request to fill the bottom frame of the
// frameset.

    strSelection = s[s.selectedIndex].value ;
    strURL = "Articles_Tech_About.asp?Record=" + strSelection;

    parent.Content.location.href = strURL;
}
-->
</SCRIPT>
</HEAD>
<BODY>
<TABLE WIDTH = "100%">
<TR>
 <TD ALIGN = "CENTER" VALIGN ="BOTTOM">
  <FORM name = "Articles">
     <select name="Category" ONCLICK="BuildURL(this)">
     <%begindetail%>
        <option value=<%insert_data_here%>><%insert_data_here%></option>
```

LISTING 23.2   Continued

```
        <%enddetail%>
      </select>
  </FORM>
  </TD>
</TR>
</TABLE>
</BODY>
</HTML>
```

The template file shown in Listing 23.2 shows the standard commented header that my company uses. You will see the JavaScript function that builds the hyperlink (URL, uniform resource locator), that is used when the client chooses an option from the selection list. The body of the template file consists of the selection list (HTML SELECT tag) with the click event associated with it. As you can see, to loop through the records returned by SQL Server 2000, you should use the <%begindetail%> <%enddetail%> syntax. To display the data, use the <%insert_data_here%> syntax. When using this syntax, the columns must be returned in the same order they're displayed. In this example, the article ID key field and then the article title are returned. In this way, the value of the key field can be placed in the value attribute of the selection list's option. The article ID is passed to my Active Server Page (ASP) file so that the correct record from the dev_articles table can be retrieved when displaying the content of the article on the ASP page.

Listing 23.3 shows the HTML page generated by SQL Server 2000 using the template file.

LISTING 23.3   Articles Listing HTML Page

```
<HTML>
<comment>
'****************************************************************
'     PROGRAMMER:      Kari Fernandez
'     PAGE NAME:       Article_Template.tpl
'     SITE NAME:       Web Developer's News and Standards Site.
'     DESCRIPTION:     Template that builds a drop-down
'                      box of Articles submitted by
'                      Web Developers.
'
'     INPUT Parameters:
'       Name                    Description
'----------------------------------------------------------------
'     OUTPUT Parameters:
```

LISTING 23.3   Continued

```
'     Name                      Description
'.........................................................................
'
'     SPECIAL CONSIDERATIONS:  None
'
'     PROCESSING RESTRICTIONS: None
'
'     PREREQUISTITES:          None
'
'     INITIATED:
'
'     Modification:
'     Date      Programmer     Description
'     ......    ..........     ...........
'     11/2000   (KAF)          Original Implementation
'
'*************************************************************************
</comment>
<HEAD>
<TITLE>Web Developers and Standards Combo Box Template</TITLE>
<SCRIPT LANGUAGE="JAVASCRIPT">
<!--
function BuildURL(s)
{
//  This function allows the user to select a record in the combo box
//  which triggers an http request to fill the bottom frame of the
//  frameset.
    strSelection = s[s.selectedIndex].value ;
    strURL = "Articles_Tech_About.asp?Record=" + strSelection;

    parent.Content.location.href = strURL;
}
-->
</SCRIPT>
</HEAD>
<BODY>
<TABLE WIDTH = "100%">
<TR>
 <TD ALIGN = "CENTER" VALIGN ="BOTTOM">
  <FORM name = "Articles">
```

LISTING 23.3　Continued

```
    <select name="Category" ONCLICK="BuildURL(this)">

        <option value=1>New Technet CDs are Available</option>

        <option value=2>ADO versus RDO:  This developer's review</option>

        <option value=4>What's ahead with SQL Server 2000</option>

        <option value=5>Check this hyperlink for new software patch</option>

        <option value=6>Registry settings for script timeout periods</option>

        <option value=7>ADO and Connection Pooling</option>

        <option value=8>SQL Server and ActiveX Data Objects</option>

    </select>
  </FORM>
 </TD>
</TR>
</TABLE>
</BODY>
</HTML>
```

In Listing 23.3, everything is the same as the template file, with one exception. Now you can see the actual values of the data returned by SQL Server 2000. Now the value attributes of the selection list options consist of the article ID, and the options displayed are the article titles. When the user clicks on a selection list option, the JavaScript function BuildURL is called. The BuildURL function builds a URL. This URL consists of an ASP page and one query string parameter (Record). Using the JavaScript object model, the location to place the ASP file can be specified. In this example, the ASP page is to be placed in the Content frame of the bottom frameset. To see an example of the article content displayed in the Content frame, refer to Figure 23.25. It shows the date the article was posted, the author, the author's contact information, and the title and content of the article.

Listing 23.4 shows the ASP file code that shows the content of the article. As you can see, a SQL Server stored procedure is called; the article ID is then passed to the stored procedure to find the unique record and its content.

LISTING 23.4   ASP Page That Shows the Article's Content

```
<%@ LANGUAGE="VBSCRIPT" %>
<%OPTION EXPLICIT%>
<!--#include FILE="../../includes/adovbs.inc"-->
<%
'**********************************************************************
'     PROGRAMMER:       Kari Fernandez
'     PAGE NAME:        Articles_Tech_About.asp
'     SITE NAME:        Web Developer's News and Standards Site.
'     DESCRIPTION:      Page that shows the content of the web
'                       developer's technical article.
'
'     INPUT Parameters:
'      Name                   Description
'---------------------------------------------------------------------
'     OUTPUT Parameters:
'      Name                   Description
'---------------------------------------------------------------------
'
'     SPECIAL CONSIDERATIONS:  None
'
'     PROCESSING RESTRICTIONS: None
'
'     PREREQUISTITES:          None
'
'     INITIATED:
'
'     Modification:
'      Date     Programmer    Description
'      ------   ----------    ----------
'      11/2000    (KAF)           Original Implementation
'
'**********************************************************************
'Local Variable Declarations
'**********************************************************************
'Dim connRecord         'ADO Connection
'Dim strDSN             'Connection String
'Dim cmdGetRecord        'ADO Command
'Dim rstMain             'ADO Recordset
'
'**********************************************************************
'Local Variable Initializations
```

LISTING 23.4   Continued

```
'*************************************************************************
'connRecord      = ""
'strDSN          = ""
'cmdGetRecord    = ""
'rstMain     = ""
%>
<HTML>
<HEAD>
<META NAME="GENERATOR" Content="Microsoft Visual InterDev 1.0">
<META HTTP-EQUIV="Content-Type" content="text/html; charset=iso-8859-1">
<TITLE>Web Developers and Standards - Technical Article</TITLE>
</HEAD>
<BODY>

<%

'*************************************************************************
'Using ADO, use the Connection, Command and Recordset objects and call
'   a stored procedure with input and/or output parameters
'*************************************************************************

    'Create the connection object
    Set connRecord = Server.CreateObject("ADODB.Connection")

    'Store the connection string to a local variable
    strDSN = Session("Dev_ConnectionString")
    strDSN = strDSN & "UID=" & Session("Dev_RuntimeUserName") & ";"
    strDSN= strDSN & "PWD=" & Session("Dev_RuntimePassword")

    'Open the connection
    connRecord.ConnectionTimeout = Session("Dev_ConnectionTimeout")
    connRecord.ConnectionString = strDSN
    connRecord.Open

    'Create a ADO Command Object
    Set cmdGetRecord = Server.CreateObject("ADODB.Command")

    'Set the Active Connection
    cmdGetRecord.ActiveConnection = connRecord
```

LISTING 23.4   Continued

```
'************************************************************************
'Set up the Calling Stored Procedure SQL using ODBC syntax for the
'call and parameters.
'************************************************************************

    cmdGetRecord.CommandText = "{call usp_Get_Tech_Article(?)}"

    cmdGetRecord.CommandType = adCmdText
    cmdGetRecord.CommandTimeout = Session("Dev_CommandTimeout")

'Name each parameter and the direction with the following syntax
    cmdGetRecord.Parameters.Append cmdGetRecord.CreateParameter _
        ("ArticleID", adInteger, adParamInput, 4)

    'Set the Input Values
    cmdGetRecord.Parameters("ArticleID") = Request("Record")

    'Create a ADO Recordset Object
    Set rstMain = Server.CreateObject("ADODB.Recordset")

    rstMain.Open cmdGetRecord, , 1, 1

    'If an error was received on open, then allow the application
    'to continue

    On Error Resume Next

    If Err Then
      Session("Message") = "Error retrieving the record: "
      Session("Message") = Session("Message") & Err.Description
      On Error Goto 0
    Else
      If (NOT(rstMain.BOF) And NOT(rstMain.EOF)) Then%>
    <HR>
      <TABLE WIDTH = "75%" topmargin = "0" Align = "Center">
      <TR>
      <TD WIDTH = "25%"><FONT FACE="Times New Roman, Arial"
        SIZE="3"><STRONG>Date Posted:</STRONG></FONT></TD>
      <TD WIDTH = "50%"><FONT FACE="Times New Roman, Arial"
        SIZE="3"><STRONG>
          <%Response.Write rstMain("dateposted")%></STRONG></FONT>
```

LISTING 23.4   Continued

```
</TD>
</TR>
<TR>
<TD WIDTH = "25%"><FONT FACE="Times New Roman, Arial"
  SIZE="3"><STRONG>Author:</STRONG></FONT>
</TD>
<TD WIDTH = "50%"><FONT FACE="Times New Roman, Arial"
  SIZE="3"><STRONG>
    <%Response.Write rstMain("author")%></STRONG></FONT>
</TD>
</TR>
<TR>
<TD WIDTH = "25%"><FONT FACE="Times New Roman, Arial"
 SIZE="3"></STRONG>Contact Information:</FONT></STRONG>
</TD>
<TD WIDTH = "50%"><FONT FACE="Times New Roman, Arial"
  SIZE="3">Email Address:
    <%Response.Write rstMain("email")%></FONT><BR>
  <FONT FACE="Times New Roman, Arial" SIZE="3">
       Telephone:
    <%Response.Write rstMain("phone")%></FONT>
</TD>
</TR>
<TR>
<TD WIDTH = "25%"><FONT FACE="Times New Roman, Arial"
    SIZE="3"><STRONG>Title:</STRONG></FONT>
</TD>
<TD WIDTH = "50%"><FONT FACE="Times New Roman, Arial"
    SIZE="3"><STRONG>
  <%Response.Write rstMain("title")%></STRONG></FONT>
</TD>
</TR>
</TABLE>
<HR>
<TABLE WIDTH = "50%" topmargin = "0" ALIGN = "Center">
<TR>
<TD><FONT FACE="Times New Roman, Arial" SIZE="2">
  <%Response.Write rstMain("content")%></FONT>
</TD>
```

LISTING 23.4   Continued

```
        </TR>
        </TABLE>

    <%Else%>

    <FONT FACE = "Times New Roman, Arial" Size = "3"><STRONG>
        No record was returned...</STRONG></FONT>
    <%End If%>



    <%End If%>
</BODY>
</HTML>
```

For your information, Listing 23.5 is the SQL Server stored procedure used by the ASP page.

LISTING 23.5   SQL Server 2000 Stored Procedure Used by ASP Page

```
/*******************************************************************/
/*                                                               */
/* Description:  Gets the Article with the                       */
/*               matching record number                          */
/* Name:         usp_Get_Tech_Article                            */
/*                                                               */
/*                                                               */
/* Called By:    Articles_Tech_About.asp                         */
/*                                                               */
/*---------------------------------------------------------------*/
/* Tips:                                                         */
/*                                                               */
/*---------------------------------------------------------------*/
/* History:                                                      */
/*---------------------------------------------------------------*/
/* 11/2000  (KAF)   Initial Implementation                       */
/*---------------------------------------------------------------*/
/*******************************************************************/
CREATE PROCEDURE usp_Get_Tech_Article

 @Record int
```

LISTING 23.5   Continued

```
AS

SELECT    CONVERT(varchar(12), A.Dateposted, 101) AS Dateposted,
          A.Title,
          A.Content,
          B.fname + ' ' + B.lname AS author,
          B.Phone,
          B.Email
FROM      Dev_Articles A, Dev_Authors B
WHERE     A.Article_ID = @Record AND
          A.Author_ID *= B.Author_ID
```

XML Integration

Extensible Markup Language (XML) is a hypertext programming language that provides a format which allows you to describe structured data. This creates the ability to precisely declare the contents of the page that can be used for viewing or updating across multiple platforms.

XML's power rests with its ability to separate the user interface from structured data. Using XML, you can define your own, unlimited number of tags that define structured data. So, you can see that by using HTML, you merely use tags to display data in a browser (setting bold and italic options for instance); whereas by using XML, you can associate elements in the XML document with elements in a database. In addition, with XML, you use style sheets such as Extensible Stylesheet Language (XSL) and Cascading Style Sheets (CSS) to show formatted data in a browser.

SQL Server 2000 is the first SQL Server release to provide integrated, native XML support. Several new features have been introduced to provide XML support such as

- The ability to access SQL Server over HTTP through a URL

- The ability to retrieve XML data using the SELECT statement and the FOR XML clause

- Support for XML-Data schemas and the ability to specify XPath queries against these schema

- The ability to write XML data using the OpenXML rowset provider in combination with two new stored procedures; sp_xml_preparedocument and sp_xml_removedocument

The HTTP access to SQL Server allows you to specify SQL queries directly in the URL, specify templates directly in the URL, specify template files in the URL, write XPath queries against the annotated XML-Data Reduced (XDR) schemas (also referred to as mapping schemas), and specify database objects directly in the URL.

The results of SELECT statements can be simply returned as XML documents. The SQL Server 2000 Transact-SQL SELECT statement has a new feature, the FOR XML clause. This clause specifies that the statement results be returned in the form of an XML document instead of a typical relational resultset. If you have complex queries or queries that need to be secured, you can be store the queries as a template in an IIS virtual root.

You can create XML views by annotating XML-Data Reduced (XDR) schemas to map the SQL Server 2000 tables, views, and columns that are associated with the elements of the schema. These XML views can then be referenced in XPath queries. XPath Queries return results from the database as XML documents. Conceptually, writing XPath queries against the mapping schemas is similar to creating views in the database using the CREATE VIEW statement and writing Transact-SQL queries against them.

If you need more than a simple XML document, maybe one that can be used for updating data, you can expose the data from an XML document as a relational rowset using the new OPENXML rowset function. This allows you to use the data in XML documents to add, modify, or delete data in the database tables, including modifying multiple rows in multiple tables in a single operation.

In addition, XML support in this version of SQL Server extends beyond the database engine. XML support in the SQL Server OLE DB provider has been enhanced to allow XML documents to be set as command text and to return XML documents as a text stream. Also, both XPath queries and a new FOR XML extension to the SELECT statement are supported.

Retrieving XML Data

The power of SQL Server 2000's XML support lies in its capability to execute SQL queries that return results as XML rather than standard rowsets.

To retrieve results, you use the FOR XML clause of the SELECT statement, and within the FOR XML clause, you specify an XML mode: RAW, AUTO, or EXPLICIT.

The FOR XML RAW returns a <row> tag for each row in the record set. This should be used in a limited fashion because it doesn't effectively use XML's capabilities for describing structured data. FOR XML AUTO names and structures the data by taking hints to how the tables are aliased and joined. FOR XML EXPLICIT allows you to specify the exact structure and naming scheme of the resulting XML. Additionally, the FOR XML EXPLICIT syntax provides several directives that help consolidate the query and speed its execution.

You can select data from a single table, but most likely you must join data from multiple tables into one XML document. You can map multiple tables in a JOIN to specific attributes or elements in XML document hierarchy. XML's intrinsic hierarchical nature (an XML document contains only one root element with all other elements nested within) makes this easy.

Here is an example of a multiple table JOIN that specifies the AUTO mode in the FOR XML clause:

```
SELECT authors.au_fname, authors.au_lname, titles.title
FROM authors INNER JOIN titleauthor ON authors.au_id = titleauthor.au_id
INNER JOIN titles ON titleauthor.title_id = titles.title_id
ORDER BY authors.au_lname
FOR XML AUTO
```

Using XPath Queries

XPath (XML Path Language) provides a syntax for locating specific elements within an XML document. The XDR schema allows the database to be treated as a giant XML document, and the XPath query merely selects a small piece of this document to return to the user. The schema describes the structure of the XML output and instructions for populating the structure, but not for restricting the query in any way—that is the role of the XPath query.

The XPath query can be specified as part of a URL or within a template. The way the schema is mapped determines the structure of this resulting document fragment, and the values are retrieved from the database.

Remember, an XML document consists of nodes such as an element node, attribute node, text node, and so on. For example, consider this XML document:

```
<root>
  <Authors au_id= "123-45-6789" lname="Bennets" fname="Abraham">
    <Titles tid="12589" au_id= "123-45-6789" title="The Busy Executive" >
    <Titles tid="891011 au_id= "123-45-6789"
      title="The Gourmet Microwave" </Titles>
  </Authors>
  <Authors au_id= "891-11-1234" lname="Carson" fname="Cheryl">
    <Titles tid="12589" au_id= "891-11-1234" title="But is it User Friendly" >
    <Titles tid="891011 au_id= "891-11-1234"
```

```
          title="You can Combat Computer Stress" </Titles>
</Authors>
</root>
```

In this document, Authors is an element node, and au_id is an attribute node.

Because XPath is a graph navigation language, it is used to select a set of nodes from an XML document. Each XPath operator selects a node-set based on a node-set selected by a previous XPath operator. For example, given a set of <Authors> nodes, XPath can select all <Titles> nodes with the title of "The Busy Executive". The resulting node-set contains all the authors with the title of "The Busy Executive".

XPath Queries Against XML-Data Reduced (XDR) Schema

XDR (XML-Data Reduced) schemas are XML documents that provide a powerful syntax for mapping database tables and columns to elements and attributes in the output XML document. The syntax used is provided by the XML Path Language (XPath) to retrieve a specific subset of the information.

To specify an XPath query against an annotated XDR schema, you must create a virtual name of schema type using the IIS Virtual Directory Management for SQL Server utility. The XDR schema specified in the URL must be stored in the directory associated with the virtual name of the schema type or one of its subdirectories.

The XPath query can be directly specified in the URL, as an example:

```
http://IISServer/VirtualRoot/SchemaVirtualName/SchemaFileName.xml/XPathQuery).
```

In this case, the schema file must be stored in the directory associated with the virtual name of schema type.

For example, consider this annotated XDR schema:

```
<?xmlversion="1.0" ?>
<Schema xmlns="urn:schemas-microsoft-com:xml-data"
        xmlns:dt="urn:schemas-microsoft-com:datatypes"
        xmlns:sql="urn:schemas-microsoft-com:xml-sql">

  <ElementType name="Author" sql:relation="Authors" >
    <AttributeType name="au_id" />
    <AttributeType name="au_lname" />
    <AttributeType name="title" />

    <attribute type="au_id" />
    <attribute type="au_lname" />
```

```
    <attribute type="title" />
  </ElementType>
</Schema>
```

For this example, this XDR schema is stored as `authorschema.xml` in the directory associated with the virtual name of schema type.

The following URL executes an XPath query against the XDR schema (`authorschema.xml`) specified in the URL. The XPath query requests all the authors with an au_id of 112-11-1234.

`http://IISServer/pubs/authorschema/authorSchema.xml/Author[@au_id="112-11-1234"]`

This is the result:

`<Author au_id="112-11-1234" au_lname="Bennets" title="The Busy Executive" />`

This document fragment is now ready for use by other documents, or it can be formatted and presented for display.

Updating Information via XML

In the last section, you learned how to use the FOR XML clause to retrieve data as an XML document; now let's see how you can use the Transact-SQL OPENXML function to add, modify, or delete data represented as an XML document. This functionality not only reduces trips to the database, but it also lets you accept input in a number of formats.

You can pass an entire XML hierarchy into a stored procedure as a varchar or text parameter and parse the hierarchy inside SQL Server to add, update, and delete multiple records in multiple tables within one stored procedure call.

OPENXML is a rowset provider similar to a table or a view, providing a rowset over in-memory XML documents. OPENXML allows access to XML data as if it is a relational rowset by providing a rowset view of the internal representation of an XML document. The records in the rowset can be stored in database tables. OPENXML can be used in SELECT and SELECT INTO statements in which a source table or view can be specified.

The following example shows the use of OPENXML in an INSERT statement and a SELECT statement. The sample XML document consists of <Authors> and <Titles> elements.

To write queries using OPENXML, you must create an internal representation of the XML document by calling sp_xml_preparedocument. The stored procedure returns a handle to the internal representation of the XML document. This handle is then passed to OPENXML, which provides rowset views of the document based on XPaths; namely one row pattern and one or more column patterns. (The internal representation of an XML document can be removed from memory by calling the sp_xml_removedocument system stored procedure).

An INSERT statement using OPENXML can insert data from such a rowset into a database table. Several OPENXML calls can be used to provide rowset view of various parts of the XML document and process them, for example, inserting them into different tables (this process is also referred to as "shredding XML into tables").

In the following example, an XML document is shredded in a way that <Authors> elements are stored in the Authors table and <Titles> elements are stored in the Titles table using two INSERT statements:

```
DECLARE @h int
DECLARE @xmldoc varchar(1000)
set @xmldoc =
'<root>
  <Authors au_id= "123-45-6789" lname="Bennets" fname="Abraham">
      <Titles tid="12589" au_id= "123-45-6789" title="The Busy Executive" >
      <Titles tid="891011 au_id= "123-45-6789" title="The Gourmet Microwave"
      </Titles>
  </Authors>
  <Authors au_id= "891-11-1234" lname="Carson" fname="Cheryl">
      <Titles tid="12589" au_id= "891-11-1234" title="But is it User Friendly" >
 <Titles tid="891011 au_id= "891-11-1234" title="You can Combat Computer Stress"
 </Titles>
</Authors>
</root>'

EXEC sp_xml_preparedocument @h OUTPUT, @xmldoc

INSERT INTO authors SELECT * FROM OPENXML(@h,'/root/authors') WITH AUTHORS

INSERT INTO titles SELECT * FROM OPENXML(@h,'/root/authors/titles',0)
WITH TITLES

EXEC sp_xml_removedocument @h
```

SQL Server 2000 provides native support of XML, making it faster with less round trips to the server. With the enhancements, you can now have the ability to access SQL Server over HTTP through a URL and integrate XML into your relational database environment. Other extended capabilities are offered by SQLXML.

SQL Server and the Web FAQ

The following section lists some commonly asked questions and answers about SQL Server 2000 and the Web.

Q What type of permissions does the SQL Server Web Assistant user have to have to create a Web Assistant Job?

A The Web Assistant user must have SELECT permissions on the table columns specified in the query and CREATE PROCEDURE permissions in the database in which the query will run. The account in which SQL Server is running must have CREATE FILE account permissions.

Q What should I enter as the path for the HTML page created by the Web Assistant Wizard?

A You can enter a local directory on the SQL Server, or alternatively you can enter any location that is accessible to the SQL Server via HTTP (Hypertext Transport Protocol), FTP (File Transport Protocol) or a UNC (Uniform Naming Convention) path.

Q How do I know if my Web Assistant jobs are running properly?

A If you created a Web Assistant job that is run periodically, at a certain time, SQL Server Agent is managing that task. Open SQL Server Agent, select your Web Assistant job, and specify an email operator to receive emails on success or failure of that Web Assistant job.

Q Are any errors captured for my Web Assistant jobs?

A You can view the error log in the SQL Server Enterprise Manager.

Summary

Use of SQL Server 2000's Web Assistant provides the novice and expert Web Assistant user with an easy way of publishing data to the Web. You can be an expert SQL Server user with little experience with the Web, or vice versa, and fair equally well when using this tool. The Web Assistant provides you with five different ways to produce your HTML pages along with formatting help if you choose not to use a template file. For HTML page updates on demand, you can re-run script that is created for you at the end of the Web Assistant Wizard (if you've saved it to a file). For HTML page updates on a regularly scheduled basis, you can monitor their success or failure through the SQL Server Agent. For HTML page updates when the SQL Server data changes, you can monitor the table triggers and make changes as required.

In addition to supporting HTML, SQL Server 2000 has introduced support for XML. The first support feature is the ability to access SQL server through HTTP (and a URL). In addition, there are several ways to retrieve and write data. To retrieve data, it's as simple as adding a FOR XML clause to any SELECT statement. Or you can retrieve XML data using the XPath query language. To write data, you can use the OpenXML rowset provider. Finally, enhancements made to the Microsoft SQL Server 2000 OLE DB provider allow XML documents to be set as command text and return resultsets as a stream.

24

Monitoring SQL Server

by Orryn Sledge

IN THIS CHAPTER

- Tools for Monitoring SQL Server
- Monitoring SQL Server FAQ

SQL Server provides several utilities that enable you to easily monitor SQL Server and its interaction with the operating system. These utilities can help a DBA isolate bottlenecks and determine hardware deficiencies.

Tools for Monitoring SQL Server

The following tools are used to monitor SQL Server:

- System Monitor
- SQL Server Enterprise Manager
- SQL Server Profiler

System Monitor

The *System Monitor* is a Windows 2000 tool for monitoring SQL Server and the Windows NT operating system (Windows NT 4.0 has a similar tool named Performance Monitor). The advantage of the System Monitor is that it is tightly integrated with the operating system. This enables you to track real-time statistics about SQL Server and Windows NT. Together, these statistics can be used to isolate bottlenecks and track performance.

> **NOTE**
>
> The System Monitor might slightly degrade system performance on older machines. The overhead incurred from the System Monitor has been found to be 5% or less on single processor machines and insignificant on multiple processor machines.

Using the System Monitor
Perform the following to utilize the System Monitor.

1. Click the Start menu found in Windows 2000.

2. Point to Settings, Control Panel.

3. From the Control Panel, double-click Administrative Tools.

4. From Administrative Tools, double-click Performance. The Performance dialog box appears.

Adding Counters
Follow these steps to add one or more counters to the System Monitor:

1. From the Performance dialog box, click the Add button on the toolbar. The Add Counters dialog box appears.

2. From the Add Counters dialog box, select the object type and counter type. Click the Add button to add the counter to the chart (see Figure 24.1).

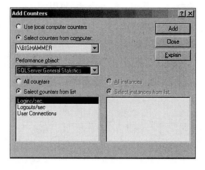

FIGURE 24.1   System Monitor dialog box for adding counters to a chart.

3. Additionally, you might need to choose the appropriate instance of a counter (see Figure 24.2).

4. Click the Close button in the Add Counters dialog box.

TIP

Pressing Ctrl+H highlights the selected counter on the chart. This is useful when the System Monitor is tracking several counters.

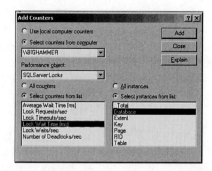

FIGURE 24.2   System Monitor dialog box for adding counters to a chart with instances.

Monitoring Key Areas

The System Monitor can be overwhelming because it provides so much information. You can track over 100 different counters (including instances) for SQL Server 2000 and hundreds of counters for Windows NT. Trying to track this much information can drive you crazy!

Instead of trying to track everything at once, you should monitor the following five key areas:

- Disk I/O

- Processor

- Memory

- User connections

- Network

TIP

One of the first things you should do after opening System Monitor is to adjust the update frequency because by the time one notices a trend, it is overwritten by the next cycle of data. To change the update frequency, click the Properties icon in the Performance toolbar. The System Monitor Properties dialog box appears. From this window, select the General tab and change the Update Automatically Every setting. For example, to slow down the System Monitor, I suggest trying 10–15 seconds instead of every second.

These five key indicators will quickly clue you in to performance bottlenecks. After you determine the general bottleneck source, you should look into the other types of counters not mentioned in this chapter (use the SQL Server Books Online).

Disk I/O   You always want to minimize disk I/O when working with SQL Server.
However, when SQL Server does read and write to the hard disk, you want to ensure
adequate disk performance. If you are not achieving adequate disk I/O, transaction
throughput suffers.

To help detect disk I/O bottlenecks, you should monitor the following two counters:

- PhysicalDisk: % Disk Time

- PhysicalDisk: Current Disk Queue Length (choose the total instance if more
  than one disk is present)

PhysicalDisk: % Disk Time Counter   The PhysicalDisk: % Disk Time counter monitors
the percentage of elapsed time that the disk is busy with read/write activity.

A consistently high value (above 2) might indicate that your disk system is a
bottleneck.

PhysicalDisk: Current Disk Queue Length Counter   The PhysicalDisk: Current Disk Queue Length counter monitors the number of outstanding requests on disk.

Sustained queue lengths greater than 3 might indicate a disk-related bottleneck. Additionally, a consistently high value for one physical disk combined with a consistently low value for your other physical disks indicates that redistributing your data might improve performance. Examine your device and segment configuration.

Processor   SQL Server is CPU intensive. Continuously high utilization rates might indicate that your CPU is the bottleneck. The best way to determine if your CPU is the bottleneck is to use the % Processor Time Counter.

Processor: % Processor Time Counter   The Processor: % Processor Time counter monitors the amount of time the CPU spends processing a thread.

A steady state value above 80–90% indicates that a CPU upgrade or additional processors might improve performance.

> **NOTE**
>
> Processor scalability (the capability to gain performance through additional processors) has continued to improve with SQL Server 2000. When running the Enterprise Editor of SQL Server 2000 on Windows 2000 Datacenter, SQL Server can effectively scale up to 32 processors.

Memory   SQL Server likes memory. It uses memory to hold data and frequently accessed objects. An increase in memory can enable SQL Server to place more data into the memory cache, which can result in better performance.

When diagnosing memory bottlenecks, the following counters are useful to monitor (see "Adding Counters," earlier in this chapter for information on adding counters):

- SQLServer: BufferManager: Buffer Cache Hit Ratio

- Memory: Page Faults/sec

- Paging File: % Usage

- SQLServer: BufferManager: Lazy writes

SQLServer: BufferManager: Buffer Cache Hit Ratio Counter   The SQLServer: BufferManager: Cache Hit Ratio counter monitors the hit rate in which data was found in the data cache. If the data is not in the data cache, the server has to read the data from disk. This counter generally provides an accurate indication of memory allocation that can be used to determine whether you have sufficient memory.

A number consistently less than 85% might indicate that you have insufficient memory. Performance can suffer because SQL Server has to read the data from physical disk. Reading data from the physical disk is an expensive operation. When evaluating this counter, it is important to base it on the type of operation being performed on the machine and the time at which the operation occurs. In a transaction-processing environment, you can probably improve the cache hit ratio by adding more memory. In a batch environment that uses very large databases, the cache hit ratio might never go above 85%. Under this scenario, additional memory might not substantially improve performance.

If there are many stored procedures on your server, the procedure cache counters might be more relevant to you than the data cache counters.

TIP

The default scale choice that System Monitor makes is not always appropriate. It is sometimes necessary to change this because the line is either above 100 or too close to zero to see significant changes. To change this line, select the Properties of the counter and choose a more appropriate vertical scale.

Memory: Page Faults/sec Counter   The Memory: Page Faults/sec counter monitors the number of times an operating system virtual page was not found in memory. When a page is not found in memory, the operating system must retrieve the page from disk. The time it takes to retrieve a page from disk is always longer than the time required to retrieve the page from memory.

After SQL Server has stabilized, this number will usually remain at or near zero. If the number is consistently greater than zero, this indicates that too much memory is allocated to SQL Server and not enough memory is allocated to Windows NT. Therefore, you should reduce the amount of memory allocated to SQL Server.

Paging File: % Usage Counter   The Paging File: % Usage counter monitors the percent of NT's paging file currently in use. If you find that a large percentage of the page file is in use, you might want to increase the size of the paging file to prevent an out-of-virtual-memory error. An alternative to increasing the page file is to add more memory to your server. Doing so will probably reduce page file utilization. With additional memory, you can improve performance because it is always faster to read data from memory than from the paging file.

Another point to consider when analyzing the paging file counter is a growing page file. A growing page file occurs when you specify an initial page file size smaller than the specified maximum size. From the NT operating system perspective, a growing page file is considered an expensive operation. It is better to set your initial page file size the same as your maximum page file size, which eliminates the need for the operating system to grow the page file.

SQLServer:Buffer Manager: Lazy Writes/sec Counter   The SQLServer: Buffer Manager: Lazy Writes/sec counter monitors the number of flushed pages per second by the Lazy Writer.

A number constantly greater than zero indicates that the Lazy Writer is constantly working to flush buffers to disk. This means that the data cache is too small, which might indicate that you have insufficient memory.

User Connections   How many times have you been hit with the following problem? System performance crawls during peak business hours. These are the hours when everyone in the company is banging away on the system. Transactions are being processed at a snail's pace and your phone is ringing off the hook with irate users.

Every DBA, at one time or another, has experienced this problem. It is no secret that as the number of active users increases, the likelihood of performance degradation also increases.

SQLServer: General Statistics: User Connections Counter   The SQLServer: User connections counter monitors the number of active user connections.

Use this counter to help determine when the number of active users exceeds the capabilities of your system.

> **TIP**
>
> The User Connections setting defaults to zero. The zero setting permits the maximum of 32,767 connections. Unless you have a good reason, it is not necessary to adjust this to have a maximum. However, monitoring the number of user connections has merit because it provides a better understanding of server load. For example, when seeing a spike in CPU utilization, is it accompanied by an increase in user connections? The follow-up question is "why?"

Network   When trying to address performance issues, do not forget to inspect the network. The following counter is useful when trying to determine if there are network related issues.

NBT Connection: Bytes Total/sec Counter   The NBT Connection: Bytes Total/sec counter monitors the number of bytes read from and written to the network.

This statistic can help you if you are not using stored procedures currently. Therefore, if you find that this counter is high and your transaction rate is low, you might be able to improve performance by implementing stored procedures. Stored procedures can help reduce the amount of network traffic. If this counter is extremely high for an extended time, you might be able to improve performance by using faster network interface cards (NICs).

User-Defined Counters

The `SQL Server: User Settable Object` enables you to create your own data that can be monitored via the System Monitor.

To create a user-defined counter, pass an integer value to one of the `sp_user_counter%` system procedures. Valid names are `sp_user_counter1` through `sp_user_counter10`.

To track the information, select the `SQLServer:User Settable` object and the corresponding instance name.

The following is an example of a user-defined counter:

```
/*
 simple example showing how to
 pass information to a user-defined counter
*/
declare @somevalue int
select @somevalue = 45


EXECUTE sp_user_counter1 @somevalue
```

If we were to inspect the `SQLServer: User Settable` object and the `User counter 1` instance, we would see the corresponding value (for this example, `45` is the value).

To take this one step further, we could create a job that automatically updates the values tracked by a user-defined counter.

Advanced Use of System Monitor   The data tracked by System Monitor can be saved into a log file for later analysis. Follow the steps for creating a log file and viewing a log file to use this feature.

Perform the following to create a log file:

1. Click the Performance Logs and Alerts section of the treeview.

2. Right-click the Counter Logs folder. From the right-mouse menu, select New Log Settings. Enter a log name and click OK.

3. Add the counters to track (see Figure 24.3). Click the OK button. This will start logging (see Figure 24.4).

4. When you are ready to stop logging, right-click the name of the log file. From the right-mouse menu, select the Stop menu option.

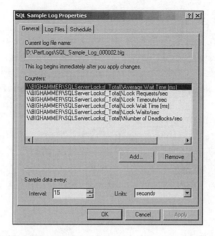

FIGURE 24.3   Adding counters to a log file.

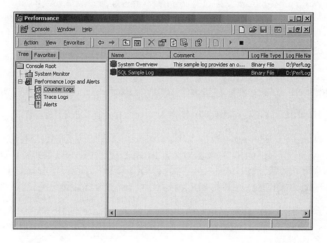

FIGURE 24.4   Counter logs.

Perform the following to view the log file:

1. Click System Monitor section of the treeview.

2. Click the View Log File Data toolbar button. The Select Log File dialog box appears. Select the log filename and click the Open button. This action will load the corresponding counters into the System Monitor.

3. Click the Add toolbar button to select an object from the log file. This enables you to graphically view the data inside the log file.

SQL Server Enterprise Manager

In addition to monitoring SQL Server activity, it might be useful to monitor individual user activity. By using the Current Activity Monitor in the Enterprise Manager, you can view user connections, locks, process numbers, and user commands. With SQL Server Profiler, you can monitor and record SQL activity and other statistics.

The Current Activity Monitor

One of the best features of the Current Activity Monitor is its capability to view more information about a process. This is a major plus for DBAs; it gives you all the information you need to know about a process. You can use this information to help kill a process or to pinpoint a query that is a burden to the system.

> **TIP**
>
> In many cases, you might find it easier simply to use the stored procedures named sp_who and sp_lock. A procedure named sp_who2 is more user friendly than sp_who. Unfortunately, sp_lock2 was removed from SQL 6.5, and it was friendly enough to tell you the name of the object. To know the name of the object in question from the output of sp_lock, you need to execute select object_name([objID]), where objID is the number found in the third column of the output.

Follow these steps to use the Current Activity Monitor:

1. Click the plus (+) sign next to the Management folder.

2. Click the plus (+) sign next to the Current Activity folder. Here you can view three types of information: Process Info, Locks/Process ID (see Figure 24.5), and Locks/Object. From these three types of information, you can view the corresponding detail by double-clicking the corresponding object.

3. When viewing details, you can view the last statement issued by the user, kill a process, and send a message to the user by right-clicking and choosing Properties (see Figure 24.6).

> **TIP**
>
> Be on the lookout for blocking when users are complaining that their transactions are hung. Select the Locks/Process ID in the Current Activity branch to view blocked processes. Another quick way of finding this information is to look at the blk column of the output from sp_who2 or run sp_blockcnt.

> **NOTE**
>
> The Send Message feature is available only for Microsoft networks.

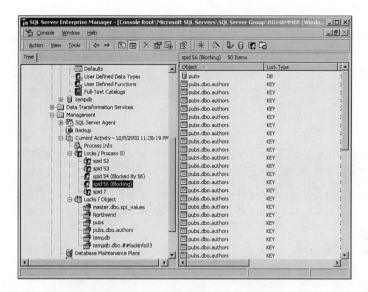

FIGURE 24.5   Locks/Process ID shows a blocked and blocking process.

FIGURE 24.6   The Process Details dialog box.

TIP

The Transact-SQL commands `sp_who`, `sp_lock`, KILL, DBCC INPUTBUFFER, and DBCC OUTPUT-BUFFER can be used to perform functions similar to those found in the User Activity Monitor.

SQL Server Profiler

SQL Server Profiler is a utility included with SQL Server that monitors Transact-SQL commands, object usage, locking, and other events. Using this utility, you can perform routines such as investigating user activity, pinpointing slow queries, and generating audit trails.

This utility is also useful for observing SQL statements generated by applications and end users. In turn, this information can be used to pinpoint poorly constructed queries or security problems. Another feature of SQL Server Profiler is its capability to save the trace information to file or a SQL Server table. This feature allows an administrator or developer to replay the queries from the trace session. Additionally, the Graphical Showplan or the Index Tuning Wizard can analyze this information. As you can see, this information can be beneficial when trying to tune queries and stored procedures.

Creating and Running a Trace

Follow these steps to use SQL Server Profiler:

1. Double-click the SQL Server Profiler icon in the Microsoft SQL Server program group. This starts the SQL Server Profiler utility.

2. Click the File menu. From the File menu, click New, Trace. The Connect to SQL Server dialog box appears. Enter the corresponding information and click the OK button to continue. The Trace Properties dialog box appears.

3. From the Trace Properties dialog box (see Figure 24.7), enter the corresponding information to trace such as General Information, Events, Trace Criteria, Capture Data, View, and so on. After entering the trace information in the Trace Properties dialog box, click the Run button to save the filter. Clicking the Run button also activates the trace you just created (see Figure 24.8).

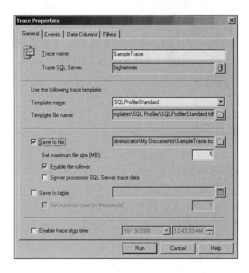

FIGURE 24.7   The Trace Properties dialog box.

4. When the trace is active, it displays the information that matches your trace criteria. As you can see, the ability to trace SQL statements provides a wealth of information that can be used to analyze SQL activity.

FIGURE 24.8   An active trace example.

TIP

The best method I've found for tracing activity is to create a trace that tightly defines the type of information you are looking for. This eliminates a lot of extraneous information that might not be of interest to you.

To include or exclude items, separate them with a semicolon (;). For example, to exclude SQL Server Profiler and MS SQL Query Analyzer, use `SQL Server Profiler%;MS SQL Query Analyzer` (see Figure 24.9).

I also recommend using the wildcard character `%` when tracing a variety of products or when you do not know the full name of the criteria. For example, to trace only Microsoft Access and Microsoft Query, you could set the Application Name to `Microsoft%` (see Figure 24.10). This works because Microsoft Access's application name is `Microsoft® Access` and Microsoft Query's application name is `Microsoft® Query`.

Advanced Analysis Using Profiler

The Profiler provides additional functionality to log its output to a file or SQL Server table. To perform advanced analysis, I recommend logging the trace information to a table. When you log a trace to a table, you can use SQL statements to extract relevant information. I often find this easier to work with as opposed to using the Profiler tool to analyze data.

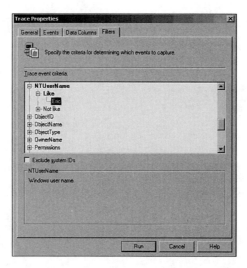

FIGURE 24.9   A dialog box that displays an example of how to enter include syntax.

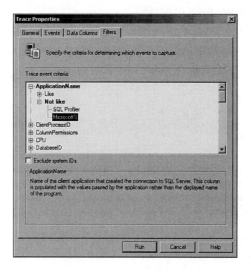

FIGURE 24.10   A dialog box that displays an example of how to enter exclude syntax.

Follow these steps to store trace information in a table:

1. Start the Profiler and create a new trace or modify an existing trace. Click the Save to Table checkbox (refer to Figure 24.7).

2. The Connect to SQL Server window appears. Enter the correct information and click OK.

3. The Destination Table window appears (see Figure 24.11). This is where you select the database and table for the Profiler to log its information. You can type in a table name if it does not exist in the table drop-down. If the table does not exist, the Profiler will automatically create the table for you.

4. Start the trace and SQL Server automatically logs the trace information to the corresponding table.

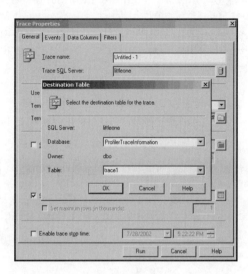

FIGURE 24.11   The Destination Table window.

TIP

Logging Profiler information to a table is an easy way to create custom reports via Excel, Microsoft Accessn or other reporting tools. I have often used Excel to create a worksheet and extract a subset of trace information. After creating the worksheet, I add several custom columns to the worksheet to keep track of the queries I have reviewed and modified. Also, this technique enables you to save off queries and perform before and after analyses.

Now that we have Profiler logging its information to a table, let's talk about how we can analyze the information.

- `TextData`, `Duration`, `Reads`, `Writes`, `CPU` columns: These columns are a great source of information when troubleshooting performance problems. For example, use the following query to determine SQL statements that run one minute or longer.

```
SELECT  TextData, Duration, Read, Writes, CPU
FROM    trace1
WHERE   EventClass = 12 -- SQL:BatchCompleted events
AND     Duration >= 100000 --1000 = 1 second, 10000 = 10 seconds, 100000 = 1
minute, etc.
```

- Start counting, grouping, and summing information: Whenever I'm brought in to troubleshoot SQL Server performance, I always want to know how many queries are really bad. An easy way to determine this information is to count the number of slow running queries, as in thus example:

```
SELECT  count(*)
FROM    trace1
WHERE   EventClass = 12 -- SQL:BatchCompleted events
AND     Duration >= 100000 --1000 = 1 second, 10000 = 10 seconds, 100000 = 1
minute, etc.
```

- Next, I will use a trick to group identical SQL statements and return the number of times they were executed. My trick involves using the `convert` statement on the `textdata` field. The reason for the `convert` syntax is that the `textdata` field is a `ntext` data type and you cannot group `ntext` fields.

```
SELECT  convert(varchar(8000),TextData), count(*), sum(duration)
FROM    trace1
WHERE   EventClass = 12 -- SQL:BatchCompleted events
AND     Duration >= 100000 --1000 = 1 second, 10000 = 10 seconds, 100000 = 1
minute, etc.
group by convert(varchar(8000),textdata)
```

- The output from the previous query also provides a sum of the duration. This is useful if you have the same query running numerous times. Based on the output from the query, you can determine the sum of the duration for each query.

- Identify read or write intensive queries: I like to use the `top` clause to determine the five most read intensive queries. The following queries use the `top` clause and sorts the result set in descending order.

```
/*
 Top 5 read operations
*/
select top 5 reads, textdata, writes, duration, cpu
from trace1
where reads is not null
order by reads desc
```

```
/*
 Top 5 write operations
*/
select top 5 writes, textdata, reads, duration, cpu
from trace1
where reads is not null
order by writes desc
```

Monitoring SQL Server FAQ

Following are some of the common questions asked by DBAs about monitoring SQL Server:

Q How do I know if the bottlenecks I'm seeing in System Monitor are reasonable?

A Experience will help here. It is important to monitor the server during normal performance to know what the range of expected values are so that when performance begins to become abnormal, you know which counters are responsible for the change.

Q Does SQL Server Profiler slow down the server?

A The answer depends on the complexity of the trace and the number of traces running concurrently. When running several complex traces, you might notice a slowdown. Therefore, you might want to limit the amount of information being traced or run individual traces instead of running multiple traces simultaneously.

Q Can I automatically start a trace whenever SQL Server is started?

A The tool is not built to function in this manner. It is built for user interaction and is not command line based.

Summary

Following is a summary of notes for monitoring SQL Server:

- The System Monitor is an excellent tool for monitoring SQL Server and the Windows NT operating system.

- Don't let the System Monitor drive you crazy! Instead of trying to track a multitude of counters, track five to eight key performance indicators. Anything over eight or ten different counters makes it difficult to determine what is happening.

- Following are some useful counters to track:

    - Processor: % Processor Time

    - SQLServer: BufferManager: Cache Hit Ratio

    - PhysicalDisk: % Disk Time

    - SQLServer: General Statistics: User Connections

    - NBT Connections: Bytes Total/sec

- Use the Current Activity Monitor to track user connections, locks, and process numbers. The Current Activity Monitor can also be used to view the SQL commands issued from each user.

- Use the SQL Server Profiler utility to trace SQL activity. This tool can monitor SQL activity and save trace information. It also can be used with the Graphical Showplan or Index Tuning Wizard.

25

SQL Mail

by Mark Spenik

IN THIS CHAPTER

- Setting Up Your SQL Server as a Mail Client

- Configuring SQL Mail

- Configuring SQL Agent Mail

- Using SQL Mail

- SQL Mail FAQ

SQL Mail is a service that enables SQL Server to utilize email functionality via any MAPI-compliant email host. SQL Mail can connect to Microsoft Exchange Server, Windows NT mail, or a POP3 server. SQL Server uses email in several different ways—SQL Mail, SQL Agent, and Data Transformation Services (DTS). SQL Mail enables you to use various stored procedures to send email within a trigger or user-defined stored procedure. SQL Mail can process email messages sent to SQL Server, including executing a query sent by email and emailing back the results. SQL Server uses email via the SQL Server Agent, to send email notifications on alerts, when performance monitor thresholds are exceeded or when scheduled jobs succeed or fail. You can include an object within a DTS package to send email notifications as packages are executed (covered in Chapter 15, "Troubleshooting SQL Server").

As you can see, SQL Server provides a rich set of functionality that enables you to integrate your SQL Server and your email functionality in the most beneficial way to your particular needs. SQL Mail is relatively easy to configure and even easier to use. The remainder of this section illustrates how you configure SQL Mail to run with your SQL Server and provides various scenarios in which you might want to use SQL Mail.

Setting Up Your SQL Server as a Mail Client

As mentioned previously, SQL Mail can utilize any MAPI-compliant email service. In order to keep this chapter manageable, however, we will only discuss SQL Mail in the context of Microsoft Exchange Server. SQL Mail works equally well with Microsoft Mail or any other MAPI-compliant software.

Before you can use SQL Mail, your SQL Server machine must be set up as a valid MAPI mail client. If you are running Microsoft Exchange, this means that you must have the Microsoft Exchange client software installed on your SQL Server, and you must have a valid mailbox established for the SQL Server user on the Exchange Server. Because this chapter is about SQL Mail and not Microsoft Exchange, it does not cover setting up a Microsoft Exchange client other than to mention a couple important points:

- As previously mentioned, your Exchange Server must have a valid mailbox for the user who is configured to run the MSSQLServer service. By default, the SQL Mail service runs under the same security context as the MSSQLServer service. To see the account under which the MSSQLServer service is running, use the Services applet under Control Panel.

- You must set up a mail profile using the Mail and Fax applet under Control Panel. This profile should be configured to point to the appropriate Microsoft Exchange Server and mailbox.

The exact details of setting up your SQL Server machine as a MAPI mail client vary depending on your email software.

TIP

You should test that your SQL Server machine is set up correctly as a mail client before going any further with SQL Mail configuration. To test this, log on to the machine under the same account that MSSQLServer will use and try to send an email message using your email client (Outlook, MS Mail, Exchange, and so on). If you cannot send an email message, SQL Server certainly won't be able to.

Configuring SQL Mail

In order to use the SQL Mail stored procedures and to process incoming email messages, you must configure the SQL Mail account used by the MSSQLServer process. Emails used by alerts and jobs statuses (that is, SQL Server Agent) are not performed by the MSSQLServer process email account but by the SQL Agent account, which must be configured separately. Let's look at how to set up the SQL Mail account first (that is, MSSQLServer process). To do this, follow these steps:

1. Open the SQL Server Enterprise Manager. Expand the appropriate Server group, and then expand the appropriate server and open the Support Services Folder. Right-click the SQL Mail icon and click Properties. You will see the dialog box shown in Figure 25.1.

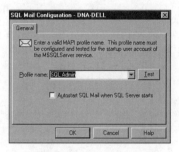

FIGURE 25.1   The SQL Mail Configuration dialog box.

2. Use the drop-down list to choose the mail profile you created when you set up your mail client. Click Test. You should see the dialog box shown in Figure 25.2.

If your mail profile was incorrectly configured, you would receive a similar dialog box that reads "Unable to start a mail session on the server with this dialog."

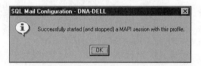

FIGURE 25.2   After testing the profile name, this message should appear.

NOTE

By default, SQL Mail must be started manually. You can do this by right-clicking the SQL Mail icon in the SQL Server Enterprise Manager and choosing Start. If you want SQL Server to automatically start SQL Mail every time SQL Server is started, simply check the Autostart check box on the SQL Mail Configuration dialog box, as shown in Figure 25.1. This is highly recommended if you want to use SQL Mail for any automated notification scenarios.

That is really all there is to configuring SQL Mail.

Configuring SQL Agent Mail

SQL Agent uses email to alert users about completed jobs or various alerts that might occur on the database server. Chapter 12, "Automating Database Administration Tasks," covers in detail setting up jobs, alerts, and operators, and how SQL Agent uses email. To configure SQL Agent with an email profile, perform the following:

1. Open the SQL Server Enterprise Manager. Expand the appropriate Server group, and then expand the appropriate server and open the Management Folder. Right-click the SQL Agent icon and select Properties. You will see the dialog box shown in Figure 25.3.

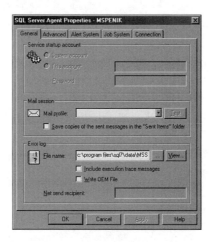

FIGURE 25.3   SQL Server Agent Properties dialog box.

2. Select the Mail Profile that you want to assign the SQL Agent from the combo box shown in Figure 25.3. Click the Test button to make sure that the account is set up properly. If you want to have all emails sent by SQL Server Agent stored in the Outlook client's Sent Items folder, check the Save Copies of the Sent Messages in the Sent Items Folder check box, as shown in Figure 25.3.

Using SQL Mail

Now that you have configured SQL Mail, it would be nice to use it. SQL Mail allows you to integrate email functionality into your SQL Server installation by enabling SQL Server to send, receive, and process email messages. The bulk of the SQL Mail functionality is implemented via a system stored procedure called sp_processmail. In addition to sp_processmail, several extended stored procedures are shipped with SQL Server that will enable you to customize SQL Mail within your databases and applications. The extended stored procedures are included in `SQLMAP70.dll`, a dynamic link library that is installed with SQL Server. A summary of these stored procedures follows:

- `xp_startmail`—Used to manually start a SQL Mail session. Remember that you can configure SQL Mail to start automatically.

- `xp_stopmail`—Used to manually stop a SQL Mail session.

- `xp_sendmail`—Used to manually send an email message to any recipient or group of recipients. This email message can contain a plain-text message, the results of a query, or even a file attachment.

- `xp_findnextmsg`—Used to find the message ID of the next message waiting in the SQL Server inbox. Remember that SQL Server can receive email messages as well as send them.

- `xp_readmail`—Used to manually read a mail message that is in the SQL Server inbox by using the message ID returned from the `xp_findnextmsg` stored procedure. Alternatively, `xp_readmail` can be used to return the entire inbox as a resultset to the client.

- `xp_deletemail`—Used to delete a mail message after it has been processed.

- `sp_processmail`—Used to process mail in the SQL Server inbox. This stored procedure uses all the extended stored procedures mentioned previously.

For a more complete explanation of these stored procedures, including all available parameters, you can refer to the Transact-SQL help.

The following sections describe how to use these stored procedures to add email functionality to your SQL Server implementation.

Sending Email from SQL Server

There are many scenarios in which you might want to use SQL Server to send email messages. Probably, the most common scenario is when system operators are automatically notified of certain database conditions. This functionality is implemented through the SQL Agent, and is discussed in detail in Chapter 12. However, the SQL Agent email functionality is limited to sending email based on events and conditions. If you want a more robust use of email, you must use the SQL Mail stored procedures.

Suppose you want to embed an email notification in a trigger so that SQL Server would automatically send an email message when a certain table is updated. For example, you might want to allow users to update information about themselves via a corporate intranet. After the user has updated his employee record, you want to send an email notification to an HR representative. This functionality could be implemented by using the SQL Mail extended stored procedures within a trigger.

To do this, simply create an UPDATE TRIGGER on the desired table that contains the following syntax:

```
CREATE TRIGGER notify ON employee
FOR INSERT, UPDATE
AS

declare @msgtext varchar(256), @employee varchar(10)

--populate message text
select @employee = inserted.emp_id
from inserted

select @msgtext = 'Please verify records for employee number: ' + @employee

--send email notification to HR Representative
EXEC xp_sendmail @recipient = 'kviers', @message = @msgtext,
@subject = 'Employee Update'
```

In this trigger, we specify that an email notification will be sent to a specific recipient anytime an employee record is updated or inserted. This email notification will include the employee ID of the record that has been affected.

The preceding code example illustrates how you can use the extended SQL Mail stored procedures within a trigger to automatically send email notifications. You could just as easily use the extended stored procedures within user-defined stored procedures to accomplish the same goal.

> **NOTE**
>
> A SQL Mail session must be started before you can run the xp_sendmail stored procedure. If you are going to use xp_sendmail from stored procedures, it is probably wise to have SQL Mail auto-start when SQL Server starts. If you do not have a SQL Mail session started, you can use the xp_startmail and xp_stopmail stored procedures to dynamically start and stop a SQL Mail session from within your stored procedure.

Processing Incoming Email

SQL Mail not only can send email messages, but also can receive and respond to them as well. A user can actually send an email message to SQL Server with a query embedded in the message text, and SQL Server can read that email and return the resultset of the query to the user.

NOTE

An incoming email message must contain a single SQL query statement in the message text of the email. The sp_processmail stored procedure will read the email message, process the query, and then return the resultset to the user as an attached file with a filename of SQL*xxx.yyy*, where *xxx* is a random number generated by SQL Server and *yyy* is the filetype specified in the sp_processmail stored procedure.

Any time a user sends an email message to the mailbox that is assigned in the SQL Mail configuration, that email is stored in the SQL Server Exchange inbox. The sp_processmail stored procedure is used to read and respond to all messages in the SQL Server Exchange inbox. The following are the parameters used to modify the behavior of the sp_processmail stored procedure:

- @subject—This parameter is used to determine which email messages to process. If this parameter is supplied, sp_processmail will only process those email messages that have a subject equal to that specified. If this parameter is not specified, sp_processmail will process all email messages in the inbox.

- @filetype—This parameter is used to specify the filetype that will be returned to the recipient(s). All query results are returned as an attached file. If this parameter is not specified, all resultsets are returned as .TXT files.

- @set_user—This parameter is used to specify the user context under which to run the queries that are being processed. If this parameter is not specified, all queries will be processed using the Guest user account.

- @dbuse—This parameter is used to specify in which database to process the query. If this parameter is not specified, all queries will be processed in the master database.

The sp_processmail stored procedure can be run manually at any time by executing the stored procedure in a SQL Query Analyzer session.

TIP

You can use SQL Agent to set up the sp_processmail stored procedure as a scheduled task that runs at set intervals to process the inbox. You can also create multiple sp_processmail tasks that each provide different parameters. This would allow you to process email differently, depending on the subject provided.

With the sp_processmail stored procedure and the extended stored procedures, there are virtually limitless ways to use SQL Mail to implement email functionality in your SQL Server scenario. The options are only limited by the imagination of the DBA.

SQL Mail FAQ

The following section contains several frequently asked questions and answers about SQL Mail.

> **Q I've had trouble setting up SQL Mail and configuring it to work. Do you have any tips to help in the future?**
>
> **A** I have found the simplest way to set up SQL Mail is to log on to the NT Server where you want to set up SQL Mail, using the NT account for the email account that you want to assign SQL Server. Then test the Outlook or mail client by sending a message to yourself. After you can verify that you can send and receive email messages via the email account, start the SQL Server Enterprise Manager (still logged in with the NT account used by the email account) and then assign SQL Mail to use the current user profile. Test SQL Mail, and it should work. You can then log off the NT server and log back on with your regular NT account.
>
> **Q What is a easy way to grant non-system admin roles the ability to use xp_sendmail?**
>
> **A** Have a system admin create a stored procedure in the master database that calls xp_sendmail. The system admin can then assign execute privileges to the non-admin users.

Summary

SQL Server provides tight integration with Microsoft Exchange or a POP3 email server that is simple to use via system stored procedures. The SQL Agent also uses email to alert various operators of alerts and job status.

26

Using SQL-DMO

by Mark Spenik

Have you ever felt that Microsoft left out a utility or some graphical display that you thought would really make your life easier? With SQL Server 2000, you might be able to write that utility yourself! "How?" you ask. The answer is an exciting feature added first to SQL Server 6.0 and extended with SQL Server 2000—SQL-DMO!

SQL-DMO stands for SQL Distributed Management Objects. SQL-DMO is based on Microsoft's Component Object Model (COM) and supports OLE automation. OLE stands for object linking and embedding, but in the past few years it has come to stand for so much more. A few years ago, Microsoft and several integrated system vendors created an open specification for application intercommunication called OLE. The OLE specifications defined more than applications communicating with one another; it also specified how applications can expose parts of their functionality as objects to be used by other applications. OLE became part of ActiveX, which is now all part of COM.

The benefits of COM include the ability of application developers to create applications that use parts of other applications to further enhance their own applications. For example, you can create an application that uses the charting capabilities of Microsoft Excel, or you can include Microsoft's Word spell checker into a text editor application.

What does all this have to do with SQL Server and database administration? Through SQL-DMO, SQL Server exposes several objects, methods, and properties that can be easily controlled programmatically to perform database administrative tasks. Using SQL-DMO, you can easily create applications, stored procedures, or Web pages that perform many DBA tasks for you!

IN THIS CHAPTER

- SQL Server's Object Model
- Why Use SQL-DMO?
- Creating Applications with SQL-DMO
- Enhancing the SQL Server DBA Assistant
- Using SQL-DMO with Stored Procedures
- SQL-DMO FAQ

Before going into more detail, here is a quick review of some OLE terminology:

- **Container/controller/client application**—An application that can create and manage OLE objects. Visual Basic is an example of a container application.

- **Server/object application**—An application that creates OLE objects. SQL Server is an object application.

- **OLE automation**—A standard that enables applications to expose their objects and methods so that other applications can use them.

- **Object**—Defining an object is a bit difficult. If the OLE definition of an object is used, the discussion gets into many other aspects of OLE, which are covered in detail in other Sams books but that confuse the topic of this book. This chapter uses a simpler definition: *An object represents some sort of data with properties and methods.* In SQL Server terms, for example, a database is an object, and a stored procedure is an object. Figure 26.1 shows an example of a database object.

  The object has attributes. (In OLE terminology, attributes are called *properties.*) In Figure 26.1, some of the properties of a database object are listed: Name, CreateDate, Size, and Status are all examples of properties of the database object.

  The Name property for the database shown in Figure 26.1 is pubs. A property tells you something about the object. You can read properties, and in some cases, you can set properties.

  Objects also have methods. A *method* is an action the object performs. Examples of database objects methods are shown in Figure 26.1. The CheckIdentityValues method, for example, can be used on the database object. If you invoked the CheckIdentityValues method of the database object named pubs, what do you think would happen? If you said, "The method would check identity columns on the tables in the pubs database," you are correct.

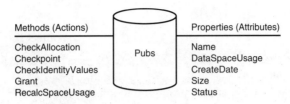

FIGURE 26.1   An example of a database object.

- **Collections**—An object that consists of items that can be referred to as a group (see Figure 26.2).

In Figure 26.2, there are several standard SQL Server databases: `master`, `pubs`, `model`, and `tempdb`. If you group all the databases shown into one large group called `databases`, you have a collection.

Collections enable you to easily perform tasks on each item in the collection. To perform a DBCC `CHECKDB` command on every database on your SQL Server, for example, you can use the collection object to get each database on the server and invoke a method to perform that DBA task.

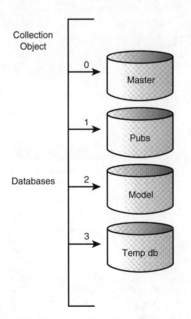

FIGURE 26.2   An example of a collection object.

SQL Server's Object Model

To use SQL-DMO, you must understand the SQL Server object model. The *object model* is the hierarchy of exposed SQL Server objects you can use programmatically.

You follow the object model as you would a file directory tree. For example, the top level of the object model is the `Application` object.

NOTE

It is standard practice when creating OLE object models from a standalone application to include an `Application` object.

To use other objects, follow the tree to the next level to find the objects you will use, for example, the SQL Server object. Object models also contain objects that are dependent upon other objects. To use a dependent object, you must first have the parent object of the dependent object. For example, getting an instance of a database object requires getting a SQL Server object first. The database object is said to be *dependent upon* the SQL Server object; that is, you must have a SQL Server object before you can use the database object.

Why Use SQL-DMO?

What benefits can you get from learning to use SQL-DMO? The real gain is that you can easily create custom solutions for your database administration environment, allowing you more free time to perform other tasks. For example, you can create a user wizard that performs a series of tasks, such as adding the user to every database based on the user's group.

Using SQL-DMO, you can create applications that you normally have to perform manually. Currently, you can automate many tasks you perform regularly by using stored procedures. The advantage SQL-DMO has over stored procedures for performing administrative task is simplicity. By using collection objects, you can easily perform DBCC commands on every database on the server, using only a few lines of code. Many transact SQL commands have been simplified. The DBCC command and the many different DBCC options become methods of different objects.

Another advantage SQL-DMO has over stored procedures is that you can use true programming languages that have more powerful programming features than transact SQL. Additionally, you can easily integrate your applications into other desktop applications (such as word processors or spreadsheets) to enhance your customized database administration applications. Following is brief list of some of the many administrative tasks you can perform with SQL-DMO. (This is a *brief* list; SQL-DMO enables you to perform almost any system administrative task.)

- Back up/restore a database

- Generate scripts

- Perform replication operations

- Perform DBCC commands such as `CheckTable`, `CheckCatalog`, and so on

- Grant and revoke privileges

- Add alerts

- Perform BCP

- Transfer data from one server to another

- Manage users

Creating Applications with SQL-DMO

You can use SQL-DMO using Transact SQL, in Active Server Pages or build entire applications around SQL-DMO. To build a SQL-DMO application or component requires a 32-bit programming language that can create OLE controller applications. Tools such as Microsoft Visual C++, a Windows-based Java tool, or Microsoft Excel for Windows NT with 32-bit VBA (Visual Basic for Applications) can easily be used. The examples and code samples shown in this chapter are based on Microsoft Visual Basic 6.0. The choice of Visual Basic is easy because it is the most popular and rapid application-development tool available. The core language of Visual Basic 6.0 is VBA and can be found in Office 2000 (that is, Access, Word, PowerPoint, and Excel) as well as Microsoft Project.

The remainder of the chapter focuses on using SQL-DMO objects to perform a variety of database administration tasks using Visual Basic.

Using Visual Basic

TIP

If you are not familiar with Visual Basic, pick up a beginner's book and learn the Visual Basic basics. After you know the basics, you can use the suggestions and examples in this chapter effectively to create your own applications. The following discussion of Visual Basic is brief and is given primarily for those who are not familiar with Visual Basic so that they can understand SQL-DMO.

Following is a brief introduction to Visual Basic to help you understand the terminology used later when creating an application that takes advantage of SQL-DMO. The main screen of Visual Basic 6.0 is shown in Figure 26.3.

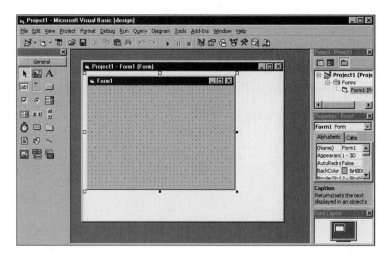

FIGURE 26.3   The Visual Basic 6.0 project design screen.

Creating Visual Basic applications consists of creating forms, adding controls to the forms using the toolbar, and adding code to modules and forms that make up the application. The forms and code modules that make up a Visual Basic application are called a *project* and can be found in the project window shown in Figure 26.3. The next sections step you through some Visual Basic rudiments you will need later to create your own SQL-DMO applications or to enhance the application provided on the book's companion Web site (the DBA Assistant).

Adding a Control to a Form and Setting Properties

A Visual Basic *control* is similar to a SQL-DMO object in that both have properties and methods. Understanding the properties and methods used with a Visual Basic control can help you better understand the concepts of SQL-DMO objects and properties. To add a control to a form, perform the following steps:

1. On the toolbar, click the icon of the control you want to add to the form. Common controls used on the toolbar are shown in Figure 26.4.

2. Place the mouse cursor on the form; while holding the left mouse button, drag the mouse down. Visual Basic begins to draw a control on the form.

3. Release the left mouse button. You have added a control to the form.

4. To set properties (such as color, name, height, width, and so on) for the control or the form, click the form or control to make it the active object and press F4. The Properties window for the object appears (see Figure 26.5).

FIGURE 26.4   The Visual Basic toolbar.

FIGURE 26.5   The Visual Basic form Properties window.

5. To change a property, select the property field and enter a new value. For example, if you want to change the name of the control, edit the Name property.

Declaring a SQL-DMO Object in Visual Basic

To use a SQL-DMO object, you must declare the object in your code. With Visual Basic, you can use the generic object type, which can hold any type of OLE object, or you can declare an object of a specific SQL-DMO object type by using the type library. To create a variable using a generic object, use the following syntax:

```
Dim Variable_Name As Object
```

To create a specific SQL-DMO, use the following syntax:

```
Dim Variable_Name As SQLDMO.SQL_DMO_OBJECT
```

In this syntax, `SQL_DMO_OBJECT` is the specific SQL-DMO object (such as `SQLServer`, `Database`, `Table`, and so on). For example, to define a SQL-DMO SQL Server object using the type library, enter the following:

```
Dim MySqlServer As SQLDMO.SQLServer
```

> **TIP**
>
> Declare SQL-DMO variables using the type library and declaring specific SQL Server objects rather than using the generic object. Using specific objects is faster and enables Visual Basic to perform *early binding* (checking that you are using proper objects and methods) during compilation rather than at runtime.

Creating a SQL-DMO Object with Visual Basic

After you declare a variable to be a SQL-DMO object, you must create the object before you can use the methods and properties of the object.

> **NOTE**
>
> Creating an object is also referred to as *getting an instance* of the object.

You can create the object with either the keyword `New` or the function `CreateObject`. Following is an example that uses the `New` keyword when declaring a variable:

```
Dim MySqlServer As New SQLDMO.SQLServer
```

You also can use the `New` keyword in code, as follows:

```
Set MySqlServer = New SQLDMO.SQLServer
```

The `CreateObject` function has the following syntax:

```
CreateObject("application_name.object_type")
```

The following code creates a new SQL Server SQL-DMO object with `CreateObject`:

```
Set MySqlServer = CreateObject("SQLDMO.SQLServer")
```

After you create an object, you can use the objects, properties, and methods to perform DBA tasks.

Releasing Objects

Just as important as creating an object is releasing the object when you are finished with it. Objects in Visual Basic are released when they go out of scope. If the object is declared in a procedure, the object is released when the procedure completes. If the object is declared in a form, the object is released when the form unloads. Global objects are not released until the application closes.

It is always good Visual Basic coding practice to release your objects in code when you are finished with them by using the keyword Nothing. The following code, for example, releases a SQL-DMO table object called MyTable:

```
Set MyTable = Nothing
```

Required SQL-DMO Files

To create SQL-DMO objects using Visual Basic, you must have the following files, which are included with the 32-bit versions of SQL Server client utilities for Windows NT and Windows 95. You can find the following files in the SQL Server 2000 home directory (C:\Microsoft SQL Server) in the directory \80\Tools\Bin:

SQLDMO.HLP	SQL-DMO help files, including object hierarchy.
SQL Server 3.70 or later ODBC files	SQL-DMO uses ODBC to connect to the server.
SQLDMO.rll	Localized resource file. The location will vary but will be in the subdirectory resources*xxxx*, in which where *xxxx* is the language of the SQL Server instance.
SQLDMO.DLL	In process SQL-DMO server.

NOTE

SQL-DMO is available only in 32-bit Windows environments (Windows NT, Windows 2000, and Windows 9*x*).

SQL-DMO Checklist

You can use the following checklist when creating SQL-DMO applications. Use this first checklist to ensure that you have the proper files and utilities required to use SQL-DMO:

❑ Have Windows NT, Windows 2000, Windows XP or Windows 9*x*.

❑ Have installed a 32-bit OLE automation controller (Visual Basic).

❑ Have an ODBC 3.70 or greater SQL Server driver (ships with SQL Server 2000)

❑ Have installed the proper SQL-DMO files from the 32-bit SQL Server Client utilities.

The next checklist includes the steps required to create SQL-DMO objects from Visual Basic:

❑   1. Include the SQL-DMO type library in the Visual Basic environment by adding `Microsoft SQLDMO Object Library` to the Visual Basic references.

❑   2. Declare a SQL-DMO `SQLServer` object.

❑   3. Create the `SQLServer` object.

❑   4. Connect the `SQLServer` object to SQL Server.

❑   5. Use the SQLServer objects, properties, and methods, and declare and create any other required SQL-DMO objects to accomplish your required DBA task.

❑   6. Release SQL-DMO objects using the keyword `Nothing` when you are done using them.

❑   7. Disconnect the `SQLServer` object.

❑   8. Release the `SQLServer` object.

Enhancing the SQL Server DBA Assistant

Now comes the real value. As you probably know by now, examples that use SQL-DMO are hard to find. SQL Server ships with a few SQL-DMO samples that are poorly documented. The overall SQL-DMO documentation contains very few descriptive examples but concentrates on describing the objects and methods.

On the Web site for this book is a Visual Basic project titled `samsdba2000.vbp`, which is the Visual Basic project file and contains all the source code for the application SQL Server DBA Assistant. The source code is included as a foundation that you can modify and enhance to meet your own needs. The following sections discuss the most important parts of the SQL Server DBA Assistant.

NOTE

The source code for the application is included on the Web site for this book. The following sections concentrate on the code that uses SQL-DMO, not the Visual Basic code that does not deal with SQL-DMO. The Visual Basic code is well documented so that you can use the code and form to easily add your own functionality to the project.

What's in the SQL Server DBA Assistant?

Before getting started on developing the SQL Server DBA application, you must decide what type of functionality you are going to put in the application. First, because the purpose of the utility is for actual DBA work and learning, you should create an application that uses several different SQL-DMO objects.

What is missing from Microsoft SQL Server 2000? Some graphical maintenance of tables as well as a non-DTS graphical BCP are missing.

To fix this oversight, the SQL Server DBA Assistant enables you to perform table maintenance on several different databases using the SQL-DMO `database` object and the `table` object. Following is a list of the functionalities of the SQL Server DBA Assistant:

- Lists all the databases in a combo box for selection

- Performs table maintenance on selected tables

- Performs BCP export on selected tables

Connecting to SQL Server

NOTE

This chapter skips a few steps here that are Visual Basic related, such as creating a new project called `samsdba` and adding controls to the logon form.

Assuming that you have all the proper files and have added the Microsoft `SQLDMO` Object Library references to Visual Basic, it is now time to declare a SQL Server object and connect to SQL Server. For logon purposes, use the form shown in Figure 26.6 (`frmLogon`).

FIGURE 26.6   The SQL Server DBA Assistant Logon form.

Using your checklist for creating a SQL-DMO application, perform Step 2: Declare a SQL-DMO object, as follows in the Visual Basic module `global.bas`:

```
Public MySqlServer As SQLDMO.SQLServer 'Global SQL Server Object
```

The next step is to create a SQL Server object. The code to create a SQL Server object is located in the Visual Basic module `sqlserv8.bas` in the procedure `main`. The code for the `main` procedure is shown in Listing 26.1.

LISTING 26.1   Procedure `main`: Creating a SQL Server Object

```
Public Sub main()
'SAMS -Microsoft SQL Server DBA Survival Guide
'
'Main - The procedure main creates a OLE SQL Server Object
'        and then prompts the user to enter the correct SQL Server
'        name.  If the user properly connects to the SQL Server
'        the main form of the application is shown.
'
'Set up Error handling

On Error GoTo Err_Main

'
'Check if the application is already running
'
If App.PrevInstance > 0 Then
    MsgBox "SQL Server DBA Assistant already running on this machine.", _
            vbCritical, "Already Running"
    End
End If

'
'Create a New SQL Server OLE Object
'
Set MySqlServer = CreateObject("SQLDMO.SQLServer")

connected = False 'Set Global to Not Connected
'
'Set SQL Server Connection Timeout Value
'
MySqlServer.LoginTimeout = 15 'Set for 15 seconds
'
```

LISTING 26.1   Continued

```
'Display the Logon Screen
'
frmLogon.Show 1
Set frmLogon = Nothing  'Reclaim Object Memory

'If We established a Connection Display the Main form
' Otherwise exit the application
If connected = True Then
    frmSplash.Show   'Display Splash Screen
    DoEvents         'Allow time to Paint the Splash Screen
    Load frmMain7    'Load the Main Form
    frmMain7.Show    'Make it Appear
    Unload frmSplash 'Make it disappear
    Set frmSplash = Nothing 'Reclaim Memory
    Exit Sub
End If
'
'Exit - If not Connected
Quit_App:

    If Not (MySqlServer Is Nothing) Then
        'Release SQL Server Object
        Set MySqlServer = Nothing
    End If
    End 'End the program
'
'Error Handler
'
Err_Main:
        '
        'Display Error Message
        MsgBox Err.Description, vbCritical, "Connection Error"
        Resume Next


End Sub
```

The following line creates a SQL-DMO SQL Server object using the function
CreateObject (as specified in Step 3 of the SQL-DMO checklist):

```
Set MySqlServer = CreateObject("SQLDMO.SQLServer")
```

When this line of code executes, the variable `MySqlServer` contains a SQL Server object.

Before you try to connect to a SQL Server by logging on, you set the login timeout value by setting the SQL Server object property `LoginTimeout`, as follows:

```
MySqlServer.LoginTimeout = 15 'Set for 15 seconds
```

You now are ready to perform Step 4 of the checklist: Establish a connection to SQL Server. The logon form appears (refer to Figure 26.6). A user enters the SQL Server, user name, and password and clicks the Logon button on the form. The code shown in Listing 26.2 executes to establish a connection to the SQL Server.

LISTING 26.2   SQL Server Connection

```
Private Sub cmdLogon_Click()

    'Set up the Error Handler
    '
    On Error GoTo Err_Logon
    '
    'Connect to the SQL Server
    '
    If txtServer <> "" Then
        Me.MousePointer = vbHourglass 'Turn Cursor to HourGlass
        '
        'Invoke Connect Method of the SQL Server Object
        '
        MySqlServer.Connect ServerName:=txtServer.Text, _
                       Login:=txtLogon.Text, _
                       Password:=txtPassword.Text
        '
        'Sql Server Connected Correctly - Unload the form
        '
        connected = True           'Set Global Connection Variable
        Me.MousePointer = vbDefault 'Turn Mousepointer back to default
        Unload Me                  'Unload the Logon form
    Else
        MsgBox "You must enter a SQL Server Name to Connect", _
            vbCritical, "Invalid Entry"
    End If
    '
```

LISTING 26.2   Continued

```
    'Exit the routine - If Not Logged In Try Again
    '
Exit_Logon:

    Exit Sub
'
' Error handler
'
Err_Logon:
    Me.MousePointer = vbDefault
    MsgBox "Error Connection to Server. Error: " & Err.Description, _
        vbCritical, "Error Connection"
    Resume Exit_Logon
End Sub
```

The following lines of code establish a connection with SQL Server using the Connection method of the SQL Server object:

```
    'Invoke Connect Method of the SQL Server Object
    '
    MySqlServer.Connect ServerName:=txtServer.TEXT, _
                    Login:=txtLogon.TEXT, _
                    Password:=txtPassword.TEXT
```

After you establish a successful connection to SQL Server, you are ready to perform Steps 5 and 6 of the SQL-DMO application checklist: Perform various tasks by creating objects, invoking methods, and setting properties.

Filling a Combo Box with Databases

To make the SQL Server DBA Assistant a useful tool during database table maintenance, you add the capability to select a database from a combo box and then read all the nonsystem tables associated with the database into a Visual Basic List Box control.

To read all the databases on the selected server into a combo box, you use the SQL Server SQL-DMO object and the databases collection. The code shown in Listing 26.3 populates a Visual Basic combo box with all the database names in your SQL Server object collection.

LISTING 26.3   Populating a Combo Box with Database Names

```
Dim Db As SQLDMO.Database

    CenterForm frmMain7
    '
    'Fill the Combo Box on the form with the
    'available databases by using the SQL Server databases collection
    '
    For Each Db In MySqlServer.Databases
        '  Make sure the database is not currently being loaded
        '

        If Db.Status <> SQLDMODBStat_Inaccessible Then
            cmbDatabase.AddItem Db.Name
            cmbBCP.AddItem Db.Name
        Else
            MsgBox "Database: """ + Db.Name _
              + " "" can not be accessed at this time.", _
              vbCritical, "Database Loading"
        End If
    Next
    Set Db = Nothing
```

To populate a list box with the tables in the database, you read the tables collection of the selected database. The code to populate the list box using the selected database is shown in Listing 26.4.

LISTING 26.4   Populating a List Box with Table Names Using a Database Object and the Tables Collection

```
Private Sub cmbDatabase_Click()
Dim WorkTable As SQLDMO.Table 'SQL-DMO Table Object

    On Error GoTo Get_Tables_Error
    frmMain7.MousePointer = vbHourglass
    '
    'Database changed - Modify Database Object
    '
    Set WorkDb = Nothing    'Clear the Work Database object
    lstTables.Clear         'Clear tables list box
    lstOperateTables.Clear 'Clear the operate tables list Box
```

LISTING 26.4   Continued

```
    'Get the currently selected database object
    '
    Set WorkDb = MySqlServer.Databases(cmbDatabase.Text)


    '
    'Fill The list box with the table names using the database
    'tables collection exclude any system tables.
    '
    For Each WorkTable In WorkDb.Tables 'Do For Each table in the database
        If Not (WorkTable.SystemObject) Then
            lstTables.AddItem WorkTable.Name 'Add to the list Box
        End If
    Next WorkTable

Exit_Get_Tables:
    Set WorkTable = Nothing
    frmMain7.MousePointer = vbDefault
    Exit Sub   'Leave the Procedure

'
' Error handler
'
Get_Tables_Error:
    Me.MousePointer = vbDefault
    MsgBox "Error reading tables collection " & Err.Description, _
        vbCritical, "Filling Combo Box Error"
    Resume Exit_Get_Tables

End Sub
```

TIP

You can begin to see that using SQL-DMO is simple after you become familiar with the SQL-DMO object model. Study the model and become familiar with the collections, objects, and the hierarchy.

Getting a list of objects is simple using the Visual Basic FOR EACH - NEXT statement. A FOR EACH - NEXT is used to read through all items of an array or collection. Examples of the FOR EACH - NEXT statement can be found in Listings 26.3 and 26.4.

Performing Table Maintenance

After a database has been selected, a database object can easily be created using the selected database name and the SQL Server object, as follows:

```
'Get the currently selected database object
    '
    Set WorkDb = MySqlServer.Databases(cmbDatabase.TEXT)
```

When the line of code executes, you have a SQL-DMO database object for the selected database. If you remember the object model for SQL-DMO, you can easily create a table object using the database object. After the table object has been created, you can perform a variety of table maintenance tasks using the different table methods. Following are some examples of the table object methods and the tasks they perform:

CheckTable	Performs the DBCC CheckTable command.
Grant	Grants table privileges to a list of SQL Server users or groups.
RecalcSpaceUsage	Recalculates the space information for the table.
Script	Generates the Transact SQL statements to create the table.
UpdateStatistics	Updates the data distribution pages used by the Query Optimizer to make proper index selection.

For the SQL Server DBA Assistant, you can select the tables on which you want to perform a table maintenance operation and then click a button to perform the appropriate action. The code that scans through the list of selected tables and invokes the method is as follows:

```
'Execute Update Statistics command on selected tables
    '
    For X = 0 To lstOperateTables.ListCount - 1
        ProgressBar1.VALUE = X
        Set WorkTable = WorkDb.Tables(lstOperateTables.List(X))
        '
        'Update Statistics on the Table - using the UpdateStatistics Method
        '
        WorkTable.UpdateStatistics
        'Release the Work Table object
        Set WorkTable = Nothing
    Next X
```

The Table Maintenance tab of the SQL Server DBA Assistant dialog box is shown in Figure 26.7.

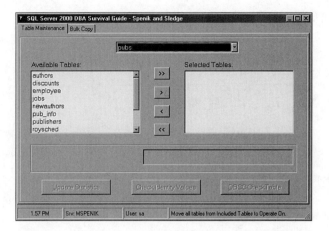

FIGURE 26.7   The Table Maintenance tab of the SQL Server DBA Assistant dialog box.

Listing 26.5 shows the code used behind the Update Statistics button (shown in Figure 26.7).

LISTING 26.5   Updating Statistics on Selected Tables

```
Private Sub cmdUpdate_Click()
Dim WorkTable As SQLDMO.Table 'SQL-DMO Table Object
Dim X As Integer

    On Error GoTo Up_Stats_Error
    frmMain7.MousePointer = vbHourglass
    '
    'Setup The Progress Bar
    ProgressBar1.Max = lstOperateTables.ListCount
    ProgressBar1.Value = 0
    lblStatus.Caption = "Updating Statistics"
    DoEvents 'Allow Screen to repaint
    '
    StatusBar1.Panels("status").Text = "Updating Statistics - Please Wait..."

    'Execute Update Statistics command on selected tables
    '
    For X = 0 To lstOperateTables.ListCount - 1
        ProgressBar1.Value = X
        Set WorkTable = WorkDb.Tables(lstOperateTables.List(X))
        '
```

LISTING 26.5   Continued

```
        'Update Statistics on the Table - using the UpdateStatistics Method
        '
        WorkTable.UpdateStatistics
        'Release the Work Table object
        Set WorkTable = Nothing
    Next X
    ProgressBar1.Value = ProgressBar1.Max

    'Cleanup and Exit
Up_Stats_Exit:
    '
    StatusBar1.Panels("status").Text = ""
    frmMain7.MousePointer = vbDefault
    ProgressBar1.Value = 0
    Exit Sub
'
' Error handler
'
Up_Stats_Error:
    Me.MousePointer = vbDefault
    MsgBox "Error Updating statistics on table " & lstOperateTables.List(X) _
        & "Error: " & Err.Description, _
        vbCritical, "Update Statistics Error"
    Resume Up_Stats_Exit

End Sub
```

TIP

We have provided you with the following three table maintenance functions already programmed and ready to use. Look on the Web site for this book; they're with the SQL Server DBA Assistant.

- Update Statistics
- Check Identity Values
- DBCC CheckTable

As stated earlier, the purpose of the SQL Server DBA Assistant is to provide you with a foundation from which you can create your own application. If you look behind each of the buttons, you will notice that the code is almost identical except for the methods added. By cutting and pasting the code into new buttons and adding new methods, you can add more functionality. You also can optimize the application by reducing the code behind the buttons by using a shared function or procedure. The list is endless—what are you waiting for?

Performing Table Exports Using Bulk Copy (BCP)

A graphical BCP utility was available in SQL Server 4.21. SQL Server 2000, of course, has the very graphical and powerful DTS services, which perform import/export services to non-SQL Server data sources, but still no graphical BCP. Because the DBA Assistant is all about tools left out of the SQL Enterprise Manager, the ability to perform graphical BCP is very important—especially if you are in environments where the data fed into SQL Server is from mainframe flat files (or vice versa). The SQL Server DBA Assistant provides you with your own graphical BCP tool by adding the ability to export data using the `BulkCopy` object in the following formats:

- Tab delimited (default)
- Comma delimited
- Native format

The `BulkCopy` object differs from the objects used so far in these sample applications because the `BulkCopy` object does not depend on other objects. To use a `BulkCopy` object, you create the `BulkCopy` object, set the various parameters of the `BulkCopy` object, and then pass the `BulkCopy` object as a parameter to a table or view object's ImportData or ExportData method. The BulkCopy object has a single method, `Abort`, to abort a running BCP; this method must be executed from another thread.

For the SQL Server DBA Assistant, the `BulkCopy` object is created when the object parameter oBCP is declared using the keyword New as follows:

```
Dim oBCP As New SQLDMO.BulkCopy
'Note BCP object is created here using New Keyword
```

After the `BulkCopy` object has been created, the next step is to set the desired properties (such as the import batch size or the number of errors to ignore before halting the bulk copy). Here is an example of setting the `BulkCopy` object's MaximumErrorsBeforeAbort property:

```
'Max Number of errors before BCP quits
    If IsNumeric(txtMaxErrors.Text) Then
        oBCP.MaximumErrorsBeforeAbort = CInt(txtMaxErrors.Text)
    Else
        'Use Default
        oBCP.MaximumErrorsBeforeAbort = 1
    End If
```

When you set the properties of the `BulkCopy` object to import or export data, you pass the BulkCopy object as a parameter to a table or view the object's ImportData or

ExportData method. The following example shows the ExportData method being used:

```
iNumRows = BCPTable.ExportData(oBCP)
```

The Bulk Copy tab of the SQL Server DBA Assistant dialog box is shown in Figure 26.8.

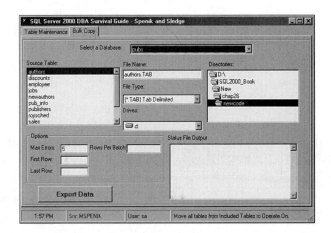

FIGURE 26.8   The Bulk Copy tab of the SQL Server DBA Assistant dialog box.

Listing 26.6 shows the code used behind the Export Data button (shown in Figure 26.8).

LISTING 26.6   Performing BCP Export on Selected Tables

```
Private Sub cmdExportData_Click()
Dim BCPTable As SQLDMO.Table      'SQL-DMO Table Object
Dim oBCP As New SQLDMO.BulkCopy   'Note BCP object is
                                  'created here using New Keyword
Dim iNumRows As Long              'Stores number of rows returned from BCP
Dim oOutputFile As CFile          'Used for file I/O
Dim sTempBuf As String, sTemp As String 'Temp variables

    'Set up a simple error handler
    On Error GoTo Export_Error

    'Setup display
    frmMain7.MousePointer = vbHourglass
```

LISTING 26.6   Continued

```
'
StatusBar1.Panels("status").Text = "Exporting Data - Please Wait..."

'Step 1 - Get a instance of the table object to perform the BCP
'
'Get the table object - to perform the export
'
Set BCPTable = WorkDb.Tables(lstBCPTables.Text)

'Step 2 - Set up the BCP objects properties
'
'(Note: A instance of the BCP object was
'created above in DIM statement
'               using the keyword New)
'
'Set the BulkCopy input/output file parameter
oBCP.DataFilePath = Dir1.Path & "\" & txtFile

'Set the error log and log file parameters
oBCP.LogFilePath = App.Path & "\sams_bcp.log"
oBCP.ErrorFilePath = App.Path & "\sams_err.log"

'
'Do some validation checking and set optional parameters
'
' Batch Size (Not used for exporting - only used in imports
'               added here for your convenience - should you modify
'               the program to do imports).
'
If IsNumeric(txtBatchSize.Text) Then
    oBCP.ImportRowsPerBatch = CInt(txtBatchSize.Text)
Else
    'Use Default
    oBCP.ImportRowsPerBatch = 1000
End If

'Max Number of errors before BCP quits
If IsNumeric(txtMaxError.Text) Then
    oBCP.MaximumErrorsBeforeAbort = CInt(txtMaxError.Text)
Else
    'Use Default
```

LISTING 26.6   Continued

```
        oBCP.MaximumErrorsBeforeAbort = 1
End If


'First Row to start BCP
If txtFirstRow <> "" Then
    If IsNumeric(txtFirstRow.Text) Then
        oBCP.FirstRow = CInt(txtFirstRow.Text)
    End If
End If


'Last Row to end BCP
If txtLastRow <> "" Then
    If IsNumeric(txtLastRow.Text) Then
        oBCP.LastRow = CInt(txtLastRow.Text)
    End If
End If


'Set the output type for the BCP- based on combo box
sTemp = cmbType.Text


Select Case sTemp
    Case "(*.CSV) Comma Delimited"
        oBCP.DataFileType = SQLDMODataFile_CommaDelimitedChar

    Case "(*.TAB) Tab Delimited"
        oBCP.DataFileType = SQLDMODataFile_TabDelimitedChar

    Case "(*.DAT) Native"
        oBCP.DataFileType = SQLDMODataFile_NativeFormat

End Select

'Step 3 - Export the Data
'
'Here is the part you have been waiting for -
'Pass the BCP object to the table ExportData method and
'away it goes!
'

iNumRows = BCPTable.ExportData(oBCP)
```

LISTING 26.6   Continued

```
    'The output results are written to a file.
    'Create a file object to read the contents
    'of the file and display the output file results in the status text box.
    '
    Set oOutputFile = New CFile
    oOutputFile.FileName = oBCP.LogFilePath
    oOutputFile.IOMode = "INPUT"
    oOutputFile.IOType = "SEQUENTIAL"
    oOutputFile.OpenFile
    If oOutputFile.Status = 1 Then
        oOutputFile.ReadAll sTempBuf
        If sTempBuf <> "" Then
            txtStatus.Text = sTempBuf
        Else
            txtStatus.Text = Str(iNumRows) & " rows exported."
        End If
    Else
        txtStatus = "Error reading BCP output file."
    End If
    oOutputFile.CloseFile

    'Report the number of rows exported
    MsgBox Str(iNumRows) & " rows exported.", vbInformation, "Bulk Copy"

    'Cleanup and Exit
Export_Exit:
    '
    Set oBCP = Nothing
    Set BCPTable = Nothing
    Set oOutputFile = Nothing
    StatusBar1.Panels("status").Text = ""
    frmMain7.MousePointer = vbDefault
    Exit Sub

Export_Error:
    MsgBox Err.Description
    Resume Export_Exit


End Sub
```

NOTE

The BCP code provided does not import data, but you can modify the code to add this feature. The value of the `BulkCopy` object property `ImportRowsPerBatch` is set and is included in the export data code—even though it is not used during BCP export—in case you want to modify the code to import data. The log and error files created when performing BCP default to the DBA Assistant application directory (that is, the directory where the DBA Assistant is executing) with the filenames `sams_bcp.log` and `sams_bcp.err`.

Using SQL-DMO with Stored Procedures

Not comfortable with Visual Basic, but you're pretty good with Transact SQL? Have you ever been writing a stored procedure and wanted to perform some administrative task during the procedure like backing up a database or exporting a table? For those of you who answered yes to any of the previous questions, Microsoft has created a set of stored procedures that enable you to invoke COM-based objects that support OLE automation (that is SQL-DMO) within a stored procedure. You can use SQL-DMO via Transact SQL or you can write your own OLE automation servers using your Windows tool of choice (for example, Visual Basic) to create components that can be invoked through Transact SQL. Creating your own components enables you to perform complex operations that might be difficult or impossible using Transact SQL. OLE automation also enables you to use existing business objects that other Windows- or COM-based applications might already be using. The following stored procedures enable you to write Transact SQL batches and stored procedures that act as OLE automation clients and can create and control OLE automation servers:

- sp_OACreate

- sp_OAGetErrorInfo

- sp_OAMethod

- sp_OAGetProperty

- sp_OASetProperty

- sp_OAStop

- sp_OADestroy

OLE Automation Procedures

Before looking at an example of using SQL-DMO using Transact SQL, take a look at each OLE automation stored procedure.

`sp_OACreate`

`sp_OACreate` creates an instance of an OLE automation object. Think of it as the Visual Basic equivalent to `CreateObject`. The syntax is as follows:

```
sp_OACreate 'ProgramID'|'classid', object_token OUTPUT [,process_context]
```

ProgramID has the form `OLEComponentName.Class`: *classid* is the class identifier of the OLE object, which has the form *nnnnnnnn-nnnn-nnnn-nnnn-nnnnnnnnnnnn*; *object_token* is the returned object token of type Transact SQL type `int`; and *process_context,* an optional parameter, specifies whether the object runs in the server process or out of process, or supports either. The procedure also returns a status. If the status returned is not `0`, an error has occurred.

For example, the following Transact SQL creates a SQL Server SQL-DMO object:

```
Declare @oSQL int
Declare @status int
@status = sp_OACreate 'SQLDMO.SQLServer',@oSQL OUT
```

`sp_OAGetErrorInfo`

When invoking the Transact SQL OLE automation stored procedures, use `sp_OAGetErrorInfo` to retrieve error status from the previous `sp_OA` call. The error status is reset each time an OLE automation stored procedure is called, except for `sp_OAGetErrorInfo`. The syntax is as follows:

```
sp_OAGetErrorInfo [object_token[,source OUTPUT[,description OUTPUT
➥[,help_file OUTPUT [,help_id]]]]]
```

The syntax breaks down as follows: *object_token* is the object token of a previously created OLE automation object; `source` is a `char` or `varchar` variable to return the source of the error; `description` is a `char` or `varchar` character that returns a description of the error; `help_file` is a `char` or `varchar` variable that returns the help file for the OLE automation object; and `help_id`, which must be a data type of `int`, is the help file context ID for the OLE automation object.

For example, the following Transact SQL creates ways to check for an error using `sp_OAGetErrorInfo`:

```
If @status <> 0
Begin
exec sp_OAGetErrorInfo @oSQL,@source OUT, @ErrorDescription OUT
end
```

NOTE

In the example code just listed, OUT is a permissible Transact SQL shortcut for OUTPUT.

sp_OAMethod

To invoke a method on an OLE automation object, use sp_OAMethod. The syntax for sp_OAMethod is as follows:

```
sp_OAMethod object_token, method_name, [,return_value OUTPUT,
➥[,@parametername=]parameter [OUTPUT] [...n]]]
```

In this case, *object_token* is the object token of a previously created OLE automation object; *method_name* is the method to invoke; *return_value* is the value returned from the method; *@parametername* is used to specify a named parameter; *parameter* is a local variable; and *OUTPUT* is required if a value is returned from the method.

sp_OAGetProperty

sp_OAGetProperty retrieves the property value of an OLE automation object. sp_OAGetProperty has the following syntax:

```
sp_OAGetProperty @object_token, property_name [,property_value OUTPUT][,index...]
```

Here, *object_token* is the object token of a previously created OLE automation object; *property_name* is the name of the property to retrieve; property_value is the variable to return the property value to; and index is an index parameter used by some OLE object properties.

If you do not specify a local variable (such as property_value parameter) to return the property, the value is returned in a resultset that consists of a single column/single row array. Multidimensional arrays and OLE objects can also be returned. The following is an example of getting the path where a BCP log file is to be written:

```
Declare @property_return varchar(255)
exec @status = sp_OAGetProperty @oBCP, 'LogFilePath', @property_return OUT
```

sp_OASetProperty

To set a property on an OLE automation object, use the stored procedure sp_OASetProperty, which has the following syntax:

```
sp_OASetProperty @object_token, property_name new_value [,index...]
```

In this case, *object_token* is the object token of a previously created OLE automation object; *property_name* is the name of the property to retrieve; new_value is the value to set the property; and index is an index parameter used by some OLE object properties.

The following is an example of setting the path where a BCP log file is to be written:

```
Declare @property_return varchar(255)
exec @status = sp_OASetProperty @oBCP, 'LogFilePath', "C:\BCP\LOG\bcp.log"
```

sp_OAStop

The first time sp_OACreate is invoked on a SQL Server, the OLE Automation
Environment is started up on that SQL Server and shared by all clients using OLE
automation via the OLE automation stored procedures. To stop the environment, use
the stored procedure sp_OAStop, which has the following syntax:

sp_OAStop

This will stop the shared environment and cause errors in any clients that were using
OLE Automation via the OLE automation stored procedures at the time of the shutdown. The next time sp_OACreate is invoked, the environment will restart. It is not
necessary to shut down the OLE automation environment because it is shut down
when SQL Server is halted.

sp_OADestroy

sp_OADestroy destroys the created OLE object (for example removes the object reference and frees up memory). The syntax is as follows:

sp_OADestroy object_token

In this case, *object_token* is the object token of a previously created OLE automation object.

> **NOTE**
>
> It is a good programming practice to call sp_OADestroy to clean up and remove any OLE
> objects you use that are not necessary. SQL Server automatically destroys any objects you use
> at the end of the Transact SQL batch.

Transact SQL Examples

The following examples show you how to use SQL-DMO within a Transact-SQL
stored procedure.

BCP Out T-SQL Example

The following example is a stored procedure that uses SQL-DMO and the OLE
automation stored procedures to perform a bulk copy operation. This example is
included because it can be used to solve a common real-world scenario. The (typical)

real-world scenario is a stored procedure that is summarizing or rolling up data. After the summarization or rollup is completed, the information is to be exported to a flat file. One of the problems you encounter in this problem is how to know that the stored procedure has successfully summarized or rolled up the information so that you can perform the BCP. The second problem then becomes how to invoke the BCP. The most elegant solution is to use SQL-DMO, which enables you to perform the BCP operation from within a Transact SQL batch, which solves both of your problems.

The code, shown in Listing 26.7, is well documented and self-explanatory. Read the comments and code to quickly see how easy it is to use SQL-DMO and the OLE automation stored procedures! The following Transact SQL script is located on the Web site in a file called TSQLBCP.sql.

LISTING 26.7   Performing BCP Export on Selected Table Using Transact SQL

```
CREATE         PROCEDURE usp_BCP_Table_Out @tablename varchar(30),
@outpath varchar(255)
 AS

/*
** This stored procedure is an example of using SQL DMO to
** export a table out.
*/

/* Declare Variables used */
Declare @oSQL int, @oBCP int  /* Used to store object tokens */
Declare @status int /* Used to check error status */
Declare @source varchar(255), @description varchar(255) /*
➥Error information output parameters */
Declare @iNumRows int     /* Number of Rows Exported */
Declare @temp varchar(255) /* Temp area to construct SQL-DMO statement */
Declare @db_name varchar(30) /* database name */
/*
** Create the SQL Server object
*/
exec @status = sp_OACreate 'SQLDMO.SQLServer', @oSQL OUT

if @status <> 0
begin
    exec @status = sp_OAGetErrorInfo @oSQL,@source,@description
    Select  @source "Source of Error", @description "Error Description"
```

LISTING 26.7   Continued

```
    return
end

/*
** Log on to the SQL Server
*/
exec @status = sp_OAMethod @oSQL, "Connect", NULL, "(local)", "sa"

if @status <> 0
begin
    exec @status = sp_OAGetErrorInfo @oSQL,@source,@description
    Select  @source "Source of Error", @description "Error Description"
    return
end

/*
** Create the BCP object
*/
exec @status = sp_OACreate 'SQLDMO.BulkCopy', @oBCP OUT

if @status <> 0
begin
    exec @status = sp_OAGetErrorInfo @oBCP,@source,@description
    Select  @source "Source of Error", @description "Error Description"
    return
end

/*
** Set some BCP Properties
*/

/*
** Path to export file to - use path passed in as a parameter
*/
exec @status = sp_OASetProperty @oBCP, 'DataFilePath',@outpath
if @status <> 0
begin
    exec @status = sp_OAGetErrorInfo @oBCP,@source,@description
    Select  @source "Source of Error", @description "Error Description"
```

LISTING 26.7   Continued

```
   return
end

/*
**Path to create error and log file
*/
exec @status = sp_OASetProperty @oBCP, 'ErrorFilePath',"C:\bcperror.txt"

if @status <> 0
begin
   exec @status = sp_OAGetErrorInfo @oBCP,@source,@description
   Select  @source "Source of Error", @description "Error Description"
   return
end

exec @status = sp_OASetProperty @oBCP, 'LogFilePath',"C:\bcplog.txt"

if @status <> 0
begin
   exec @status = sp_OAGetErrorInfo @oBCP,@source,@description
   Select  @source "Source of Error", @description "Error Description"
   return
end

/*
** Now Let's create the string - to export the table.
** We will use the SQL Server object databases collection and the
** database table collection to invoke the table ExportData method.
**
** Note: this stored procedure uses the name of the current
** database by using the DB_Name function.
*/

Select @db_name = DB_NAME()

/*
** Build SQL_DMO string
*/
Select @temp =  'Databases(' + '"' + @db_name + '"' + ').Tables('
Select @temp = @temp + '"' + @tablename + '"' + ').ExportData'
```

LISTING 26.7   Continued

```
/*
** Now execute the string using SQL Server Dynamic SQL features
*/
exec @status = sp_OAMethod @oSQL,@temp,@iNumRows OUT,@oBCP

if @status <> 0
begin
   exec @status = sp_OAGetErrorInfo @oSQL,@source,@description
   Select  @source "Source of Error", @description "Error Description"
   return
end

Select @iNumRows "Number of rows exported"

/*
** Clean up and destroy the OLE objects
*/
exec @status = sp_OADestroy @oBCP
if @status <> 0
begin
   exec @status = sp_OAGetErrorInfo @oBCP,@source,@description
   Select  @source "Source of Error", @description "Error Description"

end
exec @status = sp_OADestroy @oSQL
if @status <> 0
begin
   exec @status = sp_OAGetErrorInfo @oSQL,@source,@description
   Select  @source "Source of Error", @description "Error Description"
end
```

Show Database Size Example

The following example displays the size of all the databases on a SQL Server. The
stored procedure uses SQL-DMO as well as a Transact-SQL cursor, discussed in detail
in Chapter 22 "Using Stored Procedures and Cursors." This example is similar to the
BCP example except that integrated security is used to log on to SQL Server instead
of standard SQL Server authentication. DBAs may want to modify this example to
store the size of the database in a table for trend and capacity planning.

LISTING 26.8   Viewing Database Size Using Transact SQL

```
Create Procedure usp_GetDBSize
as
SET NOCOUNT ON
Declare @oSQL int, @oDB int          /* Used to store object tokens */Declare
@status int                  /* Used to check error status */Declare @source var-
char(255), @description varchar(255) /*Error information output parameters
*/Declare @size int
Declare @db_name varchar(40),@temp varchar(120)
/*** Create the SQL Server object*/exec @status = sp_OACreate 'SQLDMO.SQLServer',
@oSQL OUTif @status <> 0begin   exec @status = sp_OAGetErrorInfo
@oSQL,@source,@description   Select  @source "Source of Error", @description "Error
Description"end
/*** Log on to the SQL Server - Use trusted connection*/
EXEC @status = sp_OASetProperty @oSQL, 'LoginSecure','True'
IF @status <> 0
BEGIN
   EXEC sp_OAGetErrorInfo @oDB, @source OUT, @description OUT
   Select  @source "Source of Error", @description "Error Description"
   RETURN
END
exec @status = sp_OAMethod @oSQL, 'Connect',Null,'(local)','','''if @status <>
0begin   exec @status = sp_OAGetErrorInfo @oSQL,@source,@description   Select
@source "Source of Error", @description "Error Description"end

/*** Create the Database object*/exec @status = sp_OACreate 'SQLDMO.Database', @oDB
OUTif @status <> 0begin   exec @status = sp_OAGetErrorInfo @oDB,@source,@descrip-
tion   Select  @source "Source of Error", @description "Error Description"end/*
** Create a cursor of databases.
*/
declare database_crsr cursor
for
Select name
from master..sysdatabases
FOR READ ONLY

open database_crsr

fetch next from database_crsr
into @db_name
```

LISTING 26.8 Continued

```
While @@fetch_status = 0
BEGIN

/*
** Get the database using database collection
*/
Set @temp = 'Databases("' + @db_name + '")'
EXEC @status = sp_OAGetProperty @oSQL, @temp, @oDB OUT
IF @status <> 0
BEGIN
   EXEC sp_OAGetErrorInfo @oDB, @source OUT, @description OUT
   Select  @source "Source of Error", @description "Error Description"
    RETURN
END

/*
** Get the database size - using the SQL-DMO size property.
*/
EXEC @status = sp_OAGetProperty @oDB, 'Size', @Size OUT
IF @status <> 0
BEGIN
   EXEC sp_OAGetErrorInfo @oDB, @source OUT, @description OUT
   Select  @source "Source of Error", @description "Error Description"
    RETURN
END

/*
** Display the size.
*/
Select @db_name "database", @size "Size"

/*
** Get next record.
*/
fetch next from database_crsr
into @db_name

END /* End of While @@fetch_status */
/*
** Clean up cursor
*/
```

LISTING 26.8   Continued

```
close database_crsr
deallocate database_crsr


/*** Clean up and destroy the OLE objects*/
exec @status = sp_OADestroy @oDB
if @status <> 0
begin
   exec @status = sp_OAGetErrorInfo @oDB,@source,@description
   Select  @source "Source of Error", @description "Error Description"
end
exec @status = sp_OADestroy @oSQL
if @status <> 0
begin
   exec @status = sp_OAGetErrorInfo @oSQL,@source,@description
   Select  @source "Source of Error", @description "Error Description"
end
```

SQL-DMO FAQ

Following are some frequently asked questions about SQL-DMO and the COM object
stored procedures:

Q Can I Create Internet SQL-DMO applications?

A SQL-DMO is a COM-based interface, so of course you can create Web-based
applications with Web servers that support COM, such as Microsoft's Internet
Information Server's Active Server Pages. To help get you started, we include a
small Web-based Active Server Page example that enables you to log on to your
SQL Server via the Internet and view the status of scheduled tasks.

Q I'm having a hard time finding examples of SQL-DMO—any suggestions?

A SQL-DMO is one of SQL Server's hidden features. It appears that developers and
DBAs have been slow to look into SQL-DMO and use it to their advantage.
However, SQL-DMO's usefulness is starting to be noticed. Several NT and devel-
oper's magazines have run articles on SQL-DMO. You can also check
Microsoft's Web site for SQL-DMO examples as well as perform a Web search
on SQL-DMO.

Q Can I use other COM objects in my stored procedures besides SQL-DMO?

A Sure, the COM object stored procedures work with any COM-based object that can be created using ActiveX (OLE) automation. The component needs to be properly registered on the SQL Server where you want to create the object.

Summary

For the non–Visual Basic DBAs in the crowd, I hope that these explanations and code examples were easy for you to follow and that they motivated you to learn Visual Basic.

If you are unfamiliar with Visual Basic but quite comfortable with Transact SQL, the BCP example of using the OLE automation procedures and SQL-DMO provides you with an example you can learn from and use in your existing applications.

Using SQL-DMO, you can create powerful DBA tools that can be used to simplify your job!

PART XII

Replication

IN THIS PART

27 Replication

28 Transactional Replication

29 Snapshot and Merge Replication

27

Replication

by Laura Jones

Data replication is a powerful feature of SQL Server. SQL Server 7.0 provided many improvements from previous versions, and SQL Server 2000 builds on those features and adds more to increase the reliability, ease of use, and management of replication.

> **NOTE**
>
> I throw in the fact that it ships with the standard product because several other RDBMS vendors treat replication as a separate product for which you pay extra.

In a nutshell, *replication* is the capability to reliably duplicate data from a source database to one or more destination databases. Using Microsoft SQL Server replication, you can automatically distribute data from one SQL Server to many different SQL Servers through ODBC (Open Database Connectivity) or OLE DB. SQL Server 2000 enables you to replicate to non-SQL Server subscribers (heterogeneous subscribers), such as Microsoft Access or Oracle, using ODBC or OLE DB and enables support for Internet anonymous subscribers. SQL Server replication provides update replication capabilities such as immediate updating subscribers and merge replication. With all the new enhancements to SQL Server replication, the number of possible applications and business scenarios is mind-boggling. In Chapters 28, "Transactional Replication," and 29, "Merge Replication," you examine the different types of replication in detail as well as appropriate and inappropriate applications for each type. However, for starters here

IN THIS CHAPTER

- Replication Overview and Terminology

- Creating and Assigning the Distribution Database

- Configuring Replication Distribution Options

- Deleting a Distribution Database

- Configuring Replication Publishing

- Enabling Replication Subscribers

- Using the Disabling Publishing and Distribution Wizard

- Adding NonSQL Server (Heterogeneous) Subscribers

- Upgrading SQL Server Replication

- Replication FAQ

are some examples of applications or scenarios in which SQL Server replication can be used:

- To distribute the workload across servers (such as moving an *ad-hoc* query and reporting capability from a source server).

- To move specific subsets of data (such as a company department or one month's worth of data) from a main central server.

- When you have a central database that is updated and the updates must be moved out to other databases (such as a department store changing prices for an item).

- Account management/tracking applications used by salesmen or field reps using laptops in a disconnected mode that later replicate changes to a central internal server.

- A Web-based user group or subscription application that can periodically pull down database changes via the Web.

- Environments in which servers are importing flat-file information. Use a central database to import the flat file and replicate the information to the other sites.

NOTE

Some of the screens in this chapter will differ, depending on the platform and edition of SQL Server. The screens for this chapter were captured on a Windows 2000 Server using the standard version of SQL Server. You will find that on the Desktop and Personal editions, some buttons or functionality might be missing. The Desktop and Personal editions of SQL Server 2000 can be subscribers for all forms of replication, but can only be publishers for merge and snapshot replication.

Replication Overview and Terminology

As stated earlier, SQL Server 2000 has added many new enhancements to data replication. This chapter focuses on introducing you to SQL Server replication terminology and the different types of replication. Additionally it shows you how to perform standard administrative tasks such as creating a distribution database. The next two chapters will get into more detail as they walk you through transactional, merge, and snapshot replication. To become familiar with replication terminology, consider the replication scenario shown in Figure 27.1. With transactional replication, the publication is modified at the publisher's site and the changes are replicated to the subscribers of the publication.

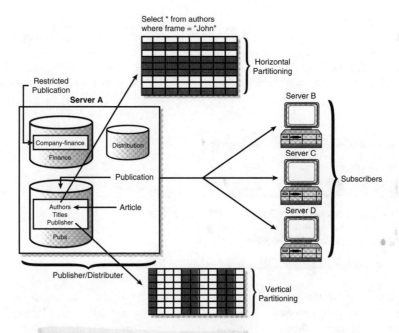

FIGURE 27.1   Overview of replication (transactional).

Publish and Subscribe

SQL Server replication uses a *publish and subscribe* metaphor. Servers publish publications to which other servers can subscribe. A good analogy of this process would be a magazine. The publishers provide subscriptions of their magazine publication. The subscribers of the magazine acquire their copies of the publication and read the articles that interest them. That is how SQL Server replication works as well. A SQL Server that makes data available to other servers for subscribing purposes is called a *publisher*. For example, Server A in Figure 27.1 is a publisher. A SQL Server that subscribes to a publication published by another SQL Server is said to be a *subscriber*. (An example of a subscription server is Server B in Figure 27.1.) A SQL Server that contains the distribution database is said to be a *distributor*. (The distribution server is Server A in Figure 27.1.)

Publication and Articles

A publisher publishes a collection of one or more articles called a *publication*. The publication shown in Figure 27.1 contains the authors, titles, and publishers table found in the SQL Server sample database, pubs. An *article* is the basic unit of replication and can be a table, a subset of the table, or stored procedures. Do you see the similarities between SQL Server replication and the magazine analogy?

NOTE

Articles are always associated with a publication and cannot be published by themselves. SQL Server 7.0 allowed subscriptions to a single article. SQL Server 2000 still supports this feature for compatibility reasons via Transact-SQL. However, it is strongly recommended that you only subscribe to publications, which is much easier to administer than a subscription to a single article.

Publications can contain one or more of the following:

- Tables
- Vertically partitioned tables
- Stored procedures (New for SQL Server 2000)
- Horizontally partitioned tables
- Horizontally and vertically partitioned tables

A *vertical partitioned table* (refer to Figure 27.1) is an article that uses a filter to select only certain columns of a table. A *horizontal partitioned table* (refer Figure 27.1) is an article that uses a filter to select only specific rows in the table.

The following cannot be published:

- The model, tempdb, and msdb databases
- The system tables in the master database

Subscriptions Types (Push and Pull)

Changes made at the publisher can be replicated to the subscribers via a push subscription or a pull subscription. With a *push subscription*, the publication server is responsible for replicating all changes to the subscribers without the subscribers asking for the changes. A push subscription is typically used when the subscribing databases want the changes as soon as they are made or a high level of security is required. With a *pull subscription*, the subscriber initiates the replication instead of the publisher. Pull subscriptions require lower overhead than push subscriptions and are better suited for situations with a large number of subscribers or lower security requirements.

Server Roles

SQL Server can play one or more of the following roles during the replication process:

- **Publisher**—A publisher server is responsible for maintaining its source databases, making the data available for replication, and sending the data to the distribution database to be replicated to subscribing servers.

- **Subscriber**—A subscriber server receives and maintains published data. Subscribers can also make changes to publications. In cases where a subscriber changes the publication, the subscriber is still a subscriber and not a publisher. (The information still has only a single publisher.)

- **Distributor**—The distribution server maintains the distribution database, which is responsible for the store and forward capabilities of SQL Server snapshot and transactional replication. The job of the distribution server is to replicate data from the distribution database to the appropriate subscribing servers.

SQL Server can participate in one or more replication roles. For example, in many cases, a publication server also serves as a distribution server and can also subscribe to other publications from other publishers (in which case, the same server that was acting as a publisher and distributor is also acting as a subscriber). It is not uncommon for a subscriber also to be a publisher. However, in all SQL Server replication cases, for a publication there exists only a single master copy of the database, which is maintained by the publisher (regardless of how many different subscribers are allowed to update the publication). For example, in a merge replication publication scenario, server A publishes the pubs database. Server B and server C are subscribers and make modifications to the database. The master copy of the database that is receiving the changes is the publisher's database, server A. Server B receives server C's changes when server B replicates with server A.

Out of the box, nonSQL Server systems, such as Oracle and Microsoft Access, can be subscribers of all types of replication (except Immediate Updating Subscribers). However, Microsoft has created an open interface to SQL Server's transaction-based replication services so that third parties can create products that allow nonSQL Server systems (that is, heterogeneous data sources) to become publishers.

Replication Types

SQL Server 2000 has several different types of replication that can be used for a variety of business applications. The next few chapters look at each different type of replication in detail and when and how to use it. The SQL Server 2000–supported replication types are as follows:

- Transactional

- Snapshot

- Merge

- Immediate Updating Subscribers

Transactional

In transactional replication, the publication is modified at the publisher's site and the changes are replicated to the subscribers of the publication. Transactional replication was part of SQL Server 6.x replication. In essence, subscribers of the publication do not modify the publication but treat the information as read-only. This does not mean that all updates to an underlying table must happen at one site. Using vertical and horizontal partitioning, you can create solutions that allow for multiple sites editing information in the same table.

The key, however, to partitioning is that each site owns a particular partition of data that can only be modified by the publishing site. SQL Server 2000 makes it possible to use bi-directional transactional replication without partitioning by using custom stored procedures and loopback detection.

However, because the majority of transactional replication essentially is used by subscribers who treat the publications as read-only or use partitioning, there is no need for conflict resolution or lost updates. Such problems are avoided by the transactional-replication model and data partitioning. Examples of good transaction-based applications/scenarios are a database of rollup information, data marts, databases with regional or divisional information, and a central sales or inventory database that is updated and replicated to different sites.

Snapshot

Snapshot replication takes a snapshot of the schema and data at a certain point in time and replicates this information to subscribing databases. Snapshot replication was also included in SQL Server 6.x and is the simplest type of replication to implement. Because the data is provided as a snapshot of information at some point in time, there is no need to worry about conflicts or loss of transactions. Examples of good snapshot-based applications/scenarios are lookup tables that do not change frequently, anonymous subscribers, static information, or information that is infrequently updated.

Merge

Merge replication enables users to subscribe to a publication and edit the same articles (tables) in the publication without any partitioning or custom procedures. When a subscriber edits the publication, the change is replicated back to the publisher. If a conflict occurs (for example, different users modify the same row at different sites after the databases are synched), the conflict is resolved either by priority-based rules or the first one to change the row wins. A good merge application or scenario is a sales tracking/call application in which a salesman uses a laptop computer in a disconnected mode to add a new customer or record a sales call. Later when the salesman is back in the office and connects the laptop to the network, the SQL Server database on the laptop merges the changes made to the central SQL Server database.

Immediate Updating Subscribers

Immediate Updating Subscribers is another form of SQL Server 2000 update replication. The Immediate Updating Subscriber is transaction-based replication (available with snapshot and transactional replication) that enables the subscriber to modify articles in the publication. The modification is then made at the publisher using the two-phase commit protocol and replicated to the other subscribers using the standard transaction-based replication mode. The two-phase commit protocol requires that the change occur immediately on all servers participating in the transaction or the transaction is rolled back. Therefore, all servers participating in the transaction must have a reliable connection to one another.

Immediate Updating Subscribers removes the complexity of requiring all sites to participate in a two-phase commit (which requires that all sites are connected) and yet still maintain transaction integrity. Good applications/scenarios for Immediate Updating Subscribers are applications with good network connections, applications that do not have high levels of OLTP (OnLine Transaction Processing), and applications that need the same number at the remote site as well as a central site.

Transactional Consistency

Transactional consistency in the context of replication means that the data will be identical across all sites with a result that could have been achieved had all transactions been performed at a single site. Replication also adds the caveat of eventuality or at some point in time because there might be a time delay from the time the change is made to the time the data is replicated to the subscribers. SQL Server 2000 replication falls into two modes of transaction consistency: guaranteed loose consistency and guaranteed no consistency. Let's look at the guaranteed tight consistency model and the compare it to the two models provided by SQL Server replication.

In a tight consistency model, all transactions are committed or rolled back on all the servers so that the data is in synch 100% of the time. A *guaranteed tight consistency* distributed data model can be accomplished with SQL Server using a two-phase commit protocol. In a loose consistency model, transactions are committed or rolled back on a source server. The transactions on the source server are then replicated asynchronously to subscribing servers. *Guaranteed loose consistency* means that the data synchronization between the source and destination servers does not occur simultaneously.

The big difference between the guaranteed tight consistency model and the guaranteed loose consistency model is that, with the guaranteed loose consistency model, there is some lag time between when changes are made to the source server and when they are replicated to the destination servers (that is, the databases are temporarily out of synch). Transactional replication and snapshot replication are all examples of the guaranteed loose consistency model. The transaction-based

Immediate Updating Subscriber model lies somewhere between guaranteed loose consistency and guaranteed tight consistency. With an Immediate Updating Subscriber, a two-phase commit (tight consistency) is used between two sites (the publisher and a subscriber) and then the standard transactional replication (loose consistency) is used to replicate the change to all other subscribers.

Merge replication falls into the guaranteed no consistency model. With *guaranteed no consistency*, the data will be identical across all sites with a result that might not have been achieved had all transactions been performed at a single site (see Chapter 29 for an actual example). Because Merge replication is for sites that are regularly disconnected, site autonomy is more important than transaction consistency. All the sites end up with the same value; however, it might be a value that would not have been achieved had all the changes been made at a single site. For an example of guaranteed no consistency when using merge replication see Chapter 29 the section "Merge Replication and Transactional Consistency."

The Problem That SQL Server 2000 Replication Cannot Solve

There is one situation which SQL Server replication cannot address (nor can any of the competition despite their update-anywhere claims). It is having multiple sites without reliable connections update data at any time with any frequency and maintain transactional integrity. The problem is that, as sites become disconnected (through, for example, unreliable connections), transaction integrity is rapidly lost. A disconnected site could make a change to a record that is deleted by another site. When the site reconnects, a problem occurs as the update fails because the record no longer exists on the master database. As you read the details about the different types of replication in the next few chapters, you will see further reasons why the problem can't be solved.

Distribution Database

The distribution database stores all the transactions to be replicated to subscribing servers (transactional replication) and acts as the store-and-forward database for replicated transactions. Transactions stay in the distribution database until all subscribers have successfully received the transaction. The distribution database is used to store publication and subscriber synchronization information as well. The following are some of the system tables that make up the distribution database:

- `MSmerge_history`—Contains historical information about previous subscriber updates.

- `MSmerge_agents`—Contains information about merge agents.

- `MSdistribution_agents`—Contains information about distribution agents.

- `MSdistribution_history`—Contains historical information for distribution agents.

- `MSlogreader_agents`—Contains information about log reader agents at the local distributor.

- `MSlogreader_history`—Contains historical information for log reader agents.

- `MSrepl_commands`—Contains replicated commands.

- `MSrepl_errors`—Contains information about failed replication.

- `MSrepl_transactions`—Contains a row for each replicated transaction.

- `MSrepl_version`—Contains a single row with the current version of replication installed.

An Overview of the SQL Server Replication Agents

To effectively administer SQL Server 2000 replication, make yourself familiar with the different agents used for replication. Chapter 28 and Chapter 29 cover each of the agents' roles in detail. The agents are as follows:

- **Log reader agent**—The *log reader agent* searches the transaction log of published databases for transaction log entries marked for replication. The log reader agent moves the marked transactions to the distribution database. All transaction-based publications have a log reader agent.

- **Merge agent**—The *merge agent* is responsible for merging incremental changes as well as applying the initial snapshot created by the snapshot agent. Each merge publication has a merge agent.

- **Snapshot agent**—The *snapshot agent* creates the snapshot files on the distributor and tracks the synchronization status in the distribution database between the published database and the subscribing databases. All publications have a snapshot agent.

- **Distribution agent**—The *distribution agent* distributes the transactions stored in the distribution database to the subscribing servers. Transactional and snapshot publications have a distribution agent for each subscriber.

- **Queue Reader agent**—The *queue reader agent* can be used with snapshot or transactional replication. It is a multithreaded process that runs on the distributor, taking messages from a queue and applying them to the appropriate publication.

SQL Server 2000 allows the merge agent and distribution agent to be executed from applications other than SQL Server using the ActiveX controls provided. Additional functionality can be added using SQL-DMO and third-party agents. Figure 27.2 shows an overview of the different interfaces and agents possible in SQL Server 2000.

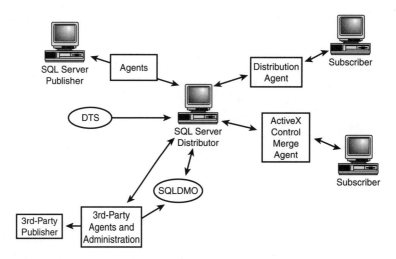

FIGURE 27.2   Overview of SQL Server replication interfaces and agents.

Synchronization Modes

The process of synchronization transfers data between the publisher and the subscribers after the initial snapshot has been applied to the subscriber. SQL Server uses the distribution agent and the merge agent to move data when changes occur at the publisher or the subscriber. The different types of synchronization used in replication are

- Transactional Synchronization
- Merge Synchronization
- Synchronizing Schema Changes
- On Demand Script Execution

With the No Synchronization option, SQL Server assumes that the articles in the source are already in synch with articles in the destination. SQL Server does nothing to verify that the databases are synchronized; that task is up to you.

Walking Through Automatic Synchronization

For this example, assume that server B selects Automatic synchronization during the subscription process. The distribution server creates two files referred to as a *synchronization set* in the replication working directory (the default is \REPLDATA off the SQL Server home directory). The synchronization set consists of a BCP data file with the actual data of the subscribed articles and the article's table schema file.

TIP

Schema files created for replication have a .SCH extension; the data files have a .BCP file extension.

After the synchronization set is created, a synchronization job is added to the distribution database. The distribution process reads the distribution database and applies the synchronization file set to the subscribing server (in this example, server B). First the schema file is applied to create the table schema. The table information is then copied to the subscribing server using BCP. The distribution server is notified that synchronization has completed, and server A can begin to replicate the publication MyPubs to server B.

NOTE

After all other subscriptions have acknowledged successful synchronization, the .BCP files are removed from the replication working directory.

Any transactions that occurred to the published articles after the subscribing server first subscribed but before the synchronization process occurred are then replicated to the subscriber.

Creating and Assigning the Distribution Database

Now that you have an overview of SQL Server replication, examine how to set up replication. First, examine how to create or specify the distribution database.

NOTE

Creating a distribution database requires sysadmin permission.

To create a distribution database, follow these steps using the SQL Enterprise Manager:

1. Select the server on which you want to install the distribution database.

2. From the SQL Enterprise Manager menu, select Tools and then select Replication. A drop-down menu appears (see Figure 27.3). Select the Configure Publishing, Subscribers, and Distribution option. You can also right-click the Replication folder and choose Configure Publishing, Subscribers, and Distribution. The Configure Publishing and Distribution Wizard dialog box appears (see Figure 27.4).

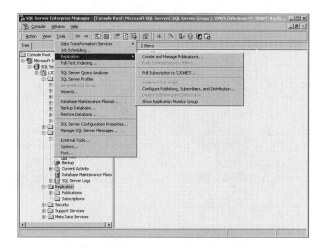

FIGURE 27.3   The Replication Configuration menu and option list.

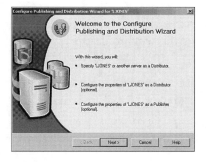

FIGURE 27.4   The Configure Publishing and Distribution Wizard dialog box.

3. The Configure Publishing and Distribution Wizard walks you through the process of creating a distribution database or a publication. To continue the process, click the Next button.

4. The Select Distributor dialog box, shown in Figure 27.5, appears.

   To make the selected server a distributor and create a distribution database on the server, select the default option, Make *Server Name* Its Own Distributor. This action creates a distribution database on the selected server. To use another server with an existing distribution database, select Use the Following Server, which Has Already Been Configured as a Distributor option, click the Add Server button, and select the server you want to use. For this example, you create a new distribution database on the selected server. Click the Next button. The Customize the Configuration dialog box appears (see Figure 27.6).

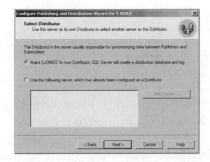

FIGURE 27.5   The Select Distributor dialog box.

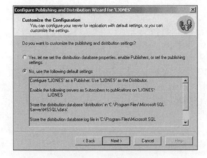

FIGURE 27.6   The Customize the Configuration dialog box.

The Configure Publishing and Distribution dialog box enables you to take the default or use a custom configuration. The custom configuration lets you configure the following options:

- Distribution database (name and location)
- Enable publishers
- Enable databases for publishing
- Enable subscribers

If you take the default, the distribution database is called distribution (unless there is more than one distribution database). The files for the data and log are located in the \Program Files\Microsoft SQL Server\MSSQL\Data directory. All registered servers are selected as eligible subscribers. No databases are published and the server that the distribution database is being installed on is enabled for publishing. After you have made your selections, custom or default (in the case of the custom install, fill in the required parameters), click the Next button and then the Finish button on the following dialog box.

NOTE

If the SQLSERVERAGENT service is configured to log on as Local System account, the distribution database will not be created. Make sure an account with sysadmin privileges is used for the SQLSERVERAGENT service to log in.

A progress dialog box appears as the distribution database is created and publishers and subscribers are added, followed by a successful creation dialog box. Another dialog box will appear to tell you that SQL Server added the Replication Monitor to the console tree. At this point the distribution database has been created. The distribution database contains the system tables described and system stored procedures used by the Distributor during replication.

Configuring Replication Distribution Options

Using SQL Enterprise Manager, you can configure the distribution database agent logon information, amount of time to hold replicated transactions, and holding time of replication performance information. Additionally you can view all the publishers using the distribution database. To set distribution database options, perform the following:

1. Select the server on which you want to configure the distribution database options.

2. From the SQL Enterprise Manager menu, select Tools and then select Replication. A drop-down menu appears; select the Configure Publishing, Subscribers, and Distribution option. The Publisher and Distributor Properties dialog box appears, with the Distributor tab, shown in Figure 27.7.

FIGURE 27.7   The Publisher and Distributor Properties dialog box—Distributor tab.

By using the Agent Profiles button of the Publisher and Distributor Properties dialog box, you can set the user account used by replication agents when they log in to the distribution database. The default option is to impersonate the SQL Server Agent account used on the distribution computer. The Publishers password text box in the Publisher and Distributor Properties dialog box allows you to set up a password to be used by non-trusted publishers to connect to the distribution database. This is not required for trusted publishers.

Click the Properties button to display the properties of the selected distribution database. The Distribution Database Properties dialog box, shown in Figure 27.8, appears.

FIGURE 27.8   The Distribution Database Properties dialog box.

The Distribution Database Properties dialog box shows the current publishers using the distribution database. Also you can use the Distribution Database Properties dialog box to set the minimum and maximum number of hours/days to store transaction records that have already been replicated before purging them. This parameter is very important when creating a backup and recovery plan for the distribution server (see Chapter 10, "Backup and Recovery"). You can also set the amount of time replication performance history is maintained (in hours or days). The Publishers tab (not shown) displays a list of publishers using the distribution database.

Deleting a Distribution Database

SQL Server 2000 enables you to create multiple distribution databases on the same server. You can delete a distribution database without disabling the server as a distributor. However, when you remove a distribution database, any publications using the database are removed. To delete a distribution database, perform the following:

1. Select the server on which you want to delete the distribution database.

2. From the SQL Enterprise Manager menu, select Tools and then select Replication. A drop-down menu appears. Select the Configure Publishing, Subscribers, and Distribution option. The Publisher and Distributor Properties dialog box appears, shown in Figure 27.9.

FIGURE 27.9   The Publisher and Distributor Properties dialog box.

3. Select the distribution database you want to remove and click the Delete button.

NOTE

Before you can delete a distribution database, you must remove all publications and disable all the publishers using the distribution database. The Delete button in the Publisher and Distributor Properties dialog box will be disabled if publishers are attached to that distribution database.

The Transact-SQL command used to remove a distribution database is *sp_dropdistributiondb*, which has the following syntax:

```
sp_dropdistributiondb 'database'
```

database is the name of the distribution database to drop. The following example drops the distribution database distribution1:

```
sp_dropdistributiondb 'distribution1'
```

sp_dropdistributiondb removes the database from SQL Server and the data and log files if they are not being used by other databases.

Configuring Replication Publishing

After the distribution database has been successfully installed, or you have been given permission to publish to a remote distribution server, you can then configure a server to be a publisher.

NOTE

To set up SQL Server as a publisher, you must have one of the following:

- A local distribution database
- Access to a remote distribution database

If you have a local distribution database on your server (that is, your server is acting as a distribution server), you can perform the following:

- Set distribution working directory
- Allow other servers access to your distribution database for publishing

Both distribution servers and publisher servers can control which servers allow access to published articles and which databases on your local server can publish articles.

Adding a Publisher to a Distribution Database

To allow a remote server to use a local server's distribution database, perform the following:

1. Select the server on which you want to add publishers to the distribution database.

2. From the SQL Enterprise Manager menu, select Tools, and then select Replication. A drop-down menu appears. Select the Configure Publishing, Subscribers, and Distribution option. The Publisher and Distributor Properties dialog box appears. Select the Publishers tab, shown in Figure 27.10.

FIGURE 27.10   The Publisher and Distributor Properties dialog box—Publishers tab.

Check the box by the server you want to grant access. Select the distribution database to which you are granting the server publication access by clicking the square to the right of the selected server. To enable all remote servers, click the Enable All button. To remove a server from a distribution database and server, uncheck the server. Click the Enable None button to remove all remote servers from publishing to the server's distribution databases. To select a distribution database for the selected publisher, click the square to the left of the selected server. The Publisher Properties dialog box, shown in Figure 27.11, appears.

FIGURE 27.11   The Publisher Properties dialog box—General tab.

If the server has more than one distribution database, use the Distribution Database combo box, shown in Figure 27.11, to select the distribution database for the publisher to use. Use the Snapshot Folder text box to set the path where snapshot information for publications is to be stored. The Replication agents on the Distributor login to the Publisher area, in Figure 27.11, allow you to set up security and accounts used by the distributor's replication agents to log in to the publisher. The default setting is to impersonate the SQL Server Agent on the publisher, which requires a trusted connection. You can also use a regular SQL Server account. The Administrative link area allows you to determine how a publisher logs in to the distributor. You can set up a trusted connection or require a password.

The Transact-SQL command to add a publisher to a distribution database is sp_adddistpublisher, which has the following syntax:

```
sp_adddistpublisher 'publisher','distribution database'
➥[,security_mode[,logon[,password']]],
'working directory'
```

publisher is the server name to add as a publisher, *distribution database* is the distribution database to add the publisher to, *security_mode* determines how the server is being administered—0 uses SQL Server authentication, 1 uses Windows NT authentication, *logon* is the user logon name (sa if security_mode = 0), *password* is the logon password and *working directory* is the path of the working directory.

Enabling a Database for Publishing and Removing a Database from Publishing

Before you can create a publication that subscribers can subscribe to, you must first enable the database for publication. Enabling a database for publication allows publications to be created within the database for replication. You can also remove a database from having publication capabilities. To enable or disable a database for publishing, perform the following steps:

1. Select the server on which you want to add a publication.

2. From the SQL Enterprise Manager menu, select Tools and then select Replication. A drop-down menu appears. Select the Configure Publishing, Subscribers, and Distribution option. The Publisher and Distributor Properties dialog box appears. Select the Publication Databases tab, shown in Figure 27.12.

FIGURE 27.12   The Publisher and Distributor Properties dialog box—Publication Databases tab.

3. To enable a database for transactional or merge publication, select the check box next to the appropriate database.

4. To remove a database from publishing, deselect the server's check box beside the name of the database you want to remove. All existing publications in the database are removed.

5. The Enable All or Enable None buttons enable you to select all the databases or deselect all the databases for transactional or merge replication.

Enabling Replication Subscribers

To allow remote servers to receive data from your server, you must enable permissions for the remote servers using the SQL Enterprise Manager.

To enable subscribers, follow these steps:

1. Select the server on which you want to add a publication.

2. From the SQL Enterprise Manager menu, select Tools and then select Replication. A drop-down menu appears. Select the Configure Publishing, Subscribers, and Distribution option. The Publisher and Distributor Properties dialog box appears. Select the Subscribers tab, shown in Figure 27.13.

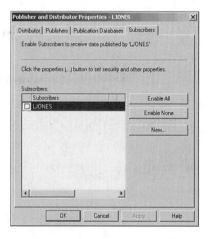

FIGURE 27.13   The Publisher and Distributor Properties dialog box—Subscribers tab.

To enable a server to subscribe, select the check box next to the server's name. To disable a server from subscribing, deselect the check box next to the server's name. To add a new server as a subscriber, click the New button. The Enable New Subscriber dialog box, shown in Figure 27.14, appears.

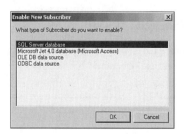

FIGURE 27.14   The Enable New Subscriber dialog box.

This dialog box allows you to add new subscribers. It is discussed in more detail in the section on "Adding NonSQL Server (Heterogeneous) Subscribers."

Using the Disabling Publishing and Distribution Wizard

To quickly remove all the distribution servers on a specific server, drop all publishers and publications using the distribution database and remove all subscriptions to the deleted publication—use the SQL Server 2000 Disable Publishing and Distribution Wizard. The Disable Publishing and Distribution Wizard disables all the publishers using the Distributor and, if possible, logs on to the publishing servers to drop the publications. The wizard also disables all the subscribers using the publications and drops the distribution databases. Of course, the wizard lets you selectively decide if you want to remove the distribution databases or leave the distribution databases and drop all the publications. To use the wizard, perform the following steps:

1. Select the server on which you want to add a publication.

2. From the SQL Enterprise Manager menu, select Tools and then select Replication. A drop-down menu appears. Select the Disable Publishing option. If the server is not set up as a publisher, select the Disable Publishing and Distribution option. The Disable Publishing and Distribution Wizard Startup dialog box, shown in Figure 27.15, appears. Read over the dialog box and click the Next button.

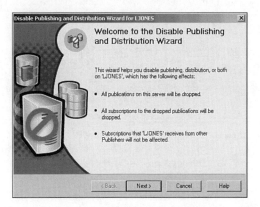

FIGURE 27.15   The Disable Publishing and Distribution Wizard Startup dialog box.

The Disable Publishing dialog box appears (see Figure 27.16). If you want to drop all the distribution databases and disable all the publishers using the distributor, select the Yes, Disable Publishing on *Server Name* option. Selecting this option disables the publishers and, if possible, drops the publications on the publishing servers and removes the distribution databases. If this is the option you want to perform, click the Next button. The wizard begins the process just described. If you select No, you are finished and the wizard completes without performing any task.

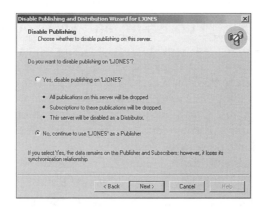

FIGURE 27.16   The Disable Publishing dialog box.

Adding NonSQL Server (Heterogeneous) Subscribers

SQL Server can replicate to nonSQL Server ODBC or OLE DB subscribers such as Microsoft Access and Oracle databases. As stated earlier, nonSQL Server ODBC sources can only be subscribers. You can use transactional and snapshot replication with all heterogeneous subscribers, merge replication with Microsoft Access subscribers, and immediate update subscribers with SQL Server. ODBC or OLE DB subscribers can be publishers using third-party software (which might or might not be available for your particular data source).

> **NOTE**
>
> Because nonSQL Server subscribers use ODBC or OLE DB, the list of possible nonSQL Server subscribers will increase. For an updated list of supported heterogeneous subscribers, refer to your Microsoft documentation or check the SQL Server forums on the Internet. Microsoft provides and supports ODBC/OLE DB drivers for Microsoft Access, Oracle, and DRDA. All other systems must have ODBC drivers that are thread safe, ODBC Level-1 compliant, transaction capable, and able to support DDL. From this point on, ODBC and OLE DB subscribers refer to nonSQL Server data sources.

Heterogeneous subscribers must be set up by the publishing server using the push subscription method (see Chapters 28 and 29 for setting up push subscriptions). Each heterogeneous subscriber participating in SQL Server replication has its own individual requirements and restrictions. For example, when creating the ODBC Data Source Name DSN with Oracle, you must include a username; with Microsoft Access

DSN, some datatypes are not supported. Check out the Microsoft SQL Server documentation for the various restrictions that apply between Microsoft SQL Server and the selected ODBC subscriber.

Here are a few known restrictions that apply to all ODBC subscribers:

- ODBC DSN must follow SQL Server naming conventions.

- The character bulk copy method must be selected for synchronization.

- The publication option Truncate Before Synchronization is not supported.

- Target server's quoted identifier, reported by the ODBC driver, is used.

- Batch statements are not supported.

- When an article is added or deleted from a publication, you must reinitialize the subscription.

The following sections describe how to set up an ODBC subscriber using Microsoft Access 2000.

Step 1: Create an ODBC Data Source Name (DSN)

The first step in setting up replication to an ODBC subscriber is to create a system (DSN) for the subscribing server. The ODBC DSN must be created on the distribution server. To create a system ODBC DSN, follow these steps:

1. Double-click the Data Sources (ODBC) icon located in the Control Panel to start the ODBC Administrator. In Windows 2000, this icon is located under the Administrative Tools folder in the Control Panel. The ODBC Data Source Administrator dialog box appears. Click the System DSN tab, shown in Figure 27.17.

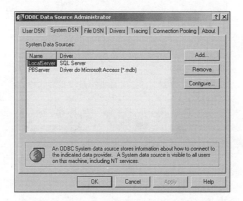

FIGURE 27.17   The ODBC Data Source Administrator dialog box—System DSN tab.

2. Click the Add button to add a new system DSN. The Create New Data Source dialog box appears (see Figure 27.18).

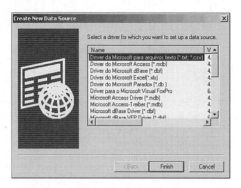

FIGURE 27.18   The Create New Data Source dialog box.

3. A list of installed ODBC drivers appears. Select the correct ODBC driver for your subscribing server (for this example, select Microsoft Access). After you select the correct ODBC driver, click Finish. The ODBC Microsoft Access Setup dialog box appears (see Figure 27.19).

FIGURE 27.19   The ODBC Microsoft Access Setup dialog box.

NOTE

The look of the ODBC Setup dialog box varies for different data sources. For this example, Microsoft Access is used. Compare the Microsoft Access Setup dialog box in Figure 27.19 to the ODBC Setup screen for SQL Server (shown in Figure 27.20).

---

4. Enter the Data Source Name for the Microsoft Access database. The Data Source Name is how SQL Server references the ODBC subscriber. Select the Access

database to push the replicated data to, and click the Advanced button. If you register an Access database that resides on a remote server, use the UNC name (\\ServerName\directory\database.mdb). After you enter the correct information, click the OK button to add the ODBC data source.

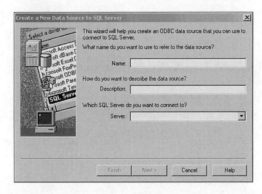

FIGURE 27.20   The ODBC SQL Server Setup dialog box.

NOTE

To replicate to Microsoft Access, subscribers require that the MSSQLServer service use the domain user account used by the SQL Agent, which must have the necessary permissions to connect to Access databases over the network.

Step 2: Register the ODBC Source as a Subscribing Server

The next step is to add the ODBC DSN to SQL Server's list of subscribing servers. To add an ODBC DSN to the list of subscribing servers, follow these steps:

1. From the folder tree in Enterprise Manager, select the server on which you want to add a publication.

2. From the SQL Enterprise Manager menu, select Tools and then select Replication. Select the Configure Publishing, Subscribers, and Distribution option from the drop-down menu that appears. The Publisher and Distributor Properties dialog box appears. Select the Subscribers tab (refer to Figure 27.13). Click the New button. The Enable New Subscriber dialog box, shown in Figure 27.21, appears.

3. Select the ODBC data source option. For OLE DB sources, select the OLE DB data source, and select SQL Server database for SQL Servers. After you have made your selection (in this example, ODBC data source), click the OK button; the Enable Subscriber—ODBC Data Source dialog box appears (see Figure 27.22).

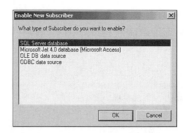

FIGURE 27.21   The Enable New Subscriber dialog box.

FIGURE 27.22   The Enable Subscriber—ODBC Data Source dialog box.

4. Select the correct ODBC DSN shown in the list. Enter the login ID and password if required. The login ID and password are optional because they might not be needed. In the case of Microsoft Access, unless you have added security, leave the login and password fields blank. To register the ODBC subscriber, click the OK button. *Note:* This action adds the DSN to the SQL Server system table sysservers.

After you register a nonSQL Server subscriber, you can add the subscriber to push subscriptions (see Chapters 28 and 29). The system stored procedures that deal with ODBC subscribers are sp_dsinfo, which retrieves information about the ODBC DSNs installed on a distribution server, and sp_enumdsn, which shows all the ODBC DSNs defined for a specific Windows NT account of a server.

Upgrading SQL Server Replication

As you begin the process of upgrading SQL on your existing servers, some of those servers might be slated for upgrades at different times. If replication is involved, things could get complicated. Keep in mind the following guidelines, and the task of upgrading SQL Server replication will be made simpler:

- The distributor must be running the highest version of SQL Server and should be upgraded first. The publishers should be the next servers to upgrade, followed by the subscribers.

- During the process of upgrading SQL 7.0 replication servers to SQL 2000, the database compatibility level must at least be temporarily set to 70 or later. The upgrade will fail if your servers are set to 65 or earlier compatibility levels.

- The sooner all servers are upgraded to SQL Server 2000, the sooner the added functionality provided by SQL 2000 can be utilized. If a publisher is running SQL 7.0 and a subscriber is running SQL 6.5, you are bound by the limitations of SQL 6.5 replication and will be unable to take advantage of the new features in SQL 7.0 or SQL 2000.

If you are using the immediate updating option with snapshot or transactional replication, new changes will affect how you upgrade. The uniqueidentifier column is now used instead of the timestamp column to detect conflicts when receiving updates from the subscriber. Changes have also been made to the triggers created to handle updates. The following steps need to be taken when upgrading SQL Servers using immediate updating:

- Upgrade both the publisher and the subscriber to SQL 2000.

- Drop all publications and subscriptions to the publications.

- Drop the timestamp column from the tables on the publisher and from the subscriber that allow subscriber updates.

- Re-create the publications and subscriptions. SQL Server will add the uniqueidentifier column to the published tables.

Replication FAQ

Following are some of the common questions asked by DBAs about SQL Server replication:

Q If I need to perform multiple updates at many sites, why not always use merge replication instead of transactional replication and partitioning?

A Merge replication is good in cases where your sites are disconnected or the data does not partition well. If your application can be partitioned between updating sites, updates can be made without worrying about conflict resolution and loose transactional consistency can be obtained instead of no consistency. (See Chapter 28 "Transactional Replication" and Chapter 29 "Merge Replication" for more details.)

Q Does the ODBC DSN for a nonSQL Server subscriber belong on the Distributor or the Publisher?

A The ODBC DSN for a nonMicrosoft SQL Server subscriber belongs on the distribution server.

Summary

Replication is an exciting technology that will play an important part in many real-world solutions. As a Microsoft SQL Server DBA, you must fully understand how to correctly set up and administer replication and how to correctly use replication to benefit your company or organization.

Following are some of the important things to remember for SQL Server replication:

- SQL Server replication is transaction based and follows a loose consistency data distribution model to a no consistency data model.

- Replication uses a publisher/subscriber metaphor.

- Subscribing databases can perform updates when using merge replication or Immediate Updating Subscribers.

- SQL Server uses ODBC or OLE DB for replication.

- A server can play multiple roles and be a subscriber, publisher, or distributor.

- To set up replication to a nonSQL Server ODBC source, add the ODBC DSN using the ODBC administrator on the distribution server.

- NonSQL Server ODBC sources can only be subscribers (without third-party software).

- The merge and distribution agents do not have to be executed via SQL Server. You can write applications that run these agents using ActiveX controls that ship with SQL Server.

- You can have multiple distribution databases on a single server.

- Different versions of SQL Server can participate in replication.

28

Transactional Replication

by Laura Jones

Transactional replication is one of three methods provided by SQL Server for distributing data from one database to each subscribing database. SQL Server monitors changes made in the publishing database and passes those changes (inserts, updates, and deletes) to the subscribers of the data. The distribution of data can take place within seconds providing a near real-time environment.

This chapter covers the different replication topology scenarios and appropriate applications for transactional replication. It also covers various components that make transactional replication work. You will be guided through the steps of creating a publication and learn how to partition the data.

> **NOTE**
>
> Publications cannot be created for transactional replication using the personal and desktop editions of SQL Server 2000; they can only participate as subscribers. All other versions of SQL Server 2000 can support all functions of transactional replication.

IN THIS CHAPTER

- Applicable Uses for Transactional Replication
- Replication Agents
- Replication Topology
- Immediate Updating Subscribers
- Recommended Topology for Updating Subscribers
- Creating a Transaction Based Publication
- Subscriptions
- Custom Stored Procedures
- Transforming Published Data
- Inline Data Validation and Reinitialization
- Generating Publication Scripts
- Replicating Stored Procedures
- Replication Monitor
- Transactional Replication FAQ

Applicable Uses for Transactional Replication

Different types of applications are complimented by transactional replication. In an environment where data needs to be distributed with little latency, transaction replication is well suited for the task.

In a manufacturing setting, different divisions within a facility might collect production data. Those divisions within that facility would then distribute their data to a central collection point for reporting. Taking that scenario one step further, the collection of data from multiple factories could be distributed to a centralized location for further analysis and reporting.

A bank with branch offices would be a well suited candidate for transactional replication. Each branch keeps track of its own records within a database. The main office subscribes to the branches to collect all the data for the organization.

Replication Agents

Following are three major components in transaction replication used to carry out the process of distributing data from the publisher to each subscriber:

- **Snapshot Agent**—Prepares schema and data files to be used to synchronize new subscribers to a publication.

- **Log Reader Agent**—Reads transactions marked for replication in the publisher's transaction log and inserts them into the distribution database.

- **Distribution Agent**—Moves the replicated transactions from the distribution database to all subscribers of the publication.

Here is how these agents work together to move the data. A publication is created specifying all data to be replicated to a subscribing database. The Snapshot Agent creates a schema file to create the table structure on a subscribing database. The Snapshot Agent also creates files containing the data in each of the articles and updates the Distribution database to reflect the synchronization task.

Flags are placed in the publisher's transaction log to distinguish all transactions being replicated to one or more subscribing databases. The Log Reader Agent reads the flagged INSERT, UPDATE, and DELETE statements in the transaction log. The agent monitors the replicated transactions on the publisher for each publication and copies them to the distribution database. The Distribution Agent will then disburse the replicated commands to all the subscribers of that publication.

After the subscribers are initially synchronized with the publisher, actual data is no longer distributed to them. Subscribers are kept up-to-date by the Distribution Agent, which relays all INSERT, UPDATE, and DELETE commands performed on the publication. It is important to understand the flow when changes made on a publisher are distributed to the subscribers. This can be very useful when it is time to troubleshoot problems with replication.

Replication Topology

Publishers, distributors, and subscribers each play a role in the distribution of data. The method of connecting all these pieces together and their relationship to one another establishes your topology. In a simple topology, the publisher and distributor are located on a single server and there can be one or more subscribers. Specific requirements for distributing data might call for a more complicated topology. If there are hundreds of subscribers to a publication, a single publisher or distributor might not have the resources necessary to manage the heavy processor load and disk I/O. By carefully arranging your publishers and distributors, you could alleviate some of the burden on a server that contains the primary source of data for distribution.

SQL Server 2000 supports only a hub-and-spoke topology. Data flows from the publisher/distributor (hub) to each subscriber (spoke). Data cannot move directly from subscriber to subscriber. If a subscriber becomes disabled, the hub and the other subscribers are not affected. If the hub becomes disabled, all data flow will cease until the problem is resolved.

The hub-and-spoke topology can be configured to accommodate different scenarios as follows:

- Central Publisher
- Central Publisher with remote distributor
- Republisher
- Central Subscriber

Central Publisher

In this scenario, the publisher and the distributor coexist on the same physical SQL Server. The subscriber resides on a different server. This is the simplest form of replication topology. Keep in mind, with this topology, the burden of transaction processing, the synchronization of the subscribers, the LogReader, and the distribution to the subscribers are all performed by the same server. If the amount of transactions or subscribers is substantial, it is recommended that you separate the distributor from the publisher. Figure 28.1 represents the central publisher scenario.

Central Publisher with Remote Distributor

As the level of replication increases, the burden of the publisher and distributor also increases. Server resources become labored and efficiency decreases. Now is the time to separate the distributor from the publisher. If low latency is a requirement, make sure that the connection between the publisher and the distributor is reliable and fast.

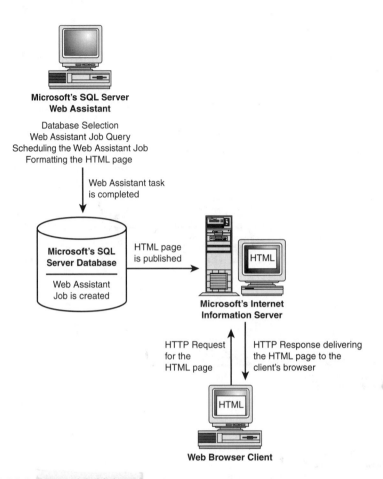

**Microsoft's SQL Server
Web Assistant**

Database Selection
Web Assistant Job Query
Scheduling the Web Assistant Job
Formatting the HTML page

Web Assistant task
is completed

**Microsoft's SQL
Server Database**

Web Assistant
Job is created

HTML page
is published

HTML

**Microsoft's Internet
Information Server**

HTTP Request
for the
HTML page

HTTP Response delivering
the HTML page to the
client's browser

HTML

Web Browser Client

FIGURE 28.1   Central Publisher.

The LogReader will scan the flagged transactions in the publishing database from across the network and copy those transactions into the distribution database. The major tasks of the LogReader—distribution and synchronization—will be performed by the distribution server, freeing resources on the publisher.

The tradeoff for this scenario is increased traffic over the network. Using Performance Monitor will help determine whether a server can bear the burden of a combined publisher/distributor scenario or whether it is necessary to separate those components. Figure 28.2 depicts the central publisher with a remote distributor scenario.

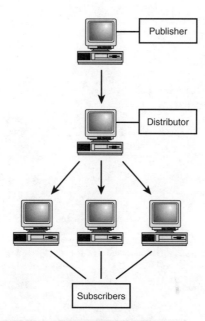

FIGURE 28.2   Central Publisher with remote distributor.

Republisher

A republisher model can be used when there is a slow or expensive network link between the original publisher of the data and the subscribers. A publisher could distribute data to a subscriber with a reliable communications link. That subscriber could then publish the same data to the remaining subscribers. The republisher would be in a better position to distribute the data than the original publisher would be. This scenario is useful when crossing continents, spanning states, or any other situation in which unfavorable network conditions exist.

It is not difficult to create this type of replication model. The original publisher and the republisher act as their own distributors. The republisher is the only subscriber to the original publication and has the same publication defined on that server. The remaining subscribers are subscribed to the republisher. Figure 28.3 is a graphic depiction of a republisher model.

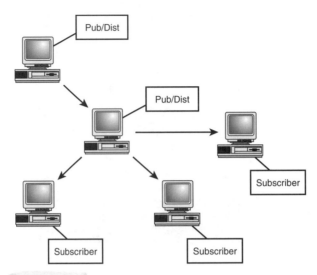

FIGURE 28.3   Republisher.

Central Subscriber

If data comes from multiple sources to populate a single, central database, you have a central subscriber scenario. This is relatively simple to implement when setting up replication. Each source of data is configured as a publisher. All publishers distribute the data to a single subscriber. In this case, the subscribing database can be used as a central reporting point.

Suppose that a company has a headquarters site as well as individual branches. Specific data corresponding to each branch is populated by the branch and then distributed to headquarters. The data collected at the central point would be readily available for reports on any branch or totals accumulated by all.

If a DBA has the ability to administer the databases for all branches, it might be prudent to use a single SQL Server as the distributor. This enables the DBA to monitor all distribution agents for all the publishers from a central location. If each branch is charged with maintaining its own data, distribution could reside on the same servers as the publishers. Figure 16.4 shows a central subscriber in which the publishers and distributors reside on single servers.

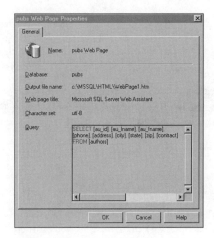

FIGURE 28.4   Central Subscriber.

Immediate Updating Subscribers

An immediate updating subscriber allows the subscriber to directly modify the published database. When a publication is created, the creator has the option of allowing a subscriber to update the copy of its local data. The updates the subscriber makes will be propagated back to the publisher, and then to the remaining subscribers of the data. The two-phase commit protocol provides assurance that the publisher has received the data and there are no conflicts. If the publisher is unable to receive the data, the transaction made by the subscriber will not be committed on the subscriber's database. The following components are used when immediate updating subscribers is enabled:

- Triggers

- Stored procedures

- Microsoft Distributed Transaction Coordinator

- Conflict detection

- Loopback detection

Triggers

Triggers are located on the subscriber. The triggers ensure that any transaction beginning on the subscriber is committed on the publisher before being committed by the subscriber. The protocol used for this type of transaction is called a two-phase commit (2PC). If the transaction is not committed by the publisher, it is rolled back on the subscriber and both databases remain synchronized.

> **NOTE**
>
> If the subscription is dropped and data will be modified at the subscriber, the triggers created for 2PC need to be manually dropped on those tables.

Stored Procedures

Stored procedures are located in the publisher. They ensure that any transactions being replicated are applied only if there are no conflicts. If there is a conflict, the transaction will be rolled back at both sites. Stored procedures are created for INSERT, UPDATE, and DELETE transactions.

> **NOTE**
>
> The logic within the stored procedures can vary depending on the method of conflict detection.

Microsoft Distributed Transaction Coordinator

Microsoft Distributed Transaction Coordinator (MS DTC) is the component that manages the two-phase commit execution between the publisher and the subscriber. A remote stored procedure call initiates MS DTC using the Begin Distributed Tran statement.

Conflict Detection

Conflict detection in SQL Server 7.0 was initiated using timestamp columns on the published tables. In SQL Server 2000, conflict detection is based on a uniqueidentifier column. The stored procedure being executed on the publisher compares the current uniqueidentifier value with the value of the row in question. If there is a conflict between the values, the transaction is rejected.

Loopback Detection

SQL Server determines if a transaction has already been applied to a server by using the loopback detection mechanism. When a subscriber initiates a change and it is propagated to the publisher, loopback detection prevents the change from being reapplied to the subscriber. If Subscriber A inserts a row, the insert is reflected on the publisher. The publisher then sends the insert command to all its subscribers. If loopback detection was not enabled, the INSERT statement would be passed along back to Subscriber A, causing a constraint violation. This violation could stop the distribution agent to that server and replication will stop. If you are not using loopback detection and problems occur, add a timestamp to the published tables and recreate publication and subscriptions.

> **NOTE**
>
> If the same transaction is used to update tables in different databases at the subscriber or tables in different databases across subscribers having immediate updating subscriptions, the information used to control loopback detection will be deleted and could cause replication to fail.

Recommended Topology for Updating Subscribers

An effective model to use for immediate updating subscribers would be a central publisher with remote distributor. Not all subscribers have to be updating subscribers. A reliable fast link is required between the publisher and subscriber.

Creating a Transaction Based Publication

SQL Server 2000 provides a Create Publication Wizard to guide when you create a publication. There are many ways you can configure replication in order to fine tune it to your needs

> **TIP**
>
> The creation of your publication will probably progress more smoothly if you have already started your SQL Server Agent and the MS DTC Agent before creating the publication.

Following are the steps you can use to create a typical transactional replication publication:

1. In Enterprise Manager, make sure that you have the correct server selected. Several SQL Servers might be registered in Enterprise Manager. From the Tools menu, select Replication, and click Create and Manage Publications. When the Create and Manage Publications dialog box appears, click the database that you are going to publish. In this case we will be using the pubs database. Click the Create Publication button. If there is already an existing publication on that database, SQL Server gives you the option of using it as a template for your new publication. This section assumes that you have not already created a publication on the pubs database.

2. The Create Publication Wizard dialog box appears. Check the option box to Show Advanced Options in this wizard. Click the Next button (see Figure 28.5).

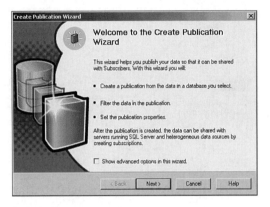

FIGURE 28.5   The Create Publication Wizard dialog box.

3. The Choose Publication Database dialog box appears (see Figure 28.6). Click the pubs database and then click the Next button. The Select Publication Type dialog box appears.

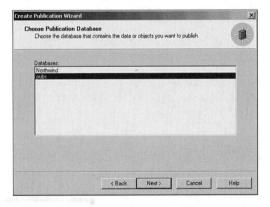

FIGURE 28.6   The Choose Publication Database dialog box.

4. Now it's time to choose the type of publication you are creating. Because this chapter is all about transactional replication, choose Transactional Publication. Click the radio button next to the appropriate option; then click the Next button (see Figure 28.7).

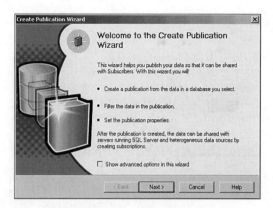

FIGURE 28.7   The Select Publication Type dialog box.

NOTE

If the Transaction Publication option is not enabled, most likely the incorrect version of SQL Server 2000 is installed. The SQL Server 2000 desktop engine and Personal edition can only participate as subscribers of transactional replication.

5. The next dialog box that appears permits you to choose to allow updateable subscriptions, and you also have the option of selecting queued updating. Based on analysis of your needs, you might have already decided whether to allow subscribers to update the articles that will be defined in your publication (see Figure 28.8). After making your selections, click Next.

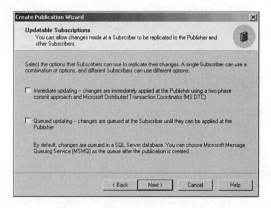

FIGURE 28.8   Updateable Subscriptions dialog box.

6. The Transform Published Data dialog appears (see Figure 28.9). If there is data to be transformed (using Data Transformation Services), this is where you will select that option. This feature allows you to create custom partitions (vertical and horizontal) as well as map datatypes between columns in the publications and subscriptions. In this case we are not doing any transformations, but you are encouraged to experiment with the options here and get to know them. Click the Next button to move on to specify subscriber types.

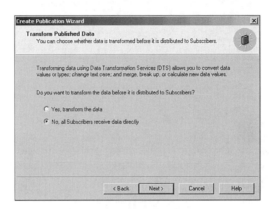

FIGURE 28.9   Transform Published Data dialog box.

7. In the Specify Subscriber Types dialog box (see Figure 28.10), choose whether you have subscribers running SQL Server 2000 databases, SQL 7.0, or if some will be non-SQL Server. After choosing the option to use SQL Servers running SQL Server 2000, click Next.

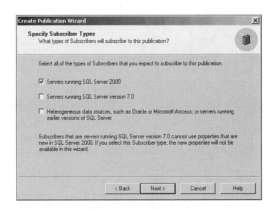

FIGURE 28.10   The Specify Subscriber Types dialog box.

8. The Specify Articles dialog box enables you to choose which tables and stored procedures you want to include as articles in your publication. Click the corresponding check boxes to include the articles. The authors, titles, and titleauthor tables would be good candidates in our example. Notice the tables that do not contain primary keys cannot be selected (see Figure 28.11).

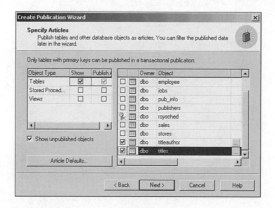

FIGURE 28.11 The Specify Articles dialog box.

9. The next dialog box is Select Publication Name and Description. Type an appropriate name and description for your publication and click the Next button (see Figure 28.12).

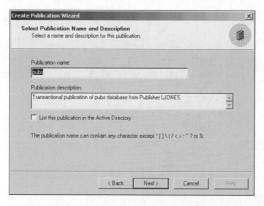

FIGURE 28.12 The Select Publication Name and Description dialog box.

10. In the Customize the Properties of the Publication dialog box, you can change default settings such as filtering columns, rows, or anonymous subscribers. If you check No here, your publication will be completed. If you check Yes, you

will be able to further define your publication by adding vertical and horizontal filters, allowing anonymous subscriptions, and scheduling the snapshot agent to run (see Figure 28.13). Let's click Yes and the Next button to customize our publication.

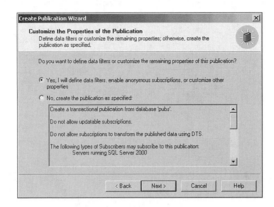

FIGURE 28.13   The Customize the Properties of the Publication dialog box.

11. The Filter Data dialog box appears (see Figure 28.14). You can choose to filter data by row (horizontally), by column (vertically), or a combination of both. Let's select the option to filter Vertically and click the Next button.

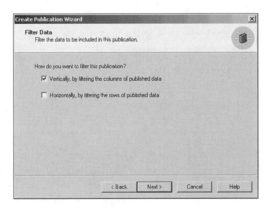

FIGURE 28.14   The Filter Data dialog box.

12. From the Filter Table Columns dialog box (see Figure 28.15), the tables you have chosen for your publication are listed in the left pane; as you click the table names, the column lists appear in the right pane. By default, all the column names are checked. Uncheck the columns you do not want to be in

the publication. In our example, click the `titles` table in the left pane. Uncheck the `advance`, `royalty`, `ytd_sales`, and `notes` columns. Click the Next button.

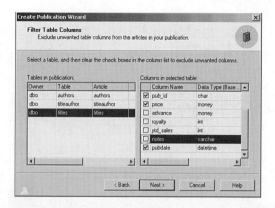

FIGURE 28.15   The Filter Table Columns dialog box.

13. The Allow Anonymous Subscriptions dialog box appears (see Figure 28.16). If you are making your publication accessible through the Internet, choose Yes. Other factors determine the need for anonymous subscribers. If your applications have a large number of subscribers and you do not want to maintain extra information at the publisher or distributor, you might want to use anonymous subscriptions. After making your selection, click the Next button.

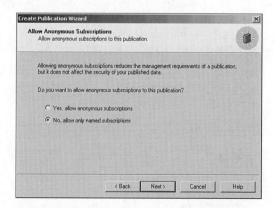

FIGURE 28.16   The Allow Anonymous Subscriptions dialog box.

14. The next dialog box to appear is the Set Snapshot Agent Schedule. If you are running database maintenance or backups during the default time, you can

choose another schedule for your Snapshot Agent (see Figure 28.17). You also have the option of creating the first snapshot immediately. After you have made the appropriate changes, click the Next button. This is the last screen of the Create Publication Wizard.

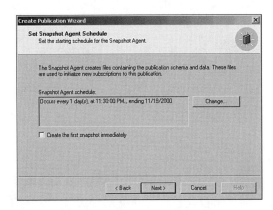

FIGURE 28.17   The Set Snapshot Agent Schedule dialog box.

15. Review your publication specifications in the Completing the Create Publication Wizard dialog box (see Figure 28.18). After you are confident with your choices, click the Finish button. When all the publication components are created, you will see a dialog box letting you know the creation of the publication was successful. The publication properties are made available to you. You can view or change the properties if you want, or just click the Close button.

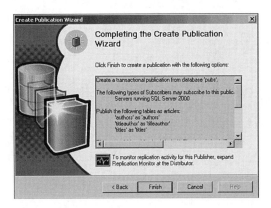

FIGURE 28.18   The Completing the Create Publication Wizard dialog box.

Subscriptions

After the publication is created, subscriptions to the data need to be initiated. The subscription can either be pulled from the subscriber or pushed by the publisher.

- **Push Subscription**—To initiate a push subscription, select the Tools menu option; then click Replication. Click Push Subscriptions to Others. Expand the database that contains the publication, and click the publication. Click the Push New Subscription button. The Push Subscription Wizard appears. Follow the instructions to select the subscription server, database, and distribution options.

- **Pull Subscriptions**—To initiate a pull subscription, select the Tools menu option; then click Replication. Click Pull Subscription to '%'. Click the Pull New Subscription button. The Pull New Subscription Wizard appears. Follow the instructions to select the publication server, publication, and destination database.

Custom Stored Procedures

Why use stored procedures during replication? Let's start with the obvious: Use stored procedures to improve the performance of the replication process. Stored procedures improve performance by using precompiled SQL statements during replication. Stored procedures also reduce network traffic because you pass only the stored procedure name and parameters rather than the entire SQL statement. You can also use stored procedures to perform custom processing on the subscribing server such as reformatting the data to simplify end-user queries. The custom stored procedures might be as simple as translating an integer status field to a character field that reports "SUCCESS" or "ERROR".

You have the option of using custom stored procedures in lieu of Transact SQL commands after at least one subscriber has been initialized. Stored procedures are created on the subscribing databases for you after you select to use them. The stored procedures SQL Server creates include parameters for columns where necessary and contain the appropriate UPDATE, INSERT, and DELETE commands. In order to view the replication stored procedures and customize them to your needs, perform the following steps after creating a publication on the pubs database:

1. From Enterprise Manager, expand the server name you are going to be using for this example. Expand the Replication folder, and then the Publications folder. Right-click the pubs publication, and then select Push New Subscription.

2. You will see the Push Subscription Wizard appear. Click the Next button.

3. Select your server from the Choose Subscribers dialog box, and then click the Next button.

4. Click the Browse or Create button. This option will create your subscribing database, and your schema can be created for the articles in the publication as well. Click the Create New button.

5. In the General tab of the Database Properties dialog box, name your database **PubsA**. Make sure that the paths to the data and transaction logs are where you want them to be by checking the Data Files and Transaction Log tabs. After this is done, click the OK button.

6. This will take you back to the Browse Databases dialog box. Make sure that PubsA is selected, and click the OK button.

7. The next dialog box is the Initialize Subscription. You have the option of letting SQL Server create the schema, or you can specify that you have the schema and the data already. In our case, we are going to stay with the default, letting SQL Server create the schema and synchronize the data. Click the Next button.

8. Verify that you have the SQLServerAgent running and click the Next button.

9. Double check your settings before clicking the Finish button, and the process is complete.

10. Now, you are ready to create SQL Server's custom stored procedures for replication.

11. From Enterprise Manager, expand the Replication folder and then expand the Publications folder. Right-click the publication and select Properties. The Publication Properties dialog box appears (see Figure 28.19).

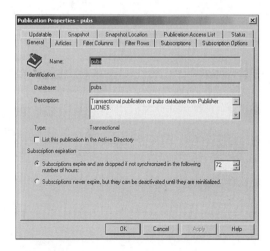

FIGURE 28.19   The Publication Properties dialog box.

12. From Publication Properties, select the Articles tab. In the Articles section, you can view the tables, stored procedures, and views in the publication article. The tables in the publication will be listed in the right pane in the window. Selecting the ellipsis (...) brings up the Table Articles Properties dialog box (see Figure 28.20).

FIGURE 28.20   The Table Articles Properties dialog box—General tab.

13. Click the Commands tab in the Table Articles Properties. If there is no Commands tab, make sure that you have a subscriber to your publication initialized. Here is where custom stored procedures are configured for replication (see Figure 28.21).

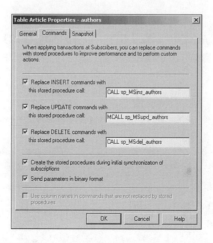

FIGURE 28.21   The Table Articles Properties dialog box—Commands tab.

14. The INSERT, UPDATE, and DELETE functions are all checked to be replaced by stored procedures. You can change the names of the stored procedures or you can keep the default procedure names. Clicking the OK button will create the stored procedures on any existing subscriptions and will also create the procedures on any new subscriptions.

15. If you open the subscribing database, you can view the stored procedures that SQL Server created. You can edit the procedures to your needs from here. The possibilities here are endless for customizing replication to a particular need.

Transforming Published Data

With snapshot and transactional replication comes the option of transforming data as it goes to the subscriber. Data can be mapped to different columns or datatypes, and it can be filtered using DTS packages.

Examples of how you can use data transformation include

- Custom vertical and horizontal partitions of published data on a per subscriber basis.

- Data transformations such as data type mappings (that is, datetime to char data type), column manipulations (that is, concatenating first name and last name columns), string manipulations, and functions.

When you create a publication, you have the option of using data transformations. After a DTS package is created, it can be used during the subscription process, attached to the subscriber to become part of replication.

Inline Data Validation and Reinitialization

A new function within SQL Server replication is inline data validation. This function helps subscribers and publishers stay synchronized by counting rows or performing checksums. Validation can be configured for merge, transactional, and snapshot replication. You can also configure all subscriptions or specify subscriptions for validation.

Checksums, if you opt to use them, are 32-bit redundancy checks performed on a column-by-column basis. This requires a lot of processing power and should be scheduled to run during the most inactive times on the server.

If you have vertical partitioning set up for replication, the checksum will not work because the columns are going to be different between the publisher and subscriber. Row count validation will not work correctly when replication is set up with horizontal partitioning because the number of rows between the publisher and subscriber are not going to match.

To set up inline data validation from Enterprise Manger, expand the Replication Monitor from the server set up as the Distributor. Expand the Publishers folder, and then expand the server containing the publication. Right-click the publication and select Validate Subscriptions. You can select to validate all subscriptions, or only for select subscriptions. Click the Validate Options button. Choose from the options provided and click OK.

Data validation will occur the next time the Distribution agent is started.

By default, the subscriber will be reinitialized if data validation fails. A job is created by SQL Server to reinitialize the subscribers. If the subscribers are not to be reinitialized, go to Jobs under the SQL Server Agent, and disable the Reinitialize subscriptions having data validation failures job.

Generating Publication Scripts

For anyone who has used Replication with SQL Server 6.x, the Scripts tab will be a welcome sight. SQL Server 2000's scripting utility allows you to generate a script that re-creates the entire publication (including articles, subscribers, filters, and so on). You can also generate a script that allows you to delete the publication as well as append the script to an existing file.

To create a replication script from Enterprise Manager, expand the Replication, and then the Publication folders. Right-click the publication, and select Generate SQL Script from the shortcut menu.

Using the script generator, you could create a single file that drops all your publications and then re-creates them. The capability to generate scripts to re-create publications is a welcome enhancement. It's hard to tell you how useful this functionality is. You might never have to re-create a publication (many of you will), but you might be required to move the publication from a test environment to a production environment. Prior to SQL Server 7.0, you either had to perform the publication re-creation manually or had to take the time to create your own scripts using the replication stored procedures.

Replicating Stored Procedures

Stored procedures can be replicated instead of Individual INSERT, UPDATE, and DELETE statements. Suppose that there is a large update on a table that is being published, and an update involves 5,000 rows. SQL Server's optimizer will change those UPDATE statements into 5,000 deletes and 5,000 inserts. These 10,000 SQL statements travel through a network to populate 10,000 rows in the Distribution database. This can dramatically affect network bandwidth because of the large amount of transactional traffic. These transactions could also fill up the Distribution database if you aren't careful about sizing it.

In order to optimize performance on the network and to prevent cluttering up your distribution database with a tremendous amount of SQL commands, you might want to replicate stored procedures to reduce your load. If the changes to the data are made on a one-time basis, replicating a stored procedure might not be applicable. If the changes are made on a fairly regular basis, a stored procedure can be very beneficial.

NOTE

Data stored in the publishing and subscribing tables should be identical when using stored procedures for replication. There will be a lot less troubleshooting in your future if you are dealing with the same data on both sides!

To define a stored procedure as an article, follow these steps:

1. Create your publication and check the Show Stored Procedures check box. Make sure that the check box to Show Unpublished Objects is checked.

2. Select the appropriate stored procedure and then click Next.

3. Follow the remaining steps in the preceding section to complete the creation of your publication.

Replication Monitor

You have defined a publication and are ready to push data to a subscriber. What if something goes wrong? SQL Server provides a tool to aid DBAs with troubleshooting replication problems. The Replication Monitor helps pinpoint problems with replication.

When a server functions as a distributor and the user is in the sysadmin role, replication monitoring is enabled. The Replication Monitor can be used for viewing publishers, publications, and all subscriptions. The following replication objects can be monitored by the Replication Monitor:

• Subscriptions to the publication

• Snapshot Agent

• LogReader Agent

• Distribution Agent

- Merge Agent

- Miscellaneous Agents (cleanup)

- Replication Alerts

If you create a publication and synchronization fails, you can use Replication Monitor to determine where the failure occurred and where the problem can be corrected. Existing tables on the subscribers might not be dropped and re-created because of foreign key constraints, or the server was unavailable at the time of synchronization. The error messages supplied by Replication Monitor provide invaluable aid in solving replication mysteries.

If an agent fails to complete a task (see preceding list), a red X will appear on the Replication Monitor icon in the SQL Enterprise Manager. When that agent is double-clicked, the Distribution Agent Error Details dialog box will contain the complete error description.

Replication Monitor is a convenient, centralized tool containing essential data for all the pieces of the replication process. You can view properties of publications, see a listing of publications, and monitor all replication agents within one interface. If you are using SQL Server replication, it will make your life much easier!

Transactional Replication FAQ

Following are some of the common questions asked by DBAs about SQL Server transaction replication:

Q How do I change my options for the Distribution Agent?

A In the Replication Monitor, you can configure options on all the replication agents. Double-click an agent folder (LogReader, Snapshot, Distribution, Miscellaneous). When the current agents populate the right pane of the Management Console, right-click the one you want to configure. Choose Agent Properties from the shortcut menu.

Q How do I unsubscribe from a publication?

A The publisher can delete a push or pull subscription from a publication. Expand the Replication folder in Enterprise Manager. Expand the Publications folder and right-click the name of the publication you want to modify. When the shortcut menu appears, click Properties. A dialog box might pop up to warn you about modifying a publication with existing subscribers. Click OK to acknowledge the warning. In the Publication Properties dialog box, click the Subscriptions tab. Click the subscription you want to unsubscribe, and click the Delete button.

If you are pulling a subscription from another SQL Server, select the Tools menu option in SQL Server Enterprise Manager. Click Replication, and then click Pull Subscription to "?". In the Pull Subscription dialog box, select the publication you want to unsubscribe, and then click the Delete Subscription button.

Q How do I view transactions that have not been delivered to the distributor?

A The sp_replshowcmds stored procedure gives you a view of transactions remaining in the transaction log of the publisher. You can view the actual commands of the transactions in the log. See SQL Server books online for further details about this stored procedure.

Q How do I modify a publication after I have already created it?

A To modify a publication, ensure that no other databases are subscribing to it. Follow the steps stated previously to remove existing subscriptions on your publication. Expand the Replication folder. Expand the Publications folder and right-click the name of the publication you want to modify. The Properties dialog box contains tabs with all the options available during the creation of a publication when using the Create Publication Wizard. Click the tabs to make the appropriate modifications to your publication. Then follow the steps described earlier in the chapter to add a subscription.

Summary

In this chapter, you learned about the various topologies of transactional replication. You saw how the replication agents act to move data from publisher to subscriber. You now have more options for configuring replication, such as updating subscribers and making use of stored procedures. The Replication Monitor is a centralized tool that enables you to view all aspects of replication and determine the cause of problems if they occur.

29

Snapshot and Merge Replication

by Laura Jones

This chapter examines the simplest form of replication, Snapshot replication and one of the more exciting SQL Server replication modes, merge replication. Snapshot replication was available in SQL Server 6.x; however, SQL Server 7.0 added the capabilities to use updating subscribers and anonymous subscribers with snapshot replication. Merge replication was introduced in SQL Server 7.0 and improved with SQL Server 2000. In this chapter, you will learn which types of applications work well with merge replication and which types of applications do not. Configuring, managing, and monitoring merge and snapshot publications are covered, as is troubleshooting. This chapter also discusses using the Internet to replicate changes or snapshots.

> **NOTE**
>
> This chapter builds on previous chapters and focuses on using snapshot and merge replication. Snapshot replication has many capabilities common to standard transactional replication, such as horizontal and vertical filtering, anonymous subscribers, and Immediate Updating Subscribers. Implementation of these features is the same as in transactional replication. If you skipped Chapter 27, "Replication," and Chapter 28, "Transactional Replication," you might want to refer to them to learn about
>
> - Setting up publishers and subscribers (Chapter 27)
> - Setting up a distribution database (Chapter 27)
> - Creating publications (Chapter 28)
> - Configuring articles (Chapter 28)

IN THIS CHAPTER

- What Is Snapshot Replication?
- Setting Up a Snapshot Publication
- What Is Merge Replication?
- Setting Up a Merge Publication
- Merge Replication and Resolving Conflicts—Hands-on Example
- Troubleshooting Merge and Snapshot Replication
- Additional Publication Options
- Alternative Synchronization Partners
- Replicating via the Web (Internet)
- Replication FAQs

What Is Snapshot Replication?

Snapshot replication takes a picture of the data (that is, copies all the data in the table as defined by the article) at a certain point in time and replicates the snapshot of data to subscribers. Snapshot replication can be thought of as a "table refresh" because all the information for the article is exported and loaded into the subscriber's table. With snapshot replication, no transactional information is kept or required. SQL Server 2000 gives you the flexibility to determine how the subscriber's tables are refreshed. Tables can be dropped and re-created, tables can be truncated (that is, all the rows are deleted) and the data refreshed, or the data can be added to an existing table without dropping the table or deleting all the records. Similar to transactional replication, snapshot replication can also use *Immediate Updating Subscribers*, which means that a subscriber can update the information in the article via a two-phase commit with the publisher. The change then replicates to the other subscribers at the scheduled synchronization time, using standard snapshot replication.

Snapshot Applications

Before going into the details of snapshot replication, take a minute to examine appropriate and inappropriate uses of snapshot replication. In general, snapshot replication is a good solution when performing a table refresh meets the business requirements and the lag time between data modifications and the table refresh is acceptable. Snapshot replication is not an appropriate solution when subscribers want to stay current with information from a publication that is being modified constantly or even several times a day. Such a scenario would require moving entire tables back and forth to reflect a single transaction! Some appropriate uses of snapshot replication are as follows:

- Static lookup tables

- Tables that change infrequently

- Information that is rolled up or summarized and then distributed on a scheduled basis (daily, weekly, monthly, and so on) to subscribers for reporting

- Subscriptions that are not transaction based (such as very limited updating) whose users might be disconnected for long periods of time

- Internet applications that want to receive information for viewing purposes

- Company information such as an employee list, a store list, a price list, or a product list that is updated at a central site and then distributed on a scheduled basis (daily, weekly, monthly, and so on) to subscribers

Inappropriate uses of snapshot replication are as follows:

- Contact management or sales force automation databases that are updated frequently offline and at multiple sites

- High-transaction-based applications that require real-time replication to subscribers

- Multisite data-entry applications

- Financial applications and other applications that require all information be up-to-date with all database changes

- Applications in which the data is changed frequently at a single site and replicated to other sites

- Applications that use data partitioning

Snapshot Replication: Step by Step

Snapshot replication is one of the simpler modes of replication to administer and maintain because the entire content of the article is replicated; you don't have to worry about applying transactions or resolving merge conflicts. As such, a log reader agent or merge agent is not required. Snapshot replication uses the snapshot agent and the distribution agent. Figure 29.1 shows an example of snapshot replication. In Figure 29.1, Server A is the publisher and distributor (you can also use a remote server as a distributor), and Server B is the subscriber. The pubs database contains a publication called *Pubs*MyPubs with a single article, the authors table. You can use Figure 29.1 to walk through the snapshot replication process; assume that a publication has been created and that the publisher is pushing the publication to a subscriber.

> **NOTE**
>
> When you create a snapshot publication, a snapshot agent and a distribution agent are created for the publication. The snapshot agent typically executes at the distributor. For push subscriptions, the distribution agent executes at the distributor. For a pull subscription, the distribution agent executes on the subscriber server. Both the snapshot agent and the distribution agent can be embedded in other applications and run outside of the SQL Server environment, using ActiveX controls provided with SQL Server 2000.

Step 1: Snapshot Agent Executes: Synchronization Set Created

When a snapshot publication is created and a subscriber subscribes to the publication, the snapshot agent executes as either part of a scheduled job or when information in the article(s) is changed. When the snapshot agent executes, the first thing the agent does is to put a read lock on all tables that make up the publication. Using Figure 29.1, a read lock would be placed on the single article, the authors table in the publication MyPubs. The snapshot agent then generates a schema file (that is, Data Definition Language [DDL]) for each table (article) in the publication. The agent then uses BCP (Bulk Copy) to copy the data out of each table. Both the schema file and the data file are written to the replication working directory of the distributor (refer to Figure 29.1). The schema file has a .SCH extension, and the data file has a .BCP extension for articles distributed to SQL Servers only (that is, native). Articles replicated to SQL Server and other data sources are copied out in text format and have the extension .TXT. The schema file and the data file are called the *synchronization set* for the article (table). Each article in the publication contains a synchronization set.

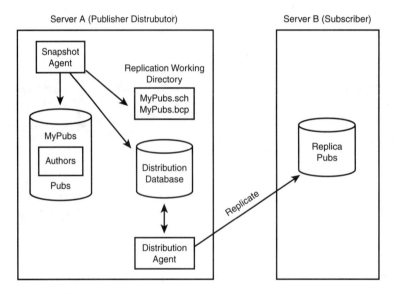

FIGURE 29.1   Snapshot replication—step by step.

CAUTION

Be careful when scheduling the update frequency of a snapshot publication. While the snapshot synchronization set is being created, read locks are placed on all the tables in the publication (that is, articles) for the entire time that schema files and data files are being created. The read locks prevent any application from obtaining an exclusive table lock on one of the articles, which could cause your application to block (wait until the synchronization sets are built). Also, the process of building a large number of synchronization sets or creating large data files for replication adds overhead to your system and can affect the performance of the distribution server (push) or subscription server (pull). You should try to schedule snapshot updates (refresh) during off-peak hours or days.

Step 2: Snapshot Agent Updates Distribution Database

After the synchronization sets are built, the snapshot agent inserts new rows in the distribution database's `MSRepl_commands` table and `MSRepl_transactions` table, shown in Figure 29.1. `MSRepl_commands` table contains information about the publisher, the article, and the location of the schema and data files. `MSRepl_transactions` contains commands that reference the subscriber's synchronization task.

Step 3: Snapshot Agent Releases Read Locks on Articles

After the synchronization sets have been created and the distribution database updated, the read locks are removed from the articles. In the case of Figure 29.1, they are removed from the `authors` table.

Step 4: Distribution Agent Checks the Distribution Table

The distribution agent, shown in Figure 29.1, checks the `MSrepl_transactions` and `MSrepl_commands` tables in the distribution database for a synchronization set for the subscriber.

Step 5: Distribution Agent Copies Data to Subscriber

When a synchronization set is found for a subscriber, the distribution agent copies the data and schema to the subscriber server. The distribution agent then places a read lock on the table(s) and applies the commands found in the distribution database, which includes importing the data. The read lock is held on the table(s) until all synchronization sets and commands are applied for the entire publication to ensure that referential integrity is maintained.

Planning and Special Design Considerations for Snapshot Replication

As stated earlier, snapshot replication is one of the simplest and easiest forms of replication to set up and administer; however, planning and design considerations are still important to ensure smooth operation and the best performance.

Unlike other forms of replication, snapshot replication (without an updating subscriber) does not require the tables being published to have a primary key.

As a publisher or distributor, you should pay special attention to the timing of the creation of synchronization sets, which add additional overhead to your server while they are being generated. If at all possible, the synchronization sets should be generated during off-peak hours. Keep in mind that while the synchronization set is being generated, the tables that make up the publication will have read locks placed on them for the duration of the synchronization set build, preventing other applications from obtaining exclusive locks.

If your publication is going to have numerous subscribers, you should consider using a pull subscription, as opposed to a push subscription. A pull subscription is more scalable and can handle a larger number of subscribers compared to a push subscription. With a pull subscription, the distribution agent executes on the subscriber server instead of the distribution server, which greatly reduces the amount of resources required on the distribution server to handle the publication/subscribers. Remember, with a push subscription, a distribution task exists on the distribution server for each subscriber.

As with all other forms of update replication, avoid using identity columns, which can produce conflicts when replicating between sites. Instead, use the unique identifier data type.

Keep in mind that snapshot replication copies entire tables over the network. So be realistic about the amount of data you want to send to each site with snapshot replication. For example, you would not want to try to replicate 100MB of data using snapshot replication between two sites with a 56KB RAS connection; however, with a T1 the time required might be acceptable.

Setting Up a Snapshot Publication

In Chapter 28, you learned how to use the Publication and Subscription Wizard to create a transaction-based publication.

TIP

SQL Server 2000 allows you to use any existing publication as a template for a new publication. This feature can come in handy for configuring different sites that use vertical or horizontal filters or very large publications. After you create the publication as a template, you can modify or remove the articles as required.

You create a snapshot publication in the same manner, using the Publication and Subscription Wizard. Instead of walking through the Wizard again, you can examine the screens that differ in transactional replication and snapshot replication.

NOTE

Some of the following screens might appear slightly different depending on the edition of SQL Server you are using. These are screens from the Desktop edition. Items disabled in the Desktop edition are enabled in the Standard and Enterprise editions.

The first screen to examine, the Select Publication Type screen, is shown in Figure 29.2.

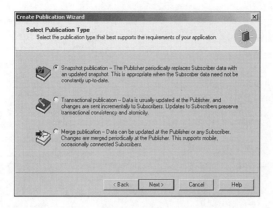

FIGURE 29.2   The Select Publication Type dialog box.

For a snapshot publication, select the Snapshot Publication radio button shown in Figure 29.2.

> **NOTE**
>
> Obviously, to create a merge replication (discussed later in this chapter), select the Merge Publication radio button.

As you walk through the wizard, you reach the Specify Articles dialog box that allows you to select the tables and stored procedures that make up the publication. To set snapshot-specific options for each article, click the square box located to the right of the selected article in the Specify Articles dialog box. The Table Article Properties dialog box appears. Click the Snapshot tab, shown in Figure 29.3.

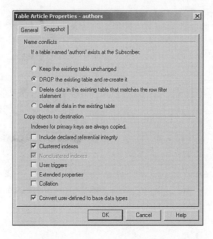

FIGURE 29.3   The Snapshot tab of the Table Article Properties dialog box.

The Snapshot tab allows you to define the behavior of the snapshot when it is loaded into the subscriber database. The following sections take a close look at each part of the dialog box.

Name Conflicts

The Name Conflicts section allows you to define what to do at the subscriber database with the snapshots synchronization set. The options are as follows:

- **Keep the Existing Table Unchanged**—To add new data to a subscriber table but leave the existing data alone, select this option.

- **Drop the Existing Table and Re-create It**—Select this option if you want to drop and re-create the tables as well as refresh the data at the subscriber server. Select this option if you want the table refreshed; the table might then undergo column changes periodically.

- **Delete Data in the Existing Table That Matches the Row Filter Statement**—If you are using vertical partitioning in defining the article, select this option so that only data being published by the article is removed from the subscriber table.

- **Delete All Data in the Existing Table (Using TRUNCATE)**—Select this option to clean out the data in the table and reload the data using the synchronization set. Select this option to perform a table refresh.

Copy Objects to Destination

This section allows you to select objects, such as indexes and triggers, to be included in your replication definition.

- **Include Declared Referential Integrity**—Check this option if you want to maintain referential integrity between tables within the publication.

- **Clustered Indexes**—This selection allows you to create clustered indexes when the publication is distributed to subscribers.

- **Nonclustered Indexes**—This selection allows you to create nonclustered indexes when the publication is distributed to subscribers.

- **User Triggers**—Choose this option to create the same triggers used in the publishing database.

- **Extended Properties**—Select this option to include extended properties from the publisher. Extended properties can be created in the Query Analyzer's object browser.

- **Collation**—This section allows you to use the same collation (code page and sorting) that the publishing database is using.

- **Convert User-Defined to Base Data Types**—Selecting this option ensures that tables implementing user-defined datatypes can be re-created without requiring the user-defined data type to be present in the subscribing database.

What Is Merge Replication?

Merge replication is the capability for multiple sites to make changes in a database (that is, publication), track the changes, and then merge the changes back in to a destination database. With merge replication, each site works by itself without having to be connected to any other site(s), and users can update, add, or delete any information in the published articles without using data partitioning or a two-phase commit. At some point, the site connects to another site (that is, destination database) and merges the changes to the destination database. If both sites update the same information, a conflict occurs. In this case, merge replication performs conflict resolution and accepts one of the changes based on the rules set up for conflict resolution.

Merge replication applications and solutions differ from the transactional solutions previously examined. Transactional solutions require that sites be connected and transaction consistency maintained. The whole idea behind merge replication is to have disconnected sites, the downside being that transactional consistency is not maintained. When I say transactional consistency is not maintained, I mean that eventually all sites will have the same results in the database. However, the results in the database might include results that could not have been achieved had all the changes been made at a single location. A demonstration of how transactional consistency is lost appears later in this section. In the meantime, don't panic! merge replication is a great solution for many applications, and it allows full site autonomy. Eventually, all databases will end up with the same result, but unlike transactional replication, the result could be one that could not have been achieved had all transactions been performed at a single site (that is, transactional consistency).

Merge Applications

Before going into the details of merge replication, here's a summary of appropriate and inappropriate uses of merge replication. In general, merge replication is a good solution for applications that require sites to be disconnected (that is, site autonomy) and require the capability to modify and make changes to the data in the database. Merge replication is not an appropriate solution when transactional consistency is required. Some appropriate uses of merge replication are as follows:

- Contact management or call-tracking databases that are frequently updated offline and at multiple sites

- Company timesheet database

- Road-warrior database solutions: salespeople, district managers, and so on who spend a lot of time out of the office (often at company or client sites) and update database applications from the field to merge back to the main company database at a later time

- Company information such as an employee list, a store list, a price list, or a product list that is updated at satellite sites and replicated to a central database

Inappropriate uses of merge replication are as follows:

- Static lookup tables

- High transaction-based applications that require real-time replication to subscribers and have a high likelihood of collisions

- Financial applications and other applications that require transactional consistency

- Applications that require transactional consistency and use data partitioning with frequent updates and changes replicated ASAP to other sites. (Note: All sites are connected.)

Merge Replication: Step by Step

Unlike snapshot replication, merge replication is not a simple form of replication. Fortunately, SQL Server hides the complexities of merge replication from the DBA and the programmers and makes it as simple to set up and administer as any other form of replication. Before walking through the merge replication process, though, you need to know what happens when you create a merge publication.

When you create a merge publication, SQL Server makes modifications to your database and the tables that make up the articles. SQL Server makes sure that all published tables have a unique column for each row in the table. SQL Server looks for and uses unique identifier columns with the ROWGUIDCOL property set. If one is not found, SQL Server adds one. SQL Server then adds triggers to track the changes made to the data in the tables and adds to the database several system tables that are used to track changes and perform conflict detection and resolution.

Because merge replication tracks when a row changes and only its final state is replicated, a log reader agent is not required (that is, one row could change 100 times, but the row would only be reconciled once). Merge replication uses the snapshot agent and the merge agent. The following sections describe the steps that occur with merge replication.

Step 1: Snapshot Agent Executes

Before the merge replication process can begin between the publisher and the subscriber, the databases must be synchronized (that is, identical). The synchronization process is performed by the snapshot agent, which copies synchronization sets from the publisher to the subscriber and applies them to the subscriber database. The process of synchronization is similar to the step-by-step snapshot replication described earlier in this chapter. For very large databases or very slow networks, you don't have to rely on the snapshot agent for the initial synchronization; the database can be synchronized manually as well. You can perform a manual synchronization of the database by using the backup and recovery utility.

Step 2: Subscriber Updates a Row in an Article

When a subscriber makes a change to a row in an article (table), a trigger on the table fires and sets the generation column for the modified row to zero.

Step 3: Merge Agent Executes

The merge agent executes and retrieves all the rows where the generation column has been set to zero and sends them to the destination database.

Step 4: Merge Agent Merges Data at the Destination Database

The merge agent examines the data changes arriving at the destination database with the existing rows in the destination database. If no conflicts are found, the change is made to the destination database. A *conflict* is a row that has been modified by more than one site since the last synchronization. Conflicts can be determined by column changes or row changes. The default conflict-tracking mode is column-based changes. If a conflict occurs, it is resolved using a priority-based system. In the priority-based system, each site participating in replication is assigned a priority with 100 being the highest priority and 0 the lowest. The default is for the highest priority to win; however, the default conflict resolution system can be overridden with a custom resolution system. In the case of two sites with equal priority updating the same row, the tie goes to the change that is already at the destination database.

Step 5: Subscribers Receive Changes at Synchronization

Other subscribers receive the changes made to the article when the subscriber synchronizes with the publication, which can be performed at any time.

Merge Replication and Transactional Consistency

Earlier in the book, the statement was made several times that merge replication did not maintain transactional consistency, but that each site's database would converge to the same result over time. So what does all this mean? The easiest way to help you understand merge replication and transactional consistency is to walk through a simple example. For simplicity sake, this example uses a table called `test` that has two columns and two rows, as shown in Table 29.1.

TABLE 29.1   Test—Initial Publishers Database

Name	State
Mark	Va
Orryn	Pa

Now assume that two different users execute the following transactions:

User1:

```
BEGIN TRANSACTION
Update Test
Set State = "Tx" where Name = "Mark" and State = "Va"
Update Test
Set State = "NC" where Name = "Orryn" and State = "Pa"
COMMIT TRANSACTION
```

User2:

```
BEGIN TRANSACTION
Update Test
Set State = "NY" where Name = "Orryn" and State = "Pa"
COMMIT TRANSACTION
```

If all the changes where made at the same site (that is, transactional consistency), the outcomes shown in Tables 29.2–29.4 would be possible.

TABLE 29.2   Test—Both Transactions Failed

Name	State
Mark	Va
Orryn	Pa

TABLE 29.3   Test—User1 Transaction Succeeds

Name	State
Mark	Tx
Orryn	Nc

TABLE 29.4 Test—User2 Transaction Succeeds

Name	State
Mark	Va
Orryn	Ny

With merge replication, all the previous outcomes are possible; however, one other outcome is possible, shown in Table 29.5, that could not have been achieved had all the changes been made at a single site (that is, transactional consistency is lost). In the case of Table 29.5, both transactions succeed at disconnected sites. When the data is merged back to the destination database, User 2 has a higher priority than User 1 has. Therefore, User 2's change to row 2 is applied, and because User 2 did not change row 1, the row 1 change made by User 1 also applies.

TABLE 29.5 Test—Database After Transactions Merged

Name	State
Mark	TX
Orryn	NY

Planning and Special Design Considerations for Merge Replication

When planning a successful merge replication application, remember to think about the amount of data that will be modified and required to travel over the network or a modem during the merge process and the frequency and ramifications of replication conflicts. Your goal should be to limit the amount of data traveling over the wire and to reduce the number of conflicts. This discussion starts with the recommended topology for merge replication, a spoke-and-hub topology as shown in Figure 29.4.

Currently, the SQL Server Enterprise Manager supports the spoke-and-hub topology only when setting up merge replication. You can use other topologies, but use them with caution and good planning. The three examples in Figure 29.4 show a simple spoke-and-hub topology and more complex examples of a spoke-and-hub topology.

Merge replication also possesses several restrictions on your table design. For starters, all timestamp columns must be removed from tables that are articles in a merge publication.

> **NOTE**
>
> This situation is a Catch-22 for client/server developers. Typically, timestamp columns are added to improve update performance to SQL Server tables when using tools such as Visual Basic and Microsoft Access via RDO, ODBC, DAO, and ADO.

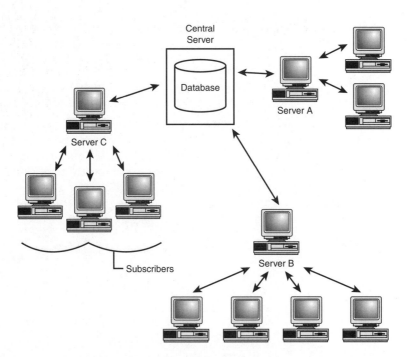

FIGURE 29.4   Recommended merge replication topology—spoke and hub.

The identity column, which is a sequential number, must be used with caution because identity columns are generated as unique sequential values for each database. Most likely, users adding the same article in disconnected sites—which use identity columns—will end up with unique identifier conflicts when the results are merged into the destination database. You are better off modifying the table to use a `uniqueidentifier` data type, which avoids such conflicts, instead of an identity column. If you must use identity columns, you might want to assign different starting values for each autonomous site and the central site to avoid the sequential number conflicts and lost transactions.

To ensure data integrity and maintain referential integrity, all lookup and reference tables must be part of the subscriber's database. One way to meet this requirement is to include them as part of the publication.

Text and image columns can be used only if the `UPDATE` statement is used to modify the text or image column. The `WriteText` and `UPDATEXT` statements do not work here.

Setting Up a Merge Publication

When creating a merge publication, you use the Publication and Subscription Wizard described in detail in Chapter 28 and select Merge as the type of publication. As stated in the Snapshot overview, instead of walking you through the wizard again, this chapter examines the screen that differs in transactional replication and merge replication. The Table Article Properties dialog box is shown in Figure 29.5.

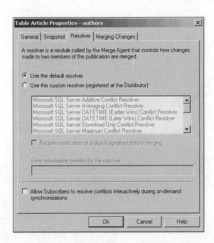

FIGURE 29.5   The Table Article Properties dialog box—Resolver tab.

The Table Article Properties dialog box can be displayed when choosing which tables to include in the publication. You place a check beside the table you want to include in the publication and then click the box to the far right of the selected table to bring up the Article Option dialog box. The Resolver tab, shown in Figure 29.5, allows you to assign a custom resolver to resolve conflicts that occur during merge replication. Custom resolvers can be written using Transact-SQL and stored procedures.

Merge Replication and Resolving Conflicts—Hands-on Example

The following section walks through creating a merge publication, subscribing to the merge publication, and using the conflict resolution manager. The following prerequisites apply to the exercise:

- Your SQL Server is configured to use a distribution database (local or remote; for details on adding a distribution database, see Chapter 27).

- The pubs database is enabled for Merge Replication publication.

In this exercise, perform the following steps:

1. Create a database called DBA_pubs.

2. Create a merge publication called test_authors.

3. Push the publication.

4. Make changes to the information in one of the articles.

5. Replicate the changes.

6. Deal with conflicts.

Step 1: Create a Database

In a SQL Query Analyzer Tool window, enter the following script and click the Execute Query button (green arrow) or use the Enterprise Manager to create the database DBA_Pubs:

```
Create Database DBA_Pubs
```

NOTE

The size and location of the database files are not specified, so they will default to the same size (data and log) of the model database with autogrow on.

In the Enterprise Manager, select the database folder and right-click to refresh the databases on the server.

Step 2: Create a Merge Publication Called test_authors

In this step, you use the Merge Publication Wizard to create a simple merge publication. The wizard greatly simplifies the process, and each step here details which selections to make on the dialog boxes:

1. Expand the Replication folder from Enterprise Manager. Right-click the Publications folder. Select New Publication. The Create Publication Wizard dialog box appears. Click the Next button.

2. The Choose Publication Database dialog box appears; Select the pubs database and click the Next button. If the Use Publication Template dialog box appears, make sure that No is selected and click the Next button.

3. The Select Publication Type dialog box appears; select the Merge publication option (which creates a merge publication) and click the Next button.

4. The Specify Subscriber Type dialog box appears; select the Servers Running SQL Server 2000 check box and click the Next button.

5. The Specify Articles dialog box appears. For this exercise, the publication contains a single article. Select the `authors` table by checking the check box next to the table name; then click the Next button. A dialog box appears stating that a new column with the `uniqueidentifier` data type needs to be added to the `authors` table for merge replication. Click the Next button.

6. The Publication Name dialog box appears. Enter **test_authors** in the Publication Name text box and click the Next button.

7. The Customize the Properties of the Publication dialog box appears. For this exercise, take the defaults (the No, Create a Publication as Specified radio button is already checked) by clicking the Next button.

8. To create the publication, click the Finish button.

The publication `test_authors` is created.

Step 3: Push the Publication

In the following steps, you use the SQL Enterprise Manager to push the publication to the database `DBA_Pubs`:

1. In the Enterprise Manager, expand the Replication folder and then click the Push New Subscription option. The Push Subscription Wizard dialog box appears (see Figure 29.6). Click the Next button.

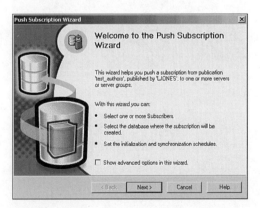

FIGURE 29.6   The Push Subscription Wizard dialog box.

2. The Choose Subscribers dialog box, shown in Figure 29.7, appears. Select the server to push the subscription. For this exercise, select your server (the one that is also the publisher) and click the Next button.

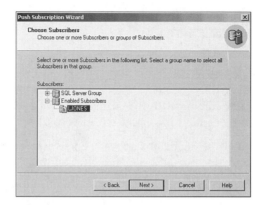

FIGURE 29.7 The Choose Subscribers dialog box.

3. The Choose Destination Database dialog box, shown in Figure 29.8, appears. Browse and select the DBA_Pubs database created earlier and click the Next button.

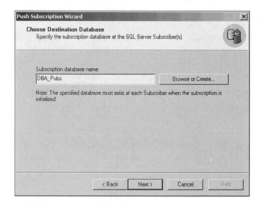

FIGURE 29.8 The Choose Destination Database dialog box.

4. The Set Merge Agent Schedule dialog box, shown in Figure 29.9, appears. Click the Next button to take the default schedule (which is to execute every hour on a daily basis) and click the Next button.

NOTE

This dialog box allows you to determine whether the snapshot of the publication should be constantly maintained on the distributor or maintained only as needed. If you select to maintain a snapshot on the distributor, you can have the synchronization set created immediately or later at a scheduled time. If you choose to maintain a snapshot only as needed, the snapshot files will be randomly generated. Scheduling the creation of the synchronization set allows you to determine the times of day the set is created (for example, off-peak hours).

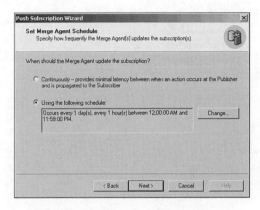

FIGURE 29.9   The Set Merge Agent Schedule dialog box.

5. The Initialize Subscription dialog box, shown in Figure 29.10, appears. Select the Yes, Initialize the Schema and Data radio button. Select the Start the Merge Agent to Initialize the Subscription Immediately check box. Click the Next button.

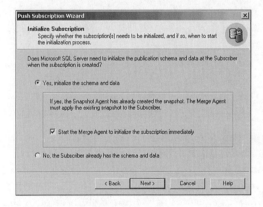

FIGURE 29.10   The Initialize Subscription dialog box.

6. The Set Subscription Priority dialog box appears, as shown in Figure 29.11. This dialog box allows you to set the priority of the subscription to be used in conflict resolution. Take the default by clicking the Next button.

7. The Start Required Services dialog box, shown in Figure 29.12, opens. Check the Agent check box to make sure that the agent is executing, and click the Next button.

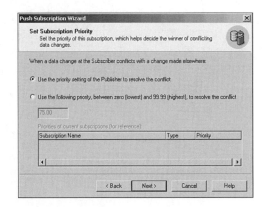

FIGURE 29.11   The Set Subscription Priority dialog box.

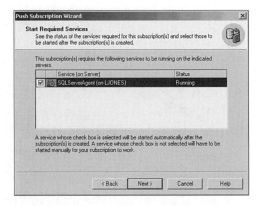

FIGURE 29.12   The Start Required Services dialog box.

8. The Completing the Push Subscription Wizard dialog box is displayed. Click the Finish button to push the publication to the DBA_Pubs database. The Merge Publication Wizard executes the required steps to push the publication to the subscriber.

Before beginning the next step, make sure that the replication snapshot agent has created the snapshot and that the push has succeeded. You can check the status of the agents by selecting the test_authors publication, located under your server name in the Publishers folder of the Replication Monitor icon of the SQL Enterprise Manager. By selecting the test_authors publication, the agents and their status will appear in the right-hand dialog box of the Enterprise Manager. If the test_authors snapshot agent does not show a status of Succeeded, select the snapshot agent, right-click, and select Start to run the agent. You can read the history of a task by double-clicking the agent to bring up the Agent History dialog box. For detailed information of the steps performed by the agent, select a history item and click the Session Details button located on the Agent History dialog box. The Latest History of Merge Agent dialog box, shown in Figure 29.13, appears.

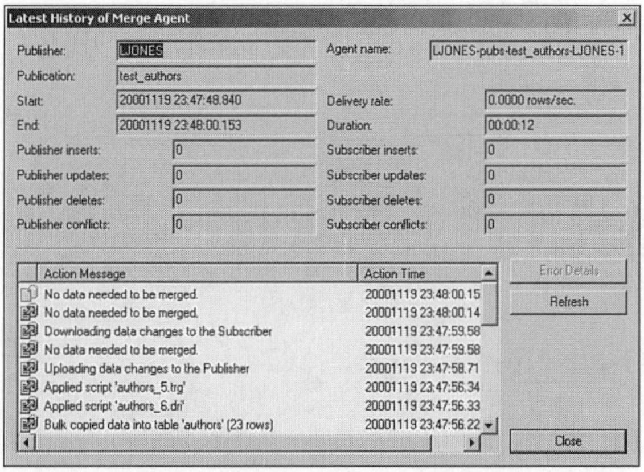

FIGURE 29.13   The Latest History of Merge Agent dialog box.

Step 4: Make Changes to the Information in One of the Articles

This step modifies two records in the pubs database and one record in the DBA_Pubs database. One of the modifications is replicated to the DBA_Pubs database without incident to show you that merge replication can copy the changes to the new database. The other change causes a conflict, which replicates and uses the default conflict rule to apply the change. In this section, you examine ways to view the conflicts and change the outcome if you so desire:

1. In the Enterprise Manager, select Tools, SQL Server Query Analyzer. The SQL Server Query Analyzer dialog box appears.

2. Using the database combo selection box (located in the right corner), select the DBA_Pubs database.

3. Enter the following SQL statement in the query window:

```
UPDATE authors
Set State = 'VA'
Where au_id = '172-32-1176'

Update authors
Set au_lname = 'AAAAA'
Where au_id = 213-46-8915'
```

4. Click the green arrow to execute the SQL statements. You have now modified two records in the DBA_Pubs database.

5. Using the database combo selection box (located in the right corner), select the pubs database.

6. Enter the following SQL statement in the query window:

```
UPDATE authors
Set State = 'PA'
Where au_id = '172-32-1176'
```

7. Click the green arrow to execute the SQL statements. You have now modified one record in the pubs database.

Step 5: Replicate the Changes

In the previous step, you modified two records in the DBA_Pubs database and one record in the pubs database. When the two databases replicate, each database should receive a copy of the changed information from the other database. However, you also produced a conflict by updating the same record and column in both databases (that is, the column state was set to VA in DBA_Pubs and PA in pubs). Using the default rule for the publication, the publisher's update carries a higher weight than the subscriber's, so PA overrides VA. In the next section, you learn how to view these conflicts and override the conflict resolution rules if desired. To replicate the changes, follows these steps:

1. Click the Replication Monitor.

2. Expand the Agents folder (by clicking the folder).

3. Select the Merge Agents folder (by clicking the folder).

4. The available merge agents appear in the right frame. If no agent is listed, right-click in the right pane and select Refresh from the shortcut menu.

5. Select the test_authors agent.

6. Right-click and select Start Agent.

The changes made to the DBA_Pubs database and the pubs database are replicated. You can verify the replication by using the SQL Query Analyzer and executing the following query in both the pubs database and the DBA_Pubs database:

```
Select au_id,state, au_lname from authors
```

Notice that the state for the record 172-32-1176 is PA and that the last name of record 213-46-8915 has been changed to AAAAA. You can also right-click the test_authors merge agent and view the history to see that the merge occurred successfully.

Step 6: Deal with Conflicts

Conflicts occur when two sites make modifications to the same information. You can define a conflict to occur whenever the same record has been modified or only if the same column has been modified. When a conflict occurs, the conflict rule is applied. By default, the rule uses a weighted system with each site carrying a certain priority value to help the conflict manager determine which changes win when a conflict occurs. You can also create your own conflict handlers. If you want to view and possibly override conflicts manually, perform the following:

1. Click the Replication Monitor.

2. Expand the Publishers folder (by clicking the folder).

3. Select your computer's publication folder.

4. Select the test_authors publication.

5. Right-click and select View Conflicts. The Microsoft Replication Conflict Viewer, shown in Figure 29.14, appears.

FIGURE 29.14   The Microsoft Replication Conflict Viewer dialog box.

6. Select the test_authors publication in the Publications drop-down box and select the authors table in the Tables list box (refer to Figure 29.14).

7. Click the View button; the Conflict Resolution dialog box appears.

You can use the Conflict Resolution dialog box to see what changes produced the conflict. Then you can leave the existing change alone, override the conflict with the change from the lower priority site by selecting the Overwrite with Conflicting Data radio button, or apply your own changes by selecting the Keep Revised Data or Overwrite with Revised Data radio button. After you make your selection, click the Resolve button to resolve the conflict. If you are happy with the default, you can select the Keep Existing Data radio button to remove the conflict from the conflict table; alternatively, you can decide to resolve the conflict later by clicking the Postpone button.

Troubleshooting Merge and Snapshot Replication

The best way to troubleshoot snapshot and merge replication is to use the Replication Monitor. The Replication Monitor visually alerts you when replication fails and provides detailed success and error messages.

NOTE

You can set up the agent to alert you via email, pager, or network message when something goes wrong. To add such capabilities to a publication agent, use the Agent Job Properties dialog box. You can bring up an Agent Job Properties dialog box by selecting the agent, right-clicking, and selecting Agent Properties. Figure 29.15 shows the Agent Job Properties dialog box with the Notifications tab selected. Use the Notifications tab to have the agent alert you via email or pager.

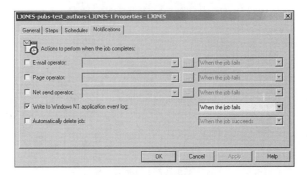

FIGURE 29.15   The Agent Job Properties dialog box—Notifications tab.

Typical failure points for snapshot and merge replication are loss of connectivity and security. The Replication Monitor should give you some error messages that can help you detect whether you are having connectivity problems. You can test connectivity and security by executing a remote stored procedure in the subscriber's database.

Snapshot and merge agents execute in the security context of the SQL Server agent. As such, the SQL security agent requires the proper permissions on the working directory of the distribution server to be capable of creating new schema and data files. The SQL Server agent also requires the proper permission to the databases involved in the snapshot replication.

Additional Publication Options

Now that you have covered the different types of replication, it's time to examine some available options and features of a publication that were not covered in previous chapters. To view publication properties, expand the Replication folder and then expand the Publications folder. Select a publication, right-click, and select Properties; the Publication Properties dialog box, shown in Figure 29.16, appears.

FIGURE 29.16   The Publication Properties dialog box—General tab.

The Publication Properties dialog box is a tabbed dialog box that allows you to view specific information relating to the publication, such as the subscribers to the publication.

The following sections examine some of the tabs on the Publication Properties dialog box not covered in earlier chapters.

General Tab

The General tab, shown in Figure 29.16, displays high-level information about the publication, such as the database the publication belongs to, the type of publication (for example, snapshot, merge), and an editable description of the publication.

The General tab also allows you to expire subscriptions that have not been synchronized within a set amount of days. You can also opt to list the publication in the Active Directory.

Status Tab

The Status tab, shown in Figure 29.17, displays the current status of the snapshot agent for the publication. The tab displays the last time the agent executed and the next scheduled time the agent is to execute. You can manually run the agent by clicking the Run Agent Now button, shown in Figure 29.17. To set the agent scheduling properties, click the Agent Properties button. To start the SQL Server agent if it is not running, click the Start Service button.

FIGURE 29.17   The Publication Properties dialog box—Status tab.

Snapshot Tab

The Snapshot tab, shown in Figure 29.18, allows you to specify Native SQL Server format or Character Mode format for your snapshots. If all subscribers are using SQL Server, Native SQL Server format will be your best option. If there are heterogeneous subscribers, you must choose Character Mode format.

This tab also allows you to use additional scripts before and after a snapshot is applied.

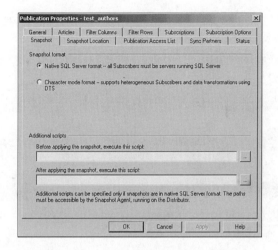

FIGURE 29.18   The Publication Properties dialog box—Snapshot tab.

Alternative Synchronization Partners

SQL Server 2000 provides the option of using alternative synchronization partners. This option allows merge subscribers to use a different server or database to synchronize with other than the publishing server or database. If you are using named subscriptions, the subscriber must be enabled at the alternative synchronization partner and a subscription must be created identical to the original subscription at the alternative synchronization partner.

To configure a subscriber to use an alternate synchronization partner, go to the Publication Properties dialog box and click the Sync Partners tab. Choose the option to allow subscribers to synchronize with other partners. A window will pop up letting you know that this option requires the SQL Server subscribers to be at SQL Server version 2000. Click the Yes button and choose your alternate synchronization partner.

Replicating via the Web (Internet)

SQL Server 2000 replication can be performed over the Internet using push, pull, and anonymous subscriptions for snapshot, merge, and transactional replication. For Web-based replication, you use the same wizards and Transact-SQL statements used to create standard publications and subscriptions. The only difference is the topology and the setup at the subscriber for pull and anonymous subscribers. The basic requirements for all types of subscribers are

- The publisher and distributor need a direct connection (that is, cannot be connected via the Internet).

- If a firewall is in place, the publisher and distributor need to be on the same side of the firewall.

- The TCP/IP protocol is enabled on all servers with distribution and merge agents.

Additional requirements for pull and anonymous subscribers are as follows:

- The distributor and Internet Information Server (IIS) need to be installed on the same server.

- The IIS FTP home directory is set to the distributor's working folder, which defaults to Program Files\Microsoft SQL Server\MSSQL\repldata\ftp.

- Configure the subscriber merge and distribution agents with the proper distributor FTP information, which includes the file, transfer type, FTP address, FTP port, FTP username, and FTP password.

NOTE

You can set the FTP properties for a distribution agent using the Distribution Agent Utility, distrib, from the DOS command prompt, which is located in the Program Files\Microsoft SQL Server\80\COM directory.

Using the Web to replicate changes really is quite simple. You can also create custom applications, using the Merge ActiveX control, that allow your applications to replicate via the Web by simply setting a few properties (for example, FTP user and password).

Replication FAQ

DBAs frequently ask the following questions when working with merge and snapshot replication:

Q Can I script an entire replication setup for a server?

A Yes, you can script an entire replication setup for a server, but to do so requires scripting each publication and appending it to a single file.

Q Can I replicate via a RAS connection?

A A common way for merge replication users to synchronize and merge their databases is RAS. To use RAS, make sure that you have RAS installed on both machines and that you have the proper security setup between the two servers. The two SQL Servers need to be in the same domain or in a trusted domain. For network selection, use the multiprotocol or named pipes. Remember, with SQL Server 2000, you can replicate using the Internet as well.

Q Can SQL Server use merge replication with an Access 98 database?

A SQL Server and Access merge replication are very similar, and Access 98 replication works with SQL Server merge replication. Using Access, as opposed to SQL Server 2000, makes sense for existing Access applications or applications using older computers that might not have the hard drive space or the processing power to run SQL Server.

Q Can I write an application that runs a merge or distribution agent via user request or when the application is started?

A Microsoft provides two ActiveX controls, a Distribution control and a Merge control with SQL Server 2000. The ActiveX controls allow you to create applications from many sources—Visual Basic, VB Script, Visual J++, .NET and so on; you can easily create applications that have no dependency on SQL Server agents and can control when replication takes place.

Summary

Following are some of the important things to remember for SQL Server snapshot and merge replication:

- Snapshot replication takes a picture of the data at a certain point in time and replicates the snapshot of data to subscribers.

- Snapshot replication is a good solution when performing a table refresh that meets the business requirements, and the lag time between data modifications and the table refresh is acceptable.

- Snapshot replication is not an appropriate solution when subscribers want to stay current with information from a publication that is being modified constantly or even several times a day.

- Merge replication is the capability to make changes in a database, track the changes, and then merge the changes back in to a destination database.

- Merge replication is a good solution for applications that require sites to be disconnected (that is, site autonomy) and require the capability to modify and make changes to the data in the database.

- Merge replication is not an appropriate solution when transactional consistency is required.

- The snapshot, merge, and distribution Agents can be executed outside of SQL Server, using the provided ActiveX controls.

PART XIII

Data Warehousing

IN THIS PART

30 Introduction to Datawarehousing

31 SQL 2000 Analysis Services

30

Introduction to Data Warehousing

by Kevin Viers

IN THIS CHAPTER

- Why Warehouse?

- What Is a Data Warehouse?

- Warehouse Data Versus Operational Data

- Data Warehousing Components

- What Is a Data Mart?

- Transforming Operational Data

- Planning the Warehouse Design

- Important Design Considerations

- Managing a Data Warehouse or Data Mart

- Microsoft and SQL Server 2000 Contributions to Data Warehousing

- Data Warehousing FAQ

You might be asking yourself, "What is a data warehouse, and what does it mean to me?" Well, data warehousing has become one of largest buzzes around the database industry today. Most organizations are either planning or embarking on some sort of data warehousing effort. Because of the large shift of organizations toward the construction of warehouses, it is imperative to the survival of DBAs to understand the concepts and procedures involved with this phenomenon.

This chapter centers on familiarizing you with the current concepts of data warehousing. It will also provide some design issues and architectural considerations for implementing a warehouse solution within your organization.

Why Warehouse?

Companies are finding that in order to be competitive, in whatever business, they must have easy access to information. Imagine that a sales manager approaches your boss and states that he needs to see the sales totals for a product across a region for the past several quarters to decide whether a certain group should be targeted for a new sales promotion. The executive knows that those doing order entry are capturing this information. He does not know that you are going to have to do some fancy pretzel-like maneuvers to pull up these sales totals. Over time, you provide him with the report and it ends up being not exactly what he wanted. The executive, now disgusted with the efforts of IT, resorts to having his secretary dump several reports from the mainframe system and selectively pick out bits of the information to be summarized in a spreadsheet. While on the plane back to his territory, the sales manager reads in a popular computing magazine how data warehousing is allowing companies to be more competitive because it gives decision makers access to information to solve problems.

The need for data warehousing stems from the fact that organizations keep their information stored in so many places and that it is difficult to report on all the information available. Because the data is on different systems, it is usually in different formats as well. Consolidation and easy access to data are major themes for warehouses. You must bring all the information together from several sources so that one can learn more about their customers buying habits, suppliers, vendors, and so on.

What Is a Data Warehouse?

A *data warehouse* is a centralized storage facility for differing types of data throughout an enterprise. This data is subject oriented, time sensitive, and organized in a way that offers simplified analysis. For example, a data warehouse might contain customer information and sales to these customers over the past five years. It might be derived from several types of disjoint production systems in the enterprise, such as an order-processing system, which resides on a mainframe, or a sales-tracking application housed on an AS400. Querying these systems for trends might prove to be a difficult task. Data warehousing is the process of collecting, aggregating, storing, and maintaining this information so that executives can use it to make accurate business decisions. Some characteristics and features of data warehousing are as follows:

- Offers one-stop shopping and provides a consolidated store of information from across the enterprise

- Supports data driven decision-making

- Precalculated summaries or aggregations offer increased speed

- Offers snapshots of time to better aid business analysis

- Regular schedule of dumps and loads from operational data stores

All these features help differentiate warehouses from typical operational database systems. This leads the warehouse to be separated from these systems and gain its own set of physical requirements. It is common to keep warehouses on separate machines that can be tuned for a lower frequency of users with different querying characteristics. Data warehouses are usually read-only based systems, aside from the periodic loading of current information.

Warehousing is not a trivial task. It involves coercing different groups across the enterprise to work together. The data can be spread across geographical as well as departmental boundaries and differing hardware/software platforms. The data warehousing development team will need a broad range of skills to become a reality. This effort can span many months to many years depending on the needs of the system and the political conflicts that are sure to erupt. The different departments must agree on common information formats such as customer or vendor account numbers. As in most development efforts, it helps to have a strong executive champion to approve budget extensions as the needs of the warehousing project increase.

Decision Support Systems (DSS)

Decision Support Systems (DSS) are applications that provide analysis on the data stored in the warehouse. They can supply trend information that can help business leaders know what customers or products they should concentrate on in the near future. Decision support systems together with data warehouses provide the following benefits:

- Aid management and decision-makers to transform raw data into information

- Help management identify key trends

- Help an enterprise foresee predictable events and act in anticipation of those events

- Assist management in understanding the big picture and thus reengineer business practices in reaction to what happened

Online Analytical Processing (OLAP)

Online Analytical Processing (OLAP) systems are a type of decision support application. They enable the user to query the data and view it from several perspectives. OLAP applications provide the following:

- Quick canned views of data (common reports).

- Advanced data analysis through pivot tables. Pivot tables are interactive views of data that let you rotate and examine the information from different summary levels, filter for specific data elements, or drill down into detail levels of interest.

- Flexible, easy reporting through *ad hoc* queries.

- Forecasting, what if analysis, prediction of future outcomes.

Using tools for DSS or OLAP for a particular knowledge, workers might ask or receive results from the following typical questions:

- Which customers shopped by catalog and waited until the last minute to buy Christmas gifts?

- What was the percentage of customer service calls made during the first few months of a particular phone service installation?

- Which customers supply 80% of the revenue? Will these customers fit the profile for the next set of planned sales promotions?

- How many times did a particular customer visit my online store before making a purchase?

- At what point are most users leaving this Web site?

The previous queries are common when doing a type of decision support called segmented profiling. Decision support also enables you to do predictive modeling and predict trends, such as the next big products or which customers might leave. Another technique called *data mining* involves asking questions that cannot be answered from the data alone, such as hidden relationships or patterns.

Data warehousing is entirely about providing easy access to information to support decision making. Supplying this information in a presentable format is possibly the most time consuming part of the process. The operational systems that store our vital day-to-day data usually is not simplified enough to help answer these types questions.

Warehouse Data Versus Operational Data

Operational database systems deal with handling many users and transactions. These are often referred to as *Online Transactional Processing* systems (or *OLTP*). Users might be constantly adding, updating, and querying information in these production systems.

An example of an OLTP is a typical order-entry application. A customer calls a sales representative and orders some products from a catalog. The sales associate can pull up the order entry screen and enter the line items the customer desires. The order is placed, which triggers inventory allocations and so on. This small part of the process has generated many records, and many transactions have taken place. This OLTP system requires transactions to be speedy and inventory levels to be accurate. The sheer volume of these diverse operations and the amount of data that is produced provide a poor environment for decision support.

In contrast, in a typical decision support system, a marketing representative can collect data about all the customers who have purchased a particular product from the catalog over the last couple of years and target these customers for a promotion that offers similar products. Because the data warehousing database consists of consolidated information on subjects such as sales, products, or customers, this proves to be a simple task. Additionally, because the operational systems archive information irrelevant to day-to-day operations, the ability for the marketing managers to query on historical events would have been arduous or impossible.

To understand the concept of data warehousing, it is often informative to differentiate it from the common operational systems from which it gains all its information. Table 30.1 lists some of the differences between OLTP and data warehousing data stores.

TABLE 30.1   Operational Versus Warehouse Data

Operational Database	Warehouse Database
Transaction oriented around entities and relationships	Subject oriented around facts and dimensions
Many tables, normalized schema	Fewer tables, denormalized schema
Users adding, updating, and deleting records	Users querying read-only records
Many users accessing records, fewer users reporting	Most users reporting
Transaction/rollback logs used	No transaction/rollback logs needed
Many detail rows	Consolidated, summarized rows
Smaller indexes for speedy updates	Vast indexes for optimized queries
Always currently accurate data, if not, can be updated	Accurate for a specific moment in time

Data Warehousing Components

Figure 30.1 represents the basic design of most data warehousing efforts.

- **Operational data stores**—The OLTP systems currently in use by the organization. They might be dispersed throughout the enterprise and provide specialized functionality to different divisions.

- **Data transformations**—The process in which data is moved out of the OLTP systems and modified, summarized, or consolidated into a format suitable for the data warehouse. These might involve splitting up a name field into first, last, middle initial, or consolidating duplicate customer records from disparate systems into one unified customer account record.

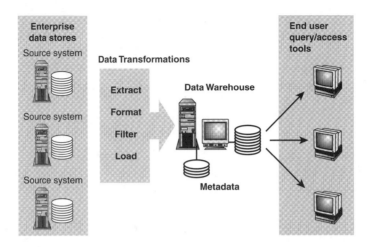

FIGURE 30.1   The data warehousing environment.

- **Metadata**—The description of the data to be stored in the data warehouse. This might include the source of the original information and the business rules or transformations that were applied when the data was loaded.

- **Data store**—The actual database and server hardware that contains the warehouse. This might consist of one central data warehouse or multiple specialized data marts.

- **End user access/query tools**—These can be third-party query reporting tools or applications built in house that provide access to the information stored in the data warehouse.

What Is a Data Mart?

A *data mart* is a repository of data gathered from operational data or other sources that is designed to serve a particular department or functional group. Does it sound like a warehouse? Yes, but you can think of a mart as being less generic than the typical warehouse. The emphasis of a data mart is on meeting the specific demands of a particular group of knowledge users in terms of analysis, content, presentation, and ease-of-use. The information is stored in the data mart in a format familiar to the users.

A common approach to using data marts is to keep data at a detail level in the data warehouse and summarize this information into the data mart for each functional group or department. Another design method includes building data marts in each departmental unit and merging departmental data into an enterprise-level data store later. Either method offers the benefit of centralizing the information for the end users. Some characteristics of data marts are as follows:

- Data specialized for a particular group of an organization

- Yields quicker return on investment

- Engineered for easy access

- Optimal response from lower volume queries

Because of the simplified and specialized nature of data marts, organizations are turning to data marts, as a quick solution to their decision-support needs. Figure 30.2 illustrates how marts and warehouses can coexist in the enterprise.

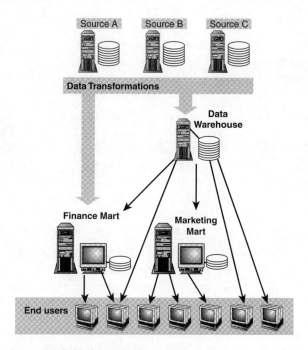

FIGURE 30.2   Data warehousing with data marts.

Warehouses Versus Marts

Data warehouses can be viewed as being similar to wholesale warehouse clubs. They contain a large inventory of items; however, they do not seem to specialize in one area in particular. Data marts are like specialized product stores, such as a coffee shop or bakery. They only deal in coffee or baked goods, and they will package it in a format that is familiar and expected for you.

A data mart and a warehouse each tend to imply the existence of the other. It is widely understood that the design of the data mart starts from the requirements of the user. The data warehouse design usually begins from the analysis of currently existing data and how it can be collected to be used later.

A data warehouse is a central aggregation of data. A data mart can be derived from a warehouse, or the warehouse can be derived from the smaller specialized marts. The mart emphasizes ease of access and usability for a particular design purpose. In general, a data warehouse tends to be strategic but often unfinished; a data mart tends to be tactical and aimed at meeting an immediate need. Table 30.2 summarizes some of the key differences between warehouses and marts.

TABLE 30.2   Key Differences Between Data Warehouses and Data Marts

Data Warehouse	Data Mart
Enterprise-wide use	Used by department or functional unit
Difficult, more time-consuming to implement	Easier, quicker to implement
Larger volume of data	Smaller, more specialized volume of data
Developed using the data currently available	Developed from the users data needs

Data marts are clearly the quick answer to a department's needs. Their lower cost and ease of use allow for quick implementation and an almost instant *return on investment (ROI)*. Often, when a single division's data mart efforts are viewed a success, others will soon follow with implementations of their own. From an enterprise perspective, the existence of several divisional marts might mean the organization is merely a step away from implementing a companywide solution.

Care must be taken when separate departments and divisions build their own data marts. It is common for many divisional companies to hold differing views of certain business concepts. If, for example, the finance and marketing department both implement their own data marts, each can keep track of sales but defines them differently. Later, if someone in marketing needs to gather some information from the finance mart, how will she resolve this difference? From a departmental point of view, a unified vision is necessary even when building data marts.

Transforming Operational Data

The key issue with developing data stores of any type is how to change the raw data you have into the information you need. This process is called *data transformation*. It is rare that the data which exists in the OLTP systems can actually be used to perform complex decision support. Generally, small bits of relevant information are extracted from a virtual sea of data. A table that consists of 50 or so fields in the operational system might contain 10 columns or less that are useful for this type of business analysis. Data transformations are a set of operations performed on the source data as it is transferred to its destination. Typical transformations include integrating data from several sources into one destination, cleaning up dirty data, mapping different definitions of information to a common model, and performing summarization on many detail records. Data transformation procedures account for the most time required to implement a warehouse or mart.

Data Integration or Consolidation

Consolidation of data from several sources is a simple but powerful concept. These differing operational sources were never designed to work together. By integrating data elements from each of these sources, you can put together a more robust informative record, maybe the best of both worlds. Consolidation can be as simple as copying the data from the different sources into one destination as is. Alternatively, you might need to massage the data a bit so that it conforms to a unified model. This type of data consolidation load would create the benefit of having all your data elements in one place for easier query development, thus speeding up response times.

With a warehouse, you can integrate the portions of each system into a common customer table. For example, you can consolidate billing addresses from the financial department's system with the service agreement information from the customer service database and contact data from the sales telemarketing tables.

Another example would be if two systems used a different data type for a similar account number. Account 000125 in system A might be customer 125 in system B. An agreement must be reached on which format offers the most informative approach to this piece of information; that is, the format that should be stored in the warehouse.

Ensuring Data Quality

A key element in gathering and storing data from operational systems is data cleansing or scrubbing. Business processes might dictate to the production users that a particular piece of information follows a particular format; however, in practice there are usually inconsistencies in the data entry. If a name field in a legacy system were to be separated into first name and last name fields in the warehouse, you would encounter many different combinations of first, last, and middle initials strewn throughout the records. Missing fields might exist in the source records, or redundant records might exist. Another example of data scrubbing involves specific validation schemes needed to ensure that all account numbers follow a required format.

A great deal of effort should be placed on this aspect of data transformation because it is here that any warehousing project can be perceived as a failure. If users see that there is an unclean data morsel in data mart, they might begin to question the validity of the other information it contains. User perception can determine whether you end up with a data warehouse or a data outhouse.

Data Mapping and Matching

Legacy systems are famous for embedding numeric values in fields to store hidden information. The priority field in a particular table might be storing values such as 1, 2, and 3. In relational systems these might be implemented as foreign key lookup tables and the true meaning might be revealed by a simple join operation. However, in flat files and nonrelational databases, the meaning is buried deep within application logic or a programmer's cranium. When this data is transformed to the data warehouse, the numerical values need to be mapped to more meaningful terms, such as a high, medium, and low priority.

A code for an account manager field might contain information regarding her region or territory. Because the warehouse or mart is designed to bring more of this information out in the open, the information tucked deep away in codes should be mapped to descriptive elements such as northeast, or even region number 10. This allows warehousing users or query applications to submit queries such as the following:

```
SELECT sum_profits FROM sales WHERE region = 10
```

instead of

```
SELECT sum_profits FROM sales WHERE SUBSTRING(accmgr_id,1,2) = '10'"
```

This example is simplified. When the data is logically organized within the warehouse, queries such as this one become less complex and can offer enhanced results.

Summarization

It is common in data warehousing to aggregate data as it is moved from the operational systems to the mart or warehouse. Pre-aggregating the data provides improved performance over applying summarization every time the same query is executed. This also reduces the amount of data that is initially stored.

Often simple aggregation is all that is required, but complex aggregations across several disjoint tables can offer results that are extremely useful in analytical processing.

Extracting, Loading, and Refreshing Data

When you have decided on information to store and the types of transformations needed, you will then be faced with the challenge of loading and periodically refreshing the warehouse. The information in the warehouse represents a slice in time of the operational data. Just how small of a slice is up to you. You might decide to load data into the warehouse on a weekly schedule, or perhaps after a certain closing or posting period during the month. It might be determined that the best time to do such a load is during a low traffic period, say after normal business hours or on weekends.

What rules do you make for extracting data? Do you extract all the data or just the part that is new or different? The ideal method involves loading only the new information into the warehouse during each interval. This, however, might not prove to be as easy as it sounds for some legacy systems. If the system does not use some form of a transaction log, similar to SQL Server, more effort will be required to identify the changes made since the last refresh. The time-sensitive information (orders, proposals, shipments, and so on) can be retrieved by simple queries specifying a date prior to the last refresh. The static information (customers, suppliers, products, and so on) might be more difficult to probe for changes. You might decide to implement some sort of audit procedure to simplify this, or you might want to simply refresh all the static tables. This is an example of the tradeoff between having efficient warehousing routines or a shortened warehouse implementation time frame.

Data extraction can involve procedures that run on the existing data sources, such as triggers or scheduled tasks. An example would be a batch job on a legacy system that exports all of the new production orders that have occurred in the last period to a dump file for loading into the warehouse. In this scenario, the data extraction and loading are separate processes. An alternative method might involve the destination data source initiating the refresh and performing the extract and load at the same time. This can be accomplished with the Data Transformation Services (DTS) in SQL Server 2000. For example, a DTS package could be scheduled to periodically run that imports all the new production orders that fall into a particular date range. After a warehouse is implemented, the most integral part of its operation are these periodic refresh routines.

Metadata

Data that eventually makes its way into the mart or warehouse could go through any number of transformations listed previously. It could also be from varying systems throughout the enterprise. How do you keep this information regarding transfer of data into the storehouse straight? Just as a normal warehouse keeps an inventory of the items it contains, a data warehouse keeps track of its contents through metadata. Its purpose is to describe the data stored in the warehouse, where it has been, what changes have been made to it, and when.

Metadata contains business semantics that explain what a certain column is with friendly names and offers descriptions of what it means to the user. In addition, it describes the data transformations that have been applied to it. This historical log that explains how an item of information was derived is called *data lineage*.

Another purpose for metadata is impact analysis. This determines what data transformations will be broken when schema changes are made to the warehouse database. These informative elements of the data warehousing architecture prove to be invaluable as the needs of the project grow and change over time.

Planning the Warehouse Design

The physical and operational requirements of warehousing solutions between traditional database efforts cause design and maintenance to be quite different. The architecture can be made up of several data marts feeding an enterprise storehouse or a warehouse supplying specialized aggregations for the smaller marts. In either solution, the basic considerations for planning the solution are as follows:

- Gather the key players interested in the warehousing results.

- Evaluate the scope, benefits, and costs of the warehousing effort.

- Determine the intended business use and relationships of data to be loaded.

- Evaluate the enterprise's key facts and subject-oriented dimensions.

- Determine the frequency at which data is to be loaded, extracted filtered, or transformed.

- Provide expectations of the finished warehouse and how it will adapt as business processes change over time.

Top Down or Bottom Up?

Which approach should you use when designing the warehouse? Should you start from the top down, designing an enterprisewide architecture and then construct data stores that conform to that architecture? Or should you implement a bottom-up method, beginning with highly focused and specialized data marts targeted at particular business functions? The key here has to do with deciding whether to address short-term issues of a particular department or to step back and look at the bigger picture of long term benefits.

The bottom-up approach deals with using the smaller, more focused applications of data warehousing, which can simplify the entire process. There are usually smaller data requirements and a limited amount of specialized queries or summarization. The bottom-up approach offers the trade-off of difficulty scaling to the entire organization for a speedier development time. Although this method can return the quickest implementation results, care must be taken to ensure that the tighter focus does not shut the door to later cross-organizational abilities. This approach can be effective because there are usually no political issues regarding data ownership when the data in question is focused at a departmental level.

For the best long-term results, choose the top-down method. The pitfalls of the bottom-up approach are avoided by determining standardized definitions of business concepts and data requirements up front. The costs, difficulty, and time required are much greater to arrive at this common understanding. Getting business leaders to cooperate without political posturing can also prove to be an arduous task. Usually the biggest questions are, "Who will own the data?" or "Who will cover the costs of development?" What can be gained, however, is a comprehensive resource that is globally accepted throughout the enterprise.

Dimensional Modeling (Stars and Snowflakes)

The traditional entity relationship (ER) model uses a normalized approach to database design. Normalization removes redundancy from the schema to optimize storage. Data warehousing is not so concerned with saving space but providing simplicity from the perspective of the user. A small amount of redundancy is usually acceptable. Dimensional modeling is a more appropriate approach to the warehouse design. It involves designing the schema so that you separate the business into logical events or facts, and a set of corresponding dimensions.

The schema that results is commonly referred to as the *star* schema. This is because the star schema utilizes few, large, centralized fact tables and many small dimension tables. Figure 30.3 describes an example of a star schema.

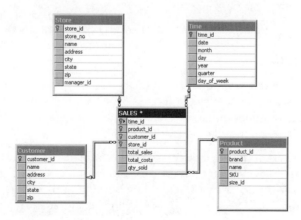

FIGURE 30.3   A sample star schema.

The following is a common query executed against the schema described previously. The results are the customers that bought a particular product in October of 1996.

```
SELECT    c.customer_ID, name, address, sum(qty_sold)
FROM      sales s, time t, product p, customer c
WHERE     month = 10 AND
       year = 1996 AND
       upc_code = 8989764 AND
       s.time_id = t.time_id AND
       s.customer_id = c.customer_id AND
       s.product_id  = p.product_id
GROUP BY     c.customer_id
ORDER BY     c.customer_id
```

Fact Tables

The central fact table usually consists of business events that can be recorded over time, such as bank transactions, sales, orders, returns, shipments, and Web site visits. They are normally made up of foreign keys to the dimension tables and a set of numerical values. The information stored in the fact tables is usually static because it is historical. The most common example of a fact table in the star schema is for sales.

Dimensions

The dimension tables consist mainly of textual information linked to fact records, such as customer names, product descriptions, suppliers, and vendors. These tables will contain fewer records than the facts tables and are not static. Records in dimension tables can be updated. For example, the customer address might be modified in the source system.

Dimension tables or tables that deal with periods of time are always used in the schema of data warehouses. This is a key element to tracking the time variant information in these types of databases.

There have been several variations upon the classic star pattern. Sometimes a more normalized approach is taken to the dimension tables. It is also common to include aggregations across dimensional hierarchies. The resulting tables are referred to as a snowflake schema or constellation (see Figure 30.4).

Snowflake schemas of this type offer the best performance when using aggregates such as the sales totaled by store in the previous example. These sales numbers could also be summarized into separate fact tables by region or district. Snowflake schema trades performance for the further complication of maintenance of the warehouse metadata and the transformations required from the source systems.

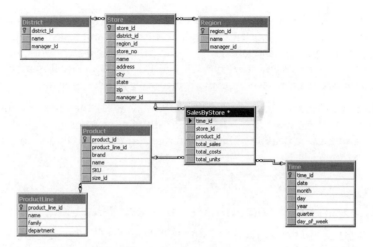

FIGURE 30.4   A sample snowflake with aggregations.

The dimensional model is a logical technique optimized for queries and reporting. It is the most common model used in current warehousing or mart efforts. It provides simplified paths for end-user features such as drill-downs and roll-ups. You can embed precalculated aggregations in the fact tables. This practice can result in rapid query-response times, which again will directly affect the user.

Important Design Considerations

It is generally understood that most first-effort warehouses will fail or not live up to the original expectations. Reasons for failure include lack of adequate corporate sponsorship to neglecting to conform to a unified enterprise model. Whatever the case, there have been several success stories as well. Following is a list of tips that can help you build a successful warehouse or mart in your organization the first time.

- **Start small**—The warehousing project is an iterative process. Build for specific applications that will offer immediate return on investment and end-user acceptance such as trend analysis, profit analysis, or expense reduction. This allows you to gain experience and still provide positive results.

- **Keep users involved**—Do not get the specifications of the project and disappear for several months. The users are the keys to the success for the warehouse. Deliver a prototype a few months into the project. Involve them in the end-user tool selection or construction. Allow the user to test canned queries and validate the data from the transformation efforts. Begin the training of new concepts in data visualization from the very beginning.

- **Get to know the data**—You will need to know the details of the information stored in the warehouse as well as the source and transformations. Remember garbage in, garbage out? The data in the warehouse is only as good as the data that is entered. Try to fix most of your data quality problems in the source systems prior to it making it into your warehouse.

- **Always think ahead**—Do not build problems for the future by committing to a specialized mart that offers no growth plan or common model. Your system must be flexible to handle success and be open enough to *scale* to the enterprise.

Managing a Data Warehouse or Data Mart

You must realize that the data warehouse will be an evolving project. After you decide to begin one, there will probably be no end in sight. The users will constantly need access to different types of information. Source systems will change, and these changes will disrupt the transformation processes. The success of any system tends to bring forth more users and more new requests, and thus put a larger load on system resources. You must be prepared to handle the following ongoing tasks:

- **Backup/Recovery**—As with any database, a solution must be reached for how frequently backups will occur. The data in warehouses can be viewed as less volatile from day to day but not less important. Because the volume of data can grow to enormous sizes, decisions should be made as to when the information is ready for archival.

- **Scheduling loads**—How frequently should information be captured from the source systems? When should these loads occur?

- **Replication**—The warehouse might be entirely published. The subscribers might be marts in several departments that gather information from a common source.

- **Query performance tuning**—Maintaining a warehouse might involve providing canned queries for users or improving response times with schema or index changes.

Microsoft and SQL Server 2000 Contributions to Data Warehousing

Microsoft is truly committed to the advancement of data warehousing using its products (see Figure 30.5). It has helped developed a Data Warehousing Framework that describes the integration of technologies (data access, metadata, transformations, end user query, and so on) throughout the cycles of building, managing, and using data warehousing. Microsoft is also providing support in its Office, BackOffice, and Visual Studio product lines for each of the components of the Warehousing Framework. Microsoft has also partnered with other warehousing vendors to form the Data Warehousing Alliance. These vendors came together to cooperate on technologies and protocols that were agreed on in the Warehousing Framework. This allows for greater interoperability among the various products on the market for data warehousing.

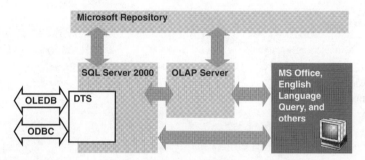

FIGURE 30.5   Microsoft tools for data warehousing.

SQL Server 2000 offers many features that can help in constructing data warehouses. Large database support, query optimizations, and replication add to its usefulness as a solution for a warehouse or mart. Heterogeneous queries allow resultsets to be combined across several disjointed OLE DB or ODBC data sources. Other additions include Data Transformation Services (DTS), use of the Repository for metadata storage, and the Analysis Services OLAP engine.

Data Transformation Services

Data Transformation Services is a flexible toolkit built into SQL Server 2000 that enables you to easily import, export, and transform data from any source to any destination, as long as both support OLE DB or ODBC. DTS can be thought of as a data pump that enables you to move source records from one place to the next. This is achieved through a simple wizard interface.

DTS provides services for importing and exporting data from a variety of data sources:

- OLE DB data sources—Oracle, SQL Server 2000, 7.0, 6.5, and others

- ODBC data sources—DB2 on MVS, AS400/data, Informix, Microsoft Access, Microsoft Excel, and more

- Text files—ASCII, fixed length, or delimited

- Simple transformations—Using the DTS Wizard approach

- Complex transformations—Using the DTS Designer

The DTS framework provides functionality for building robust data warehouses from several heterogeneous operational data stores. It contains tools for setting up regularly scheduled data loads as well as validating or transforming the data into the format required by the warehouse.

Repository

The Microsoft repository is an infrastructure for shared metadata. It permits data in the warehouse to be described in a common way. Using the repository, the data requirements can be stored independently of the data it describes and provides access from other components in the warehousing architecture. The repository's data warehousing features include the following:

- Stores star schema data models

- Catalogs relationships of data elements to source systems

- Records data transformations and data lineage

- Stores data extraction and replication rules

- Supports team development

The Microsoft Repository was designed with a generic and open object model, which has garnered support from many tool vendors. This extensive third-party support benefits the organization by enabling a large set of product choices to help with data warehousing development and maintenance.

Analysis Services

The Microsoft Analysis Services is engine for bringing the power of OLAP and information in the data warehouse to the masses. It presents the warehousing information in multidimensional cubes that allow for slice and dice data analysis.

The key features and benefits of the Microsoft Analysis Services are as follows:

- Accesses any OLE DB compliant data source

- Supports MOLAP (multidimensional online analytical processing), ROLAP (relational OLAP), and HOLAP (a hybrid between the two)

- Bridges the gap between SQL Server and Excel by support for creation of pivot tables

- Allows for mobile or disconnected analysis of information

- Scales from desktop to the enterprise

The OLAP server in DSS multiplies the value of the data stored in the warehouse or mart by providing access and features that enhance decision support. It integrates well with MS BackOffice and Office framework of applications as well as other third party products. See Chapter 31, "SQL 2000 Analysis Services," for a more complete discussion of this product.

Data Warehousing FAQ

Some common questions that DBAs new to data warehousing might encounter are as follows:

Q When should I consider a data warehousing solution?

A When users are requesting access to large amounts of historical information for reporting purposes, you should strongly consider a warehouse or mart. The user will benefit when the information is organized in an efficient manner for this type of access.

Q DBAs have always been told that having non-normalized data is bad. Why is it now okay?

A Normalization in relational databases results in an efficient use of database storage. Data warehousing is not concerned with accomplishing the same storage efficiencies. The main concern is to provide information to the user as fast as possible. Because of this, storing information in a denormalized fashion, including aggregate columns and summarization, provides the best immediate results.

Q What is the difference between data warehousing and OLAP?

A These two terms are often used interchangeably. Warehousing is primarily the organization and storage of the data such that it can be analyzed easily. OLAP deals with the particulars of the process on analyzing the data, managing aggregations, and partitioning information into cubes for in-depth visualization.

Q How often should I load data into my warehouse from my enterprise transaction systems?

A The answer to this question might depend on the needs of the users and the volume of information to be moved. It is common to schedule weekly or monthly dumps from the operational data stores, during periods of low activity (for example, nights or weekends). The longer the gap between loads, the longer processing times for the load when it does run. You will have to weigh the implications of each to come up with an ideal solution for your situation.

Q How do I get started with data warehousing?

A Build one! The easiest way to get started with data warehousing is to analyze an existing OLTP database and see what type of trends would be interesting to examine. From there you could model your new schema and load it with some current data. Although this might seem trivial, it is not. Start small and build from there. SQL Server 2000 offers excellent tools and technologies for starting any warehousing effort.

Summary

In this chapter, the concepts of data warehousing were covered. A warehouse is a central storage facility for subject-oriented data throughout an organization and data warehousing is the process involved in extracting, storing, aggregating this information to provide easy access for end users. You learned how warehousing data differs from online transactional systems and how to transform the transactional data from these systems to the warehouse. You were introduced to the concept of the data mart as a smaller, more specialized warehouse designed to satisfy a particular functional unit. You were also presented with issues related to planning, designing, and maintaining data warehouses in your own organization. Finally, you were presented the tools and services that Microsoft provides to help in the development of data warehouses.

Warehousing has truly been in the spotlight recently. It appears to be a promising method to help decision-makers sort through the abundance of information their systems have collected. It challenges developers and DBAs to shift the way they have been designing databases for the past several years. The information in this chapter should have shed the light on some of the common warehousing concepts and procedures. This should get you started on the road to providing easy access to information for users in your enterprise.

31

SQL 2000 Analysis Services

By Kevin Viers

IN THIS CHAPTER

- What Is OLAP?
- Understanding Multidimensional Data
- The Microsoft Analysis Manager
- Building an OLAP Database
- Data Storage in an OLAP Database
- Optimizing an OLAP Database
- Managing Multidimensional Data
- Microsoft SQL Server 2000 Analysis Services FAQ

Microsoft Analysis Services is the Online Analytical Processing (OLAP) database engine that Microsoft ships with SQL Server 2000. Although the name is different, it is the upgrade to the OLAP Services that shipped with SQL Server 2000. Analysis Services is a feature-rich product in its own right, with the ability to interact with virtually any relational data store. It would be possible to dedicate an entire book to this product, but because it is not the focus of this book, we use this chapter to provide the reader with a foundation of knowledge on which you can begin to effectively use this product.

What Is OLAP?

The term *OLAP* stands for *Online Analytical Processing.* As its name implies, it is a technology centered around the analysis of data. OLAP applications allow users to select, view, and analyze transactional data from a variety of sources, which allows corporations to extract additional value from their traditional Online Transaction Processing (OLTP) systems and data warehouses. OLAP is really an extension, or further refinement, of previous genres of applications such as Decision Support Systems (DSSs) and Executive Information Systems (EISs). Those types of applications are intended to provide high-level, summarized information about which decisions can be made so management can stay informed. OLAP takes that notion and expands on it by providing the ability to slice, dice, roll up, and drill down into all your corporate data.

But what really separates OLAP technology from traditional OLTP technology is its ability to provide multidimensional views of transactional data.

Understanding Multidimensional Data

Before we get too deeply into a discussion about Analysis Services, it is very important that you grasp the concept of multidimensional data and its usefulness as an analytical tool. Most of us, particularly those who are reading this book, are very familiar with relational database systems and the way data is stored and represented in those systems. As shown in Figure 31.1, typical relational database systems provide only a two-dimensional view of data (rows and columns).

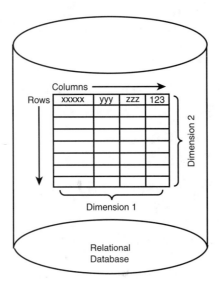

FIGURE 31.1   The traditional relational data store.

This flat representation of transactional data does not lend itself to complex data analysis scenarios that involve looking at quantitative data summarized across many different categories.

A multidimensional database, on the other hand, is capable of providing an *n*-dimensional view of the data. The number of dimensions that can be represented is theoretically unlimited. There are, however, practical storage and performance limitations that keep this number finite.

The primary building block in a multidimensional database is called the *cube*. A cube in a multidimensional database consists of a set of dimensions and measures.

> **NOTE**
>
> Don't misunderstand the definition of a cube. We were all taught in school that a cube is a three-dimensional square. Although that might be the geometric definition of a cube, there can be many more than three dimensions in a cube within a multidimensional database.

The *dimensions* of the cube are the categories across which you want to analyze and summarize your data. These dimensions are created from the tables and columns in your relational data store. Typical dimensions in an OLAP multidimensional database are time, geography, and product. Each dimension consists of a set of levels and members that further define the data.

The *measures* of the cube are the quantitative data elements that you want to analyze. Like dimensions, measures are created from the tables and columns in your relational data store. Typical measures in an OLAP multidimensional database are sales, budgets, and costs; however, virtually any quantitative data element can be included as a measure in a multidimensional cube.

Now that you have a basic understanding of multidimensional data, let's take a look at how Analysis Services can be used to create and maintain multidimensional OLAP databases.

The Microsoft Analysis Manager

The Analysis Manager is a snap-in for the Microsoft Management Console (MMC). The MMC is the standard management console for all the Microsoft BackOffice suite. The look and feel of this console will become familiar very quickly. As shown in Figure 31.2, the Analysis Manager is a very user-friendly interface with a hierarchical, tree-view representation of the server and all its components in the left pane. You can unlock most of its functionality by highlighting an item in the tree view and right-clicking the mouse.

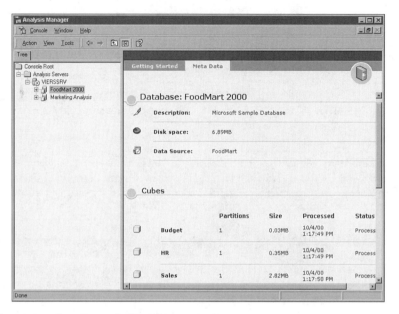

FIGURE 31.2   The Microsoft OLAP Manager.

Building an OLAP Database

Please keep in mind that the primary audience of this book is the database administrator and, as such, the focus of the chapter will be on the administrative activities required to support an OLAP database. The following discussion on creating the OLAP database, cubes, dimensions, levels, and so on is provided only to give you a basic understanding of the concepts behind the development of a multidimensional database using Analysis Services. This discussion is by no means a complete discussion of the many complexities surrounding the design and development of OLAP databases. Entire books are devoted to this subject, including *Microsoft Analysis Services Unleashed* from Sams. I would encourage you to read one of those books if you are a data warehouse designer or developer, but for the database administrator, the following discussion should provide you with a solid knowledge base on which to build.

The first step in using Analysis Services is to create your OLAP database. In order to bring some real-world value into this discussion, we will use an example throughout the remainder of this section. The example will consist of creating a multidimensional OLAP database for the marketing department of a national grocery store chain. The marketing department is concerned about shrinking sales and therefore would like to analyze sales data across a variety of demographic, geographic, and product categories.

To create an OLAP database, highlight the server icon. Right-click to display a short-cut menu. Choose New Database from the shortcut menu. You will see the dialog box shown in Figure 31.3.

FIGURE 31.3   The Database dialog box.

Enter the name of your database and click OK. When you return to the Server Manager, you see your newly created database in the list.

Creating the Data Source

Most OLAP databases do not stand alone as data storage facilities. Rather, they are utilized as a view into your relational transaction-oriented data. Therefore, any OLAP database created in Analysis Services must have a data source that provides the data to populate the dimensions and measures of the cubes.

The data source for your OLAP database can be virtually any relational data store that can expose its data via an OLE DB provider. OLE DB is Microsoft's universal data access object model. As long as your data source can expose itself to an OLE DB provider, you can access that data. SQL Server 2000 ships with several OLE DB providers, including those for Oracle, Jet, SQL Server, DB2, and Analysis Services. Many other OLE DB providers are available from various third-party vendors. A discussion of OLE DB is outside the scope of this chapter; however, it is a published standard that is available on Microsoft's Web site.

To create a data source for your OLAP database, expand the database in the Analysis Server Manager. Highlight the Data Source folder. Right-click to display a shortcut menu. Choose New Data Source from the shortcut menu. You will see the dialog box shown in Figure 31.4.

Notice that this dialog box looks slightly different from what you might have expected for a data source dialog box. Instead of showing the ODBC data sources, it gives a list of available OLE DB providers. The OLE DB provider must be installed and registered on your server in order to be available in this list. After you choose which OLE DB provider you want to use, click Next. You are then prompted for connection information. Microsoft has built intelligence into this dialog box to change the required connection information based on the OLE DB provider you choose. This is done because each OLE DB provider might require unique connection parameters in order to establish a connection to the data source. For our example, we will use the OLE DB provider for ODBC and the FoodMart ODBC data source.

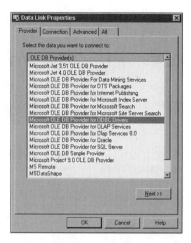

FIGURE 31.4   The Data Link Properties dialog box.

NOTE

Your OLAP database can contain multiple data sources. By using multiple data sources, you can pull data from a variety of transactional or data warehouse systems into one OLAP multi-dimensional database.

Defining the Dimensions

After you have created an OLAP database, the next step is to define your shared dimensions. A shared dimension is a dimension that is available to any cube in your OLAP database. Remember that the dimensions are categories across which you want to analyze and summarize your data. For our example, you might want to create the following dimensions: store location, customer age, customer gender, product, and time. To create a new shared dimension, expand the database. Expand the Library folder. Highlight the Shared Dimensions folder. Right-click to display a shortcut menu. Choose New Dimension from the shortcut menu. You can choose to use a wizard or go straight to the editor. For now, let's use the wizard. Click Next on the introduction screen, and you will see the dialog box shown in Figure 31.5.

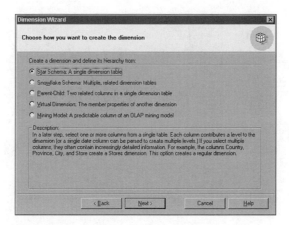

FIGURE 31.5   The Dimension Wizard.

NOTE

Wizards, wizards, everywhere! As I am sure you are aware by now, SQL Server 2000 provides more wizards than ever to walk you through routine tasks. This is true in Analysis Services as well. Virtually every operation you might want to perform involves a wizard. Even if you aren't a big fan of wizards, you will find that the wizards in Analysis Services are useful tools that provide the flexibility you need.

The wizard will ask you what type of dimension that you want to create. The dimension type will be based on the underlying source data tables for your dimension. Choose the Star Schema: single dimension table option. This is the basic dimension that uses a single underlying database table to define its characteristics. Again, a full discussion of each of the dimension types available in Analysis Services is outside the scope of this text.

After you have chosen the type of dimension to create, the next step in creating your dimension is to choose a dimension table. The *dimension table* is the table that provides the source data for your dimension. In other words, this table provides the data about the category for which your dimension is being created. To select a dimension table, click Next on the Dimension Wizard dialog box. You will see the dialog box shown in Figure 31.6.

Expand the desired data source to display a list of available tables. Remember that your OLAP database can have multiple data sources. You can even create a new data source from the Dimension Wizard by clicking the New Data Source button. You can also browse the data that is contained in the dimension table you select. Choose the appropriate table for the dimension you want to create. For our example, we will create a customer location dimension, so choose the customer table. Click Next.

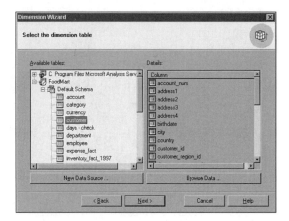

FIGURE 31.6   The Select Dimension Table dialog box.

> **NOTE**
>
> If the dimension table you select contains a date field, the Dimension Wizard asks whether you want to create a standard dimension or a time dimension. Analysis Services can automatically create time dimensions for you based on date columns by using the numeric parts of the date. A time dimension can be years, quarters, months, weeks, days, and so on.

Dimension Levels and Members

After you select a dimension table, the next step in the process is to define the levels and members within your dimension. The dialog box shown in Figure 31.7 is where you define the levels that make up the hierarchy, or summarization path, of your dimension data.

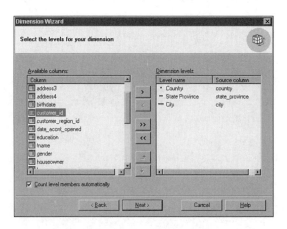

FIGURE 31.7   The Dimension Wizard Select Levels dialog box.

As shown in Figure 31.7, the Dimension Wizard allows you to create levels within the dimension. To create levels within a dimension, choose the columns from your dimension table that correspond to the levels you want to create, and click the > button. You can use the Move Up and Move Down buttons to organize your levels.

Consider the customer location dimension. This dimension is made up of geographical information about the location of each customer. There is a natural hierarchy within this dimension: Country, State, City. Each point along the hierarchy represents one level.

The levels should be organized from the most summarized to the least summarized data. It is possible that a dimension will only have one level. This is not a problem as long as that one level is the only level of summarization that is needed for your data analysis.

CAUTION

Be careful how you set up your levels. As mentioned previously, the levels must be organized within a dimension from the most summarized to the least summarized data. This implies that each parent level must contain fewer members than the level below it. This maintains an essential one-to-many relationship among the data hierarchy that ensures an accurate drill-down and roll-up. In other words, you would not want the City level above the State level in a dimension hierarchy.

Within each level are members. The members represent the actual data values within the dimensions, and the levels represent the hierarchy. For example, the country level within the customer location dimension might consist of the members: USA, Canada, and Mexico. Likewise, the State level might consist of the members: Washington, California, and Oregon.

After you have defined your levels and members, click Next through the next two wizard screens. These screens provide you with some advanced options for creating your dimensions. The default options are sufficient for this discussion. You are now done with the Dimension Wizard. At this point, you can provide a name for your dimension and preview the dimension data in the hierarchy that you defined as shown in Figure 31.8.

Click Finish and you will be taken back to the OLAP Manager. You will need to repeat the previous steps for each dimension you want to create. You should make sure that you define all the dimensions that you want before you begin creating cubes. The dimensions provide the definition for how users will be able to analyze the data that will be stored in your multidimensional database. In creating your dimensions, you should carefully consider all the ways in which your users might want to analyze the data.

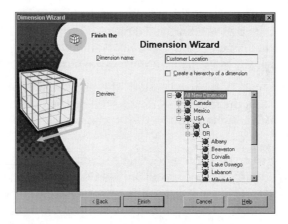

FIGURE 31.8   The Dimension Wizard Finish dialog box.

Building the Cube

After you have defined your dimensions, or the categories across which you want to analyze and summarize your data, the next step is to build your cubes. The cube is the basic building block of the multidimensional OLAP database. The cube associates the dimensions you have defined with the quantitative data you want to analyze, such as sales figures or costs.

To create a cube, expand the database and highlight the Cubes folder. Right-click to display a shortcut menu. Choose New Cube from the shortcut menu. You can choose to use the wizard or to go straight to the editor. Let's again use the wizard. Click Next on the introduction screen, and you will see the dialog box as shown in Figure 31.9.

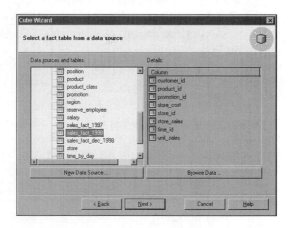

FIGURE 31.9   The Cube Wizard Select Fact Table dialog box.

The Fact Table

The cube in a multidimensional database serves to associate dimensions with quantitative data. The *fact table* is the table within your relational data store that contains the actual quantitative data you want to analyze. Typical fact data within multidimensional OLAP databases are sales, budgets, and costs.

Notice that this dialog box looks exactly like the Dimension Wizard dialog box. Simply expand the desired data source to see a list of available tables and choose the desired fact table.

Typically, the fact table is a table that contains detailed transaction-oriented records, such as sales records. Using our example, you might want to choose the sales_fact_1998 table as the fact table for your cube because it contains transactional sales data from the organization.

> **NOTE**
>
> Each cube must be based on only one fact table. If more than one table contains data that you want to analyze, you must create a separate cube for each one of those fact tables.

From the dialog box shown in Figure 31.10, click Next to define which data within the fact table you want to analyze. This data is known as the measures of the cube.

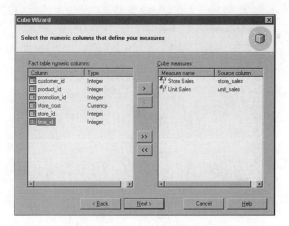

FIGURE 31.10   The Cube Wizard Define Measures dialog box.

Defining the Measures

The measures represent the columns from the fact table that contain the numeric data you want to analyze.

The Cube Wizard Define Measures dialog box, shown in Figure 31.10, functions in much the same way as the Dimension Wizard Select Levels dialog box. Simply choose the columns you want to analyze and click the > button. Unlike the dimension levels definition, there is no set order or hierarchy to the measures. You can add as many measures to the cube as you want, as long as those columns are present in the fact table.

For our example, we want to define a cube that will help us to analyze the store sales and unit sales across a variety of dimensions. To do this, we choose the store_sales and unit_sales columns as measures within our cube. The data contained in these two columns in the fact table will be the basis of all the data that is contained in this cube.

CAUTION

The Cube Wizard automatically shows all the numeric columns that are available in the fact table you have chosen. Although a store ID or customer number might be a numeric value, it is probably not a quantitative measure that you want to include in a cube.

From the dialog box shown in Figure 31.11, click Next to define the dimensions you want to include in your cube.

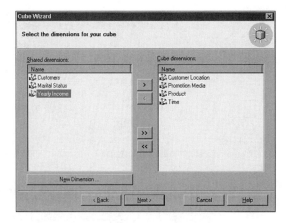

FIGURE 31.11   The Cube Wizard Select Dimensions dialog box.

Adding Dimensions to the Cube

The dimensions provide the categories that are used to analyze the measures of the cube. The dimensions will enable users to drill-down or roll up data about store sales and unit sales across any of the dimensions included in your cube. Using the wizard, you can include any of the dimensions that you have previously defined as shared dimensions as shown in Figure 31.11.

NOTE

The Cube Wizard allows you to include only those dimensions that have been previously defined as shared dimensions. After you have finished using the wizard, however, you are automatically taken to the Cube Editor. From the Cube Editor, you will be able to add additional shared dimensions or create private dimensions that are available only to the cube you are creating.

For our example, we will include the following dimensions in our cube: Customer Location, Promotion Media, Product, and Time. These dimensions apply meaning to the measures. In other words, the user will be able to use this cube to analyze store sales by quarter across each product.

After you have defined your cube dimensions and clicked Next, you are finished with the Cube Wizard.

You will see the dialog box shown in Figure 13.12.

FIGURE 31.12   The Cube Wizard Finish dialog box.

This dialog box allows you to provide a name for your cube and shows you a graphical representation of the dimensions and measures that you have defined. For our example, we will call the cube Marketing Cube. Click Finish to create your cube definition.

You can repeat the previous steps to create as many cubes as you want in your OLAP database. Each cube can have its own set of dimensions and measures. Remember that a cube can only be based on one fact table, so you need a separate cube for each individual fact table that you want to analyze.

At this point, you have seen how to create the dimensions that are used to categorize and summarize your data. You have seen how to create the cube, which defines the relationships between the quantitative data you want to analyze and the dimensions across which you want to analyze that data. At this point, however, you have simply created the definition of the cube, or the metadata, within the multidimensional OLAP database.

Before you can use the cube, it must be populated with actual data. Populating the cube involves processing all the rows and columns of your dimension tables and fact tables to produce an actual cube of data within the OLAP database. In order to fully appreciate what happens when the cube is processed and data is stored, we are going to spend some time discussing data storage within an OLAP database.

Data Storage in an OLAP Database

Remember that the multidimensional databases created in Analysis Services are all based on underlying source data that resides in other relational data stores. In most instances, this underlying relational data store is a data warehouse or data mart. When you process a cube, that source data must be stored in such a way that it can be retrieved by Analysis Services and returned as a resultset to a client application. Analysis Services supports three storage modes:

- Multidimensional OLAP (MOLAP)
- Relational OLAP (ROLAP)
- Hybrid OLAP (HOLAP)

Over the years there has been a heated debate within the OLAP community as to which of these storage methods is the superior way to store data for OLAP purposes. In the following sections, we will discuss each storage method and its implementation in Analysis Services.

MOLAP

The MOLAP storage method involves storing all the detailed cube data within a proprietary multidimensional data store. This means that the relational data stored within the dimension tables and fact tables of the underlying relational data source is written to an optimized multidimensional storage.

In addition to the detailed cube data, all aggregation data is also stored in the multidimensional data store. You are probably asking "What is an aggregation, and why do I care?" We will answer that question shortly, but for now understand that aggregation data must be stored somewhere, and in the MOLAP storage mode, it is stored in the multidimensional data store.

Within Analysis Services, the actual data storage architecture consists of records that are written to 64KB segments. Within each record is a compressed 4-byte to 8-byte key that is a pointer to a set of dimension coordinates within the cube. This storage architecture is optimized for the Analysis Services query processor and offers the best performance of any of the storage modes.

ROLAP

The ROLAP storage method involves storing all the detailed cube data and aggregation data within a relational data store. This means that all the detailed cube data found in the dimension tables and fact tables is left alone in its native relational data store. The data is not moved.

When aggregation data is stored, summary tables are created within the relational data store by Analysis Services and populated by using simple INSERT INTO SQL statements. Analysis Services creates all tables and indexes automatically. Remember that this happens only when the aggregation data is stored; the detailed cube data is left alone.

This storage method does not offer the same performance benefits as MOLAP; however, it is an extremely scalable storage mode that allows corporations to leverage existing data storage capabilities.

HOLAP

The final storage mode supported by Analysis Services is HOLAP. As you might imagine, HOLAP is a combination of MOLAP and ROLAP. This storage method involves storing all the detailed cube data within the relational data store and all the aggregation data within a multidimensional data store. This storage method might provide the best of both worlds: the performance of MOLAP and the scalability of ROLAP.

Now that you have an understanding of the three data storage methods supported by Analysis Services, let's take a look at what is involved in processing the cubes within our OLAP database. The following sections will continue to build on our Marketing Cube example by showing you how to populate the cube with data and optimize its performance within the OLAP database.

Optimizing an OLAP Database

As mentioned previously, in order to use your OLAP database, you must first process the cubes that are contained within the database. Simply stated, processing the cube populates the cube definition with actual transactional data from your data warehouse or data mart. Before you actually populate your cube, however, you need to define certain optimization definitions for your cube. Analysis Services provides two primary mechanisms for optimizing the cubes within OLAP databases:

- Aggregations
- Partitions

Aggregations

Aggregations are summaries of data that are calculated by the Analysis Server and stored in the database along with the transaction level cube data. For example, an aggregation of data would be the total sales data for all stores in the United States for a certain time period. This number must be calculated by summing all the individual sales figures from each member within the store location dimension. This calculation can occur when the cube is processed or when the client application requests the data. By creating an aggregation, the calculation is performed when the cube is processed and the total is stored in the OLAP database.

When a client application requests data from a cube, the Analysis Server first searches all the stored aggregations to determine whether the requested data already exists. If the server finds the requested data, it simply returns that data to the client with no further calculations required. If the requested data does not exist in any stored aggregation, the server must calculate the data on-the-fly. As you can see, there can be significant performance gains when you use aggregations.

There is, however, a downside to aggregations. They take up considerable storage space on your server and they might take significant time to process. When defining the aggregations to use for your cube, it is important to consider the tradeoff between performance and storage requirements.

Data Explosion

Beware of data explosion! *Data explosion* is a phenomenon of multidimensional databases which indicates that as the number of dimensions in a cube increases, the number of potential aggregations grows exponentially.

Consider a cube with 1 measure and 2 dimensions; each dimension contains 4 levels (for example, a time dimension consisting of years, quarters, months, and weeks; a geography dimension consisting of countries, regions, states and cities; and a measure consisting of sales figures). How many different ways can data be aggregated or summarized across the different levels within this cube? In this example, there are at least 16 potential aggregations or summaries for this cube.

So there are n^x potential aggregations, where n represents the number of levels within a dimension and x represents the number of dimensions in the cube. Based on this formula, a cube with 8 dimensions, each having 4 levels (which is not completely unlikely in a multidimensional OLAP scenario) has 65,536 potential aggregations! Remember that each aggregation must be stored either in the multidimensional or the relational database. Also keep in mind that each aggregation must be calculated when the cube is processed. As you can see, there are significant implications on both storage space and time required to process a cube when creating aggregations.

Now, let's take a look at how to create and process aggregations for our Marketing cube within Analysis Services.

Creating Aggregations

To create aggregations for the Marketing cube, highlight the Marketing cube within the Cubes folder in the tree-view. Right-click to display a shortcut menu. Choose Design Storage. This will launch the Storage Design Wizard. The Storage Design Wizard helps you do two things: choose a storage mode for your cube and aggregation data and design a set of aggregations for your cube.

Choosing a Storage Mode   The dialog box shown in Figure 31.13 will allow you to determine the storage mode you would like to use for the cube. Refer to the section "Data Storage in an OLAP Database" for a complete discussion of the available storage modes and an explanation of each.

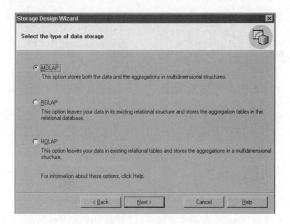

FIGURE 31.13   The Storage Design Wizard data storage dialog box.

The storage mode determines how Analysis Services stores the aggregation and detailed cube data. You are probably asking "How do I know which data storage mode to use?" This is an important, difficult-to-answer question. The answer depends on your individual situation. However, we'll try to provide some general guidelines.

As mentioned previously, MOLAP storage can provide significant performance advantages over ROLAP and HOLAP. If you have no pressing reasons to use one of the other data storage methods, you should use MOLAP. The only real drawback to MOLAP storage is that the data storage structure is proprietary to Analysis Services and, therefore, only client applications that support OLE DB for Analysis Services have access to that data.

If you have a tremendous amount of historical data that might not be accessed very frequently, it might make sense to use the ROLAP storage method because ROLAP leverages the existing relational database and leaves the detailed data in its native data store. Keep in mind, however, that every aggregation created using the ROLAP storage method results in a new table with indexes in your relational database management system (RDBMS). As mentioned earlier, a cube with 8 dimensions, each with 4 levels, could produce up to 65,536 aggregations. Do you really want to add 65,536 new tables to your database? Probably not. There is a time and place for everything, and ROLAP is no exception.

HOLAP might be an appropriate choice where you have large quantities of detailed data, but your applications need frequent access to that data. HOLAP allows you to take advantage of the scalability of your RDBMS by leaving the detailed data in its native source, but provides some performance improvement by storing aggregation data in MOLAP.

You should not take this decision lightly. Consider all the factors and choose the appropriate storage method for each cube that you are processing. Each cube can have its own storage method. This means that you could store one cube as MOLAP data and another cube as ROLAP. Again, the decision depends on a number of factors that only you, as a DBA, can know.

For our example, we will choose the MOLAP storage mode as we want maximum performance from our cube. Click Next to design the aggregations for your cube.

Designing Aggregations   The dialog box shown in Figure 31.14 allows you to design the aggregations for your cube. What you are actually doing here is telling Analysis Services how many of the potential aggregations to create for your cube. Analysis Services uses sophisticated algorithms to determine which aggregations to create. The only real control you have over this process is to specify the trade-off between disk space and performance.

Analysis Services provides the capability to perform partial preaggregation. This means that you, as a DBA, can determine the appropriate mix between storage space requirements and performance enhancement when creating aggregations.

As you can see in Figure 31.14, you have three basic aggregation design options.

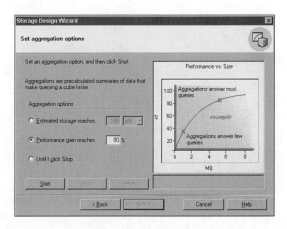

FIGURE 31.14   The Storage Design Wizard Design Aggregations dialog box.

The options tell Analysis Services to create aggregations until

- Estimated storage reaches xMB—Checking this option causes Analysis Services to create aggregations until it determines that the specified amount of disk space will be used.

- Performance gain reaches x%—Checking this option causes Analysis Services to create aggregations until it determines that a specified percentage of performance gain is reached.

- The user clicks Stop—Checking this option causes Analysis Services to create aggregations until the user clicks Stop.

As is the case with choosing the storage mode, choosing the level of aggregation optimization is really an individual DBA decision that is based on many factors. Microsoft says, however, that 80% performance optimization seems to realize the best disk space versus performance tradeoff.

For our example, we will take Microsoft's advice and allow Analysis Services to design aggregations until it determines that we will realize an 80% performance gain. From the dialog box shown in Figure 31.14, click Start. You will notice that the graph on the right side of the dialog box dynamically displays the disk space versus performance gain as the aggregations are designed. After Analysis Services has created the aggregations to satisfy the specified condition, click Next to display the dialog box shown in Figure 31.15.

FIGURE 31.15   The Storage Design Wizard Finish dialog box.

As you can see from this dialog box, you have the following choices:

- Process now—Checking this option causes Analysis Services to process all aggregations when you click Finish. By this, we mean that Analysis Services performs all data calculations and stores the data in the specified data storage mode with the cube.

- Save, but don't process now—Checking this option allows you to save the aggregation design without actually calculating or storing the data. Remember that you must process these aggregations before the data will be available to the user.

For our example, we want to choose the Process Now option and click Finish.

Depending on the level of optimization you have chosen and the complexity of your cube, this process could take a significant amount of time. Also, if you have chosen MOLAP storage, all the detail data must also be written to the multidimensional data store.

In any event, Analysis Services displays a detailed status window of all processing. This status shows any database operations that are being performed and indicates either the success or failure of those operations (see Figure 31.16).

At this point, we have created the OLAP database, defined a cube within that database, designed aggregations to optimize the cube, and processed the data that is stored within the cube. We could actually begin to use our cube now. But before we discuss how to use the cube, a few more optimization issues are worth discussing.

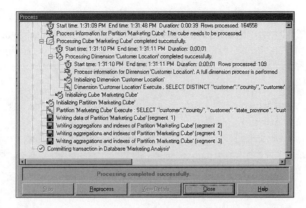

FIGURE 31.16   The Storage Design Wizard Process Status dialog box.

Usage-Based Optimization

After reading the previous sections, you might feel that designing aggregations is a less-than-exact science. You are correct. How do you know what the appropriate level of aggregation is for your cube? More importantly, how can you be sure that the aggregations you wanted were actually created? For example, you might know that your users will frequently request total sales for the Northwest region. In that case, you would like to ensure that an aggregation is created for that scenario.

Analysis Services provides a tool known as *usage-based optimization* to help you more accurately optimize your cube. To use this feature, highlight your cube in OLAP Manager. Right-click to display a shortcut menu. Choose Usage-Based Optimization to display the dialog box shown in Figure 31.17.

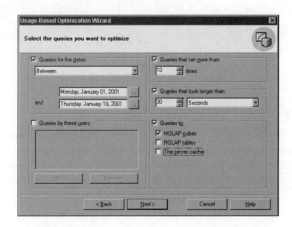

FIGURE 31.17   The Usage-Based Optimization Wizard dialog box.

As its name implies, this tool relies on previous cube access to determine which aggregations to design. In other words, you can define how aggregations are created based on actual usage patterns from your client applications. The aggregation design might be based on queries that took too long to execute or queries that were run by certain users.

For example, let's say that John Smith is the president of FoodMart, Inc. He wants to access the overall sales figures across all regions each day. You can use the Usage-Based Optimization Wizard to indicate that aggregations should be created for all queries executed by John Smith. Analysis Services will then create the appropriate aggregations and store them in the cube.

Over time, you will be able to fine-tune the optimization of your cube based on actual historical user interaction. After the initial guess at performance versus disk space aggregation design, you should always use Usage-Based Optimization.

> **NOTE**
>
> A good recommendation is to always set your first aggregation level by using a 20% performance improvement and then run the Usage-Based Optimization Wizard after the cube has been in user acceptance testing for a week or so. Make sure to keep your user community informed of your plans. They should be made aware that the performance experienced for the first week will not be indicative of the final production level performance.

Usage Analysis

Another tool that will be extremely valuable for any DBA charged with maintaining an OLAP database is the Usage Analysis Wizard. This wizard enables the DBA to print several graphs that give some indication of how the cubes within an OLAP database are being used by client applications.

To launch the Usage Analysis Wizard, highlight your cube in Analysis Manager. Right-click to display a shortcut menu. Choose Usage Analysis to display the dialog box shown in Figure 31.18.

This wizard will allow you to choose one of the following graphs or tables to determine cube usage:

- Query runtime table—Table showing the runtimes of queries executed against the cube ordered from longest to shortest in duration

- Query frequency—Table showing the frequency of queries executed against the cube, order from the most frequent to the least frequent.

- Active user table—Table showing active users and the queries they have executed against the cube.

- Query bar graph—Bar graph showing the response times for all queries executed against the cube.

- Query by hour graph—Bar graph showing queries executed against the cube grouped by hour.

- Query by date graph—Bar graph showing queries executed against the cube grouped by date.

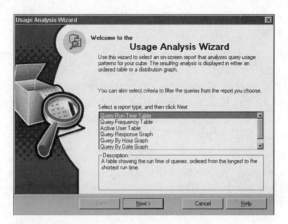

FIGURE 31.18   The Usage Analysis Wizard dialog box.

As you can see, this is quite a powerful tool and will enable the DBA to better plan aggregation and optimization strategies. Regular use of both the Usage-Based Optimization tool and the Usage Analysis tool will allow you to maintain an OLAP database with the most efficient mix of performance enhancement and storage utilization.

NOTE

Analysis Services manages the Usage-Based Optimization and Usage Analysis functions by logging queries that are sent to the Analysis Server. These queries are captured and stored in a Microsoft Access database (msmdqlog.mdb). By default, Analysis Services is set to log every tenth query that is sent to the server. To change this setting, highlight the server in the Analysis Manager, right-click, and choose Properties. From the Server Properties dialog box, choose the Logging tab. You can set the value anywhere from 1 to 10,000. Be aware that as user queries are logged more frequently, performance might be negatively impacted. I would recommend setting the query frequency to 1 during the initial performance tuning effort and changing the frequency to 10 or higher before production implementation. By setting the logging frequency to 1 during the initial tuning phase, you can be sure that Analysis Services has a complete picture of your expected usage pattern in order to most effectively and efficiently create aggregations.

Partitions

Partitions represent the physical data storage of the cube and aggregation data. The cube is the logical definition of the data. When you create a cube in an OLAP database, Analysis Services automatically creates one partition. After you have created the cube, you can go back and create new partitions. These partitions are used to physically segment the data from your logical cube definition.

The true power of partitions is that each partition can have its own storage mode and its own unique set of aggregations. In this way, one logical cube can be segmented into different physical data stores using a combination of MOLAP, ROLAP, and HOLAP and different aggregation optimizations. This might be very desirable as you find the need to archive less used historical data to a different physical storage location while still allowing cube access to that data.

NOTE

Creating user-defined partitions (those that are not automatically created by Analysis Services) requires the Enterprise Edition of Analysis Services. If you are running the standard edition, this feature is not supported.

Managing Multidimensional Data

Obviously, the transaction-oriented business does not stop once a cube has been created. So far we have discussed the cubes as if they were read-only snapshot views of transactional data. Although it is true that OLAP databases are used to perform analysis on historical transactional data, those cubes need to be updated as the underlying transactional data changes.

Analysis Services provides three primary mechanisms for updating the multidimensional data within your cubes:

- Processing the cube
- Merging partitions
- Client write back

The following sections will discuss these topics.

Processing the Cube

As mentioned earlier, in order for a cube to be populated with actual data, it must be processed. Likewise, in order to update data in a cube, it must be processed. To update your cube data, highlight the cube in OLAP Manager. Right-click to display a shortcut menu. Choose Process to display the dialog box shown in Figure 31.20.

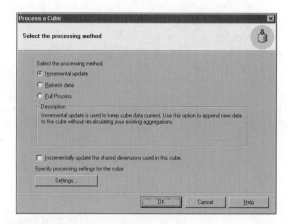

FIGURE 31.20 The Process a Cube dialog box.

Figure 31.20 shows the dialog box to process a cube with the following options:

- Incremental update—Choose this option to add only changed data to the cube. Existing cube data is left intact and aggregations are recalculated to add the new data. The incremental update can be performed while users are still connected to the database. When the update is finished, users have access to the new data.

- Refresh data—Choose this option to clear out all the data in the cube and repopulate. When you choose this option, all aggregations are re-calculated and the data is stored in the cube based on the original cube definition.

- Process—Choose this option only if the structure of your cube has changed; for example, if you have added or removed a dimension or measure to the cube. This option completely rebuilds the cube based on the current cube definitions. This process is exactly the same as the process you ran when you originally created the cube.

One of the biggest problems that many administrators encountered while processing cubes in the previous version of this tool was that while the cube is being processed, the data is unavailable for user queries. This can cause a problem if you ever need to re-process a cube during normal operational times. Analysis Services allows you to grant user access to the cubes as soon as cube data is populated and before aggregations have been calculated. This feature minimizes the time that cubes are unavailable to your users. To modify this behavior, click the Settings button as shown in Figure 31.20. You will see the dialog box shown in Figure 31.21.

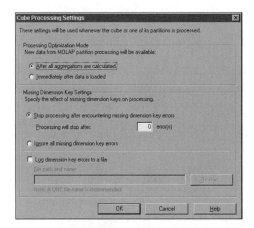

FIGURE 31.21   The Cube Processing Settings dialog box.

Choosing the Immediately After Data Is Loaded option will enable your users to access cube data before aggregations are created. Be aware, however, that query performance will be significantly worse until all aggregations have been created.

Merging Partitions

Analysis Services enables you to merge data from one partition to another. Why would you want to do this? Let's say that you create a cube to store regional sales information. The cube is created with four partitions, one in each sales region. These partitions are physically distributed, but client access is via one logical cube. At the end of the year, you want to combine all the regional sales data into one physical partition located on a central server for faster processing. You can do this by merging the partitions.

To merge partitions, highlight the source or target partition in the OLAP Manager. Right-click to display a shortcut menu. Choose Merge.

NOTE

If you intend to merge two partitions at some point in the future, you need to keep some design considerations in mind when originally creating your partitions. In order for partitions to be merged, they must have the same storage mode (MOLAP, ROLAP, or HOLAP) and have identical aggregations; and their fact tables must have identical structures.

Client Write Back

You might wonder if it is possible for a client to update the data in a cube. After all, the client is the person who is more than likely the most familiar with the data and the one who could spot data that needs to be changed. The answer to this question is yes and no.

Analysis Services allows a cube to be write-enabled. When a cube is write-enabled, users can write data back to the cube. The trick is that the data is not actually written to the cube itself or to the underlying source data. Rather, Analysis Services maintains a separate write-back table that stores all the data that is written to the cube. Users are able to browse the write-back data and they are unaware that the data is not stored in the cube. The data that is stored in the write-back table is actually the variance from the original cube value. Whenever a user queries a write-enabled cube, the changes stored in the write-back table are applied to the original cube data and presented to the user.

To write-enable a cube, highlight the cube in the Analysis manager. Right-click to display a shortcut menu. Choose Write-Enable to display the dialog box shown in Figure 31.22.

FIGURE 31.22   The Write Enable dialog box.

In this dialog box, you can enter the name of a data source and a table in which the write-back data will be stored. As far as the user can tell, this data is part of the cube.

After the cube has been write-enabled, users can actually make changes to the data while they are browsing the cube. These changes are stored in the write-back but are displayed to the user as if part of the cube.

You can convert this write-back table to a permanent partition at any point as well. After the write-back table is converted to a partition, the write-back table and all its data are deleted and the cube once again becomes read-only.

Securing Your OLAP Data

Just as with any database management system, security is a significant concern in Analysis Services. The Analysis Services server is responsible for providing data to end users and, as such, requires a mechanism by which that data can be secured.

Integrated Windows NT Security

The first level of any security scheme is user authentication. Before you even begin to determine what data a user should or should not be able to view within an OLAP database, you need to determine whether the user should have access to the Analysis Services server. Analysis Services employs integrated Windows NT security for this authentication process. In order to have access to OLAP Services, a user must be a member of the domain under which the OLAP Services was installed or be a member of one of its trusted domains.

When Analysis Services is installed, it creates a local NT group called OLAP Administrators on the server on which it is installed. By default, the user account under which the Analysis Services is installed becomes a member of that group. You can add other users to this group as long as they are part of the same or another trusted domain. This is done through the Windows NT User Manager. There is no interface within Analysis Manager to add users to the OLAP Administrators group. Those users will then have administrator privileges on the OLAP Server. Be aware that any user who is a member of the OLAP Administrator group will have full access to all cube data regardless of any specific roles or permissions that you apply through OLAP Manager.

Creating Database Roles

Now that you understand that OLAP Services uses basic NT authentication to allow users to access the server, you need to understand how to restrict access to the specific OLAP databases and cubes within those databases. The primary mechanism for creating this level of security is the role. A role provides a way to map NT user accounts and groups to specific security roles within an OLAP database.

Roles are defined at the database level and are not shared across databases. You might define as many roles as you like within each OLAP database. Once the roles have been defined at the database level, you can assign those roles to those cubes for which you want to apply security.

To create a database role, highlight the Database Roles icon in the Analysis Manager. Right-click to display a shortcut menu. Choose Manage Roles to display the dialog box shown in Figure 31.23.

The Database Role Manager allows you to create as many roles as needed within your OLAP database. The dialog box shown in Figure 31.23 displays all the roles that have been created for the specified database. You can see at a glance all the relevant information about each role, such as which Windows NT users have been assigned to the role and to which cubes the roles have been granted access.

From the Database Role Manager, click New to add a new role to the database. You will see the dialog box shown in Figure 31.24.

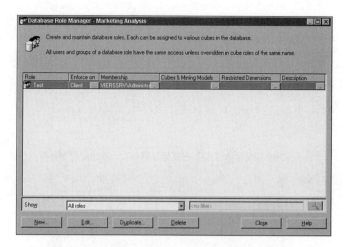

FIGURE 31.23   The Database Role Manager dialog box.

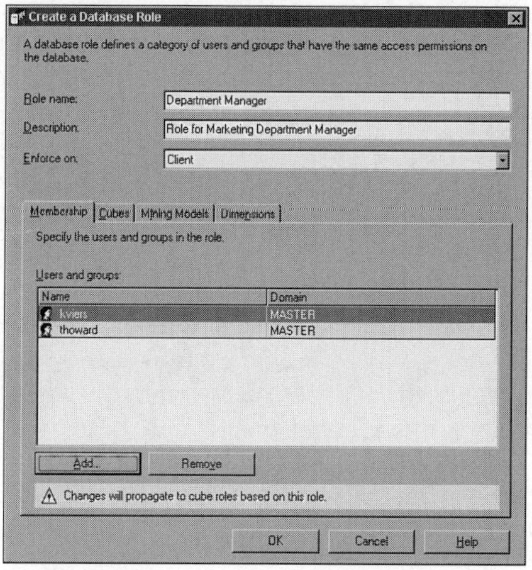

FIGURE 31.24   The Create a Database Role dialog box.

Enter the name of the role you want to create and a description in the appropriate text boxes. After you have named the new role, you need to identify the membership of that role.

When a user attempts to access data from an OLAP database, Analysis Server first validates the user using Windows NT authentication and then determines to which roles that validated user belongs. As a result, the roles within the OLAP database must be mapped to Windows NT groups or domain users. To map Windows NT groups or users to the role, click the Add button. This will display a standard Windows NT user dialog box from which you select all domain groups and users who will be assigned to the new role.

You also need to grant access to at least one cube. To grant access to specific cubes, click the Cubes tab of the Create a Database Role dialog box as seen in Figure 31.24. You will see the dialog box shown in Figure 31.25.

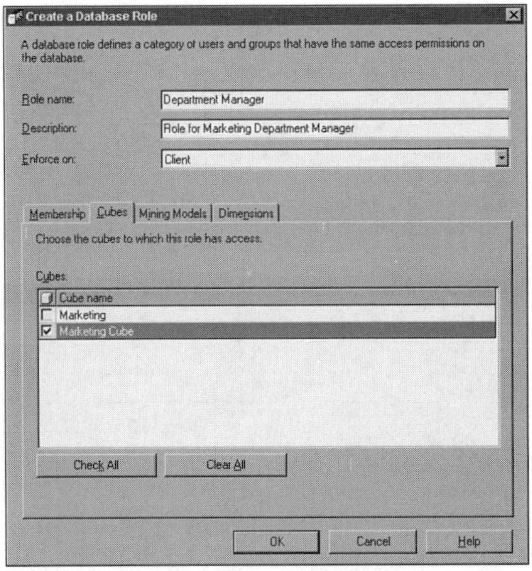

FIGURE 31.25   The Create a Database Role dialog box—Cubes tab.

On the Cubes tab, simply check each cube for which you want the role to have access. At the cube level, you are only able to grant or deny access to the cube as a whole. In other words, if a role is granted access to a particular cube, the members of that role can view all the data contained within that cube, including all dimensions, aggregations, and cell level values.

> **NOTE**
>
> When you grant access to a cube within a database role, you are actually creating a cube role within each cube for which access has been granted. The cube role is inherited from the database role, but attributes can be overwritten at the cube level. The security settings at the cube level take precedence over those set at the database level.

As you can imagine, this level of security is certainly not sufficient for a production level implementation of an OLAP database. You can provide a more granular level of security using Analysis Services by specifying both dimension level and cell level security.

Dimension Level Security

Setting dimension level security allows you to specify how a user will be able to browse through the dimensions of a cube. Suppose that one of the dimensions in your HR cube was salary. You do not want to provide access for that type of information to some users. You can use dimension level security to deny access to the salary dimension to specified database roles.

To set dimension level security, click the Dimensions tab of the Create a Database Role dialog box seen in Figure 31.25. You will see the dialog box shown in Figure 31.26.

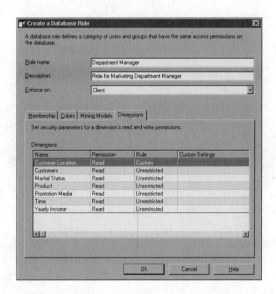

FIGURE 31.26   The Create a Database Role dialog box—Cubes Tab.

This dialog box allows you to set dimension level security for each shared dimension within your OLAP database. You have three basic options for setting dimension level security rules. Those options are as follows:

- Unrestricted—Setting this security rule indicates that all users who are members of the role will have complete read access to all levels and members of the dimension, including the measures dimension. This is the default setting for all shared dimensions.

- Fully Restricted—Setting this security rule indicates that all users who are members of the role will not be able to see any of the levels and members of the dimension. When a user belonging to the rule accesses a cube containing this dimension, he will not see the dimension at all.

- Custom—Setting this security rule allows you to provide a more customizable security setting for the dimension. To set custom dimension security, set the rule to Custom and click on the expand button under Custom Settings. You will see the dialog box as shown in Figure 31.27.

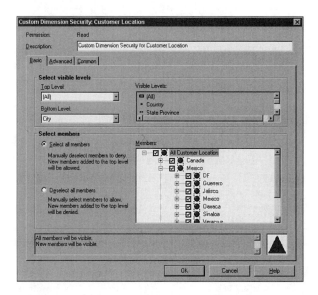

FIGURE 31.27   The Custom Dimension Security dialog box.

The Custom Dimension Security dialog box allows you to create a more customized access path for the dimension. You can use the options on this dialog box to set specific levels and members within the dimension for read access. For example, you might want to set up a security role for department managers that only allow them to view members of the employee dimension at their level and below. To do this, you set the Top Level in the Select Visible Levels to reflect the highest level in the hierarchy to grant access. Any hierarchy levels above the Top Level set here will not be available to members of the role. Additionally you can select or deselect specific members within the dimension in order to grant or deny access at an extremely granular level.

Of course, in some cases dimension level security is not flexible enough. In that case, you can set up cell level security.

Cell Level Security
The capability to restrict access to the individual data elements within a cube is a vital part of any OLAP application. This concept, known as cell level security,

enables you to create cubes that contain all your relevant data and then restrict access to that data based on various data-related criteria.

The most obvious example of why you need cell level security is seen when examining sensitive data such as salary information. You might want to create a cube that contains salary data for a department within your organization. Obviously, only certain individuals within the department will need access to that data, whereas virtually every individual within the department will need access to other data contained within the cube. Without cell level security, the only way to achieve this level of security would be to create multiple cubes for each type of user and then physically slice the data partitions to restrict certain data from users. This solution creates an administrative nightmare, redundant data storage, and any number of other disadvantages.

To solve this problem, Analysis Services enables you to define a set of permissions for each role you create that will allow various levels of access to specific data elements within your cubes. Each cube can be assigned many roles and each role can have a more granular permission assigned to restrict cell level data access. The following sections explain in more detail how to do this within your applications.

Cell level security is set at the cube role level and not at the database role level. In order to set cell level security options, expand the cube and highlight the Cube Roles icon. Right-click to display a shortcut menu. Choose Manage Roles to display the dialog box shown in Figure 31.28.

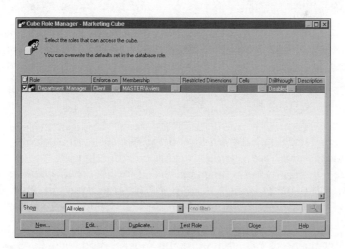

FIGURE 31.28   The Cube Role Manager dialog box.

This dialog box will show all the roles that have been granted access to this cube. To set cell level options, click the Expand button in the Cells column to display the dialog box shown in Figure 31.29.

FIGURE 31.29   Edit a Cube Role dialog box.

Three possible permission levels can be granted at the cell level. Those permission levels are

- Read Permission—This level allows users to read the data values within a cell based on a set of criteria that is defined by the *PermissionsExpression*.

- Contingent Read Permission—This level applies only to calculated members. It enables you to set read access to a cell that returns calculated members as long as the underlying data cells are readable.

- Write Permission—This level allows a cell to be written. It is only applicable for a write-enabled cube.

The key to understanding the cell-level permissions is to understand that each cell permission level can have only one rule per role. In other words, you can only define one rule to determine whether to grant read access to a cell. Whenever a user application requests data from an OLAP cube, the server evaluates the rules for every cell requested. The outcome of that rule evaluation determines if an individual cell is returned.

The default behavior is that each of the three permission levels is set to unrestricted read. This means that all cell values will be available to the members of the role. In order to restrict access to specific cells, you must define a custom rule for the desired permission level. To set a custom rule for a permission, use the Edit a Cube Role dialog box as seen in Figure 31.34. Set the Cell Security Policy to Advanced. Set the rule for the Appropriate Permission level to Custom. Click the Expand button in the Custom Settings column to display the dialog box shown in Figure 31.30.

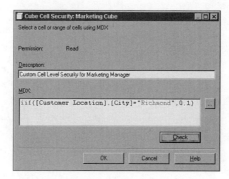

FIGURE 31.30   Cube Cell Security dialog box.

The custom rule is set by defining a multidimensional expression (MDX) for each permission level that will evaluate to True or False. MDX is the standard query language used by Analysis Services. It is analogous to SQL in the OLAP world. A discussion of MDX syntax is outside the scope of this text and is predominantly a developer issue.

For the purposes of this discussion, you should understand that each custom rule must be a valid MDX expression that will evaluate to either True or False. When a user requests data from a cube, Analysis Services will evaluate the MDX expression for each cell that is being returned to the user. If the expression evaluates to True, access to the contents of the cell is denied.

CAUTION

Be very careful about how you build your permission rules. In a typical security scenario, most administrators tend to lock everything down and then grant access to resources as needed. If you take this approach when applying cell-level security to a cube, you can get burned. In other words, if you apply a permissions rule that will only evaluate to TRUE when a given condition exists, all other data will be denied to the user. This can have consequences if you don't create your MDX statement correctly. A safer approach is to create permission rules that will evaluate to FALSE only when a given condition exists. This has the effect of keeping all data accessible accept those cells for which you explicitly want to deny access. It is up to the administrator to determine the most appropriate security strategy.

It is important to understand the order in which OLAP Services will evaluate security rules so as to determine whether to return a cell value. This can have an impact when you plan your security strategy.

If a client application requests read access to a cell, the following are evaluated:

- If no read-access rules are defined for the role, OLAP does not perform any further checks and returns the value of the cell.

- If a read-access rule applies to the cell, the rule is evaluated. If the condition is satisfied, Analysis Services returns the value of the cell and no further checks are performed.

- If a contingent-read-access rule applies to the cell, the rule is evaluated. If the condition is satisfied, Analysis Services returns the value of the cell and no further checks are performed.

- If the cell contains a calculated member (defined by the client application and not in the OLAP cube structure), Analysis Services returns the value of the cell.

- If none of these conditions is satisfied, Analysis Services returns an error.

The following is the default security behavior:

- If no read-access or contingent-read-access rules are present, read access is granted to all cells within the cube

- If no write-access rules are present, and the role has read/write permission on the parent cube, write access to all cells is granted.

Microsoft SQL Server 2000 Analysis Services FAQ

The following section lists some commonly asked questions and answers about SQL Server 2000 Analysis Services.

Q When should I consider implementing OLAP technology?

A Basically, any business process that requires you to analyze (roll up, drill down, and so on) transactional data across a variety of categories is an excellent application of OLAP technology. Loosely speaking, any time you have created an Excel pivot table, you have started to explore the power of OLAP technology.

Q What is the difference between relational and multidimensional databases?

A The primary difference between a relational database and a multidimensional database is semantics. The true differentiation is the manner in which data is represented, and not the underlying technology. Relational databases tend to represent data in a flat, two-dimensional manner, whereas multidimensional databases have the capability to represent data across many dimensions.

It is important to note that the underlying technology between the two kinds of databases does not have to be different. It is possible to create a multidimensional database using SQL Server 2000. This is a complex task, requiring sophisticated database schemas, such as star schemas, but it can be done. Likewise, it would be possible to create a standard two-dimensional relational database using Analysis Services by creating cubes with only two dimensions.

Q How do I translate my transactional data into an effective multidimensional database?

A In Analysis Services, the multidimensional database is based on a data source; typically this data source is the database that holds your transactional data. In order to create the multidimensional database, you must translate your data. Translating this relational data into an effective multidimensional database requires careful thought and a true understanding of the base data and how your users need to analyze that data.

Basically, the translation involves choosing the appropriate tables and columns within those tables to represent the dimensions and measures of your cube. As is the case with most things, this is often easier said than done. The trick to effectively translating your data is to truly understand the underlying data. In most cases, it is necessary to have many people involved in designing the cubes that make up the multidimensional database.

Q Can I analyze data that is calculated from my source data such as net profit?

A Yes, Analysis Services supports calculated members. A calculated member is essentially a measure that does not have a value explicitly stored in the underlying fact table but whose value can be derived from other values that are explicitly stored in the fact table. After you have defined a calculated member, it appears similar to any other measure within the cube and its source is invisible to the user.

Summary

As you can see, Microsoft SQL Server Analysis Services is an exciting new technology that will have a significant impact on business application development. It is expected that the OLAP and data warehousing market will be the fastest growing segment of the database market over the next five years. Microsoft is poised to become a major player in this market segment with the introduction of the Analysis Services.

PART XIV

Appendixes

IN THIS PART

A Naming Conventions

B DBCC Commands

C SQL Server Resources

APPENDIX A

Naming Conventions

by Orryn Sledge

Recommended naming conventions for SQL Server are listed in Table A.1.

TABLE A.1   Suggested Naming Conventions

Object	Naming Convention	Example
database	*(business name)*	`sales`
table	*(business name)*	`customer`
constraint		
foreign key constraint	*(table name)* + `_fk`	`customer_fk`
primary key constraint	*(table name)* + `_pk`	`customer_pk`
unique key constraint	*(table name)* + `_uniq`	`customer_uniq`
Or		
foreign key constraint	`fk_` + *(table name)*	`fk_customer`
primary key constraint	`pk_` + *(table name)*	`pk_customer`
unique key constraint	`uniq_` + *(table name)*	`uniq_customer`
index		
clustered	*(column_name)* + `_cdx`	`customer_id_cdx`
nonclustered	*(column name)* + `_idx`	`customer_id_idx`
trigger		
delete	*(table name)* + `_dtr`	`customer_dtr`
insert	*(table name)* + `_itr`	`customer_itr`
update	*(table name)* + `_utr`	`customer_utr`
insert and update	*(table name)* + `_iutr`	`customer_iutr`
Or		
delete	`dtr_` + *(table name)*	`dtr_customer`
insert	`itr_` + *(table name)*	`itr_customer`
update	`utr_` + *(table name)*	`utr_customer`
insert and update	`iutr_` + *(table name)*	`iutr_customer`
stored procedure *(style A)*	`usp_` + *(business name)* `usp_customer_inquiry` (usp stands for *user-defined stored procedure*)	
stored procedure *(style B)*	This style combines the action being performed in the stored procedure with a business name. For example, a stored procedure that deletes the customer profile has the name `del_customer`. If the stored procedure performs multiple business functions, use `oth_` + *(business name)*.	
DELETE	`del_` + *(business name)*	`del_customer`
INSERT	`ins_` + *(business name)*	`ins_customer`

TABLE A.1 Continued

Object	Naming Convention	Example
SELECT	`sel_` + *(business name)*	`sel_customer`
UPDATE	`upd_` + *(business name)*	`upd_customer`
Other types of actions	`oth_` + *(business name)*	`oth_customer`
view	*(business name)* + `_view`	`customer_view`

NOTE

To improve readability, I recommend standardizing of lower-, upper-, or mixed case. Personally, I make everything lowercase. Uppercase makes it look like someone is shouting at you!

APPENDIX B

DBCC Commands

by Orryn Sledge

DBCC stands for *Database Consistency Checker*. However, over the years DBCC has grown to include commands that display configuration information, probe SQL Server's internals, and perform other commands. Therefore, it is recommended that administrators review this appendix for commands that can detect database problems and for commands that provide other types of interesting SQL Server information.

DBCC commands are commonly used to perform the following tasks:

- **Verify database integrity**—It is good idea to periodically run the DBCC CHECKDB command. This command can help isolate database and table problems before they manifest themselves into larger issues.

- **Investigate errors**—Use DBCC to pinpoint the source of errors such as Table Corrupt or Extent not with segment. DBCC commands such as CHECKDB can help you isolate corruption, and starting with SQL Server 2000, the CHECKDB command can repair certain types of corruption.

- **Analyze SQL Server**—Several DBCC commands provide information about transactions, memory usage, and trace flag settings. These commands are often used to help fine-tune SQL Server.

IN THIS APPENDIX

- Quick Reference
- Reading the Output from DBCC Commands
- Resolving Errors Reported by DBCC
- Essential DBCC Commands
- DBCC Commands for Verification
- DBCC Commands to Return Process Information
- DBCC Commands to Return Performance Monitor Statistics
- Trace Flag Commands
- Data Cache Commands
- Transaction Commands
- Other DBCC Commands

Quick Reference

A quick syntax reference for DBCC commands is shown in Listing B.1.

LISTING B.1   Command

```
DBCC CHECKALLOC
( 'database_name'
[, NOINDEX
|
{ REPAIR_ALLOW_DATA_LOSS
| REPAIR_FAST
| REPAIR_REBUILD
}]
) [WITH {ALL_ERRORMSGS | NO_INFOMSGS}]

DBCC CHECKCATALOG [(database_name)] [WITH NO_INFOMSGS]

DBCC CHECKTABLE
    (    'table_name'
            [,     NOINDEX
                | index_id
                |    {    REPAIR_ALLOW_DATA_LOSS
                        | REPAIR_FAST
                        | REPAIR_REBUILD
                    }]
    ) [WITH {ALL_ERRORMSGS | NO_INFOMSGS}]

DBCC CHECKDB
    (    'database_name'
            [,     NOINDEX
                |    {     REPAIR_ALLOW_DATA_LOSS
                        | REPAIR_FAST
                        | REPAIR_REBUILD
                    }]
    ) [WITH {ALL_ERRORMSGS | NO_INFOMSGS}]

DBCC CHECKFILEGROUP
    (    [{'filegroup' | filegroup_id}] [, NOINDEX]
    ) [WITH {ALL_ERRORMSGS | NO_INFOMSGS}]

DBCC CHECKIDENT [(table_name)] [, { NORESEED | {RESEED
    [,new_reseed_value] } } ] )

DBCC DBREINDEX (['database.owner.table_name' [, index_name
    [, fillfactor ]]])[WITH NO_INFOMSGS]
```

LISTING B.1   Continued

```
DBCC dllname (FREE)

DBCC INPUTBUFFER (spid)

DBCC OPENTRAN ({database_name} | {database_id}) [WITH TABLERESULTS]
    [,NO_INFOMSGS]

DBCC OUTPUTBUFFER (spid)

DBCC PERFMON

DBCC PINTABLE
    (database_id, table_id)

DBCC SHOW_STATISTICS
    (table_name, index_name)

DBCC SHOWCONTIG
    (table_id, [index_id])

DBCC SHRINKDATABASE (database_name [, target_percent]  [, {NOTRUNCATE
    | TRUNCATEONLY} ])

DBCC SHRINKFILE
    (    {file_name | file_id }
           {    [, target_size]
           |    [, {EMPTYFILE | NOTRUNCATE | TRUNCATEONLY}]
           }
    )

DBCC SQLPERF (LOGSPACE)

DBCC TRACEOFF (trace# [,...N])

DBCC TRACEON (trace# [,...N])

DBCC TRACESTATUS (trace# [, trace#...])

DBCC UNPINTABLE (database_id, table_id)
```

LISTING B.1   Continued

```
DBCC UPDATEUSAGE
    (    {'database_name' | 0}
            [, 'table_name' [, index_id]
            ]
    )    [    WITH [COUNT_ROWS] [, NO_INFOMSGS ]
        ]


DBCC USEROPTIONS
```

> **TIP**
>
> When DBCC performance is a primary concern (especially when working with very large data-
> bases), use the NOINDEX argument with the following commands: CHECKALLOC, CHECKTABLE,
> CHECKDB, and CHECKFILEGROUP When the NOINDEX argument is specified, only clustered
> indexes are inspected for errors. All nonclustered indexes are ignored. This option is generally
> safe to use because damaged indexes can be dropped and re-created without affecting the
> data within a table

Reading the Output from DBCC Commands

DBCC commands often generate a great amount of output. The problem is determining what is relevant within the output. Use the following list as a guide of what
to look for in the DBCC output:

- Any message that contains the string *corrupt* (for example, Table Corrupt).

- Error messages that range from 2500 to 2599 or 7900 to 7999. DBCC error
  messages usually contain these error numbers.

- Messages that contain the string error.

> **TIP**
>
> To help reduce the amount of information returned by a DBCC command use the WITH
> NO_INFOMSGS option. By using this option, DBCC will return only relevant information such as
> error messages. For example
>
> DBCC CHECKDB (pubs) WITH NO_INFOMSGS
>
> The following DBCC commands support the WITH NO_INFOMSGS option:
> - CHECKALLOC
> - CHECKCATALOG

- CHECKDB
- CHECKFILEGROUP
- CHECKTABLE
- DBREINDEX
- OPENTRAN
- UPDATEUSAGE

Resolving Errors Reported by DBCC

When an error is reported by DBCC, you should immediately investigate it. Unresolved errors can propagate throughout a database, increasing the likelihood of permanent data corruption.

The following items provide a general guideline for investigating and resolving errors reported by DBCC:

- Save and print DBCC output. On very large databases, DBCC commands can sometimes take hours to run. Do not take a chance on forgetting an error message and having to rerun the DBCC command!

- Look up the specific error code in the "Troubleshooting" chapter in the *SQL Server Books Online*. The chapter provides error-specific solutions.

- Shut down and restart the SQL Server. This action flushes out the data cache and might resolve the problem.

- Contact Microsoft Support for additional assistance.

Essential DBCC Commands

You should run the DBCC CHECKDB and DBCC CHECKCATALOG commands to detect database and table corruption, along with structure inconsistencies. Additionally, you might want to schedule these commands prior to or immediately after running a backup. Keep in mind that these commands should be run for all databases, excluding pubs and tempdb. This includes your user-defined database and master, model, and msdb.

NOTE

Because of improved data storage and built-in, real-time data checks, Microsoft no longer recommends running CHECKDB before or immediately after performing a backup. With previous versions, it was common to schedule CHECKDB to run as part of the backup/database maintenance task.

TIP

The easiest method to automate and schedule CHECKDB and other DBCC commands is to use the Database Maintenance Plan Wizard. Selecting the Check Database Integrity prompt will automatically schedule the CHECKDB command.

DBCC Commands for Verification

The following DBCC commands are used for verification:

CHECKALLOC

CHECKCATALOG

CHECKDB

CHECKFILEGROUP

CHECKIDENT

CHECKTABLE

DBREINDEX

SHOWCONTIG

UPDATEUSAGE

CHECKALLOC

Syntax

```
DBCC CHECKALLOC
( 'database_name'
[, NOINDEX
|
{ REPAIR_ALLOW_DATA_LOSS
| REPAIR_FAST
| REPAIR_REBUILD
}]
) [WITH {ALL_ERRORMSGS | NO_INFOMSGS}]
```

CHECKALLOC scans the database to ensure that data page allocation is correct. In SQL Server 2000, CHECKALLOC should be used instead of NEWALLOC. This is ironic, because in version 6.x Microsoft told us to use NEWALLOC instead of CHECKALLOC!

See Table B.1 for an explanation on the REPAIR_ALLOW_DATA_LOSS | REPAIR_FAST | REPAIR_REBUILD options.

CHECKCATALOG

Syntax

```
DBCC CHECKCATALOG [(database_name)] [WITH NO_INFOMSGS]
```

CHECKCATALOG checks the system tables for consistency by verifying the data and relationship between the syscolumns table and the systypes table. It verifies that each table and view in the sysobjects table has one or more matching records in the syscolumns table.

Use this command to analyze the system tables within a database or when you suspect corruption within the system tables.

Example

```
DBCC CHECKCATALOG (pubs)
```

CHECKDB

Syntax

```
DBCC CHECKDB
    (    'database_name'
         [,      NOINDEX
             |    {      REPAIR_ALLOW_DATA_LOSS
                    | REPAIR_FAST
                    | REPAIR_REBUILD
             }]
    ) [WITH {ALL_ERRORMSGS | NO_INFOMSGS}]
```

CHECKDB checks all tables and indexes in a database for pointer and data page errors, that data and index pages are properly linked, that indexes match the proper sort order, and that page offsets and page information is correct. In SQL Server 2000, CHECKDB also checks text, ntext and image pages.

Example

```
DBCC CHECKDB(pubs)
```

Sample Output (output has been abbreviated and is indicated by the "..." symbol)

```
Checking pubs
Checking sysobjects
There are 97 rows in 1 pages for object 'sysobjects'.
Checking sysindexes
There are 48 rows in 1 pages for object 'sysindexes'.
Checking syscolumns
...
There are 23 rows in 1 pages for object 'authors'.
Checking publishers
There are 8 rows in 1 pages for object 'publishers'.
Checking titles
...
CHECKDB found 0 allocation errors and 0 consistency errors in database 'pubs'.
```

Example

```
DBCC CHECKDB(pubs) WITH NO_INFOMSGS
➡DBCC execution completed. If DBCC printed error messages, contact your
➡system administrator.
```

NOTE

The following are notes on the CHECKDB command.

Use this command to verify database integrity: CHECKDB validates the integrity of every database object inside a database. CHECKDB is the equivalent of running CHECKALLOC against the database and CHECKTABLE against every table in the database.

Use the NO_INFOMSGS option: CHECKDB can generate a lot of meaningless information. Therefore, I recommend using the NO_INFOMSGS option so that only relevant information is displayed.

Repair option usage: SQL Server 2000 includes the following repair options listed in Table B.1.

NOTE: The database must be in single user mode to run the repair options listed here.

TABLE B.1 Repair Options

Repair Option	Explanation

REPAIR_ALLOW_DATA_LOSS	This option removes corrupt data and attempts to resolve structural errors. It includes the functionality found in the REPAIR_REBUILD option. This option might lead to data loss. It can be part of a transaction, which can be rolled back if necessary. The following is an example of this command within a transaction:
	
	```\n/* place database in single user mode */\nsp_dboption pubs,'single user',true\ngo\nbegin transaction\ngo\ndbcc checkdb(pubs, REPAIR_ALLOW_DATA_LOSS) with\nNO_INFOMSGS\ngo\n```
	
	After the CHECKDB command has executed, you can commit the changes or roll back the changes. The following is an example of the commit and rollback logic:
	Commit Example
	```\n/* if everything is ok -> commit changes */\ncommit transaction\n```
	
	Rollback Example
	```\n/* if everything is NOT ok -> rollback changes */\nrollback transaction\n```
	
	The last step is to take the database out of single user mode, which is shown in the following example:
	```\n/* take database out of single user mode */\nsp_dboption pubs,'single user',false\ngo\n```

REPAIR_FAST	This option resolves simple errors such as nonclustered indexes containing extra columns. It will not lead to data loss.
REPAIR_REBUILD	This option rebuilds all the indexes in the database. Depending on the database size, number of indexes, and number of errors, this can be a time-consuming task. This option also includes the functionality found in the REPAIR_FAST option. It will not lead to data loss.

Ignore row count adjustment messages: You can safely ignore the following messages that are sometimes generated by CHECKDB:

```
The number of data pages in Sysindexes for this table was 9.
➡ It has been corrected to 1.                    .
The number of rows in Sysindexes for this table was 273.
➡It has been corrected to 16.
```

These messages indicate that SQL Server is performing some internal housekeeping to keep row counts accurate for the sp_spaceused command.

CAUTION

CHECKDB requires shared locks: CHECKDB will place shared locks on all tables and indexes in the database. Therefore tables, indexes, views, stored procedures, defaults, user-defined data types, users, roles, or permissions cannot be created, altered, or dropped while CHECKDB is running. Keep this in mind when you run CHECKDB on a production table! However, users can query and modify data while CHECKDB is running.

CHECKFILEGROUP

Syntax

```
DBCC CHECKFILEGROUP
    (    [{'filegroup' | filegroup_id}] [, NOINDEX]
    ) [WITH {ALL_ERRORMSGS | NO_INFOMSGS}]
```

CHECKFILEGROUP validates the integrity of tables, indexes, and data that resides in a filegroup.

NOTE

CHECKFILEGROUP is the same as running CHECKDB, except that the tables, indexes, and data that resides in a filegroup is checked. With CHECKDB, the entire database is checked.

Example

```
/* check all filegroups in the database */
use sales
go
dbcc checkfilegroup
go
```

Sample Output

```
DBCC results for 'Sales'.
DBCC results for 'sysobjects'.
There are 38 rows in 1 pages for object 'sysobjects'.
DBCC results for 'sysindexes'.
There are 29 rows in 1 pages for object 'sysindexes'.
DBCC results for 'syscolumns'.
There are 391 rows in 5 pages for object 'syscolumns'.
DBCC results for 'systypes'.
There are 24 rows in 1 pages for object 'systypes'.
DBCC results for 'syscomments'.
There are 108 rows in 11 pages for object 'syscomments'.
DBCC results for 'sysfiles1'.
There are 7 rows in 2 pages for object 'sysfiles1'.
DBCC results for 'syspermissions'.
There are 36 rows in 1 pages for object 'syspermissions'.
DBCC results for 'sysusers'.
There are 13 rows in 1 pages for object 'sysusers'.
DBCC results for 'sysdepends'.
There are 181 rows in 1 pages for object 'sysdepends'.
DBCC results for 'sysreferences'.
There are 0 rows in 1 pages for object 'sysreferences'.
DBCC results for 'sysfulltextcatalogs'.
There are 0 rows in 1 pages for object 'sysfulltextcatalogs'.
DBCC results for 'sysfilegroups'.
There are 3 rows in 1 pages for object 'sysfilegroups'.
DBCC results for 'sysallocations'.
There are 1 rows in 1 pages for object 'sysallocations'.
CHECKFILEGROUP found 0 allocation errors and 0 consistency
➥ errors in database 'Sales'.
DBCC execution completed. If DBCC printed error messages,
➥ contact your system administrator.
```

CHECKIDENT

Syntax

```
DBCC CHECKIDENT [(table_name)] [, { NORESEED |
➥{RESEED [, new_reseed_value] } } ] )
```

The CHECKIDENT command checks the IDENTITY data type in a table and will repair the identity value if it is incorrect. This command can also be used to modify the identity value. It returns the current identity value and the maximum identity value.

Example

```
DBCC CHECKIDENT(jobs)
```

Sample Output

```
Checking identity information: current identity value '14',
➡ current column value '14'.
```

Example

```
DBCC CHECKIDENT(jobs, RESEED, 1000)
```

Sample Output

```
Checking identity information: current identity value '14',
➡ current column value '1000'.
```

CHECKTABLE

Syntax

```
DBCC CHECKTABLE
    (    'table_name'
            [,     NOINDEX
                | index_id
                |    {    REPAIR_ALLOW_DATA_LOSS
                        | REPAIR_FAST
                        | REPAIR_REBUILD
                    }]
    ) [WITH {ALL_ERRORMSGS | NO_INFOMSGS}]
```

CHECKTABLE ensures that all pointers are correct, that data and index pages are properly linked, that indexes match the proper sort order, and that page offsets and page information is correct. Run this command when you suspect that a table is corrupt or as part of your periodic maintenance plan.

See Table B.1 for an explanation on the REPAIR_ALLOW_DATA_LOSS | REPAIR_FAST | REPAIR_REBUILD options.

NOTE

CHECKTABLE does not need to be run if CHECKDB is run. The functionality provided by CHECK-TABLE is encompassed in CHECKDB.

Example

```
DBCC CHECKTABLE(titles)
```

Sample Output

```
Checking titles
There are 18 rows in 1 pages for object 'titles'.
DBCC execution completed. If DBCC printed error messages,
➡ see your System Administrator.
```

DBREINDEX

Syntax

```
DBCC DBREINDEX (['database.owner.table_name' [, index_name
[, fillfactor ]]])
[WITH NO_INFOMSGS]
```

The DBREINDEX command rebuilds a table's indexes. This command is often used when a PRIMARY KEY or UNIQUE constraint needs to be rebuilt. The advantage of using this command instead of the CREATE INDEX command is that you do not have to specify the table and index information to rebuild the constraint.

Example (rebuilds all indexes for the titleauthor table)

```
DBCC DBREINDEX (titleauthor,"")
```

Example (rebuilds a particular index for the titleauthor table)

```
DBCC DBREINDEX (titleauthor,"auidind")
```

SHOWCONTIG

Syntax

```
DBCC SHOWCONTIG (table_id, [index_id])
```

SHOWCONTIG determines the amount of table fragmentation. A high degree of fragmentation can lead to poor query performance because more data pages must read by SQL Server to process a query.

Fragmentation occurs when modification statements (DELETE, INSERT, and UPDATE) are performed on a table. A table subject to many modification statements is more likely to become fragmented than a table that is seldom modified.

To determine the degree of fragmentation, inspect the `Scan Density` information. A `Scan Density` value less than `100%` indicates that some fragmentation exists. Tables that generate low values such as a `Scan Density <= 90%` will benefit from defragmentation.

To defragment a table, drop and re-create the table's clustered index. Alternatively, use `DBCC DBREINDEX` or BCP to copy out the data, drop the table, re-create the table, and use BCP again to copy in the data.

TIP

Use the `object_id()` function to determine a table's ID.

Example

```
/* get table id */
use pubs
go
SELECT object_id('authors')
-----------
117575457
/* run DBCC command */
DBCC SHOWCONTIG(117575457)
```

Sample Output

```
DBCC SHOWCONTIG scanning 'authors' table...
Table: 'authors' (117575457); index ID: 1, database ID: 5
TABLE level scan performed.
- Pages Scanned...............................: 1
- Extents Scanned.............................: 1
- Extent Switches.............................: 0
- Avg. Pages per Extent.......................: 1.0
- Scan Density [Best Count:Actual Count].......: 100.00% [1:1]
- Logical Scan Fragmentation ..................: 0.00%
- Extent Scan Fragmentation ...................: 0.00%
- Avg. Bytes Free per Page....................: 6008.0
- Avg. Page Density (full)....................: 25.77%
```

UPDATEUSAGE

```
DBCC UPDATEUSAGE ({'database_name'| 0} [, 'table_name' [, index_id]])
[WITH
[NO_INFOMSGS]
[[,] COUNT_ROWS]
```

When an index is dropped from a table, sp_spaceused might inaccurately report space utilization. Use the UPDATEUSAGE command to correct the inaccuracy.

NOTE

Generally speaking, DBCC UPDATEUSAGE is only necessary when you question the information being returned from sp_spaceused. To validate if information is correct from sp_spaceused, perform a SELECT COUNT(*) FROM table_name on the table used by the sp_spaceused command. You should run DBCC UPDATEUSAGE if SELECT COUNT(*) FROM table_name returns a row count different from the row count returned by sp_spaceused.

Dropping and re-creating the table will also resolve any inaccuracies.

Example (update a single table)

```
dbcc updateusage ('pubs','employee')
```

Sample Output

```
use pubs
go
DBCC UPDATEUSAGE: sysindexes row updated for table 'employee' (index ID 1):
        USED pages: Changed from (4) to (5) pages.
        RSVD pages: Changed from (4) to (5) pages.
```

Example (update all tables in a database)

```
dbcc updateusage ('pubs')
```

Sample Output

```
DBCC UPDATEUSAGE: sysindexes row updated for table 'syscolumns' (index ID 2):
        USED pages: Changed from (2) to (8) pages.
        RSVD pages: Changed from (2) to (8) pages.
DBCC UPDATEUSAGE: sysindexes row updated for table 'authors' (index ID 1):
        USED pages: Changed from (6) to (5) pages.
        RSVD pages: Changed from (6) to (5) pages.
DBCC UPDATEUSAGE: sysindexes row updated for table 'publishers' (index ID 1):
        USED pages: Changed from (4) to (3) pages.
        RSVD pages: Changed from (4) to (3) pages.
DBCC UPDATEUSAGE: sysindexes row updated for table 'titles' (index ID 1):
        USED pages: Changed from (6) to (5) pages.
        RSVD pages: Changed from (6) to (5) pages.
DBCC UPDATEUSAGE: sysindexes row updated for table 'titleauthor' (index ID 1):
        USED pages: Changed from (8) to (7) pages.
        RSVD pages: Changed from (8) to (7) pages.
```

```
DBCC UPDATEUSAGE: sysindexes row updated for table 'stores' (index ID 1):
        USED pages: Changed from (4) to (3) pages.
        RSVD pages: Changed from (4) to (3) pages.
DBCC UPDATEUSAGE: sysindexes row updated for table 'sales' (index ID 1):
        USED pages: Changed from (6) to (5) pages.
        RSVD pages: Changed from (6) to (5) pages.
DBCC UPDATEUSAGE: sysindexes row updated for table 'roysched' (index ID 0):
        DATA pages: Changed from (1) to (2) pages.
DBCC UPDATEUSAGE: sysindexes row updated for table 'discounts' (index ID 0):
        DATA pages: Changed from (1) to (2) pages.
DBCC UPDATEUSAGE: sysindexes row updated for table 'jobs' (index ID 1):
        USED pages: Changed from (4) to (3) pages.
        RSVD pages: Changed from (4) to (3) pages.
DBCC UPDATEUSAGE: sysindexes row updated for table 'pub_info' (index ID 1):
        USED pages: Changed from (4) to (3) pages.
        RSVD pages: Changed from (4) to (3) pages.
DBCC UPDATEUSAGE: sysindexes row updated for table 'dtproperties' (index ID 1):
        USED pages: Changed from (4) to (3) pages.
        RSVD pages: Changed from (4) to (3) pages.
```

DBCC Commands to Return Process Information

The following two DBCC commands return process information:

Syntax

```
DBCC INPUTBUFFER (spid)


DBCC OUTPUTBUFFER (spid)
```

The INPUTBUFFER and OUTPUTBUFFER commands enable a DBA to monitor process activity. The INPUTBUFFER command displays the command last executed by a process; the OUTPUTBUFFER command displays the corresponding result. Unfortunately, the information returned from the OUTPUTBUFFER command can be difficult to understand because it is displayed in hexadecimal and ASCII text.

NOTE

The INPUTBUFFER command returns the first 255 characters of syntax. If you need additional information beyond 255 characters, use the SQL Server Profiler.

TIP

Use the system procedure sp_who to determine the spid of a process.

Use the INPUTBUFFER command to diagnose blocking and resource utilization problems. When performance begins to suffer, look for data modification queries that do not contain WHERE clauses or SELECT queries that perform table scans on large tables.

Example

```
DBCC INPUTBUFFER(11)
```

Sample Output

```
EventType       Parameters EventInfo
-------------- ---------- -----------------------
Language Event 0          select * from authors
```

DBCC Commands to Return Performance Monitor Statistics

The following two DBCC commands return Performance Monitor statistics:

Syntax

```
DBCC PERFMON

DBCC SQLPERF (LOGSPACE)
```

The PERFMON command provides various statistics such as general performance, I/O statistics, and read-ahead statistics. When the SQLPERF command is used with LOGSPACE parameter, a listing of database log statistics will be displayed.

Example

```
DBCC PERFMON
```

Sample Output

```
Statistic                      Value
------------------------------ ---------------------
Reads Outstanding              0.0
Writes Outstanding             0.0

(2 row(s) affected)
```

```
Statistic                      Value
------------------------------ -----------------------
Cache Hit Ratio                99.992455
Cache Flushes                  0.0
Free Page Scan (Avg)           0.0
Free Page Scan (Max)           0.0
Min Free Buffers               331.0
Cache Size                     4362.0
Free Buffers                   46.0

(7 row(s) affected)

Statistic                      Value
------------------------------ -----------------------
Network Reads                  16992.0
Network Writes                 12644.0
Command Queue Length           0.0
Max Command Queue Length       0.0
Worker Threads                 0.0
Max Worker Threads             0.0
Network Threads                0.0
Max Network Threads            0.0

(8 row(s) affected)

Statistic                      Value
------------------------------ -----------------------
RA Pages Found in Cache        0.0
RA Pages Placed in Cache       0.0
RA Physical IO                 0.0
Used Slots                     0.0
```

Example

```
DBCC SQLPERF(LOGSPACE)
```

Sample Output

```
Database Name       Log Size (MB)        Log Space Used (%)       Status
------------------- -------------------- ------------------------ ------
distribution        3.7421875            23.68215                 0
board               4.9921875            14.152973                0
sales               1.9921875            18.995098                0
pubs                2.4921875            18.064262                0
```

msdb	1.9921875	42.965687	0
tempdb	1.9921875	33.740139	0
model	1.0	33.513779	0
master	3.9921875	24.143835	0

Trace Flag Commands

The following commands are used to turn on and off trace flags as well as to check the status of a trace flag:

Syntax

```
DBCC TRACEOFF (trace# [,...N])

DBCC TRACEON (trace# [,...N])

DBCC TRACESTATUS (trace# [, trace#...])
```

TIP

The trace flag 1200 can be useful for tracking locking behavior. You must also turn on trace flag 3604 to echo trace information to the client workstation (see SQL Server's Books Online for a complete list of trace flags).

Example

```
use pubs
go
DBCC traceon(3604)
DBCC traceon(1200)
UPDATE authors
SET au_lname = 'smith'
WHERE au_id = '172-32-1176'
go
/* turn trace flags off */
DBCC traceoff(3604)
DBCC traceoff(1200)
go
```

Sample Output from DBCC Trace Flag 1200

```
DBCC execution completed. If DBCC printed error messages,
➥ contact your system administrator.
Process 10 acquiring S lock on  DB: 1  result: OK
```

```
Process 10 acquiring S lock on KEY: 1:36:1 (924d4009008e) result: OK
Process 10 releasing lock on KEY: 1:36:1 (924d4009008e)
Process 10 acquiring S lock on KEY: 1:36:1 (924d4009008e) result: OK
Process 10 releasing lock on KEY: 1:36:1 (924d4009008e)
Process 10 acquiring S lock on KEY: 1:36:1 (e4120d0900e0) result: OK
Process 10 releasing lock on KEY: 1:36:1 (e4120d0900e0)
DBCC execution completed. If DBCC printed error messages,
➥ contact your system administrator.
Process 10 releasing all locks @10ADEABC

Process 10 acquiring IX lock on TAB: 5:117575457 [] result: OK
Process 10 acquiring IX lock on UNK: 16454:858993459:1071854387:d result: OK
Process 10 acquiring IU lock on PAG: 5:1:96 result: OK
Process 10 acquiring U lock on KEY: 5:117575457:1 (0afe9ce59186) result: OK
Process 10 acquiring IX lock on PAG: 5:1:96 result: OK
Process 10 acquiring X lock on KEY: 5:117575457:1 (0afe9ce59186) result: OK
Process 10 releasing lock reference on KEY: 5:117575457:1 (0afe9ce59186)
Process 10 acquiring X lock on KEY: 5:117575457:2 (dba93ee7e0d7) result: OK
Process 10 releasing lock reference on KEY: 5:117575457:1 (0afe9ce59186)
Process 10 acquiring IX lock on PAG: 5:1:123 result: OK
Process 10 acquiring IX lock on PAG: 5:1:123 result: OK
Process 10 acquiring IIn-Null lock on KEY: 5:117575457:2 (d5968ed3b619)
➥ result: OK
Process 10 acquiring X lock on KEY: 5:117575457:2 (f8ac17e7faf7) result: OK
Process 10 releasing lock reference on KEY: 5:117575457:2 (dba93ee7e0d7)
Process 10 releasing lock reference on KEY: 5:117575457:2 (f8ac17e7faf7)
Process 10 releasing lock reference on PAG: 5:1:96
Process 10 releasing lock reference on TAB: 5:117575457 []
Process 10 releasing all locks @10ADEABC
```

Data Cache Commands

The PINTABLE command forces a table to remain in cache until it is removed from the cache with the UNPINTABLE command. You should be careful when pinning a table in the cache. By keeping a table constantly in the cache, you can improve data access performance. However, a large table can dominate the data cache. This could reduce the amount of data held in cache for other tables, thus hindering performance.

Syntax

```
DBCC PINTABLE (database_id, table_id)

DBCC UNPINTABLE (database_id, table_id)
```

Tables that are forced into cache via the PINTABLE command will remain in cache after SQL Server is restarted. Use the UNPINTABLE command to remove the table from cache.

Example

```
use pubs
go
declare @id integer
select @id = object_id('authors')
/* 5 = pubs database */
DBCC PINTABLE (5,@id)
go
```

Sample Output

```
WARNING: Pinning tables should be carefully considered. If a pinned table
➡ is larger or grows larger than the available data cache,
➡ the server may need to be restarted and the table unpinned.
DBCC execution completed. If DBCC printed error messages, see your
➡ System Administrator.
```

Transaction Commands

Use the OPENTRAN command for information about transactions.

Syntax

```
DBCC OPENTRAN ({database_name} | {database_id})
➡ [WITH TABLERESULTS] [,NO_INFOMSGS]
```

The OPENTRAN command reports the oldest open transaction. An open transaction can stem from an aborted transaction, a runaway transaction, or poor transaction management. If necessary, you can terminate the offending transaction by issuing the KILL command with the process ID returned from the OPENTRAN command.

TIP

Long-running transactions can lead to contention for resources, which can lead to blocking. Use OPENTRAN to detect open transactions. If necessary, use the KILL command to cancel the transaction.

Example

```
DBCC OPENTRAN(pubs)
```

Sample Output

```
Transaction information for database 'pubs'.

Oldest active transaction:
    SPID (server process ID) : 10
    UID (user ID) : 1
    Name            : user_transaction
    LSN             : (7:202:1)
    Start time      : Oct 18 1998  2:42:34:480PM
```

Other DBCC Commands

The following sections cover some of the other types of DBCC commands.

SHOW_STATISTICS

Syntax

```
DBCC SHOW_STATISTICS (table_name, index_name)
```

SHOW_STATISTICS displays index distribution information.

Example

```
use pubs
go
DBCC SHOW_STATISTICS ('authors','aunmind')
go
```

Sample Output

```
Statistics for INDEX 'aunmind'.
Updated              Rows  Rows Sampled Steps  Density       Average key length
.................... ..... ............. ...... ............. ..................

Sep 13 1998  3:16AM  23    23            23     3.9697543E-2  34.956524

(1 row(s) affected)

All density              Columns
........................ ...........................................
```

```
4.7258981E-2          au_lname
4.3478262E-2          au_lname, au_fname
```

(2 row(s) affected)

```
Steps
----------------------------------------
Bennet
Blotchet-Halls
Carson
DeFrance
del Castillo
Dull
Green
Greene
Gringlesby
Hunter
Karsen
Locksley
MacFeather
McBadden
O'Leary
Panteley
Ringer
Ringer
Smith
Straight
Stringer
White
Yokomoto
```

(23 row(s) affected)

SHRINKDATABASE

Syntax

```
DBCC SHRINKDATABASE (database_name [, target_percent]
  [, {NOTRUNCATE | TRUNCATEONLY} ]  )
```

SHRINKDATABASE reduces the physical size of the database. A database can be reduced to a certain percentage of its current size by specifying a *target_percent* value (for example, 80 will reduce the database by 20% of its current size). If a *target_percent* is not specified, the database will be reduced to the smallest size possible for the database. A database cannot be shrunk beyond the amount of storage space required to store data and other types of information.

> **NOTE**
>
> A database cannot be shrunk beyond the size specified for the model database.

Example

```
DBCC SHRINKDATABASE (sales)
```

Sample Output

```
DBCC execution completed. If DBCC printed error messages,
➥ see your System Administrator.
```

SHRINKFILE

Syntax

```
DBCC SHRINKFILE
    (    {file_name | file_id }
            {    [, target_size]
            |    [, {EMPTYFILE | NOTRUNCATE | TRUNCATEONLY}]
            }
    )
```

SHRINKFILE reduces the physical size of a data file. A data file can be reduced to a certain size by specifying a *target_size* value. If a *target_size* is not specified, the data file will be reduced to the smallest size possible for the data file. A data file cannot be shrunk beyond the amount of storage space required to store data and other types of information.

Example

```
use pubs
go
/* shrink log file */
dbcc shrinkfile(pubs_log)
go
```

Sample Output

DbId	FileId	CurrentSize	MinimumSize	UsedPages	EstimatedPages
5	2	96	63	96	56

USEROPTIONS

Syntax

```
DBCC USEROPTIONS
```

The USEROPTIONS command displays the status of SET commands for the current session.

Example

```
DBCC USEROPTIONS
```

Sample Output

Set Option	Value
textsize	64512
language	us_english
dateformat	mdy
datefirst	7
ansi_null_dflt_on	SET
ansi_warnings	SET
ansi_padding	SET
ansi_nulls	SET

DBCC *dllname* (FREE)

Syntax

```
DBCC dllname (FREE)
```

This command removes a DLL (dynamic link library) from memory.

Example

```
DBCC mydll (FREE)
```

APPENDIX C

SQL Server Resources

by Orryn Sledge

Tables C.1 and C.2 contain a listing of popular SQL
Server Web sites and newsgroups.

TABLE C.1   SQL Server Web Sites

Web Site	Web Site Name	Notes
15seconds.com	15Seconds	Brief articles that are concise and well-written.
devx.com		DevX Provides SQL Server tips and tricks.
www.devx.com/ gethelp/default.asp? Area=SQL+Server	Ask the SQL Server Pro!	Provides answers to frequently asked questions and allows users to post new questions.
winntmag.com	WIN NT Magazine	Contains a forum and articles on Windows NT.
sqlmag.com/	SQL Server Magazine and articles on SQL Server.	Contains a forum
swynk.com	Swynk BackOffice Resource	SQL Server FAQ and comprehensive information on other BackOffice products.
pinpub.com/sq	SQL Server Professional Magazine	Online listing of the SQL Server Professional Magazine.
msdn.microsoft.com/ sqlserver	MSDN Online	MSDN Online SQL Server Developer Center.
microsoft.com/technet	TechNet Online	Microsoft's TechNet Web site provides technical forums and resources.
www.microsoft.com/ sql	Microsoft's SQL Server Web site	This is listed just in case you forgot the location!

TABLE C.2   SQL Server Newsgroups Sites

SQL Server Newsgroups

The following is a subset of Microsoft SQL Server newsgroups.

```
news://msnews.microsoft.com/microsoft.public.sqlserver.server
news://msnews.microsoft.com/microsoft.public.sqlserver.connect
news://msnews.microsoft.com/microsoft.public.sqlserver.odbc
news://msnews.microsoft.com/microsoft.public.sqlserver.programming
news://msnews.microsoft.com/microsoft.public.sqlserver.replication
news://msnews.microsoft.com/microsoft.public.sqlserver.datawarehouse
news://msnews.microsoft.com/microsoft.public.sqlserver.clients
```

For a complete listing of newsgroups, go to:
http://microsoft.com/sql/community/newsgroups/default.asp

Index

Symbols

* (asterisk), 573
.. (double period) syntax, 399
= (equals), 569
> (greater than), 569
>= (greater than or equal to), 569
< (less than), 569
<= (less than or equal to), 569
% character, 697
+ (plus sign), 314
# (pound sign), 399
? symbol, 389
@ symbol, 607
@@cursor_rows global variable, 619
@@ERROR global variable, 610
@@FETCH_STATUS global variable, 610, 619
@@IDENTITY global variable, 610
@@lock_timeout variable, 544
@@ROWCOUNT global variable, 610
@@SERVERNAME global variable, 610
@@TRANCOUNT global variable, 610
@@VERSION global variable, 610

Numbers

1st normal form, 472
2nd normal form, 473
2PC protocol (two-phase commit), 785
3rd normal form, 474-475
50001 (error number), code to trigger, 340-341

A

a-a switch, BCP (Bulk Copy Program), 402

Able To Restore Additional Transaction Logs
option, 280

accessing

data, roles, 882-885

data sources, syntax, 586

accounts (user)

database users, 205

database object owners, 223

DBOs (database owners), 223

domain user, 67

guest users, 206

logins

editing login information, 219-220

managing, 212-214

mixed mode security, 205

passwords, 220-221

troubleshooting, 221

viewing login information, 219

Windows Authentication, 204-205

permissions

administration tips, 226-227

combining with views, 232

granting, 206, 224-229

object permissions, 207

revoking, 206-207, 224-225, 228-229

statement permissions, 207

roles

database roles, 208-212, 216-219

server roles, 208, 215-216

system administrators, 223

actions, job steps, 324

active scripting, 315, 325-327

Active Server Pages, SQL-DMO, 715

Active user table, 876

ActiveX Data Objects. See ADO

ActiveX Script Task Properties dialog box, 384

ActiveX Script tasks

adding to packages (DTS Designer), 371

DTS packages, custom programming, 376

ActiveX scripts, 359

debugging multiple, 383

return codes for objects associated with a
step, 387

Script Debugger, 388

Workflow ActiveX Properties dialog box, 384

Add Counters dialog box, 686

Add Destination Database window, 287

adding hyperlinks to Web pages, 657-662

adding

indexes, 499-500

servers (linked), 586-588

administration

backups, 257-259, 274-277

log truncation options, 255-256

logins, 212-214

restoring, 274

databases, 278-280

transaction logs, 279

SQL-DMO. See SQL-DMO

ADO (ActiveX Data Objects)

cursor syntax, 614

recordsets, opening, 391

advanced configuration parameter, 154-156

Advanced tab (New Job Step dialog box), 318

affinity mask advanced configuration parameter,
154

Agent Job Properties dialog box, 826

Agent, Web Assistant, 662

agents, transactional replication, 780

aggregate functions, 526

aggregate functions (SQL statements), 573

aggregations

creating, 871

data explosion, 870

designing, 872

partitions, 878

processing, 874

Alert Manager

custom alerts, 337-341

event alerts, 329-330

email notifications, 332

error messages, finding, 331

performance condition alerts, 333-336

SQLServerAgent, 329

Alert Properties dialog box, 130

alerts, 329

creating, 329-332

custom, 329, 337

creating, 338-341

email messages, low inventory, 341

enabling, 332

error messages, finding, 331

event, 329

events, 329-332

managing (SQL Server Agent), 129

modifying, 332

performance, building, 333-336

performance condition, 329, 333-336

triggered, email message sent, 337

viewing, 332

aliases

columns, assigning, 573

tables, 575

allocating memory, 148

Allow Anonymous Subscriptions dialog box (Create a Publication Wizard), 793

allow updates configuration parameter, 150

ALTER PROCEDURE command, 600

alternative synchronization partners, 829

analysis, performing using Profiler, 697

Analysis Manager, 857

Analysis Services, 35

aggregations, storage, 871

creating OLAP databases, 858

building cubes, 864-867

data source connections, 860

data sources, 859

defining dimension layers and members, 862-863

defining dimensions, 860-861

data management (OLAP databases), 878

client write back, 881

merging partitions, 880

processing the cube, 879

data storage, 868

HOLAP, 869

MOLAP, 868

ROLAP, 869

designing aggregations, 872

MDX, 889

optimizing OLAP databases, 869

aggregations, 870-874

partitions, 878

usage-based optimization, 875-876

partial preaggregation, 872

securing OLAP data, 881

authentication, 882

cell level security, 887-889

dimension level security, 885

roles, 882-885

Usage Analysis Wizard, 876

wizards, 861

Analysis Services (Microsoft), 852

ANSI characters, 65

ANSI NULL Default option, 177

ANSI SQL versus T-SQL, 565

ANSI style comments, 607

Append Rows to Destination Table option (Transform dialog box), 366

AppleTalk ADSP protocol, 67

application database roles, 211-212

Application object (object model), 714

applications

creating

SQL-DMO, 714-715, 719

Visual Basic, 716

database administration, 714

Decision Support Systems (DSS), 837

OLAP, 855

OLE, 711

transactional replication, 779

troubleshooting, 445

tuning, 140

archived error logs, 436

arguments

b@old, 657

c@olheader, 657

d@ayflags, 653

f@ixedfont, 657

i@talic, 657

w@hentype, 650

articles, 753

modifying (merge replication), 823

read locks, released by snapshot agent, 807

Ask the SQL Server Pro! Web site, 926

assigning

aliases, columns, 573

domain user accounts, 88

asterisk (*), 573

Asynchronous Read Ahead, 150

Asynchronous Read-Ahead Technology, 59

Attach Database dialog box, 274

attaching databases, 190-191

auditing object permissions, 308

audits, triggers, 233-234

authentication

OLAP databases, 882

setting at server registration, 114

Windows Authentication, 204-205

Authentication Mode dialog box, 87

Auto Close option, 178

Auto Create Statistics option, 179

Auto Shrink option, 179

Auto Update Statistics option, 179

auto-incrementing IDs, 556

auto-update statistics option, 509

Automatic synchronization, 760-761

Automatically Grow File option, 169, 182

autorun utility, 81

autoshrink option (databases), 186

Avg aggregate function (SQL statements), 573

awe enabled advanced configuration parameter, 154

B

"b@old argument, 657

b-b switch, BCP (Bulk Copy Program), 400

B-Tree structure

clustered indexes, disk I/O, 489

index pages, 488

levels, reducing, 488

nonclustered indexes, 490-491

b.BCP file extension, 761

backing up databases

backup devices, 246-247

backup media integrity, 251

Backup Wizard, 257-259

cautions, 250

DBCC commands, 248

differential backups, 267

example, 262, 274-277

expiration, 252

Full Recovery model, 262-266

hot backups, 283

master

    reattaching database files, 273-274

    restoring, 271-273

msdb, 281

overwriting existing media, 259

recommendations, 282

restoring, 267-270

scheduling, 250, 280-281

steps, 248-249

TRUNCATE_ONLY option, 255

BACKUP DATABASE command, 242

Backup Device Properties-New Device dialog box, 246

backup devices

    creating, 246-247, 275

    media sets, 261-262

    parallel striped backups, 261-262

    temporary, 254

BACKUP director, 77

Backup Verification and Scheduling dialog box, 260

Backup Wizard, 257-259

backups, 239

    data warehouses, 850

    databases, 242

        incremental, 243

        maintenance plans, 307

    differential, 243

    file/filegroup, 244-245, 271

    hot backups, 283

    multiple backup devices, 262

    SQL Server 2000, 240-241

    SQL Server 6.x, 261

    system databases, 343

temporary backup devices, 254

transaction logs, 243-244, 346

    creating schedules, 280-281

    differential backups, 267

    example of, 274, 276-277

    loading, 266

    recommendations, 282

    restoring, 270

BACKUP_LOG command, NO_LOG option, 256

Banyan Vines, 66

batch processing, DTS, 380-381

BATCHSIZE switch (BULK_INSERT statement), 422

BCP (Bulk Copy Program), 355

    advantages and disadvantages, 397-399

    BULK_INSERT operations, 421-423

    cautions, 398

    character mode, 405

    common problems, 418

    decreasing load time, 394

    enforcement of objects, 417-418

    FAQs (frequently asked questions), 424

    fast mode, 414-417

    interactive mode, 405-408

    permissions, 404

    programming tips, 418-421

    sample scripts

        comma-delimited export, 411

        comma-delimited import, 411

        fixed-length export, 413

        fixed-length import, 411-412

        simple export, 410

        simple import, 410

        skipped fields on export, 414

        skipped fields on import, 413

    slow mode, 414-417

    supported file formats, 424

switches
-a, 402
-b, 400
-C, 401
-e, 400, 402-403
-F, 400
-h, 403-404
-i, 401
-k, 403
-L, 400
-m, 400
-n, 400-401
-o, 401
-P, 403
-q, 401
-r, 401
-S, 403
-t, 401, 403
-v, 403
-w, 401
syntax, 36, 399-400, 404

bcp command
switches
-a, 402
-b, 400
-C, 401
-e, 400-403
-F, 400
-h, 403-404
-i, 401
-k, 403
-L, 400
-m, 400
-n, 400-401
-o, 401
-P, 403
-q, 401

-r, 401
-S, 403
-t, 401-403
-U, 403
-v, 403
-w, 401
syntax, 399-400

BCP utility (Bulk Copy), 731
importing data, 736
listing, 732
setting path to a BCP log file, 739

BEGIN TRANsaction [] statement, 167

BEGIN...END statement, 602

BETWEEN...AND comparison operator, 569

BI (Business Intelligence), 47

BINN directory, 77

blocking, 539
diagnosis, 546
SQL Server 7.0, 546
troubleshooting, 555-556
viewing, 544-546

Books Online (Microsoft's), 433-434

boosting SQL Server priority, cautions, 160

bottlenecks
disk I/O, 59, 172-173, 688
memory, 689
triggers as, 532

bottom up design, 846

BREAK statement, 605

buffer caches, 148

building performance alerts, 333-336. *See also* restoring

Bulk Copy page (SQL Server DBA Assistant dialog box), 732

Bulk Copy Program. *See* BCP

BULK INSERT statement, decreasing load time, 394

Bulk Insert task, 360

bulk load statements, logging, 243

Bulk Recovery model, 262-266

Bulk-Logged Recovery (recovery model), 241-242, 246

Bulk-Logged recovery mode, 177

bulkadmin role, 208

BulkCopy object

   creating, 731

   exporting data, 731

   importing data, 736

   setting properties, 731

BULK_INSERT statement

   switches

      BATCHSIZE, 422

      CHECK_CONSTRAINTS, 422

      CODEPAGE, 422

      DATAFILETYPE, 422

      FIELDTERMINATOR, 422

      FIRSTROW, 422

      FORMATFILE, 422

      KEEPIDENTITY, 422

      KEEPNULLS, 423

      KILOBYTES_PER_BATCH, 423

      LASTROW, 423

      MAXERRORS, 423

      ORDER, 423

      ROWS_PER_BATCH, 423

      ROWTERMINATOR, 423

      TABLOCK, 423

   syntax, 421

Business Intelligence (BI), 47

buttons

   Error Number, 330

   Manage Error Messages, 330

   New Schedule, 318-320

   Run a Wizard, 341

C

c@olheader argument, 657

c-c option, 94

c-c switch, BCP (Bulk Copy Program), 401

C2 Audit Mode advanced configuration parameter, 155

caches

   buffer, 148

   pinning tables, 918

Can't create directory error message, 81

capturing SQL Server profiler workload, 503

Cascading Style Sheets (CSS), 676

cataloging stored procedures, 595

cells, security, 887-889

central publisher scenario (hub-and-spoke topology), 781

central publisher with remote distributor scenario (hub-and-spoke topology), 781

central subscriber scenario (hub-and-spoke topology), 784

certification, 18-19

changing. *See* editing

character mode (BCP), 405

character sets, collation setting, 65

characters, 65

Check Identity Values function, 730

CHECKALLOC command, 904

CHECKCATALOG command, 903-905

CHECKDB command, 899, 903-905

   database integrity verification, 906

   repair options, 907

   shared locks, 908

CHECKDB command (DBCC), 248

CHECKFILEGROUP command, 908, 914

CHECKIDENT command, 909

CheckIdentityValues method, 712

checksums, 798

CHECKTABLE command, 910

CheckTable method, 728

CHECK_CONSTRAINTS switch (BULK_INSERT statement), 422

choose Destination Database dialog box (Push Subscription Wizard), 820

Choose Publication Database dialog box (Create a Publication Wizard), 788

Choose Subscriber dialog box (Push Subscription Wizard), 820

classes, DBAs, 17

Client Tools, installing, 103

clients, configuring new, 104

Close Connection on Completion property (workflow), 383

CLOSE statement, cursors, 618

clustered index key value, 491

clustered indexed, finding data, 527

Clustered Indexed option, 810

clustered indexes, 488

    creating, 494-498

    disk I/O, 489-491

    DROP EXISTING option, 497

    Fill Factor, 491

    page splits, 491

    when to use, 502

CmdExec (operating system command), 315

code

    error number 50001, triggering, 340-341

    sqlmaint.exe utility, command-line parameters, 350

    stored procedures, 327-328

CODEPAGE switch (BULK_INSERT statement), 422

Collation option, 811

collation setting, 65

Collation Settings dialog box, 88

collections, 388, 713

column delimiters, 363

column list component

    CREATE TABLE statement, 582

    INSERT statement, 577

    SELECT...INTO statement, 583

column-level security, 230-231

columns

    adding to indexes, 501

    aliases, assigning, 573

    column-level security, 230-231

    computed, 498

    indexes, 491

    mapping, DTS Wizard, 366

    selecting for indexes, 494

    tables

        fixed values, setting, 579

        retrieving, 566

        values, setting, 579-580

Columns Null by Default option. See ANSI NULL Default option

COM (Component Object Model), 357, 711

combo boxes, 726

comma-delimited export script (BCP), 411

comma-delimited import script (BCP), 411

command line, starting SQL Server, 93-95

COMMAND object, 592

command-line, running packages, 393

command-line parameters, sqlmaint.exe utility, 350

command-line switches. See switches

command-line utilities, 36-38

commands. See also statements; triggers

    BACKUP DATABASE, 242

    bcp

        switches, 400-404

        syntax, 399-400

    Database Maintenance Plan Wizard, 351

    databases, 316

DBCC, 442-443, 899
   CHECKALLOC, 904
   CHECKCATALOG, 903-905
   CHECKDB, 903-905
   CHECKFILEGROUP, 908
   CHECKIDENT, 909
   CHECKTABLE, 910
   data cache, 918
   DBCC dllname (FREE), 923
   DBREINDEX, 444, 911
   INPUTBUFFER, 914
   OPENTRAN, 919
   OUTPUTBUFFER, 914
   PERFMON, 915
   reading output, 902
   returning Performance Monitor statistics, 915
   returning process information, 914
   SHOWCONTIG, 444, 911
   SHOW_STATISTICS, 920
   SHRINKDATABASE, 921
   SHRINKFILE, 922
   SWLPERF, 915
   syntax reference, 899
   trace flags, 917
   transaction, 919
   UPDATEUSAGE, 912
   USEROPTIONS, 923
   verification, 904
   WITH NO INFOMSGS option, 902
Net Send, 321
operating system (CmdExec), 315
UPDATE STATISTICS, 351
xp_sendmail, 327
commenting stored procedures, 607
COMMIT TRANsaction [] statement, 167
comparison operators, 569
compatibility level option, 180

Completing the Create Index Wizard dialog box, 495
Completing the Create Publication Wizard dialog box, 794
Completing the Index Tuning Wizard screen (Index Tuning Wizard), 520
Component Object Model (COM), 357, 711
Component Selection dialog box, Install SQL Server 2000 Components option, 82
components
   SELECT...INTO statement, 583
   statements
      DELETE, 580
      INSERT, 577
      UPDATE, 578-579
   statements (SQL), SELECT, 567
composite indexes, 528
compressed drives, cautions, 171
computed columns, 498
Computer Name dialog box, 82
Concat NULL Yields NULL option, listing, 180
concurrency issues, 462
configuration parameters (SQL Server), 150
   advanced
      affinity mask, 154
      awe enabled, 154
      C2 Audit Mode, 155
      cost threshold for parallelism, 155
      cursor threshold, 155
      default full-text language, 156
      fill factor, 156
      index create memory, 157
      lightweight pooling, 157
      max degree of parallelism, 158
      max server memory, 158
      max worker threads, 158
      media retention, 159
      min memory per query, 159
      min server memory, 159

network packet size, 159

open objects, 160

priority boost, 160

query governor cost limit, 161

query wait, 161

recovery interval, 161

scan for startup procs, 162

set working set size, 162

user connections, 162

advanced locks, 157

allow updates, 150

default language, 151

max text repl size, 151

nested triggers, 152

remote access, 152

remote login timeout, 152

remote proc trans, 153

remote query timeout, 152

show advanced options, 153

two digit year cutoff, 153

user_option, 154

Configure Publishing and Distribution Wizard, 761-763

configuring

agent logon information (distribution database), 764-765

dimension level security rules, 885

Fill Factor value, 495

hub-and-spoke topology

central publisher scenario, 781

central publisher with remote distributor scenario, 781

central subscriber scenario, 784

republisher scenario, 783

SQL Agent mail, 706

SQL Mail, 704

SQL Server, 140

database settings, 143

dynamic configuration variables, 146-147

memory options, 141

processor options, 141

server settings, 143

sp_configure, 145

user connections, 143

SQL Server Agent, 118

SQL Server Mail, 119

subscribers, alternative synchronization partners, 829

systems for SQL Server optimal performance, 61

Confirm Password dialog box, 220

conflict detection, 786

conflicts, resolving (merge replication), 817-818

Connect to SQL Server dialog box, 136

connecting to servers, 116

Connection method (SQL Server object), 725

connections

destination, importing files, 364

DTS framework, 359

SQL Server

listing, 724

from SQL Server Enterprise Manager, 117

user, monitoring, 691

consolidating data, 843

constraint violations, 787

constraints

enforcing, BCP (Bulk Copy Program), 417

naming conventions, 896

container/controller/client applications, 712

context switch, 461

CONTINUE statement, 605

Control Panel, 25

control-of-flow language, 600

BEGIN, , .END statement, 602

BREAK statement, 605

CONTINUE statement, 605

DECLARE statement, 601

GOTO statement, 602

IF...ELSE statement, 602

PRINT statement, 605

RAISERROR statement, 606

RETURN statement, 604

WAITFOR statement, 603

WHILE statement, 605

controls, 716

conventions, naming conventions (linked servers), 590

Convert User-Defined Data Types to Their Base Data Types option, 811

converting nonsearch arguments to search arguments, 533

Copy Database Wizard, 70, 97

copying

databases, 191

SQL Server 2000 database to upgrade SQL Server 7.0 databases, 95-97

corrupted databases, restoring, 267

corruption (database/table), 903

cost, memory, 58

cost threshold for parallelism advanced configuration parameter, 155

Count aggregate function (SQL statements), 573

counters

adding

log files, 693

System Monitor, 686

disk I/O bottlenecks, 688

memory monitoring, 689-690

network monitoring, 691

physical disk, 688

processor monitoring, 689

user connection monitoring, 691

user-defined, 692

CPUs, monitoring, 689

Create a Database Role dialog box, 883

Create a Publication Wizard, 787

Allow Anonymous Subscriptions dialog box, 793

Choose Publication Database dialog box, 788

Completing the Create Publication Wizard dialog box, 794

Customize the Properties of the Publication dialog box, 792

Filter Data dialog box, 792

Filter Table Columns dialog box, 793

Select Publication Name and Description dialog box, 791

Select Publication Type dialog box, 789

Set Snapshot Agent Schedule dialog box, 794

Specify Articles dialog box, 791

Specify Subscriber Types dialog box, 790

Transform Published Data dialog box, 790

Updateable Subscriptions dialog box, 789

Create Database Backup Wizard dialog box, 257

CREATE DATABASE statement permission, 171

Create Destination Table option (Transform dialog box), 366

CREATE INDEX command, options, 497

Create Index Wizard

Column Select Columns dialog box, 494

Completing the Create Index Wizard dialog box, 495

Current Index Information dialog box, 493

Database and Select Database and Table dialog box, 493

Index Options dialog box, 497

Specify Index Option dialog box, 494

Welcome dialog box, 492

Create New Data Source dialog box, 774

Create Procedure statement, 596

CREATE TABLE

command, ON filegroup_name option, 196

component (CREATE TABLE statement), 582

statement, 566, 581-583

CreateObject function, 718

creating
  alerts, 329-332
  clustered indexes, 489
  custom alerts, 338-341
  jobs, 314-322
  nonclustered indexes, 490
  procedures, stored, 584
  reports, from multiple data sources, 584
  tables, 581-583
CROSS JOIN operator, 572
cross-reference tables, searching, 571
CSS (Cascading Style Sheets), 676
Cube Editor, 867
Cube Processing Setting dialog box, 880
Cube Role Manager dialog box, 887
Cube Wizard
  adding dimensions to cubes, 867
  Define Measures dialog box, 865-866
  Finish dialog box, 867
  Select Dimensions dialog box, 866
  Select Fact Table dialog box, 864
cubes
  aggregations, 871-874
  client write back, 881
  creating, 864, 867
  defining measures, 865-866
  dimensions, 857
    adding, 866-867
    creating, 861
    dimension tables, 861
    shared, 860
  fact tables, 865
  measures, 857
  naming, 867
  partitions, 878-880
  processing, 879
  roles, 884
  Usage Analysis Wizard, 876
Current Activity dialog box, 441

Current Activity Monitor (Enterprise Manager), 694
cursor close on commit option, 181
cursor extension syntax, 615
cursor options, minimizing locking, 557
cursor threshold advanced configuration parameter, 155
cursors
  allowing updates, 616
  batch run example, 627-630
  closing/deallocating, 618
  creating, 613
  declaring, 614-615
  deleting data from tables, 624
  displaying object names and types, 622-623
  fetching, 617
  global variables, 619-620
  looping through tables, 620
  positional updates, 626
  read-only, 616
  standard, 616
custom alerts, 329, 337
  creating, 338-341
  email messages, low inventory, 341
Custom Dimension Security dialog box, 886
custom reports, creating, 699
custom stored procedures, 795
Customize the Configuration dialog box (Configure Publishing and Distribution Wizard), 763
Customize the Properties of the Publication dialog box (Create a Publication Wizard), 792

D

d@ayflags argument, 653
d-d option, 93
d@dbuse parameter (sp_processmail), 709

data, 173

aggregations, 870

analysis, Analysis Manager, 857

checksums, 798

data marts, 840

databases. *See* databases

dimensions, levels, 863

exporting, 356, 731

fact tables, 865

importing, 355

inline validation, 798

lineage, 846

linked servers, retrieving, 590-591

locks, 537

    functionality, 539

    managing, 544

    minimizing, 551-553

    nested transactions, 555

    page, 542

    physical, 541

    row-level, 541

    table, 543

    trace flags, 549

    tracking, 549

    viewing, 544-546

modification, 166-167

multidimensional, 856

nonclustered indexes, 490

normalization, 847

publishing to Web pages, Web Assistant, 660-662

relational database systems, 856

replication. *See* replication

storing, compressed drives, 171

subscriptions, 795

transactional replication, 780

transformation, 842

    data quality, 843

    extracting, loading and refreshing, 845

    integration or consolidation, 843

    mapping and matching, 844

    metadata, 845

    summarizing, 844

transforming published, 798

uniqueness, 495

updating with XML, 680-681

warehousing. *See* data warehousing

write-back, 881

XML, 677-679

data cache commands, 918-919

DATA directory, 77

Data Driven Query task, 360

data explosion, 870

data file location, 64

Data Link Properties dialog box, 860

data marts, 840

cautions, 842

managing, 850

versus data warehouses, 841-842

data mining, 838

data modification statements, exclusive locks, 544

data modification transactions, cautions, 552

data operating system files, 167

data pages, Fill Factor, 495

Data Pump

data type conversions, 367

DTS framework, 361

data scans, parallel, 150

Data Source Name (DSN), 773-775

data source/destination palette, 372

data sources (OLAP databases)

accessing, syntax, 586

connections, 860

creating, 859

multiple, 584

non-relational, manipulating, 584

Data Storage dialog box, Storage Design Wizard, 871

data stores, 840

data striping, 59, 172-173

data transformation package, managing (SQL Server Agent), 132

Data Transformation Service folder, (SQL Server Enterprise Manager), 393

Data Transformation Services (DTS). *See* DTS

Data Transformation Services folder (Enterprise Manager), 358

data transformations, 393-394, 839

data type conversions, 367

data types

    BCP (Bulk Copy Program) file storage types, 406

    restricted from index creation, 492

data warehousing, 47, 356

    components, 839

    data integration or consolidation, 843

    data marts, 840-842

    Decision Support Systems (DSS), 837

    justification, 835

    managing, 850

    metadata, 845

    Online Analytical Processing (OLAP), 837-838

    overview, 836

    planning designs, 846

        dimensional modeling, 847-849

        important considerations, 849

        top down/bottom up, 846

    SQL Server 2000, 850-852

    versus operational data, 838-839

    Warehousing Framework, 851

Database Access tab (SQL Server Login Properties dialog box), 217

database administration tasks, FAQs, 351

Database Administrator Wizard, sqlmaint.exe utility (command-line parameters), 350

database administrators. *See* DBAs

Database Backup dialog box, General tab, 248

Database Consistency Checker. *See* DBCC

Database Engine Option (SQL Server), 62

Database File Location dialog box (Copy Database Wizard), 99

Database Information Tables and Indexes dialog box, 499

Database Integrity Check dialog box, 343-344

Database Maintenance Plan Wizard, 307, 341, 343-344, 346-347, 350

    commands, 351

    dialog box, 348

    jobs, 348

    plans, running, 348

    scheduling CHECKDB command, 904

    system databases, for backups, 343

database object owners, 223

database owners (DBOs), 223

Database Properties dialog box, 168

Database Role Manager dialog box, 883

database roles, 208

    granting, 216-219

    predefined, 209

    user-defined, 210-212

database servers, DBA duties, 11

database users, 205

databases

    administration, 714

    attaching/detaching, 190-191

    backing up

        Backup Wizard, 257-259

        differential backup, 267

        example, 262

        Full Recovery model, 262-266

        hot packups, 283

        multiple backup devices, 261-262

        overwriting existing media, 259

        TRUNCATE_ONLY option, 255

        T-SQL, 252

backups, 242
  backup devices, 246
  backup devices, creating, 246-247
  backup media integrity, 251
  DBCC commands, 248
  expiration, 252
  incremental, 243
  scheduling, 250
  steps, 248-249
  troubleshooting, 243
blocking, 539
combo boxes, 726
commands, 316
Copy Database Wizard, 70
corruptions
  detecting, 903
  NO_TRUNCATE option, 256
creating, 168, 275
  backing up the master database, 171
  checklist, 172
  listing, 171
  operating system files, 172
  presizing files, 170
  size (minimum/maximum, 170
  storage location for files, 169
data, 468-469
data marts, 840
  cautions, 842
  managing, 850
data operating system files, 167
data transformation, 842
  data quality, 843
  extracting, loading and refreshing, 845
  integration or consolidation, 843
  mapping and matching, 844
  metadata, 845
  summarizing, 844

data warehousing
  components, 839
  Decision Support Systems (DSS), 837
  justification, 835
  managing, 850
  Online Analytical Processing (OLAP),
    837-838
  overview, 836
  planning designs, 846-849
  SQL Server 2000, 850-852
  versus data marts, 841-842
database roles, 208
  granting, 216-219
  predefined, 209
  user-defined, 210-212
DBCC, 442
  case example of use, 444
  error tracking, 443
  table/index fragmentation, 444-445
deadlocks, 539-540, 551-553
delete anomalies, 469
deleting, 188-189
deleting data files, 278
designing
  denormalization, 475-477
  normalization, 470-474
  problems from improper design, 467-469
dirty reads, 538
disk drives, 59
displaying size of, 743
documenting modifications, 192
enabling, replication subscribers, 770
enabling for publication, 769
expanding
  assigning new files, 183
  automatically, 182
  listing, 185
  manually, 183

filegroups, 193
    adding secondary data files to, 195
    creating indexes on, 196
    implementing, 194
    placing objects on, 196
    viewing information, 197-198
indexes, principle behind, 483
insert anomalies, 470
integrity, CHECKDB command, 906
lists of states, 391
locks, 537
    functionality, 539
    managing, 544
    minimizing, 551-553
    nested transactions, 555
    page, 542
    physical, 541
    row-level, 541
    table, 543
    trace flags, 549
locks
    tracking, 549
    viewing, 544-546
log operating system files, 167
login credential, 365
maintenance, 307
    SQL Server DBA Assistant, 721
    SQL-DMO functionality, 728
managing
    tips and tricks, 191-192
    users and objects, 124
master, 64
    reattaching database files, 273-274
    restoring, 271-273
maximum file size option, 170
merge replication, 756
    applications of, 811
    database synchronization, 813
    design considerations, 815-816

inappropriate applications of, 812
Merge publications, conflicts, 825
Merge publications, creating, 818
Merge publications, modifying articles, 823
Merge publications, pushing, 819-823
Merge publications, replicating changes, 824
Merge publications, setting up, 817
merging data at the destination database, 813
overview, 812
resolving conflicts, 817-818
subscriber updates, 813
table design limitations, 815
transactional consistency, 813-815
model, 64, 192
msdb, 64, 281
multidimensional, cubes, 857
multiple instances, 464
multiuser, 537
naming, 169
naming convention, 896
normalization, 847
NorthWind, 64
objects, 713
OLAP
    building cubes, 864-867
    creating, 858
    data explosion, 870
    data management, 878-881
    data sources, 859-860
    data storage, 868-869
    defining dimension layers and members, 862-863
    defining dimensions, 860-861
    optimizing, 869-878
    security, 881-889
    Usage Analysis Wizard, 876
operational, 839

performance
  bulk loading operations, 245
  growing the database, 170
pubs, 64
queries, table scans, 484
recovering, 241-242
renaming, 187-188
replication, 751
  applications of, 752
  articles, 753
  configuring servers to be publishers, 767
  distribution database, 758, 761-766
  Immediate updating Subscribers, 757
  overview, 752-754
  server roles, 754-755
  SQL Server 2000 limitation, 758
  transactional consistency, 757-758
  types, 755
restoring, 239, 268-269
  bulk-logged recovery method, 246
  example, 267
  example of, 274, 278-280
  file/filegroup backups, 244-245
  point in time recovery, 245
  selecting method, 245-246
  SQL Server 2000, 240-241
  T-SQL (RESTORE command), 270
retrieving from normalized databases, 476
selecting, 645
setting options, 174-175
  ANSI NULL Default option, 177-178
  Auto Close option, 178
  Auto Create Statistics option, 179
  Auto Shrink option, 179
  Auto Update Statistics option, 179
  compatibility level option, 180
  Concat NULL Yields NULL option, 180
  cursor close on commit option, 181

  Default to Local Cursor option, 181
  QUOTED IDENTIFIER option, 180
  Read Only, 176
  Recovery Model, 176
  Recursive Triggers option, 178
  Restrict Access, 176
  sp_dboption [] command, 180
  Subscribed option, 182
  Torn Page Detection option, 179
shrinking, 186, 921
snapshot replication, 756
SQL-DMO database objects, 728
stored procedures, 593
  advantages, 594
  ALTER PROCEDURE command, 600
  comments, 607
  control-of-flow language, 600-606
  creating, 595-597
  debugging, 610-612
  disadvantages, 594
  executing, 597
  global temporary, 595
  global variables, 610
  headers, 597
  local temporary, 595
  modifying, 600
  naming, 595
  parameters, 607-609
  return values, reserved, 604
  technical notes, 594
  WITH ENCRYPTION option, 597
system
  for backups, 343
  restoring, 282
system requirements, 55
tables
  deleting data with cursors, 624
  looping through with cursors, 620

updating, 913

viewing all within, 498

tempdb, 64

Test Database Integrity, 344

transaction logs, 165,

   expanding, 182-183

   shrinking, 186

   write-ahead, 167

transactional replication, 756, 779

   agents, 780

   topology, 781-783

transactions

   nested, 553-554

   understanding, 553

transformations, DTS Wizard example, 367

two-dimensional, 856

updating, anomalies, 469

upgrading, preserving existing data, 356

user, backing up, 280

verifying integrity, 899

viewing information about, 174

warehouse, 839

Databases Properties dialog box, 125

databases, MSDB, 351

DATAFILETYPE switch (BULK_INSERT statement), 422

DataSource property, 392

datatypes

CREATE TABLE statement, 582-583

mismatched, 532

user-defined, 40

DBAs (database administrators), 9, 12

backing up databases, example of, 274

certification, 18

classes, 17

database maintenance plans, 307

duties, 13-16

   database servers, 11

   file/print servers, 11

   hardware, 10

   networks, 10

   OS, 11

job maintenance plans, 308

job resources, 18

maintenance checklist, 311

overview, 13

pay, 16

restoring databases, example of, 274, 278-280

restoring transaction logs, example of, 279

SQL Server, tuning, 147

SQL-DMO, 712. *See* SQL-DMO

system maintenance plans, 301

   logins (SQL Server), 306

   monitoring error logs (SQL Server), 302-304

   recording configuration information (SQL Server), 305

table/object maintenance plans, 308

team interaction, 19-20

training, 17

Windows NT maintenance plans, 309

DBCC (Database Consistency Checker), 442

case example of use, 444

commands, 443

   CHECKALLOC, 904

   CHECKCATALOG, 903-905

   CHECKDB, 903-905

   CHECKFILEGROUP, 908

   CHECKIDENT, 909

   CHECKTABLE, 910

   data cache, 918

   DBCC dllname(IT) (FREE), 923

   DBREINDEX, 911

   INPUTBUFFER, 914

   OPENTRAN, 919

   OUTPUTBUFFER, 914

   PERFMON, 915

   reading output, 902

returning Performance Monitor statistics, 915

returning process information, 914

SHOWCONTIG, 911

SHOW_STATISTICS, 920

SHRINKFILE, 922

SHRINNKDATABASE, 921

SQLPERF, 915

syntax reference, 899

trace flags, 917

transaction, 919

UPDATEUSAGE, 912

USEROPTIONS, 923

verification, 904

WITH NO INFOMSGS option, 902

DBREINDEX command, 444

DBREINDEX statement, 502

error messages, 902

error tracking, 443

errors, resolving, 903

performance, 902

SHOWCONTIG command, 445

table/index fragmentation, 444-445

trace flags, locking behaviors, 550

DBCC CHECKDB, 351

DBCC CheckTable function, 730

DBCC commands, 248

DBCC dllname(IT) (FREE) command, 923

DBCC INPUTBUFFER(spid) command, 546

DBCC SHOW_STATISTICS command, 509

DBCC USEROPTIONS command, 558

dbcreator role, 208

DBOs (database owners), 223

DBREINDEX

command, 444, 911

statement, 502

db_accessadmin role, 209

db_backupoperator role, 209

db_datareader role, 209

db_datawriter role, 209

db_ddladmin role, 209

db_denydatareader role, 209

db_denydatawriter role, 209

db_owner role, 209

db_public role, 209

db_securityadmin role, 209

DDL, distributed queries, 585

deadlocks, 539-540

example of, 541

troubleshooting, 551-553

DEALLOCATE statement, cursors, 618

debugging

ActiveX scripts, multiple, 383

stored procedures, 610-612

Decision Support Systems (DSSs), 837, 855

DECLARE statement (T-SQL), 601, 613

declaring

cursors, 613-615

output parameters, 609

SQL-DMO, 718, 722

DEFAULD constraint, 40

default language configuration parameter, 151

Default to Local Cursor option, 181

defaults, 40

enforcing, BCP (Bulk Copy Program), 417

User Connections setting, 691

Define Measures dialog box (Cube Wizard), 865-866

defining

cube measures, 865-866

custom error messages, 430

dimensions (OLAP databases), 861-863

job schedules, 320

stored procedures as articles, 800

variables, with DECLARE statement, 601

defragmenting

tables, 912

tables/indexes, 444-445

del remove old data stored procedure, 328

delaying stored procedures, 603

delete anomalies (databases), 469

DELETE FROM component (DELETE statement), 580

Delete Rows in Destination Table option (Transform dialog box), 366

DELETE statement

    components, 580

    cursors, 618-619

    SQL, 566

    versus TRUNCATE TABLE statement, 580

deleting

    data, from tables with cursors, 624

    databases, 188-189

    distribution databases, 765-766

    indexes, 499-500

    rows (tables), 580-581

    SQL Server installations, 102

del_remove_old_data stored procedure, scheduling, 314-315

denormalization

    database, 475-477

    databases, performance, 475

DENY statement, 207

dependent objects, 714

DESC keyword, 570

Design Aggregations dialog box (Storage Design Wizard), 873

Design Table dialog box, 126

designing

    aggregations, 872

    data warehouses

        dimensional modeling, 847-849

        important considerations, 849

        top down/bottom up, 846

    databases

        data transfer with upgrades, 356

        denormalization, 475-477

        normalization, 470-474

        problems arising from improper design, 467-469

    merge replication plans, 815

destination connections, 364-365

destination databases, conflicts, 813

destination steps, 360

destination tables, 365

detaching databases, 190-191, 273

Developer Edition (SQL Server), 62

Developers Network (Microsoft), 18

diagrams, steps for jobs, 324

dialog boxes

    Confirm Password, 220

    Database Integrity Check, 343-344

    Database Maintenance Plan Wizard, 348

    Edit Recurring Job Schedule, 319

    Job Properties, 320-321

    Linked Server Properties, 588

    Linked Server Properties-New Linked Server, 586

    Maintenance Plan History, 347

    Manage SQL Server Messages, 330

    New Alert Properties, 330-333

        performance condition alerts, 334

        Response tab, 332, 335

        Responses tab, 339

    New Job Properties, 314

        General tab, 330, 333-335

        Response tab, 336

        Schedules tab, 318

        Steps tab, 335

    New Job Schedule, 318

    New Job Step, 315-316, 335

        Advanced tab, 318

        Advanced tab, output file feature, 318

    New SQL Server Message, 339

    Object Properties, 224

    Reports to Generate, 347

Select Databases, 342

Select Wizard, 341

Specify Backup Disk Directory, 345

Specify the Database Backup Plan, 344-345

Specify the Transaction Log Backup Plan, 346

Specify Transaction Log Backup Disk
Directory, 346

SQL Mail Configuration, 705

SQL Server Login Properties

Database Access tab, 217

General tab, 216

Permissions tab, 216

Server Roles tab, 215

SQL Server Login Properties - New Login, 213

Update Data Optimization Information, 343

Web Assistant Job, 646

differential backups, 243, 267

dimension level security rules, 885

dimension tables, 861

Dimension Wizard, 861-862

dimensional modeling, 847-848

dimensions

adding to cubes, 866-867

creating, 861

cubes, 857

data explosion, 870

defining (OLAP databases), 861-863

dimension tables, 861

security, rules, 885

shared, 860

directories, created on installation, 77

dirty pages, 161

dirty reads, 538

**Disable Publishing dialog box (Disable
Publishing and Distribution Wizard), 772**

disabling

Distributed Queries, 94

distribution databases, 771

**Disabling Publishing and Distribution Wizard,
771**

disconnecting from servers, 118

disk arrays, 173

disk defragmentation, Windows NT, 310

disk I/O

bottlenecks, 59

clustered indexes, 489

disk I/O monitoring (System Monitor), 688

disk space, SQL Server installation, 63

disk striping, 173-174

diskadmin role, 208

diskperf command, 688

**Display Selected Options dialog box (Backup
Wizard), 260**

displaying

rows, 659

object names and types with cursors, 622-623

process activity, 441

displaying. *See* viewing

distributed queries, 584

disabling, 94

executing, 588

restrictions, 585

troubleshooting, 586

Distributed Transaction Coordinator (DTC), 137

distribution agents, 759, 780, 805-807, 830

distribution database, 758

adding publishers, 767-768

configuring

agent logon information, 764-765

servers to be publishers, 767

creating, 761-762

deleting, 765-766

disabling, 771

enabling, 769-770

selecting, 763

Distribution Database Properties dialog box, 765

distribution databases

deleting servers, 768

nonSQL Server subscribers, 772-775

security, 768

snapshot agent updates, 807

distributor servers, 755

distributors, replication, 315

documents, XML, 680-681

domain user accounts, Windows 2000/NT, 88

DQLDMO.DLL file, 719

drives, hard drives, 58

DROP EXISTING option, 497

DROP INDEX command, 499

DROP_DATABASE command, 266

DSN (Data Source Name), 773-775

DSS (Decision Support System), 837, 855

DTC (Distributed Transaction Coordinator), 137

DTS (Data Transformation Services), 15, 355

batch processes, 380-381

COM objects, 357

data warehousing, 356, 851

exporting data from SQL Server to flat files, 389

flexibility, 357

framework, 356-357

connections, 359

Data Pump, 361

objects, 358

package, 358

steps, 360

tasks, 359-360

improvements, 48

loop control, 385

packages

ActiveX scripts, 384

creating, 371

using, 393

performance, 393

services, 357

wizards, 361

workflow, 380-381

Close Connection on completion property, 383

Execute on Main Package Thread property, 383

loop control, 385-388

properties, 382-383

DTS Designer, 357, 370-378

adding tasks and simple workflow to packages, 371, 379

DTS Package Properties dialog box, 380

overriding precedence constraints, 387

workflow solutions, 380-381

loop control, 385-388

setting properties, 382-383

DTS package operations, 359

DTS package performance, 393

DTS Package Properties dialog box, 380

General tab, 374, 381, 396

Logging tab, 382

DTS Wizard. *See also* **DTS Designer**

column delimiter, 363

destination connections, 364

example of use, 362

file format options, 363

mappings, 366

opening, 361

package actions, 368

package execution, 369

purpose of, 362

saving packages, 369

source and destination tables, 365

source connections, 363

Transform dialog box, 366

transformations, 367

dynamic configuration variables, 146-147

dynamic locking strategy, 466

dynamic memory allocation feature, 148

Dynamic Properties task, 360, 373-375

dynamic SQL, 613

E

e-e option, 93

e-e switch, BCP (Bulk Copy Program), 400-403

early binding, 718

Edit a Cube Role dialog box, 889

Edit Existing Index dialog box, 501

Edit Recurring Job Schedule dialog box, 251, 319

Edit Schedule dialog box, 250

editing

ActiveX scripts, 384

alerts, 332

login information, 219-220

passwords, 220-221

Registry, 27

stored procedures, 600

tables, indexes slowing performance, 491-492

editions (SQL Server 2000), installing, 78

EISs (Executive Information Systems), 855

email

alerting if a replication problem, 826

messages

alerts triggered, 337

extending jobs, 328

low inventory, 341

Microsoft Exchange, 704

notifications, 323, 332

SQL Agent, configuring, 706

SQL Mail, 703

configuring, 704

functionality, 706

processing mail, 708-709

sending messages, 707-708

setting up, 704

starting, 705

testing SQL Server setup, 704

SQL Mail status indicator, 321

Emergency Repair disks (ERDs), 310

Enable New Subscriber dialog box, 770, 776

enabling alerts, 332

end user access tools, 840

enforcing objects, BCP (Bulk Copy Program), 417-418

engine parameters, SQL Server 7.0, 301

Enterprise Edition (SQL Server), 62

Enterprise Manager

alerts, 332

attaching databases, 273

backups

backup media integrity, 251

DBCC commands, 248

devices, creating, 246-247

expiration, 252

multiple backup devices, 262

scheduling, 250

steps, 248-249

connecting to servers, 116

Current Activity Monitor, 694

Data Transformation Services folder, 358

disconnecting from servers, 118

DTS package operations, 359

inline data validation, 799

Push Subscription Wizard, 795

registering servers, 113

SQL Mail status indicator, 321

SQL Server configuring, 140, 143

starting, 112

Stored Procedure Wizard, 595

viewing, error logs, 437

Enterprise networks, 11

entity relationship (ER) model, 847

equals sign (=), 569

ER (entity relationship) model, 847

ERDs (Emergency Repair disks), 310

error logs

    archived, 436

    installation troubleshooting, 91-93

    managing (SQL Server Agent), 134

    monitoring (SQL Server), 302-303

    output, 437

    sample, 303

    searching for text patterns, 304

    versions, 303

    Windows NT event log, 438

error messages

    error logs, 436-438

    fatal errors, 431

    finding, 331

    Microsoft's Books Online, 433-434

    numbers, 430

    RAISERROR statement, 606

    severity levels, 431

    sysmessages system table, 432

    user-defined, 430

    viewing, with SQL Server Enterprise Manager, 432

error number 50001, code to trigger, 340-341

Error Number button, 330

error state numbers, 432

error status, checking with @@ ERROR global variable, 610

errors

    Can't create directory, 81

    checking with CHECKDB command, 899

    DBCC, 902-903

    tracking, DBCC, 443-444

event alerts, 329

event logs

    notifications, 323

    sizing, 27

    Windows NT, 310, 438

Event View, 25

Event Viewer (Windows NT), 438

Event Viewer dialog box, 438

events, locking, 549

ExampleBatchExport DTS package, 389

exclusive locks, 543

Execute on Main Package Thread property, 383

Execute Package task, 360, 379

EXECUTE permissions, stored procedures, 600

Execute Process task, 360, 372-373

Execute SQL task, executing SQL statements, 377

EXECUTE statement, dynamic SQL statements, 613

executing

    jobs, manually, 322

    packages, 358

    queries

        distributed, 588

        pass through, 584

    tasks, redirection, 387

execution paths, queries, 507

execution status, waiting, 388

Executive Information Systems (EISs), 855

examples, advanced template file example, 663-671, 674-675

expanding model database, 193

explicit locking, 558

export scripts, BCP (Bulk Copy Program)

    cautions, 398

    comma-delimited export, 411

    fixed-length export, 413

    simple export, 410

    skipped fields on export, 414

Export Wizard (DTS), 357. *See also* **DTS Wizard**

exporting

    changing filename, 392

    data, 356

        BulkCopy object, 731

        DTS Designer. *See* DTS Designer

listing, 732

SQL Server to flat files, 389

Extended Properties option, 810

extended stored procedures, 27, 328, 707

extending jobs, 326-328

Extensible Markup Language. *See* **XML**

Extensible Stylesheet Language (XSL), 676

extensions, operating system files, 172

extents, 485

extracting data, 845

F

f-f option, 94

f-f switch, BCP (Bulk Copy Program), 400

f@filetype parameter (sp_processmail), 709

f@ixedfont argument, 657

fact tables, 848, 865

FAQs (frequently asked questions)

BCP (Bulk Copy Program), 424

database administration tasks, 351

security, 234-236

fast mode (BCP), 414

backup strategies, 415

compared to slow mode, 416-417

requirements, 415

window of opportunity, 415

FAT (File Allocation Table), 60

fatal errors, 431

fault tolerance

hard drives, 59

RAID 0 systems, 174

federated database servers, 465

Federated Servers, 58

FETCH cursor syntax, 617

fibers, 461

field length (BCP), 407-408

field terminators (BCP), 408

FIELDTERMINATOR switch (BULK_INSERT statement), 422

File Allocation Table (FAT), 60

file storage types (BCP), 406

file/filegroups

backing up, 248-249

backup media integrity, 251

expiration, 252

multiple backup devices, 261-262

scheduling, 250

backups, 244-245, 254

restoring, T-SQL, 271

file/print servers, DBA duties, 11

filegroups, 193

adding secondary data files to, 195

creating indexes on, 196

implementing, 194

placing objects on, 196

viewing information, 197-198

filenames, changing at export, 392

files

format files, 408-409

moving database files, 190-191

output, Advanced tab (New Job Step dialog box), 318

shrinking, 922

T-SQL, 254

Fill Factor, 491, 495

fill factor advanced configuration parameter, 156

Filter Data dialog box (Create a Publication Wizard), 792

Filter Table Columns dialog box (Create a Publication Wizard), 793

finding error messages, 331

Finish dialog box

Cube Wizard, 867

Storage Design Wizard, 874

FIRSTROW switch (BULK_INSERT statement), 422

fixed values, columns (tables), setting, 579

fixed-length export script (BCP), 413

fixed-length import script (BCP), 411-412

flags, trace, 442-443

FOR EACH – NEXT statement, 727

format files (BCP), 408-409

FORMATFILE switch (BULK_INSERT statement), 422

formatting Web pages, Web Assistant, 654-658

fragmentation, 911-912

frequently asked questions. *See* FAQs

FROM component

    SELECT statement, 567

    UPDATE statement, 579

FTDATA directory, 77

FTP task, sending/receiving files, 378

Full Recovery mode, 176-177

Full Recovery model, 241-242, 262-268

FULL [OUTER] JOIN operator, 572

functions

    aggregate (SQL statements), 573

    OPENQUERY, 592

G

g-g option, 94

General tab

    New Job Properties dialog box, 330, 333-335

    SQL Server Login Properties dialog box, 216

Generate SQL Script dialog box, 127

generating SQL scripts, 126

global temporary, 595

global variables

    assigning parameters, 391

    cursors, 619-620

    stored procedures, 610

GOTO statement, 602

Goto Step N option (jobs), 318

Grant method, 728

GRANT statement, 206

granting

    database roles, 216-219

    permissions, 206

        object permissions, 224-226

        statement permissions, 228-229

    server roles, 215-216

graphical BCP utility, 731

    importing data, 736

    listing, 732

    setting path to a BCP log file, 739

graphical showplans, 521

greater than or equal to symbol ((gt)=), 569

greater than symbol ((gt)), 569

GREP utility, 304

GROUP BY clause (SELECT statement), 574-575

GROUP BY component (SELECT statement), 567

grouping

    results, queries, 574-576

    rows (tables), 566

guaranteed loose consistency, 757

guaranteed no consistency, 758

guaranteed tight consistency, 757

guest users, 206

H

h-h switch, BCP (Bulk Copy Program), 403-404

hard drives

    autoshrink option (databases), 179

    data striping, 172-173

    fault tolerance, 59

RAID, 59

speed, 59

SQL Server installation, 58

striping, 59

hardware

DBA duties, 10

hard drives, 58-59

Microsoft recommendations, 61

selecting, 56-57

SQL Server 2000 installation, 80

hardware-level disk striping, 174

HAVING

clause (SELECT statement), 576

component (SELECT statement), 567

headers, stored procedures, 597

heap storage, 490

heterogeneous subscribers, 772

hierarchy (security), 223-224

HOLAP (hybrid OLAP), 869

HOLDLOCK

command, cautions, 552

lock, 559

horizontal partitioned tables, 754

hot backups, 283

HTML

hyperlinks, 657-662

naming pages, 654

publishing pages, 644-662

hub-and-spoke topology, 781

central publisher scenario, 781, 784

configuring, 781

republisher scenario, 783

hybrid OLAP (HOLAP), 869

hyperlinks, Web pages, 657-662

I

i-i switch, BCP (Bulk Copy Program), 401

I/O

disk, bottlenecks, 59

measurements, 523

i@talic argument, 657

icons, Linked Servers or Tables, 589

IDENTITY data type, CHECKIDENT command, 909

identity property, 556

IDs

auto-incrementing, 556

logon, 588-589

IE 5.0 (Internet Explorer), 79

IF, , .ELSE statement, 602

IGNORE DUP KEY option, 497

Immediate Updating Subscribers, 757-758

import scripts, BCP (Bulk Copy Program)

cautions, 398

comma-delimited import, 411

fixed-length import, 411-412

simple import, 410

skipped fields on import, 413

Import Wizard, (DTS), 357. *See also* **DTS Wizard**

importing

data, 355

BCP utility, 736

DTS Designer. *See* DTS Designer

tables, DTS Wizard example, 362-366

text files, Bulk Insert, 360

IN comparison operator, 569

incident reports, Microsoft tech support, 446

Include Declarative Referential Integrity option, 810

incremental database backups, 243

Incremental update option (Process a Cube dialog box), 879

index create memory advanced configuration parameter, 157

index hints, 529-530

Index Options dialog box, 497

Index Recommendations screen (Index Tuning Wizard), 520

Index Tuning Wizard, 503

Completing the Index Tuning Wizard screen, 520

Index Recommendations screen, 520

query optimization, 512-514, 520

Schedule Index Update Job screen, 520

Specify Workload screen, 519

working with SQL Server Profiler, 517

Index Wizard (SQL Server 2000), 492-495

indexed, enforcing (BCP), 417

indexes

adding, 499-500, 514

affecting performance, 491

Auto Create Statistics option (databases), 179

Auto Update Statistics option (databases), 179

B-Tree structure, levels, 488

clustered, 488-489

creating, 494

DROP EXISTING option, 497

finding data, 527

when to use, 502

composite, 528

creating

CREATE INDEX command, 497

on computed columns and views, 498

on filegroups, 196

processor effects, 496

restricted data types, 492

selecting columns, 494

SQL Server 2000

Index Wizard, 492-495

what not to index?, 502

what to index?, 501

deleting, 499-500

disk I/O, performance enhancements, 491

dropping from tables, 913

example, 484-486

Fill Factor, 495

fragmentation, DBCC, 444-445

integrity validation, 908

names, 496

naming conventions, 896

nonclustered, 488, 490

limits, 491

minimizing, 553

number allowed in tables, 491

when to use, 502

page splits, 491

pages, 485-486

performance, 491-492

principle behind, 483

rebuilding, 911

renaming, 499-501

selection, 503

size concerns, 487

space allocation, 485

statistics, 508

structure of, 488

T-SQL index operations, 498

table design effects, 487

tuning, 503

uniqueness, 495

inequality, indicating, 568-569

information, analyzing, 699

Information Files Found dialog box (Version Upgrade Wizard), 101

Initialize Subscription dialog box (Push Subscription Wizard), 821

inline data validation, 798

INNER JOIN operator, 572

input parameters, stored procedures, 607-608

INPUTBUFFER command, 914

insert anomalies (databases), 470

INSERT INTO component (INSERT statement), 577

INSERT INTO...SELECT statement, 578

INSERT statement

    components, 577

    Fill Factor effects, 495

INSERT statement (SQL), 566

INSERT statements, reducing locks, 551

inserting rows (tables), 577-578

INSTALL directory, 77

installation, remote, 105

Installation Definition dialog box, 85

installing

    Books Online, 433

    multiple instances of SQL Server database engine, 65

    network libraries, 66

    SQL Server, 67

        Client Tools, 103

        configuring clients, 104

        data file location, 64

        dedicating a machine, 55

        directories created on installation, 77

        hard drives, 58

        memory, 58

        Microsoft hardware and software recommendations, 61

        network options, 65

        options, 63

        planning, 54

        questions, 64

        removing instances, 102

        selecting a platform, 56-57

        selecting platforms, 61

        services created on installation, 77

        system requirements, 54-55

        upgrading the existing SQL Server (single computer, 69

        user requirements, 55

        utilities created on installation, 78

    SQL Server 2000

        alongside SQL Server 7.0, 97-98, 100

        Authentication Mode dialog box, 87

        Can't create directory error message, 81

        checklist, 80

        Collation Settings dialog box, 88

        Computer Name dialog box, 82

        documentation, 79

        domain user accounts (Windows 2000/NT), 88

        editions, 78

        Installation Definition dialog box, 85

        Instance Name dialog box, 85

        License Agreement dialog box, 84

        multiple instances, 106

        Network Libraries dialog box, 88

        prerequisites, 79

        remotely, 105

        sample UDF functions, 599

        Select Components dialog box, 87

        Server Installation dialog box, 83

        Service Manager, 90

        setup program, 81

        Setup Type dialog box, 86

        Start Copying Files dialog box, 89

        troubleshooting, 91-93

        User Information dialog box, 84

Instance Name dialog box, 85

instances, 106

integrating

    CSS, 676

    data sources, multiple, 584

    XML, 676-677

    XSL, 676

integrating data, 843

integrity
   backup media, 251
   databases, 899
intent locks, 543
interactive mode (BCP)
   field length, 407-408
   field terminators, 408
   file storage types, 406
   format files, 408-409
   prefix length, 407
   prompts, 405-406
Internet, Web Assistant, 641-643
inventories, low inventory email messages, 341
Inventory Properties dialog box, 182
isolation levels, (transactions), 557-558
ISQL, 37

J

Job Properties dialog box, 129
   Notifications tab, 320-321
   Schedules tab, 320
job responsibilities, 11
   DBAs, 12-16
   network administrator, 12
   PC and tech support, 12
   system administrator, 12
   Webmasters, 12
Job Scheduler, 316
   del remove old data stored procedure, 328
   SQLServerAgent service, 314
jobs
   active scripting, 315, 325-327
   CmdExec (operating system command), 315
   creating, 314-322
   databases, commands, 316
   email messages, 328
   email notifications, 323
   event log notifications, 323
   extending, 326-328

   Goto Step N option, 318
   Last Run Status, 322
   listing, 348
   maintenance plans, 308
   managing (SQL Server Agent), 127, 314-322
   manually executing, 322
   multiserver, 351
   replication distributor, 315
   replication merge, 316
   replication snapshots, 316
   replication transact-SQL script (TSQL), 316
   replication transaction-log reader, 315
   schedule types, 319
   schedules, defining, 320
   SQL Server Agent, 313-314
   starting, 348
   step actions, 317-318
   step diagrams, 324
   steps, 323-325
   steps of, 324
   types, 315-316
   Web Assistant, 643, 646
      managing, 663
      scheduling, 649, 652-653
      triggers, 652
JOBS directory, 77
JOIN operator, 571-573
joining tables, 530, 571-573

K

k-k switch, BCP (Bulk Copy Program), 403
KEEPIDENTITY switch (BULK_INSERT statement), 422
KEEPNULLS switch (BULK_INSERT statement), 423
Kerberos, 229
keywords
   DENY, 207
   DESC, 570

GRANT, 206

REVOKE, 206

KILL command, 439

killing processes, 438-441

KILOBYTES_PER_BATCH switch (BULK_INSERT statement), 423

L

l-l option, 93

L-L switch, BCP (Bulk Copy Program), 400

Last Run Status column, creating jobs, 322

LASTROW switch (BULK_INSERT statement), 423

Latest History of Merge Agent dialog box (Push Subscription Wizard), 823

leaf level (B-Tree structure), 488

Leave Database Read-Only option, 280

less than or equal to symbol (<=), 569

less than symbol (<), 569

levels

    B-Tree index structure, 488

    dimensions, 862-863

levels of security, 222

libraries

    Microsoft SQLDMO Objects Library, 720

    network, 66

    SQLMAP70.dll, 707

License Agreement dialog box, 84

lightweight pooling, 461

lightweight pooling advanced configuration parameter, 157

LIKE comparison operator, 569

Limit the Maximum Number of Tasks Executed in Parallel option, 381

limiting rows, 659

lineage (data), 846

Linked Server Properties dialog box, 588

Linked Server Properties-New Linked Server dialog box, 586

linked servers

    adding, 586-588

    data, retrieving, 590-591

    naming conventions, 590

    queries, pass through, 592

    tables, viewing, 589

    troubleshooting, 586

Linked Servers icon, 589

list boxes, populating with table names, 726

listing jobs, 348

listings

    ActiveX Script Task code for step 1 (Loop Control example), 386

    BCP

        exports, 732, 740

        syntax, 36

    concat null yields null option, 180

    creating SQL Server object, 722

    Customer transform script, 367

    Data Transformation's Workflow ActiveX Script property, 392

    databases

        creating, 171

        expanding, 185

        inventory database, 194

    ISQL syntax, 37

    populating a combo box with database names, 726

    populating list boxes with table names, 726

    PRINT statement, 606, 610

    sample error log, 303

    secondary data files, creating, 195

    SELECT statement, debugging, 612

    setting execution status to waiting, 388

    sp_configure, output with Show Advanced options, 145

    SQL Server connection, 724

    transaction logs, expanding, 185

Update Statistics option, 729

viewing database size using transact SQL, 744

Workflow ActiveX Script property, 386

load time, decreasing, 394

loading data, 845

local temporary stored procedures, 595

Lock Counters (Performance Monitor), 548

Lock:Deadlock Chain event, 549

Lock:Deadlock event, 549

locking troubleshooting, 551-553

locks, 537

explicit, 559

functionality, 539

managing, 544

minimizing, cursor options, 557

nested transactions, 555

page, 542

physical, 541

row-level, 541

table, 543

tracking information, SQL Server Profiler, 549

viewing, 544-546

locks advanced configuration parameter, 157

LOG directory, 77

log files, 172

creating, System Monitor, 692

point of failure recovery, 245

log operating system files, 167

Log Properties dialog box, 27

log reader agent, 759, 780

log shipping

maintenance plan, deleting, 291

monitoring, 292

process, 290-291

requirements, 284

resources, 285

setting up, 285-289

troubleshooting, 292

uses of, 284

utility, 283

Log Shipping Schedules window, settings, 288

log truncation options, 255-256

logging statements, bulk load, 243

logic, read-ahead, 466

logical reads, 523

login credentials, 365

Login Properties dialog box, 122

logins

editing login information, 219-220

maintenance, 306

managing, 121, 212-214

passwords, 220-221

security, 204-205

troubleshooting, 221

viewing login information, 219

LoginTimeout property, 724

logon IDs, 588-589

logon mappings, setting, 588

logs

automatically copying, 283

data lineage, 846

error

archived, 436

managing, 134

output, 437

viewing (SQL Server), 302

generating, using performance monitor, 449-451

transaction

backing up, 346

backups, 243-244

inactive parts, 243

troubleshooting, 244

truncation options, 255-256

Windows NT event log, 438

loop control, (DTS example), 385

loopback detection, 786

loops, 605

low inventory email messages, 341

m-m option, 94

m-m switch, BCP (Bulk Copy Program), 400

Main=DTSTaskExecResult_Success statement, 386

maintenance

    databases, DBCC, 442

    OLAP databases, Usage Analysis Wizard, 876

    SQL Server, 302-306

Maintenance Plan History dialog box, 347

maintenance plans, 301-302

    checklist, 311

    databases, 307

    jobs, 308

    tables/objects, 308

    Windows NT, 309

Manage Error Messages button, 330

Manage Indexes dialog box, 500

Manage SQL Server Messages dialog box, 330

management. *See* administration

managers. *See* Alert Manager

managing

    alerts (SQL Server Agent), 129

    backups, 283

    data transformation packages (SQL Server Enterprise Manager), 132

    data warehouses/data marts, 850

    databases, 124, 191-192

    error logs (SQL Server Enterprise Manager), 134

    jobs, 314-322

    jobs and tasks (SQL Server Agent), 127

    locks, 544

    logins, 121

    multidimensional data, 878

        client write back, 881

        merging partitions, 880

        processing the cube, 879

    operators (SQL Server Agent), 129

    server configurations (SQL Server Enterprise Manager), 120

    server roles, 122

    stored procedures, 594

    user activity (SQL Server Enterprise Manager), 132

    Web Assistant jobs, 663

manipulating data sources, non-relational, 584

manually executing jobs, 322

MAPI mail clients (setting SQL Server up as), 704

mapping

    columns (DTS Wizard), 366

    data, 844

mappings, logon, setting, 588

master database, 64

    backing up

        after creating new, 171

        after deleting databases, 189

        scheduling, 280

    restoring, 271-274

matching data, 844

Max aggregate function (SQL statements), 573

max degree of parallelism advanced configuration parameter, 158

max degree of parallelism parameter, 496

max memory advanced configuration parameter, 158

max server memory parameter, 148

max text repl size configuration parameter, 151

max worker threads advanced configuration parameter, 158

MAXERRORS switch (BULK_INSERT statement), 423

.MDF files, 172

MDX (multidimensional expressions, 889

measures, cubes, 857

media retention advanced configuration parameter, 159

media sets, 261-262

memory

cost, 58

creating indexes, 157

dynamic memory allocation feature, 148

monitoring, 149, 689-690

self-tuning ability (SQL Server), 147-148

SQL Server 2000, 63

SQL Server installation, 58

too much, 149

transaction performance, 556

Memory: Page Faults/sec counter, 690

merge agent, 759

Merge Agent, execution, 813

Merge Publication Wizard, 818

Merge publications, 812

conflicts, 825

creating, 818

modifying articles, 823

pushing, 819-823

replicating changes, 824

setting up, 817

merge replication, 756

applications of, 811

database synchronization, 813

design considerations, 815-816

guaranteed no consistency model, 758

inappropriate applications of, 812

Merge Agent, merging data at the destination database, 813

Merge publications

conflicts, 825

creating, 818

modifying articles, 823

pushing, 819-823

replicating changes, 824

setting up, 817

overview, 812

resolving conflicts, 817-818

spoke-and-hub topology, 816

subscriber updates, 813

timestamp columns, 815

transaction replication (comparison), 811

transactional consistency, 813-815

troubleshooting, 826

merges, replication, 316

merging partitions, 880

Message Queue task, 360

messages

email

alerts triggered, 337

extending jobs, 328

low inventory, 341

error, finding, 331

error. *See* error messages

net send, notifications, 321

metadata, 840, 845

methods, 712

Microsoft

certification, 18

OLE DB, 356

tech support, 446

Microsoft Analysis Manager, 857

Microsoft Analysis Services, 852, 855

Microsoft Analysis Services Unleashed(IT), 858

Microsoft Analysis Services, 852

Microsoft Cluster Server (MSCS), 25

Microsoft Developer Network (MSDN), 18, 448

Microsoft Distributed Transaction Coordinator (MS DTC), 786

Microsoft English Query, 34

Microsoft Exchange, 704

Microsoft Management Console (MMC), 857

Microsoft Meta Data Services, storing packages, 358

Microsoft Replication Conflict Viewer dialog box, 825

Microsoft Solution Provider Authorized Technical Education Centers, 17

Microsoft SQL Server Professional(IT), 18

Microsoft SQLDMO Object Library, 720

Microsoft TechNet, 18, 447

Microsoft's Books Online, 433-434

Microsoft's SQL Server Web site, 926

migrating databases, on SQL Server upgrades, 70-71

Min aggregate function (SQL statements), 573

min memory per queryadvanced configuration parameter, 159

min server memory advanced configuration parameter, 159

min server memory parameter, 148

mining (data), 838

mixed mode security, 205

mixed security mode, 66

MMC (Microsoft Management Console), 857

model database, 64

    deleting, 192

    expanding, 193

    objects and settings that can be stored, 192

    viewing, 192

modes, BCP (Bulk Copy Program)

    character, 405

    fast, 414-417

    field length, 407-408

    field terminators, 408

    file storage types, 406

    format files, 408-409

    interactive, 405-409

    native, 405

    prefix length, 407

    prompts, 405-406

    slow, 414-417

modifying. *See* editing

MOLAP (multidimensional OLAP), 868, 872

monitoring

    memory, 149

    SQL Server Profiler, 695-696

    user activity, 694

monitoring SQL Server, System Monitor, 685-691

moving database files, 190-191

MS DTC (Microsoft Distributed Transaction Coordinator), 786

MSCS (Microsoft Cluster Server), 25

msdb

    backing up, 281

    database, 64, 351, 358

MSdistribution_agents table, 758

MSdistribution_history table, 758

MSDN (Microsoft Developers Network), 18, 448

MSDN Online Web site, 926

MSlogreader_agents table, 759

MSlogreader_history table, 759

MSmerge_agents table, 758

MSmerge_history table, 758

MSrepl_commands table, 759, 807

MSrepl_errors table, 759

MSrepl_transactions table, 759, 807

MSrepl_version table, 759

MSSQLServer process, setting up SQL Mail, 704

multi-instances, 47

multidimensional data, 856

multidimensional databases, 857, 860. *See also* **OLAP**

    cubes

        aggregations, 872

        creating, 864, 867

        defining measures, 865-866

        dimensions, 857, 866-867

        fact tables, 865

        measures, 857

    data explosion, 870

data management, 878
    client write back, 881
    merging partitions, 880
    processing the cube, 879
data storage
    HOLAP, 869
    MOLAP, 868
    ROLAP, 869
optimizing, 869
    aggregations, 870-874
    partitions, 878
    usage-based, 875-876
security, 881
    cell level, 887-889
    dimension level, 885
    roles, 882-885
Usage Analysis Wizard, 876
multidimensional expressions (MDX), 889
multidimensional OLAP (MOLAP), 868
multiple instances, 106, 464
multiprotocol, 66
multiserver jobs, 351
multitable queries, 575
multithreaded operating systems, 460
multiuser environments, 537
    blocking, troubleshooting, 555-556
    SQL Server configuration options, 557

N

n-n switch, BCP (Bulk Copy Program), 400-401
Name Conflicts options (Table Articles Properties dialog box), 810
named-pipes protocol, 66
names, indexes, 496
naming
    cubes, 867
    databases, 169, 187

    HTML pages, Web Assistant, 654
    stored procedures, 595
naming conventions
    linked servers, 590
    SQL Server, 895
    standardizing case, 897
narrowing queries, 568
native mode (BCP), 405
NBT Connection: Bytes Total/sec counter, 691
.NDF files, 172
nested transactions, 553-554
nested triggers configuration parameter, 152
Net Libraries (SQL Server), 105
Net Send command, 321
net send messages, notifications, 321
NET Start MSSQLSERVER command, 30
network administrators, 12
network libraries, 66
Network Libraries dialog box, 88
network packet size advanced configuration parameter, 159
networks
    DBAs, 10-16
    Enterprise, 11
    job responsibilities, 11
    monitoring (System Monitor), 691
    network administrators, 12
    PC and tech support, 12
    performance, stored procedure replication, 800
    system administrators, 12
    Webmasters, 12
New Alert Properties dialog box, 330, 333
    performance condition alerts, 334
    Response tab, 332, 335-339
New Database dialog box, 859
New Job Properties dialog box, 314
    General tab, 330, 333-335
    Response tab, 336

Schedules tab, 318

Steps tab, 335

New Job Schedule dialog box, 318

New Job Step dialog box, 315-318, 335

New keyword, 718

New Schedule button, 318-320

New SQL Server Message dialog box, 339

New Technology File System (NTFS), 60

newsgroups, SQL Server, 18, 927

NOINDEX argument, 902

NOLOCK lock, 559

non-relational data sources, manipulating, 584

Nonclustered Indexed option, 810

nonclustered indexes, 488, 490

creating, after clustered indexes, 496

DBREINDEX statement, 502

limits, 491

minimizing, 553

number allowed in tables, 491

when to use, 502

nonsearch arguments, 533

normalization, database, 470, 847

1st normal form, 472

2nd normal form, 473

3rd normal form, 474-474

NorthWind database, 64

not equal to symbol (< >), 568-569

Nothing keyword, 720

notifications

email, 323, 332

event log, 323

net send messages, 321

Notifications tab (Job Properties dialog box), 320-321

NO_LOG option, 256

NO_TRUNCATE option, 256, 265

NTSF (New Technology File System), 60

NULL values, 608

NWLink IPX/SPX protocol, 66

O

O-O option, 94

o-o switch, BCP (Bulk Copy Program), 401

Object Browser, 48

object linking and embedding. See OLE

object model, (SQL Server), 714

object permissions, 207

granting, 224-226

revoking, 224-225

Object Properties dialog box, 224

Object Search, 48

objects

active scripting, 326

BulkCopy, 731

collections, 713

COMMAND, 592

common, 39

database, 713

dependent, 714

DTS framework, 357

enforcing, BCP (Bulk Copy Program), 417-418

getting an instance of, 718

getting list of, 727

maintenance plans, 308

methods, 712

naming conventions, 896-897

permissions, 207

auditing, 308

granting, 224-226

revoking, 224-225

placing on filegroups, 196

properties, 712

releasing, 719

SQL-DMO

creating, 718-723

declaring, 722

table maintenance, 728

object_id() function, 912

ODBC (Open Database Connectivity), 356, 751

adding DSN to list of subscribing servers, 775

creating a DSN, 773-774

cursor syntax, 614

setting up subscribers using MS Access 2000, 773

tracing, 612

ODBC Data Source Administrator dialog box, 773

ODBC SQL Server Setup dialog box, 775

OLAP (Online Analytical Processing), 837-838

Microsoft Analysis Services, 855

multidimensional databases, dimensions, 857

overview, 855

OLAP Administrators group, 882

OLAP databases

creating, 858, 864

cubes

aggregations, 872

creating, 867

defining measures, 865-866

dimensions, 866-867

fact tables, 865

data explosion, 870

data management, 878

client write back, 881

merging partitions, 880

processing the cube, 879

data sources, 859-860

data storage, 868-869

defining dimensions, 860-863

dimensions, creating, 861

optimizing, 869

aggregations, 870-874

partitions, 878

usage-based, 875-876

security, 881

authentication, 882

cell level, 887-889

dimension level, 885

roles, 882-885

rules, 890

Usage Analysis Wizard, 876

OLE (object linking and embedding), 711

automation, 712

automation stored procedures, 736

bulk copy operations, 739

sp_OACreate, 737

sp_OADestroy, 739

sp_OAGetErrorInfo, 737

sp_OAGetProperty, 738

sp_OAMethod, 738

sp_OASetProperty, 738

sp_OAStop, 739

creating object models, 714

terminology, 712

OLE DB

DTS framework, 356

Execute on Main Package Thread property, 383

OLE DB providers, 585

OLTP systems (Online Transaction Processing), 838-839, 855

On filegroup_name option (CREATE TABLE command), 196

Online Analytical Processing. See OLAP

Online Transactional Processing systems (OLTP), 838-839, 855

Open Database Connectivity. See ODBC

open objects advanced configuration parameter, 160

OPENQUERY function, 592

OPENTRAN command, 919

operating system command (CmdExec), 315

operating system files, extensions, 172

operating systems. See OSs

operational data

transforming, 843

versus warehouse data, 838-839

operational data stores, 839
operational databases, 839
operations. *See* tasks
Operator Properties dialog box, 131
operators
   comparison, 569
   CROSS JOIN, 572
   FULL [OUTER] JOIN, 572
   INNER JOIN, 572
   JOIN, 571-573
   LEFT [OUTER] JOIN, 572
   managing (SQL Server Agent), 129
   RIGHT [OUTER] JOIN, 572
optimization
   indexes, 528
   OLAP databases, Usage Analysis Wizard, 877
optimizing
   OLAP databases, 869
      aggregations, 870-874
      data explosions, 870
      partitions, 878
      usage-based, 875-876
   queries
      causes of poor performance, 531-533
      search versus nonsearch arguments, 533
options
   command-line, 93
   publications, 827
ORDER BY
   clause (SELECT statement), 569
   component (SELECT statement), 567
ORDER switch (BULK_INSERT statement), 423
organizing dimension levels, 863
orphaned logins, 221
OSQL, 38
OSs (operating systems)
   DBA duties, 11
   multithreaded, 460

scalability, 57
SQL Server 2000 support, 63
SQL Server installation, 54
SQL Server support, 24
system administrators, 12
output
   DBCC command, 902
   error logs, 437
output files, Advanced tab (New Job Step dialog box), 318
output parameters, stored procedures, 609
OUTPUTBUFFER command, 914
overriding
   DTS Designer precedence constraints, 387
   query optimizer, 529
   SQL Server's default locking behavior, 558

P

P-P switch, BCP (Bulk Copy Program), 403
packages, 358
   (DTS framework), 357
   actions, 368
   building with DTS Wizard, 362
   DTS
      ActiveX scripts, 384
      creating, 371
      operations available in Enterprise Manager, 359
      using, 393
   DTS Package Properties dialog box, 380
   executing, 358
   execution, 369
   Package object collections, 388
   properties, 381
   running from command-line, 393
   saving, 369
   storing, 358, 393

PAD INDEX option, 497

Page Faults/sec counter, 149

page locks, 542

page splits, 491

pages

affected by table design, 487

dirty, 161

extents, 485

Fill Factor, 495

layout, 486

size (version differences), 462

splitting, 444

Torn Page Detection option (databases), 179

Paging File: % Usage counter, 690

PAGLOCK lock, 559

Parallel Data Scan, 150

parallel queries, 461

parallel striped backups, 261-262

Parameter Mapping dialog box, 391

parameters

assigning to global variables, 391

command-line, sqlmaint.exe utility, 350

memory configuration, 148

SQL Server configuration, 140

advanced, 154-162

allow updates, 150

default language, 151

dynamic configuration variables, 146-147

max text repl size, 151

nested triggers, 152

remote access, 152

remote login timeout, 152

remote proc trans, 153

remote query timeout, 152

show advanced options, 153

two digit year cutoff, 153

user_option, 154

stored procedures

DEFAULT clause, 608

input, 607

input, default values, 608

output, 609

partitions

merging, 880

optimizing cubes, 878

user-defined, 878

pass through queries

executing, 584

links servers, 592

passing parameters in stored procedures, 607

passwords, changing, 220-221

pausing SQL Server, 30, 111

PC support, 12

PERFMON command, 915

performance

backups, 261

bulk loading operations, 245

databases

3rd normal form design, 475

effects of growing the database, 170

filegroups, 193-194

DBCC, 902

DTS, 393

fault tolerance, 59

hard drives, data striping, 173

indexes, 488, 491

monitoring

SQL Server Profiler, 695-696

System Monitor, 687

multiuser environments, 537

OLAP databases

data explosion, 870

optimizing, 869-878

Usage Analysis Wizard, 876

processor scalability, 689

query optimization, 531-533

query optimizer, 507

SQL Server, 140, 149

SQL Server 2000, 47

stored procedures, 594

table fragmentation, 911

transactions, 57, 556

performance alerts, building, 333-336

performance condition alerts, 329, 333-336

Performance Monitor, 28

generating a log, 449-451

performance condition alerts, 333-336

returning statistics, 915

too much memory allocated, 149

tracking, lock information, 548

trend analysis, 448

Performance Monitor dialog, 450

period (.), syntax, 399

permissions

administration tips, 226-227

BCP (Bulk Copy Program), 404

cautions, 889

combining with views, 232

granting, 206

object permissions, 224-226

statement permissions, 228-229

object permissions, 207, 308

OLAP database security, 887

revoking, 206-207, 224-225, 228-229

statement permissions, 207

Permissions tab (SQL Server Login Properties dialog box), 216

Personal Edition

Authentication Mode, 87

SQL Server, 62

physical disk counters, 688

physical locks, 541

physical reads, 523

PhysicalDisk: % Disk Time counter, 688

PhysicalDisk: Current Disk Queue Length counter, 689

pinging servers, 117

PINTABLE command, 918

planning

data warehouse design

dimensional modeling, 847-849

important considerations, 849

top down/bottom up, 846

merge replication design, 815

snapshot replication, 807

SQL Server

installation, 54-55

upgrades, 68-73

plans, running, 348

platforms, selecting for SQL Server installation, 56-57

plus sign (+), 314

point in time recovery, 245

Point In Time Restore, 268

pointers, CHECKTABLE command, 910

populating tables, remote, 585

positional updates with cursors, 626

pound sign (#), 399

power users, 210-211

precedence constraints

overriding, 387

Step objects, 360

predefined database roles, 209

preemptive multitasking operating systems, 460

prefix length (BCP), 407

primary files, 172

PRIMARY KEY constraint, rebuilding, 911

primary keys, 503

PRINT statement

debugging, 611

listing, 606, 610

priority boost advanced configuration parameter, 160

Priority class property (packages), 381

procedures

extended stored, 328

stored, 233

code, 327-328

creating, 584

del remove old data, 328

del_remove_old_data stored procedure, scheduling, 314-315

sp_addlinkedserver, 586

sp_addlinkedsrvlogin, 588

Process a Cube dialog box, 879

Process Details dialog box, 695

Process Information dialog box, 442

Process option (Process a Cube dialog box), 879

Process Status dialog box (Storage Design Wizard), 875

processadmin role, 208

processes

automating, 380

blocking, 545

killing, 438-441

returning information, 914

spids, determining, 915

stages, 379

state, 379

status, 379

viewing, activity, 441

zombies, 440

processing the cube, 879

processor monitoring (System Monitor), 689

Processor: % Processor Time counter, 689

processors, affecting index creation, 496

production servers, Transact-SQL Debugger, 611

Profiler, 549, 697

Profiler information, logging to tables, 699

programming, DTS, resources, 388

programming languages, 714-715

programs. See stored procedures

projects. See applications

properties, objects, 712

protocols

AppleTalk ADSP, 67

named-pipes, 66

network, SQL Server 2000 installation, 80

NWLink IPX/SPX, 66

TCP/IP, 66

providers, OLE DB, 585

Publication and Subscription Wizard, 808

Merge publications, setting up, 817

Select Publication Type dialog box, 809

Table Article Properties dialog box, 809

Publication Properties dialog box

General tab, 827

Snapshot tab, 828

Status tab, 828

Sync Partners tab, 829

Publication Properties dialog box (Push Subscription Wizard), 796

publications, 753

articles, 754

creating, 787-794, 808

enabling, 769-770

maintaining snapshot of, 820

Merge, 812

conflicts, 825

creating, 818

modifying articles, 823

pushing, 819-823

replicating changes, 824

setting up, 817

merge replication

applications of, 811

database synchronization, 813

design considerations, 815-816

inappropriate applications of, 812

merging data at the destination database, 813

overview, 812

resolving conflicts, 817-818

subscriber updates, 813

table design limitations, 815

transactional consistency, 813-815

options, 827

publication scripts, 799

snapshot, 805

information, 768

replication, pull subscriptions, 807

setting up, 808-810

update frequency, 806

subscriber, updating local data, 785-786

subscriptions, 795

transaction based, 787-794

Publisher and Distributor dialog box, 766

Publisher and Distributor Properties dialog box, 764

Publisher Properties dialog box, 768

publisher servers, 755

publishers

adding to distribution databases, 767-768

configuring servers, 767

disabling, 771

enabling, replication subscribers, 770

enabling databases for publication, 769

merge replication, 813

nonSQL Server subscribers, 772-775

publishing HTML pages, Web Assistant Wizard, 644-662

pubs database, 64, 190

pull subscriptions, 754, 795, 807

Push Subscription Wizard, 795, 819

Choose Destination Database dialog box, 820

Choose Subscriber dialog box, 820

Initialize Subscription dialog box), 821

Latest History of Merge Agent dialog box, 823

Publication Properties dialog box, 796

Set Merge Agent Schedule dialog box, 821

Set Subscription Priority dialog box, 822

Start Required Services dialog box, 822

Table Articles Properties dialog box, 797

push subscriptions, 754, 795

pushing Merge publication, 819

Q

q-q switch, BCP (Bulk Copy Program), 401

queries

? symbol, 389

complex views, 498

composite indexes, 528-529

computed columns, 498

distributed, 584

DDL, 585

executing, 588

restrictions, 585

troubleshooting, 586

Fill Factor effects, 495

graphical showplans, 521

I/O measurements, 524

index hints, 530

indexes, 487

MDX, 889

mismatched datatypes, 532

multitable, 575

narrowing, 568

nonsearch arguments, 533

OLAP systems, 837

optimization, 507

causes of poor performance, 531-533

Index Tuning Wizard, 512-514, 520

overriding the query optimizer, 529

SET FORCEPLAN ON command, 531

Set Statistics IO query option, 524

showplans, 521

SQL Server Profiler, 514-518

statistics I/O, 523-524

Statistics Time tool, 524

suggestions, 511

tools, 511

parallel, 461

pass through, 584

performance concerns, 531

query optimizer, 507

referencing views, 532

results, 569, 574-576

search versus nonsearch arguments, 533

Set Statistics Time query option, 525

showplans, reading, 526-527

subqueries, 581

table scans, 484, 487, 526

test-based showplans, 523

Web Assistant jobs, 647

wildcards, 530

Xpath, 678

Query Analyzer, 514

improvements, 48

SQL Server, 135

Query bar graph, 876

Query by date graph, 877

Query by hour graph, 877

Query dialog box, 136

Query frequency table, 876

**query governor cost limit advanced configura-
tion parameter, 161**

query optimizer

index hints, 529-530

intelligent, 508

overriding, 529

SET FORCEPLAN ON command, 530-531

showplans, 527

SQL Server 7.0, 509-510

Query runtime table, 876

query tools, 840

**query wait advanced configuration parameter,
161**

querying sysmessages table, 432

queue reader agent, 759

QUOTED IDENTIFIER option, 180

R

r-r switch, BCP (Bulk Copy Program), 401

RA (Read Ahead), 150

**RAID (Redundant Array of Inexpensive Disks),
172**

disk configurations

RAID 0, 59

RAID 1, 60

RAID 5, 60

RAID 10, 60

filegroups, 193

level 0, 173

level 1, 174

level 2, 174

level 3, 174

level 4, 174

level 10, 173

RAISERROR statement, 606

**RDBMS (relational database management sys-
tems), 9**

Read Ahead (RA), 150

READ COMMITTED isolation levels, 557-558

read locks, releasing by snapshot agent, 807

Read Only option, 176

read statements, shared locks, 544

READ UNCOMMITTED isolation levels, 557-558

read-ahead logic, 466

read-ahead reads, 523

read-only cursors, 616

readability, stored procedures, 597

READCOMMITTED lock, 559

readers, replication transaction-logs, 315

reading

   DBCC common output, 902

   showplans, 526-527

READPAST lock, 559

READUNCOMMITTED lock, 559

Rebuild Master Utility, 272

rebuilding master database, 272

RecalcSpaceUsage method, 728

receiving email, SQL Mail, 708-709

RECONFIGURE command, 145

recording configuration information (SQL Server maintenance), 305

recovering databases, 241-242

recovery interval advanced configuration parameter, 161

Recovery Model option, 176

recovery models, 241

recovery. See restoring

Recursive Triggers option, 178

redirecting task execution, 387

Refresh data option (Process a Cube dialog box), 879

refreshing data, 845

REGEDIT.EXE, 27

Register SQL Server Wizard, 114

Registered SQL Server Properties dialog box, 117

registering server, 113

Registry, 27

relational database management systems (RDBMS), 9

relational OLAP (ROLAP), 869

reliability, SQL Server, 25

remote access configuration parameter, 152

remote login timeout configuration parameter, 152

remote proc trans configuration parameter, 153

Remote Procedure Call (RPC), 66

remote query timeout configuration parameter, 152

remote tables, populating, 585

renaming

   databases, 187-188

   indexes, 499-501

repair options (CHECKDB command), 907

REPAIR_ALLOW_DATA_LOSS option (CHECKDB command), 907

REPAIR_FAST option (CHECKDB command), 907

REPAIR_REBUILD option (CHECKDB command), 907

REPEATABLE READ isolation level, 557

REPEATABLEREAD lock, 559

REPLDATA directory, 77

replication, 751

   applications of, 752

   articles, 753

   configuring, servers to be publishers, 767

   distribution database, 758

      configuring agent logon information, 764-765

      creating, 761-762

      deleting, 765-766

      selecting, 763

   distribution databases

      adding publishers, 767-768

      disabling, 771

      enabling for publication, 769

      enabling replication subscribers, 770

   Immediate Updating Subscribers, 757

   merge, 756

      applications of, 811

      database synchronization, 813

      design considerations, 815-816

      inappropriate applications of, 812

      Merge publications, setting up, 817

      merging data at the destination database, 813

      overview, 812

resolving conflicts, 817-818

subscriber updates, 813

table design limitations, 815

transactional consistency, 813-815

nonSQL Server subscribers, 772-775

overview, 752

publications, 754

publish and subscribe metaphor, 753

server roles, 754-755

snapshot, 756, 803

agents, 806-807

applications of, 804

design considerations, 807

distribution agent functions, 807

inappropriate applications of, 805

overview, 804

publications, setting up, 808-810

synchronization sets, 806

SQL Server 2000

agents, 759

limitation, 758

synchronization modes, 760-761

stored procedures, 799

subscriptions, 754

transactional, 756,

agents, 780

applications of, 779

inline data validation, 798

publication scripts, 799

stored procedures, 795-798

topology, 781-783

transactional consistency, 757-758

types, 755

upgrading, 776

vertical partitioning, 798

Web-based, 829

replication distributor, 315

replication merge, 316

Replication Monitor (SQL Server), 800

replication snapshots, 316

replication transact-SQL script (TSQL), 316

replication transaction-log reader, 315

reports, creating from multiple data sources, 584

Reports to Generate dialog box, 347

Repository

data warehousing, 852

storing packages, 393

republisher scenario (hub-and-spoke topology), 783

resources, security, 203

Response tab

New Alert Properties dialog box, 332, 335, 339

New Job Properties dialog box, 336

RESTORE command, 270

Restore Database dialog box, 268-269

restoring

databases, 239, 269

bulk-logged recovery method, 246

differential backups, 267

example, 262, 267, 274, 278-280

file/filegroup backups, 244-245

Full Recovery model, 262-266

master, 271-274

point in time recovery, 245

Point In Time Restore, 268

selecting method, 245-246

SQL Server 2000, 240-241

system, 282

T-SQL (RESTORE command), 270

file/filegroup, T-SQL, 271

transaction logs

example of, 279

T-SQL, 270

restoring databases, force restoring option, 269

Restrict Access option (databases), 176

restrictions, queries (distributed), 585

results (queries)

grouping, 574-576

sorting, 569

resultsets, cursors, 613, 617

retrieving

columns (tables), 566

data

linked servers, 590-591

XML, 677-679

return on investment, (ROI), 842

RETURN statement, 604

return values (stored procedures), reserved, 604

returning values, summary, 573

REVOKE statement, 206

revoking, permissions, 206-207

object permissions, 224-225

statement permissions, 228-229

RIDs (Row Ids), 490

RIGHT [OUTER] JOIN operator, 572

ROI (return on investment), 842

ROLAP (relational OLAP), 869, 872

role mapping, 211

role-based security management, 229-230

roles

data access, 882-885

database roles, 208

granting, 216-219

predefined, 209

user-defined, 210-212

managing, 122

server roles

bulkadmin, 208

dbcreator, 208

diskadmin, 208

granting, 215-216

processadmin, 208

securityadmin, 208

serveradmin, 208

setupadmin, 208

sysadmin, 208

rollback statements, inner transactions, 553

ROLLBACK TRANsaction [] statement, 167

root level (B-Tree structure), 488

Row Ids (RIDs), 490

row-level locking, 466, 541

row-level security, 231

ROWLOCK lock, 559

rows

displaying, 659

limiting, 659

locators, nonclustered indexes, 490

row-level security, 231

tables

adding, 276

deleting, 580-581

grouping, 566

inserting, 577-578

ROWS_PER_BATCH switch (BULK_INSERT statement), 423

ROWTERMINATOR switch (BULK_INSERT statement), 423

RPC (Remote Procedure Call), 66

rules, 39

dimension level security, 885

enforcing, BCP (Bulk Copy Program), 417

Run a Wizard button, 341

running

packages (DTS Wizard), 369

plans, 348

Web Assistant, 643

S

s-s option, 93

S-S switch, BCP (Bulk Copy Program), 403

s.SCH file extension, 761

s@set_user parameter (sp_processmail), **709**

s@subject parameter (sp_processmail), **709**

saving packages, DTS Wizard, **369**

scalability

operating systems, 57

processor, 689

SQL Server 2000, 47

scaler UDFs, **599**

scaling out, **57**

scan count, **523**

Scan Density value, **912**

scan for startup procs advanced configuration parameter, **162**

Schedule Index Update Job screen (Index Tuning Wizard), **520**

Schedule the DTS Package dialog box (Copy Database Wizard), **100**

schedule types for jobs, **319-320**

Schedules tab, **318-320**

scheduling

active scripts, 325-326

backups, 250, 280-281

del_remove_old_data stored procedure, 314-315

stored procedures, batch run example, 627-630

transformations, 368

Web Assistant jobs, 649, 652-653

schema locks, **544**

Script Debugger, **388**

Script method, **728**

scripting, active, **325-327**

scripts

active, 315, 325-326

ActiveX, debugging, 383

BCP (Bulk Copy Program)

comma-delimited export, 411

comma-delimited import, 411

fixed-length export, 413

fixed-length import, 411-412

simple export, 410

simple import, 410

skipped fields on export, 414

skipped fields on import, 413

replication transact-SQL (TSQL), 316

SQL, generating, 126

transformation, 367

search arguments, converting from nonsearch arguments, **533**

Search tab (Microsoft's Books Online), **434**

searching tables, cross-reference, **571**

secondary files, **172**

security

database users, 205

distribution databases, 768

FAQs (Frequently Asked Questions), 234-236

guest users, 206

guidelines, 203

hierarchy, 223-224

Kerberos, 229

levels, 222

logins

editing login information, 219-220

managing, 212-214

mixed mode security, 205

passwords, 220-221

troubleshooting, 221

viewing login information, 219

Windows Authentication, 204-205

OLAP data, 881

authentication, 882

cell level, 887-889

dimension level, 885

roles, 882-885

permissions

administration tips, 226-227

combining with views, 232

denying, 207

granting, 206, 224-229

object permissions, 207

revoking, 206, 224-225, 228-229

statement permissions, 207

resources, 203

role-based security management, 229-230

roles

database roles, 208-212, 216-219

server roles, 208, 215-216

stored procedures, 233, 594

triggers, 233-234

views

column-level security, 230-231

combining with permissions, 232

row-level security, 231

securityadmin role, 208

segments, limitations, 463

Select a Destination Server dialog box (Copy Database Wizard), 98

Select a Source Server dialog box (Copy Database Wizard), 98

Select a SQL Server dialog box, 114

Select Backup Destination dialog box, 249

SELECT component

INSERT statement, 577-578

SELECT statement, 567

Select Components dialog box, 87

Select Counter dialog, 451

General Tab, 452

Log Files Tab, 452

Schedule Tab, 453

Select Database to Backup dialog box, 258

Select Databases dialog box, 342

Select Destination and Action dialog box (Backup Wizard), 259

Select Dimension Table dialog box (Dimension Wizard), 862

Select Dimensions dialog box (Cube Wizard), 866

Select Distributor dialog box (Configure Publishing and Distribution Wizard), 763

Select Fact Table dialog box (Cube Wizard), 864

SELECT INTO

component (SELECT...INTO statement), 583

statement (SQL), 566

Select Levels dialog box (Dimension Wizard), 862

Select Publication Name and Description dialog box (Create a Publication Wizard), 791

Select Publication Type dialog box

Create a Publication Wizard, 789

Publication and Subscription Wizard, 809

Select Related Objects dialog box (Copy Database Wizard), 100

SELECT statement, 612

SELECT statement (SQL), 566

components, 567

GROUP BY clause, 574-575

HAVING clause, 576

ORDER BY clause, 569

WHERE clause, 568-571

Select the Database to Move or Copy dialog box (Copy Database Wizard), 99

Select Type of Backup dialog box, 259

Select Wizard dialog box, 341

SELECT...INTO statement, components, 583

selecting

databases, 645

hard drives, 59

platforms for SQL Server installation, 56-57, 61

self-tuning, 147-148

Send Mail task, 360

sending email from SQL Server, 707-708

SERIALIZABLE isolation level, 557

SERIALIZABLE lock, 559

Server Backup dialog box, 251

Server Installation dialog box, 83

Server Properties dialog box
Connections tab, 143
Database Settings tab, 144
General tab, 141
Memory tab, 142, 144
Processor tab, 142
Server Role Properties dialog box, 123
server roles
bulkadmin, 208
dbcreator, 208
diskadmin, 208
granting, 215-216
processadmin, 208
securityadmin, 208
serveradmin, 208
setupadmin, 208
sysadmin, 208
Server Roles tab (SQL Server Login Properties dialog box), 215
server/object applications, 712
serveradmin role, 208
servers
alternative synchronization partners, 829
configuring to be publishers, 767
connecting to (Enterprise Manager), 116
databases, backups, 250
deleting from distribution databases, 768
disabling distribution databases, 771
disconnecting from (Enterprise Manager), 118
distributor, 755
enabling replication subscribers, 770
federated database, 465
linked
adding, 586-588
naming conventions, 590
pass through queries, 592
retrieving data, 590-591
troubleshooting, 586
viewing tables, 589

Mail. *See* SQL Mail
managing configurations, 121
multiserver jobs, 351
publish and subscribe metaphor, 753
publishers, 755
registering, 113
replication, 754-755
selecting groups at registration, 115
server roles
bulkadmin, 208
dbcreator, 208
diskadmin, 208
granting, 215-216
processadmin, 208
securityadmin, 208
serveradmin, 208
setupadmin, 208
sysadmin, 208
subscriber, 755
synchronization, 760-761
upgrading, SQL Server 2000, 95
services, created on SQL Server installation, 77
SET
commands, status, 923
component (UPDATE statement), 579
SET FORCEPLAN OFF command, 531
SET FORCEPLAN ON command, 530-531
SET LOCK TIMEOUT, 544
Set Merge Agent Schedule dialog box (Push Subscription Wizard), 821
SET SHOWPLAN_ALL, 522
SET SHOWPLAN_TEXT, 522
Set Snapshot Agent Schedule dialog box (Create a Publication Wizard), 794
Set Statistics IO query option, 524
Set Statistics Time query option, 525
Set Subscription Priority dialog box (Push Subscription Wizard), 822
SET TRANSACTION ISOLATION LEVEL command, 557

set working set size advanced configuration parameter, 162

setting

columns, tables, 579-580

database options, 174-175

ANSI NULL Default option, 177-178

Auto Close option, 178

Auto Create Statistics option, 179

Auto Shrink option, 179

Auto Update Statistics option, 179

compatibility level option, 180

Concat NULL Yields NULL option, 180

cursor close on commit option, 181

Default to Local Cursor option, 181

QUOTED IDENTIFIER option, 180

Read Only, 176

Recovery Model, 176

Recursive Triggers option, 178

Restrict Access, 176

sp_dboption [] command, 180

Subscribed option, 182

Torn Page Detection option, 179

mappings, logon, 588

memory allocation options, 148

workflow properties, 382-388

setup program, 81

Setup Type dialog box, 86

setupadmin role, 208

SETUSER statement, 227

severity levels (error messages), 431

shared dimensions, 860

shared locks, 543, 908

show advanced options configuration parameter, 153

SHOWCONTIG command, 444, 911

showplans

graphical, 521

output with SET FORCEPLAN ON command, 531

query optimization, 521

reading, 526-527

text-based, 522

SHOW_STATISTICS, 920

Shrink Database dialog box, 187

SHRINKDATABASE command, 921

SHRINKFILE command, 922

shutting down SQL Server 2000, 278

simple export script (BCP), 410

simple import script (BCP), 410

Simple Recovery (recovery model), 241

Simple recovery mode, 176-177

single-user mode, 94

size

databases, minimum/maximum, 170

indexes, 491

sizing event logs, 27

skipped fields on export script (BCP), 414

skipped fields on import script (BCP), 413

SL statements, TRUNCATE TABLE, 580

slow mode (BCP), 414-417

smart disk controller cards, 173

SMP (Symmetric Multiple Processors), 23, 57, 461

snapshot, 798

snapshot agents, 759, 780, 805

execution, 806

releasing read locks on articles, 807

updating distribution database, 807

snapshot publications, 806-810

snapshot replication, 756, 803

applications of, 804

design considerations, 807

distribution agent, 807

guaranteed loose consistency model, 757

Immediate Updating Subscribers, 757

inappropriate applications of, 805

overview, 804

snapshot agents, 806-807

snapshot publications, 808-810

synchronization sets, 806

troubleshooting, 826

snapshots, replication, 316

snowflake schemas (dimensional modeling), 848

software

Microsoft Exchange, 704

Microsoft recommendations, 61

software-level disk striping, 173

SORT IN TEMPDB option, 497

sorting results (queries), 569

source connections, DTS Wizard example, 363

source steps, 360

source tables, 365

SourceSafe, stored procedures, 595

Specify Articles dialog box (Create a Publication Wizard), 791

Specify Backup Disk Directory dialog box, 345

Specify Subscriber Types dialog box (Create a Publication Wizard), 790

Specify the Database Backup Plan dialog box, 344-345

Specify the Transaction Log Backup Plan dialog box, 346

Specify Transaction Log Backup Disk Directory dialog box, 346

Specify Workload screen (Index Tuning Wizard), 519

speed

backups, 261

database backups, 283

hard drives, 59

spids

determining, 915

killing, 440

spoke-and-hub topology, merge replication, 816

sp_adddistpublisher command, 768

sp_addlinkedserver stored procedure, 586

sp_addlinkedsrvlogin stored procedure, 588

sp_addumpdevice stored procedure, 247

sp_autostats system stored procedure, 509

sp_blockcnt system procedure, 546

sp_configure, 305

changing system configuration parameters, 144

listings, output with Show Advanced options, 145

sp_dboption [] command, 180

sp_detach_db stored procedure, 273

sp_dropdistribtiondb command, 766

sp_helpdb [] command, 174

sp_indexoption system procedure, 544

sp_lock system procedure, 544

sp_OACreate stored procedure, 737

sp_OADestroy stored procedure, 739

sp_OAGetErrorInfo stored procedure, 737

sp_OAGetProperty stored procedure, 738

sp_OAMethod stored procedure, 738

sp_OASetProperty stored procedure, 738

sp_OAStop stored procedure, 739

sp_processmail, 707-709

sp_recompile stored procedure, 596

sp_rename system stored procedure, 500

sp_who command, 439

sp_who system procedure, 544-545

sp_who2 system procedure, 546

SQL

cursors

allowing updates, 616

closing/deallocating, 618

creating, 613

declaring, 614-615

fetching, 617

read-only, 616

standard, 616

UPDATE and DELETE statements, 618-619

dynamic, 613

statements
    BULK_INSERT, 421-423
    CREATE TABLE, 566, 581-583
    DELETE, 566, 580
    IF...ELSE statement, 603
    INSERT, 566, 577
    INSERT INTO...SELECT, 578
    SELECT, 566-567
    SELECT INTO, 566
    SELECT...INTO, 583
    UPDATE, 566, 578-580
stored procedures, 593

SQL Agent, email, 706-707

SQL Executive, 67

SQL Mail, 703
configuring, 704
functionality, 706-709
MSSQLServer process, 704
setting up, 704
starting, 705
testing SQL Server setup, 704

SQL Mail Configuration dialog box, 705

SQL Mail status indicator, 321

SQL scripts, 126, 359

SQL Server 2000 indexes, performance enhancements, 491

SQL Server
Agent, 662
architecture, 23
backups. *See* backups
-c option, 94
certification, 19
command-line utilities, 36-38
companion products, 34-35
configuration, FA, 163
configuration parameters
    advanced, 154-162
    allow updates, 150

    default language, 151
    max text repl size, 151
    nested triggers, 152
    remote access, 152
    remote login timeout, 152
    remote proc trans, 153
    remote query timeout, 152
    show advanced options, 153
    two digit year cutoff, 153
    user_option, 154
configuring, 140
    database settings, 143
    dynamic configuration variables, 146-147
    memory options, 141
    processor options, 141
    server settings, 143
    sp_configure, 145
    user connections, 143
connections, from SQL Server Enterprise Manager, 117
cursors
    batch run example, 627-630
    CLOSE or DEALLOCATE statements, 618-619
    deleting data from tables, 624
    displaying object names and types, 622-623
    FETCH statement, 617
    global variables, 619-620
    looping through tables, 620
    positional updates, 626
data modification, 166
databases
    adding new files, 183
    attaching/detaching, 190-191
    Automatically Grow File option, 169
    creating, 168-172
    data operating system files, 167
    deleting, 188-189

expanding, 182-183

log operating system files, 167

managing, 124

presizing files, 170

renaming, 187-188

setting options, 174-182

shrinking, 186

size (minimum/maximum), 170

viewing information about, 174

DBCC

case example of use, 444

error tracking, 443

table/index fragmentation, 444-445

deadlocks, 540

defaults, 40

determining running version, 284

disk arrays, 173

dynamic locking strategy, 466

editions, 62, 752

email, SQL Mail, 703-709

Enterprise Manager

connecting to servers, 116

disconnecting from servers, 118

registering servers, 113

starting, 112

error logs, 436-438

error messages

Microsoft's Books Online, 433-434

numbers, 430

severity levels, 431

sysmessages system table, 432

user-defined, 430

viewing with SQL Server Enterprise
Manager, 432

Event Viewer, 25

exporting, data to flat files, 389

extents, 485

file groups, 464

Fill Factor value, 495

history of, 45

importing, text files, 360

importing data, 355

index pages, 489

Index Tuning Wizard, 503

indexes, 483

B-Tree structure, 488

example, 486

pages, 485

principle behind, 483

processor differences, 496

selection, 503

size concerns, 487

structure of, 488

types of, 488

installing, 67

Client Tools, 103

configuring clients, 104

data file location, 64

dedicating a machine, 55

directories created on installation, 77

hard drives, 58

memory, 58

network options, 65

options, 63

planning, 54

questions, 64

removing instances, 102

selecting platforms, 56-57, 61

services created on installation, 77

system requirements, 54-55

user requirements, 55

utilities created on installation, 78

Job Scheduler, 316

join orders, 530

lock manager, 543

locks, 537
    functionality, 539
    managing, 544
    minimizing, 551-553, 557
    overriding default locking behavior, 558
    page, 542
    physical, 541
    row-level, 541
    table, 543
    trace flags, 549
    viewing, 544
maintenance plans, 301
    logins, 306
    monitoring error logs, 302-304
    recording configuration information, 305
managing, logins, 121
MAPI mail client, 704
max degree of parallelism parameter, 496
Microsoft hardware and software recommen-
    dations, 61
monitoring
    memory, 149
    System Monitor, 685-691
    user activity, 694
MSCS, 25
multiple instances, 464
multiuser configuration options, 557
naming conventions, 895
Net Libraries, 105
network independence, 24
network options, 65
new features for SQL Server 2000, 46
newsgroups, 927
object model, 714
objects, 39
operating system support, 24
OS requirements, 54
packages, saving, 369

pages, 486-487
pausing, 30, 111
performance, 140, 149
Performance Monitor, 28
priority, 160
processor requirements, 24
publish and subscribe metaphor, 753
Query Analyzer, improvements, 48
query optimizer, 507, 511
read-ahead logic, 466
registering, setting authentication mode, 114
Registry, 27
reliability, 25
replication, 751
    applications of, 752
    articles, 753
    overview, 752-754
    server roles, 754-755
roles, managing, 122
rules, 39
security modes, 66
self-tuning ability, 139, 147-148
showplans, 521, 526-527
SMP, 23
snapshot replication, troubleshooting, 826
SQL-DMO, 711. *See* SQL-DMO
starting, 30
    default instance, 95
    from command line, 93-95
    single-user mode, 94
    troubleshooting, 94
starting/stopping, 111
stored procedures, 42
table scans, 487
tables, 39
taskbar, 25
thread scheduling, 461
trace flags, 442-443

transaction completeness, 166

transactional replication

  agents, 780

  applications of, 779

  inline data validation, 798

  publication scripts, 799

  stored procedures, 795-798

  topology, 781-783

transactions

  isolation levels, 557-558

  nested, 554

  user interaction, 555-556

triggers, 41

troubleshooting

  applications, 445

  FAQ, 453

  resources, 446-448

tuning, 140

Typical Installation, 86

upgrading

  fall back plans, 73

  plans, 68-71

  steps, 72

  Version Upgrade Wizard, 70-71

user groups, 448

user processes, 438-441

user-defined datatypes, 40

version differences, 45

  architectural changes, 459

  Parallel Data Scan, 150

  thread scheduling, 460

versions, support, 24

views, 40

visual administration tools

  Enterprise Manager, 30

  Profiler, 33

  Query Analyzer, 31

  Service Manager, 29

  SQL Server Setup, 31

  Version Upgrade Wizard, 34

Web sites, 925

Windows 2000 support, 47

Windows NT Authentication, 28

worker threads, 158

workloads, capturing, 503

SQL Server 2000, 9

AppleTalk ADSP protocol, 67

backups. *See* backups

Banyan Vines, 66

collation setting, 65

conflict detection, 786

Create a Publication Wizard, 787

data warehousing, 850-852

Database Maintenance Plan Wizard, 307

databases

  restoring, 240-241, 267-270

  shrinking, 187

editions, 78

graphical BCP utility, 731

graphical maintenance, fixing with SQL-DMO, 721

hardware platforms supported, 62

heap storage, 490

importing/exporting text files, 357

Index Wizard, creating indexes, 492-495

indexes

  creating on computed columns and views, 498

  Fill Factor, 495

installing

  alongside SQL Server 7.0, 97-100

  Authentication Mode dialog box, 87

  Can't create directory error message, 81

  checklist, 80

  Collations Settings dialog box, 88

  computer Name dialog box, 82

  documentation, 79

domain user accounts (Windows 2000/NT), 88

editions, 78

Installation Definition dialog box, 85

Instance Name dialog box, 85

License Agreement dialog box, 84

multiple instances of SQL Server database engine, 65

Network Libraries dialog box, 88

prerequisites, 79

Select Components dialog box, 87

Server Installation dialog box, 83

Service Manager, 90

setup program, 81

Setup Type dialog box, 86

Start Copying Files dialog box, 89

troubleshooting, 91-93

User Information dialog box, 84

log truncation options, NO_TRUNCATE option, 256

master database

reattaching database files, 273-274

restoring, 271-273

memory, 58, 63

merge replication

applications of, 811

database synchronization, 813

design considerations, 815-816

inappropriate applications of, 812

Merge publications, 818-825

merging data at the destination database, 813

overview, 812

resolving conflicts, 817-818

subscriber updates, 813

table design limitations, 815

transactional consistency, 813-815

troubleshooting, 826

merge replication, 756

Microsoft Analysis Services, 855

named-pipes protocol, 66

network options, 65

operating system support, 63

query optimizer, 508

Rebuild Master Utility, 272

recovery models, 241

replication, 751

agents, 759

configuring servers to be publishers, 767

distribution database, 758, 761-765

distribution databases, adding publishers, 767-768

distribution databases, deleting, 765-766

distribution databases, disabling, 771

distribution databases, enabling for publication, 769

enabling subscribers, 770

Immediate Updating Subscribers, 757

limitation, 758

nonSQL Server subscribers, 772-775

overview, 752

snapshot, 803

transactional consistency, 757-758

types, 755

upgrading, 776

Web-based, 829

scripting utility, 799

shutting down, 278

Simple recovery mode, 176

snapshot replication, 756

applications of, 804

design considerations, 807

distribution agent functions, 807

inappropriate applications of, 805

overview, 804

snapshot agents, 806-807

snapshot publications, setting up, 808-810

synchronization sets, 806

SQL Server Agent, 67
Standard edition, limitations, 79
statistics, 508
stored procedures, 610-612
synchronization, 760-761
tables, viewing all within databases, 498
TCP/IP, 66
transaction logs, restoring, 270
Transaction Publication option, 789
transactional replications, 756, 779-781
UDFs (user-defined functions), sample, 599
upgrading, 95
    from SQL Server 6.5, 101-102
    from SQL Server 7.0, 96
Web Assistant, 641-643
Web Publishing, 641-643
WHERE clauses, changing, 390
XML integration, 676-677
SQL Server 2000 Books Online, 388
SQL Server 3.70 file, 719
SQL Server 6.0, upgrading, 69
SQL Server 6.5
heap storage, 490
stored procedures, debugging, 611
upgrading, 95, 101-102
SQL Server 6.x
backups, 261
dynamic locking strategy, 466
page size, 462
read-ahead logic, 466
segments, 463
thread scheduling, 461
SQL Server 7.0
blocking, 546
conflict detection, 786
cursors, 616
Data Transformation Services (DTS), 355
disk I/O and data management, 462

engine parameters, 301
file groups, 464
index performance enhancements, 491
locks, 537
query optimizer, 509-510
replication, articles, 754
stored procedures, debugging, 611
upgrading, 69, 95-96
SQL Server Agent, 67, 118
Alert Manager, 329
alerts
    custom, 337-339, 341
    email notifications, 332
    error messages, finding, 331
    events, 329-332
    performance condition, 333-336
jobs, 313
    active scripting, 325-327
    creating, 314-322
    email messages, 328
    email notifications, 323
    event log notifications, 323
    extending, 326-328
    Last Run Status, 322
    managing, 314-322
    schedule types, 319
    step actions, 317-318
    step diagrams, 324
    steps, 323-325
    types, 315-316
managing
    alerts, 129
    jobs and tasks, 127
    operators, 129
Performance Monitor
    custom alerts, 337
    performance condition alerts, 333-336

SQL Server Agent Error Log, 309

SQL Server Authentication, 213

SQL Server Books Online dialog box, 433

SQL Server Client Network Utility dialog box, 104

SQL Server Collation Settings dialog box, 88

SQL Server Computer Name dialog box, 82

SQL Server DBA Assistant

  BulkCopy object, 731

  enhancing, selecting a database from a combo box, 725

  graphical BCP utility, 731

  overview, 721

  table maintenance, 721, 728

SQL Server DBA Assistant dialog box

  Bulk Copy page, 732

  Table Maintenance page, 728

SQL Server Debugger, 612

SQL Server Enterprise Manager, 30

  common tasks, 120

  Data Transformation Service folder, 393

  Database Properties dialog box, 168

  DTS package operations, 359

  generating SQL scripts, 126

  indexes, 498-500

  managing

    alerts, 129

    data transformation packages, 132

    database users and objects, 124

    databases, 124

    error logs, 134

    jobs and tasks, 127

    logins, 121

    operators, 129

    server configurations, 121

    server roles, 122

    user activity, 132

  SQL Server configurations, 140, 143

viewing

  database information, 174

  error logs, 302, 437

  error messages, 432

  locks and blocking, 546

  SQL Server Agent Error Log, 309

SQL Server License Agreement dialog box, 84

SQL Server Login Properties - New Login dialog box, 213

SQL Server Login Properties dialog box

  Database Access tab, 217

  General tab, 216

  Permissions tab, 216

  Server Roles tab, 215

SQL Server Magazine Web site, 926

SQL Server Magazine (IT), 18

SQL Server Mail, 119

SQL Server Network Libraries dialog box, 88

SQL Server News Group, 18

SQL Server Performance Monitor, tracking, lock information, 548

SQL Server Professional Magazine Web site, 926

SQL Server Profiler, 33, 695-696

  debugging stored procedures, 612

  query optimization, 514-518

  tracking, lock information, 549

SQL Server Query Analyzer, 31, 135, 514

  executing stored procedures, 597

  graphical showplans, 521

  sp_lock system procedure, 544

  sp_who system procedure, 545

  stored procedure debugger, 611

  text-based showplans, 522

SQL Server Replication Monitor, 800

SQL Server Select Components dialog box, 87

SQL Server Server Installation dialog box, 83

SQL Server Service Manager, 30, 90, 111

SQL Server Setup, 31

SQL Server Start Copying Files dialog box, 89

SQL Server: User Settable Object, 692

SQL statements, aggregate functions, 573

SQL-92 cursor syntax, 614

SQL-DMO (SQL Distributed Management Objects), 711

applications, 715, 719

availability, 719

benefits, 714

declaring variables, 718

enhancing SQL Server DBA Assistant, selecting a database from a combo box, 725

functionality, 714

objects

creating with Visual Basic, 718-723

database, 728

declaring, 722

declaring in Visual Basic, 717

LoginTimeout property, 724

releasing, 719

programming languages, 714

SQL Server object model, 714

stored procedures, 736, 739

table maintenance, 728

SQLDMO.HLP file, 719

SQLDMO.rll file, 719

sqlmaint.exe utility, command-line parameters, 350

SQLMAP70.dll, 707

SQLPERF command, 915

SQLServer: Buffer Manager: Lazy Writes/sec counter, 691

SQLServer: BufferManager: Buffer Cache Hit Ratio counter, 689

SQLServer: General Statistics: User Connections counter, 691

SQLServerAgent, Alert Manager, 329

SQLSERVERAGENT service, distribution databases, 764

SQLServerAgent service, Job Scheduler, 314

SQL_DMO objects, creating, 717

Sqynk BackOffice Resource Web site, 926

stages (processes), 379

standard database roles, 210-211

Standard edition (SQL Server 2000), limitations, 79

Standard Edition (SQL Server), 62

star schema (dimensional modeling), 847-848

Start Copying Files dialog box, 89

Start Required Services dialog box (Push Subscription Wizard), 822

starting

Enterprise Manager, 112

jobs, 348, 646

SQL Mail, 705

SQL Server, 30

command line, 93-95

default instance, 95

single-user mode, 94

troubleshooting, 94

SQL Server Agent, 118

SQL Server Mail, 119

Web Assistant Wizard, 645

state (processes), 379, 391

state numbers (errors), 432

statement permissions, 207

granting, 228-229

revoking, 228-229

statements. See also commands

bulk load, logging, 243

BULK_INSERT, 421-423

control-of-flow, 600

CREATE TABLE, 581-583

DELETE, 580

DENY, 207

GRANT, 206

INSERT, components, 577

INSERT INTO...SELECT, 578

locks, 544

processing, showplans, 521

query optimizer advantages, 507

renaming database cautions, 188

REVOKE, 206

SELECT...INTO, components, 583

SETUSER, 227

showplans, reading, 526-527

T-SQL, debugging stored procedures, 611

TRUNCATE TABLE, 580

UPDATE, 578-580

Visual Basic, FOR EACH - NEXT, 727

statements (SQL)

aggregate functions, 573

CREATE TABLE, 566

DELETE, 566

INSERT, 566

SELECT, 566

components, 567

GROUP BY clause, 574-575

HAVING clause, 576

ORDER BY clause, 569

WHERE clause, 568-571

SELECT INTO, 566

UPDATE, 566

states, adding new to tables, 391

statistics, 508-509

statistics I/O, query optimization, 523-524

STATISTICS NORECOMPUTE option, 497

Statistics Time tool, query optimization, 524

status (processes), 379

don't execute, 387

execution, waiting, 388

status = WAIT message, 545

step actions for jobs, 317-318

step diagrams, for jobs, 324

Step object, DTS framework, 360

steps, redirecting task execution, 387

steps for jobs, 323-325

Steps tab (New Job Properties dialog box), 335

Stop Selected Traces dialog box, 517

stopping

SQL Server Agent, 118

SQL Server Mail, 119

storage

cubes and aggregations, 871

data marts, 840

data quality, 843

data warehouses, 836-838

components, 839

versus data marts, 841-842

distribution database, 758

configuring agent logon information, 764-765

creating, 761-762

deleting, 765-766

selecting, 763

stored procedures, 595

Storage Design Wizard

Data Storage dialog box, 871

Design Aggregations dialog box, 873

Finish dialog box, 874

Process Status dialog box, 875

Stored Procedure Wizard, 595

stored procedures, 42, 233

adding backup devices, 247

advantages, 594

ALTER PROCEDURE command, 600

batch run example, 627-30

changing, system configuration parameters, 144

code, 327-328

comments, 607

control-of-flow language, 600

BEGIN...End statement, 602

BREAK statement, 605

DECLARE statement, 601

GOTO statement, 602

IF...ELSE statement, 602

PRINT statement, 605

RAISERROR statement, 606

RETURN statement, 604

WAITFOR statement, 603

WHILE statement, 605

control-of-flow languageCONTINUE statement, 605

creating, 584, 595-597

debugging, 610

ODBC tracing, 612

SQL Server Debugger, 612

SQL Server Profiler, 612

Transact-SQL Debugger, 611

defined, 593

defining as an article, 800

del remove old data, 328

del_remove_old_data stored, scheduling, 314-315

disadvantages, 594

executing, 597

extended, 328, 707

global temporary, 595

global variables, 610

headers, 597

local temporary, 595

managing, 594

modifying, 600

monitoring user activity, 694

naming, 595

naming conventions, 896

OLE automation, 736-739

OLE automation clients, 736

parameters, 607-609

passing values, 607

replicating, 799

return values, reserved, 604

SourceSafe, 595

sp_addlinkedserver, 586

sp_addlinkedsrvlogin, 588

SQL Mail, 706

SQL-DMO, 736

bulk copy operations, 739

comparison, 714

technical notes, 594

transactional replication, 786, 795-798

Web Assistant, 675

WITH ENCRYPTION option, 597

WITH RECOMPILE option, 596

storing

database files, 169

packages, 358

strategies (security)

role-based security management, 229-230

stored procedures, 233

triggers, 233-236

views, 230-232

striped sets, 173

striping (hard drives), 59

subqueries, 581

Subscribed option, 182

subscriber servers, 755

subscribers

alternative synchronization partners, 829

Automatic synchronization, 760-761

heterogeneous, 772

merge replication, 813

nonSQL Server, 772

updating

local data, 785-786

recommended topology, 787

subscriptions, 753

Enable New Subscribers dialog box, 770

nonSQL Server subscribers, 772-775

pull, 754, 795, 807

push, 754, 795

Sum aggregate function (SQL statements), 573

summarizing data, 844

summary values, returning, 573

supporting XML, 676-677

switches

    BCP (Bulk Copy Program

        -a, 402

        -b, 400

        -C, 401

        -e, 400-403

        -f, 400

        -h, 403-404

        -i, 401

        -k, 403

        -L, 400

        -m, 400

        -n, 400-401

        -o, 401

        -P, 403

        -q, 401

        -r, 401

        -S, 403

        -t, 401-403

        -U, 403

        -v, 403

        -w, 401

    BULK_INSERT statement

        BATCHSIZE, 422

        CHECK_CONSTRAINTS, 422

        CODEPAGE, 422

        DATAFILETYPE, 422

        FIELDTERMINATOR, 422

        FIRSTROW, 422

        FORMATFILE, 422

        KEEPIDENTITY, 422

        KEEPNULLS, 423

        KILOBYTES_PER_BATCH, 423

        LASTROW, 423

        MAXERRORS, 423

        ORDER, 423

        ROWS_PER_BATCH, 423

        ROWTERMINATOR, 423

        TABLOCK, 423

Symmetric Multiple Processors (SMP), 23, 57, 461

synchronization

    alternative partners, 829

    Automatic, 760-761

synchronization sets, 806

syntax

    data sources, accessing, 586

    DBCC SHOW_STATISTICS command, 509

    explicit locking, 560

    READ UNCOMMITTED transaction isolation level, 558

    sp_who system procedure, 545

    text-based showplans, 522

sysadmin role, 208

sysmessages system table, 432

system administrators, 12, 223

system configuration parameters, changing, 144

system databases

    for backups, 343

    restoring, 282

System Monitor, 685

    adding counters, 686

    advanced uses, 692

    default scale choice, 690

    key area monitoring, 687

        disk I/O, 688

        memory, 689-690

        networks, 691

        processor, 689

        user connections, 691

    update frequency, 687

    user-defined counters, 692

    viewing log files, 693

system performance, processors, 57

system procedures, undocumented (blocking diagnosis), 546

system requirements, SQL Server installation, 54-55

T

T-SQL

adding publishers to distribution databases, 768

backing up

databases, 252

files/filegroups, 254

transaction logs, 253

checking for errors, 737

CREATE INDEX command, 497

databases, 189-190

debug statements, 611

DECLARE statement, 601

deleting

distribution databases, 766

indexes, 499

detaching databases, 273

expanding databases and logs, 185

index operations, 498

OLE automation stored procedures, 737

renaming indexes, 500

restoring, 270-271

shrinking databases, 187

sp_dboption [] command, 180

sp_helpdb [] command, 174

SQL-DMO, 715, 736

versus ANSI SQL, 565

viewing filegroup information, 198

T-T option, 94

t-t switch, BCP (Bulk Copy Program), 401-403

Table Articles Properties dialog box, 797, 809-810, 817

table locks, 543

Table Maintenance page (SQL Server DBA Assistant dialog box), 728

table scans, 484, 487

caused by queries with wildcards, 530

inefficiencies, 527

tables, 39

aliases, 575

columns

column-level security, 230-231

retrieving, 566

setting to fixed values, 579

setting values, 579-580

corruption

CHECKTABLE command, 910

detecting, 903

creating, 275, 581-583

cross-reference, searching, 571

deleting data with cursors, 624

destination, 365

dimension, 861

fact, 865

fragmentation

DBCC, 444-445

SHOWCONTIG command, 911

granting privileges, 728

horizontal partitioned, 754

IDENTITY data type, CHECKIDENT command, 909

importing, DTS Wizard example, 362-366

indexes

adding, 514

clustered, 489, 527

composite, 528

dropping, 913

Fill Factor, 495

heavy transaction processing, 492

rebuilding, 911

selecting, 501

size concerns, 487

slowing performance, 491-492

what not to index?, 502

what to index?, 501

integrity validation, 908

joining, 530, 571-573

linked servers, viewing, 589

looping through with cursors, 620

maintenance, 728-730

maintenance plans, 308

Merge publications, 812

naming convention, 896

nonclustered indexes, 490-491

pinning in the cache, 918

populating list boxes with table names, 726

query optimizer, 528

remote, populating, 585

rows

adding, 276

deleting, 580

grouping, 566

inserting, 577-578

row-level security, 231

segments, limitations, 463

SET FORCEPLAN ON command, 530

sizing, 487

source, 365

space allocation, 485

timestamp columns, merge replication, 815

updating, 913

Usage Analysis Wizard, 876

vertical partitioned, 754

Web Assistant, 656

Tables icon, 589

TABLOCK

lock, 559

switch (BULK_INSERT statement), 423

TABLOCKX lock, 559

tape drives, backup devices, 246

tasks

adding to packages (DTS Designer), 371

control, 387

database administration, FAQs, 351

don't execute status, 387

DTS framework, 359-360

execution control, changing, 387

managing (SQL Server Agent), 127

TCP/IP, 66, 117

tech support, 12, 446

TechNet (Microsoft), 18, 447

TechNet Online Web site, 926

tempdb database, 64

tempdb in Ram option, 148

terminators, BCP (Bulk Copy Program), 404

templates

file example, 663-671, 674-675

Web Assistant, 654-658, 663-671, 674-675

Test Database Integrity, 344

testing

database backup/recovery strategy, 307

SQL Server, as MAPI mail client, 704

test_authors Merge Publication, 818

text files, importing (determining file format), 363

text patterns, searching error logs for, 304

text-based showplans, syntax, 522

TEXTCOPY, 38

thread scheduling, 461

threads, 460-461

Tile Transfer Protocol task, 360

titles, Web Assistant pages, 654

time, updating indexes, 492

time quantum, 461

timestamp columns, merge replication, 815

tools. *See* utilities

top down design, 846

topologies

hub-and-spoke, 781-784

spoke-and-hub, merge replication, 816

updating subscribers, 787

Torn Page Detection option, 179

TPC-C, 465

trace, 696

trace flags, 442

commands, 917

locking behavior (SQL Server), 549

starting SQL Server, 94

turning on, 443

trace information, logging to tables, 697

Trace Properties dialog box, 516, 696

traces, query data, 516-517

tracking locking behavior, 550

training

certification, 19

DBAs, 17

Transact-SQL, UDFs, 49

Transact-SQL Debugger, production server cautions, 611

transaction

commands, 919

understanding, 553

Transaction Isolation Matrix, 558

transaction logs, 165

backing up, 248-249, 346

backup media integrity, 251

creating schedules, 280-281

differential backups, 267

example of, 274-277

expiration, 252

Full Recovery model, 262-266

loading, 266

multiple backup devices, 261-262

NO_TRUNCATE option, 265

recommendations, 282

scheduling, 250

T-SQL, 253

backups, 243-244

data modification, 166

expanding

assigning new files, 183

automatically, 182

listing, 185

manually, 183

inactive parts, 243

NO_LOG option, 256

Recovery Model option, 177

restoring

example of, 279

T-SQL, 270

shrinking, 186

transactional replication, 780

troubleshooting, 244

truncation options, 255-256

write-ahead, 167

transactional consistency

merge replication, 813-815

replication, 757-758

transactional data, analyzing, 856

transactional replication, 756. *See also* **replication**

agents, 780

applications of, 779

conflict detection, 786

hub-and-spoke topology, 781-784

Immediate Updating Subscribers, 757

inline data validation, 798

loopback detection, 786

merge replication (comparison), 811

overview, 752

publication scripts, 799

publications

creating, 787-794

subscriptions, 795

stored procedures, 786, 795-798

topology, 781-783

transforming published data, 798

transactions

blocking, 539

deadlocks, 540

dirty reads, 538

distribution database, 758

adding publishers, 767-768

configuring agent logon information, 764-765

configuring servers to be publishers, 767

creating, 761-762

deleting database, 765-766

disabling, 771

enabling for publication, 769

enabling replication subscribers, 770

selecting, 763

distribution databases, nonSQL Server subscribers, 772-775

isolation levels, 557-558

locks

minimizing, 551-553

trace flags, 549

viewing, 546

long-running (cautions), 552

nested, 553-554

physical locks, 541

publications (transaction based), 787-794

rollback statements, 553

status = WAIT message, 545

user interaction, 555-556

Transcender tests, 19

Transfer SQL Server Objects task, 360

Transform Data Task Properties dialog box, 390

Transform dialog box, 366

Transform Published Data Dialog box (Create a Publication Wizard), 790

Transform task, 360

transformations

DTS Designer, 370-379

packages, 358-359

repeating data transformation step, 393

scheduling, 368

scripts, listing, 367

source connections, 363

Transform dialog box, 366

trend analysis, performance monitor, 448

triggering error number 50001, code, 340-341

triggers, 41, 233-234, 785

as bottlenecks, 532

enforcing, BCP (Bulk Copy Program), 417

naming conventions, 896

Web Assistant, 652, 662

troubleshooting

applications, 445

backups, databases, 243

batch processing concerns, 380-381

BCP (Bulk Copy Program), 418

blocking, 539, 555-556

bottlenecks, 173

database/table corruption, 903

databases

corruption, 256, 264

management tips and tricks, 191-192

renaming, 188

DBCC, 442

case example, 444

error tracking, 443

table/index fragmentation, 444-445

deadlocks, 539-540, 551, 553

error messages

error log, 436-437

Microsoft Books Online, 433-434

numbers, 430

severity levels, 431

sysmessages system table, 432

viewing with SQL Server Enterprise Manager, 432

errors, reported by DBCC, 903

FAQ, 453

hardware platform problems, 56

improper database design, 467-469

index performance, 488

installation, 91-93

killing user processes, 439

log shipping, 292

logins, 221

merge replication, 826

nonsearch arguments, reducing the use of, 533

overriding query optimizer, 529

queries, distributed, 586

query optimization, 511

resources

Microsoft Developer Network, 448

Microsoft TechNet, 447

tech support, 446

servers, linked, 586

snapshot replication, 826

SQL Server, 4, 969

stored procedures, debugging, 610-612

table scans, 527

torn pages, 179

trace flags, 442-443

transaction logs, 244

trigger bottlenecks, 532

upgrading, SQL Server 6.5, 101-102

TRUNCATE TABLE statement, versus DELETE statement, 580

TRUNCATE_ONLY option, 255

TSQL (replication transact-SQL script), 316

tuning, 140

two digit year cutoff configuration parameter, 153

two-phase commit protocol, 785

Type Name and Description for Backup dialog box, 258

types of jobs, 315-316

Typical Installation, 86

U

U-U switch, BCP (Bulk Copy Program), 403

UDFs (user-defined functions), 49, 599

UMS, SQL Server threads, 462

Unicode characters, 65

UNIQUE constraint, rebuilding, 911

uniqueness, indexes, 495

UNIX, GREP utility, 304

UNPINTABLE command, 918

UPDATE component (UPDATE statement), 579

Update Data Optimization Information dialog box, 343

update frequency, System Monitor, 687

update locks, 543

UPDATE statement, 580

components, 578-579

cursors, 618-619

Fill Factor effects, 495

SQL, 566

UPDATE STATISTICS command, 351, 508

Update Statistics, 729-730

Updateable Subscriptions dialog box (Create a Publication Wizard), 789

UpdateStatistics method, 728

UPDATEUSAGE command, 912

updating

cursors, 618-619

databases, anomalies, 469

indexes during data modification, 492

information with XML, 680-681

local subscriber data, 785-786

statistics, 509

subscribers, recommended topology, 787

system tables, cautions, 151

tables, 913

UPDLOCK lock, 559

Upgrade directory, 77

UPGRADE subdirectory, 102

upgrading

checklist, 95

from 7.0 to SQL Server 2000, 96

replication, 776

servers, SQL Server 2000, 95

SQL Server

fall back plans, 73

planning, 68-71

questions, 64

steps, 72

Version Upgrade Wizard, 70-71

SQL Server 6.5, 95, 101-102

SQL Server 7.0, 69, 96

Usage Analysis Wizard, 876

usage-based optimization, 875-876

Usage-Based Optimization Wizard, 875

user accounts

database object owners, 223

database users, 205

DBOs (database owners), 223

guest users, 206

logins

editing login information, 219-220

managing, 212-214

mixed mode security, 205

passwords, 220-221

troubleshooting, 221

viewing login information, 219

Windows Authentication, 204-205

permissions

administration tips, 226-227

combining with views, 232

granting, 206, 224-229

object permissions, 207

revoking, 206-207, 224-229

statement permissions, 207

roles

database roles, 208-212, 216-219

server roles, 208, 215-216

system administrators, 223

user connections, monitoring (System Monitor), 691

user connections advanced configuration parameter, 162

user databases, backing up, 280

user groups, SQL Server, 448

User Information dialog box, 84

user processes, 438-441

user requirements, SQL Server installation, 55

User Triggers option, 810

user-defined counters, 692

user-defined database roles, 210-212

user-defined datatypes, 40

user-defined error messages, 430

user-defined functions (UDFs), 49, 599

user-defined partitions, 878

user-defined transactions, specifying the beginning of, 167

USEROPTIONS command, 923

users

databases, managing, 124

managing activity, (SQL Server Agent), 132

monitoring activity, 694

processes, killing, 439

tracing activities, 697

user_option configuration parameter, 154

usp_Batch_Run stored procedure, 627, 630

utilities. *See also* **SQL Server Agent**

BCP (Bulk Copy Program), 397-398

advantages and disadvantages, 397-399

BULK_INSERT operations, 421-423

cautions, 398

character mode, 405

common problems, 418

enforcement of objects, 417-418

FAQs (frequently asked questions), 424

fast mode, 414-417

interactive mode, 405-409

permissions, 404

programming tips, 418-421

sample scripts, 410-414

slow mode, 414-417

supported file formats, 424

switches, 400-404

syntax, 399-400, 404

command-line, 36-38

command-line parameters, sqlmaint.exe, 350

created on SQL Server installation, 78

DTS. *See* DTS (Data Transformation Service)

monitoring SQL Server, 685

query optimization, 511

Index Tuning Wizard, 512-514, 520

showplans, 521

SQL Server Profiler, 514-518

statistics I/O, 523-524

Statistics Time tool, 524

SQL Server Profiler, 695-697

V

v-v option, 94

v-v switch, BCP (Bulk Copy Program), 403

**value list component (INSERT statement),
577-578**

values

columns (tables), setting, 579-580

retrieving, using Dynamic Properties task,
374

summary, returning, 573

w@hentype argument, 650

VALUES component (INSERT statement), 577

**variables, defining with DECLARE statement,
601**

VBA (Visual Basic for Applications), 715

Version Upgrade Wizard, 34, 70-71

Informational Files Found dialog box, 101

upgrading SQL Server 6.5, 95

vertical partitioning

checksums, 798

tables, 754

viewing

alerts, 332

database information, 174

error logs, 437

information on filegroups, 197-198

locks, 544

log files, (System Monitor), 693

login information, 219

model database, 192

package properties, 381

process activity, 441

SQL Server Agent Error Log, 309

SQL Server error logs, 302

statistic update information, 509

tables, 498, 589

views, 40

combining with permissions, 232

creating indexes on, 498

security, 230-231

visual administration tools

SQL Server Enterprise Manager, 30

SQL Server Profiler, 33

SQL Server Query Analyzer, 31

SQL Server Service Manager, 29

SQL Server Setup, 31

Version Upgrade Wizard, 34

Visual Basic

combo boxes, populating with database
names, 726

controls, 716

CreateObject function, 718

creating

applications, 716

SQL-DMO objects, 718-720

SQL-DMO objects, 721-723

declaring SQL-DMO objects, 717

early binding, 718

FOR EACH – NEXT statement, 727

learning the basics, 715

New keyword, 718

Nothing keyword, 720

overview, 715

releasing objects, 719

Visual Basic for Applications (VBA), 715

Visual Basic form Properties window, 717

W

w-w switch, BCP (Bulk Copy Program), 401

w@hentype argument, 650

WAITFOR statement, 603

waiting execution status, 388

WAL Server 2000, NWLink IPX/SPX protocol, 66

warehouse databases, 839

Warehousing Framework, 851

warehousing. See data warehousing

Web Assistant Job dialog box, 646

Web Assistant (SQL Server 2000), 641-643

adding hyperlinks, 657-662

databases, 645

formatting Web pages, 654-658

jobs, 643, 646

managing, 663

scheduling, 649, 652-653

limiting rows, 659

publishing pages, from data, 660-662

starting, 643

stored procedures, 675

tables, 656

templates, 654-658, 663-671, 674-675

triggers, 662

Web Assistant Wizard, 642, 663-671, 674-675

publishing pages, 644-662

starting, 645

Web FAQs, chapter 23, 682

Web masters, 12

Web sites

DBA salary surveys, 17

Microsoft Developer Network, 448

Microsoft SQL Server News Group, 18

Microsoft TechNet, 18, 447

MSDN, 18

newsgroups, 927

SQL Server, 18

SQL Server Magazine, 18

SQL Server resources, 925

TPC-C benchmarks, 465

Transcender tests, 19

Web-based replication, 829

Web pages

formatting, Web Assistant, 654-658

hyperlinks, 657-662

publishing, Web Assistant Wizard, 644-662

titles, 654

Web Publishing (SQL Server 2000), 641-643

WHERE clause

changing, SQL Server 2000, 390

DELETE statement, 581

SELECT statement, 568-571

WHERE component

DELETE statement, 580

SELECT statement, 567

UPDATE statement, 579

WHILE statement, 605

WIN NT Magazine Web site, 926

WIN32 thread priorities, changing, 381

Windows 2000, System Monitor, 685

adding counters, 686

key area monitoring, 687-691

update frequency, 687

Windows Authentication, 204-205, 213

Windows NT

authentication, 66

disk defragmentation, 310

disk striping, 173

diskperf command, 688

event log, 310, 438

FAT, 60

fibers, 461

hardware platforms, 56

maintenance plans, 309

NTFS, 60

paging file monitoring, 690

Service Control Manager, bypassing, 94

setting up domain users, 67

Windows NT Authentication, 28

Windows NT FINDSTR.EXE utility, 304

WITH ENCRYPTION option, example, 597

WITH GRANT OPTION option, 226

WITH NO INFOMSGS option (DBCC commands), 902

WITH OVERRIDE parameter, 145

WITH RECOMPILE option, when to use, 596

Wizard Selection dialog box, 492

wizards

Copy Database, 70

Database Maintenance Plan, 307

Database Maintenance Plan Wizard, 341-347, 350

commands, 351

jobs, 348

plans, running, 348

DTS, 361

SQL Server 2000, 48

Version Upgrade, 70-71

Web Assistant, 642-671, 674-675

worker threads, 158

workflow

adding to packages (DTS Designer), 371

Close Connection on Completion property, 383

DTS, 380-381

loop control, 385-388

properties, 382-383

Execute on Main Package Thread property, 383

processing, 379

Workflow ActiveX Properties dialog box, 384

Workflow ActiveX Script property, 385-388

Workflow Properties dialog box, Options tab, 383

workloads, capturing, 503

Write Enable dialog box, 881

write-ahead transaction logs, 167

write-enabling cubes, 881

writing stored procedures, success values, 604

X-Z

XDR (XML-Data Reduced), 679

XML (Extensible Markup Language), 676

    retrieving data, 677-679

    SQL Server 2000 support, 46

    updating data with, 680-681

    Xpath queries, 678

XML-Data Reduced (XDR), 679

Xpath queries, 678

XSL (Extensible Stylesheet Language), 676

x-x option, 94

xp_deletemail, 707

xp_findnextmsg, 707

xp_logevent, 27

xp_readmail, 707

xp_sendmail, 707

xp_sendmail command, 327

xp_startmail, 707

xp_stopmail, 707

y-y option, 95

zombie processes, 440